Human Relations for Career and Personal Success

Third Canadian Edition

Andrew J. DuBrin
Rochester Institute of Technology

Terri Geerinck
Sir Sandford Fleming College

Toronto

For Rod, Adelaide, and Skyler.

National Library of Canada Cataloguing in Publication

DuBrin, Andrew J.
Human relations for career and personal success / Andrew J. DuBrin, Terri Geerinck. — 3rd Canadian ed.

Includes bibliographical references and index.
ISBN 0-13-123996-1

1. Interpersonal relations. 2. Success in business. I. Geerinck, Terri, 1958– II. Title.

HF5386.D78 2004 158.2 C2003-904471-8

ISBN 0-13-123996-1

Vice President, Editorial Director: Michael J. Young
Acquisitions Editor: Marianne Minaker
Marketing Manager: Toivo Pajo
Supervising Developmental Editor: Suzanne Schaan
Editorial Coordinator: Söğüt Y. Güleç
Copy Editor: Martin Townsend
Proofreader: Julie Fletcher
Production Coordinator: Anita Heyna
Page Layout: Janette Thompson (Jansom)
Art Director: Julia Hall
Cover and Interior Design: David Cheung
Cover Image: Getty Images

Photo Credits
p. 2: Bill Bachman/Courtesy of Stock Boston; p. 55: John Coletti/Courtesy of Stock Boston; p. 88: Michael Newman/Courtesy of PhotoEdit; p. 120: Scott Barrow/International Stock Photography, Ltd.; p. 149: Spencer Grant/Courtesy of PhotoEdit; p. 206: M. Ferguson/Courtesy of PhotoEdit; p. 258: Digital Vision; p. 308: Johnny Stockshooter/International Stock Photography, Ltd.; p. 333: Rafael Macia/ Courtesy of Photo Researchers, Inc.; p. 384: Gale Zucker/Courtesy of Stock Boston; p. 406: Willie L. Hill, Jr./Courtesy of Stock Boston.

Statistics Canada information is used with the permission of the Minister of Industry, as Minister responsible for Statistics Canada. Information on the availability of the wide range of data from Statistics Canada can be obtained from Statistics Canada's Regional Offices, its World Wide Web site at http://www.statcan.ca, and its toll-free access number 1-800-263-1136.

1 2 3 4 5 08 07 06 05 04

Printed and bound in Canada.

Contents

Human Relations Case Studies

Preface

Welcome to the third Canadian edition of *Human Relations for Career and Personal Success*. The purpose of this book is to show you how you can become more effective in your work and personal life through knowledge of and skill in human relations. A major theme of this book is that success in work and success in personal life are related. Success on the job often leads to success in personal life, and success in personal life can lead to job success. To progress in your career, you need to deal effectively with yourself and other people. Dealing effectively with people is an enormous asset in both work and personal life.

One major audience for this book is students who will meet human relations problems on the job and in personal life. The text is designed for human relations courses taught in colleges, career schools, vocational–technical schools, and other post-secondary schools. Another major audience for this book is managerial, professional, and technical workers who are forging ahead in their careers.

Organization of the Book

The text is divided into three parts, reflecting the major issues in human relations. Part 1 covers aspects of understanding and managing yourself: Chapter 1 focuses on self-understanding and the interrelationship of career and personal success; Chapter 2 explains how to use goal setting and other methods of self-motivation to improve your chances for success; Chapter 3 explains the basics of solving problems and making decisions with an emphasis on creativity; Chapter 4 deals with achieving wellness by managing stress and burnout; Chapter 5 focuses on dealing with personal problems such as substance abuse, counterproductive habits, and other forms of self-defeating behaviour; and Chapter 6 provides key ideas for finding happiness and enhancing your personal life.

Part 2 examines the heart of human relations—dealing effectively with other people. The topics in Chapters 7 through 12 are, respectively, communicating with people, improving intercultural competence, handling conflict with others and being assertive, getting along with your manager, getting along with your co-workers and customers, and developing self-confidence and leadership skills.

Part 3 provides information to help career-minded people capitalize on their education, experience, talent, and ambition. The topics of Chapters 13 through 16 are choosing a career, developing a portfolio career, conducting a job search, developing good work habits, and getting ahead in your career.

Human Relations for Career and Personal Success, Third Canadian Edition, is both a text and a workbook of experiential exercises, including role plays and self-assessment quizzes related to the text. (An experiential exercise allows for learning by doing, along with guided instruction.) Each chapter contains one or more exercises and ends with a human relations case study. The experiential exercises, which can all be completed during a class session, emphasize human interaction and thinking while keeping class paperwork to a minimum.

Changes in the Third Canadian Edition

The third Canadian edition continues to emphasize Canadian content, with even more references to Canadian research and Canadian companies. It also features more Canadian illustrations applicable to our culture and current economic environment, including information from the latest Canadian census. The text has more emphasis on the internet, and each chapter contains an online skill-building exercise called an Internet Skill Builder. Also, websites are referred to throughout the text.

Chapter 1 contains more information on the importance of self-esteem. Chapter 2 has better coverage of risk taking and thrill seeking, and discusses generational differences in needs. Chapter 3 includes information about emotional intelligence and decision making, asking "but not" questions to sharpen problem solving. Chapter 4 describes how the body mass index relates to health, the tend-and-befriend explanation of stress, emotional labour as a stressor, sick buildings and job stress, and creating your own stress triggers. Chapter 5 contains information about online addictions and eating disorders. Chapter 6 has some additional information on love relations.

Chapter 7 adds more information about nonverbal behaviour, including indicators of lying, as well as more extensive sections on the effects of computer-mediated communication and using presentation technology. In Chapter 8, the focus continues to be on developing intercultural competence, but with updated statistics and more strategies to overcome cultural barriers. Chapter 9 includes more information on harassment and workplace violence, using meta-communication to resolve conflicts, mediation, and the relationship between decisiveness and assertiveness. Chapter 10 includes emotional intelligence, more coverage of ethics, a section on becoming a good organizational citizen, and a new section on bullying. Chapter 11, on getting along with co-workers and customers, includes a new area on barriers to effective teams, ineffective team roles, and more strategies to assist in becoming an effective team member. Chapter 12 now includes information on servant leadership as well as emotional intelligence and its relationship to effective leadership.

Chapter 13 describes job shadowing as a way of choosing a potential career. Chapter 14 adds new research about the relative importance of job-finding approaches. Chapter 15 describes how perfectionism contributes to procrastination and provides a quiz for measuring perfectionism. Chapter 16 adds information about cyber-networking and developing a personal board of directors.

Several more complex cases have been added, many self-assessment exercises have been revised, and many new ones added. Over 50 percent of the cases and examples are new. As well, there are several new Canada Today features and others have been updated with the most recent data available at the time of writing.

Many of the new additions were a direct result of Canadian research on the employability skills that will be required for workers now and in the future. Today's workplace looks very different from the workplace of 20 years ago. This book provides students with the skills required for this new workplace as well as the foundation for building a satisfying personal life.

Instructor's Manual and Test Item File

The Instructor's Manual for this text contains over 750 test questions, chapter outline and lecture notes, answers to discussion questions and case problems, and comments about the exercises.

Acknowledgments

This book was certainly not written in isolation and could not have been accomplished without the assistance of many people. Many thanks go to the team that helped put this book together, which includes Marianne Minaker, Andrew Simpson, Söğüt Y. Güleç, Martin Townsend, and Julie Fletcher. I am sure there are many others behind the scenes who also deserve my gratitude.

On my work front at the college, Debora Windover also deserves mention as an exemplary team leader and supporter of my writing endeavours. I would also like to thank many of my co-workers who supported me through this and offered many wonderful ideas.

Thanks to the outside reviewers, Gary Anderson, Camosun College; Denise Blay, Fanshawe College; Anne Gelsheimer, Seneca College; Terry Macklem, Oulton's Business College; and Elizabeth Skitmore, Algonquin College, who provided many suggestions for improving this book.

Thanks also to my family members and friends, whose emotional and spiritual support also assisted me in this project. Without all of you this book would have not been possible.

About the Authors

An accomplished author, Andrew J. DuBrin, Ph.D., brings to his work years of research experience in business psychology. His research has been reported in *Entrepreneur, Psychology Today, The Wall Street Journal,* and over 100 national magazines and local newspapers. An active speaker, Dr. DuBrin has appeared as a guest on over 350 radio and television shows. He has published numerous articles, textbooks, and well-publicized professional books. Dr. DuBrin received his Ph.D. from Michigan State University and is currently teaching management and organizational behaviour at the Rochester Institute of Technology.

Terri Geerinck is a faculty member in the Interdisciplinary Studies Centre at Sir Sandford Fleming College. She teaches several courses including Introductory Psychology, Social Psychology, and Interpersonal and Group Dynamics. As part of a team, she has also delivered human relations training to business and industry with a particular emphasis on problem solving, interpersonal communication skills, and conflict management. Her teaching interests are instructional design, methodology, prior learning assessment, and course conversion to web-based formats. Before teaching at Sir Sandford Fleming, she held various consulting positions in several communities in Ontario. Terri Geerinck's formal education includes a Bachelor of Arts degree in psychology and sociology from Brock University and a master's degree in education from Central Michigan University.

Human Relations and Yourself

Learning Outcomes

After studying the information and doing the exercises in this chapter, you should be able to

- explain the meaning of human relations
- pinpoint how work and personal life influence each other
- explain how the self-concept influences behaviour
- summarize the nature and consequences of self-esteem
- describe how to improve your self-concept and self-esteem
- be aware of the dangers of preoccupation with the self

Bryant, a computer operator, works effectively with other people in computer operations. He is quiet, but sincere and hardworking. Bryant's job doesn't require much conversation because he is always caught up in running computers. Off the job, he is a loner. He would like to make friends, but he doesn't take the initiative to reach out to people. Bryant prefers work to personal life, largely because he deals better with people in a computer centre than in a social setting.

Tony, a youth services worker, has difficulty dealing with co-workers at the group home where he works days. He resents the low wages and recent government cutbacks in services. At times, he takes his anger out on clients. Tony's supervisor wrote on his last performance evaluation that "Tony is too short with people to last very long with us." Off the job, Tony's personality becomes more positive. He can be mildly sarcastic at times, but his friends and family realize that Tony's sharpness is a small price to pay for his devotion and friendship.

Linda, a restaurant manager, is a likeable person who interacts well with people both on and off the job. Linda is only 20 years old, while several of the people who work for her are in their mid-20s. As one of them puts it, "Who cares if Linda is young? The woman is a natural leader." Despite Linda's nontraditional working hours, she has many friends with whom she shares her free time. Her friends include day-shift people and night-shift people. They are particularly impressed with her smooth and confident manner and her ability to be a good listener at the same time.

The three people just described tell us something about the meaning of human relations. Bryant practises a limited type of human relations. He deals effectively with people primarily on the job. Tony is the opposite. He is effective with people primarily in social settings. Linda practises the type of human relations emphasized in this book—she is effective with people in both work and personal settings.

In the context used here, **human relations** is the art of using systematic knowledge about human behaviour to improve personal and career effectiveness. In other words, you can accomplish more in dealing with people in both personal and work life. You can do so by relying on guidelines developed by psychologists, counsellors, and other human relations specialists.

This book presents a wide variety of suggestions and guidelines for improving your personal relationships both on and off the job. Most of them are based on systematic knowledge about human behaviour. Our main concern, however, will be with the suggestions and guidelines themselves, not the methods by which these ideas were discovered.

How Work and Personal Life Influence Each Other

Most people reading this book will be doing so to improve their careers. Therefore, the book focuses on relationships with people in a job setting. Keep in mind that human relationships in work and personal life have much in common. If we followed the cases of Bryant and Tony over an extended period of time, we would probably discover certain similarities in their relationships with people on and off the job. As Bryant continued to develop confidence in his role as a computer operator, he would slowly become more effective in handling people off the job. Impressed with his job skills, a few of his co-workers might begin to invite him to social gatherings. As Tony became increasingly bitter about his job, some of his bitterness would probably spill over into his personal relationships. His occasional sarcasm might turn into a steady flow of verbal abuse toward others.

A recent US study based on a nationwide sample supports the close relationship between job satisfaction and life satisfaction. The study found that job satisfaction and life satisfaction influence each other. Life satisfaction significantly influenced job satisfaction, and job satisfaction significantly influenced life satisfaction. The relationship between job and life satisfaction is particularly strong at a given time in a person's life. However, being satisfied with your job today has a smaller effect on future life satisfaction.[1]

Work and personal life influence each other in a number of specific ways. First, the satisfactions you achieve on the job contribute to your general life satisfactions. Conversely, if you suffer from chronic job dissatisfaction, your life satisfaction will begin to decline. Career disappointments have been shown to cause marital relationships to suffer. Frustrated on the job, many people start feuding with their partners and other family members.

Second, an unsatisfying job can also affect physical health, primarily by creating stress and burnout. Intense job dissatisfaction may even lead to heart disease, ulcers, intestinal disorders, and skin problems. People who have high job satisfaction even tend to live longer than those who suffer from prolonged job dissatisfaction.[2] Finding the right type of job may thus add years to a person's life.

Third, the quality of your work relationships influences the quality of your personal relationships, and vice versa. If you experience intense conflict in your family, you might be so upset that you will be unable to form good relationships with co-workers. Conversely, if you have a healthy, rewarding personal life, it will be easier for you to form good relationships on the job. People you meet on the job will find it pleasant to relate to a seemingly positive and untroubled person.

Relationships on the job also influence personal relationships. Interacting harmoniously with co-workers can put one in a better mood for dealing with family and friends after hours. Crossing swords with employees and customers during working hours can make it difficult for you to feel comfortable and relaxed with people off the job.

Fourth, certain skills contribute to success in both work and personal life. For example, people who know how to deal effectively with others and get things accomplished on the job can use the same skills to enhance their personal lives. Similarly, people who are effective in dealing with friends and family members, and who can organize things, are likely to be effective supervisors.

Can you think of other ways in which success in work and success in personal life are related?

Another way of understanding how work life and personal life influence each other is to be aware of what employers are doing to help workers balance work and family demands. During the last decade, companies have established a variety of programs that make it easier for employees to meet the demands of career and family life. A major rationale for these programs is that workers who have their personal lives under control can concentrate better at work. As a result, they will be more productive. In addition, workers who have family obligations running smoothly will attend work more regularly. The challenge of balancing work and family demands is particularly intense for employees who are part of a two-wage-earner family, a group that includes 80 percent of the workforce in Canada. As well, the challenge may be even more difficult for a single working parent.

Eddie Bauer, the casual lifestyle retailer with locations in both the United States and Canada, is an example of a company that recognizes the close connection between work and personal life. Balance between home and work is a strong corporate value at Eddie Bauer. The company uses its work/life programs to help its associates (the company term for employees) lead more productive and balanced lives. Management at Eddie Bauer believes that physical and mental fitness contribute to a productive and satisfied workforce. The various programs help associates to be more focused at work because they know resources are available to help them manage the demands of their personal lives. Over the past several years, the company has introduced more than 20 programs to help associates run their lives more smoothly. For example, Balance Days are offered—a free day intended for associates to schedule a "call in well" absence, once a year. Also, the company offers a Customized Work Environment program that enables associates to choose job-sharing (where one job is divided between two people), a compressed work week (such as working 40 hours in four days), or working at home.[3]

Many other companies offer similar programs and arrangements that allow better personal balancing of home and work demands. Many companies, such as IBM Canada, offer *flextime* arrangements. With flextime, all employees must be present for a certain number of core hours (such as 10 a.m. to 3 p.m.), but the employees design the rest of their days or hours according to their own schedule. According to Human Resources Development Canada, flextime is widespread in Canada.[4] Almost one-fifth of the paid Canadian workforce reported being on a flextime arrangement in 1995, up significantly from previous years.[5]

Compressed work weeks are another work option that some employers offer. According to Human Resources Development Canada, between 14 and 24 percent of Canadian workplaces offer this type of work, but only one-fifth to one one-third of employees take advantage of this offer.[6]

Teleworking, another work arrangement, entails working at a location outside the workplace, usually at home. This type of work, also known as *telecommuting*, can be part-time or full-time and may involve the use of computers, the internet, and other electronic processing of information. See the Canada Today feature below to learn more about this work alternative.

Two studies by Health Canada, however, offer evidence that argues against the notion of supportive work arrangements by concerned and sensitive employers.[7] For example, one finding of these studies is that one in four employees work more than 50 hours per week— up from one in ten in 1991. Also, employees donate a significant amount of time to unpaid overtime work and spend more time doing work at home after hours. The results from studies such as these indicate more than ever that you need to develop a variety of skills and facilities to balance the increasing demands of the workplace while seeking personal life satisfaction. One such facility is self-understanding.

Telecommuting as an Alternative Work Arrangement

Now that advances in technology—from voice mail to email to the internet—have made telecommuting possible, you would think that people would flock to this type of work! You don't have to dress up, no one notices if you are late, there is no commuting, you save money, and you can take a break when you feel like it. The advantages of telecommuting include these:

- **Teleworkers can set their own pace.**
- **They save money on fuel, tolls, transit fares, food, and clothing (you can work in your PJs!).**
- **They have the opportunity to balance their work and family lives better.**
- **They enjoy more flexible scheduling.**
- **They are less exposed to office politics.**

So has telecommuting become popular? In fact, the numbers haven't changed much over the last few years. In 2001, the number of people who worked at home in Canada via telecommuting was only 6.3%, down one-tenth of a percent since 1991. So the number of teleworkers has remained relatively stable even with the technological advances in the last few years. Working at home is more popular in British Columbia—Victoria being the leader—than in the metropolitan Toronto area.

So why aren't more people taking advantage of this work arrangement when it is offered? According to two different sources, some of the disadvantages of telecommuting outweigh the advantages.

- **Some teleworkers may feel socially isolated and miss the social interaction of the office. The social isolation is worsened if office-bound colleagues are jealous of the opportunity to telework.**
- **Professional isolation may also be a problem. When you are not at the office, you may have less influence because you are not there when a problem occurs or a decision is made. The teleworker may also have fewer career and promotional opportunities because of decreased visibility. In an era of downsizing and layoffs, many workers don't want to skip the office atmosphere.**
- **Other people may lack the focus to telework and get easily distracted.**

The bottom line may be personal fit. If you like to work on your own, do not get easily distracted, feel secure in your job, and can do your job via teleworking, you may want to examine this alternative. You can start by visiting the Canadian Telework Association website at **www.ivc.ca**.

NOTES:

"Advantages and Disadvantages of Telework for Teleworkers," at **www.ivc.ca/proteleworkers.html**.

Statistics Canada, 2001 Census, Where Canadians Work and How They Get There, #96F0030XIE2001010.

Lorrayne Athony, " 'Telecommuting' trend hasn't taken off," *The Peterborough Examiner*, February 21, 2003, p. A6.

The increasing availability of such different types of work may lead to many questions as we choose or change careers. If you had to choose an alternative work arrangement, which one would you select? What do you see as advantages and disadvantages of each type of arrangement? With the increased presence of the internet, do you think teleworking will be a great wave in the future?

Human Relations Begins with Self-Understanding

Before you can understand other people very well, you must understand yourself. All readers of this book already know something about themselves. An important starting point in learning more about yourself is self-examination. Suppose that instead of being about human relations, this book were about dancing. The reader would obviously need to know what other dancers do right and wrong. But the basic principles of dancing could not be fully grasped unless they were seen in relation to your own style of dancing. Watching a videotape of your dancing, for example, would be helpful. You might also ask other people for comments and suggestions about your dance movements.

Similarly, to achieve **self-understanding**, you must gather valid information about yourself. (Self-understanding refers to knowledge about oneself, particularly with respect to mental and emotional aspects.) Every time you read a self-help book, take a personality quiz, or receive an evaluation of your work from a manager or instructor, you are gaining some self-knowledge.

In achieving self-understanding, it is helpful to recognize that the **self** is a complex idea. It generally refers to a person's total being or individuality. However, a distinction is sometimes made between the self a person projects to the outside world and the inner self. The **public self** is what the person is communicating about himself or herself, and what others actually perceive about the person. The **private self** is the actual person that one is.[8] To avoid making continual distinctions between the various selves throughout this text, we will use the term *self* to refer to an accurate representation of the individual.

Although an entire chapter in this book is devoted to the self, that is not meant to imply that the other chapters do not deal with the self. Most of this text is geared toward using human relations knowledge for self-development and self-improvement. Throughout the text you will find questionnaires designed to improve insight. The self-knowledge emphasized here deals with psychological characteristics (such as personality traits and thinking style) rather than physical ones (such as height and blood pressure).

Here we discuss six types of information that contribute to self-understanding:

- General information about human behaviour
- Informal feedback from people
- Feedback from employers, managers, and team leaders
- Feedback from co-workers
- Feedback from self-assessment quizzes
- Insights gathered in psychotherapy and counselling

General Information about Human Behaviour

As you learn about people in general, you should also be gaining knowledge about yourself. Therefore, most of the information in this text is presented in a form that should be useful to you personally. Whenever general information is presented, it is your responsibility to relate such information to your particular situation. Chapter 7, for example, discusses some causes of conflicts in personal relationships. One such general cause is limited resources; that is, not everyone can have what he or she wants. Consider how this general principle applies to you. An example involving others is, "That's why I've been so angry with Melissa lately. She was the one given the promotion, while I'm stuck in the same old job."

In relating facts and observations about people in general to yourself, be careful not to misapply the information. Feedback from other people will help you avoid the pitfalls of introspection (looking into oneself).

Informal Feedback from People

As just implied, **feedback** is information that tells you how well you have performed. You can sometimes obtain feedback from the spontaneous comments of others, or by asking them for feedback. A materials-handling specialist grew one notch in self-confidence when co-workers began to call him "Lightning." He was given this name because of the rapidity with which he processed orders. His experience illustrates that a valuable source of information for self-understanding is what the significant people in your life think of you. Although feedback of this type might make you feel uncomfortable, when it is consistent, it accurately reflects how you are perceived by others.

With some ingenuity you can create informal feedback. (In this sense, the term *informal* refers to not being part of a company-sponsored program.) A student enrolled in a human relations course obtained valuable information about himself from a questionnaire he sent to 15 people. Here are his directions:

> I am hoping that you can help me with one of the most important assignments of my life. I want to obtain a candid picture of how I am seen by others—what they think are my strengths, weaknesses, good points, and bad points. Any other observations about me as an individual would also be welcome.
>
> Write down your thoughts on the enclosed sheet of paper. The information that you provide will help me develop a plan for personal improvement that I am writing for a course in human relations. Mail the form back to me in the enclosed envelope. It is not necessary for you to sign the form.

A few sceptics will argue that friends never give you a true picture of yourself, but rather say flattering things about you because they value your friendship. Experience has shown, however, that if you emphasize the importance of their opinions, most people will give you a few constructive suggestions. You also have to appear to be sincere. Since not everyone's comments will be helpful, you may have to sample many people.

Feedback from Employers, Managers, and Team Leaders

Virtually all employers provide employees with formal and/or informal feedback on their performance. A formal method of feedback is called a *performance appraisal.* During a performance appraisal your manager or team leader will convey to you what he or she thinks you are doing well and not so well. These observations become a permanent part of your personnel record. Informal feedback occurs when a manager or team leader discusses your job performance with you but does not record these observations.

The feedback obtained from managers in this way can help you learn about yourself. For instance, if two different managers say that you are a creative problem solver, you might conclude that you are creative. If several managers told you that you are too impatient with other people, you might conclude that you are impatient.

Given that work life consumes so much of a working adult's time, it becomes a valuable source of information about the self. Many people, in fact, base much of their identity on their occupations. Next time you are at a social gathering, ask a person "What do you do?" Most likely, the person will respond in terms of an occupation or a company affiliation. It is a rare person in our culture who responds, "I sleep, I eat, I watch television, and I talk to friends."

Feedback from Co-Workers

A growing practice in organizations is to carry out **peer evaluations**, a system in which co-workers contribute to an evaluation of a person's job performance. Although co-workers under this system do not have total responsibility for evaluating each other, their input is taken seriously. The amount of a worker's salary increase could thus be affected by peer judgments about his or her performance. The results of peer evaluations can also be used as feedback for learning about yourself. Assume that co-workers agree on several of your strengths and needs for improvement. You can conclude that you are generally perceived that way by others who work closely with you.

Customer service technicians (people who service and repair photocopying machines) at Xerox Corporation use an elaborate system of peer evaluations. A group of peers indicates whether a particular aspect of job performance or behaviour is a strength or a *developmental opportunity.* "Developmental opportunity" is a positive way of looking at a weakness. The five factors rated by peers are shown in Exhibit 1-1. The initials under "Peer Evaluations" are those of the co-workers who are doing the evaluations. The person being rated thus knows who to thank (or kick) for the feedback.

In addition to indicating whether a job factor is a strength or an opportunity, raters can supply comments and developmental suggestions. For example, CJ made the following written comment about Leslie Fantasia: "Missed 50 percent of our work group meetings. Attend work group member training and review our work group meeting ground rules."

Feedback from Self-Examination Quizzes

Many self-help books, including this one, contain questionnaires and quizzes that you fill out by yourself, for yourself. The information that you pick up from these questionnaires often provides valuable clues to your preferences, values, and personal traits. Such self-examination questionnaires should not be confused with the scientifically researched tests you might take in a counselling centre or guidance department, or when applying for a job.

exhibit 1-1

Peer Evaluation of Customer Service Technician

PERSON EVALUATED: Leslie Fantasia

Skill Categories and Expected Behaviours	*Peer Evaluations for Each Category and Behaviour*					
	TR	JP	CK	JT	CJ	ML
Customer Care						
Takes ownership for customer problems	O	S	S	S	S	S
Follows through on customer commitments	S	S	S	S	S	S
Technical Knowledge and Skill						
Engages in continuous learning to update technical skills	O	S	S	S	S	O
Corrects problems on the first visit	O	O	S	S	S	S
Work Group Support						
Actively participates in work group meetings	S	S	S	S	O	S
Backs up other work group members by taking calls in other areas	S	O	O	S	S	S
Minimal absence	S	O	S	S	O	S
Finance Management						
Adheres to work group parts expense process	S	S	S	O	S	S
Passes truck audits	S	S	S	O	S	S

NOTE: S refers to a strength, O refers to developmental opportunity.

The amount of useful information gained from self-examination questionnaires depends on your candour. Since no outside judge is involved in these self-help quizzes, candour is usually not a problem. An exception is that we all have certain blind spots. Most people, for example, believe that they have considerably above-average skills in dealing with people.

As a starting point in conducting self-examination quizzes, fill out Human Relations Self-Assessment Quiz 1-1. The quiz will help get you into the self-examination mode.

Insights Gathered in Psychotherapy and Counselling

Many people seek self-understanding through discussions with a psychotherapist or other professional counsellor. **Psychotherapy** is a method of overcoming emotional problems through discussion with a mental health professional. However, many people enter into psychotherapy with the primary intention of gaining insight into themselves. A representative area of insight would be for the therapist to help the client detect patterns of self-defeating and self-destructive behaviour. For example, some people unconsciously do something to ruin a personal relationship or perform poorly on the job just when things are going well. The therapist might point out this self-defeating pattern of behaviour. Self-insight of this kind often—but not always—leads to useful changes in behaviour.

Your Self-Concept: What You Think of You

Another aspect of self-understanding is your **self-concept**, or what you think of you and who you think you are. A successful person—one who is achieving his or her goals in work or personal life—usually has a positive self-concept. In contrast, an unsuccessful person often has a negative self-concept. Such differences in self-concept can have a profound influence on your career.[9] If you see yourself as a successful person, you will tend to engage in activities that will help you prove this view of yourself right. Similarly, if you have a limited view of yourself, you will tend to engage in activities that prove that limited view right. For example, you may often look for convenient ways to prevent yourself from succeeding.

Self-concepts are based largely on our perceptions of what others have said about us and others' reactions to us. This process of incorporating what others have said about us into our self-concept is known as **reflected appraisal**. Reflected appraisal tends to occur most often when the same thing is told to us by many different people. If enough people tell you that you are "terrific," after a while you will have the self-concept of a terrific person. When people tell you that you are not a worthwhile person, after a while your self-concept will become that of a not-worthwhile person. People who say "I'm OK" are expressing a positive self-concept. People who say "I'm not OK" have a negative self-concept.

We also compare ourselves with others to examine how different we are from others. Through this process of **social comparison**, we describe ourselves in terms of the ways in which we stand out from others around us. These comparisons also become part of our self-concept. For example, you ask others in your class how

The Written Self-Portrait

A good starting point in acquiring serious self-knowledge is to prepare a written self-portrait in the major life spheres (or aspects). In each of the spheres listed below, describe yourself in about 25–75 words. For example, under the social and interpersonal sphere, a person might write: "I'm a little timid on the surface. But those people who get to know me well understand that I'm filled with enthusiasm and joy. My relationships with people last a long time. I'm on excellent terms with all members of my family. And my spouse and I have been together for five years. We are very close emotionally, and should be together for a lifetime."

A. *Occupational and School:*

____

____

____

____

B. *Social and Interpersonal:*

____

____

____

____

C. *Beliefs, Values, and Attitudes:*

____

____

____

____

D. *Physical Description (body type, appearance, grooming):*

____

____

____

____

they did on the last test. Your grade is far better than others in your class. If this is a pattern (your grades higher than others' grades), then you may describe yourself as smarter (at least academically) than the majority of the students in your business program.

Another important fact about the self-concept is that it usually has several components. Many people, for example, have an academic self-concept and a nonacademic self-concept.[10] One person might feel proud and confident in a classroom yet quite humble and shaky on the job. Another person might feel unsure and uneasy in the classroom yet proud and confident on the job. Following the same logic, a person's self-concept with respect to personal life may differ from his or her career self-concept.

The experiences that we have, our changing abilities and knowledge, and our interactions with others create a complex self-concept. The self-concept can change and we can improve how we feel about ourselves. Several strategies to improve your self-concept and self-esteem will be reviewed later in the chapter.

The Self-Concept and Self-Confidence

A strong self-concept leads to self-confidence, which has many important implications for job performance. People who are confident in themselves are more effective in leadership and sales positions. Self-confident workers are also more likely to set higher goals for themselves and to persist in trying to reach their goals.[11]

Why some people develop strong self-concepts and self-confidence while others have weak self-concepts and self-confidence is not entirely known. One contributing factor may be inherited talents and abilities. Assume that a person quickly learns how to perform key tasks in life such as walking, talking, swimming, running, reading, writing, computing, and driving a car. This person is likely to be more self-confident than a person who struggled to learn these skills.

Another contributing factor to a positive self-concept and self-confidence is lifelong feedback from others (as mentioned above). If, as a youngster, your parents, siblings, and playmates consistently told you that you were competent, you would probably develop a strong self-concept. However, some people might find you to be conceited.

Self-confidence also contributes heavily to leadership ability. How to build self-confidence will therefore be described in Chapter 12, which deals with becoming a leader.

Your Body Image as Part of Your Self-Concept

Our discussion of the self-concept so far has emphasized mental traits and characteristics. Your **body image**, or your perception of your body, also contributes to your self-concept.[12] The current emphasis on physical fitness stems largely from a desire on the part of people to be physically fit and healthy. It is also apparent that being physically fit contributes to a positive self-concept, and being physically unfit can contribute to a negative self-concept. The relationship between the self-concept and physical fitness also works the other way: If your self-concept is positive it may push you toward physical fitness. Conversely, if you have a negative self-concept you may allow yourself to become physically unfit.

A distorted body image can result in severe problems such as anorexia nervosa. Anorexic people have such an intense fear of obesity that they under-eat to the point of malnutrition and illness. About five percent will die from their disorder. Having a positive body image is obviously important for personal life. For example, some people who are dissatisfied with their bodies will not engage in sports or attend activities where too much of their bodies is revealed. Also, having a positive body image helps one be more confident in making new friends.

A positive body image can also be important for work life. Employees who have a positive body image are likely to feel confident performing jobs that require customer contact, such as sales work. Many business firms today expect their managers to appear physically fit and to present a vigorous, healthy appearance. Managers and customer-contact workers with these qualities would generally have positive body images.

Group Identification and the Self-Concept

Similar to the process of social comparison, another important source of the self-concept is the small groups people join. People not only compare themselves with others, but choose groups that are attractive to them. For example, if you feel that you are athletic you may join sports groups. As part of a baseball team or some other team, you begin to identify yourself as a baseball player as well as a member of this specific team.

Also, according to research by social psychologist Marilynn Brewer, people join small groups to achieve some degree of individuality and identity.[13] People develop much of their self-concepts by comparing their own group with others. The group you identify with becomes part of your psychological self. Joining the group satisfies two conflicting needs. A person wants to retain some individuality, so being a member of a mega-group like students or General Motors employees does not quite do the job. Yet people also yearn to have some group affiliation. So joining a small group that is distinctive from others is a happy compromise.

The smaller group the person joins becomes part of the self-image and self-concept for many people. A sampling of the kinds of groups that could become part of a person's self-concept might include athletic teams, church groups, street gangs, musical bands, volunteer committees, and internet chat rooms. What group memberships have become part of your self-concept?

The Nature and Consequences of Self-Esteem

Although the various approaches to discussing the self may seem confusing and overlapping, all of them strongly influence your life. A particularly important role is played by **self-esteem**, which refers to appreciating self-worth and importance, being accountable for your own behaviour, and acting responsibly toward others.[14] People with positive self-esteem have a deep-down, inside-the-self feeling of their own worth. Consequently, they develop a positive self-concept. Before reading further, you are invited to measure your current level of self-esteem by taking our

Human Relations Self-Assessment Quiz 1-2. We look next at the nature of self-esteem and many of its consequences.

The Nature of Self-Esteem

The definition just presented tells a lot about self-esteem, yet there is much more to know about its nature. According to Nathaniel Branden, self-esteem has two interrelated components: self-efficacy and self-respect.[15] **Self-efficacy** is confidence in your ability to carry out a specific task in contrast to generalized self-confidence. When self-efficacy is high, you believe you have the ability to do what is necessary to complete a task successfully. Being confident that you can perform a particular task well contributes to self-esteem.

Self-respect, the second component of self-esteem, refers to how you think and feel about yourself. Self-respect fits the everyday meaning of self-esteem. Many street beggars are intelligent, able-bodied, and have a good physical appearance. You could argue that their low self-esteem leads them to beg. Also, people with low self-respect and self-esteem allow themselves to stay in relationships where they are frequently verbally and physically abused. These abused people have such low self-worth they think they deserve punishment.

Part of understanding the nature of self-esteem is knowing how it develops. As with the self-concept, self-esteem comes about from a variety of early-life experiences. People who were encouraged to feel good about themselves and their accomplishments by family members, friends, and teachers are more likely to enjoy high self-esteem. A widespread explanation of self-esteem development is that compliments, praise, and hugs alone build self-esteem. Yet many developmental psychologists seriously question this perspective. Instead, they believe that self-esteem results from accomplishing worthwhile activities and then feeling proud of these accomplishments. Receiving encouragement, however, can help the person accomplish activities that build self-esteem.

Psychologist Martin Seligman argues that self-esteem is caused by a variety of successes and failures. To develop self-esteem people need to improve their skills for dealing with the world.[16] Self-esteem therefore comes about through genuine accomplishments, followed by praise and recognition. Heaping undeserved praise and recognition on people may lead to a temporary high, but it does not produce genuine self-esteem. The child develops self-esteem not from being told he or she can score a goal in soccer, but from scoring that goal.

The Consequences of Self-Esteem

One of the major consequences of high self-esteem is good mental health. People with high self-esteem feel good about themselves and have a positive outlook on life. One of the links between good mental health and self-esteem is that high self-esteem helps prevent many situations from being stressful. Few negative comments from others are likely to bother you when your self-esteem is high. A person with low self-esteem might crumble if somebody insulted his or her appearance. A person with high self-esteem might shrug off the insult as simply being the other person's point of view. If faced with an everyday setback such as

The Self-Esteem Checklist

Indicate whether each of the following statements is Mostly True or Mostly False, as it applies to you.

	Mostly True	Mostly False
1. I am excited about starting each day.	______	______
2. Most of any progress I have made in my work or school can be attributed to luck.	______	______
3. I often ask myself, "Why can't I be more successful?"	______	______
4. When I'm given a challenging assignment by my manager or team leader, I usually dive in with confidence.	______	______
5. I believe that I am working up to my potential.	______	______
6. I can set limits to what I will do for others without feeling anxious.	______	______
7. I regularly make excuses for my mistakes.	______	______
8. Someone else's bad mood will affect my good mood.	______	______
9. I care very much how much money other people make, especially when they are working in my field.	______	______
10. I feel like a failure when I do not achieve my goals.	______	______
11. Hard work gives me an emotional lift.	______	______
12. When others compliment me, I doubt their sincerity.	______	______
13. Complimenting others makes me feel uncomfortable.	______	______
14. I find it comfortable to say, "I'm sorry."	______	______
15. It is difficult for me to face up to my mistakes.	______	______
16. My co-workers think I should not be promoted.	______	______
17. People who want to become my friends usually do not have much to offer.	______	______
18. If my manager praised me, I would have a difficult time believing it was deserved.	______	______
19. I'm just an ordinary person.	______	______
20. Having to face change really disturbs me.	______	______

Scoring and Interpretation: The answers in the high-self-esteem direction are as follows:

1. Mostly True	6. Mostly True	11. Mostly True	16. Mostly False
2. Mostly False	7. Mostly False	12. Mostly False	17. Mostly False
3. Mostly False	8. Mostly False	13. Mostly False	18. Mostly False
4. Mostly True	9. Mostly False	14. Mostly True	19. Mostly False
5. Mostly True	10. Mostly False	15. Mostly False	20. Mostly False

17–20: You have very high self-esteem. Yet if your score is 20, it could be that you are denying any self-doubts.
11–16: Your self-esteem is in the average range. It would probably be worthwhile for you to implement strategies to boost your self-esteem (described in this chapter) so that you can develop a greater feeling of well-being.
0–10: Your self-esteem needs bolstering. Talk over your feelings about yourself with a trusted friend or with a mental health professional. At the same time, attempt to implement several of the tactics for boosting self-esteem described in this chapter.

losing keys, the high-self-esteem person might think, "I have so much going for me, why fall apart over this incident?"

Although people with high self-esteem can readily shrug off undeserved insults, they still profit well from negative feedback. Because they are secure, they can profit from the developmental opportunities suggested by negative feedback.

Workers with high self-esteem develop and maintain favourable work attitudes and perform at a high level. These positive consequences take place because such attitudes and behaviour are consistent with the personal belief that they are competent individuals. Mary Kay Ash, the legendary founder of a beauty-products company, put it this way, "It never occurred to me I couldn't do it. I always knew that if I worked hard enough, I could." Furthermore, research has shown that high-self-esteem individuals value reaching work goals more than do low-self-esteem individuals.[17]

The combined effect of workers having high self-esteem helps a company prosper. Long-term research by Branden suggests that self-esteem is a critical source of competitive advantage in an information-based society. Companies gain the edge when, in addition to having an educated workforce, employees have high self-esteem, as shown by behaviours such as the following:

- Being creative and innovative
- Taking personal responsibility for problems
- Feeling independent while still wanting to work cooperatively with others
- Trusting one's own capabilities
- Taking the initiative to solve problems[18]

Behaviours such as these help workers cope with the challenge of a rapidly changing workplace where products and ideas become obsolete quickly. Workers with high self-esteem are more likely to be able to cope with new challenges regularly because they are confident they can master their environment.

A major consequence of low self-esteem is poor mental health. People with low self-esteem are often depressed, and many people who appear to have "paranoid personalities" are suffering from low self-esteem. A store manager who continually accused store associates of talking behind his back finally said to a mental health counsellor, "Face it, I think I'm almost worthless, so I think people have negative things to say about me."

Schoolchildren with low self-esteem are more likely to be delinquents. These same students generally have a poor relationship with teachers and parents.[19] Workers with low self-esteem often develop and maintain unfavourable work attitudes and perform below average. These negative behaviours are consistent with the self-belief that they are people of low competence.[20]

How to Enhance Self-Esteem

Improving self-esteem is a lifelong process because self-esteem is related to the success of your activities and interactions with people. Following are four approaches to enhancing self-esteem that are related to how self-esteem develops.

Legitimate Accomplishment and Self-Esteem

To emphasize again, accomplishing worthwhile activities is a major contributor to self-esteem in both children and adults. Recent social science research suggests this sequence of events: Person establishes a goal → person pursues the goal → person achieves the goal → person develops esteem-like feelings.[21] The opposite point of view is this sequence: Person develops esteem-like feelings → person establishes a goal → person pursues the goal → person achieves the goal.

The comments of columnist Mona Charen support years of psychological research: "Self-esteem does not come in a jar. To be real, self-esteem must be based on something true. A child doesn't get a sense of accomplishment and pride by being told, 'You can ride a bicycle.' She gets it by riding the bike."[22] Similarly, giving people large trophies for mundane accomplishments is unlikely to raise self-esteem. More likely, the person will see through the transparent attempt to build his or her self-esteem and develop negative feelings about the self. What about you? Would your self-esteem receive a bigger boost by (1) receiving an A in a course in which 10 percent of the class received an A, or (2) receiving an A in a class in which everybody received the same grade?

Awareness of Strengths and Self-Esteem

Another method of improving your self-esteem is to develop an appreciation of your strengths and accomplishments. Research with over 60 executives showed that their self-concepts became more positive after one month of practising this exercise for a few minutes every day.[23] A good starting point is to list your strengths and accomplishments on paper. This list is likely to be more impressive than you expected. The list of strengths and accomplishments requested in the Human Relations Self-Assessment Quiz 1-3 can be used for building self-esteem.

You can sometimes develop an appreciation of your strengths by participating in a group exercise designed for such purposes. A group of about seven people meet to form a support group. All group members first spend about ten minutes answering the question, "What are my three strongest points, attributes, or skills?" After each group member has recorded his or her three strengths, that person discusses them with the other group members.

Each group member then comments on the list. Other group members sometimes add to your list of strengths or reinforce what you have to say. Sometimes you may find disagreement. One member told the group: "I'm handsome, intelligent, reliable, athletic, self-confident, and very moral. I also have a good sense of humour." Another group member retorted, "And I might add that you're unbearably conceited."

Minimize Settings and Interactions That Detract from Your Feelings of Competence

Most of us have situations in work and personal life that make us feel less than our best. If you can minimize exposure to those situations, you will have fewer feelings of incompetence. The problem with feeling incompetent is that it lowers your self-esteem. An office supervisor said she detested company picnics, most of all because she was forced into playing softball. At her own admission, she had less aptitude for athletics than any able-bodied person she knew. In addition, she felt uncomfortable with the small-talk characteristic of picnics. To minimize dis-

The Self-Knowledge Questionnaire

Complete the following questionnaire for your personal use. You might wish to use a worksheet before putting your comments in final form.

I. Education

1. How far have I gone in school?
2. What is my major field of interest?
3. Which are (or have been) my best subjects?
4. Which are (or have been) my poorest subjects?
5. What further educational plans do I have? Why?
6. What extracurricular activities have I participated in?
7. Which ones did I enjoy? Why?

II. Work Experience

8. What jobs have I held since age 16?
9. What aspect of these jobs did I enjoy? Why?
10. What aspect of these jobs did I dislike? Why?
11. What were my three biggest accomplishments on the job?
12. What kind of employee am (was) I?
13. What compliments did I receive from my managers, co-workers, or customers?
14. What criticisms or suggestions did I receive?
15. What would be an ideal job for me?

III. Attitudes toward People

16. The kind of people I get along best with are...
17. The kind of people I clash with are...
18. How many close friends do I have? What is it I like about each one?
19. Would I prefer working mostly with men or women? Why?
20. How much contact with other people do I need?
21. My arguments with other people are mostly about...

IV. Attitudes toward and Perceptions of Myself

22. What are my strengths?
23. What are my weaknesses or opportunities for improvement?
24. What do I think of me?
25. What do I worry about most?
26. What is my biggest problem?
27. What things in life do I dislike?
28. What have I accomplished in life so far?
29. Has this been enough accomplishment?
30. So far, what has been the happiest period of my life? Why?
31. What gives me satisfaction in life?
32. In what ways do I make life miserable for myself?
33. What motivates me?

V. How People outside of Work See Me

34. What is the best compliment my spouse (or a good friend) has paid me?
35. In what ways would my spouse (or a good friend) like me to change?
36. What do my friends like best about me?
37. What do my friends dislike about me?

VI. Hobbies, Interests, Sports

38. What activities, hobbies, interests, sports, and so forth do I actively participate in?
39. Which one of these do I really get excited about? Why?

VII. My Future

40. What are my plans for further education and training?
41. What positions would I like to hold within the next five years?
42. What are my career goals beyond five years?
43. Where would I like to be at the peak of my career?
44. What activities and interests would I like to pursue in the future?
45. What goals do I have relating to friends, family, and marriage?

Additional Thoughts

1. What other questions should have been asked of you in the Self-Knowledge Questionnaire?
2. To what use can you put all or part of this information?
3. What impact did completing this questionnaire have on your self-understanding?

comfort, the woman attended only those picnics she thought were absolutely necessary. Instead of playing on the softball team, she volunteered to be the equipment manager.

A problem with avoiding all situations in which you feel lowly competent is that it might prevent you from acquiring needed skills. Also, it boosts your self-confidence and self-esteem to become comfortable in a previously uncomfortable situation.

Talk and Socialize Frequently with People Who Boost Your Self-Esteem

Psychologist Barbara Ilardie says that the people who can raise your self-esteem are usually those with high self-esteem themselves. They are the people who give honest feedback because they respect others and themselves. Such high-self-esteem individuals should not be confused with yes-people who agree with others just to be liked. The point is that you typically receive more from strong people than weak ones. Weak people will flatter you but will not give you the honest feedback you need to build self-esteem.[24]

Potential Disadvantages of Preoccupation with the Self

We have emphasized the importance of understanding the self as a starting point in developing good human relations skills. Much of this chapter was also devoted to the importance of developing self-esteem. Despite the soundness of this advice, a person must also guard against becoming too caught up in the self. A recent study of the self proposes that the modern individual is burdened with a too-weighty self. For many people, the self has too many components, aspiration levels, and hard-to-meet expectations.[25]

Too much attention to the self can lead a person to be self-centred, self-conscious, and uninterested in other people and the outside world. You have met people who include in almost every conversation a statement about their health, and whether they feel hot or cold. The same people are likely to inform others when they are fatigued, even when nobody asked.

Preoccupation with the self can lead to unattainable aspirations. As a consequence of not attaining these aspirations, the person develops a negative self-evaluation. According to one theory, these negative self-evaluations prompt the person to escape the self. The path chosen to escape the self is often alcoholism, drug abuse, and binge eating (bulimia).[26] More will be said about personal problems in Chapter 5.

The right balance is to be concerned about yourself, your self-esteem, and your personal growth yet still focus on the world outside you. Focusing on the outside world can ultimately strengthen the self, because you develop skills and interests that will enhance your self-esteem. Rowan, a supervisor of electronics technicians, explains how his outside interests helped him achieve high self-esteem:

> I used to worry a lot about myself. I used to obsess over the fact that many people my age earned more money and owned better cars. I also used to worry too much about my appearance. Sometimes I would weigh myself several times a day, always hoping that I had shed a pound or two.

It hit me one day that I had the most fun when I could get outside myself and not think so much about me. I then plunged myself further into my hobby of producing home videos. After shooting a scene, such as a trip to Niagara Falls, I would edit the tape to make the production smooth. I showed my edited tapes to a few friends. Before long, many friends and acquaintances were calling me for help in editing their tapes. My reputation as a video expert spread. I felt great about myself that my hobby enabled me to help others.

How Studying Human Relations Can Benefit You

A person who carefully studies the information in this book and incorporates its suggestions into his or her way of doing things should derive the five benefits discussed next. Knowledge itself, however, is not a guarantee of success. Since people differ greatly in learning ability, personality, and life circumstances, some will get more out of this book than will others.

You may, for example, be getting along so well with co-workers or customers that the chapter on this topic is unnecessary from your viewpoint. Or you may be so shy at this stage of your life that you are at present unable to capitalize on some of the tips for being assertive with people. You might have to work doubly hard to reap benefit from that particular chapter.

The major benefits from studying human relations are

- *Acquiring valid information about human behaviour.* To feel comfortable with other people and to make a favourable impression (both on and off the job), one needs to understand how people think and act. This book will provide you with some basic knowledge about interpersonal relationships such as the meaning of emotional security, openness, and nonverbal messages. You will even learn about such things as mimicking another person's body movements in order to improve rapport with that person.
- *Developing skills in dealing with people.* Anyone who aspires to high-level jobs or an enriched social life needs to be able to communicate with others, resolve conflict, and behave in a confident manner. Relating well to diverse cultural groups is also an asset. Studying information about such topics in this book, coupled with trying them out in practice, should help you develop such interpersonal skills.
- *Coping with job problems.* Almost everyone who holds a job inevitably runs into human relations problems. Reading about these problems and suggestions for coping with them could save you considerable inner turmoil. Among the job survival skills that you will learn about in the following chapters are how to cope with job stress and how to overcome what seems to be an overwhelming workload.
- *Coping with personal problems.* We all have problems. An important difference between the effective and ineffective person is that the effective person knows how to manage them. Among the problems this book will help you cope with are shyness, finding a job when you are unemployed, overcoming low self-confidence, and managing stress.

- *Capitalizing on opportunities.* Many readers of this book will someday spend part of their working time taking advantage of opportunities rather than solving daily problems. Every career-minded person needs a few breakthrough experiences in order to make his or her life more rewarding. Toward this end, the book discusses how to get ahead in your career and how to become a leader.

Summary

Human relations is the art and practice of using systematic knowledge about human behaviour to improve personal, job, and career effectiveness.

Work and personal life often influence each other in several ways. A high level of job satisfaction tends to spill over to one's personal life. Conversely, an unsatisfactory personal life could lead to negative job attitudes. Another close tie between work and personal life is that one's job can affect physical and mental health. Severely negative job conditions may lead to a serious stress disorder, such as heart disease.

The quality of one's relationships with people in work and the quality of one's personal relationships influence each other. Also, certain skills (such as the ability to listen) contribute to success in work and personal life.

To be effective in human relationships, you must first understand yourself. Six methods for gaining self-understanding are: (1) acquire general information about human behaviour and apply it to yourself; (2) obtain informal feedback from people; (3) obtain feedback from superiors; (4) obtain feedback from co-workers; (5) obtain feedback from skill-building exercises and self-assessment quizzes; and (6) gather insights in psychotherapy and counselling.

An important aspect of self-understanding is your self-concept, or what you think of you and who you think you are. The self-concept is based largely on what others have said about us. A strong self-concept leads to self-confidence, which is a basic requirement for being successful as a leader or in sales.

Natural abilities contribute to a person's self-concept and level of self-confidence. Your body image, or your perception of your body, also contributes to your self-concept. A positive body image can help you in both your work and personal life because it enhances your self-concept.

Self-esteem refers to appreciating self-worth and importance, being accountable for your own behaviour, and acting responsibly toward others. People with high self-esteem develop a positive self-concept. Self-esteem has two interrelated components: self-efficacy (a task-related feeling of competence) and self-respect. Self-esteem develops from a variety of early-life experiences. People who were encouraged to feel good about themselves and their accomplishments by key people in their lives are more likely to enjoy high self-esteem. Most significantly, self-esteem also results from accomplishing worthwhile activities, and then feeling proud of these accomplishments. Praise and recognition for accomplishments also help develop self-esteem.

Good mental health is one of the major consequences of high self-esteem. One of the links between good mental health and self-esteem is that high self-esteem helps prevent many situations from being stressful. Workers with high self-esteem develop and maintain favourable work attitudes and perform at a high level.

A major consequence of low self-esteem is poor mental health. Schoolchildren with low self-esteem are more likely to be delinquents. Workers with low self-esteem often develop and maintain unfavourable work attitudes and perform below expectations.

Self-esteem can be enhanced in many ways. Accomplishing worthwhile activities is a major contributor to self-esteem in both children and adults. Developing an appreciation of your strengths and accomplishments is another self-esteem builder. It is also important to minimize settings and interactions that detract from your feelings of competence. In addition, talk and socialize frequently with people who boost your self-esteem.

Despite the importance of self-understanding, guard against becoming too caught up in the self. Too much attention to the self can lead a person to be self-centred, self-conscious, and uninterested in other people and the outside world.

Questions and Activities

1. Why is it difficult for a person with poor human relations skills to succeed in business?
2. How important are human relations skills in an era of high technology in the workplace?
3. Many companies now provide child-care facilities for children of employees. What does this employment practice tell you about the relationship between work and personal life?
4. How do some people attempt to combine work and personal life?
5. Give an example from your own experience of how work life influences personal life and vice versa.
6. Whom can a person turn to as the most reliable source of feedback about himself or herself?
7. Of the six sources of information about the self described in this chapter, which one do you think is likely to be the most accurate? Why?
8. How can your self-concept affect your career?
9. Interview a person whom you perceive to have a successful career. Ask that person to describe his or her self-concept. Be prepared to discuss your findings in class.

Internet Skill Builder

Reducing Work/Personal Life Conflict

Search the internet for useful ideas about reducing the conflict between work and personal life or work and family. As a starting point, insert into your search engines phrases like "work/life programs," "work/family conflict," and "balancing the demands of work and family life." Attempt to find at least three practical suggestions you can use to balance these two major demands in the lives of many people.

What Is Human Relations?

Although this text offers a working definition of *human relations,* the term has different meanings. Use the internet to find at least two meanings of the term *human relations.* Because you are using a search engine to chase down an abstract idea, you might have to approach the task from several different directions. You might enter a phrase into your search engine, such as "What is the meaning of human relations?" Or you might search by the term "human relations" or related terms. The idea of this exercise, and subsequent ones in the text, is to help you sharpen your search skills and learn more about specific topics within human relations. Good internet search skills are helpful in many jobs.

Weblinks

www.selfgrowth.com
A site devoted to self-knowledge, self-growth, and self-help. Here you can join up for a free newsletter and read articles about topics devoted to the "self." There is no fee to join this site.

www.mindbodysoul.com
This site is also devoted to self-knowledge, self-growth, and self-help but also includes some different topics, such as astrology. You can obtain a free newsletter from this site as well. However, there are also some areas that you must pay for, for instance if you want your horoscope.

www.hrdc-drhc.gc.ca
This is the site for Human Resources Development Canada. This is a very extensive site which you will want to explore for information on career skills, how to write résumés, and other information on jobs including actual employment listings. There is also a library area where you can look up statistics and articles.

www.utexas.edu/student/cmhc/selfest.html
Consequences of low self-esteem.

Human Relations Case Study

SELF-ESTEEM BUILDING AT PYRAMID REMANUFACTURING

Pyramid Remanufacturing opened for business ten years ago in a cinder block building with four employees. Today Pyramid is housed in an old factory building in a low-rent district. The company has 100 full-time employees and about 50 part-timers. The nature of the company's business is to salvage parts from used or broken equipment sent to them by other companies. One of Pyramid's remanufacturing projects is to salvage the workable parts from single-use cameras and recycle the balance of the plastic parts. Another large company contract is to salvage parts from children's toys that purchasers have returned to retailers because they do not function properly. Both contracts also call for making new single-use cameras and toys, incorporating the salvaged parts.

The basic remanufacturing jobs can be learned in several hours. The work is not complex, but it is tedious. For example, a remanufacturing technician would be expected to tear down, salvage, and assemble about 100 single-use cameras per day. The jobs pay about twice the minimum wage, and full-time workers receive standard benefits.

Derrick Lockett, president and founder of Pyramid, believes that his company plays an important role in society. As he explains, "First of all, note that we are *remanufacturers.* We are helping save the planet. Think of the thousands and thousands of single-use cameras that do not wind up in landfills because of our recycling efforts. The same goes for plastic toys. Consider also that we hire a lot of people who would not be working if it were not for Pyramid. A lot of our employees would be on welfare if they were not working here. We hire a lot of people from the welfare rolls. We also hire a lot of troubled teenagers and seniors who can't find employment elsewhere.

"Some of our other employees have a variety of disabilities which make job-finding difficult for them. Two of our highest producers are blind. They have a wonderful sense of touch, and they can visualize the parts that have to be separated and assembled. Another source of good employees for us is recently released prisoners."

Lockett was asked if all Pyramid manufacturing employees were performing up to standard. He explained that about one-fourth of the workforce were either working so slowly or doing such sloppy work that they were a poor investment for the company. "Face it," said Lockett, "some of our employees are dragging us down. After a while we have to weed out the workers who just don't earn their salary."

Next, Lockett gave his analysis of why some remanufacturing technicians are unable to perform properly. "Lots of reasons," said Lockett. "Some can't read; some have a poor work ethic; some have attention deficit disorders. But the big problem is that many of the poor performers have such rotten self-esteem. They don't believe in themselves. They think nobody wants them and that they are incapable of being valuable employees."

Lucy Winters, the director of human resources and administration, explained what Pyramid was attempting to do about the self-esteem problem. "You have to realize," she said, "that it's not easy for a company to build the self-esteem of entry-level employees. Derrick and I would both like to save the world, but we can't do everything. But we are taking a few initiatives to build the self-esteem of our employees.

"One approach is that our supervisors give out brightly coloured badges imprinted with the words 'I'm a real remanufacturer.' The supervisors are supposed to give out the badges when a technician looks to be down in the dumps. We also have a newsletter that features stories about our remanufacturing technicians. Each month we choose somebody to be 'Remanufacturer of the Month.' Usually it's an employee whose self-esteem appears to be hurting.

"Another approach is more informal. We ask our supervisors to remember to be cheerleaders. They're supposed to lift the spirits of employees who don't think much of themselves by saying things like 'I know you can do it,' or 'I believe in you.'"

When asked how the self-esteem-building program was working, Winters and Lockett both said it was too early to tell with certainty. Winters did say, however, "I see a few bright smiles out there among our technicians. And the turnover rate is down about five percent. So the program might be working."

Questions

1. What is your evaluation of Lockett's analysis that low self-esteem could hurt the work performance of entry-level remanufacturing technicians?
2. What is your evaluation of the self-esteem-building program at Pyramid?
3. What other suggestions can you offer for building the self-esteem of the Pyramid employees who appear to be having a self-esteem problem?

Self-Motivation and Goal Setting

Learning Outcomes

After studying the information and doing the exercises in this chapter, you should be able to

- explain how needs and motives influence motivation
- identify several needs and motives that could be propelling you into action
- pinpoint how the hierarchy of needs could explain your behaviour
- explain why and how goals contribute to self-motivation
- describe how to set effective goals
- specify the problems sometimes created by goals
- apply the self-discipline model to achieve your goals

Gary Rogers is the president of Jasco Tools, a company that employs 300 people. He thinks that the employee work ethic is a big problem. According to Rogers, job applicants come to the firm asking what's in the job for them, not what they can do to make the company a success. "It used to be that you would find job applicants dressed up for an interview. They would wear a suit and tie or dress and try to make a good impression. Now they come in jeans and hats turned around backwards." Rogers said that Jasco tries to teach virtues such as punctuality and teamwork. But basic attitudes won't change until schools and parents start to instill a work ethic.[1]

Whether or not you agree with Gary Rogers that the work ethic (belief in the dignity of work) is declining, his comments emphasize an important truth. You have to be motivated to achieve success in work. Strong motivation is also important for personal life. Unless you direct your energies toward specific goals, such as improving your productivity or meeting a new friend, you will accomplish very little. Knowledge of motivation and goal setting, when applied, can therefore pay substantial dividends in improving the quality of your life. Understanding motivation and goal setting is also important when attempting to influence others to get things accomplished. Motivating others, for example, is a major requirement of a manager's job.

Being well motivated is also important just to meet the demands of employers. Even when unemployment is low, most organizations insist on high productivity and quality from workers at all levels. Assuming you have the necessary skills, training, and equipment, being well motivated will enable you to achieve high productivity and quality. Furthermore, workers in professional-level positions are often expected to work about 55 hours per week, which includes doing work at home.

The general purpose of this chapter is to present information that can help you sustain a high level of motivation by focusing on the importance of needs and goals.

How Needs and Motives Influence Motivation

According to a widely accepted explanation of human behaviour, people have needs and motives that propel them toward achieving certain goals. Needs and motives are closely related. A **need** is an internal striving or urge to do something, such as a need to drink when thirsty. It can be regarded as a biological or psychological requirement. Because the person is deprived in some way (such as not having enough fluid in the body), the person takes action toward a goal. In this case the goal might be simply getting something to drink.

A **motive** is an inner drive that moves a person to do something. The motive is usually based on a need or desire, and results in the intention to attain an appropriate goal. Because needs and motives are so closely related, the two terms are

Figure 2-1 Drive Theory of Motivation

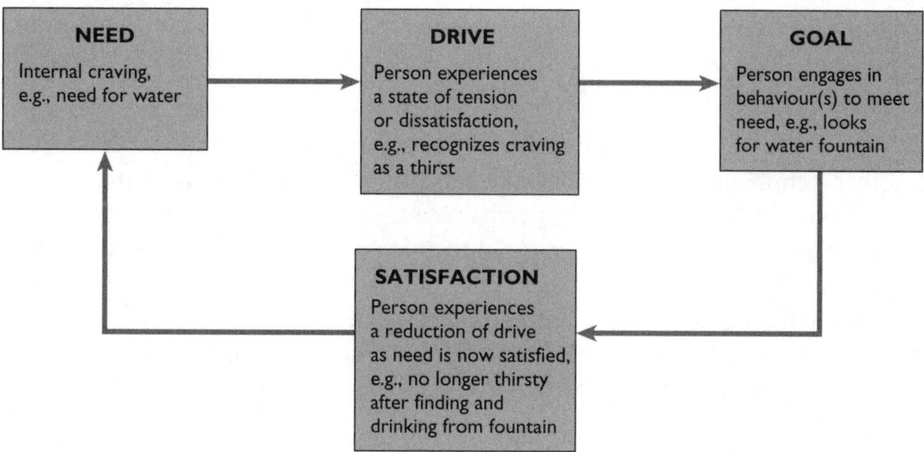

often used interchangeably. For example, "recognition need" and "recognition motive" refer to the same thing.

The Drive Theory of Motivation

The central idea behind drive theory is that unsatisfied needs, whether physiological or psychological, motivate us until they become satisfied. When people are dissatisfied or anxious about their present status or performance, they will try to reduce this anxiety.[2] This drive cycle is shown in Figure 2-1. Assume that you have a strong need or motive to achieve recognition. As a result, you experience tension that drives you to find some way of being recognized on the job. The action you take is to apply for a position as the team leader of your group. You reason that being appointed as team leader would provide ample recognition, particularly if the team performs well.

You are appointed to the position, and for now your need for recognition is at least partially satisfied as you receive compliments from your co-workers and friends. Once you receive this partial satisfaction, two things typically happen. Either you will soon require a stronger dose of recognition, or you will begin to concentrate on another need or motive, such as achievement.

In either case, the drive cycle will repeat itself. You might seek another form of recognition, or satisfaction of your need for power. For example, you might apply for a position as department manager. Ideally in this situation your boss would give you more responsibility. This could lead to more satisfaction of your recognition need and to some satisfaction of your need for achievement. (The needs mentioned so far, and others, are defined next.)

Important Needs and Motives People Attempt to Satisfy

Work and personal life offer the opportunity to satisfy dozens of needs and motives. In this and the following section, we describe important needs that propel people into action. As you read these needs and motives, relate them to yourself. For example, ask yourself, "Am I a power-seeking person?"

Achievement People with a strong achievement need find joy in accomplishment for its own sake. The achievement motive or need is especially important for self-employed people and employees occupying high-level managerial positions.[3] The achievement need can be satisfied by such activities as building things from the ground up or by completing a major project.

Power People with a high power need feel compelled to control resources, such as other people and money. Successful executives typically have a high power motive and exhibit three dominant characteristics: (1) they act with vigour and determination to exert their power; (2) they invest much time in thinking about ways to alter the behaviour and thinking of others; and (3) they care about their personal standing with those around them.[4] The power need can be satisfied through occupying a high-level position or by becoming a highly influential person. (Or you can buy newspaper chains, following the lead of Conrad Black.)

Affiliation People with a strong affiliation need seek out close relationships with others and tend to be loyal as friends or employees. The affiliation motive is met directly through belonging to the "office gang," a term of endearment implying that your co-workers are an important part of your life. Many people prefer working in groups to individual effort because of the opportunity the former provides for socializing with others.

Recognition People with a strong need for recognition want to be acknowledged for their contribution and efforts. The need for recognition is so pervasive that many companies have formal recognition programs in which outstanding or long-time employees receive gifts, plaques, and jewellery inscribed with the company logo. The recognition motive can be satisfied through means such as winning contests, receiving awards, and seeing one's name in print.

Dominance People with a strong need for dominance want to influence others toward their way of thinking, often by forceful methods. People driven by a dominance motive often take over in meetings, volunteer to be leaders, and are good at the "hard sell." A need for dominance could therefore be satisfied by taking control over any situation in which you are placed.

Order People with a strong need for order have the urge to put things in order. They also want to achieve arrangement, balance, neatness, and precision. The order motive can be quickly satisfied by cleaning and organizing one's work or living space. Occupations offering the opportunity to satisfy the order motive almost every day include accountant, computer programmer, and paralegal.

Risk Taking and Thrill Seeking Some people crave constant excitement on the job and are willing to risk their lives to achieve thrills. The need to take risks and pursue thrills has grown in importance in the high-technology era. Many people work for employers, start businesses, and purchase stocks with uncertain futures. The search for giant payoffs and the desire for daily thrills motivate these individuals.[5] A strong craving for thrills may have some positive consequences for the organization, including willingness to perform such dangerous feats as setting explosives, capping an oil well, controlling a radiation leak, and introducing a new product in a highly competitive environment. However, extreme risk takers and thrill seekers can also create problems such as being involved in a disproportionate

Human Relations Self-Assessment

Quiz 2-1

The Risk-Taking Scale: We Dare You to Take This Quiz

How can you size up your capacity for risk and thrills? Here's an informal quiz. Although some of the questions seem obvious, your final score reflects the range of risk that you are comfortable with, not just whether you like taking risks or not. Answer True or False:

	True	*False*
1. I don't like my opinions being challenged.	☐	☐
2. I would rather be an accountant than a TV anchor.	☐	☐
3. I believe that I can control my destiny.	☐	☐
4. I am a highly creative person.	☐	☐
5. I like a variety of romantic partners.	☐	☐
6. I don't like trying exotic foods.	☐	☐
7. I would choose bonds over growth stocks.	☐	☐
8. Friends would call me a thrill seeker.	☐	☐
9. I like to challenge authority.	☐	☐
10. I prefer familiar things to new things.	☐	☐
11. I'm known for my curiosity.	☐	☐
12. I would not like to be an entrepreneur.	☐	☐
13. I'd rather not travel abroad.	☐	☐
14. I am easily bored.	☐	☐
15. I wouldn't like to be a stand-up comedian.	☐	☐
16. I've never gotten speeding tickets.	☐	☐
17. I am extremely adventurous.	☐	☐
18. I need a lot of stimulation in my life.	☐	☐
19. I would rather work for a salary than a commission.	☐	☐
20. Making my own decisions is very important to me.	☐	☐

Give yourself 1 point each time your answer agrees with the key. If you score 16 to 20, you are probably just back from hang gliding in the Himalayas; from 10 to 15, you're a sushi eater who'd skip the trip to Japan; from 5 to 10, don't forget the umbrella (it might rain); from 0 to 5, so, how long have you been in life insurance?

(continued)

1. F	6. F	11. T	16. F
2. F	7. F	12. F	17. T
3. T	8. T	13. F	18. T
4. T	9. T	14. T	19. F
5. T	10. F	15. F	20. T

number of vehicular accidents and making imprudent investments. Take Human Relations Self-Assessment Quiz 2-1 to measure your tendency toward risk taking.

Generational Differences in Needs

Popular opinion strongly suggests that the various generations have different needs, which are based on their values. A **value** is the importance a person attaches to something that serves as a guide to action. If you value cleanliness, you will strive to keep your work area neat. Values are also tied in with needs. If you value love, your need for love and affection will be strong. Generational differences in needs and values are reflected in the stereotypes about differences between older people (Baby Boomers) and younger people (Generation X and Generation Y, or the Net generation). Older people will more frequently have strong needs for security. In contrast, younger people might have a stronger need for thrill seeking.[6] This is one of several reasons that middle-aged people are more likely to be hired as pilots of large commercial airplanes.

Exhibit 2-1 summarizes stereotypes about generational differences in values. The values in turn can be translated into needs. For example, "appreciating hierarchy" may be based on a need for order and security. Keep in mind, of course, that not everybody fits these stereotypes. Some 70-year-olds enjoy skydiving, and some 23-year-olds are looking for secure, low-risk jobs.

Maslow's Need Hierarchy

The best-known categorization of needs is **Maslow's need hierarchy**. At the same time, it is the most widely used explanation of human motivation. According to psychologist Abraham H. Maslow, people strive to satisfy the following groups of needs in step-by-step order:

1. *Physiological needs* refer to bodily needs, such as the requirements for food, water, shelter, and sleep.
2. *Safety needs* refer to actual physical safety and to a feeling of being safe from both physical and emotional injury.
3. *Social needs* are essentially love or belonging needs. Unlike the two previous levels of needs, they centre on a person's interactions with other people.

exhibit 2-1

Value Stereotypes for Several Generations of Workers

Baby Boomers (1946–1964)	*Generation X (1965–1977)*	*Generation Y (1978–1984)*
Uses technology as necessary tool Appreciates hierarchy Tolerates teams but values independent work	Techno-savvy Teamwork very important Dislikes hierarchy	Techno-savvy Teamwork very important Culturally diverse Dislikes hierarchy
Strong career orientation	Strives for work/life balance but will work long hours for now	Strives for work/family balance but will work long hours for now
More loyalty to organization	Loyalty to own career and profession	Believes in informality Wants to strike it rich quickly Highly regards start-up companies
Favours diplomacy Favours old economy	Candid in conversation Appreciates old and new economy	Candid in conversation Prefers the new economy
Expects a bonus based on performance	Would appreciate a signing bonus	Expects a signing bonus

SOURCE: Several of the ideas in this table are from Robert McGarvey, "The Coming of Gen X Bosses," *Entrepreneur*, November 1999, pp. 60–64; Joanne M. Glenn, "Teaching the Net Generation," *Business Education Forum*, February 2000, pp. 6–14; Charlene Marmer Solomon, "Ready or Not: Here Come the Kids," *Workforce*, February 2000, pp. 62–68.

4. *Esteem needs* represent an individual's demands to be seen by others as a person of worth.
5. *Self-actualizing needs* are the highest levels of needs, including the needs for self-fulfillment and personal development.[7]

A diagram of the need hierarchy is presented in Figure 2-2. Notice the distinction between higher-level and lower-level needs. With few exceptions, higher-level needs are more difficult to satisfy. A person's needs for affiliation might be satisfied by being a member of a friendly work group. Yet to satisfy self-actualization needs, such as self-fulfillment, a person might have to develop an outstanding reputation in his or her company.

The need hierarchy implies that most people think of finding a job as a way of obtaining the necessities of life. Once these are obtained, a person may think of achieving friendship, self-esteem, and self-fulfillment on the job. When a person is generally satisfied at one level, he or she looks for satisfaction at a higher level.

Figure 2-2 Maslow's Need Hierarchy

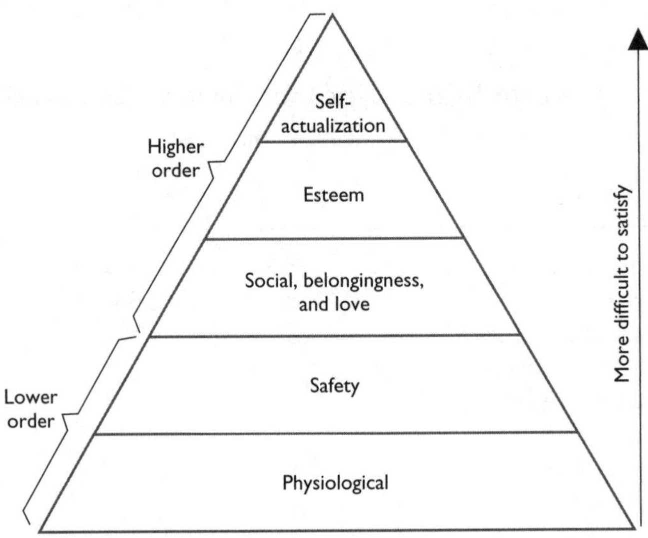

As Maslow describes it, a person is a "perpetually wanting animal." Very few people are totally satisfied with their lot in life, even the rich and famous.

How do Maslow's needs and the other needs described in this chapter relate to self-motivation? First you have to ask yourself, "Which need do I really want to satisfy?" After answering the question honestly, concentrate your efforts on an activity that will most likely satisfy that need. For instance, if you are hungry for power, strive to become a high-level manager or a business owner. If you crave self-esteem, focus your efforts on work and social activities that are well regarded by others. The point is that you will put forth substantial effort if you think the goal you attain will satisfy an important need. Many business people still use Maslow's need hierarchy to guide their thinking about motivation in the workplace, and many university and college courses teach it as a method of understanding how needs influence motivation.

Goals and Motivation

One writer says this about success: "All truly successful men or women I have met or read about have one thing in common. At some point in their lives, they sat down and wrote out their goals. The first great key to success begins with you, a piece of paper, and a pencil."[8] This statement indicates why goal setting is so important. A **goal** is an event, circumstance, object, or condition a person strives to attain. A goal thus reflects your desire or intention to regulate your actions. Here we look at two related topics: (1) the advantages of goals, and (2) the underlying reasons why they are motivational.

Advantages of Goals

Goal setting is well accepted as a motivational tool. Substantial research indicates that setting specific, reasonably difficult goals improves performance.[9] Goals are useful for several reasons. First, when we guide our lives with goals, we tend to focus our efforts in a consistent direction. Without goals, our efforts may become scattered in many directions. We may keep trying, but we will go nowhere unless we happen to receive more than our share of luck.

Second, goal setting increases our chances for success, particularly because success can be defined as the achievement of a goal. The goals we set for accomplishing a task can serve as a standard to indicate when we have done a satisfactory job. A sales representative might set a goal of selling $300,000 worth of merchandise for the year. By November she might close a deal that places her total sales at $310,000. With a sigh of relief she can then say, "I've done well this year."

Third, goals serve as self-motivators and energizers. People who set goals tend to be motivated because they are confident that their energy is being invested in something worthwhile. Aside from helping you become more motivated and productive, setting goals can help you achieve personal satisfaction. Most people derive a sense of satisfaction from attaining a goal that is meaningful to them. The sales representative mentioned above probably achieved this sense of satisfaction when she surpassed her quota.

Cognitive and Neurological Reasons Why Goals Are Effective

The advantages of goals just described provide some explanation of why goals help motivate people. Yet to fully understand the contribution of goals, it is important to dig deeper by uncovering the cognitive (or mental) and neurological reasons for the contribution of goals to motivation.

One cognitive explanation of the effectiveness of goals states that they are not motivational by themselves. Rather, the discrepancy between what individuals have and what they aspire to achieve creates dissatisfaction. (The need cycle described earlier also deals with such discrepancies between a person's ideal and actual state.) The self-dissatisfaction serves as an incentive. People respond to reduce the discrepancy. A positive self-evaluation results from achieving the goal.[10]

An example will help clarify this cognitive explanation of why goals are motivational. Bob might be working as a telemarketer (a person who sells over the phone). He sets a goal of being promoted to an outside sales position where he can call on customers and earn a bigger commission. Having set this goal, he is now dissatisfied with the discrepancy between his present job and being an outside sales representative. Bob's dissatisfaction prompts him to work extra hard to perform well as a telemarketer. Because of this, his manager might offer him a promotion.

The motivational effects of goal setting also have a neurological (nervous system) explanation. A building block for this explanation is that many of our actions are influenced by an arousal mechanism. The strength of the arousal moves along a continuum from a low point during sleep to a high point of frantic effort or excitement. (Have you ever observed a sports fan watch his or her team win the "big game" at the buzzer?) The state of being aroused is associated with activity in the sympathetic nervous system. The sympathetic nervous system readies the body for action. It also governs the amount of energy and effort available for performing a task.[11]

Arousal is linked to goals because setting a goal often arouses the sympathetic nervous system to action. Assume that on Monday, university student Carla establishes the goal of completing all the research on two term papers by the following Monday. The goal is a stretch for Carla, but not impossible. Her nervous system will be activated to gear up for the task. By having extra energy to meet these demands, Carla will in essence be well motivated. A problem, however, is that if the task is too demanding, the goal may produce over-arousal. As a result, the person may be too "hyper" to perform well and will back away from getting the task accomplished.

The Learning and Performance Orientations toward Goals

Another useful perspective on understanding how goals influence motivation is that goals can be aimed at either learning or performing.[12] A learning-goal orientation means that an individual is focused on acquiring new skills and mastering new situations. For example, you might establish the goal of learning how to develop skill in making a computerized-presentation package. You say to yourself, "My goal is to learn how to use PowerPoint (or similar software)."

A performance-goal orientation is different. It is aimed at wanting to demonstrate and validate the adequacy of your competence by seeking favourable judgments about your competence. At the same time, you seek to avoid negative judgments. For example, your goal might be to make PowerPoint presentations that would highly impress whoever watched them. Your focus would be on looking good and avoiding negative evaluations of your presentations.

A person's goal orientation usually affects his or her desire for feedback. People with a learning-goal orientation are more likely to seek feedback on how well they are performing. In contrast, people with a performance-goal orientation are less likely to seek feedback. If you focus too much on setting performance goals, you might have a tendency to overlook the value of feedback. Yet the feedback could help you improve your performance in the long run. It is also important to recognize that if you, the goal setter, seek feedback, you will create a good impression.

Goal orientation is also important because it can affect work performance. Attempting to master skills often leads to better results than does attempting to impress others. A study of the effects of the two different goal orientations was conducted with 167 salespeople working for a medical supplies distributor. The salespeople were paid mostly on the commission of the gross profits they generated. The researchers found that a learning-goal orientation was associated with higher sales performance. In contrast, a performance-goal orientation was unrelated to sales performance. An important implication of the study for managers and workers is that a focus on skill development, even for an experienced workforce, is likely to lead to higher performance.[13]

Before studying more about goals, do Human Relations Self-Assessment Quiz 2-2. It gives you an opportunity to think through your readiness to accept goals as part of your life.

Quiz 2-2

Are You Ready for Goal Setting?

Answer each of the following questions spontaneously and candidly. As with all self-help quizzes, if you try to answer the question in a way that will put you in a favourable light, you will miss some potentially valuable diagnostic information. For each question answer 1 for strongly disagree, 2 for disagree, 3 for a neutral attitude, 4 for agree, and 5 for strongly agree.

1. I almost always know what day of the month it is. ____
2. I regularly prepare to-do lists. ____
3. I make good use of my to-do lists. ____
4. I can tell you almost precisely how many times I engaged in my favourite sport or hobby this year. ____
5. I keep close tabs on the win and lose record of my favourite athletic team. ____
6. I have a reasonably accurate idea of the different income tax brackets. ____
7. I use a budget to control my personal expenses. ____
8. I know how much money I want to be making in five years. ____
9. I know what position I want to hold in five years. ____
10. Careful planning is required to accomplish anything of value. ____

Total ____

Scoring and Interpretation: Add up your point score. If your score is 40 points or higher, you are probably already convinced of the value of goal setting. If your score is between 20 and 39 points, you are in the middle range of readiness to incorporate goal setting into your life. You probably need to study more about goal setting to capitalize on its value. If your score is between 10 and 19 points, you are far from ready to accept goal setting. Carefully review the information about the advantages of goal setting mentioned previously. Until you change your attitudes about the contribution of goals to your life, you will not become an active goal setter and planner.

Goal Setting on the Job

If you are already well into your career, you have probably been asked to set goals or objectives on the job. Virtually all modern organizations have come to accept the value of goal setting in producing the results they want to achieve.

In most goal-setting programs, executives at the top of the organization are supposed to plan for the future by setting goals such as "Improve profits ten percent this year." Employees at the bottom of the organization are supposed to go along with such broad goals by setting more specific goals. An example is "I will decrease damaged merchandise by ten percent this year. I will accomplish this by making sure that our shelving is adequate for our needs."

An interesting aspect of goal-setting programs on the job is that they lead you to pursue goals set by both your employer and yourself. The firm or company establishes certain goals that are absolutely essential to staying in business. A bank, for example, might impose the following goal on the tellers: "Shortages and overages of cash must be kept within two percent of transactions each week." The tellers will thus work extra hard to be sure that they do not give customers too much or too little money. Similarly, the top management of a hospital might impose the following goal (or objective) on all ward personnel: "All prescription drugs must be accounted for with 100 percent accuracy."

You participate in the goal-setting process by designing goals to fit into the overall mission of the firm. If you were a teller in the bank mentioned above, you might set a personal goal of this nature: "During rush periods, and when I feel fatigued, I will double-count all the money that I handle." In some goal-setting programs, employees are requested to set goals that will lead to their personal improvement. A federal auditor set this goal for herself: "Within the next 12 months, I will enroll in and complete a supervisory training course in a local college." This woman aspired to become a supervisor.

An important part of goal setting, both on and off the job, is priority setting. You pursue with more diligence those goals that can have the greatest impact on performance or are most important to top management. Suppose that one of a purchasing associate's goals for the month is to trim the number of email messages, letter files, and data files stored in his computer. He rightfully assumes that if he cleans up his computer files, he will be able to think more clearly. Yet he is also working on a goal of much more interest to top management—finding new sources of supply for a precious metal used in manufacturing a key product. The purchasing associate should temporarily set aside his need for order and work on the precious metal goal.

To increase the motivational impact of goals, some managers encourage workers to track their own performances. One approach is to use a bar chart as a data-collecting tool. In this way, as employees fill in the boxes, they can see their progress immediately. The fill-in-the-bar-chart approach shows workers at a glance where to concentrate more effort as well as areas in which they are not performing well.[14] A portion of the bar chart for the purchasing associate might look like that shown in Figure 2-3.

A sample set of work goals is shown in Figure 2-4. The service and repair shop supervisor who set these objectives took into account the requirements of his boss and the automobile dealership. Even if you set goals by yourself, they must still

Figure 2-3 Bar Graph Showing Progress against Goal

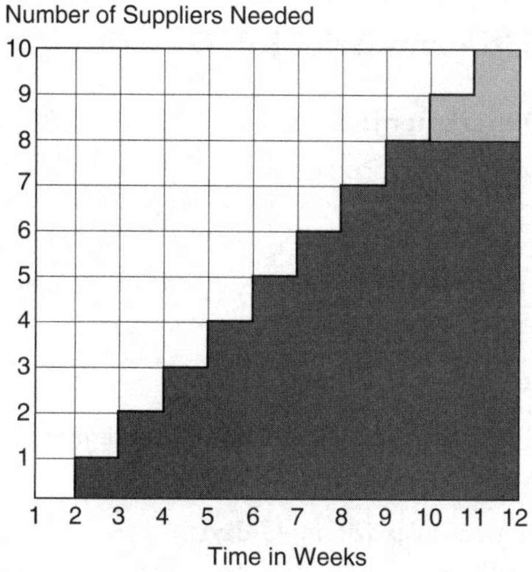

take into account the needs of your employer. As you read through the goals listed in Figure 2-4, see if they conform to the suggestions made in the section "Guidelines for Goal Setting" (below).

Personal Goal Setting

Personal goals are important in their own right. If you want to lead a rewarding personal life, your chances of doing so increase if you plan it. Personal goals heavily influence the formulation of career goals as well. For this reason it is worthwhile to set personal goals in conjunction with career goals. Ideally, they should be integrated. Two examples follow.

- A young man may have a strong interest in hiking, camping, skiing, and appreciating nature. One personal goal he might formulate is to have enough money for this lifestyle and to live in an area where it would be available. His occupational goals should then include developing skills that are needed in smaller and more remote communities. Another personal goal may be to learn wilderness and survival skills. His career planning might then focus on obtaining employment in a geographic location such as northern British Columbia, where skiing and hiking are readily accessible.
- A woman might develop a preference early in life for the outdoors, particularly for hunting, fishing, and camping. She might also be interested in raising a large family. Part of her career planning should include developing skills that are in demand in rural areas where her preferences are easier to satisfy than in a city. When she learns that many manufacturing facilities have been developed in rural and semi-rural areas, her career planning might then include the goal of developing job skills that are in demand in a factory or mill. Computer skills, of course, are in demand everywhere. Another alternative for this woman might be to develop technical computer skills so that she could work for a city company through teleworking.

Figure 2-4 Memo Form Used in Automobile Dealership for Statement of Goals

Job Title and Brief Job Description

Manager, Service Department:

Responsible for supervision of service department of automobile dealership. Responsible for staffing service department with appropriate personnel and for quality of service to customers. Work closely with owner of dealership to discuss unusual customer problems. Handle customer complaints about mechanical problems of cars purchased at dealership.

Objectives for Scott Gilley

1. By December 31 of this year, decrease by 10 percent customer demands for rework.
2. Hire two general mechanics within 45 days.
3. Hire two body specialists within 45 days.
4. Decrease by 30 percent the number of repairs returned by customers for rework.
5. Reduce by 10 percent the discrepancy between estimates and actual bills to customers.

Types of Personal Goals

Personal goals can be subdivided into those relating to social and family life, hobbies and interests, physical and mental health, and finances. Examples of each type follow:

Social and family: "By age 30 I would like to have a spouse and two children." "Have my own apartment by age 23."

Hobbies and interests: "Become a black belt in karate by age 28." "Qualify as a downhill ski instructor by age 21."

Physical and mental health: "Be able to run four miles without stopping or panting for breath by April 15 of next year." "Get my dermatitis under control within six months from now." "Maintain normal blood pressure for the indefinite future."

Financial: "Within the next four years be earning $40,000 per year, adjusted for inflation." "Build my mutual fund accounts into a total value of at least $20,000 within five years."

The Human Relations Skill-Building Exercise 2-1 accompanying this discussion will give you an opportunity to set both work and personal goals. Ideally, reading this chapter and doing the exercises in it will start you on a lifelong process of using goals to help you plan your life. But before you can capitalize on the benefits of goal setting, you need a method for translating goals into action.

Exercise 2-1

Goal-Setting and Action Plan Worksheet

The purpose of this activity is to help you gain some experience in setting both work and personal goals and action plans to accompany them. Before writing down your actual goals, consult "Guidelines for Goal Setting" (below). For each of the following levels of goals, set a work goal, a personal goal, and a brief action plan for each. If you are not currently employed, set up hypothetical goals and action plans for a future job.

Long-Range Goals (beyond five years)

Work: ____________________

Action plan: ____________________

Personal: ____________________

Action plan: ____________________

Medium-Range Goals (two to five years)

Work: ____________________

Action plan: ____________________

Personal: ____________________

Action plan: ____________________

Short-Range Goals (within two years)

Work: ____________________

Action plan: ____________________

Personal: ____________________

Action plan: ____________________

Action Plans to Support Goals

An **action plan** describes how you are going to reach your goal. The major reason you need an action plan for most goals is that without a method for achieving what you want, the goal is likely to slip by. Few people ever prepare a road map or plan that will lead them to their goal. If your goal were to build your own log cabin, part of your action plan would be to learn how to operate a buzz saw, to read a handbook on log cabin building, to learn how to operate a tractor, and so forth.

Some goals are so difficult to reach that your action plan might encompass hundreds of separate activities. You would then have to develop separate action plans for each step of the way. If your goal is to lead a rewarding and satisfying career, the techniques presented in this book can help you formulate many of your action plans. Among these skill-building techniques are assertiveness, resolving conflict, developing good work habits, and managing stress.

Some immediate goals do not really require an action plan. A mere statement of the goal may point to an obvious action plan. If your goal is to start painting your room, it will not be necessary to draw up a formal action plan such as: "Go to hardware store to purchase paint, brush, and rollers; borrow ladder and drop cloth from Ken; put furniture in centre of room"; and so on.

Guidelines for Goal Setting

Goal setting is an art in the sense that some people do a better job of goal setting than others. The following paragraphs provide suggestions on setting effective goals—those that lead to achieving what you hoped to achieve.

Formulate Specific Goals A goal such as "To attain success" is too vague to serve as a guide to daily action. A more useful goal would be to state specifically what you mean by success and when you expect to achieve it. For example, "I want to be the manager of customer service at a telephone company by January 1, 2006."

Formulate Concise Goals A useful goal can usually be expressed in a short, punchy statement. An example: "Decrease input errors in bank statements so that customer complaints are decreased by 25 percent by September 30 of this year." People new to goal setting typically commit the error of formulating lengthy, rambling goal statements. These lengthy goals involve so many different activities that they fail to serve as specific guides to action.

Describe What You Would Actually Be Doing If You Reached Your Goal An effective goal specifies the behaviour that results after the goal is achieved. A non-specific goal for a sales representative would be "become a more effective salesperson." A more useful goal would be "increase the percentage of leads I turn into actual sales." The meaning of a "more effective salesperson" is specified in the second goal (a higher conversion rate for leads).

Similarly, if your goal is to "get into good shape," you need to specify what signifies "good shape." It could mean such things as "weigh between 88 and 90 kilograms," "run a kilometre in less than five minutes," or "decrease the amount of time lost from work due to illness."

Describing what you will be doing implies writing down your goal statements. It is helpful to choose lively verbs to direct your efforts.[15] Instead of writing, "I will fix my website," you might write, "I will revitalize (or sharpen) my website." Human Relations Skill-Building Exercise 2-2 gives you an opportunity to improve your goal-setting skills.

Set Realistic Goals A **realistic goal** is one that represents the right amount of challenge for the person pursuing the goal. On the one hand, easy goals are not very motivational—they may not spring you into action. On the other hand, goals that are too far beyond your capabilities may lead to frustration and despair

Goal Sharing and Feedback

Each person in the class selects one work-related and one personal goal from Human Relations Skill-Building Exercise 2-1, exactly as stated on the worksheet, that he or she would be willing to share with other members of the class. Other class members have the opportunity of providing feedback to the person sharing his or her goals. Here are a few types of errors commonly made in goal setting that you should avoid:

1. Is the goal much too lengthy and complicated? Is it really a number of goals rather than one specific goal?
2. Is the goal so vague that the person will be hard-pressed to know if he or she has reached the goal (e.g., "I intend to become a good worker.")?
3. Is the action plan specific enough to serve as a useful path for reaching that goal?
4. Does the goal sound sincere? (Admittedly, this is a highly subjective judgment on your part.)

because there is a good chance you will fail to reach them.[16] The extent to which a goal is realistic depends upon a person's capabilities. An easy goal for an experienced person might be a realistic goal for a beginner.

Set Goals for Different Time Periods As just implied, goals are best set for different time periods, such as daily, short-range, medium-range, and long-range. Daily goals are essentially a "to do" list. Short-range goals cover the period from approximately one week to one year into the future. Finding a new job, for example, is typically a short-range goal. Medium-range goals relate to events that will take place within approximately two to five years. They concern such things as the type of education or training you plan to undertake and the next step in your career.

Long-range goals refer to events taking place five years into the future and beyond. As such they relate to the overall lifestyle you wish to achieve, including the type of work and family situation you hope to have. Although every person should have a general idea of a desirable lifestyle, long-range goals should be flexible. You might, for example, plan to stay single until age 40. But while on vacation next summer you might just happen to meet the right partner for you.

Include Some Fantasy in Your Personal Goal Setting Breakthrough goals greatly enlarge your horizons. Fantasy goals take you one step further. Such fantasies can bridge the gap between personal and career goal setting. A fantasy goal would be difficult to attain at any stage in your life. Fantasy goals also reflect your vision of the ideal type of life you would like to lead. They help you dream the impossible dream. However difficult they may be to attain, some people *do* eventually live out their wildest dreams.

Here is a sampling of fantasy goals found in the career reports of students in a career development course:

- "I'd like to become a big tycoon by owning about ten office buildings in Toronto along with the Maple Leafs and the Argonauts."
- "I hope to become a freelance photographer for major news magazines. My specialty would be shooting civil unrest and border wars."
- "I hope to become a millionaire philanthropist and have a high school named after me in a poor neighbourhood."

Aside from being exciting to pursue, fantasy goals are important for another reason. Research suggests that your fantasy life can help with personal adjustment and overcoming stress. A well-developed fantasy can result in a pleasurable state of physical and mental relaxation. Furthermore, fantasy goals can help you cope with an unpleasant current situation by giving you hope for the future.[17]

Specify What Is Going to Be Accomplished, Who Is Going to Accomplish It, When It Is Going to Be Accomplished, and How It Is Going to Be Accomplished A comprehensive suggestion for effective goal setting is to specify the "what," "who," "when," and "how" of your goal. This suggestion includes many of the previous points about the characteristics of an effective goal. Here is a work goal that meets these requirements: "The VCR sales manager will increase the number of sales by 40 percent within 15 months by selling to dealers with sat-

Setting Goals May Be Kids' Business—At Least for These Three Pals!

Have you heard of the Air Hog? If not, you must not be into, or have kids who are into, the latest fast-moving toys. It is one of the latest inventions of Spin Master Toys, a Toronto-based company, headed up by three college pals. Following on the heels of their other successful inventions, the Earth Buddy and the three-rod juggling game called Spin Master Devil Sticks, their latest invention is an airplane that flies hundreds of metres on air power.

Where did they come up with their goals for this toy? First, after the success of Devil Sticks, they decided to focus their energies on designing toys. Second, they also decided that they were going to design and manufacture their own product. The Air Hog came onto the scene in February 1996 at an annual New York event called The Toy Fair, which attracts hundreds of toy makers, retailers, and inventors. At the fair, they were approached by the inventors (Dixon-Manning Ltd., an English firm) and eventually the inventors mailed the prototype of the Air Hog to Toronto. Much to their dismay, they found out that other big companies like Hasbro and Mattel had turned down the Air Hog. But these three had a goal to make it a best-selling toy and pursued it over several hurdles. In the spring of 1999, the Air Hog was on the shelf—an amazing achievement considering that at that time, the staff numbered 25, including two PR people.

Since 1999, Spin Master Toys has remained a strong and growing business. After success with their line of air-pressured cars, they have come up with a line of air-powered aircraft including the Air Hog Sky Patrol. Along a slightly different line, another new toy invention is Catch-a-Bubbles, which are tough bubbles that you can catch and stack. Recently, the company won the Best Outdoor Toy of the Year Award, and these three guys continue to come up with more amazing ideas for "kid fun."

SOURCES: Shawna Steinberg and Joe Chidley, "Fun for the Money," *Canadian Business*, December 11, 1998. Used with permission.

www.spinmaster.com.

isfactory credit records. Returns and nonpayments will be subtracted from the total number of sales."

Specifying that sales must be made to qualified dealers and that returns and nonpayments will not be counted focuses on the "how." It implies that sales should not be increased by pushing the VCRs on unqualified dealers who have low volume or are poor credit risks.

Review Your Goals from Time to Time A sophisticated goal setter realizes that all goals are temporary to some extent. In time one particular goal may lose its relevance for you and therefore may no longer motivate you. At one time in your life you may be committed to earning an income in the top 10 percent of the population. Along the way toward achieving that goal, some other more relevant goal may develop. You might decide that the satisfactions of being self-employed are more important than earning a particular amount of money. You might therefore open an antique store with the simple financial goal of "meeting my expenses."

Problems Sometimes Created by Goals

Despite the many advantages of goals, they can create problems. A major problem is that *goals can create inflexibility.* If you become so focused on achieving a 90 percent in one course, you may neglect your other courses. Goals can also make a person inflexible with respect to missing out on opportunities. Some people may actually miss out on career opportunities as an offered job is not in their chosen field. Rather than seeing this position as a possible stepping stone, they flat out refuse the opportunity.

Goals can contribute to a *narrow focus, thus neglecting other worthwhile activities.* While studying hard is a worthy goal, some students miss out on physical fitness or other activities to help maintain health and well-being. In other words, when a goal becomes the primary focus of all efforts, other important areas of life can become neglected.

Another problem is that *performance goals can sometimes detract from an interest in the task.* People with a performance-goal orientation (focusing on being judged as competent) will sometimes lose interest in the task. The loss of interest is most likely to occur when the task is difficult.[18] This potential problem could be stated in another way. If you focus too much on success (as being defined by reaching your goal), you will become frustrated when the means to reaching the goal is difficult. For example, assume that your primary goal for working as a salesperson is to perform well enough so that you will be in line for promotion. If you encounter some hurdles selling your product, you may easily become frustrated with selling. However, if your orientation is primarily to learn how to sell effectively, you will not be readily frustrated when you encounter problems. You might even look on it as a learning opportunity!

Consider also that *goals can interfere with relaxation.* A preoccupation with goals makes it difficult to relax. Instead of improving one's life, goals then become a source of stress. In the words of one purchasing agent, "Ever since I caught on to goal setting as a way of life, I feel as if I'm racing from one end of the court to the other. Even worse, nobody ever calls a time out." If the person is already under pressure, taking on another goal may be overwhelming.[19]

Despite the problems that can arise in goal setting, goals are valuable tools for managing your work and personal life. Used with common sense, and according to the ideas presented in this chapter, they could have a major positive impact on your life.

Techniques for Self-Motivation

Many people never achieve satisfying careers and never realize their potential because of low motivation. They believe they could perform better but admit, "I'm just not a go-getter" or "my motivation is low." Earlier we described how identifying your most important needs could enhance motivation. Here we describe six additional techniques for self-motivation.

1. Set goals for yourself.
2. Find intrinsically motivating work.
3. Get feedback on your performance.
4. Apply behaviour modification to yourself.
5. Improve your skills relevant to your goals.
6. Raise your level of self-expectation.
7. Develop a strong work ethic.

1. Set Goals for Yourself As shown throughout this chapter, goal setting is one of the most important techniques for self-motivation. If you set long-range goals and back them up with a series of smaller goals set for shorter time spans, your motivation will increase.

2. Find Intrinsically Motivating Work A major factor in self-motivation is to find work that is fun or is its own reward. **Intrinsic motivation** refers to the natural tendency to seek out novelty and challenges, to extend and use one's capacities, to explore, and to learn.[20] The intrinsically motivated person is involved in the task at hand, such as a netizen surfing the web for hours at a time. With some serious introspection (and assisted by the Self-Knowledge Questionnaire in Chapter 1), you should be able to find work you perceive to be intrinsically motivating. Next, find a job that offers your motivators in ample supply. For example, you might have good evidence from your past experience that the opportunity for close contact with people is a personal motivator. Find a job that involves working in a small, friendly department or team.

Owing to circumstances, you may have to take whatever job you can find, or you may not be in a position to change jobs. In such a situation, try to arrange your work so you have more opportunity to experience the reward(s) that you are seeking. Assume that solving difficult problems excites you, but that your job is 85 percent routine. Develop better work habits so that you can take care of the routine aspects of your job more quickly. This will give you more time to enjoy the creative aspects of your job.

3. Get Feedback on Your Performance Few people can sustain a high level of motivation without receiving information about how well they are doing. Even if you find your work to be challenging and exciting, you will need feedback. One reason feedback is valuable is that it acts as a reward. If you learn that your efforts achieved a worthwhile purpose, you will feel encouraged. For example, if a graphics display you designed was well received by company officials, you would probably want to prepare another graphics display.

4. Apply Behaviour Modification to Yourself **Behaviour modification** is a system for motivating people that emphasizes rewarding them for doing the right things and punishing them for doing the wrong things. In recent years, behaviour modification has been used by many people to change their own behaviour. Specific purposes include overcoming eating disorders, tobacco addiction, nail biting, and procrastination.

To boost your own motivation through behaviour modification you would have to first decide what specific motivated actions you want to increase (such as working 30 minutes longer each day). Second, you would have to decide on a suitable set of rewards and punishments. You may choose to use rewards only, since rewards are generally better motivators than punishments.

5. Improve Your Skills Relevant to Your Goals The **expectancy theory of motivation** states that people will be motivated if they believe that their efforts will lead to desired outcomes. According to this theory, people hold back effort when they are not confident that their efforts will lead to accomplishments. For example, some people are hesitant to attempt to operate a new piece of software because they suspect they will flounder. One way to increase their effort (motivation) toward learning the software would be to give them step-by-step training, thus increasing their skills.

Expectancy theory has an important implication for self-motivation. Seek adequate training to ensure that you have the requisite abilities and skills to perform your work. The training might be provided by the employer or through a course or self-study. Appropriate training gives you more confidence that you can perform the work. The training also increases your feelings of self-efficacy (as described in Chapter 1).[21] By recognizing your ability to mobilize your own resources to succeed, your self-confidence for the task will be elevated.

6. Raise Your Level of Self-Expectation A final strategy for increasing your level of motivation is to simply expect more of yourself. If you raise your level of self-expectation, you are likely to achieve more. Because you expect to succeed, you do succeed. The net effect is the same as if you had increased your level of motivation.

The technical term for improving your performance through raising your own expectations is the **Galatea effect**. In one experiment, for example, the self-expectations of subjects were raised in brief interviews with an organizational psychologist. The psychologist told the subjects they had high potential to succeed in the undertaking they were about to begin (a problem-solving task). The subjects who received the positive information about their potential did better than those subjects who did not receive such encouragement.[22]

High self-expectations and a positive mental attitude take a long time to develop. However, they are critically important for becoming a well-motivated person in a variety of situations.

7. Develop a Strong Work Ethic A highly effective strategy for self-motivation is to develop a strong work ethic. If you are committed to the idea that most work is valuable and that it is joyful to work hard, you will automatically become strongly motivated. A person with a weak work ethic cannot readily develop a strong one, because the change requires a profound value shift. Yet if a person gives a lot of serious thought to the importance of work and follows the right role models, a work ethic can be strengthened. The shift to a strong work ethic is much like a person who has a casual attitude toward college or a job who then becomes conscious of the quality of his or her schoolwork or job activities.

Developing the Self-Discipline to Achieve Goals and Stay Motivated

Another perspective on achieving goals and staying motivated is that it requires **self-discipline**, the ability to work systematically and progressively toward a goal until it is achieved. The self-disciplined person works toward achieving his or her goals without being derailed by the many distractions faced each day. Self-discipline incorporates self-motivation, because it enables you to motivate yourself to achieve your goals without being nagged or prodded with deadlines. Recent articles suggest that self-discipline is a requirement for many new jobs.[23] For example, teleworking requires self-motivation, the ability to set goals, and the ability to discipline yourself in order to achieve those goals.[24] Our discussion of how to develop self-discipline follows the model shown in Figure 2-5. You will observe that the model incorporates several of the ideas about goals already discussed in this chapter. Without realizing it, you have already invested mental energy into learning the self-discipline model.

Component 1. *Formulate a mission statement.* Who are you? What are you trying to accomplish in life? If you understand what you are trying to accomplish in life, you have the fuel to be self-disciplined. With a mission, activities that may appear mundane to others become vital stepping stones for you. An example would be learning Spanish grammar to help you become an international business person. To help formulate your mission statement, answer two questions: What are my five biggest wishes? What do I want to accomplish in my career during the next five years?

Component 2. *Develop role models.* An excellent method of learning how to be self-disciplined is to model your behaviour after successful achievers who are obviously well disciplined. To model yourself on another person does not mean you will slavishly imitate every detail of that person's life. Instead, you will follow the general pattern of how the person operates in spheres related to your mission and goals. An ideal role model is the type of person whom you would like to become, not someone you feel you could never become.

Component 3. *Develop goals for each task.* Your mission must be supported by a series of specific goals that collectively will enable you to achieve your mission. Successfully completing goals eventually leads to fulfilling a mission. Each small goal achieved is a building block toward larger achievements.

Component 4. *Develop action plans to achieve goals.* Self-disciplined people carefully follow their action plans because they make goal attainment possible. It is helpful to chart your progress against the dates established for the sub-activities.

Figure 2-5 The Self-Discipline Model

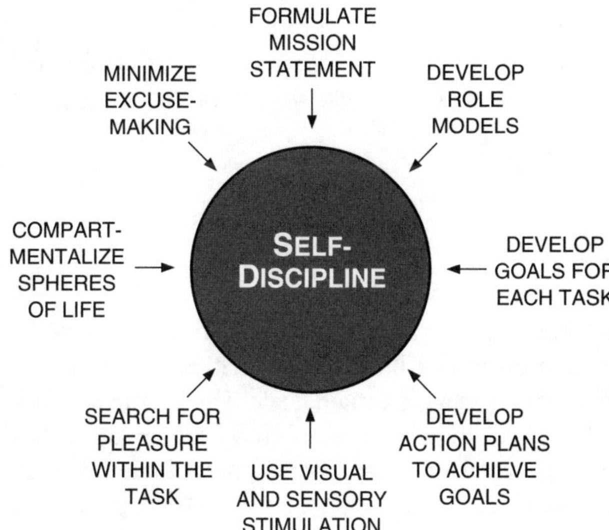

SOURCE: Andrew J. DuBrin, *Getting It Done: The Transforming Power of Self-Discipline* (Princeton, NJ: Peterson's, 1995), p. 18.

Component 5. *Use visual and sensory stimulation.* A self-disciplined person relentlessly focuses on a goal and persistently pursues that goal. To accomplish this consistent focus, self-disciplined people form images of reaching their goals—they actually develop a mental image of the act of accomplishing what they want. As mysterious as it sounds, visualization helps the brain convert images into reality. The more senses you can incorporate into your visual image, the stronger its power. Imagine yourself seeing, tasting, hearing, smelling, and touching your goal. Can you imagine yourself sitting in your condo overlooking the ocean, eating a great meal to celebrate the fact that the business you founded now has 10,000 employees?

Component 6. *Search for pleasure within the task.* A self-disciplined person finds joy, excitement, and intense involvement in the task at hand and therefore finds intrinsic motivation. Instead of focusing on the extrinsic (or external) reward, the love of the task helps the person in pursuit of the goal. An axiom of becoming wealthy is not to focus on getting rich. Instead, focus on work. If the task at hand does not thrill you, at least focus on the pleasure from the most enjoyable element within the task. An expressway toll collector might not find the total task intrinsically motivating, but perhaps he or she enjoys meeting so many people on the job!

Component 7. *Compartmentalize spheres of life.* Self-disciplined people have a remarkable capacity to divide up (or compartmentalize) the various spheres of their lives to stay focused on what they are doing at the moment. While working, develop the knack of concentrating on work and putting aside thoughts about personal life. In the midst of social and family activities, concentrate on them rather than half-thinking about work. This approach will contribute to both self-discipline and a better integration of work and family life.

Component 8. *Minimize excuse making.* Self-disciplined people concentrate their energies on goal accomplishment, rather than making excuses for why work is not accomplished. Instead of trying to justify why they have been diverted from a goal, high-achieving, self-disciplined people circumvent potential barriers. Undisciplined people, in contrast, seem to look for excuses. If you are an excuse maker, conduct a self-audit, writing down all the reasons blocking you from achieving any current goal. Be brutally honest in challenging each one of your excuses. Ask yourself, "Is this a valid excuse, or is it simply a rationalization for my getting sidetracked?"

Summary

Self-motivation is important for achieving success in work and personal life. A well-accepted explanation of human behaviour is that people have needs and motives propelling them toward achieving certain goals. The central idea behind drive theory is that unsatisfied needs motivate us until they become satisfied. After satisfaction of one need, the person usually pursues satisfaction of another, higher need.

Work and personal life offer the opportunity to satisfy many different needs and motives. Among the more important needs and motives are achievement, power, affiliation, recognition, dominance, and order. The need for risk taking and thrill seeking is also important for some people.

According to Maslow's need hierarchy, people have an internal need pushing them on toward self-actualization. However, needs are arranged into a five-step ladder. Before higher-level needs are activated, certain lower-level needs must be satisfied. In ascending order, the groups of needs are physiological, safety, social, esteem, and self-actualization (such as self-fulfillment).

Need theory helps in self-motivation. First identify which needs you want to satisfy, and then focus your efforts on the activities that will satisfy those needs.

A goal is an event, circumstance, object, or condition a person strives to attain. Goals are valuable because they (1) focus effort in a consistent direction, (2) improve one's chances for success, and (3) improve motivation and satisfaction.

One explanation for the contribution of goals is that they create a discrepancy between what individuals have and what they aspire to achieve. Self-dissatisfaction with this discrepancy serves as an incentive to achieve. Goals are also said to create a state of arousal, which readies people for accomplishment.

Goals can be aimed at either learning or performing. A learning-goal orientation means that an individual is focused on acquiring new skills and mastering new situations. A performance-goal orientation is aimed at wanting to demonstrate and validate the adequacy of your competence by seeking favourable judgments of competence. People with a learning-goal orientation are more likely to seek feedback on how well they are performing.

Goal setting is widely used on the job. Goals set by employees at lower levels in an organization are supposed to contribute to goals set at the top. Frequently, individual employees are asked to participate in goal setting by contributing ideas of their own. An important part of goal-setting, both on and off the job, is priority setting. To increase the motivational impact of goals, some managers encourage workers to track their own performance.

Goal setting in personal life can contribute to life satisfaction. For maximum advantage, personal goals should be integrated with career goals. Areas of life in which personal goals may be set include (1) social and family, (2) hobbies and interests, (3) physical and mental health, and (4) financial. To increase their effectiveness, goals should be supported with action plans.

Effective goals are specific and concise. You should describe what you would actually be doing if you reached your goal, and goals should be realistically challenging. Set goals for different time periods, and include some fantasy in your personal goal setting.

Goals have some problems associated with them. They can create inflexibility and can lead you to a narrow focus, thus causing you to neglect other worthwhile activities. Too much focus on goals can lead to missed opportunities. People may also neglect other aspects of the job because they are not included in the goals. Goals can also interfere with relaxation.

Techniques for self-motivation include (1) set goals for yourself; (2) engage in intrinsically motivating work; (3) get feedback on your performance; (4) apply behaviour modification to yourself; (5) improve your skills relevant to your goals; (6) raise your level of self-expectation; and (7) develop a strong work ethic.

Achieving goals and staying motivated require self-discipline. A model presented here for developing self-discipline consists of eight components: (1) formulate a mission statement; (2) develop role models; (3) develop goals for each task; (4) develop action plans; (5) use visual and sensory stimulation; (6) search for pleasure within the task; (7) compartmentalize spheres of life; and (8) minimize excuse making.

Questions and Activities

1. How would the drive theory of motivation explain the fact that, shortly after being promoted, many people begin thinking about their next possible promotion?
2. How might a strong need for power be satisfied off the job?
3. How might having a strong need for affiliation damage a person's career advancement?
4. Give an example from your own life of how a lower-level need had to be satisfied before you were able to concentrate on a higher-level need.
5. Identify any self-actualized person you know, and explain why you think that person is self-actualized.
6. Why does a learning-goal orientation often contribute to more peace of mind than a performance-goal orientation?
7. Describe any possible differences in an effective approach to self-motivation for a Baby Boomer versus a member of either Generation X or Generation Y.
8. How can a person be an ardent goal setter yet get around the potential problem of goals interfering with his or her relaxation?
9. What sacrifices might a high self-discipline person have to make in contrast to a low self-discipline person?
10. Ask a person who has achieved career success how much self-discipline contributed to his or her success.

Internet Skill Builder

What Motivates the Surfers?

Millions of people worldwide are strongly motivated to spend long hours surfing the internet, usually visiting websites or participating in chat rooms. Some chat rooms entail visiting members with a common interest, such as World War II buffs. Your assignment is to analyze why people surf so much (their motivation). What needs are they satisfying? Use your intuition, and communicate with others online. For example, you might visit a few chat rooms and ask some of the participants why they spend so much time online. You might obtain fruitful answers by asking informal questions such as "What keeps you glued to your computer?" or "What keeps you hanging out online?" Relate your answer to an explanation of motivation presented in this chapter.

Weblinks

www.vlib.org/Overview.html
This is the virtual library with access to thousands of articles on psychology, sociology, and other social sciences including some Canadian articles. Check out the material on motivation.

www.canbus.com
This is the site for *Canadian Business* magazine, an excellent resource for researching what is happening on the business scene.

www.workplaceissues.com/motivate.htm
This site is about self-motivation.

www.timedoctor.com/motivation.htm
This site is about time management and motivation.

Human Relations Case Study

THE MOTIVATED RETAIL WORKER

Barbara Harris faced a career setback when the fashion store she worked for was bought by a nationwide firm and converted into a subsidiary. The new owner's initial move was to replace existing management with its own people. Because of this, Barbara was on the verge of losing her job as assistant manager. Harris explains what happened:

"One week after I graduated with a degree in fashion merchandising, I obtained a job as a sales associate in a local retail outlet. Within a year I was promoted to assistant manager, and business was quite good. Three months after I was promoted, we were informed that a new company was buying the store. We were told not to worry about our jobs being disturbed.

"What we didn't know was that our job security was not guaranteed by the terms of the sales agreement between the companies. Upon acquiring our store, the new owner decided to move its own people into key positions. You can imagine the chaos that hit when we were told our jobs had been virtually eliminated with the stroke of a pen!

"The day the new company representative came to give us exit interviews we were told that the sales associates would be let go but that Julie (the store manager) and I would be able to work as sales associates. We were told that if we worked up to their standards, we might be reappointed as assistant managers in the future. Julie considered the offer to be a slap in the face after seven years in the business. She submitted her resignation that day. Who could blame her?

"I told them I'd like the weekend to consider my options and would give them my decision the following Monday morning. I spent Friday and Saturday fuming about the callous way we were all treated. By Sunday I got down to serious business, trying to understand what these changes meant to my career. I came to the conclusion that, because it was still early in my career, I had nothing to lose by accepting the company's offer. My one stipulation was that I be hired as a management trainee with the same pay and benefits as before.

"As I explained to the representative that Monday, I had a degree and nearly two years of merchandising experience. My experience included supervisory experience over sales associates. I felt I was overqualified for an associate's position. I knew I had much information to offer regarding local customer attitudes, behaviour, likes and dislikes, and preferred lifestyles.

"I can't believe how bold I was. I told that man I had no qualms about learning another style of management and that working for his company could only add to my career development. I wanted the chance to broaden my experience base. I could think of no reason why the company and I couldn't enjoy a mutually beneficial association.

"I couldn't believe my nerve, and I guess he couldn't either. I was hired that day as a manager trainee. I have to confess, I never thought my pitch would work. But you never know until you try. It's five years later and I am now the assistant regional manager for this chain. My boss is that same manager who was sent to reorganize the outlet I originally worked in."

Questions

1. What evidence can you find in this case that Barbara Harris is well motivated?
2. Identify several of Harris's strongest needs, and justify your answer.
3. What evidence do you find that Harris engaged in goal setting?

Problem Solving and Creativity

Learning Outcomes

After studying the information and doing the exercises in this chapter, you should be able to

- understand how personal characteristics influence the ability to solve problems and make decisions
- explain the four major decision-making styles as defined by the Myers-Briggs Type Indicator
- apply the problem-solving and decision-making steps to complex problems
- summarize the characteristics of creative people
- describe various ways of improving your creativity

With one month to go until graduation from career school, Jenny was having Sunday dinner with her parents. Her dad said, "Jenny, I hope you've made up your mind by now. Your mom and I want you to take over as office manager of our printing business. We need you. With the excellent training you've received in office procedures and office automation, you're a natural for the job. Besides that, why would any rational person walk away from a good job in a family business?"

Jenny felt a surge of emotion. She now faced a major problem. Her parents' proposal placed an obstacle in her path to leading the type of life she wanted for now. She wanted to move to British Columbia, where she and her boyfriend would both look for jobs. Jenny thought to herself, "If I say yes to my folks, that will mean that I will be pinned here in Ontario. Rick [her boyfriend] will think I don't love him because I won't move to British Columbia.

"If I say no to my folks, I will make Rick happy. And I'll also fulfill a dream of moving to the west. Yet I'll run the risk of hurting my parents. I'll also be walking away from a high-paying, interesting job. Who knows what position I'll find in British Columbia?

"I have to commit myself one way or another. I can't evade the issue any longer."

As Jenny's situation illustrates, problem solving and decision making are closely related. You have a problem to solve when an obstacle blocks the path you want to take. Worded in another way, a **problem** is a gap between what exists and what you want to exist. Jenny would like to please her parents, yet she wishes to move to British Columbia after graduation. If she does not join the family business she will displease her parents—an unwanted state of affairs. If she does join the family business, her desire to move to British Columbia will be frustrated, and she will displease Rick.

Decision making means selecting one alternative from the various alternative solutions or courses of action that can be pursued. Jenny can say *yes, no*, or *maybe* to her parents. Or perhaps she can choose the rude alternative solution of evading the question. Being faced with a problem forces you to make a decision. Decision making takes place after you recognize that a problem exists.

The general purpose of this chapter is to help you become a more effective problem solver when working individually or in groups. Recent research by the Conference Board of Canada listed the ability to think critically and solve problems as a requirement for successful employees.[1] Companies require workers who can solve problems and make effective and smart decisions. Whether you are solving problems by yourself or as part of a group at work or home, most of the principles apply equally well. Most of the information in this chapter is designed to help you make unique and/or major decisions such as developing a new product, purchasing major equipment, or weighing a job offer.

Personal Characteristics That Influence Your Problem-Solving Ability

Many personal characteristics and traits influence the type of problem solver and decision maker you are now or are capable of becoming. Fortunately, some personal characteristics that influence your decision-making ability can be improved through conscious effort. For instance, if you make bad decisions because you do not concentrate on the details of the problem, you can gradually learn to concentrate better. Most of the personal characteristics described next and outlined in Figure 3-1 can be strengthened through the appropriate education, training, and self-discipline.

Cognitive Intelligence, Education, and Experience

In general, if you are intelligent, well-educated, and experienced you will make better decisions than people without these attributes. Cognitive intelligence helps because, by definition, intelligence denotes the ability to solve problems. (The term *cognitive intelligence* refers to the intellectual, or traditional, type of intelligence that is necessary for such tasks as solving math problems and conjugating verbs.) Education improves the problem-solving and decision-making process because it gives you a background of principles and facts to rely on.

Experience facilitates decision making because good decisions tend to be made by people who have already faced similar situations in the past. This is one of the many reasons that experienced people command higher salaries. All things being equal, would you prefer to take your computer problem to an experienced or inexperienced specialist?

Figure 3-1 Influences on Problem-Solving Skill

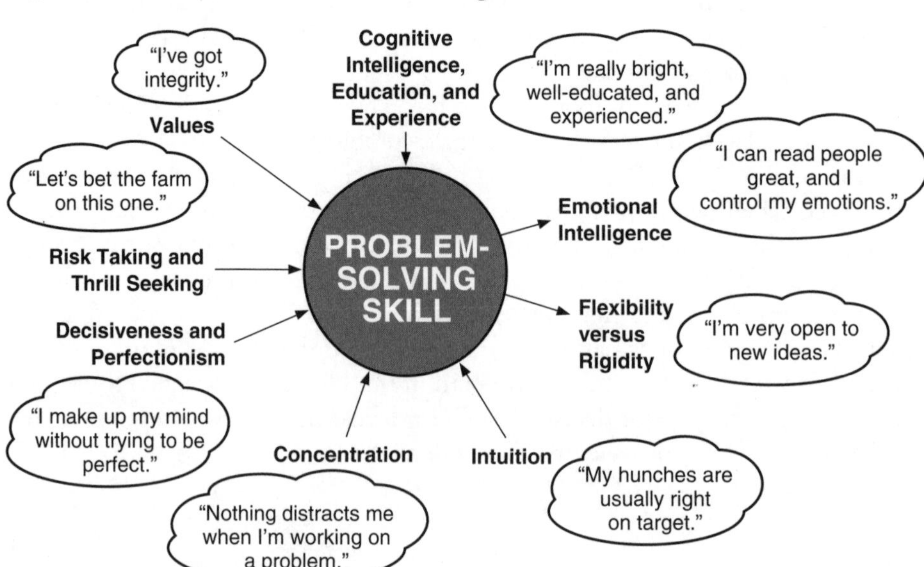

Emotional Intelligence

Being able to deal effectively with your feelings and emotions and those of others can help you make better decisions. **Emotional intelligence** refers to qualities such as understanding one's own feelings, empathy for others, and the regulation of emotion to enhance living. This type of intelligence has to do with the ability to connect with people and understand their emotions. A worker with high emotional intelligence would be able to engage in such behaviours as sizing up people, pleasing others, and influencing them.[2]

Emotional intelligence is important for decision making because effectiveness in managing your feelings and reading other people can affect the quality of your decisions. For example, if you cannot control your anger you are likely to make decisions that are motivated by retaliation, hostility, and revenge. An example would be shouting and swearing at your team leader because of a work assignment you received. Your emotional intelligence could also influence your career decision making. If you understand your own feelings, you are more likely to enter an occupation or accept a position that matches your true attitude.

Flexibility versus Rigidity

Some people are successful problem solvers and decision makers because they approach every problem with a fresh outlook. They are able to avoid developing rigid viewpoints. Flexible thinking enables the problem solver to think of original—and therefore creative—alternative solutions to solving a problem. Another perspective on the same issue is that being open-minded helps a person solve problems well. For example, a person might face the problem of wanting to purchase a high-quality PC but lacks sufficient funds. So the person keeps searching for a high-quality PC at a bargain price. If the person were more open-minded, he or she might investigate a "Net PC." Such a computer is low-priced because, instead of having a hard drive of its own, it temporarily downloads programs from the internet. The link between flexibility and creativity will be described in more detail in the discussion of the characteristics of creative people.

Intuition

Effective decision makers do not rely on careful analysis alone. Instead, they also use their **intuition**, a method of arriving at a conclusion by a quick judgment or "gut feel." Intuition takes place when the brain gathers information stored in memory and packages it as a new insight or solution. Intuitions, therefore, can be regarded as stored information that is reorganized or repackaged.[3] Developing good intuition may take a long time because so much information has to be stored. Considerable attention has been drawn to the importance of intuition in managerial decision making. Managers must still analyze problems systematically. Cognitive psychologist Gary Klein explains it this way:

> We sometimes think that experts are weighted down by information, by facts, by memories—that they make decisions slowly because they must search through so

> much data. But in fact, we've got it backward. The accumulation of experience does not weight people down—it lightens them up. It makes them fast.[4]

Interviews with 60 high-level professional employees emphasized the link between intuition and experience. It was found that employees who have more experience, who are older, or who hold managerial positions tend to use intuition more. The researchers claimed that upper-level executives need to apply intuition more than others because of their need to see the bigger picture and to deal with the long term.[5] Yet having good intuition helps you make better decisions in almost all professional jobs and at any stage in your career. For example, a 25-year-old credit analyst can profitably use intuition to help size up credit risks. (She or he can watch out for those notorious beady eyes, in addition to methodically evaluating the loan applicant's credit history!)

To use intuition to your advantage, you have to know when to rely on facts and figures and when to rely on intuitive skills. Intuition is often required when the facts and figures in a situation still leave you with uncertainty. One way of sharpening your intuition is to keep an idea journal. Whenever an insight comes to you, record it on paper or electronically. If you notice that you shut off these insights without carefully processing them, you will know that you must learn to give them more careful thought.[6]

Concentration

Mental concentration is an important contributor to making good decisions. Many people who solve problems poorly do so because they are too distracted to immerse themselves in the problem at hand. In contrast, effective problem solvers often achieve the **flow experience**—total absorption in their work. When flow occurs, things seem to go just right. The person feels alive and fully attentive to what he or she is doing. As a by-product of the flow experience, a good solution to a problem may surface. If you fail to concentrate hard enough you may overlook an important detail that could affect the outcome of the decision. For example, a person about to purchase an automobile might be excited about the high gas mileage but forget to research the vehicle's ability to withstand a crash.

Some people are ill-suited to solving problems and making decisions because they are fearful of committing themselves to any given course of action. "Gee, I'm not sure, what do you think?" is their typical response to a decision forced upon them. If you are indecisive, this characteristic will have to be modified if you are to become a success in your field. A manager has to decide which person to hire. And a photographer has to decide which setting is best for the subject. As the old saying goes, at some point you have to "fish or cut bait."

People can be indecisive because they are perfectionists. With regard to decision making, **perfectionism** is a pattern of behaviour in which the individual strives to accomplish almost unattainable standards of flawless work. Psychologist J. Clayton Lafferty explains that "Perfectionism is a way of thinking and behaving that seems like a search for excellence and perfection but actually brings great unhappiness, poor health, and massive imperfection."[7] Perfectionism leads people toward indecisiveness and delay in making decisions because they usually believe that they need more information before making a choice. Have you ever noticed how a perfectionist goes about purchasing an expensive piece of consumer electronics equipment? He or she might visit many stores, ask the opinions of many people, and search for extensive written material before making a choice. At the electronics store, the person barrages the store associate with a long series of picky questions.

The combination of being indecisive and a perfectionist can lead to procrastination. Also, being a procrastinator can make one indecisive. Perfectionism contributes to delayed decision making because the person keeps working on a project before deciding to submit it to somebody else. Have you noticed any students or work colleagues with this type of procrastination? Chapter 15, about work habits, examines procrastination in depth.

Risk Taking and Thrill Seeking

The need for taking risks and seeking thrills is yet another personality characteristic that influences problem-solving skill. For some types of problems, the risk taker and thrill seeker is at an advantage. Firefighters have to take risks to save people from burning buildings and to remove people trapped in collapsed buildings. An information technology specialist might have to engage in a risky manoeuvre to salvage data from a crashed hard drive. Risk taking and thrill seeking can also lead to poor problem solving and decision making, such as a merchandiser buying a huge inventory of highly original fashions. The experienced decision maker needs to know when to take high risks and seek thrills and when to be more conservative.

Values of the Decision Maker

Values influence decision making at every step. The right values for the situation will improve problem solving and decision making, whereas the wrong values will lead to poor decisions. Ultimately, all decisions are based on values. A manager who places a high value on the well-being of employees tries to avoid alternatives that create hardships for workers. Another value that significantly influences problem solving and decision making is the pursuit of excellence. A worker who embraces the pursuit of excellence (and is therefore conscientious) will search for the high-quality alternative solution.

Attempting to preserve the status quo is a value that can negatively influence problem solving. Clinging to the status quo is perceived as a hidden trap in decision making that can prevent making the best decisions. People tend to cling to the status quo because, by *not* taking action, they can prevent a bad decision.[8] If you value the status quo too highly, you may fail to make a decision that could bring about major improvements. For example, an executive might not bother offering dependent-care benefits to employees because he or she has not received complaints. However, by not offering these benefits, the company may be losing out on some talented prospective employees.

So You've Decided to Be a CEO (Chief Executive Officer)—How Do You Get There?

A recent article in *Canadian Business* went looking for and found five of the brightest young executives in Canada. All five were young, powerful, driven, and very ambitious, often with their sights on attaining a CEO position within the next few years. The five included Andrew Nevin, Managing Director of TD Green Line Investor Services for the Asia-Pacific Region; Michael McCain, President and COO (Chief Operating Officer), Maple Leaf Foods Inc.; Dawn Farrell, VP, independent power projects, TransAlta Corp.; Paula Zivot, Marketing Manager of private brands, Zellers Inc.; and Kathy McLaughlin, VP, Western Canada Microcell Telecommunications Inc. These five people have all worked hard in school and since leaving school. Another common characteristic that stands out in this article is their ability to not only manage change, but to embrace and be excited by changes in their various industries. They all meet challenges head on and demonstrate flexibility and creativity. For example, Paula Zivot was pivotal in the successful launch of the Martha Stewart and Cherokee lines at Zellers.

This article also included "A Brilliant Career Path," a graph of where a number of experts think you should be at specific points in your life to launch your CEO career. If you want to attain these milestones, you will have to make many decisions and solve many problems. You should complete your MBA (if you plan to get one) by your early 30s. It can be too difficult to take time off and get it later on. If you want to take time off and travel or do other things, do them in your early 20s. In your 20s and 30s you should be changing jobs and titles regularly. Before the age of 40, you need to get noticed and start earning the big money; as a general rule, you should be making about two-and-a-half times your age. By your early 40s you should be at least vice-president and have headhunters trying to get you to switch firms. If this has not happened by your early 40s, you may want to set your sights on something else.

However, take note: this is just one article on CEOs. The key is to make effective decisions once you have some ideas about where you want to be in your career. Many of us may not want to be CEOs, but if you do, you may want to jot a few of these ideas down or, better yet, read the complete article.

Source: David Berman, "Looking Great for 2008," *Canadian Business*, July 31/August 14, 1998, pp. 40–71. Used with permission.

Problem-Solving Styles

A well-documented observation is that people go about solving problems in various ways. You may have observed, for example, that some people are more analytical and systematic while others are more intuitive. The most widely used method of classifying problem-solving styles is the Myers-Briggs Type Indicator (MBTI).[9] A key aspect of the MBTI is to understand how people gather and evaluate information to solve problems.

To solve problems it is necessary to gather information. Styles of information gathering range from sensation to intuition. **Sensation-type individuals** prefer routine and order. They search for precise details when gathering information to solve a problem. These people would prefer to work with established facts rather than search for new possibilities. **Intuitive-type individuals** prefer an overall perspective—the big picture. Such people enjoy solving new problems. In addition, they dislike routine and would prefer to look for possibilities rather than work with facts.

When shopping for an automobile, a sensation-type individual would want to gather a large number of facts about such matters as kilometres per litre, provisions of the warranty, finance charges, and resale value. In contrast, the intuitive-type individual would be more concerned about the overall style of the car and how proud he or she would be as the owner.

The evaluation aspect of problem solving involves judging how to deal with information after it has been collected. Styles of information evaluation range from an emphasis on feeling to an emphasis on thinking. **Feeling-type individuals** have a need to conform, and they attempt to adapt to the wishes of others. Because of these tendencies, they try to avoid problems that might result in disagreements. **Thinking-type individuals** rely on reason and intellect to deal with problems. They downplay emotion in problem solving and decision making.

Assume that a manager asks a group of employees their opinions on an idea for a new product. Feeling-type people in the group are likely to look for the good in the proposal and express approval for the new project. Thinking-type group members are likely to be more independent in their evaluation of the new product idea. As a result, they will express their opinion even if it is not what the manager wants to hear.

The two dimensions of information gathering and evaluation are combined to produce a four-way classification of problem-solving styles, as shown in Exhibit 3-1. The four styles are (1) sensation-thinking, (2) sensation-feeling, (3) intuitive-thinking, and (4) intuitive-feeling. Listed below each type are examples of occupations well suited for people of that particular type.

If you take the Myers-Briggs Type Indicator assessment, often available in career centres, you will discover your type. You can also study these four types and make a tentative judgment as to your problem-solving style. Recognizing your problem-solving style can help you identify work that you are likely to perform well. For example, a person with an intuitive-feeling style is likely to be skillful in resolving customer complaints. The same person might not be well suited by temperament to bookkeeping.

Problem-Solving and Decision-Making Steps

Before moving on to the steps of problem solving and decision making, let's make sure we understand the differences between the two processes. Some problems are relatively simple and do not require any sort of step-by-step process. For example, if I have a sliver in my thumb, the solution to this painful experience is rather obvious. However, other problems may be more complex and you may need to generate and evaluate several solutions. Coming up with all the alternatives is part of both problem solving and decision making. Problem solving can be thought of as a complex decision-making process whereby a group or person analyzes a problem and develops a plan of action to solve the problem or reduce the effects of the problem. The actual decision-making component of the process is the part of this problem-solving model where you generate alternatives, weigh the various alternatives, and finally choose one or more alternatives to solve your problem.

The steps in this model are similar to the systematic approach used in the scientific method. Although based on the scientific method, the decision-making and

exhibit 3 - 1

Four Problem-Solving Styles and Work Matchup[10]

Sensation-Thinking: decisive, dependable, alert to details
Accounting and bookkeeping
Computer programming
Manufacturing technology

Intuitive-Thinking: creative, progressive, perceptive
Design of systems
Law, paralegal work
Middle manager

Sensation-Feeling: pragmatic, analytical, methodical, and conscientious
Supervision
Selling
Negotiating

Intuitive-Feeling: colourful, people person, helpful
Customer service
Business communications
Human resources

problem-solving steps presented here do not exclude the role of intuition. Rather, finding creative alternatives to your problem is actually at the heart of this method. Paying attention to this model is important because deviating too far from the model will often result in decision failure. Paul C. Nutt studied 356 decisions in medium to large organizations in the United States and Canada. He found that one-half of these decisions failed, mostly because the decision makers did not take a systematic approach, such as searching for many alternative solutions. The managers involved also committed the human relations error of not involving enough other people in helping with the decisions.[11]

Figure 3-2 summarizes the steps involved in problem solving and decision making. It is based on the assumption that decision making and problem solving should take place in an orderly flow of steps.

Awareness of the Problem

Problem solving and decision making begin when somebody is aware that a problem exists. In most decision-making situations, problems are given to another person. Jenny was presented with the problem of what to do with her parents' proposal. At other times, people create their own problems to solve, or they find problems. When one man decided that there were too many potholes in the streets of his town, he campaigned for the town supervisor to take decisive action on the problem.

Figure 3-2 Problem-Solving and Decision-Making Steps

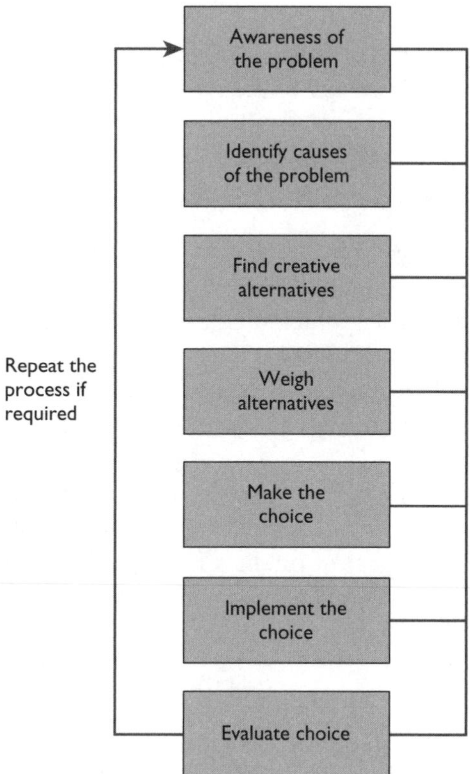

After you have identified the problem, recognize that it may represent an important opportunity. Paul Hawken, a company founder and author, says that "a mess is a pile of opportunities."[12] For example, if you are bothered enough by a problem facing your company, you might volunteer to be the person in charge of overcoming the problem.

Identify Causes of the Problem

The causes of problems should be diagnosed and clarified before any action is taken because they are not always what they seem to be on the surface. Some problems may be more complicated than suspected. You may even be facing the wrong problem—not the one you need to solve in a particular situation. The person who found the potholes was thinking about treating the symptoms and not the real problem. Although it certainly would be advisable for the town to patch its potholes, the best solution would be to attend to the cause of potholes. The town would never be able to change the weather conditions, of course, but it could strengthen all new pavement. One petroleum company, for example, has developed a type of webbing that dramatically reduces potholes when placed beneath the surface of a street.

Identifying the root cause of a problem can sometimes be facilitated by asking a series of questions. Five key elements to ask questions about (along with some sample questions) are as follows:

- *People.* What do the people involved contribute to the problem? Are they competent? Do they have an attitude problem?
- *Materials.* Do we have the right materials available? Is the quality of the materials adequate?
- *Machines and facilities.* Do we have the right machines and facilities to do the job? Have the machines and facilities changed?
- *Physical environment.* Is anything wrong with the environment (such as toxic fumes making people sick)? Has the environment changed?
- *Methods.* Are the processes and procedures adequate? Have new methods been introduced that workers do not understand?

An associate in a consumer electronics shop used the above questions to quickly identify why a customer's brand-new CD player played music with such a muffled sound. In asking about the physical environment, the associate identified the fact that the customer placed the CD player on a thick carpet—the cause of the problem.

Even when you have identified the general source of a problem, you may still need to dig further to discover what, when, and where a problem *did not* occur. Suppose a friend talks about a fear of public speaking. By asking a few "but not" questions, you might be able to identify a major cause of the problem. Let's try out the method:

Your friend: I'm horribly afraid of public speaking. I hate going up in front of the class.
You: But have you ever not been afraid of speaking to a group of people?
Your friend: Yes, I can remember once feeling OK speaking at a victory dinner for my high school soccer team. We came in first in the region.
You: What did you talk about?
Your friend: I told a cute story about how my mother and father put a soccer ball in my crib. I hugged it every day like it was a teddy bear.
You: So why weren't you afraid of giving that talk?
Your friend: I knew what I was talking about. I didn't have to rehearse.
You: What else was different about the talk?
Your friend: It wasn't like talking to strangers. I was just there with my buddies and our coaches.
You: What you are really telling me is that public speaking is OK when you are well prepared and you are in comfortable surroundings.
Your friend: Thanks for helping me understand my problem.

Find Creative Alternatives

Here creativity and imagination enter into problem solving and decision making. Successful decision makers have the ability to think of different alternatives. The person who pushes to find one more alternative to a problem is often the person who finds a breakthrough solution. Creativity plays such an important role in decision making that it will be discussed again in the next two major sections of this chapter.

Weigh Alternatives

This stage refers simply to examining the pros and cons of the various alternatives in the previous stages. In a major decision, each alternative would have to be given serious consideration. In practice, weighing alternatives often means jotting down the key good and bad points of each possible choice. Part of Jenny's list might read something like this:

> **Alternative 1: Agree to enter family business**
> On the plus side, I would have a high-paying, secure job. My parents would be forever grateful to me, and I would avoid a family feud. I could also save money for Rick and I to get married someday.
>
> On the negative side, I would miss out on fulfilling my dreams of moving to British Columbia. Even worse, my relationship with Rick might go down the tubes. It's hard to keep a relationship alive long-distance.

A source of error when weighing alternatives is to rely too much on the first information you receive. The information anchors some people to their first alternative, thereby overshadowing data and impressions that come later.[13] Anchoring can be somewhat minimized by remembering that decision making is incomplete until many alternatives have been explored.

Make the Choice

The essence of decision making is selecting the right course of action to follow. You have to choose an alternative, even if it is not to go ahead with a new plan of action. For instance, after conducting a job campaign you could decide not to change jobs. Experienced business executives have often criticized well-educated young people for their lack of decisiveness. Instead of coming to a decision, the young people are accused of over-analyzing a problem. Do you suffer from "analysis paralysis," or do you make up your mind after a reasonable amount of thought?

In choosing an alternative, it is helpful to remember that most problems really have multiple solutions. You therefore do not have to be overly concerned with finding the only correct answer to your problem. For instance, there might be several effective ways of reducing the costs of running a department.

Implement the Choice

After you decide which course of action to take, you have to put the choice into effect. Some decisions are more difficult to implement than others. Decisions made by top management, for example, are sometimes so difficult to implement that they have to be reversed. An executive announced a new policy that all employees would be restricted to 45-minute lunch breaks. Few employees took the edict

seriously, and most continued to spend about 60 minutes at lunch. The executive gave up and reconsidered the decision in terms of its effect on morale. The general point is that to implement many decisions, the human element must be taken into consideration.

Evaluate the Choice

The decision-making sequence is not complete until the decision has been evaluated. Evaluation may take a considerable period of time because the results of your decision are not always immediately apparent. Suppose you receive two job offers. It might take several months to a year to judge whether you are satisfied with the job you accepted. It would be necessary to look at the factors you think are most important in a job. Among them might be "Is there opportunity for advancement?" "Are the people here friendly?" "Is the work interesting?" Evaluating your choice would be further complicated by the difficulty of determining how you might have fared in the job you didn't accept. Now and then you might obtain some information to suggest what that alternative held in store for you, as did a woman who turned down a job offer with a new and promising company. She questioned that decision until she read one morning a year later that the company had gone into bankruptcy.

What happens when your evaluation of a decision is negative? You go back to the drawing board, as the line and arrow on the left-hand side of Figure 3-2 indicates. Since your first decision was not a good one, you are faced with another problem situation.

A helpful decision-making aid is to visualize what you would do if the alternative you chose proved to be dreadful—the **worst-case scenario**. Suppose, for example, you choose a job that proves to be unsuited to your talents. Would you resign as soon as your mistake became apparent, or would you sweat it out for a year in order to show some employment stability? Or would you retain the job while starting to look around for a more suitable job? Developing a worst-case scenario helps prevent you from becoming overwhelmed by the fear of making a bad decision.

An important benefit of applying the problem-solving and decision-making steps is that they can be used to tackle subparts of a larger problem. Two partners may decide that they would like to attempt self-employment. A problem of this nature is so complex that it might best be resolved by approaching various components: (1) "What business should we enter?" (2) "How would we obtain financing?" (3) "Would it be better to start our business part-time rather than quit our day jobs?"

To gain practice in developing your skills in making major decisions, do Human Relations Skill-Building Exercise 3-1. You will be given some additional practice in using the problem-solving method in the end-of-chapter case study.

Creativity in Decision Making

Creativity is helpful at any stage of decision making, but it is essential for recognizing problems, analyzing them, and searching for creative alternatives. Simply put, **creativity** is the ability to develop good ideas that can be put into action. Finding a creative idea usually involves a flash of insight about how to solve a problem. If you have above-average creativity you will be more adept at solving problems in both work and personal life.

When people see or hear the word *creativity,* many think of a rarefied talent. A more helpful perspective is to recognize that not all creativity requires wild imagination. According to creativity expert Michael Kirton, two types of creativity exist. *Adaptive creativity* involves improving an existing system, such as identifying what is wrong in a customer billing system and correcting the problem. *Innovative creativity* involves creating something new. Instead of trying to correct the invoicing system, the person using innovative creativity would discard it and start all over.[14]

The emphasis here is on creativity applied to business and personal life rather than on creativity in science, technology, and the arts. Creativity is important for companies of all sizes, not only for large firms. According to a survey conducted by American Express Small Business Services, three-quarters of small-business owners acknowledge that creative thinking is either "very important" (54 percent) or "crucial" (20 percent) to the success of their firms. About three-quarters of the respondents block out time for idea generation, anywhere from less than one hour per week up to one day per week.[15]

Using the Problem-Solving Process

Imagine that you have received $1,000,000 in cash. The only stipulation is that you will have to use the money to establish some sort of enterprise, either a business or a charitable foundation. Solve this problem, using the worksheet provided below. Describe what thoughts you have or what actions you will take for each step of problem solving and decision making.

1. *Awareness of the problem:* **Have you found your own problem or was it given to you?**

2. *Identify causes of the problem:* **What is your underlying problem? What is the true decision that you are facing?**

3. *Find creative alternatives:* **Think of the many alternatives facing you. Let your imagination flow and be creative.**

4. *Weigh alternatives:* **Weigh the pros and cons of each of your sensible alternatives.**

	Alternatives	Advantages	Disadvantages
a.			
b.			
c.			
d.			
e.			

5. *Make the choice:* **Based on your analysis in step 4, choose the best alternative.**

6. *Implement the choice:* **Outline your action plan for converting your chosen alternative into action.**

7. *Evaluate the choice:* **Do the best you can here by speculating how you will know if the decision you reached was a good one.**

Measuring Your Creative Potential

One way to gain an understanding of creativity is to try out exercises used to measure creative potential, such as those presented in Human Relations Self-Assessment Quizzes 3-1 and 3-2. Do not be overly encouraged or dejected by any results you achieve on these exercises, as both of them only measure creativity based on verbal ability. Human Relations Skill-Building Exercise 3-2 (the solution can be found near the end of this chapter) demonstrates how visualizing objects and shapes is important for creative problem solving. In order to solve this problem, you will need to rely on intuition. Persistence alone will not lead to a correct solution. Remember that these activities are designed to give only preliminary insights into whether your thought processes are similar to those of creative individuals, so do not be discouraged if you have some problems. This is just a starting point for you to learn and then develop your own creativity.

Quiz 3-1

Creative Personality Test

The following test will help you determine if certain aspects of your personality are similar to those of a creative individual. Since our test is for illustrative and research purposes, proceed with caution in mind. This is not a standardized psychological instrument. Such tests are not reprinted in general books. Answer each of the following statements as "mostly true" or "mostly false." We are looking for general trends; therefore, do not be concerned if you answer true if they are not entirely true and false if they are not entirely false.

	Mostly True	*Mostly False*
1. I think novels are a waste of time, so I am more likely to read nonfiction books.	_______	_______
2. You have to admit, some crooks are very clever.	_______	_______
3. People consider me to be a fastidious dresser. I despise looking shaggy.	_______	_______
4. I am a person of very strong convictions. What's right is right; what's wrong is wrong.	_______	_______
5. I enjoy it when my boss hands me vague instructions.	_______	_______
6. Business before pleasure is a hard and fast rule in my life.	_______	_______
7. Taking a different route to work is fun, even if it takes longer.	_______	_______
8. Rules and regulations should not be taken too seriously. Most rules can be broken under unusual circumstances.	_______	_______

(continued)

	Mostly True	Mostly False
9. Playing with a new idea is fun even if it doesn't benefit me in the end.	______	______
10. People say that I have an excellent sense of humour.	______	______
11. Writers should try to avoid using unusual words and word combinations.	______	______
12. Detective work would have some appeal to me.	______	______
13. Crazy people have no good ideas.	______	______
14. Why write letters to friends when there are so many clever greeting cards available in the stores today?	______	______
15. Pleasing myself means more to me than pleasing others.	______	______
16. If you dig long enough, you will find the true answer to most questions.	______	______

Scoring the Test: The answer in the creative direction for each question is as follows:

1. Mostly False	5. Mostly True	9. Mostly True	13. Mostly False
2. Mostly True	6. Mostly False	10. Mostly True	14. Mostly False
3. Mostly False	7. Mostly True	11. Mostly False	15. Mostly True
4. Mostly False	8. Mostly True	12. Mostly True	16. Mostly False

Give yourself a point for each answer you gave that agreed with the keyed answers.

Interpreting Your Score: A score of 12 or more suggests that your personality and attitudes are similar to those of a creative person. A score of 5 or less suggests that your personality is dissimilar to that of a creative person. You are probably more of a conformist (and somewhat categorical) in your thinking, at least at this point in your life. Don't be discouraged. Most people can become more creative.

Rhyme and Reason[16]

A noted creativity expert says that exercises in rhyming release creative energy; they stir imagination into action. While doing the following exercises remember that rhyme is frequently a matter of sound and does not have to involve similar or identical spelling. This exercise deals with light and frivolous emotions. After each "definition," write two rhyming words to which it refers.

Examples:

1.	Large hog	Big	pig
2.	Television	Boob	tube
3.	A computer control for the home	House	mouse

Now try these:

1. Happy father ______ ______
2. False pain ______ ______
3. Formed like a simian ______ ______
4. Highest-ranking police worker ______ ______
5. Voyage by a large boat ______ ______
6. Corpulent feline ______ ______
7. Melancholy fellow ______ ______
8. Clever beginning ______ ______
9. Heavy and unbroken slumber ______ ______
10. Crazy custom ______ ______
11. Lengthy melody ______ ______
12. Weak man ______ ______
13. Instruction at the seashore ______ ______
14. Criticism lacking in effectiveness ______ ______
15. A person who murders for pleasurable excitement ______ ______
16. Musical stringed instrument with full, rich sounds ______ ______
17. Courageous person who is owned as property by another ______ ______
18. Mature complaint ______ ______
19. Strange hair growing on the lower part of a man's face ______ ______
20. Drooping marine crustacean ______ ______
21. A computer whiz with a bizarre sense of humour ______ ______

Answers and Interpretation: The more of these rhymes you were able to come up with, the higher your creative potential. You would also need an advanced vocabulary to score very high (for instance, what is a "simian" or a "crustacean"?). Ten or more correct rhymes would tend to show outstanding creative potential, at least in the verbal area. Here are the answers:

1. Glad dad
2. Fake ache
3. Ape shape
4. Top cop
5. Ship trip
6. Fat cat
7. Sad lad
8. Smart start
9. Deep sleep
10. Mad fad
11. Long song
12. Frail male
13. Beach teach
14. Weak critique
15. Thriller killer
16. Mellow cello
17. Brave slave
18. Ripe gripe
19. Weird beard
20. Limp shrimp
21. Absurd nerd

If you can think of a sensible substitute for any of these answers, give yourself a bonus point.

Characteristics of Creative Workers

Creative workers tend to have different intellectual and personality characteristics from their less creative counterparts. In general, creative people are more mentally flexible than others, which allows them to overcome the traditional ways of looking at problems. This flexibility often shows up in practical jokes and other forms of playfulness. Laurie, a computer whiz, knew that Sergio, one of her co-workers, had been working for a month on an inventory project. Laurie decided to play a high-tech joke on Sergio. One day when he booted his computer, a message flashed across the screen: "Sorry Sergio, your files have been dumped by the Great Computer Virus." After a five-second pause, another message flashed: "Sorry to frighten you Sergio. Everything is back to normal now. Press return to continue." Later that morning, Laurie confessed to her prank. Sergio said he went through five seconds of agony but had a good laugh when he realized that he was the victim of a practical joke.

The characteristics of creative workers can be grouped into three broad areas: knowledge, intellectual abilities, and personality.[17]

Knowledge

Creative thinking requires a broad background of information, including facts and observations. Knowledge supplies the building blocks for generating and combining ideas. This is particularly true because some experts say that creativity always comes down to combining things in a new and different way. For example, a fax machine is a combination of a telephone and a photocopier.

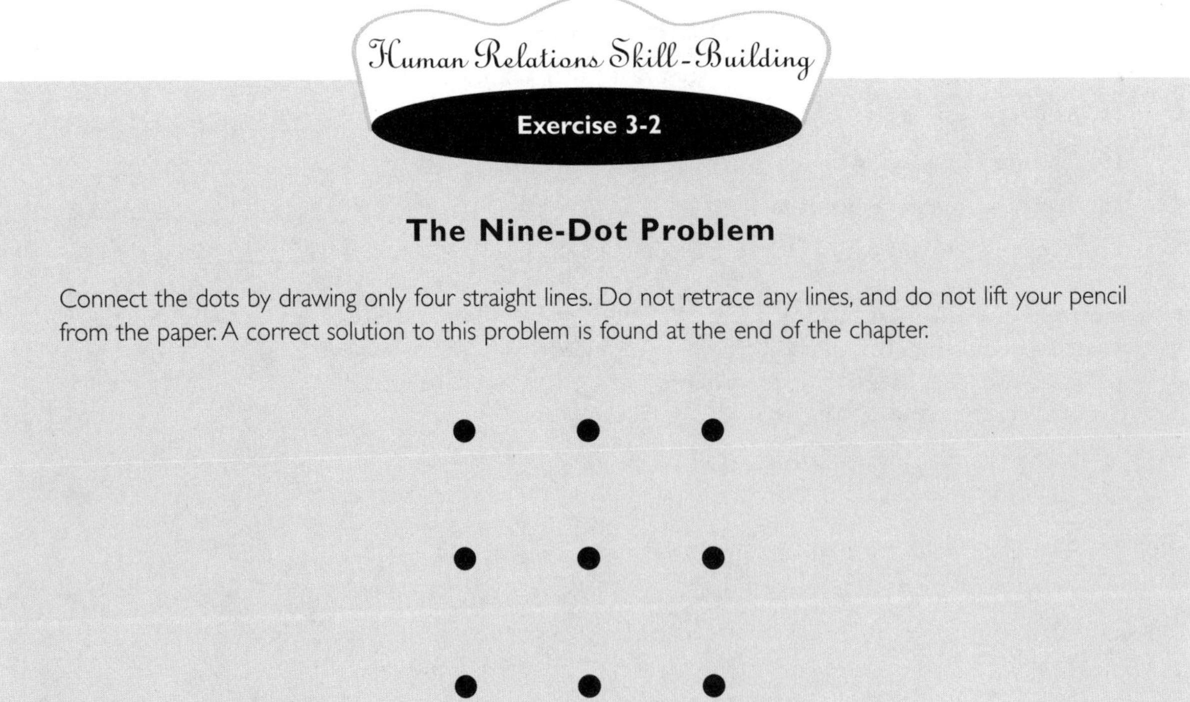

Human Relations Skill-Building

Exercise 3-2

The Nine-Dot Problem

Connect the dots by drawing only four straight lines. Do not retrace any lines, and do not lift your pencil from the paper. A correct solution to this problem is found at the end of the chapter.

Intellectual Abilities

In general, creative workers tend to be bright rather than brilliant. Extraordinarily high intelligence is not required to be creative. Yet creative people are good at generating alternative solutions to problems in a short period of time. Creative people also maintain a youthful curiosity throughout their lives. And the curiosity is not centred on just their own field of expertise. Instead, their range of interests encompasses many areas of knowledge, and they generate enthusiasm toward almost any puzzling problem. It has also been observed that creative people are open and responsive to feelings and emotions in the world around them.

Creative people are able to think divergently. They can expand the number of alternatives to a problem, thus moving away from a single solution. Yet the creative thinker also knows when it is time to think convergently, narrowing the number of useful solutions. For example, the divergent thinker might think of 27 different names for a website that sells high-fashion buttons. Yet at some point he or she will have to converge and choose the best URL, such as **www.chicbutton.com**.

Creativity can stem from both *fluid intelligence* and *crystallized intelligence*. Fluid intelligence depends on raw processing ability, or how quickly you learn information and solve problems. Like raw athletic ability, fluid intelligence begins to decline by age 30, particularly because nerve conduction slows. Crystallized intelligence is accumulated knowledge that increases with age and experience.[18]

Personality

The emotional and other nonintellectual aspects of a person heavily influence creative problem solving. Creative people tend to have a positive self-image without being blindly self-confident. Because they are self-confident, creative people are able to cope with criticism of their ideas. Creative people have the ability to tolerate the isolation necessary for developing ideas. Talking to others is a good source of ideas. Yet at some point the creative problem solver has to work alone and concentrate.

Creative people are frequently nonconformists, and do not need strong approval from the group. Many creative problem solvers are thrill seekers who find developing imaginative solutions to problems to be a source of thrills. Creative people are also persistent, which is especially important for seeing that a new idea is implemented. Selling a creative idea to the right people requires considerable follow-up. Creative people enjoy dealing with uncertainty and chaos. A creative person, for example, would enjoy the challenge of taking over a customer service department that was way behind schedule and ineffective. Less creative people become frustrated quickly when their job is unclear and disorder exists.

The Conditions Necessary for Creativity

Creativity is not just a random occurrence. Well-known creativity researcher Teresa M. Amabile has summarized 22 years of her research about creativity in the workplace. Her findings are supported by others.[19] Creativity takes place when three components come together: expertise, creative thinking skills, and the right type of motivation.

Expertise refers to the necessary knowledge to put facts together. The more ideas floating around in your head, the more likely you are to combine them in some useful way. *Creative thinking* refers to how flexibly and imaginatively individuals approach problems. If you know how to keep digging for alternatives and how to avoid getting stuck in the status quo, your chances of being creative multiply. Along these same lines, you are much more likely to be creative if you are intentionally seeking ideas, such as always being on the lookout for money-saving ideas. Persevering, or sticking with a problem to a conclusion, is essential for finding creative solutions. A few rest breaks to gain a fresh perspective may be helpful, but the creative person keeps coming back until a solution emerges.

The right type of *motivation* is the third essential ingredient for creative thought. A fascination with or passion for the task is much more important than searching for external rewards. People will be most creative when they are motivated primarily by the satisfaction and challenge of the work itself. A Dutch psychologist attempted to analyze what separated chess masters from chess grand masters. He subjected groups of each to a variety of mental ability tests, but found no difference between the two groups. The only difference found was in motivation: Grand masters simply loved chess more and had more passion and commitment for the game.[20]

Passion for the task and high intrinsic motivation contribute to a total absorption in the work and intense concentration, resulting in the flow experience. (Refer to the section in Chapter 2 about self-motivation.) Flow also means *being in the zone*. A creative businessperson, such as an entrepreneur developing a plan for worldwide distribution of a product, will often achieve the experience of flow.

In addition to the internal conditions that foster creativity, four factors external to a person are key:

1. An environmental need must stimulate the setting of a goal. This is another way of saying that necessity is the mother of invention. Here's an example for animal lovers:

> A dairy farmer in Ontario, Canada, was concerned that his cows suffered so many diseases from the bacteria that accumulate in their surroundings. Bacteria is also hazardous because it can contaminate milk. Another adverse environmental condition the farmer noticed was that cows took too many falls, often suffering serious injuries. The farmer's solution to the problem was a cow mattress. (Just think of the size of the untapped market.) Farmers in Canada, the east coast of the United States, and Europe have been the biggest customers for the mattresses because they are especially effective in cold, rainy climates. The mattresses, made of thick tarp and stuffed with ground-up auto tires, are installed on slanted concrete foundations. The slant keeps rainwater and manure from collecting and becoming a breeding ground for bacteria. The rubber-filled columns on the mattresses serve as shock absorbers that prevent the cows from slipping and injuring themselves.
>
> A California dairy farmer observed that after installing the mattresses, milk production increased, diseases decreased, and the cows were more blissful. Pointing to a cow lying on a mattress and lazily chewing her feed, the farmer said, "See how peaceful and stress-free she looks? That's a happy cow."[21]

2. Another condition that fosters creativity is enough conflict and tension to put people on edge. Jerry Hirschberg, founder and president of Nissan Design International, says that a person should be asked to simultaneously hold apparently conflicting ideas. Understanding opposing ideas helps you gain a new perspective. Some automobile designers were arguing about how to satisfy the conflicting consumer demands of having more storage space in an SUV without adding length. The demands seemed incompatible until one engineer flashed on an answer—a simple vertical rack of shelves that would provide ample storage space without increasing the length.[22]
3. Another external factor for creativity is encouragement, including a permissive atmosphere that welcomes new ideas. A manager or team leader who encourages imagination and original thinking and does not punish people for making honest mistakes is likely to receive creative ideas from people. For example, 3M is highly regarded as a company with many innovations including Scotch Tape and Post-it® Notes. The company encourages creativity in many ways, such as granting people time off from regular responsibilities just to think about new ideas.
4. Finally, humour is a key environmental condition for enhancing creativity. Humour has always been linked to creativity. Humour gets the creative juices flowing, and effective humour requires creativity. Thomas Edison started every workday with a joke-telling session. Mike Vance, chairman of the Creative Thinking Association of America, says that "Humour is unmasking the hypocritical. What makes us laugh often is seeing how things are screwed up—then sometimes seeing how we can fix them. Whenever I go into a company and don't hear much laughter, I know it's not a creative place."[23]

Improving Your Creativity

Because of the importance of creative problem solving, many techniques have been developed to improve creativity. Let us look at both specific techniques and general strategies for becoming more creative. The goal of these experiences is to think like a creative problem solver. Such a person lets his or her imagination wander. He or she ventures beyond the constraints that limit most people.

Concentrate Intensely on the Task at Hand

The ability to concentrate was mentioned earlier as a characteristic that contributes to effective problem solving in general. The ability to eliminate distractions also contributes mightily to generating new ideas. At times we think we are thinking intently about our problem (such as how to make cows more comfortable), yet in reality we may be thinking about something that interferes with creativity.[24] Among the office distractions that interfere with concentration are phone calls, a computer beep informing you of an incoming message, a fax machine in the receiving mode, and a friendly hello from a work associate walking past your cubicle. All of the following methods for enhancing creativity require concentration.

Overcome Traditional Mental Sets

An important consequence of becoming more intellectually flexible is that you can overcome a **traditional mental set**, a fixed way of thinking about objects and activities. Overcoming traditional mental sets is important because the major block to creativity is perceiving things in a traditional way. All creative examples presented so far in this chapter illustrate the power of overcoming a traditional mental set. In the anecdote about the storage space in the SUV, the designer solved an apparently impossible problem by thinking in a mental set different from that suggested by the original request. Instead of adding another six inches of room, the designer reframed the question: "How can we find more storage space?"

An effective way of overcoming a traditional mental set is to challenge the status quo. If you want to develop an idea that will impress your boss or turn around an industry, you must use your imagination. Question the old standby that things have always been done in a particular way. To make the information superhighway possible, many old standby assumptions had to be questioned. Among them were that (1) the only way to obtain videos for home use is to bring a videocassette into the home, and (2) only telephone cables can be used to transmit digital information.

Human Relations Self-Assessment Quiz 3-3 gives you an opportunity to examine your tendencies toward overcoming traditional mental sets.

Discipline Yourself to Think Laterally

A major challenge in developing creative thinking skills is to learn how to think laterally in addition to vertically. **Vertical thinking** is an analytical, logical process that results in few answers. The vertical thinker is looking for the one best solution to a problem, much as if he or she were solving an equation in algebra. In contrast, **lateral thinking** spreads out to find many different alternative solutions to a problem. In short, critical thinking is vertical and creative thinking is lateral.

A vertical thinker might say, "I must find a part-time job to supplement my income. My income is not matching my expenses." The lateral thinker might say, "I need more money. Let me think of the various ways of earning more money. I can find a second job, get promoted where I am working, cut my expenses, run a small business out of my home...."

To learn to think laterally, you have to develop the mental set that every problem has multiple alternative solutions. Do not leave the problem until you have sketched out multiple alternatives. Use a pencil or pen and paper or a computer screen, but do not walk away from your problem until you have thought of multiple alternatives.

Conduct Brainstorming Sessions

The best-known method of improving creativity is **brainstorming**, a technique by which group members think of multiple solutions to a problem. Using brainstorming, a group of six people might sit around a table generating new ideas for a product. During the idea-generating part of brainstorming, potential solutions are not criticized or evaluated in any way. In this way spontaneity is

Human Relations Self-Assessment

Quiz 3-3

How Well Do You Think outside the Box?

Creativity and marketing speaker Floyd Hunt has developed a test to see whether you have been lulled into complacency and therefore are not thinking creatively.
For each statement, rank yourself on the following 10-point scale:

I can't remember	**1–2 points**
Not in the past year	**3–4 points**
Sometime in the past year	**5–6 points**
In the past month	**7–8 points**
It happens often	**9–10 points**

The last time I remember...

1. Someone saying to me, "You've never done that before!" ________
2. Changing my routine for no particular reason other than I just wanted to ________
3. Rearranging my office, living room, or sock drawer, just for fun ________
4. Someone telling me "It can't be done," and my trying anyway ________
5. Fighting for an idea ________
6. Feeling that I was way out on a limb ________
7. Being told "You're wrong" because I tried something new ________
8. Being wrong ________
9. Doing something that made me nervous ________
10. Feeling afraid and exhilarated at the same time ________

Scoring

Less than 20: Get your head out of the sand.

21–50: You have potential, but your routines need to be shaken up.

51–80: You've either reached or are heading for success; watch out for becoming too complacent.

81–100: Let me get out of your way!

SOURCE: "Success Quiz," *Success*, November 1998, p. 22.

encouraged. The original device for programming VCRs by simply punching one number was a product of brainstorming. The product retails for about $75. It is designed for people who are unable or unwilling to learn how to program a VCR. Rules for brainstorming are presented in Exhibit 3-2. Brainstorming has many variations, including an electronic approach, creative twosomes, brainwriting, and forced associations.

Electronic Brainstorming

In electronic brainstorming, group members simultaneously enter their suggestions into a computer. The ideas are distributed to the screens of other group members. Although the group members do not talk to each other, they are still able to build on each other's ideas and combine ideas.

Electronic brainstorming helps overcome certain problems encountered in traditional brainstorming. Shyness, domination by one or two members, and participants who loaf tend to be less troublesome than in face-to-face situations. An experiment indicated that, with large groups, electronic brainstorming produces more useful ideas than the usual type.[25]

exhibit 3-2

Rules and Guidelines for Brainstorming

1. Use groups of about five to seven people.
2. Encourage the spontaneous expression of ideas. All suggestions are welcome, even if they are outlandish or outrageous. The least workable ideas can be edited out when the idea-generation phase is completed.
3. Quantity and variety are very important. The greater the number of ideas, the greater the likelihood of a breakthrough idea.
4. Encourage combination and improvement of ideas. This process is referred to as "piggybacking" or "hitchhiking."
5. One person serves as the secretary and records the ideas, perhaps posting them on a chalkboard.
6. In many instances, it pays to select a moderator who helps keep the session on track. The moderator can prevent one or two members from dominating the meeting. If the moderator takes notes, a secretary is not needed.
7. Do not overstructure by following any of the above rules too rigidly. Brainstorming is a spontaneous process.
8. To broaden idea generation, think about how a characteristic of something might be if it were modified: how something might be if it were larger or more frequent; if it were smaller or less frequent; or if something else could be used instead.

Creative Twosomes

Some of the advantages of brainstorming can be achieved by thinking through a challenging problem with a partner. As Michael LeBoeuf observes, creative twosomes are a favourite in the music business (for example, Rodgers and Hammerstein). Many researchers work in twosomes. Part of the creative-twosome technique is to audiotape your problem-solving session. After exhausting your ideas, return and listen to your tape together. Listening to previous ideas helps spur new thoughts. The next time you face a creative assignment, try teaming up with a compatible partner and a tape recorder.[26]

Brainwriting

In many situations brainstorming by yourself produces as many or more useful ideas as does brainstorming in groups. **Brainwriting**, or solo brainstorming, is arriving at creative ideas by jotting them down yourself. The creativity-improvement techniques discussed so far will help you to develop the mental flexibility necessary for brainstorming. After you have loosened up your mental processes, you will be ready to tackle your most vexing problems. Self-discipline is very important for brainwriting because some people have a tendency to postpone something as challenging as thinking alone.

An important requirement of brainwriting is that you set aside a regular time (and perhaps place) for generating ideas. The ideas discovered in the process of routine activities can be counted as bonus time. Even five minutes a day is much more time than most people are accustomed to spending thinking creatively about job problems. Give yourself a quota with a time deadline.

Forced Associations

A widely used method of releasing creativity is the **forced-association technique**. Using this technique, individuals or groups solve a problem by making associations between the properties of two objects. A link is found between the properties of the random object and the properties of the problem object. The forced association is supposed to help solve the problem. An individual (working alone or in a group) selects a word at random from a dictionary or textbook. If you happen to choose a preposition, try again until you find a noun to give you something more to work with. Next, the person (or group) lists many of the properties and attributes of this word. Assume you randomly chose the word *ladder*. Among its attributes are "durable," "foldable," "aluminum or wood," "moderately priced," and "easy to use." If you were trying to improve a bow tie to increase sales, for example, you might make the tie more durable and easier to use.

In the various types of brainstorming just discussed, collecting wild ideas is just the start of the process. After ideas are collected, the group or each member carefully evaluates and analyzes the various alternatives. It is usually important to also specify the implementation details. For example, how do you make a bow tie easier to use other than by adding a clip?

Human Relations Skill-Building Exercise 3-3 will give you an opportunity to practise brainstorming in an area familiar to every reader of this book.

1-800-Insight

Using conventional brainstorming or one of its variations, huddle in small groups. Your task is to develop 800, 888, or 900 telephone numbers for firms in various fields. Keep in mind that the best 800 (or 888, or 900) numbers are easy to memorize and have a logical connection to the goods or services provided. After each group makes up its list of telephone numbers (perhaps about three for each firm on the list), compare results with the other groups. Here is the list of enterprises:

- A nationwide chain of funeral homes
- An air conditioning firm
- A software problem help line for Microsoft Corp.
- A used-car chain
- A prayer service (a 900 number)
- An introduction (dating) service (a 900 number)

Borrow Creative Ideas

Copying the successful ideas of others is a legitimate form of creativity. Be careful, however, to give appropriate credit. Knowing when and which ideas to borrow from other people can help you behave as if you were an imaginative person. Creative ideas can be borrowed through such methods as:

Speaking to friends, relatives, classmates, and co-workers

Reading newspapers, newsmagazines, trade magazines, textbooks, nonfiction books, and novels, and surfing the internet

Watching television and listening to radio programs

Subscribing to computerized information services (expensive but worth it to many ambitious people)

Business firms borrow ideas from each other regularly as part of quality improvement. The process is referred to as *benchmarking* because another firm's product, service, or process is used as a standard of excellence. Benchmarking involves representatives from one company visiting another to observe firsthand the practices of another company. The company visited is usually not a direct competitor. It is considered unethical to visit a competitor company for the purpose of appropriating ideas.

It is difficult to capitalize on your creative ideas unless you keep a careful record of them. A creative idea entrusted to memory may be forgotten under the pressures of everyday living. An important new idea kept on your list of daily errands or duties may become lost. Because creative ideas carry considerable weight in propelling your career forward, they deserve to be recorded in a separate notebook, such as a daily planner.

Challenge Your Ruts

A major hurdle to thinking creatively is getting locked into so many habits and routines that our thinking becomes too mechanical. According to Kathleen R. Allen, "We do the same things, the same way, every day. This is a primary barrier to creativity. Often we need to feel a little uncomfortable—we need to experience new things—to get creative sparks."[27] Challenging your ruts, or habitual way of doing things, can assist you in developing mental flexibility. Anything you do that forces you out of your normal environment will help you see things in new and different ways. Here is a sampling of everyday ruts worth challenging:

- Eating lunch with the same friends at work or school
- Watching the same television shows or reading only the same sections of the newspaper
- Restricting your internet browsing to the same few bookmarks
- Befriending only those people in your same demographic group, such as age range, race, and ethnic background
- Engaging in the same pastimes exclusively
- Using the same form of physical exercise each time you exercise
- Your turn to select a rut: ______________________________

Avoiding ruts is closely associated with overcoming traditional mental sets, as measured in Self-Assessment Quiz 3-3. Traditional mental sets are essentially mental ruts.

Play the Roles of Explorer, Artist, Judge, and Lawyer

A method for improving creativity has been proposed that incorporates many of the suggestions already made. The method calls for you to adopt four roles in your thinking.[28]

First, be an explorer. Speak to people in different fields and get ideas that you can use. For example, if you are a telecommunications specialist, speak to salespeople and manufacturing specialists.

Second, be an artist by stretching your imagination. Strive to spend about five percent of your day asking "what if" questions. For example, a sales manager at a fresh-fish distributor might ask, "What if some new research suggests that eating fish causes intestinal cancer in humans?" Also, remember to challenge the commonly perceived rules in your field. For example, a bank manager challenged why customers needed their cancelled cheques returned each month. This questioning led to some banks not returning cancelled cheques unless the customer paid an additional fee for the service. (As a compromise, some banks send customers photocopies of about ten cheques on one page.)

Third, know when to be a judge. After developing some wild ideas, at some point you have to evaluate them. Do not be so critical that you discourage your own imaginative thinking. However, be critical enough to prevent attempting to implement weak ideas.

Fourth, achieve results with your creative thinking by playing the role of a lawyer. Negotiate and find ways to implement your ideas within your field or place of work. The explorer, artist, and judge stages of creative thought might take only a short time to develop a creative idea. Yet you may spend months or even years getting your brainstorm implemented. For example, it took a long time for the developer of the electronic pager to finally get the product manufactured and distributed on a large scale.

Summary

Problem solving occurs when you try to remove an obstacle that is blocking a path you want to take, or when you try to close the gap between what exists and what you want to exist. Decision making takes place after you encounter a problem. It refers to selecting one alternative from the various courses of action that can be pursued.

Many traits and characteristics influence the type of problem solver you are now or are capable of becoming. Among them are (1) flexibility versus rigidity; (2) cognitive intelligence, education, and experience; (3) emotional intelligence; (4) intuition; (5) concentration; (6) decisiveness and perfectionism; (7) risk taking and thrill seeking; and (8) values.

The Myers-Briggs Type Indicator is a widely used method of determining problem-solving styles. Information gathering is divided into two main types. Sensation-type individuals prefer routine and order. Intuitive-type individuals prefer an overall perspective. Information evaluation is also divided into two types. Feeling-type individuals have a need to conform. Thinking-type individuals rely on reason and intellect to deal with problems. The two dimensions of information gathering and evaluation are combined to produce a four-way classification of problem-solving styles. Recognizing your problem-solving style can help you identify work you are likely to perform well. (See Exhibit 3-1.)

The decision-making process outlined in this chapter uses both the scientific method and intuition for making decisions in response to problems. Decision making and problem solving follow an orderly flow of events:

1. You are aware of a problem or create one of your own.
2. You identify causes of the problem.
3. You find creative alternatives.
4. You weigh the alternatives.
5. You make the choice.
6. You implement the choice.
7. You evaluate whether you have made a sound choice. If your choice was unsound, you are faced with a new problem and the cycle repeats itself.

Creativity is the ability to develop good ideas that can be put into action. Being creative helps you in both work and personal life. Adaptive creativity involves improving an existing system, whereas innovative creativity involves creating something new. Creative workers tend to have different intellectual and personality characteristics from their less creative counterparts. In general, creative people are more mentally flexible than others, which allows them to overcome the traditional way of looking at problems.

Creative thinking requires a broad background of information, including facts and observations. Creative workers tend to be bright rather than brilliant. The emotional and other nonintellectual aspects of a person heavily influence creative problem solving. For example, creative people are frequently nonconformists and thrill seekers. Creativity takes place when three components come together: expertise, creative thinking skills, and the right type of motivation. Creative thinking refers to being flexible and imaginative. The right type of motivation refers to passion for the task and intrinsic motivation. Four factors external to a person play a key role in fostering creativity: an environmental need, enough conflict and tension to put people on edge, encouragement from management, and the presence of humour.

Methods of improving your creativity include (1) concentrating intensely on the task at hand, (2) overcoming traditional mental sets, (3) disciplining yourself to think laterally (instead of only vertically), (4) conducting brainstorming sessions, (5) borrowing creative ideas, (6) challenging your ruts, and (7) playing the roles of explorer, artist, judge, and lawyer.

Brainstorming has many variations, including electronic brainstorming in which people enter ideas into a computer. Creative twosomes involve interaction with a partner, and brainwriting is solo brainstorming. The forced-association technique requires problem solving by making associations between the properties of two objects.

Questions and Activities

1. What would be some of the symptoms or signs of "rigid thinking"?
2. How might being a perfectionist create performance problems for a team leader? For a paralegal? For a computer programmer?
3. Why does concentration improve problem solving?
4. Why is intuition referred to as the "sixth sense"?
5. Which of the four problem-solving styles shown in Exhibit 3-1 would you prefer to be characteristic of your boss? Explain your reasoning.
6. How might you use the internet to improve major decisions you face on the job and in your personal life?
7. Give two examples of decisions you have faced, or will face, that justify running through the problem-solving and decision-making steps.
8. Think of the most creative person you know. Describe his or her personal characteristics and compare them with the characteristics of creative people presented in this chapter.

9. Ask an experienced manager or professional how important creative thinking has been in her or his career. Report back to the class with your findings.
10. Give an example of one work problem and one personal problem for which brainstorming might be useful.

Internet Skill Builder

Learning about Creativity Training

Use the internet to learn more about what companies are doing to enhance employee creativity. Be specific when you make an entry in your search engine to avoid being deluged with a choice of websites far removed from your topic. A sample phrase to enter into your search engine would be "creativity training program." When you have located one or two sites that give some details about a training program, compare the information you have found to the information in this chapter about creativity enhancement. Note similarities and differences, and be prepared to discuss your findings in class.

About 5,000 web search engines are now in operation. Two effective engines you might have overlooked are **www.northernlight.com** and **www.google.ca**.

Weblinks

www.thinksmart.com
This is a fun and interesting site. You can test your creativity with an absurd and fun test and go into the "Idea Workout Gym."

www.jamming.com
Currently under reconstruction at the time of writing, this site is devoted to creativity.

www.gov.on.ca/OPP
This is the site for the Ontario Provincial Police. From this site, you can access the PARE method of problem solving used by the OPP in their "How Do We Do It?" manual and see how "crime problems" can be solved.

Solution to the Nine-Dot Problem

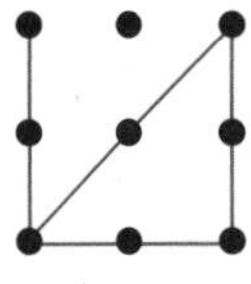

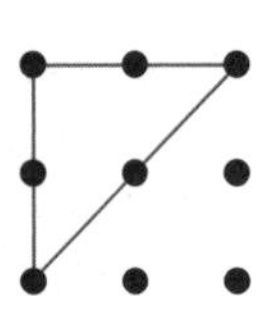

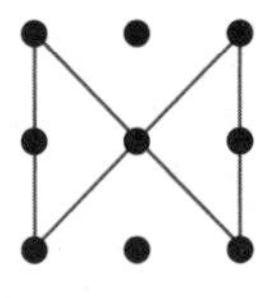

Incorrect solutions

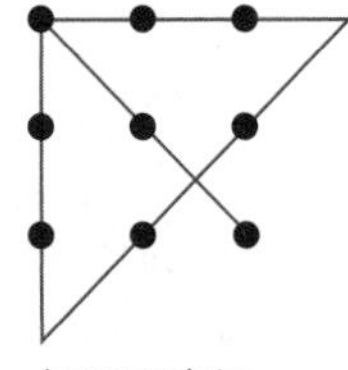

A correct solution

Human Relations Case Study

THE THINKING EXPEDITION

"This is *not* a meeting. This is *not* a training session. This is *not* an exercise," shouts Rolf Smith, who is standing before the Face 2005 Team—22 chemical engineers, biologists, and project leaders from Procter & Gamble Inc. (P&G). Smith says, "This is an expedition. And there will be no whining. No snivelling. No excuses. Please take off your watches and place them in this basket. We will give them back to you in five days." A former US Air Force officer, 59-year-old Smith was known throughout the ranks as "Colonel Innovation."

The Challenge and Rationale for the Expedition

The 22 P&G employees from Hunt Valley, Maryland, are part of a company effort to double the company's revenue by 2005. The team's mandate is to develop new products that will redefine the future of cosmetics. Cathy Pagliaro, 34, an associate director of product development, is responsible for launching this expedition. She says, "Our CEO has declared that Organization 2005 is about three things: stretch, innovation, and speed. The challenge for our small group is to help make those words a reality. My department has a charter to do new and different things to help fulfill our revenue goal. The only way we can change is if we start to think differently."

Rolf Smith's job is to help the team begin to think differently—and to turn what can feel at times like a crushing burden into a thrilling intellectual adventure. A thinking expedition combines creative problem solving with challenging outdoor experiential learning. According to Smith, "The days are intense, full, and demanding. There are no scheduled meals and no scheduled breaks. We deliberately design the expedition to push people out of their 'stupid zone'—a place of mental and physical normalcy—so that they can start to think differently, explore what they don't know, and discover answers to mission-critical problems."

Smith believes that breakthrough ideas come from the edge—that uncomfortable point at which levels of stress, tension, and exhaustion are pushed beyond the comfort zone. "People like to complain that they don't think well when they're tired or hungry. I take those people aside and tell them, 'That's the whole point. We don't want you to think well. We want you to think differently.'"

The Expedition Itself

"You are not who you were yesterday," Smith tells the members of the P&G team, now outfitted in safari vests. The first day of the expedition, which ended at 11:30 p.m., is now behind them. Team members have been briefed on the mission, the rules, and their roles. The main objective is not to solve the specific product-development challenges that the team faces—no one is going to invent new mascara or face cream in the next five days. Rather it is to define and refine the challenge itself ("the mess") that the team faces as it tries to invent new products.

Smith and the P&G team began working on the mess long before they arrived here. Each participant filled out an Expedition Visa, a detailed questionnaire with open-ended and fill-in-the-blank questions. The answers to the questions gave Smith and his team leaders insight into designing the expedition. Cathy Pagliaro didn't tell anyone what they were doing, where they were going, or what to expect. All she told them was to block off several days to go off-site. A lot of people couldn't handle not knowing, but the whole idea was to knock them out of the comfort zone.

To capture ideas, Smith distributes blue slips—pieces of light blue paper measuring two and three-quarter inches by four and one-quarter inches (deliberately not three by five)—that expedition members carry with them at all times. The key to capturing an idea, emphasizes Smith, is to write it down. The hundreds of blue-slip ideas that the Face 2005 Team will generate over five days are gathered into the "Trail Ahead Travel Log." The log is divided into sections that list the team's discoveries, results, vision, concepts of operation, and ways to keep the sense of expedition alive when they return to the office. During the expedition, Smith keeps up a barrage of questions. Some are intentionally vague and seemingly silly, such as "What's a thought that you've never thought before?"

On one hot, humid, and overcast day, the agenda is rock climbing. Harnessed, helmeted, and with all the appropriate legal waivers signed, the Face 2005 Team starts hiking down a narrow path in Virginia's Great Falls Park toward the Potomac River—and toward a sheer rock face at the water's edge.

It's dark as the team hikes back up the steep trail after hours of climbing. Some made it to the top of the cliff, others did not, and some fell off trying, avoiding serious injury or death via the safety ropes. Still, everyone is pumped. Despite groans from a blue-slip-fatigued group, Smith offers the usual flurry of pointed questions. One woman shares her insight: "We're conditioned to think that small steps aren't good enough. But I realize that small steps are just what you need to get to the top."

The trip back down the mountain, called the "long trek home," represents the work required to turn the big ideas that were generated at the summit into useful action items that can be implemented when the team returns. During descent, team members are tired, they want to get home, and worse, they stop thinking. The danger is that they may return to their offices with the "high" of climbing but without the "how" of getting things done differently.

The P&G team experienced several breakthroughs but also breakdowns. A 50-year-old research psychologist on the team wound up in the emergency room with severe rope burns on her hands. She tried a rope swing at 2 a.m. when she lacked the strength to hold on. At 11 p.m. on the second night, one of the subteams acted so arrogant about its capabilities that tensions exploded. There was crying, pouting, yelling, finger-pointing, and some door slamming.

Cathy Pagliaro thought that the blowout was one of her biggest take-aways. "The troublemakers had no idea how they were being perceived," she says. "And the rest of the group was ticked off because they felt undervalued, cut off, and unappreciated. This stuff happens all the time in the real world of work. For me, there was no clearer way to demonstrate the power of differences among teams. And once you understand that power, you can leverage it when forming teams or tackling a problem."

Questions

1. What creativity principles does the thinking expedition illustrate?
2. How can a company justify a creativity improvement program that results in physical injury to even one member and the potential injury to many others?
3. How do you think going on a thinking expedition would benefit you?

SOURCE: Adapted from Anna Muio, "Idea Summit," *Fast Company*, January/February 2000, pp. 150–164.

Achieving Wellness and Managing Stress

Learning Outcomes

After studying the information and doing the exercises in this chapter, you should be able to

- define and understand the meanings of wellness and stress
- explain the major strategies for achieving wellness
- identify several positive and negative consequences of stress
- pinpoint potential stressors in personal and work life
- describe key methods for managing the potential adverse effects of stress

To be successful in a competitive business world it is not enough simply to cope with job pressures and overcome health problems. You also have to feel and be at your best. Similarly, treating and curing physical and mental health problems is still important, but considerable emphasis is now being placed on preventing illness and staying well. Well people are not simply those who are not sick. Instead, they are vibrant, relatively happy, and able to cope with life's problems. Many companies have come to the realization that prevention rather than intervention is important to company productivity and company success. Therefore, there has been an increase in companies that offer company programs aimed at maintaining employees' wellness. **Wellness** is thus a formalized approach to preventive health care. By promoting health, company wellness programs help prevent employees from developing physical and mental problems often associated with excessive job pressures.

An excellent example of a wellness program is the state-of-the-art wellness centre at Husky Injection Molding Systems Ltd. in Bolton, Ontario. The facility houses a daycare centre for employees' children, a fully equipped weight and training room, and a library of health care books and videos. It is staffed and equipped with offices and treatment rooms for a physician, chiropractor, fitness-management specialist, massage therapist, naturopath (who is also an acupuncturist and dietician), and nurses. According to Dr. Angelo Pinto, the centre's physician, Husky has one of the lowest rates of absenteeism and industrial injuries. The team at the centre work closely together and thus provide a fuller range of care than traditional medical practice only.[1]

Companies that embrace family-friendly policies have a more holistic focus, believing that stress-free workers are more productive and productive employees are good for the company. For example, Pfizer Canada Pharmaceutical Group in Kirkland, Quebec, has daycare on-site and provides flexibility for employees trying to balance family and work life. B.C. Biomedical Laboratories in Surrey, British Columbia—rated as the best Canadian workplace—encourages innovation and flexibility with such options as job-sharing.[2]

One of the primary challenges in achieving wellness is to understand and manage stress. As the term is currently used, **stress** is an internal reaction to any force that threatens to disturb a person's equilibrium. The internal reaction usually takes the form of emotional discomfort. Notice that in general use the term *stress* typically refers to the stimulus or force that creates the problem.[3]

A **stressor** is the external or internal force that brings about the stress. The fact that something is dangerous, challenging, or disturbing in any way makes it a stressor. Your perception of an event or thought influences whether or not a given event is stressful. Your confidence in your ability to handle difficult situations also influences the amount of stress you experience. Most people find speaking in front of an audience to be a stressor, yet some experienced speakers can breeze through such an event with "no sweat." These people have learned how to handle the challenges involved in giving a talk.

Despite the importance of a person's size-up of an event, there are certain universal stressors. Almost everybody on a passenger plane experiences heavy stress when told to prepare for a crash landing. Can you think of a few other universal stressors?

In this chapter we describe the achievement of wellness and managing work stress. In the next chapter we continue with a stress-related topic: coping with personal problems.

Strategies for Achieving Wellness

The increasing costs of health care and recent cutbacks to medical care in many provinces are causing people to listen more carefully to ideas that many health care professionals and psychologists have advocated for years. An increasing number of people believe that we can live longer, healthier lives if we choose to do so.

An important principle of behavioural medicine is now widely accepted: that the body and mind must work together for a healthy lifestyle.[4] Consider also that lifestyle decisions contribute to seven of the ten principal causes of mortality. And about half of the deaths resulting from these causes could be prevented by changes in behaviour.[5] A person who smokes two packs of cigarettes per day, eats mostly fatty food and sweets, drinks a litre of wine per day, and leads a sedentary life has a below-average life expectancy. Note that all of these life-threatening activities are under the person's control.

In this section we describe achieving wellness through exercise, diet, competence, resilience, developing a health-prone personality, and minimizing health and safety risks. Another key component of achieving wellness—stress management—is described later.

Exercising Properly

The right amount and type of physical exercise contributes substantially to wellness. A recent poll from Statistics Canada about recent measures that individuals are taking to improve their health indicated that more than half of the men and women polled exercise more than three times weekly.[6] To achieve wellness it is important to select an exercise program that is physically challenging but that does not lead to overexertion and muscle injury. Competitive sports, if taken too seriously, can actually increase a person's stress level. In 1998–1999, 22 percent of Canadians in the household population over 11 years old engaged in some sort of vigorous activity that included such activities as walking for an hour, biking for 45 minutes, or jogging for 20 minutes.[7] The most beneficial exercises are those classified as aerobic, because they make you breathe faster and raise your heart rate.

Most of a person's exercise requirements can be met through everyday techniques such as walking or running upstairs, vigorous housework, yard work, or walking for several minutes each day. Avoid the remote control for your television;

even getting up to change the channel can burn off a few calories! Another exercise freebie is to park your car in a remote spot in the parking lot. The exercise you receive from walking to and from your car is an investment in your wellness.

The physical benefits of exercise include increased respiratory capacity; increased muscle tone; reduced risk of heart disease; improved circulation; reduced cholesterol level; increased energy; increased rate of metabolism; reduced body weight and improved fat metabolism; and slowed-down aging process. Of enormous importance, physical activity strengthens the heart and reduces harmful cholesterol (LDL) while increasing the level of beneficial cholesterol (HDL).

The mental benefits of exercise are also plentiful. A major benefit is the euphoria that often occurs when morphine-like brain chemicals called *endorphins* are released into the body. This experience is often referred to as "runner's high." Other mental benefits of exercise include increased self-confidence; improved body image and self-esteem; improved mental functioning, alertness, and efficiency; release of accumulated tensions; and relief from mild depression.[8]

New research suggests that people who find intrinsic motivation in exercise are the most likely to maintain a successful program. The idea is to shift the focus from long-term, external outcomes like losing weight to positive, internal experiences you can enjoy now. Exercise, like work, is the most fun when it leads to the flow experience. When exercise is fun for its own sake, you are more likely to persist and therefore derive the many benefits already mentioned.[9] A note of caution is that exercise can become too much fun. A person might become habituated to exercise, thereby incurring frequent injuries and neglecting other important life activities.

Sleeping Adequately

Getting enough sleep plays a major role in wellness, yet about 80 million people in the United States and Canada suffer from sleep deprivation. Work-related problems such as increased stress, inattention, and lowered productivity are caused by workers getting too little sleep or poor-quality sleep. Also, sleep deprivation is a major contributor to vehicular accidents. The average person requires seven and a half hours of sleep per 24 hours, yet the average amount of sleep is six and a half hours. (Some people require more sleep, others less.)

According to John Shepard, head of the Sleep Disorders Center at the Mayo Clinic, you are not getting enough sleep when you rely on an alarm clock to wake you up. He defines adequate sleep as "that amount which, when you attain it on a steady basis, produces a full degree of daytime alertness and a feeling of well-being the next day."[10] Sleep deprivation appears to be cumulative, resulting in *sleep debt*. If you need eight hours of sleep per night and only get seven, by the end of the week your sleep debt is five hours. (Also, you may have noticed that some people sleep until noon on Saturday or Sunday!)

A survey conducted by the National Sleep Foundation found that 44 percent of the 1,014 adults surveyed said they slept more on the weekends—about 40 extra minutes. Yet it is better for wellness to have a fixed sleep pattern, going to bed at the same time each night and waking up at the same time each morning, weekends included. Here are some suggestions for staying alert and getting a wellness advantage from sleep:

- At home, set a regular bedtime and observe it carefully.
- Near bedtime, avoid exercise, caffeine, and heavy food.
- Don't consume any alcohol within two hours of bedtime.
- Generally eat healthy snacks and avoid eating too much or too little.
- At work, exercise during breaks. Exercise improves mood and promotes alertness.[11]

As implied by the preceding bit of wisdom, exercise, diet, appropriate sleep, and wellness are linked to each other.

Maintaining a Healthy Diet

Eating nutritious foods is valuable for mental as well as physical health. To illustrate, many nutritionists and physicians believe that eating fatty foods such as red meat contributes to colon cancer. Improper diet, such as consuming less than 1,300 calories per day, can weaken you physically. In turn, you become more susceptible to stress.

The subject of proper diet has been debated continuously. Advice abounds on what to eat and what not to eat. Some of this information is confusing and contradictory, partly because not enough is known about nutrition to identify an ideal diet for each individual. For example, many people can point to an 85-year-old relative who has been eating the wrong food (and perhaps consuming considerable alcohol) most of his or her life. The implication is that if this person has violated sensible habits of nutrition and has lived so long, how important can good diet be? But whether we can point to this 85-year-old relative or not, it is clear that people are eating better and paying more attention to their diet.

The food requirements for wellness differ depending on age, sex, body size, physical activity, and other conditions such as pregnancy and illness. Canada's Food Guide to Healthy Eating is an excellent resource for improving and maintaining the healthy eating habits that help promote physical well-being. (See Figure 4-1.)

The guide consists of five categories. The first category is grain products and includes breads, cereal, rice, and pasta. Five to twelve servings from this category are recommended daily. The second category is fruit and vegetables, which should comprise five to ten servings per day. Grain products and vegetables and fruit should make up a large part of an individual's diet. Milk products comprise the third category and two to four servings should come from this category daily. Meat and alternatives comprise the fourth category and two to three servings are recommended daily. The fifth category consists of foods that do not fall into any of the four categories. Examples of these foods include butter, margarine, oils, salad dressings, sugar, sweets, many snack foods, beverages like soft drinks, herbs, spices, and condiments. Foods from this category should be consumed in moderation.[12]

Alcohol should also be used only in moderation. Alcoholic beverages are high in calories and low in nutrients. Heavy drinkers, especially those who also smoke, frequently develop nutritional deficiencies. They also develop more serious diseases such as cirrhosis of the liver and certain types of cancer. However, one standard-size drink per day appears to cause no harm in normal healthy, non-

Figure 4-1 Canada's Food Guide to Healthy Eating

Health Canada Santé Canada
CANADA'S
Food Guide
TO HEALTHY EATING
FOR PEOPLE FOUR YEARS AND OVER
Enjoy a variety of foods from each group every day.
Choose lower-fat foods more often.
EVAP MILK
POWDER
SKIM MILK CHEESE
YOGOURT 2.2%
0.1%
2%
SKIM
TOFU
Grain Products
Choose whole grain and enriched products more often.
Vegetables and Fruit
Choose dark green and orange vegetables and orange fruit more often.
Milk Products
Choose lower-fat milk products more often.
Meat and Alternatives
Choose leaner meats, poultry and fish, as well as dried peas, beans and lentils more often.
Canada

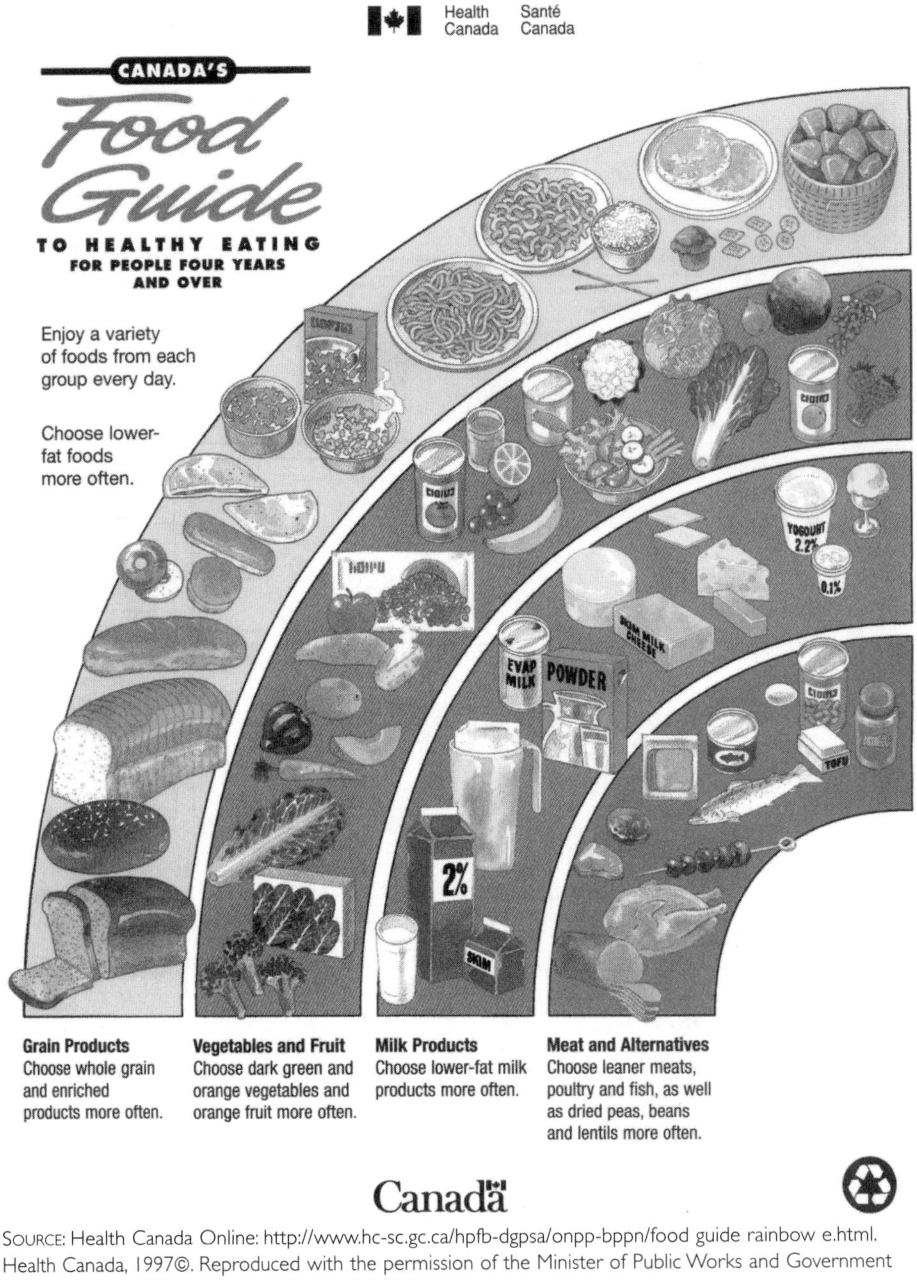

SOURCE: Health Canada Online: http://www.hc-sc.gc.ca/hpfb-dgpsa/onpp-bppn/food guide rainbow e.html. Health Canada, 1997©. Reproduced with the permission of the Minister of Public Works and Government Services Canada, 2003.

pregnant adults. Some medical specialists believe that moderate doses of alcohol actually help prevent heart disease by preventing arteries from becoming clogged with fatty deposits. Of special interest here is some recent information concerning Canadian wines, which contain greater amounts of resveratrol, a substance that decreases the risk of heart attacks, than most wines produced elsewhere in the world. Wine is also a powerful antioxidant, "eliminating free radicals which cause aging and other degenerative problems." Consuming moderate amounts of wine also increases the "good cholesterol," HDL, which removes other damaging types of cholesterol from the blood.[13]

These dietary guidelines are intended only for populations with eating habits similar to those of people in Canada. Also, the guidelines are for people who are already healthy and do not require special diets because of diseases or conditions that interfere with normal nutritional requirements. No guidelines can guarantee health and well-being. Health depends on many things in addition to diet, including heredity, lifestyle, personality traits, mental health, attitudes, and the environment. However, good eating habits based on moderation and variety keep you healthy and can even improve your health.

In addition to eating the right types of food, workers should stop to eat during the day to maintain high energy and alertness. Getting away from the desk to eat can also serve as a break necessary to revitalize energy. A major problem with skipping lunch is that it fosters overeating at home. A related problem is that when workers take only brief lunch breaks, they are likely to load up on less nutritious fast foods.[14]

A current approach to estimating whether you are achieving the right balance of food intake and exercise is the *body mass index (BMI)*, an estimation of body fat based on a person's height and weight. The National Heart, Lung and Blood Institute developed this approach to estimating body fat. People who measure high on the scale are supposedly more at risk for such ailments as heart disease, high blood pressure, and some cancers. According to the Statistics Canada Health Report in 2001, close to one-third of Canadians are overweight, and 14 percent are considered obese.[15]

Exhibit 4-1 provides a chart for determining your BMI, along with the actual method of calculation. According to the BMI categories endorsed by the World Health Organization, a normal BMI is 18.6 to 24.9; overweight is 25 to 29.9; and obesity is 30 or higher. Having a large frame or being muscular is likely to elevate your BMI. One reason is that muscle weighs more than fat. When interpreting your BMI, recognize also that many factors other than body fat influence your susceptibility to disease. Among them are blood pressure, cholesterol level, and family history.

Developing Competence

Emory L. Cowen, a major contributor to the wellness movement, says that **competence** is an important part of wellness. Competence refers to both job skills and social skills, including the ability to solve problems and control anger. The presence of these skills has been shown to be related to wellness, and their absence to poor adaptation to one's environment. Although acquiring such capabilities is a lifelong undertaking, Cowen recommends that childhood is the best time to lay the groundwork for competency.[16] If you are a well-rounded person who has performed satisfactorily in school and on the job, and you have a variety of friends, you have probably achieved competency.

The importance of competence in developing wellness illustrates how different wellness strategies produce similar results. Developing competence improves self-confidence and self-esteem. Physical exercise also contributes to enhanced self-confidence and self-esteem.

exhibit 4-1

Calculating Your Body Mass Index (BMI)

Body Mass Index: Does your weight put you at risk of health problems?

Height \ Weight	110	115	120	125	130	135	140	145	150	155	160	165	170	175	180	185	190	195	200	205	210	215	220	225	230	235	240	245	250
5′0″	21	22	23	24	25	26	27	28	29	30	31	32	33	34	35	36	37	38	39	40	41	42	43	44	45	46	47	48	49
5′1″	21	22	23	24	25	26	26	27	28	29	30	31	32	33	34	35	36	37	38	39	40	41	42	43	43	44	45	46	47
5′2″	20	21	22	23	24	25	26	27	27	28	29	30	31	32	33	34	35	36	37	37	38	39	40	41	42	43	44	45	46
5′3″	19	20	21	22	23	24	25	26	27	27	28	29	30	31	32	33	34	35	35	36	37	38	39	40	41	42	43	43	44
5′4″	19	20	21	21	22	23	24	25	26	27	27	28	29	30	31	32	33	33	34	35	36	37	38	39	39	40	41	42	43
5′5″	18	19	20	21	22	22	23	24	25	26	27	27	28	29	30	31	32	32	33	34	35	36	37	37	38	39	40	41	42
5′6″	18	19	19	20	21	22	23	23	24	25	26	27	27	28	29	30	31	31	32	33	34	35	36	36	37	38	39	40	40
5′7″	17	18	19	20	20	21	22	23	23	24	25	26	27	27	28	29	30	31	31	32	33	34	34	35	36	37	38	38	39
5′8″	17	17	18	19	20	21	21	22	23	24	24	25	26	27	27	28	29	30	30	31	32	33	33	34	35	36	36	37	38
5′9″	16	17	18	18	19	20	21	21	22	23	24	24	25	26	27	27	28	29	30	30	31	32	32	33	34	35	35	36	37
5′10″	16	17	17	18	19	19	20	21	22	22	23	24	24	25	26	27	27	28	29	29	30	31	32	32	33	34	34	35	36
5′11″	15	16	17	17	18	19	20	20	21	22	22	23	24	24	25	26	26	27	28	29	29	30	31	31	32	33	33	34	35
6′0″	15	16	16	17	18	18	19	20	20	21	22	22	23	24	24	25	26	26	27	28	28	29	30	31	31	32	33	33	34
6′1″	15	15	16	16	17	18	18	19	20	20	21	22	22	23	24	24	25	26	26	27	28	28	29	30	30	31	32	32	33
6′2″	14	15	15	16	17	17	18	19	19	20	21	21	22	22	23	24	24	25	26	26	27	28	28	29	30	30	31	31	32
6′3″	14	14	15	16	16	17	17	18	19	19	20	21	21	22	22	23	24	24	25	26	26	27	27	28	29	29	30	31	31
6′4″	13	14	15	15	16	16	17	18	18	19	19	20	21	21	22	23	23	24	24	25	26	26	27	27	28	29	29	30	30

The Actual Calculation: To calculate your BMI, follow these steps:

1. Divide your weight in pounds by your height in inches squared.
2. Multiply the result by 704.5.

For example, the BMI of a 5-foot 11-inch, 185-pound person would be calculated as follows:

$$5 \text{ ft } 11 \text{ in} = 71 \text{ in}$$
$$71^2 = 5{,}041$$
$$185 \text{ lb} \div 5{,}041 = 0.0367$$
$$0.0367 \times 704.5 = 25.85 \text{ (rounded to 26 for the chart)} = \text{low to moderate risk}$$

SOURCE: National Institutes of Health, 1998.
NOTE: People under 5 feet or over 6 feet 4 inches will have to extrapolate the data.

Developing Resilience

The ability to overcome setbacks is an important characteristic of successful people. It therefore follows that **resilience**, the ability to withstand pressure and emerge stronger for it, is a strategy for achieving wellness.[17] Most people at times in their lives experience threats to their wellness. Among these threats are the death of a loved one, having a fire in one's home, a family breakup, or a job loss.

Recovering from such major problems helps a person retain wellness and become even more well in the long term. Learning how to manage stress, as described later in this chapter, is an important part of developing resilience.

Resilience also deals with being challenged and not breaking down. The ability to bounce back from a setback, resilience is another aspect of emotional intelligence. In the context of emotional intelligence, resilience refers to being persistent and optimistic when faced with setbacks.[18] Learning how to manage stress, as described later, is an important part of developing resilience. Being resilient is also closely associated with self-confidence, as described in Chapter 12.

Human Relations Self-Assessment Quiz 4-1 gives you an opportunity to examine your level of resilience.

Quiz 4-1

Find Out How Resilient You Are

On a scale of 1 to 5, rate how much each of the following applies to you (1 = very little, 5 = very much):

1 2 3 4 5 You are curious. You ask questions, want to know how things work, experiment.

1 2 3 4 5 You constantly learn from your experience and the experience of others.

1 2 3 4 5 You need and expect to have things work well for yourself and others. You take good care of yourself.

1 2 3 4 5 You play with new developments, find the humour, laugh at yourself, chuckle.

1 2 3 4 5 You adapt quickly to change and are highly flexible.

1 2 3 4 5 You feel comfortable with paradoxical qualities.

1 2 3 4 5 You anticipate problems and avoid difficulties.

1 2 3 4 5 You develop better self-esteem and self-confidence every year. You develop a conscious self-concept of professionalism.

1 2 3 4 5 You listen well and read others, including difficult people, with empathy.

1 2 3 4 5 You think up creative solutions to challenges, invent ways to solve problems, and trust your intuition and hunches.

1 2 3 4 5 You manage the emotional side of recovery. You grieve, honour, and let go of the past.

1 2 3 4 5 You expect tough situations to work out well, and you keep on going. You help others and bring stability to times of uncertainty and turmoil.

(continued)

1 2 3 4 5 You find the gift in accidents and bad experiences.

1 2 3 4 5 You convert misfortune into good fortune.

Add numbers to get your total: If you scored 60 to 70, you're highly resilient; 50 to 60, you're better than most; 40 to 50, adequate; 30 to 40, struggling; under 30, seek help! *Note:* To improve your resilience, practise more of the preceding traits.

SOURCE: Adapted from Al Siebert, *The Survivor Personality* (Encitas, CA: Perigree/Berkeley Books 1999).

Minimize Obvious Risks to Health and Safety

Part of staying well is staying alive. Perhaps the most effective strategy for achieving wellness is to minimize exposure to activities that can readily contribute to disease, injury, and death. The list of these environmental threats is endless, including riding in helicopters, skydiving, bungee jumping, inhaling cleaning fluid or rubber cement, playing "highway chicken," walking in a high-crime area at night, or having unprotected sex with prostitutes and intravenous drug users. Add to the list drunken driving, not wearing seat belts, and motorcycle riding or bicycle riding without a helmet. All of the activities just mentioned have a common element: They are conscious behavioural acts that can in almost all cases be avoided.

To relate the concept of wellness and stress to yourself, take Human Relations Self-Assessment Quiz 4-2. Taking the inventory will give you many useful ideas for improving your well-being.

The Physiology and Consequences of Stress

An important aspect of learning about stress is to understand its underlying physiology and its consequences to the person. The physiological changes taking place within the body are almost identical for both positive and negative stressors. Riding a roller coaster, falling in love, or being fired, for example, make you feel about the same inside. The experience of stress helps activate hormones that prepare the body to either fight or run when faced with a challenge. This battle against the stressor is referred to as the **fight-or-flight response**. (The "response" is really a conflict because one is forced to choose between struggling with the stressor or fleeing from the scene.) This response helps you deal with emergencies.

Recent studies suggest the possibility that women, along with females of other species, react differently to major stressors. Instead of the fight-or-flight response typical of males, they *tend and befriend.* When stress levels mount, women are more likely to protect and nurture their children (tend) and turn to social networks of supportive females (befriend). The researchers speculate that the tend-and-befriend behaviour became prevalent over the centuries because women who tended and befriended were more likely to have their offspring survive and pass on their mother's traits. The tend-and-befriend response can be traced to a hormone, oxytocin, produced in the brain. Although this research may not be politically correct, it has stimulated the interest of many scientists.[19]

The Wellness Inventory

Answer Yes or No to each question.

1.	I rarely have trouble sleeping.	Yes	No
2.	My energy level is high when I get up in the morning and it stays high until bedtime.	Yes	No
3.	In the past year, I've been incapacitated by illness less than five days.	Yes	No
4.	I am generally optimistic about my chances of staying well.	Yes	No
5.	I do not smoke or drink alcoholic beverages habitually.	Yes	No
6.	I am pain-free except for minor ailments, which heal quickly.	Yes	No
7.	I am generally considered to be slim, not fat.	Yes	No
8.	I am careful about my diet. I restrict my intake of alcohol, sugar, salt, caffeine and fats.	Yes	No
9.	I am moderate in food and drink, and I choose fresh, whole foods over processed ones.	Yes	No
10.	I strenuously exercise at least three times a week for at least 20 minutes.	Yes	No
11.	I do not need any medicine (prescribed or self-prescribed) every day or most days to function.	Yes	No
12.	My blood pressure is 120/80 or lower.	Yes	No
13.	I am concerned about the future, but no one fear runs through my mind constantly.	Yes	No
14.	My relationships with those around me are usually easy and pleasant.	Yes	No
15.	I have a clear idea of my personal goals and choices.	Yes	No
16.	Disappointments and failures might slow me down a bit, but I try to turn them to my advantage.	Yes	No
17.	Taking care of myself is a high priority for me.	Yes	No
18.	I spend at least 20 minutes a day by myself, for myself.	Yes	No
19.	I know how much sleep I require, and I get it.	Yes	No
20.	I accept the fact that daily life can be stressful, and I am confident I can handle most problems as they arise.	Yes	No
21.	I have at least one hobby or form of creative expression (e.g., music, art, or gardening) that is a passion for me.	Yes	No
22.	I can share my feelings with others and allow them to share their feelings with me.	Yes	No
23.	I enjoy and respect my connection to nature and the environment.	Yes	No

(continued)

24. I am aware of what my body feels like when I am relaxed and when I am experiencing stress. Yes No

25. I find meaning in life and generally anticipate death with minor fear. Yes No

Score: ____________

Scoring: Give yourself four points for each Yes answer.
88–100: Excellent health/wellness awareness. You are probably well adapted to handle stress.
76–88: Good awareness, but there are areas where improvement is needed. Look at your No answers again.
Less than 76: You need to evaluate your health and lifestyle habits to improve the quality of your life and your ability to handle stressful situations.

SOURCE: Anita Schambach, Wellness Coordinator of the Holistic Health & Wellness Center at Mercy Hospital Anderson, Cincinnati, Ohio. Reprinted with permission

Another useful explanation of how stress affects people is that, when faced with stress, the brain acts much like a thermostat. When outside conditions deviate from an ideal point, the thermostat sends a signal to the furnace to increase heat or air-conditioning. The brain senses stress as damage to well-being and therefore sends out a signal to the body to cope. The purpose of coping is to modify the discrepancy between ideal (low-stress) and actual (high-stress) conditions.[20] The brain is thus a self-regulating system that helps us cope with stressors.

The activation of hormones when the body has to cope with a stressor produces a short-term physiological reaction. Among the most familiar reactions are increases in heart rate, blood pressure, blood glucose, and blood clotting. To help you recognize these symptoms, try to recall the internal bodily sensations you felt the last time you were almost in an automobile accident or heard some wonderful news. Less familiar changes are a redirection of the blood flow toward the brain and large muscle groups and a release of stored fluids from places throughout the body into the bloodstream.

If stress is continuous and accompanied by these short-term physiological changes, annoying and life-threatening conditions can occur. A stressful life event usually leads to a high cholesterol level (of the unhealthy type) and high blood pressure. Men who respond most intensely to mental stress run a higher risk of blocked blood vessels. The result is a higher risk of heart attack and stroke. One explanation of this problem is that mental stress may over time injure blood vessels and foster the buildup of arterial plaque.[21] Other conditions associated with stress are cardiac disease, migraine headaches, ulcers, allergies, skin disorders, and cancer. To make matters worse, stress can hamper the immune system, thus increasing the severity of many diseases and disorders. For example, people whose stress level is high recover more slowly from colds and injuries, and are more susceptible to sexually transmitted diseases. Stress symptoms vary considerably from one person to another. A sampling of common stress symptoms is listed in Exhibit 4-2.

Despite all the problems just mentioned, stress also plays a positive role in our lives. The right amount of stress prepares us for meeting difficult challenges and spurs us on to peak intellectual and physical performance. An optimum of stress exists for most people and most tasks.

exhibit 4-2

A Variety of Stress Symptoms

Mostly Physical

Shaking or trembling
Dizziness
Heart palpitations
Difficulty breathing
Chronic fatigue
Unexplained chest pains
Frequent teeth grinding
Frequent nausea and dizziness
Upper- and lower-back pain
Frequent headaches
Low energy and stamina
Stomach problems
Constant cravings for sweets
Increased alcohol or cigarette consumption
Frequent need to eliminate

Mostly Emotional and Behavioural

Difficulty concentrating
Nervousness
Crying
Anorexia
Declining interest in sex
Anxiety or depression
Forgetfulness
Restlessness
Frequent arguments with others
Feeling high-strung much of the time

In general, performance tends to be best under moderate amounts of stress. If the stress is too great, people become temporarily ineffective; they may freeze or choke. Under too little stress, people may become lethargic and inattentive. Figure 4-2 depicts the relationship between stress and performance. An exception to this relationship is that certain negative forms of stress are likely to lower performance even if the stress is moderate.[22] For example, the stress created by an intimidating boss or a fear about radiation poisoning—even in moderate amounts—will not improve performance.

The optimum amount and type of stress is a positive force that is the equivalent of finding excitement and challenge. Your ability to solve problems and deal with challenge is enhanced when the right amount of adrenalin flows in your blood to guide you toward peak performance. In fact, highly productive people are sometimes said to be hooked on adrenalin.

Where does burnout fit into the stress picture? One of the major problems of prolonged stress is that it may lead to **burnout**, a condition of emotional, mental, and physical exhaustion in response to long-term job stressors. The burned-out person often becomes cynical. Burnout is most likely to occur among those whose jobs call for frequent and intense interactions with others, such as a social worker, teacher, or customer service representative. Yet people in other occupations also suffer from burnout, especially when not much support from others is present and the rewards are few.[23] Also, a hostile work environment, such as being harassed by co-workers and managers, is a major contributor to burnout.[24] Students can also experience burnout because studying is hard work. Conscientiousness and perfectionism also contribute to burnout because people

Figure 4-2 The Relationship between Stress and Job Performance

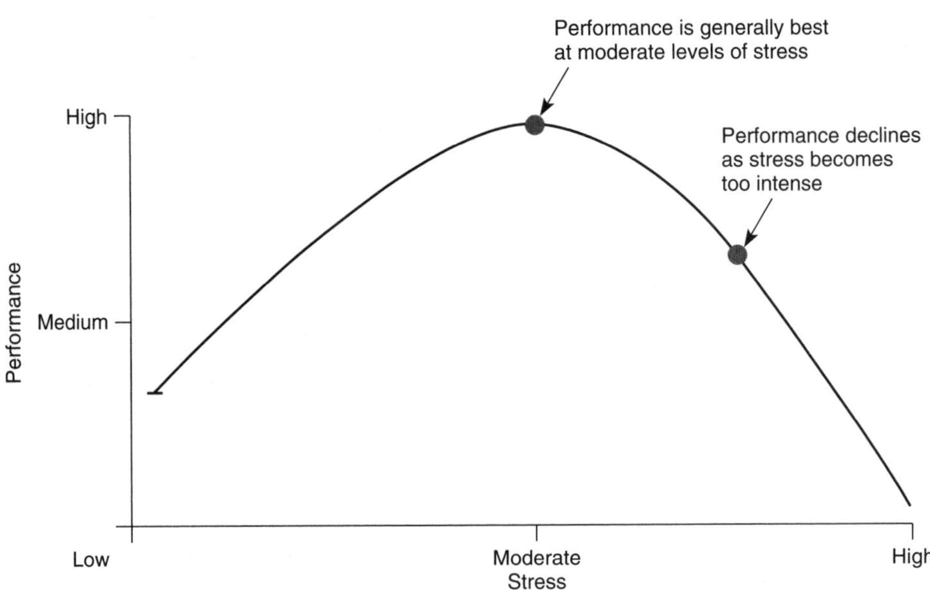

with these characteristics feel stressed when they do not accomplish everything they would like.

Burnout can be treated in many ways, just as with the negative effects of stress. Showing gratitude for hard work by employees is particularly helpful in preventing and treating burnout, because many cases of burnout are caused by intense feelings of being unappreciated.

Sources of Stress in Personal Life

Almost any form of frustration, disappointment, setback, inconvenience, or crisis in your personal life can cause stress. The list is dynamic because new sources of stress emerge continuously. For example, legislation in Quebec forbids new drivers from having even one alcoholic beverage before driving. Drinkers there who recently obtained an operator's licence have something new to worry about. Our life stage also helps determine which events are stressors. Being snubbed by a friend at age 16 may be more stressful than being snubbed at age 40. Also, although we have separated work and personal life stressors into discrete categories, in reality they overlap. According to Edward Pennington, executive director of the Canadian Mental Health Association, "There's no doubt that stress is getting worse right now." He states that in the current economic climate where people may have fewer options, stress is likely to increase.[25] In such a climate, stressors at work and in personal life may affect us at the same time to give us an overall effect of feeling "stressed out." Seven different sources of stress encountered in personal life are described here.

Canadians: Stress at Home and Work

No matter what you want to call it, many Canadians are feeling stressed, and they are feeling stressed in both life and at work. Data from the National Population Health Survey, conducted by Statistics Canada in 1994 and 1995, indicates some interesting trends. Personal stress was defined as "trying to take on too much at once; feeling pressure to be like other people; feeling that others expect too much; feeling that your work around home was not appreciated; and feeling that others are too critical of you."

The survey reported that 26 percent of Canadians rated themselves as experiencing high chronic stress. Women were more likely than men to report a high stress level in their lives, with the most stress being felt by women between the ages of 20 and 24. As people age, stress both in life and at work appears to decline. Also, people with higher levels of educational attainment were not as stressed as those with lower levels of education. People in Manitoba and Ontario reported higher levels of life stress than those from other provinces. Newfoundland reported the least amount of life stress. Single parents also reported more stress than individuals who are unattached or couples with children.

What about work stress? According to the National Population Health Survey, work stress stems from a number of sources including physically demanding labour, low support from co-workers and managers, job strain, and job insecurity. About 40 percent of workers aged 15 to 64 reported that their jobs were physically demanding, 30 percent reported low support, and 20 percent experienced job strain. Job strain was caused by such factors as conflicting job demands and having little freedom in controlling the pace of work. Also, substantial numbers of those surveyed felt that their jobs were insecure (18 percent).

A more recent international survey of over 9,000 employees echoed many of the earlier findings, finding that Canadian workers feel the most stressed, with 41 percent of the respondents stating that they "often" or "almost always" experience stress at work. According to the researchers the main cause of work-related stress is long working hours. The more hours that you work, the more stress you are likely to experience. The second largest stressor found in this study was demanding job content or dangerous work conditions. Other job conditions that led to stress included poor communication between co-workers and management, lack of support, conflicting work roles, career concerns such as job insecurity, and unpleasant environmental conditions. People experiencing high levels of job stress were also more likely to be absent and more likely to quit or have intentions of leaving.

With so much reported stress in our home and work lives, stress management becomes critical to maintaining wellness. Visualizing pleasant experiences, exercise, eating right, getting proper rest, massages, and deep breathing all have beneficial effects. It seems that in such a fast-paced society, the answer may be in learning how to "gear down" for at least a few minutes each day!

NOTES:

Statistics Canada, *Health Reports*, Volume 12 (3), April 2001, Catalogue No. 82-003-XPE, XIE.

The Federal, Provincial, and Territorial Advisory Committee on Population Health, *Statistical Report on the Health of Canadians.* Prepared for the Meeting of Ministers of Health, September 1999. Statistics Canada Catalogue No. 82-570-X1E.

Statistics Canada, *Health Reports.*

"Canadian Workers among Most Stressed," *Worklife (14)2*, pp. 8–10, 2002.

Significant Life Change

A general stressor that encompasses both work and personal life is having to cope with significant change. According to many years of research conducted by Thomas Holmes and Richard Rahe, the necessity of a significant change in an individual's life pattern creates stress. The more significant the change you have to cope with in a short period of time, the greater the probability of experiencing a stress disorder.[26] As shown in Exhibit 4-3, the maximum negative change is the death of a spouse. Twenty-four other stressors created by change are listed in the table, in decreasing order of impact. Individual differences are important in understanding the stressful impact of life changes. The rank order shown in Exhibit 4-3 represents averages that do not hold true for everybody. For example, a person who could fall back into working for a family business might not find being fired from the job (number 8) to be so stressful.

Low Self-Esteem

A subtle cause of stress is having low self-esteem. People who do not feel good about themselves often find it difficult to feel good about anything. Low self-esteem has several links to stress. One is that being in a bad mood continually

exhibit 4-3

The Top 25 Stressors as Measured by Life-Change Units

1. Death of a spouse
2. Divorce
3. Marital separation
4. Jail term/imprisonment
5. Death of a family member
6. Personal injury or illness
7. Marriage
8. Fired from the job
9. Marital reconciliation
10. Retirement
11. Change in health of family member
12. Pregnancy
13. Sexual difficulties
14. Change in financial status
15. Number of arguments with spouse
16. Major mortgage
17. Foreclosure of a loan
18. Change in responsibilities at work
19. Son or daughter leaves home
20. Trouble with in-laws
21. Outstanding personal achievement
22. Spouse begins or stops work
23. Begin or end school
24. Change in living conditions
25. Revision of personal habits

SOURCES: These stressors have changed over time. This version is from Thomas H. Holmes And Richard H. Rahe, "The Social Adjustment Rating Scale," *Journal of Psychosomatic Research*, 15, 1971, pp. 210–23, with an interview updating from Sue Macdonald, "Battling Stress," *The Cincinnati Enquirer*, October 23, 1995, p. C4.

functions like a stressor. People with low self-esteem drag themselves down into a funk, which creates stress. Another link between low self-esteem and stress-proneness is that people with low self-esteem get hurt more by insults. Instead of questioning the source of the criticism, the person with self-doubt will accept the opinion as valid.[27] An insult accepted as valid acts as a stressor because it is a threat to our well-being.

Low self-esteem is linked to stress in yet another way. People with low self-esteem doubt their ability to work their way out of problems. As a result, minor challenges appear to be major problems. For example, a person with low self-esteem will often doubt he or she will be successful in conducting a job search. As a result, having to conduct a job search will represent a major stressor. A person with high self-esteem might feel better prepared mentally to accept the challenge. (As you will recall, your perception of an event influences whether it is stressful.)

Everyday Annoyances

Managing everyday annoyances can have a greater impact on your health than can major life catastrophes. "Sweating the small stuff" can hurt you more than dealing with the significant changes mentioned above, according to several studies.[28] Everyday annoyances that create stress for many people include concerns about weight, the health of a family member, crashing a computer file, overcrowded schedules, yardwork and home maintenance, taxes, crime, and physical appearance. Several of these hassles are discussed here as separate categories.

An important finding of these studies is that people who are able to cope well with daily hassles tend to have good health. They are resilient enough to tailor-make a coping strategy for each hassle they face, such as overcoming a billing error made by a credit-card company. Another method of coping with this general category of stress is to recognize that these annoyances happen to everybody. You are not being singled out for harassment; you are not a loser; it's just part of modern living.

Social and Family Problems

Friends and family are the main source of love and affection in your life. But they can also be the main source of stress. Most physical acts of violence are committed among friends and family members. One of the many reasons we encounter so much conflict with friends and family is that we are emotionally involved with them.

Physical and Mental Health Problems

Prolonged stress produces physical and mental health problems, and the reverse is also true. Physical and mental illness can act as stressors—the fact of being ill is stressful. Furthermore, thinking that you might soon contract a life-threatening disease is stressful. Many people who find they are HIV positive (yet do not have AIDS) experience overwhelming stress. If you receive a serious injury, that too can create stress. The stress from being hospitalized can be almost as severe to some patients as the stress from the illness or injury that brought them to the hospital.

Stress operates in a cycle: stress can bring about illness and injury; the illness and injury, in turn, serve as stressors themselves, thus exacerbating the discomfort. You must learn to break the cycle by using the appropriate method of stress management.

Financial Problems

A major life stressor is financial problems. Although you may not be obsessed with money, not having enough money to take care of what you consider the necessities of life can lead to anxiety and tension. If you do not have enough money to replace or repair a broken or faulty personal computer or automobile, the result can be stressful. Even worse, imagine the stress of being hounded by bill collectors. Lack of funds can also lead to embarrassment and humiliation (both stressors).

School-Related Problems

The life of a student can be stressful. Recent research has indicated that many college students find campus life stressful and often perceive their experiences as being quite traumatic.[29] Among the stressors to cope with are exams in subjects you do not understand well, having to write papers on subjects unfamiliar to you, working your way through the complexities of registration, or having to deal with instructors who do not see things your way. Another source of severe stress for some students is having too many competing demands on their time. On most campuses you will find someone who works full-time, goes to school full-time, and has a family. This type of three-way pull often leads to marital problems. You do not have to be a middle-aged executive to develop ulcers!

Personality Factors and Stress-Proneness

Some people are more stress-prone than others because of personality factors. Three key personality factors predisposing people to stress are Type A behaviour, belief that one's life is controlled by external forces, and a negative disposition.

Type A Behaviour

People with **Type A behaviour** characteristics have basic personalities that lead them into stressful situations. Type A behaviour has two main components. One is a tendency to try to accomplish too many things in too little time. This leads the Type A individual to be impatient and demanding. The other component is free-floating hostility. Because of this combined sense of urgency and hostility, these people are irritated by trivial things. On the job, people with Type A behaviour are aggressive and hard-working. Off the job, they keep themselves preoccupied with all kinds of errands to run and things to do.

Certain features of the Type A behaviour pattern are related to coronary heart disease. Hostility, anger, cynicism, and suspiciousness lead to heart problems, whereas impatience, ambition, and being work-driven are not associated with coronary disease.[30] Many work-driven people who like what they are doing—including many business executives—are remarkably healthy and outlive less competitive people.

Belief in External Locus of Control

If you believe that your fate is controlled more by external than internal forces, you are probably more susceptible to stress. People with an **external locus of control** believe that external forces control their fate. Conversely, people with an **internal locus of control** believe that fate is pretty much under their control.

The link between locus of control and stress works in this manner: If people believe they can control adverse forces, they are less prone to the stressor of worrying about them. For example, if you believe that you can always find a job, you will worry less about unemployment. At the same time, the person who believes in an internal locus of control experiences a higher level of job satisfaction. Work is less stressful and more satisfying when you perceive it to be under your control.

The everyday problem of lost computer files illustrates the importance of an internal locus of control. When a hard drive crashes or a valuable file is lost in some other way, the externally oriented person blames the computer or the software for the stressful event. An internally oriented person, in contrast, would most likely have created backup files along the way. When a crash occurs, that person is less stressed because he or she has lost relatively little data.

What about your locus of control? Do you believe it to be internal? Or is it external?

Negative Affectivity

A major contributor to being stress-prone is **negative affectivity**, a tendency to experience aversive (intensely disliked) emotional states. In more detail, negative affectivity is a predisposition to experience emotional stress that includes feelings of nervousness, tension, and worry. Furthermore, a person with negative affectivity is likely to experience emotional states such as anger, scorn, revulsion, guilt, and self-dissatisfaction.[31] Such negative personalities seem to search for discrepancies between what they would like and what exists. Instead of attempting to solve problems, they look for them. Although negative affectivity is a relatively stable personality characteristic, new research suggests that the circumstances a person faces can trigger such behaviour.[32] For example, a four-hour wait in an airplane parked on the tarmac might trigger a person's mild tendencies toward negative affectivity.

People with negative affectivity are often distressed even when working under conditions that co-workers perceive as interesting and challenging. In one company, a contest was announced that encouraged customer-contact workers to compete against each other in terms of improving customer service. An employee with a history of negative affectivity said: "Here we go again. We're already hustling like crazy to please customers. Now we're being asked to dream up even more schemes to make sure the customer is right. It's about time the company thought of ways to please employees as well as customers."

Sources of Stress in Work Life

No job is without potential stressors for some people, and dozens of sources of stress on the job have been identified. Here we discuss six major job stressors you might encounter or might already have encountered, as listed in Figure 4-3.

High Job Demands—Low Job Control

Many workers experience stress when they are faced with a heavy workload combined with limited ability to control key features of the job.[33] Among these features would be how many phone calls to handle, when to perform certain tasks, and how fast to perform the work. Imagine being required to write more reports than you thought you could handle, yet being unable to concentrate on them for more than a few minutes at a time. The impediments to your concentration might include demands from customers, co-workers, and your boss.

Why a combination of high demand and low control creates stress can be explained as follows: High job demands produce a state of arousal that is typically reflected in such responses as increased heart rate and flow of adrenalin. When the worker has low control the arousal cannot be properly channelled into a coping response. As a result, the physiological stress reaction is even larger and persists for a longer time.[34]

Self-efficacy can influence the impact of high job demands with low control. A study of health professionals showed that having high self-efficacy (being confident of one's abilities) softens the stress consequences (as measured by blood pressure) of demanding jobs. However, people with high self-efficacy were disturbed by having low control because it conflicts with their feelings of wanting to be in control. Also, people with low self-efficacy were stressed by demanding jobs even when they had control. The responsibility of having control was stressful for those workers with low self-efficacy.[35]

Figure 4-3 Six Major Job Stressors

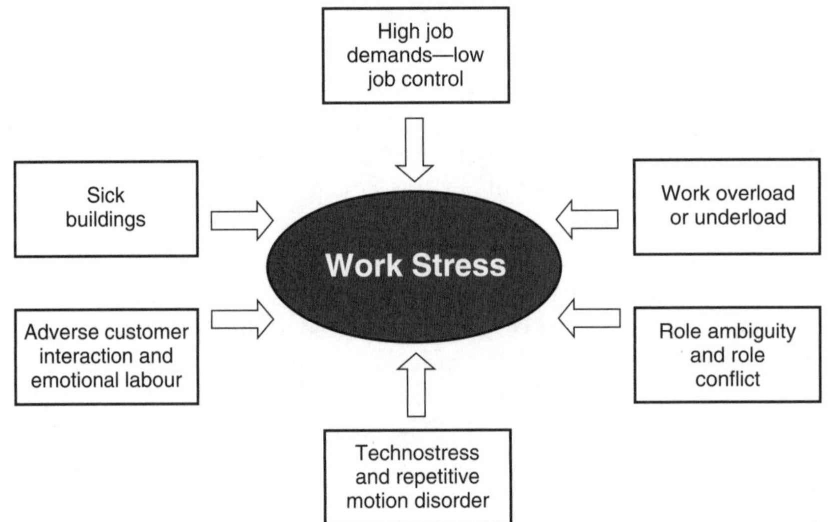

The high job demands–low job control model is illustrated by a service station mechanic suffering from migraine headaches. Asked by a health professional if he was experiencing job stress, the mechanic replied: "My job is killing me. Half the time we're shorthanded. That means while I'm doing repair work I also have to work the cash register. Sometimes I have to pump gas for the people who don't use self-serve. Every time the bell rings I have to stop what I'm doing. I can't do decent repair work when I'm being jerked around like this."

Work Overload or Underload

As just described, having limited control over a heavy workload creates job stress. A heavy workload itself, however, can also be a stressor. **Role overload**, a burdensome workload, can create stress for a person in two ways. First, the person may become fatigued and thus be less able to tolerate annoyances and irritations. Think of how much easier it is to become provoked over a minor incident when you lack proper rest. Second, a person subject to unreasonable work demands may feel perpetually behind schedule, a situation that in itself creates an uncomfortable, stressful feeling.

Another form of work overload is demanding higher and higher speed from workers. Speed is important to companies because delivering goods and services very quickly brings a competitive edge. Making matters worse is that a sagging economy (or one that goes up and down) has forced employers to make increasing demands on employees.[36] One of the main causes of such demands is the effects of **downsizing**. A company first downsizes (reduces its workforce to operate more efficiently and save money). Next, the remaining workers are expected to carry a heavier workload, at a faster pace than previously. The combination of additional responsibility and high speed can be a major stressor. Among the problems are that the hurried employees have very little time to ask for help, or to carefully study what they are doing.

A disruptive amount of stress can also occur when people experience **role underload**, or too little to do. Some people find role underload frustrating, because it is a normal human desire to want to work toward self-fulfillment. Also, making a contribution on the job is one way of gaining self-respect. As with any facet of human behaviour, there are exceptions. Some people find it relaxing not to have much to do on the job. One direct benefit is that it preserves their energy for family and leisure activities.

Role Ambiguity and Role Conflict

Not being certain of what they should be doing is a stressor for many people. **Role ambiguity** is a condition in which the job holder receives confusing or poorly defined expectations. A typical complaint is "I'm not really sure I know what I'm supposed to be doing around here." You will recall, however, that creative people enjoy ambiguity because they can define problems for themselves when clear directions are lacking. Role ambiguity is related to job control. If you lack a clear picture of what you should be doing, it is difficult to get your job under control.

Role conflict refers to having to choose between two competing demands or expectations. Many workers receive conflicting demands from two or more managers. Imagine being told by your manager to give top priority to one project. You then receive a call from your manager's manager, who tells you to drop everything and work on another project. It's often up to you to resolve such a conflict. If you don't, you will experience stress.

Technostress and Repetitive-Motion Disorder

The computerization of the workplace and home, especially information technology, has created a significant stressor labelled as **technostress**. The condition refers to a stress reaction caused by an inability to cope with computer technologies in a constructive manner.[37] One contributor to technostress is the demand for continuous learning as software changes so rapidly. At the same time, software problems surface at unpredictable times, often leaving the computer operator feeling incompetent and helpless. (What to do when the computer screen freezes and you have not saved your valuable data or words, and no one else available knows how to help?)

Another contributor to technostress is that computer work can become so consuming that the person loses interest in human interaction. As a result, interpersonal relationships suffer. (The next chapter includes a section about one of the worst computer-related problems, online addictions.) Working at a computer monitor for prolonged periods of time can lead to adverse physical and psychological reactions. The symptoms include headaches; fatigue; and hot, tired, watery eyes and blurred vision.

Technostress also comes in the form of a repetitive-motion disorder as a consequence of prolonged keyboarding. The repetitive-motion disorder (or repetitive-stress disorder) most frequently associated with keyboarding, and the use of optical scanners, is **carpal tunnel syndrome**. The syndrome occurs when repetitive flexing and extension of the wrist causes the tendons to swell, thus trapping and pinching the median nerve. Carpal tunnel syndrome creates stress because of physical pain. The thought of having to permanently leave a job requiring keyboarding is another potential stressor.

Many repetitive-motion disorders can be prevented by taking frequent rest breaks and using a well-designed combination of the worktable, chair, and monitor. Being comfortable while working prevents much physical strain. Figure 4-4 presents the basics of a workstation designed on ergonomic principles. (Ergonomics has to do with making machines and equipment fit human capabilities and demands.)

Adverse Customer Interaction and Emotional Labour

In one study, interviews conducted with 93 employees revealed that interactions with customers can be a major stressor. Stressful events frequently cited were customers losing control, using profanity, badgering employees, harassing employees, and lying. The employees interviewed said that these adverse interactions with

Figure 4-4 How to Minimize Cumulative Trauma Disorder

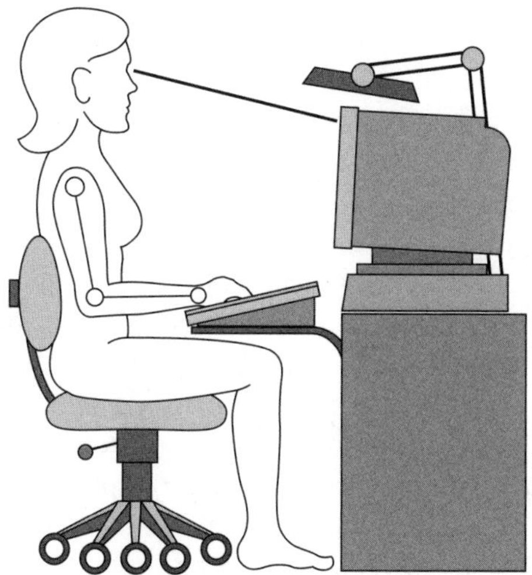

An Ergonomic Workstation

- Keep the screen below your eye level.
- Keep your elbows on the same level with home-key row, with your wrists and lower arms parallel to floor.
- Support your back and thighs with a well-constructed chair.
- Position your feet flat on the floor.
- Use lamp to supplement inadequate room lighting.

customers negatively affected the quality of their work environment.[38] Part of the problem is that the sales associate often feels helpless when placed in conflict with a customer. The sales associate is told that "the customer is always right." Furthermore, the store manager usually sides with the customer in a dispute with the sales associate.

Related to adverse customer interaction is the stressor of having to control the expression of natural emotion in order to please, or avoid displeasing, a customer. Imagine having to smile at a customer who belittles you or makes unwanted sexual advances. Alicia A. Grandey defines **emotional labour** as the process of regulating both feelings and expressions to meet organizational goals.[39] The process involves both surface acting and deep acting. Surface acting means faking expressions such as smiling, whereas deep acting involves controlling feelings, for instance suppressing anger toward a customer whom you perceive to be annoying. Sales workers and customer service representatives carry the biggest emotional labour among all workers because so often they have to fake facial expressions and feelings to please customers.

Engaging in emotional labour for prolonged periods of time can lead to job dissatisfaction, stress, and burnout. A contributing cause is that faking expressions and emotion takes a physiological toll, such as the intestines churning. Workers who engage in emotional labour may also develop cardiovascular problems and weakened immune systems.

Sick Buildings

A stressor of major concern in the modern workplace is the sick building. The problem is that some office buildings contain a diverse range of airborne particles, vapours, moulds containing toxic fungal spores, and gases that pollute the indoor environment. The result can be headaches, nausea, and respiratory infections, which function as stressors in addition to being annoying by themselves.

The World Health Organization estimates that one-third of workers may be toiling away in a workplace that makes them ill. Dozens of factors contribute to indoor air pollution in addition to those just mentioned. Many of these dangers go undetected, including carbon monoxide that is sucked into a building when air-intake vents overhang exhaust-filled loading docks and parking garages. Pesticides used indoors may contain carcinogens. Even the smoke from people smoking cigarettes at building entrances often gets sucked back into the building by revolving doors. And an indoor environment is a fertile ground for the development of moulds.[40]

The general solution to this type of stressor is for companies to pump ample fresh, clean air into buildings. However, if you are fortunate enough to work in a building with windows that open, the sick-building syndrome can be avoided.

Managing Stress

Because potentially harmful stressors surround us in work and personal life, virtually everybody needs a program of stress management in order to stay well. Stress management techniques are placed here into two categories: attacking the source of stress, including getting close to people, and relaxation techniques.

Dealing with Stress by Attacking Its Source

Stress can be dealt with in the short range by indirect techniques such as exercise and relaxation. However, to manage stress in the long range and stay well you must also learn to deal directly with stressors. Several of these techniques are described in the next few paragraphs.

Eliminate or Modify the Stressor The most potent method of managing stress is to eliminate the stressor that is giving you trouble. For example, if your job is your primary stressor, your stress level would be reduced if you found a more comfortable job. At other times, modifying the stressful situation can be equally helpful. Using the problem-solving method, you search for an alternative that will change the stressor. Here is a useful model to follow:

> A retailing executive repeatedly told her boss that she wanted to open a new branch of the business. He agreed with her, but took no action. Feeling rejected, frustrated, and stressed, she took another approach to the problem. She drew up the plans for opening a new branch, presented them to her boss, and informed him she was ready to move ahead. To the executive's surprise, he said, "Great! I was only hesitating to ask you to do this because I thought you were overworked."
>
> Everything worked out just as she wanted after she pursued the alternative of restating her plans in writing.[41]

Place the Stressful Situation in Perspective Stress comes about because of our perception of the situation. If you can alter your perception of a threatening situation, you are attacking the source. A potentially stressful situation can be put into perspective by asking, "What is the worst thing that could happen to me if I fail in this activity?"[42]

The answer to the above question is found by asking a series of questions, starting with the grimmest possibility. For instance, you are late with a report that is due this afternoon. Consider the following questions and answers:

- Will my reputation be damaged permanently? *(No.)*
- Will I get fired? *(No.)*
- Will I get reprimanded? *(Perhaps, but not for sure.)*
- Will my boss think less of me? *(Perhaps, but not for sure.)*

Only if the answer is yes to either of the first two questions is negative stress truly justified. The thought process just described allows stressful situations to be properly evaluated and kept in perspective. You therefore avoid the stress that comes from overreacting to a situation.

Gain Control of the Situation As implied in the discussion of low job control, feeling that a bothersome situation is out of control is almost a universal stressor. A key method of stress management is therefore to attack the stressor by gaining control of the situation. A multipurpose way of gaining control is to improve your work habits and time management, as described in Chapter 14. By being "on top of things," you can make heavy work and school demands less stressful.

Find the Humour in the Situation An indirect way of gaining control of the situation to reduce stress is to find the humour in the situation. By finding humour in the potentially stressful situation, the situation becomes less threatening and therefore less likely to produce stress. Quite often situations that were frustrating at the time become funny after time has passed. An example would be thinking back to how funny it was to have called in sick on your first day of work at your present job.[43] Humour is a stress reliever also because it deepens breathing, lowers blood pressure, loosens tight muscles, and releases endorphins.

Reduce Stress through Social Support An ideal way of managing stress is one that provides side benefits. Getting close to people falls into this category. You will reduce some of your tension and form healthy relationships with other human beings in the process. Closeness suggests getting in touch with your feelings or tuning into others. By getting close to others you build a **support system**, a group of people you can rely on for encouragement and comfort. The trusting relationship you have with these people is critically important. People you can go to with your problems include family members, friends, co-workers, and other students. In addition, some people in turmoil reach out to strangers to discuss personal problems. An effective way of developing a social support network is to become a good listener so others will reciprocate when you need to talk through your problems. Recent research findings indicate that having good work relations with colleagues and/or management significantly reduces workplace stress.[44] Working with people that you enjoy being with and can talk to regularly can lend you support right where the stress occurs!

The usual method of reducing stress is to talk over your problems while the other person listens. Switching roles can also help reduce stress. Listening to other people will make you feel better because you have helped them. Another advantage to listening to the feelings and problems of others is that it helps you get close to them.

Relaxation Techniques for Handling Stress

"You ought to relax" is the advice family physicians, relatives, and friends have always offered the stressed individual. Stress experts today give us similar advice but also offer specific techniques. Here we describe four do-it-yourself techniques that can help you to relax and consequently reduce stress and its accompanying tension. In addition, Exhibit 4-4 from the Canadian Mental Health Association lists a variety of tips to reduce stress and tension, many of which are relaxation-oriented. Recognize that several of these techniques are aimed at achieving wellness. Pick and choose from these brief suggestions and those presented in more detail for dealing with stressors.

exhibit 4-4

18 Tips for Dealing with Stress and Tension

1. Recognize your symptoms of stress.
2. Look at your lifestyle and see what can be changed—in your work situation, your family situation, or your schedule.
3. Use relaxation techniques—yoga, meditation, deep breathing, or massage.
4. Exercise—Physical activity is one of the most effective stress remedies around!
5. Time management—Do essential tasks and prioritize the others. Consider those who may be affected by your decisions, such as family and friends. Use a check list so you will receive satisfaction as you check off each job as it is done.
6. Watch your diet—Alcohol, caffeine, sugar, fats, and tobacco all put a strain on your body's ability to cope with stress. A diet with a balance of fruits, vegetables, whole grains, and foods high in protein but low in fat will help create optimum health. Contact your local branch of the Heart and Stroke Foundation for further information about healthy eating.
7. Get enough rest and sleep.
8. Talk with others—Talk with friends, professional counsellors, support groups, or relatives about what is bothering you.
9. Help others—Volunteer work can be an effective and satisfying stress reducer.
10. Get away for awhile—Read a book, watch a movie, play a game, listen to music, or go on vacation. Leave yourself some time that's just for you.
11. Work off your anger—Get physically active, dig in the garden, start a project, get your spring cleaning done.

12. Give in occasionally—Avoid quarrels whenever possible.
13. Tackle one thing at a time—Don't try to do too much at once.
14. Don't try to be perfect.
15. Ease up on criticism of others.
16. Don't be too competitive.
17. Make the first move to be friendly.
18. Have some fun! Laugh and be with people you enjoy!

Used with the permission of the Canadian Mental Health Association, Toronto Branch. Visit their website at **www.toronto.cmha.ca**. Visit the National site at **www.cmha.ca**.

Relaxation Response

A standard technique for reducing stress is to achieve the relaxation response. The **relaxation response** is a bodily reaction in which you experience a slower respiration and heart rate, lowered blood pressure, and lowered metabolism. The response can be brought about in several ways, including meditation, exercise, or prayer. By practising the relaxation response you can counteract the fight-or-flight response associated with stress.

According to cardiologist Herbert Benson, four things are necessary to practise the relaxation response: a quiet environment, an object to focus on, a passive attitude, and a comfortable position. You are supposed to practise the relaxation response for 10 to 20 minutes, twice a day. To evoke the relaxation response, Dr. Benson advises you to close your eyes. Relax. Concentrate on one word or prayer. If other thoughts come to mind, be passive, and return to the repetition.[45] Human Relations Skill-Building Exercise 4-1 gives you an opportunity to practise the relaxation response.

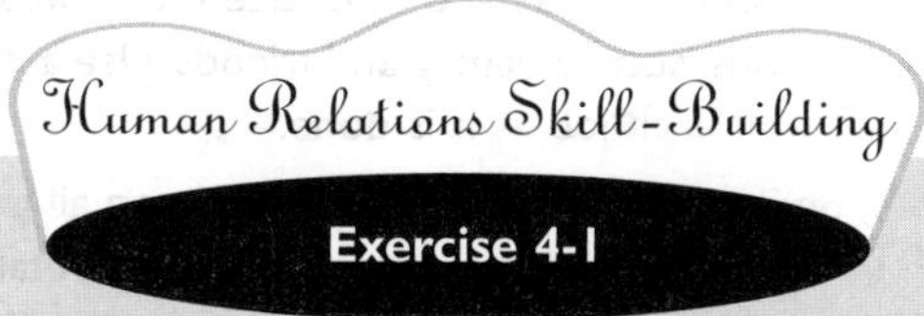

The Relaxation Response

Think of one of the most stressful moments you have experienced in recent weeks. Visualize yourself as experiencing stress. If you are currently experiencing significant stress, visualization will not be necessary. Now carry out the relaxation response. Close your eyes. Relax. Concentrate on one simple word. Repeat the word several times.

Describe to yourself, in writing, how effective this technique has been in reducing your stress. Share experiences with the rest of the class. Discuss what you see as the strengths and limitations of this technique.

Similar to any other relaxation technique, the relaxation response is harmless and works for most people. However, some very impatient people find it annoying to disrupt their busy day to meditate. Unfortunately, these may be the people who most urgently need to learn to relax.

Deep Breathing

The natural process of inhaling and exhaling slowly, filling your lungs with air and slowly letting it escape is a powerful stress reducer for many people. Deep breathing has immediate and long-term benefits. It lowers the heart rate and blood pressure and increases your skin temperature. Deep breathing also relaxes you emotionally and helps you gain perspective. The following steps explain how to use deep breathing for stress reduction.

1. Sit or lie down in a quiet spot. Place one hand on your waist, the other in the centre of your chest. Breathe several times. The hand on your belly should move more because it indicates you are breathing from your diaphragm.
2. Now inhale slowly, filling up the lungs. As you exhale slowly, push air out from the bottom of your lungs.
3. Take long, slow breaths. If you become dizzy or lightheaded, you are breathing too fast.
4. As you inhale, elevate your shoulders and collarbone slightly to fill the lungs fully with air.
5. After you have mastered the breathing technique, with each outward breath blow out your worrisome thoughts and pains. Breathe in relaxation and calmness.[46]

Create Your Own Relaxation Triggers

Marriage and family therapist Jeff Herring has developed a relaxation technique that allows you to relax anywhere, any time. It derives from a widely used visualization technique. Three simple steps are involved:

Step 1. Visualize yourself in a very relaxing place. Create as much detail as you can in the image, making it bright and colourful. Make sure you are seeing the scene through your own eyes, as if you were there. See it, hear it, and feel it.

Step 2. While you are picturing yourself in this place, create an immediate trigger that will instantly remind you of the relaxed feeling. It could be a snap of the fingers, a word or phrase, or a mental picture. It can be anything that quickly and strongly reminds you of your relaxing place.

Step 3. When you find yourself in a stressful situation, simply go for your relaxation trigger, fire it off, and feel the almost instant relaxation.[47]

Human Relations Skill-Building Exercise 4-2 will give you and your classmates an opportunity to learn more about what stress-management techniques others use.

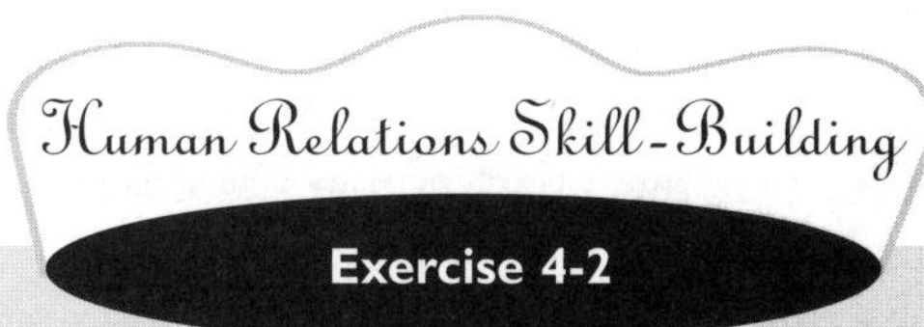

Exercise 4-2

The Stress-Buster Survey

Each class member thinks through carefully which techniques he or she uses to reduce work or personal stress. Class members then come to the front of the room individually to make a brief presentation of their most effective stress-reduction technique. After the presentations are completed, class members analyze and interpret what they heard. Among the issues to explore are:

1. **Which are the most popular stress-reduction techniques?**
2. **How do the stress-reduction techniques used by the class compare with those recommended by experts?**

Summary

Wellness is a formalized approach to preventive health care. By promoting health, company wellness programs help prevent employees from developing physical and mental problems often associated with excessive job pressures.

Six strategies for achieving wellness were described in this chapter. First, the right amount and type of physical exercise contributes substantially to wellness. Second, getting adequate sleep also contributes substantially to wellness. Third, maintaining a healthy diet is valuable for mental and physical health. Canada's Food Guide to Healthy Eating (Figure 4-1) contains many useful suggestions. Fourth, developing competence, including both job and social skills, helps us stay well. Fifth, being resilient is another wellness strategy. And sixth, minimizing obvious risks to health and safety improves the chance of achieving wellness.

The body's battle against a stressor is the fight-or-flight response. Stress always involves physiological changes such as an increase in heart rate, blood cholesterol, and blood pressure. The right amount of stress can be beneficial. Performance tends to be best under moderate amounts of stress, yet certain negative forms of stress almost always decrease performance. Prolonged stress may lead to burnout, a condition of emotional, mental, and physical exhaustion in response to long-term job stressors.

Almost any form of frustration, disappointment, setback, inconvenience, or crisis in your personal life can cause stress. The categories of situations that can produce stress include significant life changes; low self-esteem; everyday annoyances; social and family problems; physical and mental health problems; financial problems; and school-related problems.

Personality factors contribute to stress-proneness. People with Type A behaviour are impatient and demanding, and have free-floating hostility, all of which lead to stress. Another personality factor related to stress is locus of control. If you believe that your fate is controlled more by external than internal forces, you are more susceptible to stress. Another major contributor to stress-proneness is negative affectivity (a predisposition to negative mental states).

Sources of job stress are quite varied. Among them are high job demands and low job control; work overload or underload; role ambiguity and role conflict; technostress and repetitive-motion disorder; adverse customer interaction and emotional labour; and sick buildings.

To successfully manage stress in the long range you have to deal with stressors directly. Four direct approaches are eliminate the stressor; put the situation into proper perspective; gain control of the situation; and find humour in the situation.

Getting close to people in order to develop a support system is another useful strategy for managing stress. Discussing your problems with others can reduce your tension.

Three relaxation techniques for reducing stress are the relaxation response; deep breathing; and creating your own relaxation triggers.

Questions and Activities

1. How can a company wellness program improve profits and productivity?
2. If exercise contributes so much to wellness, why are so many athletes stressed out?
3. How does a person judge the strength or impact of a stressor he or she is facing?
4. Does a "well person" ever eat such foods as pizza, hamburgers, and hot dogs, and drink milkshakes and beer? Explain.
5. What responsibility should an employer have in helping employees minimize obvious risks to health and safety?
6. Identify several stressors created by cellular phones. What can be done to lessen these stressors?
7. How does carefully choosing a career help a person reduce stress?
8. Do students tend to suffer from the stress of high job demands and low job control with respect to their schooling? Explain your reasoning.
9. How can a person who suffers from technostress compete in the modern world?
10. Get in touch with a person you consider to be much more relaxed than most people. Ask your contact which (if any) of the relaxation or stress-busting techniques listed in this chapter he or she uses. Report your findings back to the class.

Internet Skill Builder

Learn Something New about Your Health

Connect with Health Canada (**www.hc-sc.gc.ca**). From this link, investigate an area of interest that pertains to material in this chapter, such as exercise or proper diet. Find one interesting piece of research, health tip, or fitness idea that you did not know prior to this investigation and share it with a class member.

Weblinks

www.selfhelp.com/bootstraps.html
This site has a series of columns about self-help and strategies for achieving wellness, managing stress, and so on.

www.statcan.ca
From this site you can access the entire results of the survey *Report on the Health of Canadians*.

www.pressanykey.com/stresstest.html
This is a self-assessment about life-event stress, and evaluates your stress resistance.

Human Relations Case Study

THE NEW MARKETING ASSISTANT

One year ago Wanda Diaz returned enthusiastically to the workforce after 12 years of being a full-time homemaker and a part-time direct sales representative for beauty products. Diaz's major motive for finding a full-time professional job was to work toward her career goal of being a marketing manager in a medium-size or large company. To help prepare for this career, Diaz completed a business administration degree over a five-year period.

Another compelling reason for returning to full-time employment was financial need. Diaz's husband owned and operated an appliance and electronics store that was becoming less profitable each year. Several large appliance stores had moved into the area, which resulted in fewer customers for Northside Appliances (the name of the family business). Diaz and her husband, Miguel, concluded that the family could not cover its bills unless Wanda earned the equivalent of a full-time income.

After three months of searching for full-time employment, Wanda responded to a newspaper ad for a marketing assistant position. The ad described the position as part of a management training program with an excellent future. Ten days after submitting her cover letter and résumé, Wanda was invited for an interview. The company proved to be a national provider of long-distance telephone service. The human resources interviewer and hiring manager both explained that Wanda's initial assignment would be as a telemarketer. Both people advised Wanda that large numbers of people were applying for these telemarketing positions.

Wanda would be required to telephone individual consumers and small-business owners and make a sales pitch for them to transfer their long-distance telephone service to her company. The company supplied an almost inexhaustible computerized list of names and telephone numbers across the country. In this way Wanda could take advantage of time-zone differences to telephone people during their dinnertime, as well as other times. Wanda would receive a small commission for customers who made the switch to her company. Her major responsibilities in addition to telephone soliciting would be to enter the results of her conversations into a computer and to prepare summaries.

One week after the interviews, Wanda was offered a job. She accepted, despite some concern that the position was a little too far removed from the professional marketing position she sought. Wanda was assigned to a small cubicle in a large room with about 25 other telemarketers. She found the training program exciting, particularly with respect to techniques for overcoming customer resistance. Wanda reasoned that this experience combined with her direct selling of beauty products would give her excellent insights into how consumers think and behave. For the first two weeks, Wanda found the calls to be uplifting. She experienced a surge of excitement when a customer agreed to switch to her company. As was the custom in the office, she shouted "Yes" after concluding each customer conversion to her company.

As the weeks moved slowly on, Wanda became increasingly restless and concerned about the job. Her success ratio was falling below the company standard of a three percent success rate on the cold calls. A thought kept running through Wanda's mind: "Even if I'm doing well at this job, 97 percent of people I call practically hang up on me. And I can't stand keyboarding all these worthless reports explaining what happened as a result of my calls. It's a horrible waste of time."

Wanda soon found it difficult to sleep peacefully, often pacing the apartment after Miguel had fallen asleep. She also noticed that she was arguing much more with Miguel and their two children. Wanda's stomach churned so much that she found eating uncomfortable. She often poked at her food, but she drank coffee and diet soft drinks much more than previously. After six months of working at the long-distance carrier, her weight plunged from 135 pounds to 123 pounds. Wanda's left thumb and wrists were constantly sore. One night when Miguel asked her why she was rubbing the region below her thumb, Wanda said, "I keep pushing around the mouse so much during the day that my thumb feels like it's falling off."

During the next several months, Wanda spoke with her supervisor twice about her future in the company. Both times the supervisor explained that the best telemarketers become eligible for supervisory positions, providing they have proved themselves for at least three years. The supervisor also cautioned Wanda that her performance was adequate but not exceptional. Wanda thought to herself, "I'm banging my head against the wall, and I'm considered just average."

As Wanda approached a full year in her position, she and Miguel reviewed the family finances. He said, "Sales at the store are getting worse and worse. I predict that this year your salary will be higher than profits from the store. It's great that we can count on at least one stable salary in the family. The kids and I really appreciate it."

Wanda thought to herself: "Now is the worst time to tell Miguel how I really feel about my job. I'm falling apart inside, and the family needs my salary. What a mess."

Questions

1. What aspects of work stress are revealed in this case?
2. What suggestions can you make to the company for decreasing the stressors in the position of telemarketer?
3. What advice can you offer Wanda to help her achieve wellness?

Dealing with Personal Problems

Learning Outcomes

After studying the information and doing the exercises in this chapter, you should be able to

- recognize how self-defeating behaviour contributes to personal problems
- explain the nature of addictive behaviour and its link to craving for dopamine
- explain how alcohol abuse and drug abuse interfere with career and personal success, and understand how to deal with these problems
- develop insights into dealing with the loss of a relationship
- recognize the career impact of absenteeism and tardiness
- describe the effects of depression, neurobiological disorders, and eating disorders and how they can lower job productivity
- develop a strategy for managing anger

Larry, an automotive technology student, had a well-paying part-time job as an automobile mechanic. A year-and-a-half later he dropped out of school and lost his job. Larry hoped to someday become a service manager in a large automobile dealership. He first showed his talents for automotive repair at age 10, when he helped his father do simple car repairs. Larry also developed an interest in computers at around the same time. His software library contained about 40 different computer games plus the latest joy sticks.

At school, Larry was allowed almost unlimited access to the computer laboratory. After completing his computer course work, Larry would stay at the lab for additional exploration. Soon he began visiting different websites related to automotive technology. Then came a search for websites about sports, automotive clubs, stock market information, chat rooms, and airline reservation systems. To give himself more time to surf the web, Larry convinced his parents to buy a computer for the home. After coming home from the lab at 9 p.m., Larry would surf for a few more hours at home. Soon he drifted into a pattern of staying up all night, except for a few brief naps, several times a week. Larry rarely left his computer on weekends.

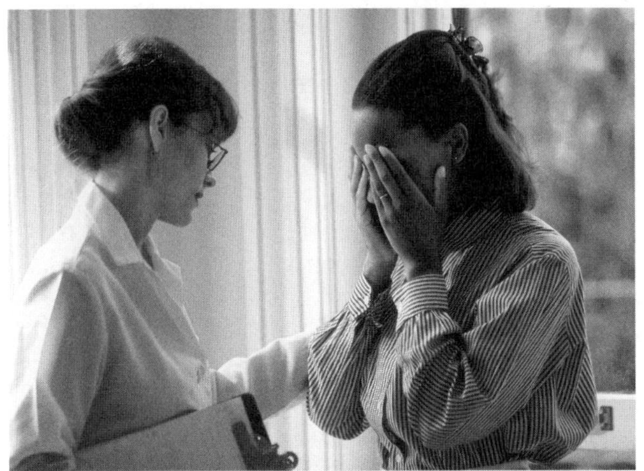

Next Larry started skipping classes and lab assignments so that he could stay in his room and stay online. He also began missing work, or showing up in such a state of fatigue that his manager sent him home. Now Larry had one more excuse to stay online: He could conduct his job search by computer. Larry's friends stopped calling him or dropping by, because he only wanted to communicate by internet. Larry skipped so many meals that he lost 20 pounds.

As Larry became more and more isolated from the outside world, his parents persistently urged him to get help for his problems. Larry finally enrolled in the Centre for Online Addiction. The psychologist running the program thinks Larry's chances for recovery are reasonably good. Soon he might be able to spend time online without it consuming his life.

Larry's addictive behaviour is but one of the personal problems described in this chapter that can wreak havoc on work and personal life. Until Larry conquers his problems, he cannot achieve wellness or manage his stress. How many people have you known or heard about who damaged their career or an important relationship because of personal problems?

Our approach to understanding and overcoming personal problems will be to first describe the self-defeating behaviour in general, and how to reverse the trend. We then describe major forms of self-defeating behaviour. Among them are alcohol abuse, substance abuse, family and financial problems, tardiness, and absenteeism. We also describe three types of personal problems that are much less under a person's control: depression and neurobiological disorders (such as attention deficit disorder), and eating disorders. Finally, we describe dealing with anger.

Self-Defeating Behaviour

Many problems on the job and in personal life arise because of factors beyond our control. A boss may be intimidating and insensitive, an employer might lay you off, or a significant other might abruptly terminate your relationship. Nevertheless, many personal problems arise because of **self-defeating behaviour**. A person with self-defeating tendencies intentionally or unintentionally engages in activities or harbours attitudes that work against his or her best interests. A person who habitually is late for important meetings is engaging in self-defeating behaviour. Dropping out of school for no reason other than being bored with studying is another of many possible examples. Let's examine several leading causes of self-defeating behaviour, and how to reverse the pattern.

Why People Engage in Self-Defeating Behaviour

Many different forces lead people to work against their own best interests, often sabotaging their careers. The major cause of self-defeating behaviour is a *loser life script.*[1] Early in life, our parents and other influential forces program our brains to act out certain life plans. These plans are known as *scripts*. People fortunate enough to have winner scripts consistently emerge victorious. When a tough assignment needs doing, they get the job done. For example, they figure out how to fix a jammed computer program that baffles everybody else in the office.

In contrast, others have scripts that program them toward damaging their careers and falling short of their potential. Much of this damage paradoxically occurs just when things seem to be going well. For example, a person might steal equipment from a company shortly after receiving an outstanding performance appraisal.

The simplest explanation for self-defeating behaviour is that some people suffer from a personality that fosters defeat. People with a *self-defeating personality pattern* have three notable characteristics. First, they repeatedly fail at tasks they have the ability to perform. Second, they place themselves in very difficult situations and respond helplessly. Third, they typically refuse to take advantage of escape routes, such as accepting advice and counsel from a manager.[2]

Self-defeating beliefs put many people on the road to career self-sabotage. In this context, a self-defeating belief is an erroneous belief that creates the conditions for failure. For example, some people sabotage their job campaigns before even starting. They think to themselves: "I lack the right experience," "I'm not sharp enough," "I'm too old," "I'm too young," and so forth.

Fear of success is yet another contributor to career self-sabotage. People who fear success often procrastinate to the point of self-defeat. The same people worry that being successful will lead to such negative outcomes as an overwhelming workload or loss of friends. They also worry that success will bring about unrealistic expectations from others, such as winning a big award every year.

To examine your present tendencies toward self-defeating behaviour, take the self-sabotage quiz presented in Human Relations Self-Assessment Quiz 5-1. Taking the quiz will help alert you to many self-imposed behaviours and attitudes that could potentially harm your career and personal life.

Quiz 5-1

The Self-Sabotage Questionnaire

Indicate how accurately each of the statements below describes or characterizes you, using a five-point scale: (0) very inaccurately, (1) inaccurately, (2) midway between inaccurately and accurately, (3) accurately, (4) very accurately. Consider discussing some of the questions with a family member, close friend, or work associate. Another person's feedback may prove helpful in providing accurate answers to some of the questions.

		Answer
1.	Other people have said that I am my own worst enemy.	_______
2.	If I don't do a perfect job, I feel worthless.	_______
3.	I am my own harshest critic.	_______
4.	When engaged in a sport or other competitive activity, I find a way to blow a substantial lead right near the end.	_______
5.	When I make a mistake, I can usually identify another person to blame.	_______
6.	I have a sincere tendency to procrastinate.	_______
7.	I have trouble focusing on what is really important to me.	_______
8.	I have trouble taking criticism, even from friends.	_______
9.	My fear of seeming stupid often prevents me from asking questions or offering my opinion.	_______
10.	I tend to expect the worst in most situations.	_______
11.	Many times I have rejected people who treat me well.	_______
12.	When I have an important project to complete, I usually get sidetracked and then miss the deadline.	_______
13.	I choose work assignments that lead to disappointments even when better options are clearly available.	_______
14.	I frequently misplace things, such as my keys, then get very angry at myself.	_______
15.	I am concerned that if I take on more responsibility people will expect too much from me.	_______
16.	I avoid situations, such as competitive sports, where people can find out how good or bad I really am.	_______
17.	People describe me as the "office clown."	_______
18.	I have an insatiable demand for money and power.	_______
19.	When negotiating with others, I hate to grant any concessions.	_______
20.	I seek revenge for even the smallest hurts.	_______
21.	I have an overwhelming ego.	_______
22.	When I receive a compliment or other form of recognition, I usually feel I don't deserve it.	_______

23. To be honest, I choose to suffer. ______
24. I regularly enter into conflict with people who try to help me. ______
25. I'm a loser. ______

Total score ______

Scoring and Interpretation: Add your answers to all the questions to obtain your total score. Your total score provides an approximate index of your tendencies toward being self-sabotaging or self-defeating. The higher your score, the more probable it is that you create conditions to bring about your own setbacks, disappointments, and failures. The lower your score, the less likely it is that you are a self-saboteur.

0–25: You appear to have very few tendencies toward self-sabotage. If this interpretation is supported by your own positive feelings toward your life and yourself, you are in good shape with respect to self-defeating behaviour tendencies. However, stay alert to potential self-sabotaging tendencies that could develop at later stages in your life.

26–50: You may have some mild tendencies toward self-sabotage. It could be that you do things occasionally that defeat your own purposes. Review actions you have taken during the past six months to decide if any of them have been self-sabotaging.

51–75: You show signs of engaging in self-sabotage. You probably have thoughts, and carry out actions, that could be blocking you from achieving important work and personal goals. People with scores in this category characteristically engage in negative self-talk that lowers their self-confidence and makes them appear weak and indecisive to others. People in this range frequently experience another problem. They sometimes sabotage their chances of succeeding on a project just to prove that their negative self-assessment is correct. If you scored in this range, carefully study the suggestions offered in this chapter.

76–100: You most likely have a strong tendency toward self-sabotage. (Sometimes it is possible to obtain a high score on a test like this because you are going through an unusually stressful period in your life.) Study this chapter carefully and look for useful hints for removing self-imposed barriers to your success. Equally important, you might discuss your tendencies toward undermining your own achievements with a mental health professional.

Strategies and Techniques for Overcoming and Preventing Self-Defeating Behaviour

Overcoming self-defeating behaviour requires hard work and patience. Here we present six widely applicable strategies for overcoming and preventing self-defeating behaviour. Pick and choose among them to fit your particular circumstance and personal style.

Examine Your Script and Make the Necessary Changes Much importance has been attached to the influence of early-life programming in determining whether a person is predisposed to self-defeat. Note carefully the word *predisposed*. A person may be predisposed to snatch defeat from the jaws of victory, but that does not mean the predisposition makes defeat inevitable. It does mean that the person will have to work harder to overcome a tendency toward self-sabotage. A good starting point is to look for patterns in your setbacks:

- Do you blow up at people who have the authority to make the administrative decisions about your future?

- Do you get so tense during your command performances (stumbling over your words in an important presentation, for instance) that you are unable to function effectively?
- Do you give up in the late stages of projects, saying, "I just can't get this done"?

Stop Blaming Others for Your Problems Blaming others for your problems contributes to self-defeating behaviour and career self-sabotage.[3] Projecting blame onto others is self-defeating because doing so relieves you of most of the responsibility for your setback and failure. Consider this example: If someone blames favouritism for not receiving a promotion, he or she will not have to worry about becoming a stronger candidate for future promotions. Not to improve one's suitability for promotion is self-sabotaging. If you accept most of the blame for not being promoted, you are more likely to make the changes necessary to qualify in the future.

An underlying theme to the suggestions for preventing and overcoming self-defeating behaviour is that we all need to engage in thoughts and actions that increase our personal control. This is precisely the reason that blaming others for our problems is self-sabotaging. By turning over control of your fate to forces outside yourself, you are holding them responsible for your problems.

Solicit Feedback on Your Actions Feedback is essential for monitoring whether you are sabotaging your career or personal life. A starting point is to listen carefully to any direct or indirect comments from your superiors, subordinates, co-workers, customers, and friends about how you are coming across to them. Consider the case of Bill, a technical writer:

> Bill heard three people in one week make comments about his appearance. It started innocently with "Here, let me fix your collar." Next, an office assistant said, "Bill, are you coming down with something?" The third comment was, "You look pretty tired today. Have you been working extra hard?" Bill processed this feedback carefully. He used it as a signal that his steady late-night drinking episodes were adversely affecting his image. He then cut back his drinking enough to revert to his normal healthy appearance.

An assertive and thick-skinned person might try the technique described for soliciting feedback described in Chapter 1. Approach a sampling of people both on and off the job with this line of questioning: "I'm trying to develop myself personally. Can you think of anything I do or say that creates a bad impression in any way? Do not be afraid of offending me. Only people who know me can provide me with this kind of information."

Take notes to show how serious you are about the feedback. When someone provides any feedback at all, say, "Please continue, this is very useful." Try not to react defensively when you hear something negative. You asked for it, and the person is truly doing you a favour.

Learn to Profit from Criticism As the above example implies, learning to profit from criticism is necessary to benefit from feedback. Furthermore, to ignore valid criticism can be self-defeating. People who benefit from criticism are able to stand outside themselves while being criticized. It is as if they are watching the criticism from a distance and looking for its possible merits. People who take criticism personally experience anguish when receiving negative feedback. The following are several specific suggestions for benefiting from valid criticism.[4]

1. *See yourself at a distance.* Place an imaginary glass shield between you and the person making the criticism. Attempt to be a detached observer looking for useful information.
2. *Ask for clarification and specifics.* Ask politely for more details about the negative behaviour in question, so you can change if change is warranted. If your boss is criticizing you for being rude with customers, you might respond: "I certainly don't want to be rude. Can you give me a couple of examples of how I was rude? I need your help in working on this problem." After asking questions you can better determine if the criticism is valid.
3. *Decide on a response.* An important part of learning from criticism is to respond appropriately to the critic. Let the criticizer know what you agree with. Apologize for the undesirable behaviour, saying something like, "I apologize for being rude to customers. I know what I can do differently now. I'll be more patient, so as not to appear rude." If the feedback was particularly useful in helping you overcome self-defeating behaviour, thank the person for the constructive feedback.

Stop Denying the Existence of Problems Many people sabotage their careers because they deny the existence of a problem and therefore do not take appropriate action. Denial takes place as a defensive manoeuvre against a painful reality. An example of a self-sabotaging form of denial is to ignore the importance of upgrading one's credentials despite overwhelming evidence that it is necessary. Some people never quite complete a degree program that has become an informal qualification for promotion. Consequently, they sabotage their chances of receiving a promotion for which they are otherwise qualified. Many people in recent years have damaged their chances for career progress by not upgrading their computer skills.

Visualize Self-Enhancing Behaviour Visualization is a primary method for achieving many different types of self-improvement. It is therefore an essential component of overcoming self-defeating behaviour. To apply visualization, program yourself to overcome self-defeating actions and thoughts. Imagine yourself engaging in self-enhancing, winning actions and thoughts. Picture yourself achieving peak performance when good results count the most.

A starting point in learning how to use visualization for overcoming career self-sabotage is to identify the next job situation you will be facing that is similar to ones you have flubbed in the past. You then imagine yourself mentally and physically projected into that situation. Imagine what the room looks like, who will be there, and the confident expression you will have on your face. Visualization is akin to watching a video of yourself doing something right. An example:

> Matt, an actuary in a life insurance company, has an upcoming meeting with top management to discuss his analysis of how insurance rates should be changed to factor in the impact of AIDS on mortality rates. Based on past experience, Matt knows that he becomes flustered and too agreeable in high-level meetings about controversial topics (such as rate increases). Matt also knows that to behave in this way is self-defeating.

As he prepares for the meeting, he visualizes himself calmly listening to challenges to his analysis. In response, he does not back off from his position, but smiles and presents his findings in more detail. Matt visualizes the people who challenged him changing their attitudes as he knowledgeably explains his case. By the end of the meeting Matt is warmly thanked for his recommendations on making rate changes to meet the incidence of AIDS in the population. The president congratulates him on how well he stood up to the challenges to his forecasts.

Understanding and Controlling Addictions

Wellness is blocked by a variety of addictions, and addictive behaviour is also a personal problem. Furthermore, people with personal problems often seek relief by lapsing into addictive behaviour. An **addiction** (or **substance dependence**) is a compulsion to use substances or engage in activities that lead to psychological dependence and withdrawal symptoms when use is discontinued. A caffeine addict would suffer adverse symptoms such as headaches and tension if deprived of caffeine for an entire day. A person with a work addiction would feel ill at ease and tense if forced to stay away from work for several days.

Recent research about brain chemistry and behaviour helps explain why addictions to substances are so widespread. The moment a person ingests a substance such as tobacco, alcohol, marijuana, or chocolate, trillions of strong molecules surge through the bloodstream and into the brain. The molecules trigger a flood of chemical and electrical events that result in a temporary state of pleasure and euphoria.

The common thread to all these mood-altering drugs is their ability to elevate levels of a chemical substance in the brain called **dopamine**, a neurotransmitter that is associated with pleasure and elation. (A neurotransmitter is a molecule in the brain that transports messages from one neuron in the brain to another. It moves across the connectors among brain cells called synapses.) Dopamine is so effective that it is regarded by some scientists as the master molecule of addiction.[5] The chemical is elevated by the common addictive drugs such as heroin, amphetamines, cocaine and crack, marijuana, alcohol, nicotine, and caffeine. However, dopamine can also be elevated by a hug, sexual attraction, praise from a key person, and presumably by finding an exciting new website or book. In short, people develop addictions to get their shot of dopamine.

The balance of our study of **substance abuse** (the overuse of any substance that enters the bloodstream) and addictions concentrates on the abuse of alcohol and a variety of other drugs. Other forms of substance abuse include inhaling intoxicants such as rubber cement or cleaning fluid. Nicotine, caffeine, chocolate, and sugar could be added to the list. With the exception of nicotine, however, their symptoms are not life threatening. For convenience, our discussion will focus on alcohol and drug problems separately. Recognize, however, that alcohol is commonly regarded as a drug. This section will end with a relatively new abuse: internet addiction.

Alcohol Abuse

In Canada, about one-third of the population consumes alcohol at least once per week. Binge drinking (defined as drinking at least five alcoholic drinks in one sitting) is far more common among men than women. One report found that nearly 24 percent of men indulged in binge drinking at least once per month, compared with seven percent of women. Binge drinking was strongly related to age, especially among men, with binge drinking at least once per month by 44 percent of men in the 18 to 24-year age group.[6] Although the number of heavy drinkers has declined since an earlier survey, it appears that many Canadians (14 percent) can be classified as regular and heavy drinkers.[7]

A major concern about consuming such large amounts of alcohol is that health may be adversely affected. What constitutes a large amount of alcohol depends on a person's size and tolerance level. For the average-size adult, more than four alcoholic beverages per day would be considered a large amount. Alcohol consumption leads to marked changes in behaviour. Even low doses significantly

Alcohol: Use or Abuse by University Students?

Are you a university or college student? Do you know any university or college students? If so, some recent surveys may be of some interest to you.

In 1995 the Addiction Research Foundation released the findings of a study on alcohol use by Ontario university students, and some of the results were startling. Alcohol use appears to be on the increase, and one-third of Ontario university students "drink at a level that puts them at risk of health and other problems." Almost one-third of undergraduates reported consuming more than 15 drinks per week and over 50 percent reported consuming more than five drinks at a single sitting in the week before the survey. Also of interest, slightly over 15 percent of the surveyed students drank more than 28 drinks in a week. First-year students, those living in residence, and males were the heaviest drinkers.

Many of the respondents also reported more problems related to alcohol than students in a 1988 study. Some of these problems included hangovers, missed classes, lower grades, vomiting, memory loss, and fighting.[a]

More recent Canadian surveys also indicate that regular and heavy drinking is most common among young people. According to one report, over one-third of those between the ages of 20 and 24 drank five or more drinks at once at least 12 times in the previous year.[b] And one in ten of these young people reported drinking heavily 52 or more times in the previous year. The age group between 18 and 24 continues to be the group that consumes the most alcohol on a regular basis.[c]

However, the good news may be that while many may overindulge in their university and college years, those people having a university degree were least likely to report regular heavy drinking. So while many young people drink heavily during college or university, this seems to decrease after they obtain degrees.[d]

However, we need to be aware that campus drinking is a problem. One suggestion is that a college culture that encourages drinking must be altered drastically. What other suggestions would you make to university and college campuses about decreasing students' heavy drinking?

SOURCES: [a] "University Student Drug Use and Lifestyle," Addiction Research Foundation, News Release, February 2, 1995.

[b] The Federal, Provincial, and Territorial Advisory Committee on Population Health. *Statistical Report on the Health of Canadians*, Prepared for the Meeting of the Ministers of Health, September 1999, Statistics Canada, Catalogue No. 82-570-XIE.

[c] Statistics Canada, *Health Reports*, Volume 12, Issue 3, Ottawa: Ministry of Industry, April 2001, Catalogue No. 82-003.

[d] The Federal, Provincial, and Territorial Advisory Committee on Population Health.

impair the judgment and coordination required to drive an automobile safely, potentially leading to injury and death.

Moderate to high doses of alcohol cause marked impairment in higher mental functions. The brain damage that results can severely alter a person's ability to learn and remember information. Very high doses of alcohol cause respiratory depression and death. Heavy alcohol consumption over a prolonged period of time contributes to heart disease. (Consuming up to three alcoholic beverages a day, however, may help prevent heart disease by stimulating the heart and unclogging arteries.)

Long-term consumption of large quantities of alcohol, particularly when combined with poor nutrition, can lead to permanent damage to vital organs such as the brain and liver. Drinking large quantities of alcohol during pregnancy may result in newborns with fetal alcohol syndrome. These infants have irreversible physical abnormalities and mental damage.

As with other drugs, repeated use of alcohol can lead to dependence. Abrupt cessation of alcohol consumption can produce withdrawal symptoms including severe anxiety, tremors, hallucinations, and convulsions. Severe withdrawal symptoms can be life threatening.

Work and Personal Life Consequences of Alcohol Abuse

Heavy consumption of alcohol has many adverse consequences for a person's career and personal life. Heavy drinking will eventually interfere with work performance, resulting in some of the following behaviours:[8]

- Low productivity and quality of work
- Erratic performance
- Erratic and unusual behaviour such as swearing at co-workers during a meeting
- Excessive tardiness and absenteeism
- Increased difficulty in working cooperatively with supervisors
- Increased difficulty in working cooperatively with co-workers
- Carelessness, negligence, or apathy

Alcohol consumption is potentially disruptive to personal and family life. Many people who quit drinking reported that they did so because it adversely affected their family life.[9] Even moderate doses of alcohol increase the incidence of a variety of aggressive acts, including partner and child abuse. Purchasing alcoholic beverages can lead to family problems because household bills may go unpaid. Many alcoholics lose friends because their friends are uncomfortable being around them when they are drinking. Sexual desire and performance often decline with heavy alcohol abuse. Many male drinkers suffer from impotence. Alcohol abuse often leads to divorce and other broken relationships.

Overcoming Alcohol Abuse

A person's approach to overcoming alcohol abuse depends to some extent on whether he or she regards alcoholism as a disease or as maladaptive behaviour. Regarding alcoholism as a disease is the majority viewpoint among mental health specialists and the general public. People who regard alcoholism as a disease are likely to seek medical or psychological help. To conquer alcoholism they would therefore seek help from physicians and counsellors. Such help might consist of outpatient visits to mental health practitioners, often at clinics for substance abusers. A person with severe alcoholism might volunteer to become an in-patient at a hospital specializing in the treatment of alcoholism.

Another viewpoint is to regard alcoholism as self-defeating behaviour that is somewhat under a person's control. People who accept the *bad habit* view of alcohol abuse might seek professional assistance with their problem. Yet the thrust of their efforts to overcome alcoholism will be to discipline themselves to change their counterproductive ways. Looking upon alcoholism as maladaptive behaviour runs contrary to the thinking of groups such as Alcoholics Anonymous. Such groups label alcoholism as a sickness over which the victim has no control, and therefore they insist on abstinence.[10] A person who believes that his or her alcohol abuse is under control could take the following precautions to prevent a major drinking problem:[11]

- Limit the consumption of alcoholic beverages to three on any given day, but average no more than two per day. Remember that popular alcoholic beverages are ranked as follows in order of increasing strength: wine cooler, beer, wine, and hard liquor. Hard liquor should therefore be consumed in smaller quantities than the other three types of beverages.
- Abstain from alcoholic beverages for at least two consecutive days each week.
- Drink only standard-size beverages: one ounce of hard liquor in a mixed drink; 12 ounces of beer; or five ounces of wine.
- Don't drink on an empty stomach.
- Drink slowly and intersperse alcoholic beverages with nonalcoholic beverages while at parties.
- When you have the urge for an alcoholic beverage, on occasion substitute a glass of fruit juice or water.
- Make friends with people whose social lives do not revolve around drinking alcoholic beverages. Associate with responsible drinkers.
- Regard drinking before 6 p.m. as a personal taboo.

The above suggestions are useful because they assume that mature adults can enjoy moderate alcohol consumption without falling prey to alcohol abuse. The same suggestions can be used to convert problem drinking into relatively safe drinking. Implementing these suggestions requires considerable self-discipline, as do approaches to overcoming other forms of self-defeating behaviour.

Drug Abuse

Another major personal problem many people face is drug abuse. The use of cannabis, cocaine or crack, and heroin continues to be a serious concern for federal, provincial, and territorial governments.[12] The use of illegal drugs is often perceived more harshly than alcohol abuse because alcohol use is legal. Similarly, the abuse of prescription drugs is not considered as wrong as the abuse of illegal drugs. The health effects and personal life consequences of abusing both illegal and prescription drugs are similar to those of alcohol abuse. Human Relations Self-Assessment Quiz 5-2 will help sensitize you to the many similarities of the behaviour consequences of drug and alcohol abuse. Here we will summarize the effects of four major categories of drugs, and then describe how drug abusers can be helped.

Uses and Effects of Controlled Substances

The term *drug* refers to a variety of chemicals with different chemical compositions and effects. One individual might inject heroin for recreational use, while another person might sniff paint thinner to achieve the same effect. There are four major categories of drugs based on their psychological effects.[13] Each of the four categories of drugs has different possible effects and different consequences for overdoses. Each category of drug has both illegal and legitimate uses. For example, stimulants include both crack cocaine and a legal drug with the trade name Dexedrine.

Opiates An **opiate** is a drug that dulls the senses, facilitates sleep, and is addictive with long-term use. Well-known opiates include opium, morphine, codeine, and heroin. The possible effects of opiates include euphoria, drowsiness, and decreased breathing. An opiate user may also experience constricted pupils and nausea. Overdosing on opiates may lead to slow and shallow breathing, clammy skin, convulsions, and coma. Death is also possible. People who use opiates frequently do severe damage to their careers and personal lives in the long run.

Depressants A **depressant** is a drug that slows down vital body processes. Barbiturates are the best-known depressant (or sedative). Alcohol is also classified as a depressant. Heavy doses of depressants can lead to slurred speech and disorientation. A depressant user will show drunken behaviour without the odour of alcohol. An overdose of depressants leads to shallow breathing, clammy skin, and dilated pupils. With extreme overdoses, the person may lapse into coma and then death.

Many anxious people are convinced they must take legally prescribed sedatives to calm down. The trade-off is the risk of lacking the mental alertness to perform at their peak. Frequent users of depressants make poor companions because they lack vitality.

Stimulants The class of drugs known as **stimulants** produces feelings of optimism and high energy. Cocaine and amphetamines are the two best-known stimulants. Taking stimulants leads to increased alertness, excitation, and euphoria. The user will also experience increased pulse rate and blood pressure, insomnia, and loss of appetite. (Many diet pills are really stimulants.) Overdoses of stimulants lead to agitation, increased body temperature, hallucinations, convulsions, and possible death. Stimulant abusers are regarded by others as being “hyper,” and may be too agitated to do high-quality work. The Addiction Research Foundation reports that stimulant use is on the increase by Canadian university students.[14]

Hallucinogens and Psychedelics In small doses the class of drugs known as **hallucinogens** produces visual effects similar to hallucinations. Three well-known hallucinogens are LSD, mescaline, and peyote. Hallucinogens lead to illusions (misperceptions) and poor perception of time and distance. Overdoses of hallucinogens can produce "trip" episodes, psychosis (severe mental disorder), and possible death. While under the influence of a hallucinogen, a person is unfit for work. The bizarre behaviour of hallucinogen abusers leads to a deterioration of their relationships with people.

Marijuana is the most widely used psychedelic drug, and its use appears to be on the increase in Canada, especially among young males between the ages of 15 and 24.[15] Marijuana use leads to feelings of euphoria, relaxed inhibitions, and increased appetite. The same drug may cause disorientation. Marijuana abuse may lead to fatigue, paranoia, and possible psychosis. Because marijuana is used as a

Quiz 5-2

Symptoms of Alcohol and Drug Abuse

People with alcohol or drug abuse problems are often poor judges of the extent of their problem. Nevertheless, it is helpful to use the symptoms mentioned below as a checklist to help identify an alcohol or drug problem you might be experiencing. Review the symptoms listed below and indicate whether each one applies to you.

Alcohol Abuse	**Yes**	**No**
Sudden decreases in my job performance	_______	_______
Decreases in my mental alertness	_______	_______
Many long lunch hours	_______	_______
Tardiness for work and social appointments	_______	_______
Wobbling instead of walking straight	_______	_______
Many absences from work or school	_______	_______
Comments by others that my speech is slurred	_______	_______
Frequent use of breath freshener	_______	_______
Frequent depressed moods	_______	_______
Trembling of my hands and body	_______	_______
Errors in judgment and concentration	_______	_______
Many financial problems because of my drinking	_______	_______
Comments by others that my eyes look sleepy	_______	_______
Much lost time due to physical illness	_______	_______
Elaborate excuses for not getting work done on the job or at home	_______	_______
Denying a drinking problem when I know I have one	_______	_______

Interpretation: If five or more of the above symptoms fit you, you may have a problem with alcohol abuse. Act on the remedial measures described in this chapter.

(continued)

Drug Abuse	**Yes**	**No**
Sudden decreases in my job performance	_______	_______
Decreases in my mental alertness	_______	_______
Hiding out on company premises	_______	_______
Many absences from work or school	_______	_______
My pupils appear dilated when I look in the mirror	_______	_______
Unusual bursts of energy and excitement	_______	_______
Prolonged and serious lethargy	_______	_______
States of apathy and elation I cannot explain	_______	_______
Errors in concentration and judgment	_______	_______
Many financial problems because of drug purchases	_______	_______
Comments by others that my eyes look sleepy	_______	_______
Frequent sniffling	_______	_______
People telling me that I look "out of it"	_______	_______
Elaborate excuses for not getting work done on the job or at home	_______	_______
Frequent dry, irritated coughing	_______	_______
Denying a drug problem when I know I have one	_______	_______
Not showing up for many work and social appointments	_______	_______

Interpretation: If five or more of the above symptoms fit you, you may have a problem with drug abuse. Act on the remedial measures described in this chapter.

cigarette, it may cause lung cancer and cardiovascular damage. Used in moderate doses, marijuana does much less damage to career and personal life than the other drugs described here.

Getting Help for Drug Abuse Problems

Many forms of assistance are available for drug abusers. The comments made earlier in relation to alcohol abuse also apply to drug abuse. Drug abusers can seek help from physicians and from mental health specialists (some of whom are physicians). At the same time, the drug abuser may view his or her problem as a form of maladaptive behaviour that can be controlled through concentrated effort. Assume, for example, a person says, "I simply cannot get through the day without an amphetamine pill. Life is too boring for me if I don't have an upper."

The antidote is for the person to say something to the following effect: "This week, I won't take an amphetamine on Monday. Next week, no amphetamine on Monday or Tuesday. I'll keep adding a day until I have gone an entire week drug-free." Self-management of this type can work for many people.

An avenue of help for an employed person with a drug abuse problem is the company employee assistance program. A major purpose of these programs is to help employees overcome personal problems that drain productivity. Typically, the assistance program coordinator refers the troubled employee to an outside treatment facility. Some larger organizations have their own treatment facilities located on or off company premises. The program is confidential, sometimes to the extent that the company does not know which employees have referred themselves for help.

Many of the problems dealt with by the employee assistance program involve forms of self-defeating behaviour in addition to drug abuse. Among them are other forms of substance abuse, cigarette addiction, compulsive gambling, financial problems, and physical and emotional abuse of family members. Employees can also spend one or two sessions with the assistance counsellor to talk about self-defeating behaviour in general. If the counsellor thinks multiple sessions are required, an appropriate referral is made.

Seeking help from an assistance counsellor rather than going to a mental health practitioner on one's own has an important advantage. Employee assistance counsellors work regularly with people whose personal problems are hurting job performance. Also, the company usually pays the entire fee.

Internet Addiction

A major new addiction, or at least a very strong habit, is the problem of feeling compelled to spend lengthy periods of time surfing the internet as a pastime. An **internet addiction** (or **dependence**) is a condition whereby a person spends so much time on the internet that other work suffers and the person experiences sleep deprivation and neglects human contact. Symptoms of pathological internet use are presented in Human Relations Self-Assessment Quiz 5-3. A concern about the social consequences of internet dependence is that many users, caught in maintaining contact with so many people with similar interests, seem to be substituting weak online friendships for stronger real-life relationships.[16] (This does not imply that nobody ever develops solid interpersonal relationships over the internet. Many people find life partners and business associates online.)

About five to ten percent of internet users develop problem behaviours—about the same frequency as for people who drink alcohol or gamble. Because so many people have problems with excessive time devoted to the internet, many abuse treatment centres have evolved. Among the specific problems treated are extensive amounts of time viewing pornography, online affairs, and addictive day trading (buying and selling the same security in a single day) on the internet. One approach to helping people overcome internet dependence is to treat it like binge eating, where the individual frequently engages in the activity to be restricted. Clients are taught how to set limits on internet use and schedule time, without having to go cold turkey.[17]

Coping with the Loss of a Relationship

A major personal problem many people encounter is the loss of a valued personal relationship. The loss may take the form of separation, divorce, or the breakup of a nonmarried couple. A more subtle loss is when a couple stays together, yet the intimacy in the relationship vanishes. Loneliness and conflict result from the lost intimacy. The next chapter presents ideas on maintaining and revitalizing relationships. Our attention here is directed toward specific suggestions for dealing with the loss of an important personal relationship.

Warning Signs of Excessive Internet Use

Psychologist Kimberly Young has identified several warning signs of excessive internet use. **Behaviours** that signal concern include

- *staying* online longer than you intended
- admitting that you *can't stop* yourself from signing on
- *neglecting* loved ones, chores, sleep, reading, television, friends, exercise, hobbies, sex, or social events because of the internet
- spending *38 hours* or more a week online
- feeling *anxious,* bored, sad, lonely, angry, or *stressed* before going online, but feeling happy, excited, loved, calmed, or confident while on the internet
- favouring *chat rooms,* games, and multi-user dungeons over other internet activities

Although this quiz does not have a scoring key, the more of these behaviours you have exhibited, the more severe your internet addiction. Get help before you end up losing your job, flunking out of school, or losing an important relationship.

SOURCE: Reprinted from Carol Potera, "Trapped in the Web," *Psychology Today,* March/April 1998, p. 68.

When you are emotionally and romantically involved with another person, the loss of that relationship usually has a big impact. Even if you believe strongly that splitting up is in your best interest, the fact that you cared at one time about that person leads to some hurt. The major reason we need tactics for dealing with lost relationships is that many upsetting feelings surface in conjunction with the loss.

A newly unattached person might feel lonely, guilty, angry, or frightened. Your role in the breakup will usually dictate which emotion surfaces. For instance, if you dumped your partner, you will probably experience guilt. If you were the person dumped, you will probably experience anger. If you survive a spouse, you might feel guilty about not having been nice enough to your partner during your years together.

A number of suggestions to help a person recover from a lost relationship are presented below.[18] Choose the tactics that seem to fit your personality and circumstances. As with the other personal problems described in this chapter, professional counselling may be helpful in making a recovery.

1. *Be thankful for the good in the relationship.* An excellent starting point in recovering from a broken relationship is to take stock of what went right when the two of you were together. Looking for the good in the relationship helps place the situation in proper perspective. It also helps prevent

you from developing the counterproductive attitude that your time together was a total waste.

2. *Find new outlets for spare time.* Some of the energy you were investing in your partnership can now be invested in spare-time activities. This activity provides a healthy form of the defence mechanism called *compensation* or *substitution*.
3. *Get ample rest and relaxation.* A broken relationship is a stressor. As a result, most people need rest and relaxation to help them overcome the emotional pain associated with the departure of a partner.
4. *Pamper yourself.* Pampering involves finding little ways of doing nice things for yourself. These could take the form of buying yourself a new outfit, taking a weekend vacation, eating pizza at midnight, or getting a body massage.
5. *Seek emotional support.* Friends and relatives can also be an important source of emotional support to help you cope with post-separation blues. Be careful, however, not to let your loss of a relationship dominate conversations with friends to the point of boring them. Another source of emotional support is groups specifically designed to help people cope with recent separation or divorce. Parents Without Partners is an example of such a group. A caution here is that some people stay too long with such groups rather than taking the initiative to find a new partner.
6. *Get out and go places.* The oldest suggestion about recovering from a lost relationship is perhaps the most valid—keep active. While you are doing new things you tend to forget about your problems. Also, as you go places and do things, you increase your chances of making new friends. And friends are the only true antidote to the loneliness of being unattached.
7. *Give yourself time to heal.* The greater the hurt, the more time it will take to recover from the broken relationship. Recognizing this fact will help to curb your impatience over disentangling yourself emotionally from the former spouse or partner.
8. *Anticipate a positive outcome.* While you are on the path toward rebuilding your social life, believe that things will get better. Also believe that all the emotional energy you have invested into splitting and healing will pay dividends. Self-fulfilling prophecies work to some extent in social relationships. If you believe you will make a satisfactory recovery from a broken relationship, your chances of doing so will increase. The underlying mechanism seems to be that if you believe in yourself, you exude a level of self-confidence that others find appealing.

Absenteeism and Tardiness

Absenteeism and tardiness are the leading causes of employee discipline. Developing a poor record of attendance and punctuality is also a form of career self-sabotage. Employees who are habitually absent or late develop a poor reputation and receive negative employment references. It becomes difficult to find a good job with another employer after having established a poor record of attendance and punctuality. Maintaining good attendance and punctuality is more important today than ever, because worldwide competition has forced many private organizations to trim costs. Government organizations are also under constant pressure to control costs. The person who is habitually absent or late therefore risks termination.

Here we will first look at data about absenteeism and tardiness standards. We will then discuss how a person might overcome the problem of high absenteeism and tardiness.

During a person's career, many unexpected situations arise in which it is necessary to be absent or late. Accidents, illnesses, severe family problems, and family deaths all may require time away from the job. A serious-minded worker should therefore strive to attain near-perfect attendance and punctuality when not faced with an emergency. Some suggestions follow to help a person develop the right mental set for achieving an excellent record of attendance and punctuality.

1. *Recognize that not to have excellent attendance and punctuality is self-defeating.* For reasons already described, poor attendance and punctuality can lead to a poor reputation and job loss. Why self-handicap your chances for career success?
2. *Look upon your job as self-employment.* Few people operating their own business will take a day off, or begin late, for no valid reason. The smaller the business, the better the attendance and punctuality, because so little help is available. You can therefore improve your attendance and punctuality by imagining that your area of responsibility is your own business.
3. *Regard your job responsibilities as equally important to those of the person in charge of opening the bank's doors in the morning.* People in charge of opening banks, department stores, movie theatres, and other retail businesses have excellent records of attendance and punctuality. A poor performance in these areas would create panic, especially in the case of the bank. To improve your attendance and punctuality, think of your responsibilities as being as important as opening the doors in the morning.
4. *Reward yourself for good attendance and punctuality and punish yourself for the opposite.* Following the suggestions for self-motivation described in Chapter 2, modify your behaviour in relation to attendance and punctuality. Treat yourself after six months of excellent attendance and punctuality. Punish yourself for a poor record. For example, if you miss one day of work for a flimsy reason, punish yourself by working all day on a national holiday.
5. *Think through carefully the consequences if all company employees were absent and late frequently.* Some people argue that they are entitled to take the maximum number of sick days allowable under company policy. If everybody took the maximum number of sick days and was late as often as possible without incurring discipline, companies would suffer. Customer service would deteriorate, productivity would decrease, and more people would have to be hired just to cover for employee "no-shows." Less money might be available for salary increases and employee benefits. Even worse, the company might have to lay off employees because of low profits.

6. *Think of the consequences to co-workers if you are absent and late frequently.* Being absent or late may hurt the company. The same behaviour can adversely affect your relationships with co-workers. Co-workers become annoyed and irritated quickly when they have to cover for a negligent peer. The worker who is frequently absent or late runs the risk of losing the cooperation of co-workers when he or she needs assistance.

Depression, Neurobiological Disorders, and Eating Disorders

Many employees perform poorly on the job because of reasons beyond their control. They would like to perform well, but disturbed emotions or brain malfunctioning interfere with handling some aspects of their job responsibilities well. To illustrate this kind of obstacle, we describe two problems faced by many workers: depression and neurobiological disorders. Here we have also added a new section on eating disorders, a growing problem in North America.

Depression

Depression is a widespread emotional disorder. A depressed person has difficulties such as sadness, changes in appetite, sleeping difficulties, and a decrease in activities, interests, and energy. Depression is the most commonly diagnosed mental illness. It has been estimated by the Canadian Mental Health Association that "15 percent of the population will experience a major depressive episode at some time in their lives."[19] In 1998–1999 an estimated four percent of Canadians of age 12 or older reported symptoms that would suggest that they had suffered at least one episode of major depression during the previous year. Also, women were twice as likely to report depression, and their depressive episodes last longer.[20]

Most cases of depression are believed to be caused primarily by a chemical imbalance in the brain whereby the functioning of the neurotransmitters is disturbed. A person's psychological makeup also contributes to susceptibility to depression. People with low self-esteem, who are pessimistic, and who manage stress poorly are prone to depression. To treat depression successfully, antidepressant medication usually needs to be accompanied by psychotherapy and counselling.

In recent years, much attention has been paid to **seasonal affective disorder (SAD)**, a form of depression that develops during the fall and winter months and disappears as the days lengthen in the spring. Because darkness stimulates the production of melatonin, some researchers believe that people who experience SAD may produce an excess of melatonin or may be particularly sensitive to the hormone. SAD sufferers become lethargic in the winter and fall, and show other symptoms of depression. In one survey study done in Toronto, almost three percent of respondents indicated that they suffered from SAD.[21] "Winter blues" is the everyday term for this problem.

The farther north of the equator you live, the more likely you are to experience SAD. However, people who enjoy outdoor winter activities like skiing, ice skating, curling, and shovelling snow are less prone to SAD (based on one author's observations).

Being depressed on the job creates many problems. Depression drains energy and reduces productivity and quality. The reduced effectiveness triggers a cycle of failure. As effectiveness decreases, the person's thinking, acting, and feeling become more damaged. As relationships with co-workers and job performance deteriorate, the person becomes more depressed.[22] Here is an example of how depression affects job behaviour:

> A sales manager known for his exuberance and enthusiasm slowly began to withdraw from face-to-face contact with team members. During one team meeting the manager abruptly terminated the meeting, telling the group, "I'm just too emotionally drained to continue today." Soon, he rarely communicated with others in the firm except through email. At times he was observed just staring out the window. Reports of his unusual behaviour soon reached his manager, who in turn urged the sales manager to visit a mental health professional. A combination of antidepressant drugs and psychotherapy helped the sales manager to overcome his problems enough to function satisfactorily on the job.

Human Relations Self-Assessment Quiz 5-4 will help you better appreciate the symptoms of depression as they apply to the job. These symptoms are easier to recognize in another person than in oneself. Having more than a few of these symptoms is an indicator that treatment by a mental health professional is important. Many people who commit suicide are extremely depressed.

Neurobiological Disorders

Personal problems on the job are sometimes the result of a **neurobiological disorder**, a quirk in the chemistry or anatomy of the brain that creates a disability. The quirk is usually inherited, but could also be caused by a brain injury or poisoning, such as exposure to harmful vapours. The disabilities take the form of reduced ability to control one's behaviour, movements, emotions, or thoughts.[23] If you experience sudden changes in your job behaviour, a thorough neurological examination is strongly recommended. The most common neurobiological disorders on the job are described next. Depression, described in the previous section, is sometimes classified as a neurobiological disorder when it stems from chemical or anatomical factors.

Attention Deficit Disorder People with this disorder have difficulty concentrating that may be accompanied by hyperactivity. The person might therefore engage in a flurry of activity on the job, yet much of the activity might be wasted effort. Many children's difficulties in paying attention in school are attributed to attention deficit disorder.

Obsessive-Compulsive Disorder People with this disorder have uncontrollable and recurring thoughts or behaviour relating to an unreasonable fear. A job example of obsessive-compulsive disorder would be a person who becomes obsessed with cleaning his or her work area. The person could be motivated by fear of being contaminated by impurities in the ventilation system.

Symptoms of Depression on the Job

Workers suffering from depression often experience a combination of one or more of the following symptoms. Not every depressed person will experience them all. (Most of these symptoms are also present off the job.)

- Slow movement, drooped posture
- Decreased energy, fatigue, and frequent complaints of being tired
- Decreased ability to concentrate, remember, or make decisions
- Taking an unusually long time to complete tasks
- Speaking only when spoken to
- Crying on the job
- Attributing any personal successes to luck
- Loss of interest in activities that were once enjoyable, such as having lunch with co-workers
- Mentions of suicide, even in a joking manner
- Deterioration in grooming such as rumpled clothing, unkempt hair, neglected facial shaving
- Increased absenteeism
- Alcohol and drug abuse
- Increasing intensity and frequency of any of the above symptoms

SOURCES: Canadian Mental Health Association, 1995; *Health Guide*, America's Pharmaceutical Research Companies, 1996 (**www.phrma.org**); John Lawrie, "Coping with Depression on the Job," *Supervisory Management*, June 1992, pp. 6–7.

Narcolepsy People with this disorder have uncontrollable sleepiness, even after receiving adequate sleep. A person with narcolepsy may fall asleep at the desk, or while driving a company vehicle or operating dangerous machinery.

Tourette's Syndrome People suffering from this disorder experience uncontrollable movement or utterances, and often shout profanities at inappropriate times. A person with Tourette's syndrome is often misinterpreted as consciously attempting to create a disturbance.

Although damaging to work performance, neurobiological disorders can be treated successfully. In addition to the proper medication, the person usually needs a supportive environment both at home and on the job. Most people with neurobiological disorders can function close to normally after appropriate medication is prescribed and they are taught how to cope with their symptoms.

Training others to understand their condition is an important part of the treatment. The person with Tourette's syndrome, for example, should explain to co-workers that at times he or she may appear insulting and abusive. Furthermore, co-workers can be advised not to take such behaviour seriously, and that the behaviour is under medical control and may soon disappear entirely. Discussing a personal problem with co-workers may help to reduce their fears about your problem and lead to better understanding.

Eating Disorders

More difficult to categorize, eating disorders are on the rise in Western countries (including Canada) while the age of onset of these disorders is decreasing.[24] The quest for "thin as beautiful" in Western society has helped to propel many people into the spiral of dieting and for some, into eating disorders.[25] While most prevalent among females, the incidence is also rising for males.[26] These disorders include *anorexia nervosa*, *bulimia nervosa*, and *binge eating disorder*.

Anorexia nervosa is the refusal to maintain normal body weight and usually includes fears of gaining weight or becoming fat accompanied by misperception of body size. People with anorexia have their body weight tied up as a large part of their self-evaluation and self-worth. Bulimia consists of bingeing on large amounts of food often followed by purging the food through such methods as vomiting or overuse of laxatives. Individuals with bulimia often feel they cannot control these binges. Binge eating disorder, or compulsive eating, may be described as food intake that is emotionally "driven" to the point of physical discomfort or beyond, often occurs in secret, is experienced as comforting to the individual and may be a continuation of a regular meal or initiated apart from meals. This type of behaviour is different from bulimia in that it is not followed by any form of purging.[27]

A recent Canadian study found disordered eating attitudes and behaviours were present in over 25 percent of girls of ages 12 to 18. These behaviours and attitudes increased gradually throughout adolescence. Behaviours and attitudes included dieting, using diet pills and self-induced vomiting. Laxatives and diuretics were not common practice.[28] Media that promote "thin as in" may be partly to blame for this North American dream of success as equal to being thin, but many people are no longer buying into this sometimes dangerous preoccupation. A healthy diet balanced with exercise is far healthier and will leave you with the energy to be successful both on and off the job. Human Relations Self-Assessment Quiz 5-5 lists some of the symptoms of eating disorders. If you display some of these symptoms, it may be time to seek some help and rethink the reasons you are behaving in these less-than-healthy ways.

Dealing with Anger

Limited ability to manage anger damages the career and personal life of many people. **Anger** is a feeling of extreme hostility, displeasure, or exasperation. The emotion of anger creates stress, including the physiological changes described in Chapter 4. One noticeable indicator of anger is enlargement of the pupils, causing the wide-eyed look of people in a rage. Blood may rush to the face, as indicated by reddening in light-skinned people. Anger often leads to aggression, which is the verbal or physical attacking of another person, animal, or object. Workplace violence, such as an ex-employee shooting a former boss who fired him, is an

Do You Have the Symptoms of an Eating Disorder?

You can be fairly certain that you have an eating problem if your eating behaviour or attitudes about weight interrupt your life and take pleasure out of it. Typically, people with eating problems are preoccupied with their weight, shape, and the food they are consuming. You may have an eating problem if you experience some of the following:

- Excessive concern about weight, shape, and calories
- Unusual eating habits
- Irregular menstruation or ceasing of menstruation
- Depression or irritability
- Guilt or shame about eating
- Strict avoidance of certain foods, particularly those considered fattening
- Feeling fat when not "overweight"
- Use of laxatives, diuretics, purgatives
- Excessive exercise
- Vomiting to purge food
- Noticeable weight loss in anorexia
- Frequent weight fluctuation in bulimia
- Extreme concern about appearance, both physical and behavioural

SOURCE: The National Eating Disorder Information Centre, **www.nedic.ca**. Used with permission.

extreme example of expressing anger. What angry behaviour have you observed on the job?

The ability to manage anger is an important interpersonal skill, now considered to be part of **emotional intelligence**. This concept refers to qualities such as understanding your feelings, empathy for others, and the regulation of emotion to enhance living.[29] A person who cannot manage anger well cannot take good advantage of his or her regular intelligence. As an extreme example, a genius who swears at the boss regularly will probably lose his or her job despite being so talented. Our concern here is with several suggestions that will help you manage (not necessarily eliminate) anger so it does not jeopardize your career or personal success.

A starting point is to recognize that at its best, *anger can be an energizing force*. Instead of being destructive, channel your anger into exceptional performance. If you are angry because you did not get the raise you thought you deserved, get even by performing so well that there will be no question you deserve a raise next time. Develop the habit of *expressing your anger before it reaches a high intensity*. Tell your companion that you do not appreciate his or her using a cell phone while you are having dinner together the first time the act of rudeness occurs. If you wait too long, you may wind up grabbing the cell phone and slamming it to the floor.

As you are about to express anger, *slow down*. (The old technique of counting to ten is still effective.) Slowing down gives you the opportunity to express your anger in a way that does not damage your relationship with the other person. Following your first impulse, you might say to another person, "You're a stupid fool." If you slow down, this might translate into, "You need training on this task." Closely related to slowing down is saying to yourself as soon as you feel angry, "Oops, I'm in the anger mode now. I had better calm down before I say something or do something I will regret later." To gauge how effectively you are expressing your anger, ask for feedback. Ask a friend, co-worker, or manager, "Am I coming on too strong when I express my negative opinion?"[30]

Anger has also become widespread throughout society and we have even labelled it depending upon where it occurs—we have "road rage," "air rage," and uncivil workplaces. Anger can erupt into violence. Many companies have been asking ill-tempered employees to attend anger management classes. Anger management is often included in drug treatment and couples counselling. A major part of these classes is to help clients learn self-control by such means as thinking through the consequences of unchecked anger. Another approach is to help people learn to look at the big picture and not let little things bother them. These classes are a start, but overcoming anger issues may take most people at least one year.[31] Human Relations Skill-Building Exercise 5-1 will give you an opportunity

Learning to Manage Anger

The next few times you are really angry with somebody or something, use one or more of the good mental health statements described below. Each statement is designed to remind you that you are in charge, not your anger. For starters, visualize something that has made you angry recently. Practise making the statements below in relation to that angry episode.

- **I'm in charge here, not my emotional outbursts.**
- **I'll breathe deeply a few times and then deal with this.**
- **I feel _____ when you _____.**
- **I can handle this.**
- **I'm going to take time out to cool down before I deal with this.**
- **Yes, I'm angry and I'll just watch what I say or do.**

Now describe the effect making the above statements had on your anger.

SOURCE: Based on Lynne Namka, "A Primer on Anger: Getting a Handle on Your Mads," **http://members.aol.com/angriesout/grown2.htm** (July 7, 1997), p. 4.

to develop your anger-management skills. However, the exercise will require some work outside class.

Summary

Unless personal problems are kept under control, a person's chances of achieving career and personal success diminish. Many personal problems arise out of self-defeating behaviour. The major cause of this behaviour is a loser life script, a life plan of coming out a loser in important situations. Other causes of self-defeating behaviour include a self-defeating personality pattern, self-defeating beliefs, and fear of success. Approaches to overcoming and preventing self-defeating behaviour include these strategies:

1. Examine your "script" and make the necessary changes.
2. Stop blaming others for your problems.
3. Solicit feedback on your actions.
4. Learn to profit from criticism.
5. Stop denying the existence of problems.
6. Visualize self-enhancing behaviour.

Wellness is blocked by a variety of addictions, and addictive behaviour is also a personal problem. Addictive behaviour toward substances such as alcohol and marijuana comes about because they elevate dopamine, a chemical substance in the brain that is associated with pleasure and elation. Dopamine can also be elevated by psychological events such as a hug.

Alcohol abuse often adversely affects health. Moderate to high doses of alcohol cause marked impairment in mental functions. Alcohol consumption is associated with heart and liver disease and fetal alcohol syndrome. Very high doses of alcohol cause respiratory depression and death. Alcohol abuse adversely affects job performance and career success. Alcoholism can be treated as a disease or as maladaptive (counterproductive) behaviour. Precautions can be taken to prevent alcohol abuse, such as not drinking during the day.

The health effects and personal life consequences of abusing both illegal and prescription drugs are similar to those of alcohol abuse. The various categories of drugs have different possible effects and different consequences for overdoses. The four drug categories are (1) opiates, (2) depressants, (3) stimulants, and (4) hallucinogens and psychedelics. Many forms of professional help are available for drug abusers, yet self-management of the problem is also an important form of help. Employee assistance programs sponsored by employers can help with drug abuse problems.

A major personal problem many people encounter is the loss of a valued personal relationship. Suggestions for dealing with this problem include the following: (1) be thankful for the good in the relationship, (2) find new outlets for spare time, (3) get ample rest and relaxation, (4) pamper yourself, (5) seek emotional support, (6) get out and go places, (7) give yourself time to heal, and (8) anticipate a positive outcome.

Absenteeism and tardiness are the leading causes of employee discipline, and thus can be a major personal problem. Workers must develop the right mental set to achieve excellent attendance and punctuality. For example, a person might look upon the job as self-employment.

Many employees perform poorly on the job because they are depressed. Depression drains energy and reduces productivity and quality. As job performance deteriorates, the person becomes more depressed. Many job problems are also caused by neurobiological disorders, a quirk in the chemistry or anatomy of the brain that creates a disability. The disabilities take the form of reduced ability to control one's behaviour, movements, emotions, or thoughts. Major neurobiological disorders are attention deficit disorder, obsessive-compulsive disorder, narcolepsy, and Tourette's syndrome. These disorders can be treated with medication, but a supportive environment is also needed. In addition, eating disorders are becoming more prevalent in Western society. A healthy diet and exercise are recommended rather than these unhealthy approaches to weight loss.

Limited ability to deal with anger damages the career and personal lives of many people. Eating disorders can also have an impact on a person's life and can cause severe health problems.

The ability to manage anger is an important interpersonal skill, considered to be a component of emotional intelligence. To manage anger well, recognize that it can be an energizing force. Express anger before it reaches a high intensity. As you are about to express anger, slow down, and then express it in a constructive way. Ask others for feedback on how well you are expressing anger. Anger management classes are also an option for coping with anger.

Questions and Activities

1. What is the difference between making a bad mistake once and self-defeating behaviour?
2. Describe a person you know who appears to have a "winner" life script, and justify your reasoning.
3. If it is really true that chocolate releases dopamine in the blood the same as nicotine and alcohol do, is munching chocolate a way to curb cigarette and alcohol abuse? Explain your reasoning.
4. Most people know that large amounts of alcohol are hazardous to health. Why then is alcohol abuse such a major problem throughout the world?
5. How can looking upon substance abuse as a bad habit help substance abusers overcome their problem?
6. Some companies offer awards for good attendance. Why is this necessary from a motivational standpoint?
7. Do you think people who have poor attendance records in school will probably have poor attendance records on the job? Explain your reasoning.
8. What is the difference between having a depression disorder and "having the blues"?
9. What are some effects that an eating disorder could create for a person on the job? Should employers have programs in place to help employees eat well, just as many employers have substance abuse programs? Explain your answer.

10. Why is it that hockey players become so angry that they regularly physically attack their opponents, whereas tennis and golf players almost never act this way?

Internet Skill Builder

The Virtual Couch

Investigate the kind of mental health services a person can receive online. In other words, what type of psychotherapy and counselling can a person receive over the internet? A good starting point would be to visit these sites: **www.metanola.org/imhs**, **www.concernedcounseling.com**, and **www.masteringstress.com**. What is your opinion about the quality of these services compared with those of a mental health professional seen in person?

Weblinks

www.helpself.com/eqtest.htm
Take an EQ (emotional intelligence) test and see how emotionally intelligent you are. Also, this site has more information on emotional intelligence.

www.camh.net/addiction/pims/evaluate_your_drinking.html
This is the site for the Centre for Addiction and Mental Health. Here you can access a questionnaire where you can evaluate your drinking behaviour and compare your behaviour with that of other Canadians.

www.ontario.cmha.ca
This is the site for the Ontario Mental Health Association. From this site you can access a wide variety of information on mental health and the mental health associations in other provinces.

www.mentalhealth.com/mag1/p51-str.html
An informative site about stress where you can find out ways of managing stress, learn more about stress, and access other references about stress. This is also a Canadian site.

http://depression.mentalhelp.net
This is a site devoted to depression and includes information on how to get to help for depression.

www.cami.org
This is the website of the Canadian Association for the Mentally Ill.

Human Relations Case Study

A CONCERN ABOUT VIOLENCE

Vernon Bigsby is the CEO and owner of a large soft-drink bottling company in Vancouver. The company invests money periodically in training to help the management and supervisory staff stay abreast of important new trends in technology and managing human resources. Bigsby recently became concerned about workplace violence. Although the company had not yet experienced an outbreak of violence, Bigsby was intent on preventing violence in the future. To accomplish his goal, Bigsby hired a human resources consultant, Sara Toomey, to conduct a seminar on preventing workplace violence.

The seminar was given twice, with one-half the managers and supervisors attending each session. Chad Ditmar, a night-shift supervisor, made the first wisecrack during the seminar. He said, "What are we here for? To prevent workers from squirting 'pop' at each other?" Toomey responded, "My job would be easy if I were here only to prevent horseplay. Unfortunately the reality is that there are thousands of lethal weapons going past your workers everyday. Just think how much damage one angry worker could do to an innocent victim with one slash of a broken bottle." The laughter in the room quickly subsided.

About one hour into the seminar, Sara Toomey projected a PowerPoint slide outlining characteristics of a worker with potential for violence. She said, "Recognize that not every person who has many of these characteristics will become violent. However, they do constitute early-warning signals. I would watch out for any worker with a large number of these traits and behaviours."

Ditmar supervises 45 workers directly involved in the bottling of three company brands of soft drinks. The workers in his department range in age from 18 to 57. The nature of the job can usually be learned within three days, so the workers are classified as semiskilled. After his initial wisecrack, Ditmar took the seminar quite seriously. He made extensive notes on what the consultant said and took back to his office a printed copy of the computer slide, which looked something like this:

Profile of the Violent Employee

- Socially isolated (a loner) white male between the ages of 30 and 40
- Fascination with the military and weapons
- Temper control problem with history of threats
- Alcohol and/or drug abuser
- Makes unwanted sexual advances toward other employees
- Accepts criticism poorly and holds grudge against the criticizer
- Shows paranoid thinking and believes that management is out to get him (or her)
- Blames others for his problems
- Makes violent statements, such as spoken threats about beating up other employees

The morning following the seminar, Chad sent an email to Gary Bia, the vice-president of operations. Chad said, "I must see you today. I'm worried about a potentially explosive personnel problem." Bia made arrangements to see Ditmar at 5:45 p.m., before Ditmar's shift began.

"What's up, Chad?" said Bia.

"Here's what's up," said Ditmar. "After attending the seminar on violence, I think I've found our suspect. As you know, you do get some strange types working the night shift. Some of them don't have a normal life. I've got this one guy, Freddie Watkins. He's a loner. He wears his hair weird with pink-colored spikes. He's got a tattoo and a huge gun collection that he brags about. I doubt the guy has any friends. He talks a lot about how he plays violent video games. Freddie told about how he once choked to death a dog that bit him.

"What really worries me is that Freddie once said he would punch out the next person who made a smart comment about his hair.

"Do you agree or not that we might have a candidate for workplace violence right here in my department? I'm talking to you first, Gary, but maybe I should be speaking to the antiviolence consultant or to our security officer. What should we do next?"

Bia said, "I'm happy that you are bringing this potential problem to my attention, but I need some more facts. First of all, have you had any discipline problems yet with Freddie?"

Chad responded, "Not yet, Gary, but we're talking about a potential killer right here on my shift. I think we have to do something."

Bia said, "Chad, I'm taking your concerns seriously, but I don't want to jump too fast. Let me think over your problem for at least a day."

Questions

1. What actions, if any, should Gary Bia take?
2. What evidence does Chad Ditmar have that Freddie Watkins has significant personal problems?
3. What career advice can you offer Freddie Watkins?

Finding Happiness and Enhancing Your Personal Life

Learning Outcomes

After studying the information and doing the exercises in this chapter, you should be able to

- explain how happiness is contingent on keeping the various spheres of life in balance
- specify factors that contribute to personal happiness
- describe a plan for meeting a romantic partner
- pinpoint several principles for working through issues with a partner
- explain how partners can meet the challenge of being a dual-income couple
- choose among techniques for keeping a relationship of yours vibrant

A satisfying and rewarding personal life is an important end in itself. It also contributes to a satisfying and rewarding career. If your personal life is miserable, you will have difficulty concentrating on your work. Also, a barren personal life leads one to question the meaning of one's work. As a lonely investment banker said to a bartender he had never met before, "What's this all about? Why am I working 65 hours a week, 50 weeks a year? I have no wife and no close friends. Nobody cares about me. What's my purpose?"

In this chapter, we look at some of the major issues involved in leading an enriched personal life. In addition, we offer a number of concrete suggestions that may help some people enhance their personal lives. We begin by summarizing some modern ideas about happiness.

Achieving Happiness

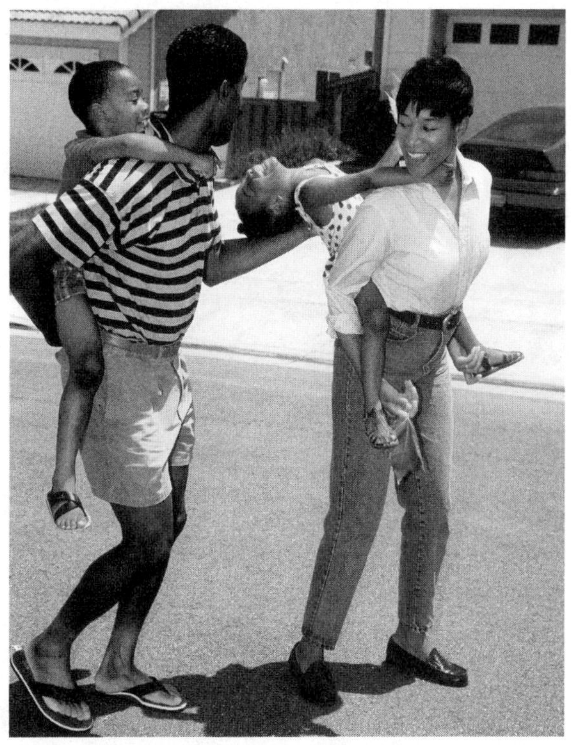

When asked what is the most important thing in life, most people respond, "happiness." Research and opinion on the topic indicate that people can take concrete steps to achieve happiness. Planning for happiness is possible because it appears to be somewhat under people's control. Unhappiness, in contrast, seems to be more predetermined by genes. Sadness tends to run in families.[1] Our approach to the unlimited topic of understanding how to achieve happiness involves a model of happiness, a listing of keys to happiness, and the five principles of psychological functioning.

The Spheres of Life and Happiness

A practical way of understanding happiness is that it is a by-product of having the various components of life working in harmony and synchrony. To understand this approach, visualize about six gears with teeth, spinning in unison. As long as all gears are moving properly (and no teeth are broken), a state of equilibrium and fluid motion is achieved. Similarly, imagine that life has six major components. The exact components will differ among people. For most people, the components would be approximately as follows:

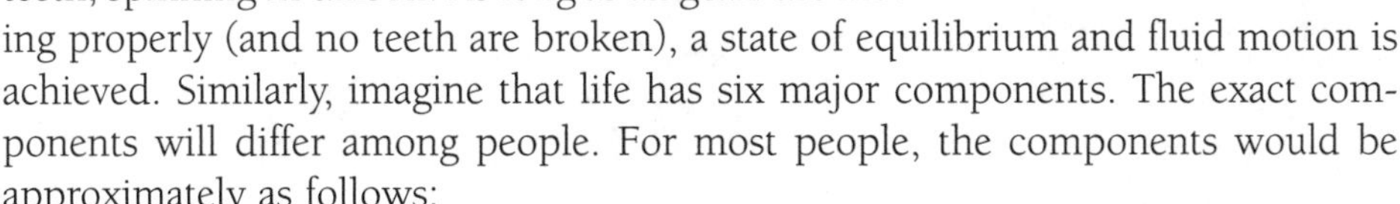

1. Work and career
2. Interpersonal life including loved ones and romantic life
3. Physical and mental health
4. Financial health
5. Interests and pastimes, including reading, surfing the internet, and sports
6. A spiritual life or belief system including religion, science, or astrology

When a person has ample satisfactions in all six spheres, he or she achieves happiness. However, when a deficiency occurs in any of these six factors, the person's spheres are no longer in harmony, and dissatisfaction, or unhappiness, occurs. Yet sometimes if a person is having problems in one sphere, satisfaction in the other spheres can compensate temporarily for a deficiency in one. For the long range, a state of happiness is dependent on all six spheres working in harmony. In short, the theme of this book surfaces again: Work and personal life are mutually supportive. Figure 6-1 presents the spheres-of-life model of happiness.

People vary as to how much importance they attach to each sphere of life. A person with intense career ambitions, for example, might place less weight on the interests sphere than would a more leisure-oriented person. However, if any of these spheres are grossly deficient, total happiness will not be forthcoming. Another source of variation is that the importance people attach to each sphere may vary according to the stage of life. A full-time student, for example, might need just enough money to avoid worrying about finances. However, after about ten years of full-time career experience, a person's expenses might peak. The person would then attach more importance to the financial sphere.

Figure 6-1 The Spheres-of-Life Model of Happiness

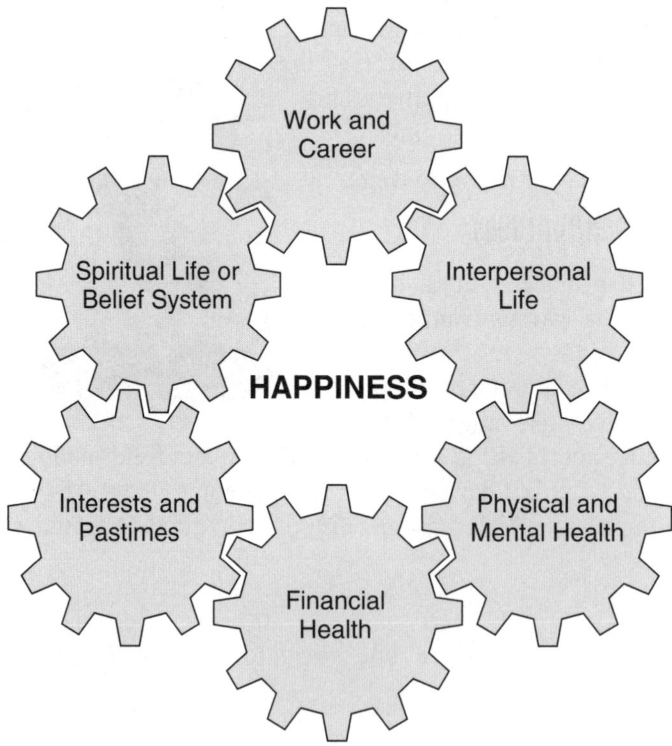

The Keys to Happiness

Many people, including psychologists and other human relations specialists, have conducted research and made observations about the ingredients of happiness. If you are aware of these contributors to happiness, you might be able to enhance your happiness. The spheres-of-life model of happiness also furnishes direction for the person seeking happiness: Strive for acceptable levels of achievement in all six spheres. Here we summarize and synthesize a wide range of research and opinion on the keys to happiness.[2]

1. *Give high priority to the pursuit of happiness.* Discover what makes you happy and make the time to pursue those activities. Spending time doing what you enjoy contributes directly to happiness.
2. *Experience friendship and love, and find a life partner.* A happy person is one who is successful in personal relationships, who exchanges care and concern with loved ones. Happy people are able to love and be loved. Hugging people you like, or being hugged by them, is an important part of having enjoyable personal relationships. Married adults, in general, are happier than unmarried ones, and the results are similar for men and women.[3] Despite the consistency of this finding, it must be interpreted cautiously. It takes a satisfying marriage to bring happiness, and unmarried partners who have a long-term, caring relationship are also likely to be happy.
3. *Develop a sense of self-esteem.* Self-love must precede love for others. High self-esteem enables one to love and be loved. Developing a good self-image leads to the self-esteem required for loving relationships. A feeling of self-worth is important because it helps prevent one from being overwhelmed by criticism. An important part of developing self-esteem is not wanting financial success more than other things. Insecure people often seek society's approval in the form of purchasing consumer goods and accumulating investments.[4]
4. *Work hard at what you enjoy.* Love may be the most important contributor to happiness, with staying involved in work you like coming in second. To achieve happiness, it is necessary to find a career inside or outside the home that fits your most intense interests. Hard work contributes to happiness. A fundamental secret of happiness is accomplishing things and savouring what you have accomplished. A contributor to unhappiness is comparing one's successes, or lack of them, with those of other people. To be happy you must be happy with what *you* achieve.
5. *Appreciate the joys of day-to-day living.* Another key to happiness is the ability to live in the present without undue worrying about the future or dwelling on past mistakes. Be on guard against becoming so preoccupied with planning your life that you neglect to enjoy the happiness of the moment. The essence of being a happy person is to savour what you have right now.
6. *Be fair, kind, and helpful to others.* The Golden Rule is a true contributor to happiness: "Do unto others as you would have them do unto you." It is also important to practise charity and forgiveness. Helping others brings

personal happiness. Knowing that you are able to make a contribution to the welfare of others gives you a continuing sense of satisfaction and happiness. Related to fairness and kindness is trusting others. Happy people have open, warm, and friendly attitudes.

7. *Have recreational fun in your life.* A happy life is characterized by fun, zest, joy, and delight. When you create a time for fun, you add an important element to your personal happiness. However, if you devote too much time to play, you will lose out on the fun of work accomplishments. In choosing fun activities, don't overplan. Because novelty contributes to happiness, be ready to pursue an unexpected opportunity or to try something different.
8. *Learn to cope with grief, disappointment, setbacks, and stress.* To be happy one must learn how to face problems that occur in life without being overwhelmed or running away. It is also important to persevere in attempting to overcome problems, rather than to whine or engage in self-pity. Once you have had to cope with problems you will be more able to appreciate the day-to-day joys of life.
9. *Live with what you cannot change.* Psychologist Martin Seligman says that attempting to change conditions unlikely to change sets us up for feeling depressed about failing. Weight loss is a prime example. Nineteen out of twenty people regain the weight they lose. It is therefore better to worry less about weight loss and concentrate on staying in good physical condition by engaging in moderate exercise. Good conditioning contributes much more to health than does achieving a weight standard set primarily to achieve an aesthetic standard.[5] You can then concentrate on being happy about your good physical condition instead of being unhappy about your weight.
10. *Energize yourself through physical fitness.* Engage in regular physical activity, such as dancing or sports, that makes you aerobically fit. Whether it is the endorphins released by exercise, or just the relaxed muscles, physical fitness fosters happiness.
11. *Satisfy your most important values.* Based on a survey of over 6,000 individuals, Steven Reiss concluded that people cannot find lasting happiness by aiming to have more fun or seeking pleasure. Instead, you have to satisfy your basic values or desires and take happiness in passing. To increase your value-based happiness, you have to first identify your most important desires and then gear your life toward satisfying these values. Among these key values are curiosity, physical activity, honour, power, family, status, and romance.[6] For example, if power and romance are two of your basic values, you can achieve happiness only if your life is amply provided with power and romance.

The Five Principles of Psychological Functioning

According to Richard Carlson, the best way to achieve inner serenity (or happiness) is to follow the five principles of psychological functioning.[7] These principles act as guides toward achieving a feeling of inner happiness. The first is *thinking*, which creates the psychological experience of life. Feelings come about only after you think about something or somebody. If you think of another person as attractive, it will lead to a warm feeling toward that person. People who learn to direct their thinking in positive directions will contribute to their own happiness. Remember that you produce your own thoughts.

The second principle is *moods*, meaning that the positive or negative content of your thinking fluctuates from moment to moment and day to day. Practise ignoring your low (bad) moods rather than analyzing them, and you will see how quickly they vanish. Developing this skill will contribute substantially to healthy psychological functioning. The third principle is *separate psychological realities*. Because each person thinks in a unique way, everyone lives in a separate psychological reality. Accept the idea that others think differently from you, and you will have much more compassion and fewer quarrels. As a result you will be happier. Also, if you accept the principle of separate realities, you will waste less time attempting to change people. At the same time, others will like you more, thus contributing to your happiness.

The fourth principle of psychological functioning is *feelings*. Combined with emotions, feelings are a built-in feedback mechanism that tells us how we are doing psychologically. If your feelings turn negative suddenly, you know that your thinking is dysfunctional. It is then time to make a mental readjustment. If you feel discontented, for example, it is necessary to clear the head and start thinking positively. As a consequence, you will experience contentment and happiness. A key point is that the person will maintain a sense of well-being as long as he or she does not focus on personal concerns.

The fifth principle is *the present moment*. Learning to pay attention to the present moment and to your feelings enables people to live at peak efficiency, without the distraction of negative thinking. Much like the flow experience, the present moment is where people find happiness and inner peace. Carlson advises, "The only way to experience genuine and lasting contentment, satisfaction, and happiness is to learn to live your life in the present moment."[8] (This supports happiness key number 5.)

Now that you have studied attitudes and activities that contribute to happiness, you are invited to do Human Relations Skill-Building Exercise 6-1. It is designed to bring about a state of happiness.

A Planned Approach to Finding a Relationship

How many people have you heard complain about a poor social life because of circumstances beyond their control? Such complaints take various forms: "The women in this school are all unappreciative," "The men at my school don't really respect women," "There's absolutely nobody to meet at work," or "This is the worst town for meeting people."

Some of the people expressing these attitudes are systematic when it comes to handling business or technology problems. Under those circumstances they use the problem-solving method. But when it comes to their social lives, they rely heavily on fate or chance.

Achieving Happiness

The following exercises will help you develop attitudes that contribute mightily to happiness.

1. **Start the day off right.** Begin each day with five minutes of positive thought and visualization. Commit to this for one week. When and how do you plan to fit this into your schedule?

2. **Make a list of five virtues you believe in.** Examples would include patience, compassion, and helping the less fortunate.

3. **Each week, for the next five weeks, incorporate a different virtue into your life.** On a simple index card, write this week's virtue in bold letters, such as "helping the less fortunate." Post the card in a prominent place. After you have completed one incident of helping the less fortunate, describe in about 10 to 25 words what you did. Also record the date and time.

4. **Look for good things about new acquaintances.** List three students, customers, or co-workers you have just met. List three *positive* qualities about each.

5. **List the *positive* qualities of fellow students or co-workers you dislike or have trouble working with.** Remember, keep looking for the good.

6. **Think of school assignments or job tasks you *dislike*, and write down the *merits* of these tasks.** Identify the benefits they bring you.

____

____

____

7. **Look at problems as opportunities.** What challenges are you now facing? In what way might you view them that would inspire and motivate you?

____

____

____

SOURCE: Adapted from Stu Kamen, "Turn Negative into Positive," *Pryor Report Success Workshop*, May 1995, pp. 1–2.

The approach recommended here is to use your problem-solving skills to improve your personal life. Whatever the problem, try to attack it in a logical, step-by-step manner. We are not ruling out the influence of emotion and feeling in personal life. We are simply stating that personal life is too important to be left to fate alone. With good fortune you might form a relationship with a stranger you meet at a rapid-oil-change-and-lubrication centre. Unfortunately, such good fortune is infrequent.

Too many people leave finding a new relationship to chance or to a few relatively ineffective alternatives. Too many unattached adults lament, "Either you go to a bar or you sit at home." In reality, both men and women can find dates in dozens of constructive ways. It is a matter of identifying some of these alternatives and trying out a few that fit your personality and preferences. See Exhibit 6-1 for more details.

exhibit 6 - 1

In Search of a Date?

Every relationship begins with one person meeting another. In order to find one good relationship, you may need to date more than a dozen people. Next is a sampling of potentially effective methods for making a social contact.

Highly Recommended

1. Participate in an activity that you do well and enjoy. For example, if you are a good Frisbee player, use Frisbee playing as a vehicle for meeting people.
2. Get involved in your work or another activity not logically related to dating. People naturally gravitate toward a busy, serious-minded person.* Besides, the workplace has now become the number-one natural meeting place for singles.
3. Take courses in which the male–female ratio is in your favour, such as automotive technology for women and cooking for men.
4. Ask your friends for introductions and describe the type of person you are trying to meet—but don't be too restrictive.
5. Get involved in a community or political activity in which many single people participate. A good example is to become a political-party worker.
6. For men, join almost any formal singles group. The membership of these clubs is overwhelmingly female.
7. For women, join an armed forces reserve unit. The membership of these units is overwhelmingly male.
8. Take advantage of every social invitation to a party, picnic, breakfast, or brunch. Social occasions are natural meeting places.
9. Place a personal ad in a local newspaper or magazine, stating the qualifications you are seeking in a companion and how you can be reached. Personal ads have achieved such popularity that several national magazines now accept them. Personal ads are frequently integrated with voice mail. (You leave a voice message for the person who placed the ad.) Under many systems, your personal ad consists of a voice message to which people respond.
10. Participate in internet chat rooms (*cyberdating*). Many people rely on the internet as their exclusive method of finding romance. Chat rooms can be selected according to interests, including movie fans, gays and lesbians, and astrology believers. After exchanging emails or instant messages, the two people arrange for an in-person meeting. Many of the people you meet might live in a faraway location. Another problem is that many chat room participants badly misrepresent themselves, and a few have proved to be deranged sex criminals. Dating services on the internet are modestly priced and offer the advantage of sorting people out by geographic area.
11. Join special-promotion singles groups such as indoor tennis for singles or a singles ski weekend. Similarly, join singles groups associated with churches, temples, or mosques. Singles groups outside of religious institutions are also worth exploring.

At Least Worth a Try

1. While networking for career purposes, also prospect for social companions.
2. Join an introduction (dating) service, particularly one that has an established reputation.
3. Shop at supermarkets from 11 p.m. to 2 a.m. You will frequently find other single people shopping at that time.
4. Spend a lot of time in laundromats and rapid-oil-change service centres.
5. Strike up a conversation while waiting in line for tickets at the movies or concerts.
6. Congregate, or float around, in large gatherings such as rallies for causes, registration for courses, or orientation programs.
7. Organize a singles party, and require each person invited to bring along an unattached person of the opposite sex—no regular couples allowed.
8. Find valid reasons for visiting other departments at your place of work. Chance meetings at photocopying machines, for example, have allegedly spawned thousands of romances.

*Although these suggestions are primarily geared to meeting people of the opposite sex, these same principles will also apply to meeting people and making friends of the same sex.

An important consideration in searching for a relationship is to recognize when you are experiencing **quest fatigue**. This is the feeling of demoralization and disappointment that takes place when all our efforts at finding a date or mate fail.[9] When quest fatigue sets in, give yourself some time off from the search. Enjoy your activities without a partner, and revitalize yourself before resuming the quest.

The steps to take after making contact with someone are not clear-cut. Some people recommend that you have at least two phone conversations before arranging a meeting. This advice is particularly applicable when you have not seen the person, as when meeting through an ad or introduction service, or through the internet such as through a chat room. It is generally recommended that the first date be informal and in a public place, such as meeting for coffee and dessert, or a glass of wine.

Susan Page, who runs singles workshops, recommends several actions to take after the initial meeting.[10] First, cast a wide net. "Most of your catches will be tossed back in the sea." Nevertheless, the more people you meet, the better the chances of one sharing your interests and values. Second, limit the first date to about one or two hours. Mention that you have a prior commitment. The limited time frame guards against the unpleasantness of an uncomfortable first date. If the date is pleasant, you will look forward with strong anticipation to the next date. Third, screen for compatibility with what you are looking for in a relationship. Initial physical attraction is important, but also look for clues to the type of relationship the person is seeking. Talk about your own general opinions and desires in a relationship and see how your new prospective friend responds.

Why People Are Attracted to One Another

As part of enriching social life, it is helpful to understand why people are attracted to each other. Understanding these forces may help in choosing a compatible person for a long-term relationship. Three different psychological explanations of why two people develop a strong attraction to each other are balance theory, exchange theory, and the need for intimacy. Attraction can also be attributed to chemical or hormonal reasons. All four of these explanations can apply in a given situation.

Balance Theory of Attraction

According to **balance theory**, people prefer relationships that are consistent, or balanced. If we are very similar to another person, it makes sense (it is consistent or balanced) to like that person. We are also attracted to similar people because they reinforce our opinions and values. It is usually reassuring and rewarding to discover that another person agrees with you or has similar values.[11]

Balance theory explains why we are eager to stay in a relationship with some people, but it does not explain why opposites often attract each other. People sometimes get along best with those who possess complementary characteristics. A talkative and domineering person may prefer a partner who enjoys listening. The explanation is that a dominant person needs someone to dominate and therefore might be favourably disposed toward submissive people.

Social Exchange Theory of Attraction

A long-standing explanation of why two people become a couple is **social exchange theory**, the idea that human relationships are based mainly on self-interest. This research shows that people measure their social, physical, and other assets against a potential partner's. The closer the match, the more likely they are to develop a long-term relationship.

Exchange theory has been able to predict the permanence of a relationship based on the way each partner feels he or she stacks up against the other. One study of 537 dating men and women found that partners who thought they were getting far more in exchange for what they were giving felt guilty and insecure. In comparison, those who believed they gave more than they got were angry.

The giving was mostly psychological. It included such things as being more physically attractive than the partner, kinder, or more flexible. The greater the imbalance, the more likely the couple was to split up; the more equitable the partners believed the exchange to be, the more likely they were to remain partners. A researcher on the topic of love offered this explanation of the findings just presented:

> It's terribly corroding if one person feels taken advantage of. And it is just as disturbing to feel you can take advantage of your partner.[12]

Need for Intimacy

For some, the balance and exchange theories of mutual attraction are too mechanical and logical. Psychologist David McClelland proposes instead that love is an experience seated in the nonrational part of the brain (the right side). People who believe that they are in love have a strong **need for intimacy**. This craving for intimacy is revealed in the thoughts of people in love who are asked to make up stories about fictitious situations. Their stories reveal a preoccupation with harmony, responsibility, and commitment, and a preference for a relationship that includes warmth and intimacy.

McClelland and his associates say that these themes show up repeatedly in many guises in the stories told by people who say they are in love. The same stories are told by people in situations where love feelings run high, such as just having seen a romantic movie.[13]

The concept of love is part of the need for intimacy, as well as a key part of understanding personal relationships. Every reader has an idea of what love means to him or her. Harry Stack Sullivan, the famous psychiatrist, developed a particularly useful description of love, as follows:

> When the satisfaction or the security of another person becomes as significant to one as is one's own satisfaction or security, then the state of love exists. So far as I know, under no other circumstance is a state of love present, regardless of the popular usage of the word.

A Biochemical Explanation of Attractiveness

Another explanation of why certain people are attracted to one another is based on chemicals and specifically hormones. According to this theory, our hormones direct us to sense or screen potential mates. After the initial biochemical attraction, our conscious, psychological preferences—like, Does he enjoy action movies and golfing?—come into play. The interests and lifestyle preferences of the potential mate carry more weight after the initial attraction. While the biochemical factors are at work, the brain is processing the external clues people use to measure sex appeal. Among these personality factors are appearance, clothing, makeup, scent, body language, and voice.[14]

A more specific explanation of attraction between people is based on the presence of pheromones. These are chemical substances released by a person (or animal) to influence the behaviour of another member of the same species. A person who emits high doses of pheromones will therefore attract more partners. Conversely, we are physically attracted to people with high doses of pheromones.

The pheromone theory is particularly geared toward explaining why one person is strongly attracted to another person at first sight. After the initial physical attraction, however, other more rational factors (e.g., Is this person employed?) enter into the picture. Several companies sell cologne that allegedly contains pheromones, thus making it easier for you to attract Prince or Princess Charming. Because these "attractant" substances are considered cosmetics, and not drugs, they are free from government regulation. Buyer beware.

The Importance of Choosing a Partner Carefully

Having a plan for meeting a partner and understanding why people are attracted to each other should be regarded as helpful information for making the right choice. A principal problem in many poor relationships is that the couple used faulty judgment in choosing each other. Of course, it is difficult to be objective when choosing a partner. Your needs at the time may cloud your judgment. Many people have made drastic mistakes in choosing a spouse because they were lonely and depressed when they met the person they married. Being on the rebound from a relationship that went bad makes you particularly vulnerable.

The problem of mate selection is indeed complicated. Do you marry for love, companionship, infatuation, or all three? It has been pointed out that the success rate of the arranged marriages still practised in a few countries is about as good as that of nonarranged marriages. Since most people have only a limited amount of time to invest in finding the ideal mate, they are content to marry a good fit.

An in-depth study of 300 happy marriages provides a practical clue about mate selection. The most frequently mentioned reason for an enduring and happy marriage was having a generally positive attitude toward each other.[15] If you view your partner as your best friend and like him or her "as a person," you will probably be happy together. As obvious as it sounds, choose only a life partner whom you genuinely like. Some people deviate from this guideline by placing too much emphasis on infatuation.

Recent research about selecting the right partner emphasizes finding a mate with a similar *love story.* According to Robert J. Sternberg, love between people follows a story. To understand love, it is necessary to understand the stories that dictate our beliefs and expectations of love. These stories form in childhood and become the basis for romance in later life. The story indicates how people describe love. For example, a person who strongly agrees with the statement, "I believe that in a good relationship, partners change and grow together" tells a travel story (in the sense that the partners are taking a journey together). A person who agrees strongly with the statement, "I enjoy making sacrifices for the sake of my partner" believes in a sacrifice story.

Sternberg contends that the key to compatibility with a romantic partner is whether their stories match, such as two people believing the business story of love (i.e., marriage as a partnership with divided responsibilities). To determine if your story matches that of a prospective partner's, you would first have to study the many stories contained in the research about love stories.[16] Should you meet someone with an incompatible love story who would otherwise make an excellent mate, another option exists. You can learn to modify your stories until they fit. However, the change would have to be sincere and involve a different way of looking at love.

Human Relations Self-Assessment Quiz 6-1 gives you an opportunity to sample a love story analysis. The love story evaluated has proven to be a workable one for many people. Also, see the Canada Today below about relationship trends in Canada. The message here is to recognize that when you are contemplating choosing a life partner, you are facing one of life's major decisions. Put all of your creative resources into making a sound decision.

Working Out Issues within Relationships

People emotionally involved with each other often find themselves in conflict over a variety of issues, especially when they are emotionally dependent upon each other. Without conflict, relationships would be artificial.

Quiz 6-1

What's Your Love Story?

Rate each statement on a scale from 1 to 9, with 1 meaning that it doesn't characterize your romantic relationships at all and 9 meaning that it describes them extremely well. Then average your scores for the story below. In general, averaged scores of 7 to 9 are high, indicating a strong attraction to a story, and 1 to 3 are low, indicating little or no interest in the story. Moderate scores of 4 to 6 indicate some interest, but probably not enough to generate or keep a romantic interest.

1. **I believe that close relationships are partnerships.**
2. **I believe that in a romantic relationship, just as in a job, both partners should perform their duties and responsibilities according to their "job description."**
3. **Whenever I consider having a relationship with someone, I always consider the financial implications of the relationship as well.**

Score: _______

A business story has several potential advantages, not the least of which is that the bills are more likely to get paid than in other types of relationships. That's because someone is always minding the store. Another potential advantage is that the roles tend to be more clearly defined than in other relationships. The partners are also in a good position to get ahead in terms of whatever they want.

One potential disadvantage occurs if only one of the two partners sees their relationship as a business story. The other partner may quickly become bored and look for interest and excitement outside the marriage. The story can also turn sour if the distribution of authority does not satisfy one or both partners. If the partners cannot work out mutually compatible roles, they may find themselves spending a lot of time fighting for position. It is important to maintain the option of flexibility.

SOURCE: Robert J. Sternberg, "What's Your Love Story?" *Psychology Today,* July/August 2000, pp. 55, 57.

Human relations specialists have formulated some ground rules for resolving the many types of conflicts that frequently occur in relationships. These rules supplement the techniques for conflict resolution presented in Chapter 9.

1. *Listen carefully and give feedback.* Many conflicts intensify because the people involved never stop to listen carefully to what the other side is trying to say. After listening to your partner's point of view, express your feelings about the issue. Expressing your feelings leads to more understanding than expressing your judgments. It is therefore preferable to say "I feel left out when you visit your mother" than to say "You're insensitive to my needs; look at the way you visit your mother all the time."

   To help improve understanding, provide mutual feedback. Although you may disagree with your partner, communicate your understanding: "From your point of view it's frivolous of me to spend so much money on bowling. You would prefer that I invest that money in baby furniture."

Changing Patterns in Conjugal Relationships

There is little doubt that times are changing and so are our love relationships. Data from the General Social Survey conducted in 1995 show some interesting trends. A comprehensive survey of 11,000 respondents aged 15 years and over remains one of the best sources for data on relationships. The survey collected statistics on all marital and common-law unions, separation (not the legal one), divorce, and the death of a partner, along with a wide range of background information.

Whether born in the 1920s or the 1960s, over 94 percent of all women, ranging in age from 30 to 69, have been in a marriage or common-law relationship. While the tendency to form unions has remained fairly constant, the real change is the choice of the relationship. Although marriage still accounts for the majority of relationships, common-law has become more popular and has become the most favoured type of first conjugal relationship for younger people. Of women aged 20–29, 52 percent started their conjugal lives with common-law partners, compared with only one percent of the women aged 60–69.

How does this newer and more popular type of first-time union fare over time? Well, according to the statistics, not as well as marriage. For example, in the 30–39 age group, 63 percent of those whose first relationship was common-law had separated by 1995, compared with 33 percent of those who had married first. In general, recent research shows that common-law relationships tend to be temporary and transitory, that they rarely transform into marriage, and that men are more likely to end this type of relationship. Women who have a better economic status are the least likely to marry a common-law partner. While choosing to live together over marriage may seem to be a better option, it appears that it is also the most temporary option.

SOURCE: Celine Le Bourdais, Ghyslaine Neill, and Pierre Turcotte with collaboration of Nathalie Bachon and Julie Archambault, "The Changing Face of Conjugal Relationships," *Canadian Social Trends*, Spring 2000, Statistics Canada, Catalogue No. 11-008.

2. *Use more positive than negative behaviours during arguments.* A ten-year study of arguments between partners in relationships, involving hundreds of couples, supported several basic ideas about good human relations. Some negative emotions used in arguments are more toxic than others. At the top of the corrosive list are criticism, contempt, defensiveness, and stonewalling (withdrawing from a discussion). On the positive side, the team of researchers found that happy couples use five times more positive behaviours in their arguments than negative behaviours. One way to be positive is to use humour to ease the tension in an argument. The humour is considered an effort to mend the conflict.[17] To illustrate, Jennifer might be upset that her husband Larry spent most of his time at an office party they attended together talking to other women. On their way home, Jennifer said, "I don't know whether to be angry at you for flirting all evening or to compliment you for networking with every woman at the party sharp enough to have a future in business."
3. *Define the real problem.* What your partner or you grumble about at first may not be the real issue in the conflict. It will require mutual under-

standing combined with careful listening and sympathy to uncover the real problem. A man might be verbally attacking a woman's dress when he really means that she has gained weight. A woman might verbally attack a man's beer drinking when her real complaint is that he should be out in the yard raking leaves instead of sitting inside playing video games.

4. *Don't hit below the belt.* The expression "below the belt" refers to something that is unfair. Some issues are just plain unfair to bring up in a marital dispute. When you are intimate with another person, you are bound to know one or two vulnerable areas. Here are two below-the-belt comments:

   > "You're lucky I married you. What other woman would have married a man who was so much of a loser that he had to declare bankruptcy?"
   >
   > "Don't complain so much about being mistreated. Remember, when I married you, you were down on your luck and had no place to live."

   Is anyone really as cruel as the above quotes would suggest? Yes, in the heat of a tiff between partners, many cruel, harsh things are said. If two people want to live harmoniously after the conflict, they should avoid below-the-belt comments.

5. *Be prepared to compromise.* For many issues compromise is possible. The compromise you reach should represent a willingness to meet the other person halfway, not just a temporary concession. On some issues the only compromise can be letting the other person have his or her way now, and waiting to have your turn later. Among such issues that cannot be split down the middle are whether to have children, whether to live in an apartment or a house, whether to go to Miami or London for a vacation, or whether to run a kosher or nonkosher household. Several of these issues should be settled before marriage or living together, since no real compromise on the basic issue is possible in these instances.

6. *Minimize an accusatory tone.* You lessen the accusatory tone when you make "I" statements instead of "you" statements. The door to dialogue is opened when you make a statement such as, "I felt really disappointed when you did not call me to ask about how my promotion interview went." You shut off dialogue when you say, "You don't care about my happiness. You didn't even call to ask about how my promotion interview went."

7. *Use email as a substitute for face-to-face confrontations.* At times, a couple may be so emotionally charged that resolving conflicts face-to-face is not possible. To back off temporarily from the difficulty of in-person conflict resolution, it may be worthwhile to correspond through email, messaging, or hard-copy letters. According to Andrew Christensen and Neil Jacobsen, the written message can help the couple avoid raising their voices and escalating the conflict.[18] While sending notes to each other, it is valuable to put down in writing what you think the other side is angry about. For instance, "You are ticked off at me because I think your family is intolerant of people who are not like themselves." After dealing with the conflict in writing, the couple may be calm enough to move on to a face-to-face discussion.

8. *Be alert to gender differences in communication style.* As will be described in more detail in Chapter 8, men and women tend to have differences in communication style. One example is that men are more likely to focus on objects and things, and thus will gloss over feelings. In contrast, women are more likely to focus on interpersonal relationships and are eager to communicate feelings. If a couple does face these forms of stereotyped behaviour, it is helpful not to devalue the other side for simply acting in a gender-appropriate way. In dealing with the differences just described, the man should not be angry with the woman for focusing too much on feelings and wanting open communication. The woman should not be angry with the man for being somewhat tightlipped about feelings. Instead, the partners should accept these gender differences and not expect major changes in communication style. As well, when not in a conflict situation, partners can help each other to overcome gender barriers in communication. The man can help the woman understand his discomfort with feelings, and the man can learn more about sharing feelings from the woman.

Meeting the Challenges of Being a Dual-Income Couple

The number of couples in which both partners have full-time jobs continues to increase. In 1997, dual-earner families comprised over 61 percent of families. Families where only one partner worked comprised just over 21 percent.[19] Two critical factors influencing this steady growth are women's career aspirations and the high cost of living. Housing, in particular, costs more today than in the past. Many families need two incomes to own their own home.

If the couple has children, women, more than men, may have the most difficulty trying to manage a home life and a work life. In families, women report more time-stress than men, as they still are the primary caregivers in the home.[20] Mothers, in particular, who try to balance the demands of earning a paycheque while still maintaining a traditional homemaker role may feel especially stressed.[21] The division of labour in two-income families has virtually remained unchanged.[22] Women are still doing the bulk of home management and child management. Therefore, women in particular may have to learn new strategies and behaviours to manage this additional stress in their lives. Managing a home, children, and a career can be extremely stressful for the dual-income couple, and both partners need to take responsibility for the family. Even without children, two-income partners may experience stress as they try to balance work, home lives, and responsibilities.

It is challenging to run a two-income household in a way that will enhance the couple's personal life. In Chapter 9 we present information about using organizational support systems to help reduce work–family conflicts. Following are some suggestions that couples themselves can implement to increase the chances of a dual-income couple or family running more smoothly.

1. *Establish priorities and manage time carefully.* A major contributor to the success of a dual-income relationship is careful time management.[23] Each partner must establish priorities, such as ranking quality time together ahead of adding a community activity to the schedule. Or both partners might inform their employer of a certain date they would be taking as a vacation day to celebrate their wedding anniversary.
2. *Deal with feelings of competitiveness.* Feelings of competitiveness between husband and wife about each other's career often exist even when both have a modern outlook. Competitive feelings are all the more likely to surface when both parties are engaged in approximately the same kind of work. One man became infuriated with his wife when she was offered a promotion before he was. They had both entered the same big company at the same time in almost identical jobs. In contrast, the working couple with traditional views is less likely to have a problem if the husband outdistances his wife in career advancement.

   The familiar remedy of discussing problems before they get out of hand is offered again here. One partner might confess to the other, "Everybody is making such a fuss over you since you won that suggestion award. It makes me feel somewhat left out and unimportant." A sympathetic spouse might reply, "I can understand your feelings. But don't take all this fuss too seriously. It doesn't take away from my feelings for you. Besides, two months from now maybe people will be making a fuss over you for something."
3. *Share big decisions equally.* A distinguishing characteristic of today's two-income families is that both partners share equally in making important decisions about the domestic side of life. Under such an arrangement, neither has exclusive decision-making prerogatives in any particular area. One may make a decision without consulting the other over some minor matter (such as the selection of a plant for the living room). The other may make the decision the next time a plant is to be selected for inside the house. But on major decisions—such as relocating to another town, starting a family, or investing in the stock market or real estate—both partners collaborate.
4. *Divide household tasks equitably.* Many women who work outside the home rightfully complain that they are responsible for too much of the housework. As stated previously, they often have the equivalent of two full-time jobs. Under this arrangement, conflict at home is highly probable. The recommended solution is for the working couple to divide household tasks in some equitable manner. Equity could mean that tasks are divided according to preference or the amount of effort required. In one family, the husband might enjoy food shopping while the wife enjoys cleaning. Assignments could be made accordingly. Each couple should negotiate for themselves what constitutes an equitable division of household tasks.
5. *Take turns being inconvenienced.* In a very traditional family, the woman assumes the responsibility for managing inconvenient household tasks even if she, too, has a job outside the home. The underlying assumption

may be that her work is less important than his work. For more modern couples, a more equitable solution is to take turns being inconvenienced. If Sue has to go to work late one day to be around for the plumber, Ted can go to work late when the dog has to be taken to the veterinarian. A working couple with children will frequently have to miss work because of a child's illness or accident, parent–teacher conferences, or school plays.

6. *Develop adequate systems for child care.* Any working couple with a young child or children will attest to the challenge of adequately balancing work and child demands. Imagine this scenario: Your spouse has already left for work, and you discover that your four-year-old child has a fever of 39°C. The child-care centre will not accept a sick child, nor will your neighbour who helps out occasionally. She fears contaminating her own children. The logical solution is to stay home from work, but you have a crucial work meeting scheduled for 11 a.m.

   One solution to dilemmas of this nature, and less serious problems, is to have a diverse support system. Make arrangements with at least three people, including relatives, who could help you out in an emergency. Retired people, for example, often welcome the challenge of helping out in an emergency.

7. *Share parenting roles.* A dual-income family functions best when both parents take an active interest in child-rearing. Mother and father have to regard spending extensive amounts of time with their child or children as an appropriate activity.

8. *Decide who pays for what.* Unfortunately, the problem of negotiating who pays for what arises for many two-income families. Many couples find that the additional expenses of being a working couple prevent them from getting ahead financially. Child-care expenses are often involved; restaurant meals become more frequent; and a second car is usually a necessity.

   A division of income that minimizes conflict for many two-income families is to allocate some money for common expenses (such as rent or mortgage payments) and some money for personal expenses. The specific allocation of the latter does not have to be discussed with the partner. For instance, one partner is free to buy a new CD player with his or her personal money. But an item like new draperies would be a joint expense and a joint decision. Another helpful practice is to have one joint chequing account and two personal chequing accounts.

Keeping Your Relationship Vibrant

One of the major challenges in personal life is to keep a relationship with a partner alive, healthy, and vibrant. For many people, relationships that begin with enthusiasm, rapport, and compatibility end in a dull routine or in splitting up. Human Relations Self-Assessment Quiz 6-2 pinpoints some of the symptoms of a relationship gone bad. Here we will describe major factors in achieving a mutually rewarding long-term relationship.

Quiz 6-2

Early Warning Signs of a Relationship in Trouble

You know your relationship is in trouble, and in need of revitalization, when several or more of the indicators below are present. The term "partner" refers to a spouse, boyfriend, girlfriend, or significant other.

- You observe that your partner has terrible table manners.
- You perceive that your partner is not as attractive or cute as you thought previously.
- The sound your partner makes with his or her teeth annoys you.
- Your conversation is confined to routine matters such as "Did you put gas in the car?" or "Why are you 15 minutes late?"
- A significant change in routine takes place, such as the partner calling every other day instead of at least once a day.
- You rarely plan ahead for social occasions, such as parties, dinner, or movies, but decide to go out at the last moment—such as making plans for Saturday night at 4 p.m. that day.
- You spend progressively less time together.
- You nitpick each other frequently, and all your partner's quirks begin to bother you.
- You touch each other less and less, including holding hands while walking or driving the car.
- Your fights are more frequent and last longer.
- Small tokens of affection, such as sending love notes, almost disappear.
- You rarely mention your partner favourably to a third party.
- You notice frequent criticisms including backhanded compliments such as, "You look nice today for a person with so little taste in clothing."
- You jump into binding commitments with little planning, such as having a baby, moving, or buying a house. (Quite often partners think that such major joint activities will save a sinking relationship.)
- You look for an opportunity to spend time with your friends, watching television, or surfing the internet rather than with your partner.
- You rarely look forward to spending time alone with your partner.
- Neither partner ever says "I love you" any longer.

SOURCE: Several of the signs were collected from relationship experts by Elaine Gross, "Love on the Edge," Gannett News Service story, March 12, 1996, and from "The Relationship Quiz" used by Worldwide Marriage Encounter (undated).

Keep Romantic Love in Proper Perspective

A speaker told an audience that you can tell you are infatuated with your partner if your heart begins pounding at a chance meeting with him or her. An 80-year-old in the audience responded, "I know just what you mean. The Mrs. and I have been married for 55 years, and that's exactly how I feel whenever I run into her downtown." This happy husband is an exception; although infatuation or romantic love is vital in getting a relationship started, it usually cools down within several years. When infatuation declines, instead of being disappointed, the couple should realize that the relationship has grown more mature and lasting.

A relationship counsellor observes that as full of rapture and delight as the first phase of a relationship is, it is essentially a trick of nature designed to bring us together. Nature knows that without the illusion of perfection, we might not choose each other. After the emotional bond is secure, nature lifts the veil.[24] To avoid discouragement and disillusionment, it is important to keep romantic love in proper perspective. It helps launch a relationship, but does not have to be kept at its initial high intensity for a relationship to endure. However, the spark should not be extinguished.

Another significant key to keeping romantic love in perspective is to review your expectations in the relationship. Over the years, the expectations for relationships have increased. People want more from marriage than in times past. Fifty years ago, for example, more people thought of a marriage as an institution primarily to raise a family and gain economic security. According to marriage therapist Rita DeMaria, many more people today want marriages to be gratifying and satisfying and intimate. When these expectations are not met, one or both partners may become discouraged.[25] In reviewing your expectations, you might decide that you have set the bar too high and are therefore creating the opportunity for disappointment.

Have Communication Sessions

Good communication is vital for creating and maintaining a loving relationship. Therefore, one way to keep a relationship alive is to hold formal communication sessions in which you tell each other almost anything on your mind. The topics can be both positive and negative. A man may want to tell his partner of something she did that he appreciated very much. Or a woman may want to talk about the way her partner offended her in public. Or a couple may want to discuss concerns about finances, a child, in-law relations, or anything else.

One of many reasons that communication sessions are important is that many couples have different perceptions about what is good and bad in their relationship. The communication sessions help clear up misperceptions. A study of 119 couples conducted by James Deal revealed that partners with more similar perceptions of their marriage and family life were more satisfied with their relationship.[26]

A vital aspect of these sessions is that both facts and feelings are expressed. The statement "I am really afraid we are drifting apart" communicates much more than "You and I haven't been talking too much lately." The role play at the end of this chapter explores the type of communication that can keep a relationship thriving.

Communication sessions are also important because they can sometimes revive a failing relationship. This is true because communication breakdowns often lead to failed relationships. Typically, in the early stages of a relationship, the couple is keenly attuned to each other's thoughts and feelings. The partners look for small verbal and nonverbal signals of contentment and discontent in each other.

After the relationship seems secure, couples often replace the intense monitoring of the early stages with a nonrevealing style of communication. For example, the man and woman may mechanically say to each other, "How was your day?" or

"Love ya." This shorthand style of communication obstructs the sending and receiving of messages that could indicate the relationship is in trouble.[27] Introducing communication sessions can make it possible for the couple to deal with subtle problems in the relationship.

Strive for Novelty in Your Relationship

An unfortunate aspect of many relationships is that they drift toward a routine. A married couple might go to the same place for vacation, meeting the same family and friends for years on end. A man dating a woman might call her every night at the same time. Or a couple's sex life may turn into a routine. Many people have suggested that you try pleasant surprises to keep your relationship vibrant and fun. Make up a list of your own, but here are a few ideas to jog your thinking:

- Ask your mate out for dinner on a *Monday* evening.
- Write your partner a poem instead of sending a commercial greeting card.
- Take up a new activity together in which you are both beginners (such as country dancing or scuba diving) and learn with each other.

Maintain a Nonpossessive Relationship

A **nonpossessive relationship** is one in which both partners maintain separate identities and strive for personal fulfillment, yet are still committed to each other. Such a relationship is based on interdependent love—love involving commitment with self-expression and personal growth.[28] A nonpossessive relationship does not mean that the partners have sexual relationships with other people.

A nonpossessive relationship is helpful because some people find the traditional form of marriage stifling. For example, many married people feel compelled to give up a hobby or interest because the partner does not share the interest. In a nonpossessive relationship, the couple can take many separate paths and pursue different interests and have friends of their own. Unfortunately, if couples pursue nonpossessive relationships too far, they can wind up drifting away from each other. The reason is that happy partners spend considerable time with each other enjoying shared activities. Each couple must find the right balance between maintaining separate identities yet spending sufficient time together to remain close.

Maintain a Differentiation of Self

Closely related to having a nonpossessive relationship is for each partner to achieve a reasonable degree of autonomy by maintaining a **differentiation of self**. The term refers to an individual who is secure and not desperate for signals of approval and affection from others. If you have a differentiation of self, you are not so subject to social pressures from your partner and other family members. Another key characteristic of a person with high differentiation of the self is that he or she is not highly judgmental and not obsessed with his or her place in the family hierarchy.[29] As a consequence, the person is not so demanding and can appreciate the reality that he or she does not dominate the partner's life. The person with self-differentiation can comfortably say, "I'm happy that you are going out to dinner with your co-workers. I'll use that time this evening for learning more about digital photography."

This sense of autonomy and laid-back nature makes the person easier to live with, thus avoiding some of the conflict over affection and control that takes place in many relationships. In turn, the relationship has a chance to remain more vibrant. A mildly detached person is easier to live with; however, the same caution about nonpossessive relationships is in order. If your differentiation of self and detachment are too pronounced, you will not participate in the closeness required of a vibrant relationship.

To further develop your sensitivity to keeping a relationship vibrant, do Human Relations Skill-Building Exercise 6-2.

Summary

A satisfying and rewarding personal life can help a person absorb a career setback and also contributes to a satisfying and rewarding career. Planning for happiness is somewhat under a person's control. A practical way of understanding happiness is that it is a by-product of having the spheres of life working in harmony and synchrony. For most people these spheres would be: (1) work and career; (2) interpersonal life, including romance; (3) physical and mental health; (4) financial health; (5) interests and pastimes; and (6) a spiritual life or belief system.

Contributors or keys to happiness are somewhat under a person's control. They include (1) giving priority to happiness; (2) experiencing love and friendship; (3)

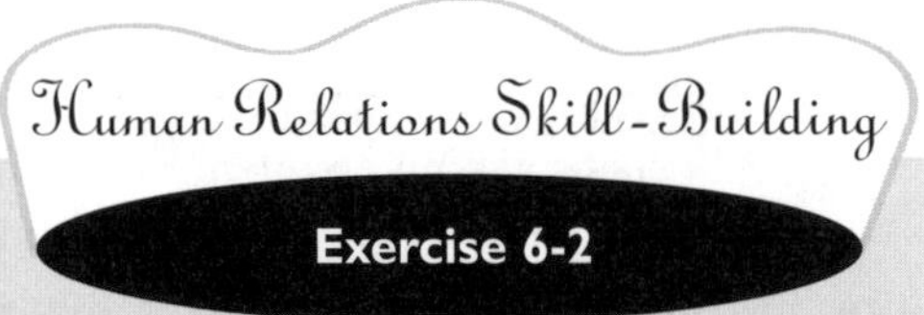

Keeping Your Relationship Vibrant

The role-playing exercise described here will help you experience the type of communication and interaction required for keeping a relationship vibrant. As with any other role play, visualize yourself in the role briefly described. Try to develop the feel and the flavour of the person depicted.

The man in this relationship is becoming concerned that his wife does not enthusiastically participate in activities involving his family. He prefers that he and his wife spend their Sunday afternoons with his parents and other relatives. He thinks they are all loads of fun and cannot imagine why his wife is beginning to drag her heels about spending time with them. Twice in the last month she has come up with excuses for not going along with him to visit his folks on Sunday.

The woman in this relationship still loves her husband but thinks his preference for Sunday afternoons with his folks is unreasonable. She prefers to pursue her own interests on Sunday afternoons. She plans to confront her husband about the situation this evening.

Two people act out this role play for about five to ten minutes. Other members of the class can act as observers. Among the observation points will be: (1) How well did the couple get to the key issues? (2) How much feeling was expressed? (3) Do they appear headed toward a resolution of this problem?

developing self-esteem; (4) working hard at things enjoyed; (5) appreciating the joys of day-to-day living; (6) being fair, kind, and helpful to others; (7) having fun; (8) coping with grief, disappointment, setbacks, and stress; (9) living with what you cannot change; (10) energizing yourself through physical fitness; and (11) satisfying your most important values.

According to Richard Carlson, the best way to achieve inner serenity (or happiness) is to follow the five principles of psychological functioning. First is thinking, which brings about feelings. Second is moods, including the idea that you can ignore bad moods. Third is separate psychological realities, meaning that each person thinks in a unique way. Fourth is feelings, which can be turned from negative to positive. Fifth is the present moment, which is where people find happiness and inner peace.

A good social life begins with finding the people you want to date. Such an important activity in life should not be left to chance or fate alone. Instead, use a planned approach that includes exploring many sensible alternatives.

Understanding why people are attracted to one another helps in choosing a compatible partner. The balance theory of attraction contends that people prefer relationships that are consistent or balanced, and therefore they are comfortable with people similar to themselves. According to social exchange theory, people seek relationships in which there is an even match of personal assets. A third explanation is that people are attracted to each other because their need for intimacy prompts them to fall in love. A fourth explanation is based on biochemistry, suggesting that our hormones direct us to sense or screen potential mates. After the initial biochemical attraction, our conscious, psychological preferences come into play.

Whatever the basis for attraction, choose a partner carefully. One factor in mate selection is choosing a person with a similar *love story,* or description of love.

To keep intimate relationships healthy, you should resolve issues as they arise. Suggestions for accomplishing this include: listen carefully and give feedback; define the real problem; avoid old wounds; don't hit below the belt; be willing to go the extra mile; and be alert to gender differences in communication.

Dual-income couples are subject to unique pressures. To sustain a good relationship, a two-income couple should consider these approaches: (1) establish priorities and manage time carefully; (2) deal directly with feelings of competitiveness; (3) share big decisions equally; (4) divide household tasks equitably; (5) take turns being inconvenienced; (6) develop adequate systems for child care; (7) share parenting roles; and (8) decide who pays for what.

Keeping a relationship vibrant is a major challenge. Among the strategies proposed to meet this goal are (1) keep romantic love in perspective; (2) have communication sessions; (3) strive for novelty in your relationship; (4) maintain a nonpossessive relationship; and (5) maintain a differentiation of self.

Questions and Activities

1. After reading this chapter, do you believe a person can learn how to be happy?
2. What are some of the skills involved in being happy?
3. How do your "spheres of life" compare with those in Figure 6-1?

4. In this chapter you were told that the office has become the best place to meet a mate. In Chapter 11 you will be cautioned about the hazards of an office romance. How will you integrate these two opinions?
5. What is your reaction to the practice of having a third party conduct a background investigation of a prospective mate? Also, should the prospective mate be informed of the investigation after it is completed?
6. What do you perceive to be the advantages and disadvantages of finding a romantic relationship over the internet?
7. In Chapter 7, devoted to communication, you will be told that a problem with email is that it may not be well-suited to conveying feelings. In this chapter, email is recommended as a way of dealing with some of the emotional issues in a relationship. How do you reconcile this apparent contradiction?
8. When one person in a two-income couple loses a job, should that person be responsible for all the household chores? Explain your reasons.
9. Find a couple that has been together for 20 years or more. Ask them what they perceive to be the secret of their successful relationship. Share your findings with class members.

Internet Skill Builder

Finding Romance on the Net

Search for five different methods of finding romance online. Evaluate which one of these methods offers the greatest promise of finding romance while minimizing the chance of being deceived by another person.

Weblinks

www.cmha.ca
This is the website for the Canadian Mental Health Association. This site has many links to other mental health sites as well as advice for achieving happiness in everyday life.

www.statcan.ca
This is the site for Statistics Canada. A very large site, it houses all kinds of statistical information on Canada and also includes research papers.

www.surpassyourdreams.com
Coaching to help achieve happiness. Includes career coaching.

www.dating.com
A free dating service from London, Ontario.

Human Relations Case Study

THE LOVE LAB

Psychologist John Gottman began his research on the quality of marital relationships 30 years ago. Since then, his University of Washington laboratory, called the "Love Lab," has focused on determining exactly what makes marriages thrive or fail. The conversation that follows is taken from the records of the Love Lab. Valerie, 24, and Mark, 25, have a young baby. They have recently moved, and both have new jobs.

Valerie: (Laughter) We don't go that long without talking.
Mark: I know, I just start going stir-crazy.
Valerie: The problem...
M: Huh?
V: ... is, you told me that when you took the job as manager at Commonwealth that you'd come home in the afternoons and spend some time with us.
M: That's right, but I did not say that it would start in the first week when I'm trying to do two different jobs. I gotta get myself replaced. Right now, I'm not just a manager.
V: It's been three weeks.
M: Well, I just don't go out on the street and say, "Hey you. Want to sell insurance?" It's not that easy. There's two people in the program. One of them is probably gonna be hired within the next couple of weeks. But in the meantime it's tough. It's just the way it's gotta be.
V: I realize that.
M: Okay.
V: But.
M: At midnight when you get off work and you're all keyed up, I'm all worn out.
V: I realize that. That doesn't bother me that much, you going to sleep at night.
M: I'll just be starting to go to sleep and you'll go "Are you listening to me?" I'll be trying to stay awake...
V: I'm laughing about it usually. I'm not upset about it.
M: I don't know by then. I'm half out.
V: But now with me having a car, you'll be able to go to sleep early and get up with Stephanie a little bit. That's one of my big problems. I'm not getting any sleep. I don't get to sleep until two.
M: I've been getting up with her.
V: You've been real good about that.
M: Okay.
V: I guess I just wish that you didn't have to go in early.
M: Yeah, we don't get a whole lot of time together.
V: When I have the car, I can get out and get stuff then. I feel like I'm stuck at home and here you are...
M: I'll be able to meet you for lunch and stuff. I guess that wasn't any big problem.
V: It is a problem. It seems like we talk about it every day.
M: Yeah, we do.
V: That's about the only thing we really complain about.

M: Yeah. The last couple of nights I tried to take you out to the lake and look at the stars and stuff, so...
V: I know.
M: We just need to get used to our schedules.
V: That first week I was so, I was real upset 'cause it seemed like all I did was stay home with Stephanie all morning till three and just work all evening. I wasn't doing anything. It didn't seem like we had family gatherings every weekend. We never had time to go out, just the two of us.
M: I got a little surprise for ya next weekend.
V: Yeah, it's always next weekend. It's never this weekend.
M: Eight weekends in a row.
V: I just went from not working at all and being home. We've both been through major job changes and all.
M: And I can't breathe.
V: But we're getting used to it and I feel so much better about going to work at three (o'clock), three-thirty now than I did that first week.
M: Um.
V: I just wish I had more time to do what I wanted to do. I, it's just being...
M: I'll be able to stay...
V: ... a wife and mother.
M: ... to stay at home during the days a little bit more. I'll have to go in early but then I can take a couple of hours off in the afternoons.
V: Do you have to go in early every day?
M: 'Cause there are things I need to do every morning.
V: I think you just like going in to your office.
M: You don't know a thing about it then. Randy was in there early every day, tell me why?
V: Yeah, but he was home at a decent hour too.
M: He stays out late.
V: Eight to eight or eight to nine every day.
M: Every day.
V: Now, then, I don't want you taking that job. You forget it.
M: No.

Questions

1. What evidence do you find in this transcript that Valerie and Mark have conflict and low levels of marital satisfaction?
2. What evidence do you find that Valerie and Mark have reasonably good marital satisfaction?
3. What recommendations can you offer Valerie and Mark to improve their relationship?

SOURCE: John Gottman and Sybil Carrere, "Welcome to the Love Lab," *Psychology Today,* September/October 2000, pp. 44–45. Reprinted with permission.

Communicating with People

Learning Outcomes

After studying the information and doing the exercises in this chapter, you should be able to

- understand the importance of effective communication for your career and personal life
- explain the basic communication process
- describe the nature and importance of nonverbal communication in the workplace
- identify the challenges to interpersonal communication created by computer-mediated communication
- identify and overcome many roadblocks to communication
- enhance your listening skills

The president of a chain of sporting and athletic goods stores was touring several of the chain's stores located in one province. The chain itself was doing very well, but some stores were showing more profits than others. The president visited one store where profits had been consistently lower than elsewhere. While not contemplating closure of this location, the president was interested in an overall picture of it, including how it was being run, what the sales targets were, and what the possible problems were. The store's manager, who had requested a promotion to a larger store with more responsibilities, greeted the president. The president asked the manager, Dominique, about the possible reasons for the lack of profit at this location. Dominique replied, "Like, I'm not really sure. It's a really busy mall and it gets pretty crazy, if you know what I mean. Like, there's lots of reasons, eh? See where I'm coming from?" The president did not know where Dominique was coming from, but he knew one thing: Dominique was not going to get her promotion.

You may feel sorry for Dominique. After all, it was only one interaction. Maybe she was nervous. Yet one thing is very clear. Communication barriers can easily be created between yourself and key people in your organization. There are side effects for choosing the wrong communication style. Not communicating properly on and off the job can have serious consequences.

Communication is so vital that it has been described as the glue that holds organizations and families together. Most job foul-ups and marital tiffs are considered to be communication problems. **Communication**, as the term is used here, is the sending and receiving of messages. Furthermore, to be successful in work or personal life, you usually have to be an effective communicator. You can't make friends or stand up against your enemies unless you can communicate with them. And you can't accomplish work through others unless you can send and receive messages effectively.

In this chapter we explain several important aspects of communication between and among people. A few sections of the chapter deal specifically with improving communication skills. As with other chapters in this text, however, explanation should also lead to skill improvement. If you understand the steps involved in getting a message across to another person, for example, you may be able to prevent many communication problems.

How Communication Takes Place

A convenient starting point in understanding how people communicate is to look at the steps involved in communicating a message. A diagram of how the process takes place is shown in Figure 7-1. The theme of the model is that two-way communication involves three major steps and that each step is subject to interference, or noise.[1]

Figure 7-1 The Communication Process

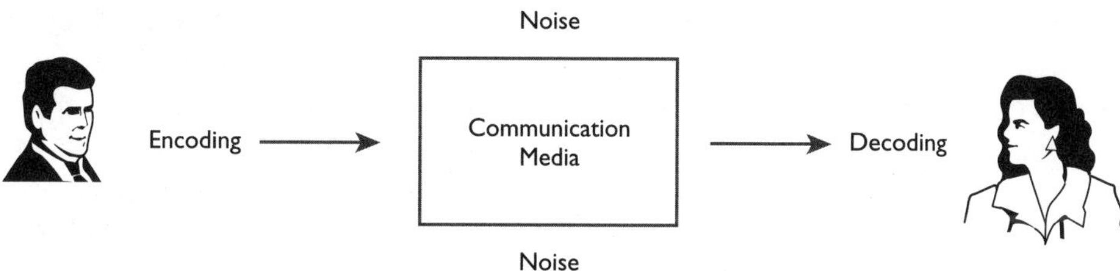

Assume that Tony, a customer, wishes to inform Crystal, a used-car sales representative, that he is willing to make an offer of $5,000 on a used car. The price tag on the car is $5,500.

Step 1: Encoding the Message **Encoding** is the process of organizing ideas into a series of symbols, such as words and gestures, designed to communicate with the receiver. Word choice has a strong influence on communication effectiveness. The better a person's grasp of language, the easier it is for him or her to encode. Tony says, "Crystal, this car obviously is not in excellent condition, but I am willing to give you $5,000 for it."

Step 2: Transmission over Communication Media The message is sent via a communication medium, such as voice, telephone, paper, or email. It is important to select a medium that fits the message. It would be appropriate to use the spoken word to inform a co-worker that he swore under his breath at a customer. It would be inappropriate to send the same message through email. Many messages on and off the job are sent nonverbally, through the use of gestures and facial expressions. For example, a smile from a superior during a meeting is an effective way of communicating the message, "I agree with you." Tony has chosen the oral medium to send his message.

Step 3: Decoding In **decoding**, the receiver interprets the message and translates it into meaningful information. Decoding is the process of understanding a message. Barriers to communication are most likely to surface at the decoding step. People often interpret messages according to their psychological needs and motives. Crystal wants to interpret Tony's message as saying that he is very eager to purchase this car. She may therefore listen attentively for more information demonstrating that he is interested in purchasing the car.

Decoding the message leads naturally to action—the receiver does something about the message. If the receiver acts in the manner the sender wants, the communication has been successful. If Crystal says, "It's a deal," Tony had a successful communication event.

Unfortunately, not all communication experiences are so successful. Many missteps can occur between encoding and decoding a message. **Interference**, or **noise**, often distorts or blocks a message and leads to misinterpretation by the receiver. If Tony has an indecisive tone and raises his voice at the end of his statement, it could indicate he is not really serious about offering a maximum of $5,000 for the car. Yelling may be perceived as anger. But someone may not realize he or she is yelling after finishing listening to loud music. Even email and paper communication can generate interference as we attempt to read between the lines. Has anyone ever said to you that someone's email was bossy or arrogant?

Noise is usually divided into three main types.[2] *Physical noise* is interference with the physical transmission of a message. An example would be trying to listen to someone in a loud and noisy restaurant. *Psychological noise* is interference inside a person that produces barriers in the decoding and processing of information, such as if you are distracted while trying to listen to someone. *Semantic noise* is interference created when the receiver does not decode the message as it was intended by the sender. If you do not know the meaning of a word, it makes it more difficult to decode the message.

A final note about this process. The diagram shows an arrow going one way from sender to receiver. Most communication between people is ongoing, with messages being sent back and forth. At any point, problems can occur in the process. These problems may be caused by interference as mentioned above. Psychological noise as well as other internal characteristics or problems can create many types of interference. Our thoughts, personalities, current physiological state, health, and other internal characteristics affect our encoding and decoding of messages. For example, have you ever found it hard to listen to someone when you have a really bad cold or have just received other disturbing information? Other sources of interference may be cultural differences, values, and beliefs. In some cultures people do not maintain eye contact during conversation. Some people may perceive this behaviour as being inattentive or rude. One office manager reported that while working in Toronto, this cultural difference took time to get used to as he had been taught to look at those in authority when they were addressing him. In fact, many of us may have been punished for not demonstrating this behaviour!

Nonverbal Communication (Sending and Receiving Silent Messages)

So far we have been talking mostly about spoken communication. However, much of the communication among people consists of messages that are neither spoken nor written. These nonverbal signals are a critical part of everyday communication. According to Albert Mehrabian,[3] in the verbal communication of a message, only seven percent of the meaning of a message is verbal content. This means that 93 percent of what we communicate to others is through nonverbal channels. Nonverbal behaviours (physical cues), for instance, account for 55 percent of our meaning. These include facial expressions, movement and gestures, territory and space, touch, and personal appearance, to name a few. Vocal cues, which include voice volume, tone, pitch, and intensity, are referred to collectively as **paralanguage**. These make up the remaining 38 percent of communication.[4] As a case in point, *how* you say "Thank you" makes a big difference in the extent to which your sense of appreciation registers. In **nonverbal communication** we use our body, voice, or environment in numerous ways to help put a message across. Sometimes we are not aware how much our true feelings colour our spoken message.

One problem of paying attention to nonverbal signals is that they can be taken too seriously. Just because some nonverbal signals (such as yawning or looking away from a person) might reflect a person's real feelings, that doesn't mean that every signal can be reliably connected with a particular attitude. Jason may put his hand over his mouth because he is shocked; Parmo may put her hand over her mouth because she is trying to control her laughter about the message; and Ken may put his hand over his mouth as a signal that he is pondering the consequences of the message. Here we will look at six categories of nonverbal communication. While we are dividing these types into discrete categories, be aware that usually these cues occur simultaneously. Much of the content below is based on North American studies that did not include cultural differences. Not all of these rules and examples will apply to all cultures.

The Environment around Us: Personal Appearance, Artifacts, and Time

Your external image plays an important role in communicating messages to others. Clothing and personal appearance constitute one of the most personal ways in which we state things about ourselves to others. Job seekers show recognition of this aspect of nonverbal communication when they carefully groom for a job interview. People pay more respect and grant more privileges to people they perceive as being well dressed and attractive. Furthermore, some research indicates that a favourable personal appearance leads to higher starting salaries and, later, salary increases.[5] In other words, we are judged by how we look, and projecting a positive image by paying attention to how we look is important.

Artifacts are the personal objects that we select and display to announce who we are and to personalize our environments. Artifacts also help to personalize and claim our space. Often personal areas are jammed with objects that are important to us and reflect our values, ideas, and beliefs. If an individual values home and family, pictures of family members and pets may be displayed. Religious individuals often decorate their homes and offices with religious symbols. A doctor may have her office decorated with pictures of all the babies she has delivered over several years. In residence, students decorate their rooms with objects that remind them of home, pictures of current musical groups, and other items that are important to them to personalize an often drab room. The next time you are in an office of a teacher or other professional, see what artifacts are present and try to determine what this says about the person.

Also surrounding us, much as our physical space does, is time. **Chronemics** refers to how we perceive and use time. We use time to define identities, interaction, and even status.[6] In the fast-paced Western society, time is highly valued and therefore so is speed. We often talk about the fast pace of life and look for ways to manage this pace. We want faster computers, faster highways, faster food, and so on. Being used to this fast pace and the high value placed on time and speed can be frustrating for Westerners who visit other cultures that don't share this value.

The Space around Us

All of us carry around an invisible bubble that is called our personal space. **Proxemics**, the study of spatial communication, was pioneered by Edward T.

Hall.[7] Often, we are not aware of our invisible bubble until someone gets too close or does not get close enough. In fact, many of our sayings use space to demonstrate feelings. "Get out of my face," "too close for comfort," and "get off my back" are just a few of the statements that we use when people are overstepping their boundaries in a relationship. When people we do not know get too close, we feel uncomfortable and we will attempt to increase the distance to regain our comfort. According to Hall, there are four interpersonal distances or circles that correspond to types of relationships: intimate, personal, social, and public (see Figure 7-2).

Intimate Distance *Intimate distance* ranges from actual touching to 46 centimetres. This distance is for close and intimate relationships where touching is important. When strangers cross over into intimate distance, we feel threatened or very uncomfortable. For instance, in a crowded elevator, we do not look at each other and focus our eyes ahead on the floor numbers.

Personal Distance Within *personal distance*, your comfort zone is from 46 centimetres to a far range of one metre. Many of our friendly relations and friendly business relations stay in this zone. At 46 centimetres you can still touch a person, such as by shaking hands or patting backs, but the zone is less intimate.

Social Distance Ranging from one to four metres, *social distance* is the distance at which we conduct impersonal business and have less personal interaction. Conducting business across a desk is usually in this zone, and many office areas are designed to maintain this distance.

Figure 7-2 Four Interpersonal Distances

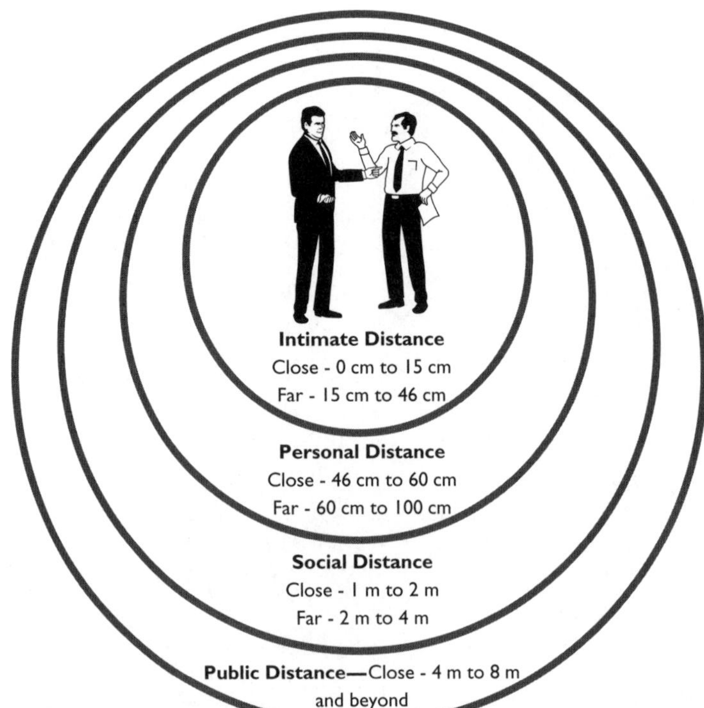

Public Distance *Public distance* ranges from four to eight metres and beyond—the outer limit being defined as the distance at which the speaker can no longer be heard. If someone is behaving in a bizarre manner, you will choose this as your safe distance because at this distance you can readily flee from a situation. Stage productions, lectures, and speeches are given using this distance.

These distances are general distances and are not always followed in interaction. For example, some cultures are more comfortable with closer contact. To illustrate, a French male is likely to stand closer to you than a British male, even if they have equally positive attitudes toward you.

Body Language: Posture, Gestures, and Movement

Think back to a time when you were really happy. Maybe it was the phone call that landed you a job you really wanted. What did you do after you hung up the phone? Some people literally jump up and down with joy! Your **body language** reflected your mood and feelings at that moment in time. Your posture can also indicate how you feel about yourself. People who walk and stand erectly, hold their heads up, and do not slouch appear calm and self-assured. On the other hand, people who shuffle along, slouch over, and keep their heads down appear to be unsure of themselves. Students who do not want to participate in a discussion often slouch over, look down, and avoid looking at the teacher. We also use posture to let others know whether or not we wish to interact. We may sit slightly forward and smile to invite interaction. Flirting signals our sexual or romantic interest to a prospective partner and involves postures and other nonverbal behaviours such as women swaying their hips and men swaying their pelvises.[8]

Related to posture are the nonverbal signals sent by standing versus sitting. Sitting down during a conversation is generally considered to more intimate and informal than standing. If you do sit down while conversing, be sure to stand up when you wish the conversation to end. Standing up sends a message to the other person that it is time to leave. It also gives you the chance to be more attentive and polite in saying goodbye.[9]

Gestures are used to emphasize or replace verbal communication and are culturally determined. In North America, "thumbs-up" means "great" or "way to go," making an "o" with your thumb and forefinger means "OK," nodding your head up and down means "yes," and displaying your middle finger up is a gesture of aggressive contempt. To illustrate the cultural determination of gestures, the North American gesture for OK means a big zero in Germany and a part of female or male anatomy in Russia.[10]

Head, Face, and Eye Signals

Since the face helps to make up 55 percent of our communication when we speak to others, it deserves special consideration. When used in combination, the head, face, and eyes provide the clearest indications of attitudes toward other people. Your face can assume a vast number of expressions, and much research has been devoted to the expression of emotion. Lowering your head and peering over your glasses, for instance, is the nonverbal equivalent of the expression, "You're putting me on." As is well known, maintaining eye contact with another person usually improves communication with that person. In order to maintain eye contact, it is usually necessary to correspondingly move your head and face. Moving your head, face, and eyes away from another person is often interpreted as a defensive gesture or one suggesting a lack of self-confidence. Would you lend money to someone who didn't look at you directly?

The face is often used as a primary source of information about how we feel. We look for facial clues when we want to determine another person's attitude. You can often judge someone's current state of happiness by looking at his or her face. The expression "sourpuss" attests to this observation. Happiness, apprehension, anger, resentment, sadness, contempt, enthusiasm, and embarrassment are but a few of the emotions that can be expressed through the face.

Blinking is a specific eye movement that communicates meaningful messages. According to experiments conducted by John Stern, blinks are punctuation marks. People blink at psychologically important times. After they have listened to and understood a question, people typically take time out for a blink. People in control of a situation, such as a pilot in control of an aircraft, are less likely to blink.[11] Many people use rapid blinking to send the message "I have no idea what you are talking about."

Facial clues can also be used to determine whether or not someone is telling the truth. Key facial clues that often reveal lying are as follows:[12]

Crooked smile. Genuine smiles are usually symmetrical, whereas phony smiles tend to be lopsided. A phony smile suggests lying about true feelings.

An overlong smile, frown, or look of disbelief. Genuine expressions last only four or five seconds, so if you smile continuously your veracity will come into question.

Failure to look you in the eye. Avoiding eye contact is often an indicator of lying but can also reflect the desire to avoid scrutiny. Also, in some Asian cultures looking a superior in the eye is considered rude.

Forced eye contact. Trying too hard to maintain eye contact may mean the person is trying to fake a sign of truth telling. Check out potential indicators of facial tension.

Frequent rubbing of the nose. Combined with other cues, rubbing of the nose may indicate a falsehood (or itching, or nervousness).

Facial shift. A facial shift is a fleeting expression, such as a frown, that is quickly replaced by another expression, such as a smile or serene face.

Touch

Touch is the earliest sense to develop and is the primary way that babies learn about their world. Touch can communicate many emotions and feelings that we have about another person. Touch can express affection, sexual interest, caring, dominance, aggression, and power. In business settings, most forms of contact are usually frowned upon except for handshakes and congratulatory pats on the back.

Being overly "touchy" is perceived as unprofessional conduct and could also be misperceived by the receiver.

Cultural rules for touching may also lead to different types of touching and different comfort levels. In some cultures, it is acceptable for male friends to greet each other with hugs and kissing the cheek, something most male college students in Canada would not do when greeting a friend at the campus library. While North Americans use handshakes to greet each other, some Asian cultures do not like to shake hands right away, particularly with strangers. East Asians also do not engage in interpersonal touching, and in particular, frown upon cross-sex touching in public.[13] We will examine cultural rules in more depth in Chapter 8. Exhibit 7-1 integrates some of the information about nonverbal communication by giving you advice about using a positive basic body vocabulary.

Paralanguage

Paralanguage is the part of vocal communication that is outside the domain of words. More significance is often attached to the *way* something is said than *what* is said. A forceful voice with a consistent tone and no vocalized pauses connotes power and control. Closely related to voice tone are volume, pitch, and rate of speaking. Voice volume (from whispering to shouting), tone, murmurs, gasps, sighs, rhythm,

exhibit 7-1

Body Basics

Patricia Ball, former president of the National Speakers Association and founder of a corporate communications consulting firm, believes strongly in body language. She says that any basic body vocabulary should include the most positive body language you can muster. When you're on a sales call or in negotiations and want to say or hear an affirmative, here are the signals to look for or send:

- *Leaning forward.* Leaning back sends the message of aloofness or rejection.
- *No leg crossing.* Keep your feet flat on the floor (both men and women).
- *A vertical handshake.* Some people shake with the palm down, forcing the other person to hold his or her palm up in a submissive, uncomfortable position.
- *An appropriate smile.* Smiling continuously may be interpreted as powerlessness.
- *Direct eye contact.* A direct look is permissible in the United States and Canada, but in many Asian and Middle Eastern cultures, a direct look is disrespectful.
- *Mirroring the other person's body language.* Ball warns against being an obvious mimic. However, if the other person has his or her leg crossed toward you and is leaning toward you, then crossing your leg in his or her direction and assuming that person's body language posture basically says, "I think like you. I'm with you."

SOURCE: Adapted from Mark Hennricks, "More Than Words," *Entrepreneur,* August 1995, p. 55.

pitch, inflection, accents, sentence complexity, and how we pronounce words are all paralanguage. When we ask a question, we use inflection at the end of the sentence. Our voices can communicate many feelings. Sarcasm is usually picked up due to the use of paralanguage. For instance, saying "Yeah, I really want to go" with sarcasm communicates the opposite of the sentence's direct meaning.

Avoiding an annoying voice quality can make a positive impact on others. The research of voice coach Jeffrey Jacobi provides some useful suggestions. He surveyed a sample of 1,000 American men and women, asking, "Which irritating or unpleasant voice annoys you the most?" The most irritating quality was a whining, complaining, or nagging tone.

Jacobi notes that we are judged by the way we sound. He also notes that careers can be damaged by voice problems such as those indicated in the survey. Jacobi continues: "We think about how we look and dress. And that gets most of the attention. But people judge our intelligence much more by how we sound than how we dress."[14] Human Relations Self-Assessment Quiz 7-1 provides more detail about his findings.

Computer-Mediated Communication

Homes and workplaces have been greatly affected by the introduction of the computer and computer-mediated communication. **Computer-mediated**

Voice Quality Checkup

Jacobi's study of voice quality (cited in the text) ranked voice quality, in decreasing order of annoyance, as follows:

- Whining, complaining, or nagging tone—44.0%
- High-pitched, squeaky voice—15.9%
- Numblers—11.1%
- Very fast talkers—4.9%
- Weak and wimpy voice—3.6%
- Flat, monotonous tone—3.5%
- Thick accent—2.4%

Ask yourself, and two other people familiar with your voice, if you have one or more of the above voice-quality problems. If your self-analysis and feedback from others does indicate a serious problem, get started on self-improvement. Tape your voice and attempt to modify the biggest problems. Another avenue of improvement is to consult with a speech coach or therapist.

communication (CMC) refers to the communication that takes place between people through the medium of computers. More and more people are using computers for work as well as to develop and maintain interpersonal relationships. Many nonverbal cues that were just discussed are missing in CMC, which has in some ways limited the richness of this type of communication. However, we still gather information and gain impressions of others through CMC. These rapid advances in information technology have enabled workers to communicate more easily and quickly than they could even a few years ago.[15] Quite often the influence has been positive, but at other times the effectiveness of interpersonal communication has decreased. Here we explore the types of computer-mediated communication, compare CMC with face-to-face communication, and provide suggestions to improve communication via CMC.

There are four major types of CMC: bulletin boards, chat rooms, email, and instant messaging. *Bulletin boards* allow people to post messages on the internet, where anyone can read them. Many bulletin boards have themes or topic areas that draw people who are interested in the same subject. For example, there are many health bulletin boards where people can read and post questions or answers about health-related problems. Often threads develop between a few people who respond almost exclusively to each other. There are often significant delays between bulletin board postings. People log on and off a bulletin board whenever they wish, and it may be hours or days before they revisit it. When people do not see each other and have views that others may view as controversial, "flaming" can erupt with people calling each other names or hurling insults. Recently, in books by such authors as Virginia Shea, rules of internet etiquette, or "netiquette," recommend that individuals learn how to communicate in cyberspace. To learn more about online etiquette and avoid miscommunicating on the internet, refer to the Internet Skill Builder at the end of the chapter to access some rules of conduct for cyberspace.

Chat rooms, unlike bulletin boards, involve the immediate sending and receiving of messages. People are actively involved in the process, responding to each other much as they would face to face in a small group discussion. One intriguing aspect of these chat rooms is that people often pair up and ignore other "chatters," responding only to each other. This can be rather confusing to a new person, but things usually become clear over time.

Aside from the telephone, *email* (electronic mail) is the information technology system with the most dramatic impact on interpersonal communication. Email is frequently used as an efficient substitute for telephone calls, letters, hard-copy memos, and in-person visits. For both work and personal life, email is typically less formal than a letter but more formal than a telephone conversation. The major impact of email on interpersonal communication is that written messages replace many telephone and in-person exchanges. Team members often keep in regular contact with each other without having lengthy meetings or telephone conversations. Email will inevitably continue to grow in importance and is likely to expand into a form of communication that will incorporate not only still drawings and photographs, but audio, video, and chunks of voice mail.

Several potential communication problems created by email should be kept in mind to minimize their impact. One major problem with email is that it encourages indiscriminate sending of messages. Some managers receive an average of 300 email messages per day. An executive in a telecommunications firm sends weekly email messages of his "thoughts for the week" to each company employee. Some company-wide email announcements describe a battered file cabinet that is available to a "good home." Some workers conduct virtual joke-telling contests via email, with some of the jokes being perceived as offensive by many other workers. Others constantly send "spam" (multiple unwanted messages) to others. The proliferation of electronic junk mail has prompted some company officials to take corrective action, such as warning employees about the problems with mass mailings and restricting the use of email during certain hours.

Email has become a new tool for office politicians who search for ways to look good themselves and make others look bad. Many office politicians use email to give credit to themselves for their contributions to a project, perhaps using a company-wide distribution list. When something goes wrong, such as a failed project, the office politician will inform hundreds of people that it was not his or her fault.

Some managers, and others whose jobs should involve considerable personal contact, prefer to remain in their offices or cubicles, firing off email messages to people. Such behaviour resembles a mild form of online addiction. As one systems analyst said, "I only see my boss about once every two months. She only relates to me by email."

Many supervisors and other workers use email to reprimand others because, by sending a message over the computer, they can avoid face-to-face confrontation. A telecommunications consultant has noted that "email is perfect for managers who would rather do anything other than walk down the hall."[16] Harsh messages sent over email create several problems. First, it is shocking to be reprimanded or insulted in writing. Second, the person receiving the message cannot offer a defence except by writing back an email message explaining his or her position. Third, the recipient, not knowing what to do about the harsh message, may brood and become anxious.

A final caution about email is that it can breed indecisiveness. Rather than making an independent decision, the worker sends an email to the boss, asking him or her to choose the best alternative. Even though the worker has the authority to make the decision, he or she sends a message to the boss wanting a recommendation. An example: "The purchasing agent at Hunt Systems wants to cancel an order for $1,500 worth of merchandise that we already shipped. What should I tell her? I have to respond by 5:00 this afternoon." The message sender would be less likely to telephone the boss, send a hard-copy memo, or request an in-person visit over the same issue.

Instant messaging (IM) is a fast-growing variety of CMC that is most likely familiar now to all of us. IM is also the quickest of all such communication methods and more closely imitates a phone call, as the sending and receiving of messages is more like the turn-taking that we experience while using the phone. Using IM, you and the people on your "buddy" list can exchange messages immediately on the computer screen without having to go through the process of sending and receiving. The technology is a hybrid of email and chat that enables real-time, one-on-one conversations online. Instead of picking up messages at times you choose, you are exposed to them whenever you are at the computer. A major problem with IM is that you may be involved with another activity (like doing homework) when someone contacts you.

Home-Office Systems

Home-office systems are configurations of electronic equipment that make it easier for employees to work at home. Because of home-office systems, telecommuting is possible. A **telecommuter** or teleworker is an employee who works at home full-time or part-time, and sends output electronically to a central office. In a recent survey, 62 percent of Canadian employers reported that teleworking had increased since 1993 and more than half predicted that teleworking could continue to increase in the future.[17] Statistics Canada has also reported that in 2001 more people were working from their homes at least some of the time.[18] Electronic equipment for telecommuters includes computers, printers, fax machines, telephones, modems, and video hookups for teleconferencing. Such equipment allows many employees the opportunity to work from home at least some of the time.

Teleworkers can communicate abundantly via electronic devices, but they miss out on the face-to-face interactions so vital for dealing with complex problems. Another communication problem teleworkers face is feeling isolated from activities at the main office, and missing out on the encouragement and recognition that take place in face-to-face encounters. (Of course, many teleworkers prefer to avoid such contact.) Many teleworkers have another communications problem: Because they have very little face-to-face communication with key people in the organization, they may believe they are passed over for promotion.

Roadblocks to Communication

Communication rarely proceeds as swiftly or as effectively as we would like. Many different factors filter our message on its way to the intended receiver. In this section we will look at some of the human, rather than physical or mechanical, roadblocks to communication. If you are aware of their presence, you will be better able to overcome them.

Routine or neutral messages are the easiest to communicate. Communication roadblocks are most likely to occur when a message is complex or emotionally arousing, or clashes with the receiver's mental set. An emotionally arousing message would deal with such topics as a relationship between two people, or money. A message that clashes with a receiver's mental set requires that person to change his or her familiar pattern of receiving messages. The next time you order a meal in a restaurant, order dessert first and an entrée second. The server will probably not "hear" your dessert order because it deviates from the normal ordering sequence.

Limited Understanding of People

If you do not understand people very well, your communication effectiveness will be limited. To take a basic example, if you frame your message in terms of what can be done for you, you may be in trouble. It's much more effective to frame your message in terms of what you can do for the other person. Suppose a person in need of money wants to sell magazine subscriptions to a friend. Mentioning financial need is a very self-centred message. It could be made less self-centred:

- *Very self-centred:* "You've got to buy a few subscriptions from me. I can't meet my credit card payments."
- *Less self-centred:* "Would you be interested in subscribing to a few magazines that would bring you enjoyment and help you get ahead in your career? If your answer is yes, I can help you."

Limited understanding of people can also result in false assumptions about the receiver. The false assumption serves as a communication roadblock. A supervisor might say to a telemarketer (a person who sells over the phone), "If you increase sales by 15 percent, we will give you an outside sales position." When the telemarketer does not work any harder, the supervisor thinks the message did not get across. The false assumption the supervisor made was that the telemarketer wanted an outside sales position. What false assumptions have you made lately when trying to communicate with another person? Guidelines for helping a person overcome a limited understanding of people are presented in Exhibit 7-2.

One-Way Communication

Effective communication proceeds back and forth. An exchange of information or a transaction takes place between two or more people. Person A may send messages to person B to initiate communication, but B must react to A to complete the communication loop. One reason written messages (including electronic mail) fail to achieve their purpose is that the person who writes the message cannot be sure how it will be interpreted. One written message that is subject to many interpre-

exhibit 7-2

A Short Course in Human Relations

- **The six most important words are "I admit I made a mistake."**
- **The five most important words are "You did a good job."**
- **The four most important words are "What is your opinion?"**
- **The three most important words are "If you please."**
- **The two most important words are "Thank you."**
- **The one most important word is "We."**
- **The one least important word is "I."**

Some people react negatively to this "short course" when they first read it. Among their reservations are that "It is corny," "It's so obvious; anybody with common sense knows that," or "Good for people in kindergarten." Yet if you put these seven rules into practice, you will find they do help overcome the communication roadblock called limited understanding of people. As one example, if you use "I" too frequently in your conversation, you will create communication roadblocks.

tations is "Your idea is of some interest to me." (How much is *some*?) Face-to-face communication helps to clarify meanings.

Instant messaging helps overcome the one-way barrier because the receiver reacts immediately to your message. An example: "You said ship the first batch only to good customers. What do you consider to be a *good* customer?" Ten seconds later comes the reply, "A good customer bought at least $4,000 worth of goods last year and is up to date on payments." Three seconds later, the first person writes, "Got it."

Different Interpretation of Words (Semantics)

Semantics is the study of the meaning and changes in the meaning of words. These different meanings can create roadblocks to communication. Often the problem is trivial and humorous; at other times, semantic problems can create substantial communication barriers. Consider first an example of trivial consequence:

> Two American first-time visitors to Montreal entered a restaurant for dinner. After looking over the menus, the husband suggested they order the shrimp cocktail entrées. He said to his wife, "A whole shrimp dinner for $9.95 Canadian is quite a deal. I guess it's because Montreal is a seaport." When the entrées arrived, the visitors were sadly disappointed because the entrées were the size of an appetizer.
>
> The husband asked the server why the entrées were so small in Montreal. With a smile, the server replied: "You folks must be Americans. In French-speaking countries the entrée is the beginning of the meal, like the word *enter*. In the United States it's just the reverse: the entrée is the main meal. Are you now ready to order your main meal?"

Of greater consequence is the experience of a trainer of airplane pilots who inadvertently contributed to a crash. As a rookie pilot navigated down the runway, the trainer shouted, "Takeoff power." The pilot shut off the engine and skidded off the runway. What the trainer really meant was to *use* takeoff power—a surge of energy to lift the airplane off the ground. He was using "takeoff" as an adjective, not a verb.

Credibility of the Sender and Mixed Signals

The more trustworthy the source or sender of the message, the greater the probability that the message will get through clearly. In contrast, when the sender of the message has low credibility, many times it will be ignored. Has someone ever lied to you? If so, the next time this person asked you to believe him or her, you probably had more trouble trusting what you were being told. He or she had lost some credibility and may have had to work to achieve it once again.

Communications can also break down as the result of a subtle variation of low credibility. The disconnect occurs from **mixed signals**—sending different messages about the same topic to different audiences. For example, a company might brag about the high quality of its products in its public statements. Yet on the shop floor and in the office the company tells its employees to cut corners whenever possible to lower costs. Another type of mixed signal occurs when you send a message to a person about desired behaviour yet behave in another way yourself. As a team leader, you might tell others that a tidy worker is a productive worker. However, your own cubicle contains a four-month supply of empty soft drink cans, and old papers consume virtually every square inch of your desk.

Distortion of Information

A great problem in sending messages is that people receiving them often hear what they want to hear. Without malicious intent, people modify your message to bolster their self-esteem or improve their situation. An incident that occurred between Jennifer and her mother is fairly typical of this type of communication roadblock. Jennifer asked her mother if she might have a 35mm camera system for Christmas. Regarding the request as far-fetched and beyond her means, Jennifer's mother replied, "Why should I buy you a camera system like that when you never even take pictures of your little brother with your present camera?"

Jennifer *heard* her mother say, "If you take pictures of your little brother, I will then buy you that camera system." Three weeks later Jennifer presented her mother with a surprise gift—a small album containing 20 photographs of her little brother. "Mom," said Jennifer, "Here's the album you ordered. Now let me tell you in more detail about that 35mm outfit you said you would get me for Christmas." Her mother replied, "I never said that. Where did you get that idea?"

The reason some people are so difficult to criticize or insult is that they ward off your message just as a duck sheds water. What message of yours has someone not heard recently? Can you think of any messages that bounced off you lately?

Different Perspectives and Experiences (Where Are You Coming From?)

People perceive words and concepts differently because their experiences and vantage points differ. On the basis of their perception of what they have heard, many Latino children believe that the opening line of the "Star-Spangled Banner" is "José, can you see..." (note that few children have *seen* the US national anthem in writing).

Young people with specialized training or education often encounter communication barriers in dealing with older workers. A minority of older workers think that young people are trying to introduce impractical and theoretical ideas. It takes time to break down this type of resistance to innovation and the application of current knowledge.

Emotions and Attitudes

Have you ever tried to communicate a message to another person while that person is emotionally aroused? Your message was probably distorted considerably. Another problem is that people tend to say things when emotionally aroused that they would not say when calm. Similarly, a person who has strong attitudes about a particular topic may become emotional when that topic is introduced. The underlying message here is try to avoid letting strong emotions and attitudes interfere with the sending or receiving of messages. If you are angry at someone, for example, you might miss the merit in what that person has to say. Calm down before proceeding with your discussion or attempting to resolve the conflict.

Improper Timing

Many messages do not get through to people because they are poorly timed. You have to know how to deliver a message, but you must also know when to deliver it. Sending a message when the receiver is distracted with other concerns or is rushing to get somewhere is a waste of time.[19] Furthermore, the sender may become discouraged and therefore will not repeat the message later.

The art of timing messages suggests not to ask for a raise when your boss is in a bad mood, or to ask a new acquaintance for a date when he or she is preoccupied. On the other hand, do ask your boss for a raise when business has been good. And do ask someone for a date when you have just done something nice for that person and have been thanked.

Communication Overload

A major communication barrier facing literate people is being bombarded with information. **Communication (or information) overload** occurs when people are so overloaded with information that they cannot respond effectively to messages. As a result, they experience work stress. Workers at many levels are exposed to so much printed, electronic, and spoken information that their capacity to absorb it is taxed. The problem is worsened when low-quality information is competing for your attention.[20] One example is receiving a lengthy letter informing you that you are one of 100 select people to receive a sweepstakes prize. (All you need to do is send $24.95 to cover the shipping and handling costs for your valuable prize.) An influx of irrelevant emails, usually advertisements, can load up your email in-box and require time and effort to sort through and delete. Software packages can be purchased to block out many of these messages and are often well worth the investment. The human mind is capable of processing only a limited quantity of information at a time.

Poor Communication Skills

A message may fail to register because the sender lacks effective communication skills. The sender might garble a written or spoken message so that the receiver finds it impossible to understand. Also, the sender may deliver the message so poorly that the receiver does not take it seriously. Communication barriers can also result from deficiencies within the receiver. A common barrier is a receiver who is a poor listener. Improving listening skills is such a major strategy for improving communication that it receives separate mention later in this chapter.

One area where poor communication skills rarely go unnoticed is the use of the written word in internet interactions and email. The ability to encode thoughts quickly and into writing is not a skill that everyone is good at. Not only do writing skills affect your ability to communicate in cyberspace, but how you write affects the perception of the receiver. Look at the following email messages and think about your perceptions of both writers:

Hotman: "Hey, sweetie! What you doing? Were shud we go to night? now what I think Id like to do?"

HonestEd: "Hi there! What a day I have had! How about we just rent a movie and stay home tonight? What are your thoughts?"

What were your impressions of the two speakers, and what created them? Did the grammar and spelling errors affect your impression of the first writer? And what about the different user names (often referred to as nicknames)? Perhaps, without realizing it, we may mistakenly give impressions to others by our writing skills. It is always wise to proofread your emails before sending them (especially at work), and you should also give careful consideration to any nicknames that you select for yourself.

Building Bridges to Communication

With determination and awareness that communication roadblocks and barriers do exist, you can become a more effective communicator. It would be impossible to remove all barriers, but they can be minimized. The following techniques are helpful in building better bridges to communication.

1. Appeal to human needs and time your messages.
2. Have an empowered attitude.
3. Repeat your message, using more than one channel.
4. Discuss differences in paradigms.
5. Check for comprehension and feelings.
6. Minimize defensive communication.
7. Counter information overload.
8. Use bias-free language and have bias-free attitudes.
9. Use mirroring to establish rapport.
10. Improve your telephone and voice-mail communication skills.
11. Use presentation technology to your advantage.

Appeal to Human Needs and Time Your Messages

People are most receptive to messages that promise to do something for them. In other words, if a message promises to satisfy a need that is less than fully satisfied, you are likely to listen. The hungry person who ordinarily does not hear low tones readily hears the whispered message, "How would you like a pizza with everything on it?" Somehow, we have always been able to communicate this message to our class: "Unfortunately the class will not meet a week from today." We wonder to which need we have been appealing.

Timing a message properly is related to appealing to human needs. If you deliver a message at the right time, you are taking into account the person's mental condition at the moment. A general principle is to deliver your message when the person might be in the right frame of mind to listen. The right frame of mind includes such factors as not being preoccupied with other thoughts, not being frustrated, being in a good mood, and not being stressed out. (Of course, all this severely limits your opportunity to send a message!)

Have an Empowered Attitude

According to Sharon Lund O'Neill, a person's communication effectiveness is directly proportional to his or her attitude. The point is that a positive attitude helps a person communicate better in speaking, in writing, or nonverbally. *Empowerment* is involved here because the person takes charge of his or her own attitude.[21] Developing a positive attitude is not always easy. A starting point is to see things from a positive perspective, including looking for the good in people and their work. If your work is intrinsically motivating, you are likely to have a positive attitude. You would then be able to communicate about your work with the enthusiasm necessary.

Repeat Your Message, Using More Than One Channel

In general, you can overcome roadblocks to communication by repeating your message several times. It is usually advisable to say the same thing in different ways so as to avoid annoying the listener with straight repetition. In any case, your message may not have been understood in its first form. If there is too much repetition, however, people no longer listen to the message. They think they already understand the message.

Repetition, like any other means of overcoming communication roadblocks, does not work for all people. Many people who repeatedly hear the message "Drinking and driving do not mix" are not moved by it. It is helpful to use several methods of overcoming roadblocks or barriers to communication.

A generally effective way of repeating a message is to use more than one communication channel. For example, follow up a face-to-face discussion with a letter or telephone call or both. Your body can be another channel or medium to help impart your message. If you agree with someone about a spoken message, state your agreement and also shake hands over the agreement. Can you think of another channel by which to transmit a message?

Discuss Differences in Paradigms

Another way of understanding differences in perspectives and experiences is to recognize that people often have different paradigms that influence how they interpret events. A **paradigm** is a model, framework, viewpoint, or perspective. When two people look at a situation with different paradigms, a communication problem may occur. For instance, one person may say, "Let's go to Montreal for the computer show." The other person may respond, "A ridiculous idea. It costs too much money and takes too much time. Besides, the company would never approve." These objections are based on certain unstated beliefs:

- Air travel is the most suitable mode of transportation.
- Travelling over 800 kilometres a day by auto is fatiguing and dangerous.
- Travelling over a weekend for business and using vacation days cannot be considered seriously.
- Paying for such a trip with personal money is out of the question.

The other person has a different set of unstated beliefs:

- It is possible, travelling on expressways and using two drivers, to cover 800 kilometres in one day.
- Travelling over a weekend and taking vacation days is sensible.
- Paying for the trip with personal money is a sound educational investment.

The solution to this communication clash is to discuss the paradigms. Both people live by different rules or guidelines (a major contributor to a paradigm). If the two people can recognize that they are operating with different paradigms, the chances for agreement are improved. Keep in mind that people can change their paradigms when the reasons are convincing.[22] For example, the first person in the preceding situation may never have thought about using personal funds for a trip as being an educational investment.

Check for Comprehension and Feelings

Don't be a hit-and-run communicator. Such a person drops a message and leaves the scene before he or she is sure the message has been received as intended. It is preferable to ask receivers their understanding or interpretation of what you said. For example, you might say after delivering a message, "What is your understanding of our agreement?" Also use nonverbal indicators to gauge how well you delivered your message. A blank expression on the receiver's face might indicate no comprehension. A disturbed, agitated expression might mean that the receiver's emotions are blocking the message.

In addition to looking for verbal comprehension and emotions when you have delivered a message, check for feelings after you have received a message. When a person speaks, we too often listen to the facts and ignore the feelings. If feelings are ignored, the true meaning and intent of the message are likely to be missed, thus creating a communication barrier. Your boss might say to you, "You never seem to take work home." To clarify what your boss means by this statement, you might ask, "Is that good or bad?" Your boss's response will give you feedback on his or her feelings about getting all your work done during regular working hours.

When you send a message, it is also helpful to express your feelings in addition to conveying the facts. For example, "Our defects are up by 12 percent [fact], and I'm quite disappointed about those results [feelings]." Because feelings contribute strongly to comprehension, you will help overcome a potential communication barrier.

Minimize Defensive Communication

Distortion of information was described previously as a communication barrier. Such distortion can also be regarded as **defensive communication**, the tendency to receive messages in such a way that our self-esteem is protected. Defensive communication is also responsible for people sending messages to make themselves look good. For example, when criticized for achieving below-average sales, a store manager might shift the blame to the sales associates in her store.

Overcoming the barrier of defensive communication requires two steps. First, people have to acknowledge the existence of defensive communication. Second, they have to try not to be defensive when questioned or criticized. Such behaviour is not easy because of **denial**, the suppression of information we find uncomfortable. For example, the store manager just cited would find it uncomfortable to think of herself as being responsible for below-average performance.

Counter Information Overload

You will recall that a flood of information reaching a person acts as a communication barrier because people have a tendency to block out new information when their capacity to absorb information becomes taxed. You can decrease the chances of suffering from communication overload by such measures as carefully organizing and sorting information before plunging ahead with reading. Speed-reading may help, provided you stop to read carefully the most relevant information. Or you can scan through hard-copy reports, magazines, and websites looking for key titles and words that are important to you. Recognize, however, that many subjects have to be studied carefully if you are to derive benefit. It is often better to read a few topics thoroughly than to skim through lots of information.

Being selective about your email and internet reading goes a long way toward preventing information overload. Suppose you see an email message titled "Car Lights Left On in Parking Lot." Do not retrieve the message if you distinctly remember having turned off your lights or you did not drive to work. Email programs and internet search software are available to help users sort messages according to their needs. You can help prevent others from suffering from communication overload by being merciful in the frequency and length of your messages. Also, do not join the ranks of pranksters who send loads of jokes on email, or be misled those who prepare bogus websites that look authentic but are unofficial (and unreliable) sources of information.

Use Bias-Free Language and Have Bias-Free Attitudes

An important implication of semantics is that certain words are interpreted by some people as signs of bias. A **bias** is a prejudgment about another person or group based on something other than fact.[23] The use of biased words is thus a form of discrimination. To avoid this type of discrimination, attempt to use bias-free language. An obvious example of a biased statement would be for a supervisor to say, "I need a real man for this job." The bias-free statement expressing the same thought would be, "I need a courageous person for this job."

Selecting bias-free terms is complex for several reasons. One problem is that terms preferred by specific groups to refer to themselves change frequently. For example, although the term "Hispanic" is still used, many people of Latin American origin now prefer the term "Latino." Another problem is that some bias-free terms are technically incorrect. For instance, there is a substantial difference between being "blind" and being "visually impaired." A third problem is that the labels we use to refer to a group can affect our perceptions of and attitudes toward that group in a positive or negative way.[24] A recent study that examined labels and the effects that these labels had on attitudes toward Native Canadians indicated that the words we use to refer to a group can influence attitudes.[25]

Recognize, however, that you cannot please everybody. It is best to avoid terms that refer to people's race, religion, or physical status unless the information is needed for purposes of identification.

Using bias-free language is equivalent to being "politically correct," or choosing words and terms carefully to avoid offending anyone. Some people are concerned that political correctness can go too far. At times we may assume that we are offending someone who belongs to a group or culture, when in fact no offence has been taken. Exemplifying this is the story of reaction to a newspaper article about "Canucks," this chapter's Canada Today feature.

Having bias-free attitudes requires the same type of open-mindedness as using bias-free language. Even if you cannot overcome your biases completely, at least be

Canuck or Not Canuck?

A newspaper article in 1999 discussed the use of the word "Canuck" to describe Canadians. According to the article, a writer for a campus newspaper had used the word when referring to the large number of Canadians moving into American entertainment. The newspaper, *The Statesman*, is the paper at Indiana State University. Because of this incident and other prior incidents that were not reported, the writer was fired. However, the writer was rehired later after the editor received many letters from Canadians saying that they were not offended by the use of the term. Interestingly, Merv Hendricks, the university's director of student publications, had complained that the term was a derogatory label for French Canadians.

There appears to have been some confusion at the university as to what the term "Canuck" means and whether or not it is offensive or politically incorrect. As mentioned in the article, the Vancouver Canucks is one of our hockey teams. "Canuck" has been around for at least a century. Johnny Canuck was a cartoon character that appeared in papers in the 1860s. During World War II, he became a cartoon hero in comic books, protecting Canadians from the Nazi threat. If you are looking for Canadian content on the internet, many sites have "Canuck" in their address or title. There is even a Canuck site of the day! So is the label of Canuck offensive? It would appear that Canadians themselves use this term to describe much about their own country and the people who inhabit this nation. What do you think? Is this an offensive term or is it OK to call ourselves Canucks?

SOURCES: "'Canuck' No Slur, Editor Rehired," *Peterborough Examiner*, Sunday, February 28, 1999, reprinted with permission from the Associated Press; and Andrew Phillips, "Fear and Hope at Home: Social Changes Caused by WWII," *Maclean's*, June 6, 1994.

willing to look at situations in a new perspective. Images of men and women exemplify the importance of bias-free attitudes. In traditional (or biased) thinking, photographs of children on a female manager's desk mean that children come first. Similar photographs on a male manager's desk are likely to evoke the reaction, "It's nice to see that he cares about his family."

Another workplace bias is that people over age 50 are either unable or unwilling to learn about technology. In reality, some older people have aptitude for and strong interest in technology. Clubs have been formed in Canada to accommodate the interests of "high-tech seniors." These are retired people who work with computers as a pastime. Many of these people send electronic messages to each other late into the night, and also develop new programs.

Bias-free attitudes improve communication because messages flow back and forth more freely when you have an open mind toward another person or group. For example, if you do not prejudge older people as disliking technology you are more apt to listen to their opinions about software.

Use Mirroring to Establish Rapport

Another approach to overcoming communication barriers is to improve rapport with another person. A form of nonverbal communication called **mirroring** can be used to establish such rapport. To mirror someone is to subtly imitate another's breathing pattern. If you adjust your own breathing rate to someone else's, you will soon establish rapport with that person. Mirroring sometimes takes the form of imitating the boss in order to communicate better and win favour. Many job seekers now use mirroring to get in sync with the interviewer. Is this a technique you would be willing to try?

Mirroring will take practice before it can contribute to overcoming communication barriers. It is a subtle technique that requires a moderate skill level. If you mirror (or match) another person in a rigid, mechanical way you will appear to be mocking that person. And mocking, of course, erects rather than tears down a communication barrier.

Improve Your Telephone and Voice-Mail Communication Skills

A direct way of overcoming communication barriers is to use effective telephone and voice-mail communication skills, since these two communication media often create communication problems. Also, many businesses attract and hold onto customers because their representatives interact positively with people through the telephone and voice mail. Many other firms lose money, and nonprofit organizations irritate the public because their employees have poor communication and voice-mail skills. Furthermore, despite the widespread use of computer networks, a substantial amount of work among employees is still conducted via telephone and voice mail. Most of the previous comments about overcoming communication barriers apply to telephone communications. A number of suggestions related specifically to improving telephone and voice-mail communications are also worth considering. The general goal of the suggestions presented in Exhibit 7-3 is to help people who communicate by telephone sound courteous, cheerful, cooperative, and competent.[26]

exhibit 7 - 3

Effective Telephone and Voice-Mail Communication Skills

1. When answering the telephone, give your name and department. Also give the company name if the call is not a transfer from a main switching centre.
2. When talking to customers or clients, address them by name, but not to the point of irritation.
3. Vary your voice tone and inflection to avoid sounding bored or uninterested in your job and the company.
4. Speak at a moderate pace of approximately 150 to 160 words per minute. A rapid pace conveys the impression of impatience, while a slow rate might suggest lack of interest.
5. Smile while speaking on the phone—somehow a smile gets transmitted over the telephone wires or optic fibres!
6. If the caller does not identify him- or herself, ask "Who is calling, please?" Knowing the caller's name gives a human touch to the conversation.
7. Be particularly tactful in your choice of words because you cannot look at the caller's face to determine if he or she is irked by your phrases. For example, the statement "I'll tell you once more" can sound even harsher over the phone than in person.
8. Use voice mail to minimize "telephone tag" rather than to increase it. If your greeting specifies when you will return, callers can choose to call again or to leave a message. When you leave a message, suggest a good time to return your call. Another way to minimize telephone tag is to assure the person you are calling that you will keep trying.
9. Place an informative and friendly greeting (outgoing message) on your voice mail (or answering machine). Used effectively, a voice-mail greeting will minimize the number of people irritated by not talking to a person.
10. When leaving a voice-mail message, give specific, relevant information. As in the suggestions for minimizing telephone tag, be specific about why you are calling and what you want from the person called. The probability of receiving a return call increases when you leave honest and useful information. If you are selling something or asking for a favour, be honest about your intent.
11. When leaving your message, avoid the most common voice-mail error by stating your name and telephone number clearly enough to be understood. Most recipients dislike having to listen to a message several times to pick up identifying information.
12. Use upbeat, modern language. Given that it's more difficult to make a positive impression over the phone than in person, sprinkle your phone conversation with modern "in" words. For example, you might say that some of your customers like "modern primitive." It refers to the revival of body modification processes like tattooing and piercing. Or try "dead tree edition" when referring to the paper version of a newspaper or magazine that also appears in electronic form.

Use Presentation Technology to Your Advantage

Speakers in all types of organizations supplement their talk with computer slides and overhead transparencies, often organizing their presentation around them. Many people want presentations reduced to bulleted items and eye-catching graphics. (Have you noticed this tendency among students?) The communication challenge here is that during an oral presentation the predominant means of connection between sender and receiver is eye contact. When an audience is constantly distracted from the presenter by movement on the screen, sounds from the computer, or lavish colours, eye contact suffers and so does the message.

One of the biggest challenges is to learn how to handle equipment and maintain frequent eye and voice contact at all times. Jean Mausehund and R. Neil Dortch offer these sensible suggestions for overcoming the potential communication barrier of using presentation technology inappropriately:

Reveal points only as needed. Project the overhead transparencies or computer slides only when needed, and use a cursor, laser pointer, or metal pointer for emphasis.

Talk to the audience and not the screen. A major problem with computer slides is that the presenter as well as the audience is likely to focus continually on the slide. If the presenter minimizes looking at the slide, and spends considerable time looking at the audience, it will be easier to maintain contact with the audience.

Keep the slide in view until the audience gets the point. A presenter will often flash a slide or transparency without giving the audience enough time to comprehend the meaning of the slide. It is also important for presenters to synchronize the slides with their comments.[27]

Enhancing Your Listening Skills

Although many workers spend more time at computers than they do communicating orally, face-to-face communication is still a major part of life. Improving your receiving of oral messages is another part of developing better communication skills. Unless you receive messages as they are intended, you cannot perform your job properly or be a good companion. Listening has even been described as our primary communication activity. About 45 percent of the time we spend communicating with people is spent listening. Listening is a particularly important skill for anybody whose job involves troubleshooting, since you need to gather information in order to solve problems.

Another reason that improving employee listening skills is important is that insufficient listening is extraordinarily costly. Listening mistakes lead to reprocessing letters, rescheduling appointments, reshipping orders, and recalling defective products. Effective listening also improves interpersonal relationships because the people listened to feel understood and respected.

A major component of effective listening is being an active listener. The **active listener** listens intensely, with the goal of empathizing with the speaker. **Empathy** is simply understanding another person's point of view. If you know "where the other person is coming from," you will be a better receiver and sender of messages. Empathy does not necessarily mean that you sympathize with the other person.

For example, you may understand why some people are forced to beg in the streets, but you may have very little sympathy for their plight.

A useful way of showing empathy is to accept the sender's figure of speech. This makes the sender feel understood and accepted. Also, if you reject the person's figure of speech by rewording it, the sender may become defensive. Many people use the figure of speech "I'm stuck" when they cannot accomplish a task. You can facilitate smooth communication by a response such as "What can I do to help you get unstuck?" If you respond with something like "What can I do to help you think more clearly?" the person is forced to change mental channels and may become defensive.[28]

As a result of listening actively, the listener can feed back to the speaker what he or she thinks the speaker meant. Feedback of this type relies on both verbal and nonverbal communication. Active listening also involves **summarization**. When you summarize, you pull together, condense, and thereby clarify the main points the other person communicates. Here are two examples of summarization statements:

> "What I heard you say during our meeting is that..."
> "As I understand it, your position is that..."

To be an active listener, it is also important to **paraphrase**, or repeat in your own words, what the sender says, feels, and means. You might feel awkward the first several times you paraphrase. Therefore, try it with a person with whom you feel comfortable. With some practice, it will become a natural part of your communication skill kit. Here is an example of how you might use paraphrasing:

Other Person: I'm getting ticked off at working so hard around here. I wish somebody else would pitch in and do a fair day's work.

You: You're saying that you do more than your fair share of the tough work in our department.

Other Person: You bet. Here's what I think we should be doing about it...

Human Relations Skill-Building Exercise 7-1 gives you an opportunity to practise your listening skills.

Summary

Communication is the sending and receiving of messages. Therefore, almost anything that takes place in work and personal life involves communication. The steps involved in communication are encoding, transmission over a communication medium, and decoding.

Nonverbal communications, or silent messages, are important parts of everyday communication. Aspects of nonverbal communication include the environment; distance or space from the other person; body language; head, face, and eye signals; and paralanguage.

Despite its many advantages, information technology and computer-mediated communication can create many communication problems. The widespread use of bulletin boards, chat rooms, email and instant messaging creates some problems. One problem is that it encourages indiscriminate sending of messages. Email

Active Listening

Before conducting the following role plays, review the suggestions for active listening in this chapter. The suggestions about paraphrasing the message are particularly relevant because the role plays involve emotional topics.

The Elated Co-worker. One student plays the role of a co-worker who has just been offered a promotion to supervisor of another department. She will be receiving ten percent higher pay and be able to travel overseas twice a year for the company. She is eager to describe full details of her good fortune to a co-worker. Another student plays the role of the co-worker to whom the first co-worker wants to describe her good fortune. The second worker decides to listen intently to the first worker. Other class members will rate the second student on his or her listening ability.

The Discouraged Co-worker. One student plays the role of a co-worker who has just been placed on probation for poor performance. His boss thinks that his performance is below standard and that his attendance and punctuality are poor. He is afraid that if he tells his girlfriend, she will leave him. He is eager to tell his tale of woe to a co-worker. Another student plays the role of a co-worker he corners to discuss his problems. The second worker decides to listen intently to his problems but is pressed for time. Other class members will rate the second student on his or her listening ability.

is also used for such negative purposes as making oneself look good and others look bad. Some managers and other workers use email to avoid direct contact with people, including discipline. Some people find it difficult to handle harsh messages sent over email. Another problem with email is that it can breed indecisiveness because a worker can readily consult the boss about every decision.

Teleworkers can communicate abundantly via electronic devices, but they miss out on the face-to-face interactions so vital for dealing with complex problems. Teleworkers can also face the problem of having so little face-to-face communication with people in the office that they are passed over for promotion.

Many potential roadblocks or barriers to communication exist. These roadblocks are most likely to occur when messages are complex, emotional, or clash with the receiver's mental set. Communication roadblocks can result from limited understanding of people; one-way communication; semantics; low credibility of the sender and mixed messages; distortion of information; different perspectives and experiences; emotions and attitudes; improper timing; communication overload; and poor communication skills.

Strategies to overcome communication roadblocks include appealing to human needs, timing your messages, and having an empowered attitude; repeating your message using more than one channel; discussing differences in paradigms; checking for comprehension and feelings; minimizing defensive communication; countering information overload; using bias-free language and having bias-free attitudes; and using mirroring to establish rapport. Also, a direct way of overcoming communication barriers is to use effective telephone, voice-mail, and internet communication skills and presentation technology, because these media often create communication problems. Unless you receive messages as intended, you cannot perform your job properly or be a good companion. A major component of effective listening is to be an active listener. The active listener uses empathy and can feed back to the speaker what he or she thinks the speaker meant. Active listening also involves summarizing the speaker's key ideas and paraphrasing what the speaker says, feels, and means.

Questions and Activities

1. How can knowing the three major steps in communication help a person communicate more effectively?
2. Why is nonverbal communication so important for the effectiveness of a manager or sales representative?
3. Would you classify a handshake as a form of nonverbal communication? Explain your reasoning.
4. In what ways might an email message contain nonverbal communication?
5. How might instant messaging distract you while you are doing homework or other work on the internet? What are some suggestions that you might offer to reduce these distractions?
6. What barriers to communication typically exist in a classroom? What can be done to reduce these barriers?
7. Based on your own observations, identify a term or phrase that creates semantic problems.
8. During your next three work- or school-related phone calls, analyze what the people you speak to are doing right and wrong from the standpoint of telephone communication. Be prepared to report your findings to the class.
9. Why is a high level of face-to-face speaking skill very important for a successful business career?

Internet Skill Builder

Test Your Online Etiquette

To reinforce your understanding of the importance of good communication skills on the internet, visit the website of Albion, the home of Netiquette, at **www.albion.com**. Once on the site, try the quiz to test your knowledge of network etiquette. You will receive a score out of ten. After learning your score and which questions that you answered incorrectly, examine some of the suggestions on the site to help improve your skills.

Weblinks

http://members.aol.com/nonverbal2/diction1.htm
From A to Z, this is a complete dictionary of nonverbal terms and phrases.

http://zzyx.ucsc.edu/~archer
This site on nonverbal communication includes a series of pictures whose nonverbal messages you can try to "read."

www.fastcompany.com/online/07/124present.html
This site offers tips to improve your presentation skills.

Human Relations Case Study

JUST CALL ME "KAT"

Katherine Matthews had worked for many years in a variety of retail positions, including a three-year assignment as an assistant manager at a woman's clothing store. Matthews was then involved in an automobile accident while a passenger in a friend's car. Although she was wearing a seat belt, Matthews was severely injured. Her right leg and ankle were broken as the door on her side caved in upon impact with a tree.

After four months of rehabilitation, Matthews walked well with the assistance of a cane. Yet she could not walk for long without enduring pain. Katherine and the team of medical specialists assisting her agreed that an on-the-feet job was not appropriate for her in the foreseeable future. Katherine assessed her financial situation and decided she needed to return to work soon, as her disability payments were ending and her savings were depleted down to $350.

To make the transition back to full-time employment in a different field, Katherine signed on with Office Temps, a well-established temporary-placement agency. Katherine explained that she sought work that was mentally challenging but not physically demanding on her right leg and ankle. After carefully assessing Katherine's capabilities and experiences, the employment interviewer, Jack Radison, created a computer file for her. Radison said, "I'll call you as soon as I find a suitable assignment."

One week later Radison called Katherine with good news. He had located a nine-month assignment for her as a telephone interviewer for a market research firm. The market research firm was hiring several people to conduct telephone interviews with dealers and retailers about the acceptability of a relatively new product, a personal air cooler. The cooler is about the size of the central processing unit on a personal computer and fits easily on a desk or adjacent to a television set. The air cooler evaporates water, thereby lowering the temperature by about seven degrees Celsius in a seven-foot area. Using an air cooler, a person would have less need for air-conditioning. With the cooler operating, a person could either eliminate air-conditioning or set it at a higher temperature. The manufacturer of the cooler was interested in estimating the potential market for the product, now being sold primarily by mail order.

Katherine's task was to telephone specific people (usually store managers or owners) from a long list of names. Completing an interview would require about 30 minutes and involved obtaining answers to 20 separate questions. Each market research interviewer was given a quota of six completed interviews per day.

As the interviewers perceived the task, a major challenge was to keep the interviewee on the line long enough to answer all the detailed questions. Quite often, the interviewer had to dig for additional information (such as sales of room air conditioners and fans) or request that the interviewee search his or her files for appropriate information. The several interviewers also agreed that an even bigger challenge was to get the people on the list to cooperate. Among the problems were reaching a voice-mail system instead of the actual person, excuses about being too busy to be interviewed, and outright rejection and rudeness.

Closely following the script provided by the market research firm, Katherine began her pitch in this manner: "Hello this is Katherine from Garson Research Associates in Chicago. I'm asking for your cooperation to participate in an important study about an exciting new product, personal coolers. My interview should take only approximately 30 minutes. May we conduct the interview right now, or would you prefer another time in the next few days?"

Four weeks into the job, Katherine was behind quota by an average of two interviews per day. Feeling fatigued one day, she slipped into introducing herself as "Kat," the name used by family members and close friends. The interviewee prospect responded, "Oh sure, Kat, I can talk now." Two days later, after having made a personal call to a friend and thus being prompted to think of herself as "Kat," Katherine again inadvertently introduced herself as "Kat" to someone on her list. Again, the prospective interviewee responded with enthusiasm: "Hey, Kat, I'm ready to talk."

Prompted by the second cooperative response, Katherine then shifted to introducing herself as "Kat." The percentage of prospects willing to be interviewed jumped from 10 percent to 20 percent. Katherine explained this unusual result to her supervisor, who said that using a nickname and achieving good results was probably just a coincidence, that maybe she had simply become more confident. The increased confidence was therefore responsible for the higher success ratio in obtaining interviews.

Katherine responded, "I'm not so sure. There must be some other reasons that "Kat" gets more interviews than "Katherine."

Questions

1. How can information about overcoming communication barriers help explain why "Kat" gets more interviews than "Katherine"?
2. How might the sex of the receiver be related to the different success ratios of "Kat" and "Katherine" in obtaining interviews?
3. Based on Kat's good results, what recommendations can you offer the research firm to help them increase the percentage of people who agree to be interviewed?

Developing Intercultural Competence

Learning Outcomes

After studying the information and doing the exercises in this chapter, you should be able to

- define culture
- define beliefs and values
- identify six major ways in which cultures differ from one another
- identify barriers to effective intercultural communication
- appreciate and understand gender differences in communication
- identify and be able to practise various strategies to reduce cross-cultural barriers

Leanne was very excited when she was chosen to fly to China to discuss the details of a tender that her company had succeeded in obtaining. The company that she worked for builds intricate measuring equipment used in mining and other geographic and geologic operations. As part of the marketing division, Leanne was to fly to China and meet with company officials for the final signing of all documentation and to become familiar with the company in China.

Leanne had learned in similar dealings elsewhere in Canada and the United States that the giving of a small gift when being treated to a meal is proper business etiquette. And she had brought an elegant gift wrapped in beautiful white and black paper just in case such an occasion arose. The contracts had all been signed, and she had done the necessary tours and become familiar with the operation, when, on her last evening she was invited out to dinner with Yen Lo, the owner, and his wife. Pleased with her gift of a carving done by a Canadian artist, she was surprised with the stony reception of her gift. The rest of the evening was not very pleasant. When Leanne returned home, she decided to approach an Asian friend of hers. When she told her about the gift, her friend suddenly interjected, "Oh my, you gave them a gift for mourning. We wrap gifts in black and white paper for those who have had a loved one die!"

Leanne made a common mistake when interacting with those from other cultures. She assumed that there were few differences between people with a North American upbringing and those with an Asian upbringing. People often assume that with technology, a global marketplace, and instant communication, differences between people are diminishing. And while this may be true in some cultures, this assumption may hurt future business. Cultures still have differences and work to maintain their own unique set of beliefs, ideas, and ways of doing things, including how to do business. Being part of a global economy and the global marketplace means that employees will need to be more aware of cultural differences and other issues in diversity. A competent employee would have researched China before landing at the airport. With some prior knowledge of cultures, Leanne would not have made such an embarrassing, and perhaps costly, mistake.

While many employees may have the opportunity to visit other countries, an extensive knowledge of cultural differences and diversity is also required in our own country. There is little doubt that Canada is a diverse nation. Canada is made up of people from diverse cultures with diverse lifestyles, and a wide range of needs and challenges. Human Relations Self-Assessment Quiz 8-1 will provide you with the opportunity to assess how ready you are to work in a culturally diverse environment.

Understanding and managing diversity and developing intercultural competence will help you become a better worker and better citizen, as many of your co-workers and clients will be very different from you. When you complete this chapter you will have an increased depth of understanding and will be better prepared to manage the diverse relationships that you will undertake both on and off the job. The facts and statistics in Exhibit 8-1 illustrate the powerful changes that are occurring in our population with regard to cultural diversity.

Keep in mind that cultures include a number of different groups, peoples, and lifestyles, including individuals with a different sexual orientation, people of the opposite gender, people with different religious affiliations and beliefs, people with disabilities, people older or much younger, and other groups that are different from your own group. For the first part of this chapter, we will explore cultural differences. Then, the barriers to effective intercultural communication will be explored. The chapter will conclude with several strategies to assist in communicating with people from diverse backgrounds, including a special section on gender differences.

Cross-Cultural Skills and Attitudes

Here are some skills and attitudes that various employers and cross-cultural experts think are important for relating effectively to co-workers in a culturally diverse environment.

	Applies to Me Now	Not There Yet
1. I have spent some time in another country.	_______	_______
2. At least one of my friends is deaf, blind, or uses a wheelchair.	_______	_______
3. Currency from other countries is as real as the currency from my own country.	_______	_______
4. I can read a language other than my own.	_______	_______
5. I can speak a language other than my own.	_______	_______
6. I can write a language other than my own.	_______	_______
7. I can understand people who speak a language other than my own.	_______	_______
8. I use my second language regularly.	_______	_______
9. My friends include people of races different from my own.	_______	_______
10. My friends include people of different ages.	_______	_______
11. I feel (or would feel) comfortable having friends with a sexual orientation different from mine.	_______	_______
12. My attitude is that cultures different from my own are equally as good.	_______	_______
13. I would be willing to (or already do) hang art from different countries in my home.	_______	_______

(continued)

14. I would accept (or have already accepted) a work assignment of more than several months in another country. ________ ________

15. I have a passport. ________ ________

Interpretation: If you answered Applies to Me Now to 10 or more of the preceding questions, you most likely function well in a multicultural work environment. If you answered Not There Yet to 10 or more questions, you need to develop more cross-cultural awareness and the skills to work effectively in a multicultural work environment. Notice that being bilingual gives you at least five points on this quiz.

SOURCE: Several ideas for statements in this quiz are derived from Ruthann Dirks and Janet Buzzard, "What CEOs Expect of Employees Hired for International Work," *Business Education Forum*, April 1997, pp. 3–7; and Gunnar Beeth, "Multicultural Managers Wanted," *Management Review*, May 1997, pp. 17–21.

Understanding Culture

Culture comes in many shapes and sizes. **Culture** can be defined as a learned and shared system of knowledge, behaviour, **beliefs**, attitudes, **values**, and norms. Culture in many ways refers to the lifestyle or way of living of a group. This system or way of life is shared by a group of people. Beliefs are the ways in which you structure your view or understanding of reality: what is true and what is false. For instance, you may have a religious belief that Jesus was the son of God. Values are more enduring than beliefs and are central to who you are. They can be defined as a set of central and enduring goals in life and ways of living that you feel are important, right, and true. The belief in Jesus may be part of a much larger value that you have in Christianity as an important part in your life. Others may have different religious beliefs and a different religious value system. Religions are part of a cultural heritage for many people. Your cultural background and all the things that make up your culture affect how you communicate with others.

Your culture came from others around you as you grew up. Through a process of **enculturation**, culture is passed on or transmitted from one generation to another. We learn our culture through the teachings of our parents, teachers, peers, various institutions, and government agencies.[1] But as we come into contact with other cultures and other cultures come into contact with us, acculturation occurs. **Acculturation** is the process through which a person's culture is modified by contact with another culture. Through contact with people from other cultures—intercultural communication—our own beliefs, values, attitudes, and ideas may change. If we look at North American culture today, there are many examples of acculturation. Many of us undergo acupuncture, take part in karate and judo, enjoy East Indian foods, eat hot dogs and watch baseball, or other things that were not initially part of our "home culture." Intercultural communication can occur between many different types of cultures and co-cultures (cultures within a culture, such as women who are also Hindu). Communication can occur between different religions, different cultures, different races, different nations, different co-cultures, and different groups within a culture. However, we need to be aware that as we communicate with others from different cultures, we are always communicating from our own cultural perspective. For example, many Western women

exhibit 8-1

The Facts and Statistics of a Culturally Diverse Population

- As of May 15, 2001, 18.4% of the Canadian population were born outside the country.
- Of those who immigrated in the 1990s, 58% were born in Asia (including the Middle East), 20% in Europe, 11% in the Caribbean and Central and South America, 8% in Africa, and 3% in the United States.
- The People's Republic of China was the leading country of birth among individuals who immigrated to Canada in the 1990s.
- 13.4% of the population identified themselves as members of visible minorities in 2001. Visible minorities are defined as "persons, other than Aboriginal peoples, who are non-Caucasian in race or non-white in colour" according to the Employment Equity Act.
- The three largest visible minority groups in 2001 were Chinese, South Asian and African Canadians, together accounting for two-thirds of the visible minority population.
- People who identified themselves as Aboriginal in 2001 accounted for 3.3% of the nation's total population, up from 2.8% in the 1996 census.
- 73% of immigrants live in three census metropolitan areas: Toronto, Vancouver, and Montreal.
- Calgary and Ottawa-Hull are emerging as centres of attraction for new immigrants, who now account for 3% of the labour force there, similar to the share of the labour force in Montreal.
- Canada is becoming more multilingual, with more than 100 native tongues spoken in significant numbers.
- Chinese is Canada's most common native tongue after English and French.
- Between 1996 and 2001, language groups from the Middle East and Asia recorded the largest gains.

SOURCES: Statistics Canada, *The Daily*, Catalogue 11-001, January 21, 2001; Statistics Canada, "The Changing Profile of Canada's Labour Force," *2001 Census: Analysis Series*, Feb. 2003, Catalogue No. 96F0030XIE2001009; Statistics Canada, "The 2001 Census of Population: Language, Mobility, and Migration," *The Daily*, Catalogue 11-001, December 10, 2002; **www.statcan.ca/Daily/English/021210/d021210a.html**.

criticize the wearing of hijab by Muslim women due to their Western views. On the other hand, Muslim women who wear hijab believe that Western women are slaves to their appearance and see their own choice of dress as being more liberated. Both sides are expressing their beliefs based on their cultural perspective.

Dimensions of Cultural Differences

Although cultures can be very different, research has identified six dimensions (or facets) of cultural values that help us understand how cultures differ from one another.[2] In other words, various cultures value different types of behaviour.

Materialism versus Concern for Others

Some cultures emphasize more materialistic values with an emphasis on assertiveness, material wealth, and achievement. Other cultures emphasize more concern for others. These cultures value relationships, caring for and nurturing others, particularly those less fortunate or able, and the quality of life.[3] The older, more traditional cultures of much of Europe, Asia, and North America are more materialistic in their cultures. Scandinavian countries all emphasize caring as a national value.

Tolerance of Uncertainty versus Avoidance of Uncertainty

Some cultures are more tolerant of ambiguity and uncertainty than other cultures. Cultures that value avoiding uncertainty are more likely to have more rigid rules for social behaviour, develop more elaborate codes of conduct, and value formality and ceremony. Workers in Latin countries highly value formality, such as lavish public receptions and processions. Cultures that are highly tolerant of uncertainty are more relaxed with rules of conduct and more permissive and casual regarding what is acceptable conduct. Americans, Canadians, and Scandinavians are much more informal. Casual observation suggests that most of the industrialized world is becoming more informal through such practices as using only first names during business introductions.

Concentrated versus Decentralized Power

Some cultures accept that power is hierarchical and that some people should have more power than others. In such cultures there are more bureaucracies that are based on power, with those higher on the ladder having more power than those lower on the ladder. People with this cultural value accept the idea that members in an organization have different levels of power and authority. The boss, therefore, makes the decisions and group members accept these decisions and comply with directions from those higher up the ladder. The cultures of Russia, France, and China are strong on the value of concentrated power.[4] Recent studies continue to indicate that this notion is reflected in a wide range of institutions including schools and businesses.[5] The cultures of the United States, Australia, Sweden, and Israel value more decentralized power and tend to minimize power differences between people. In these cultures, there is less acceptance of power and authority, and directions are accepted only when group members think the boss is right or they feel threatened.

Individualism versus Collectivism

At one end of the continuum is individualism, a mental set in which people see themselves first as individuals and believe that their own interests take priority. Individualistic cultures emphasize the individual person and give priority to personal goals over the goals of the group. Members of society who value individualism are more concerned with their careers than with the goals of their employers. Western cultures such as those of the United States, Canada, and Great

Britain emphasize the importance of individual goals and being responsible to oneself and one's immediate family.[6] Collectivistic cultures emphasize the importance of larger social groups, and individual identity is based on one's identity within a unit or group. Priority is given to group goals over personal or individual goals.[7] Members of a collectivist society are typically more concerned with the organization or the work group than with themselves. Japan and Mexico are among the countries that strongly value collectivism. Interestingly, some research indicates that African Americans tend to be more oriented to collective interests such as family than European North Americans.[8]

Urgent Time Orientation versus Casual Time Orientation

Individuals and nations value time differently. People with an urgent time orientation perceive time as a scarce resource and tend to be impatient. People with a casual time orientation view time as an unlimited resource and tend to be patient. Americans are noted for their urgent time orientation. They frequently impose deadlines and are eager to get started doing business. Asians and Middle Easterners, in contrast, are patient negotiators.

High-Context Cultures versus Low-Context Cultures

People from high-context cultures rely heavily on context and nonverbal cues in their interaction with others. Cultures that are characterized as more low-context rely on verbal language to communicate messages to others. Low-context cultures use fewer nonverbal cues to send and interpret messages.[9] To more fully understand the difference between high- and low-context cultures, think of eating at a familiar restaurant (context) that you and your friends enjoy every Friday night after work. You are well-known at this establishment by the servers. You simply have to catch the eye of a server, and lift your arm and wave. At this signal, the server comes back with your favourite before-dinner beverage. This is a high-context situation. But suppose there is a new server. You wave your arm and he or she waves back with a smile. Suddenly, you are now in a low-context situation and you will have to verbally indicate what you would like (or you may just get smiles and waves for a while and be very thirsty). Some cultures that are more high-context may use such nonverbal cues as dress, jewellery, hairstyles, and body marking to enhance messages for others within the culture. The Anglo-American (Canadian) culture is considered to be medium-low context.

Other Cultural Differences

In addition to these well-publicized dimensions of cultural values, many other cultural differences exist in the workplace that require consideration. These differences include religion, sexual orientation, lifestyle choices, and other cultural practices. An important example is that differences in religious practices often affect when people are willing to work or not work. One potential cultural clash is that the rights of an individual to freely practise and observe religious beliefs sometimes collide with company demands. Differences in religious practices must be recognized because the number of different religions in the workplace has increased substantially. A similar set of cultural differences that may affect the workplace consists of other cultural celebrations such as the Chinese New Year and various Aboriginal celebrations and ceremonies.

The key is to be alert to cultural differences and to be sensitive to how they could affect your dealings with people. Recognize that not everybody fits the same stereotype; adjust your assumptions accordingly. A furniture store manager who viewed the world with a *heterosexual bias* made the following mistake: A customer said he wished to return an end table because, after he brought it home, his partner said the table just didn't fit. The store manager responded, "What didn't your wife like about the table?" The customer replied angrily, "My partner is a man, and he said the design is atrocious." The customer then demanded a refund instead of a merchandise exchange.

How might you use this information about cultural differences to improve interpersonal relationships on the job? A starting point would be to recognize that a person's national values might influence his or her behaviour. Assume that you wanted to establish a good working relationship with a person from a high-context culture. An effective starting point would be to emphasize body language when communicating with that individual. A related point is that people from high-context cultures are more likely to touch and kiss strangers. As Fernando, who was raised in the Dominican Republic and is studying in the United States, said, "In my country I hug people I meet for the first time. When I do it here, they think I'm very rude."

Since the focus of this chapter is to improve intercultural competence, let's focus now on the skills required to manage in a diverse society by examining the barriers to effective intercultural communication. While we will largely focus on major cultures, keep in mind that these barriers can also exist between co-cultures and other groups.

Barriers to Effective Intercultural Communication

In a multicultural and multigroup society, problems in communication are bound to happen as we attempt to communicate with those different from ourselves. It is not the struggle that occurs as we attempt to understand others' messages that creates true problems; it is the barriers that we consciously or even unconsciously erect. Let's examine some of these barriers in more detail.

Perceptual Expectations

Achieving good cross-cultural relations is hampered somewhat by people's predisposition to discriminate. They do so as a perceptual shortcut, much like stereotyping. Psychologist Diane Halpern explains how the process works: "Even if you have absolutely no prejudice, you are influenced by your expectations. A small woman of colour doesn't look like a corporate executive. If you look at the heads of corporations, they are tall, slender, white males. They are not fat. They are not in a wheelchair. They are not too old. Anything that doesn't conform to expectations is a misfit."[10]

Halpern made this comment several years ago, and it is still generally true. However, many women today occupy top-level positions in business, there are many overweight male executives, and many executives are old. Yet the message about perceptual expectations is important. We have to overcome this form of discrimination to enhance cross-cultural relations.

Positive expectations or stereotypes can also create some barriers to cross-cultural relations. Two company representatives were entertaining Sophie, a work associate from Jamaica. They assumed that because Sophie was black and Jamaican, she enjoyed dancing, so they invited her to a dance club. Sophie was a little taken aback and said, "What makes you think I like to dance? Not every Jamaican lady has natural rhythm." Similarly, on the job, we sometimes think that everybody from a certain national group has the characteristics of that group. For example, not all Chinese workers are methodical and precise, and have good eye-hand coordination and exceptional math skills.

Stereotypes, Prejudice, and Discrimination

Stereotypes are formed as part of the categorization process of perception. When we **stereotype**, we place people into categories or groups based on broad generalizations and assumptions that we perceive about a particular group. The problem with stereotypes is that we "lump" large numbers of people into the same category, often with a minimum of knowledge and experience about that particular category. For example, if you were to find out that Terri wears glasses, had extremely high marks during high school, and writes textbooks, you might categorize her as a "brain" or "nerd." Such an assumption would not be based on knowledge of all the other things that make up her personality. Exhibit 8-2 below lists some common cultural stereotypes.

Once we have a stereotype of a person, we tend to treat him or her according to this stereotype, and so our responses to that person become biased and limited. For example, if a sales associate has identified a prospective customer as

exhibit 8-2

Common Cultural Stereotypes

Jews are good with money.
All women are soft.
All cops are pigs.
Arabs are sneaky.
Asian students are smart.
Blacks have rhythm.
Mentally ill people are violent.
Gay men are effeminate.
All Italians are Mafia.
Young people are troublemakers.
Native Canadians are drunks.
Sikhs are terrorists.
Jamaican men are drug dealers.
Bikers are gang members.

Source: Adapted from Robert Stansfield, *Issues in Policing: A Canadian Perspective* (Toronto: Thompson Educational Publishing, 1996), p. 136.

"poor," the associate may not give the individual the same service he or she would have if the customer had been identified as "rich." When the sales associate notices the person browsing through a rack of reduced-price merchandise, this is used to support the stereotype of "poor."

If we start to treat someone differently due to this stereotyping, we have developed a prejudicial attitude and may discriminate against members of this group. **Prejudice** is an unjustifiable negative attitude toward a group and its members; **discrimination** is the resulting unjustifiable negative behaviour based on this attitude.[11] Such behaviour may include verbal expressions of dislike, avoidance of group members, actual discriminatory practices such as excluding group members from certain activities or rights, and physical attacks. At the furthest extreme is the extermination of a group, as Adolf Hitler attempted during World War II.

Ethnocentrism

When you belong to a certain culture or group, you usually prefer the way that things are done within that group. For example, many people celebrate a holiday on December 25 that involves a figure called Santa Claus who brings toys and presents to children. More gifts are exchanged among friends and family, a tree is covered in decorations, a meal is served complete with a roasted stuffed bird, and special songs are sung. If you are part of this culture (or maybe even if you are not), you know that this is called "Christmas."

Other cultures also celebrate this time of year, but their celebrations do not involve gift-giving. You may have heard people say that children should receive gifts anyway because it would be unfair if these children were denied presents. This type of thinking is an example of **ethnocentrism**. Ethnocentrism is a belief or conviction that your cultural traditions, beliefs, ideas, and convictions are somehow superior to others'. When we state that others' ideas and beliefs about how to celebrate a holiday are erroneous, we are making the assumption that our way is better, more just, more fair, or right. This means that their way is worse, unjust, unfair, or wrong. If you want to erect a barrier, voicing ethnocentric views such as this one is one good way to do it!

Verbal and Nonverbal Communication Barriers—Different Words, Gestures, and Symbols

In Chapter 7 we discussed a number of problems with words. Words can have different meanings. This may be especially true when they are translated into another language. In Roger Axtell's book *Do's and Taboos of Hosting International Visitors*, he presents a number of examples of advertising "gone bad" because of mistranslated advertisements.[12] Here are just two examples:

> Pepsi's slogan "Come Alive with Pepsi" translated to "Pepsi brings your ancestors back from the grave" in the Taiwanese market.
>
> Parker Pen's famous "Jotter" ballpoint pen translated into something like the "jockstrap" pen in some languages and so could not be advertised as a "Jotter" in some cultures.

The meanings of gestures also vary depending on culture. Chapter 7 presented a couple of examples of how an appropriate gesture in one culture may have an inappropriate meaning in another culture. Giving the "thumbs up" sign in much of North America means "way to go" or "great"; in other cultures it translates to "up yours."

Just imagine a situation where a foreign visitor asks you for directions in almost nonexistent English. You basically sign the direction using gestures and pointing. He smiles and nods thank-you, and you feel good for helping someone. As the foreigner walks away in the right direction, he turns around and you give him the "thumbs up" gesture. Imagine your feelings when he screams back at you, gives you the same gesture (or one you do not understand) and storms on down the street!

Other symbols of what is important or cherished by one culture may also be misunderstood by another culture. Remember that symbols represent objects, concepts, and thoughts, as was discussed in Chapter 7. People who are Christians value the symbol of the cross and display or wear crosses as symbols of their beliefs. The Star of David is an important religious symbol to those of the Jewish faith. The turban and the kirpan (a kind of dagger that is a religious symbol) worn by Sikhs are important to their faith.[13] On and off the job, people different from us may value different ideas represented by various symbols.

Different Norms and Codes of Conduct

Norms are guidelines (usually unwritten) that govern the behaviour of members in a specific group. It should come as no surprise to you that different groups have norms that may differ from those of other groups. Also, what is permissible conduct in one group may be frowned upon and even punished in another group. Human Relations Skill-Building Exercise 8-1 presents some information about business and social etiquette in China.

At times, we may also make the mistake of assuming that others are similar to us and then become confused when they act differently from our expectations. We may unknowingly insult others from a different culture or they may unknowingly insult us. If you are from a culture that highly values time such as the Austrians, the Swiss, or the English, you may feel anger when your new Italian acquaintance arrives 30 minutes late for a party. Since most Italians do not adhere to rigid time schedules for social events, you have just experienced a clash of different cultural norms.

Gender Differences in Communication Style

Before we move on to discussing strategies for improving intercultural competence, we need to examine gender differences. If there are differences in how the genders communicate, an understanding of these differences will help us to communicate with the opposite sex. Despite the movement toward equality of sexes in the workplace, substantial interest has arisen in identifying differences in communication style between men and women. Interest in this topic was fuelled by the extraordinarily successful book *Men Are from Mars, Women Are from Venus*.[14]

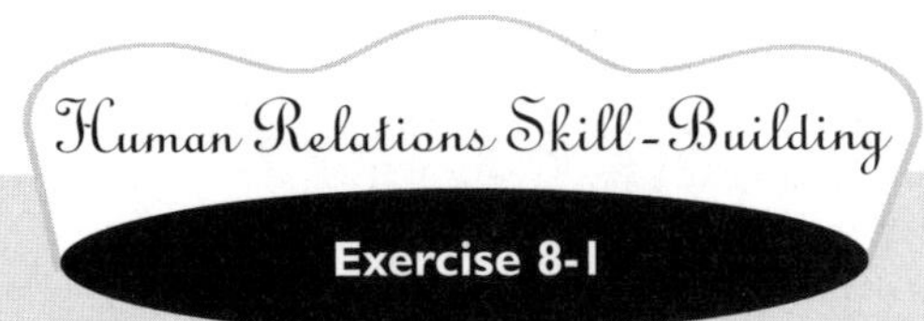

Business and Social Etiquette in China

Part of developing skills to deal successfully with individuals from other cultures is to understand and appreciate differences. Below are a few rules from China. Read the rules and then reply with the rule or norm from your culture.

When greeting a Chinese person, use his or her family name only. The Chinese family name comes first. For example, a man named Ling Pan Fu would be addressed as Mr. Ling.

Your group? ______________________________

____

The Chinese way of greeting is a nod or slight bow.

Your group? ______________________________

____

At a dinner, always leave something on your plate.

Your group? ______________________________

____

Never wrap a gift in plain black and white paper, as these are the colours of mourning.

Your group? ______________________________

____

Deny a compliment graciously.

Your group? ______________________________

____

SOURCE: Sunun Setboonsarng, Greater China and Southeast Asia Trade Development Officer, *Business and Social Etiquette in China*, Oregon Economic Development Department, 1999. Visit the website at **www.econ.state.or.us/oregontrade/chinabt.htm**.

People who are aware of these differences face fewer communication problems between themselves and members of the opposite sex. As we describe these differences, recognize that they are group stereotypes. Individual communication styles are usually more important than group ones (men versus women). Furthermore, many research studies fail to show significant gender differences in communication style.[15] Here we will describe the major findings of gender differences in communication patterns.[16]

1. *Women prefer to use conversation for rapport building.* For most women, the intent of conversation is to build rapport and connections with people. It has been said that men are driven by transactions while women are driven by relations. Women are therefore more likely to emphasize similarities, to listen intently, and to be supportive.
2. *Men prefer to use talk primarily as a means to preserve independence and status by displaying knowledge and skill.* When most men talk, they want to receive positive evaluation from others and maintain their hierarchical status within the group. Men are therefore more oriented to giving a report while women are more interested in establishing rapport.
3. *Women want empathy, not solutions.* When women share feelings of being stressed out, they seek empathy and understanding. If they feel they have been listened to carefully, they begin to relax. When listening to a woman sharing these feelings, a man may feel blamed for her problems or that he has failed the woman in some way. To feel useful, the man might offer solutions to the woman's problem.
4. *Men prefer to work out their problems by themselves, whereas women prefer to talk out solutions with another person.* Women look on having and sharing problems as an opportunity to build and deepen relationships. Men are more likely to look on problems as challenges they must meet on their own. One communication consequence of these differences is that men may become uncommunicative when they have a problem.
5. *Men tend to be more directive and less apologetic in their conversation, while women are more polite and apologetic.* Women are therefore more likely to frequently use the phrases "I'm sorry" and "Thank you," even when there is no need to express apology or gratitude. Men less frequently say they are sorry for the same reason they rarely ask directions when they are lost while driving: They perceive communications as competition, and they do not want to appear vulnerable.
6. *Women tend to be more conciliatory when facing differences, while men become more intimidating.* Again, women are more interested in building relationships, while men are more concerned about coming out ahead.
7. *Men are more interested than women in calling attention to their accomplishments or hogging recognition.* One consequence of this difference is that men are more likely to dominate discussion during meetings. Another consequence is that women are more likely to help a co-worker perform well. In one instance a sales representative who had already made her sales quota for the month turned over an excellent prospect to a co-worker. She reasoned, "It's somebody else's turn. I've received more than my fair share of bonuses for the month."
8. *Men and women interrupt others for different reasons.* Men are more likely to interrupt to introduce a new topic or complete a sentence for someone else. Women are more likely to interrupt to clarify the other person's thought or offer support.
9. *Women are more likely to use a gentle expletive, while men tend to be harsher.* For example, if a woman locks herself out of the car she is likely to say,

"Oh dear." In the same situation a man is likely to use a more "colourful" four-letter word. (Do you think this difference really exists?)

How can the information just presented help overcome communication problems on the job? As a starting point, remember that gender differences often exist. Understanding these differences will help you interpret the communications behaviour of people. For example, if a male co-worker is not as polite as you would like, remember that he is simply engaging in gender-typical behaviour. Do not take it personally.

A woman can remind herself to speak up more in meetings because her natural tendency might be toward holding back. She might say to herself, "I must watch out to avoid gender-typical behaviour in this situation." A man might remind himself to be more polite and supportive to co-workers. The problem is that, although such behaviour is important, his natural tendency might be to skip saying "thank you."

A woman should not take it personally when a male co-worker or subordinate is tight-lipped when faced with a problem. She should recognize that he may need more encouragement to talk about his problems than a woman would. If a man persists in not wanting to talk about the problem, the woman might say: "It looks like you want to work out this problem on your own. Go ahead. I'm available if you want to talk about it."

Men and women should recognize that when women talk over problems, they might not be seeking hard-hitting advice. Instead, they may simply be searching for a sympathetic ear so they can deal with the emotional aspects of the problem.

Improving Intercultural Communication and Fostering Understanding

Depending on where you choose to work, your contact with various cultures and groups will vary. If you work in a large urban centre, the cultural and ethnic diversity will be more pronounced than in a more rural setting. However, all settings will have a large diversity of groups. It is in your best personal and professional interest to learn skills that will help you communicate in this diverse nation.

Actively Seek Knowledge and Information

Ignorance of different groups and their codes of conduct or other characteristics is often at the root of communication problems and barriers. We all have our views of the world and how it works, but we must remember that this view was taught to us within the confines of our home culture. In order to understand other groups, you need to prepare yourself by gaining knowledge and information.

This knowledge and information can be gained from many sources, including books about different countries, travel brochures, art, geography books and maps, and the internet. If you travel as part of your career, time spent researching today may make it unnecessary to spend time tomorrow regretting your major breach of etiquette in a particular country. The previous box about business and social etiquette in China was accessed via the internet. Before we launch into criticism or expressing our own ethnocentric views, we should take the time to research the differences. Such knowledge will often lead to better understanding. Human Relations Skill-Building Exercise 8-2 may be a good way to start learning about another culture. Many companies offer training courses in diversity. Other companies offer tuition or other incentives to learn about cultures or to learn another language.

Demonstrate Empathy and Respect

When you meet or deal with an individual from a different background, try to put yourself in his or her place. Listen and respond actively, using the skills from Chapter 7. The person may have trouble with your language and you may have trouble with his or her language. Your nonverbal communication may be more important than words, as you may have to rely on gesturing and pointing (just be careful of how you gesture!). The key is to try to understand the person and his or her point of view. Understanding and empathy do not necessarily mean agreement, but understanding and empathy will create the groundwork for mutual respect.

This respect comes from the belief that another person's culture, however different from yours, is equally as good as yours. Respecting other people's customs can translate into specific attitudes, such as respecting one co-worker for wearing a yarmulke on Friday and another for wearing an African costume to celebrate Kwanza. Another way of being respectful would be to listen carefully to the opinion of a senior worker who says the company should never have replaced human phone-answerers with voice mail (even though you disagree).

A Plan for Learning

Identify a culture, race, or group that you have had very little experience with and limited knowledge about. Develop a plan that will help you learn the following things about this culture:

- How do they greet friends and strangers?
- What are some special holidays and celebrations?
- What is the structure of the family?
- What are the foods they typically eat and how do they organize their meals?
- Are there significant religious practices or rites of passage in this culture?

While these are only a few questions, you may want to add a few of your own. Where can you get this information? Consult the library or travel agencies, conduct personal interviews of members of this culture, telephone community associations, or try the internet. You may be surprised by what you learn, and you'll have developed at least one skill (knowledge) to help you adapt to diversity!

An aspect of respecting all workers that has won attention recently is the importance of respecting the rights of majorities, particularly white males. Gillian Flynn, a human resource professional, states the problem this way: "These days things aren't so easy for white males. They've been under attack for a long time, en masse, for the problems of women and minorities. And some should be, certainly. But it's ironic that a movement that demands equal treatment for individuals often lumps all men into one troublesome bundle."[17] Following this logic, a true cross-cultural person would not have negative attitudes toward a person just because that person is a white male.

Do Not Be Afraid to Ask Questions

Sometimes we are afraid to ask questions. We engage in negative self-talk and say things to ourselves such as "I don't want to appear stupid," "This will be too embarrassing," or "What if I offend her?" If you have travelled, you may have found yourself in the uncomfortable position of not knowing what to do next. So you try watching and copying and then end up feeling foolish. Most people are rarely offended if you ask questions. For instance, the request "I'm not sure how I am supposed to do this. Could you show me?" rarely causes alarm. In fact, many people are pleased and complimented by your desire to learn their traditions or way of doing things. Many immigrants to Canada are also willing to share their stories of their countries and why they chose to immigrate. Read the Canada Today feature below for an interview with a recent Canadian immigrant who was willing to share his story.

Canada Today

An Immigrant's Story: A Soft Landing

During a search for information about immigration to Canada, an interesting website popped up. The website "Soft Landings" quotes the interesting president of the organization's Canadian chapter, Harris Abro. His story of immigration is an interesting one, and of special interest is the design of "Soft Landings" to help others who immigrate to Canada (or one of several other countries) or who are thinking about immigration. This is his story, most of it in his own words via telephone and email interviews.

> I came to Canada because I was living in a country with an uncertain future. Crime and violence was a problem in South Africa and there was little respect for people's rights or their property. I wanted to move to a society where people showed respect to others and valued personal freedoms and liberties. It was wonderful to walk down the streets in a Canadian city without any fear. It was great to see houses with no fences and no security alarms. In this country, children can be seen playing in the streets, women walking or jogging alone without the fear present in my mother country.
>
> Why did I choose Canada as my country for immigration? The truth is that I was single and had no family or friends in any other countries throughout the world. My previous profession (lawyer) was also extremely limiting in allowing me to apply for immigration in most countries (including Canada). There was initially no prospect of practising as a lawyer in Canada without vigorous obstacles that needed to be over-

come (qualifying for and going back to law school, doing articles and also writing the Bar exam—at best probably a three-year procedure. (It should be noted that this procedure has now been simplified to an extent.) My sister and brother-in-law were immigrating to Canada so I decided that I would go to a country where I at least had my family.

On arriving in Canada, I soon realized how different things were to be. A change in profession, a separation from friends and family, adaptation to new weather conditions, and one or two bad business experiences taught me that this was not an easy transition. If only someone had told me what to expect; if only I'd had a network of people to support and advise me on how differently things worked in this new country; if only I had been better prepared for being in this country.

For example, after arriving in Canada, unsure of what I would do, I was approached by a realtor introduced by an acquaintance. The realtor advised a group of us about a "revolutionary" business opportunity that would take the Vancouver market by storm. It involved a home delivery service that was just starting out. It was a franchise operation and sounded very interesting. Obviously as new immigrants we were extremely vulnerable and had no one to turn to for general advice. We accordingly did our due diligence as best we could, but not knowing the market or opportunities, or having any contacts, we were limited in our knowledge. We relied to a large extent on the advice of the realtor and the franchiser. It turned out that many of the "facts" were misrepresented to us and after we invested in this venture, it went bust. A lesson learned.

However, I did find gainful employment. Initially, when I started business (on my own, on a commission basis) I had absolutely no "natural market"—not knowing anybody in the city. My first three sales were to my brother-in-law, my sister and myself! I gradually started meeting more and more ex-South Africans and getting support from them. Today I have developed a fairly extensive client base of people from all over the world, and also many Canadians. For the past nine years, I've been involved in the insurance and financial planning industry. I was recruited as an insurance agent and began my career with Canada Life. Since then my knowledge and experience have developed in this industry and today I am with a very well-known and established firm in Vancouver.

About a year after arriving here, I went to South Africa with an immigration lawyer friend and spoke at some seminars that were being hosted for prospective immigrants. I also developed a relationship with personnel at the Canadian High Commission. They were very encouraging about my efforts and were comfortable to allow informal distribution of the first Soft Landings brochure in 1994 at their office. I continued to visit South Africa over the years that followed and held many information sessions there. Our aim is to provide a support network and assistance for immigrants to Canada.

With no real experiences of prejudice or discrimination other than the local people having difficulty with the South African accent and the way they speak, there are still difficulties and issues such as having no "Canadian experience," no credit history in Canada, no references, no driver's licence. As an immigrant it's therefore very difficult to get a rental suite, purchase property without a significant down-payment, apply and compete in the job market unless you have specialist skills, apply for a credit card or even get a telephone.

Harris does have some advice for those who are new immigrants or those who are considering immigration:

Be prepared to adapt to life in Canada and the Canadian lifestyle and habits. Don't try and change Canadians to be like you, but rather accept that they are different and do things differently. Be prepared to change. Try and understand that the process that you will go through is different from any experience that you have ever had in your life. Saying goodbye to friends and family will be extremely traumatic. Be prepared for this. Canada will offer you a wonderful life and lifestyle. It may take a while to get used to the differences, so be patient. In the end it will all be worthwhile and a wonderful life-enhancing experience.

I think the hardest thing about being an immigrant is that you're always split between two lives: the life that you lived pre-immigration and the new life that you've developed post-immigration. It's hard to imagine that things are still continuing in your "old life": people that you knew, places that you were familiar with—life still carries on as normal. Yet you are far, far away and starting a new life that's totally new and different.

So for the most part you develop a sort of "defence mechanism"—a way to deal with things. You try to forget about the old life, the way things were, and get on with your new life. But every once in a while, sometimes more often than not, you're brought back to your old life. A call from a family member, an email from a friend, news of someone in hospital, someone ill or someone passing away brings you back to that old life. Or happy events such as a friend's wedding or a new baby also make you realize how much you sometimes miss your old life. Then there's the guilt that is often present as you feel that you have left parents far behind, "abandoned" friends, careers, and people that depended on you. Also, there is that constant fear of receiving that devastating phone call telling you that someone is sick—"come back as soon as you can."

And then, as time goes by, it's the new life, the new friends, the new family in your adopted country that make your life here worthwhile and wonderful. It's quite a challenge and it can be quite an emotional roller coaster to deal with everything. But with a site such as Soft Landings, some of that roller coaster ride may be avoided and your landing may be a little "softer."

Soft Landings is well worth a visit—and a pleasant journey in itself. To explore this interesting site designed to assist immigrants, go to **www.softlandings.com**.

SOURCE: This story has been published with the permission of Harris Abro, President and Founder, Soft Landings International.

Develop Tolerance and Sensitivity

In this context, tolerance does not mean that you stoically put up with something whether you like it or not, such as tolerating going to the lectures for a course you do not like. In this context, **tolerance** means being aware of and acknowledging that cultural differences exist. This kind of tolerance is based on empathy and knowledge that will allow you to cope with cultural and group differences. If your son or daughter comes home from a new friend's house and exclaims that Sam has two moms, you can use this opportunity to explain about same-sex couples (depending on the age of your son or daughter) in a positive and enlightened manner. This kind of tolerance depends on your flexibility and your willingness to understand how others are different.

When working with people from different cultures, even from one's own country, one must be patient, adaptable, tolerant, flexible, and willing to listen and learn. These characteristics are part of **cultural sensitivity**, an awareness of and a willingness to investigate why people of another culture act as they do.[18] A person with cultural sensitivity will recognize certain nuances in customs that will help build better relationships with people from different cultural backgrounds. Keep in mind the cultural differences that have been discussed in this chapter. Try to understand and even use your knowledge of some of these differences. For example, on a business trip you are invited to the manager's home for dinner. You notice that she takes off her street shoes upon entering the house. By also doing so, you are establishing rapport with your manager.

Avoid Making Negative Judgments

"Here we go again, another customer from welfare alley!" is a negative and prejudiced statement. First, because the customer is from an area where many people have low incomes, an assumption has been made that this customer is on welfare. Second, this statement also indicates how the person feels about individuals who receive social assistance. Third, it also assumes that individuals who receive social assistance are somehow not as valued as customers who do not receive assistance. Could this attitude then lead to different treatment of the customer? Possibly and probably.

There is evidence that attitudes can influence behaviour. For example, according to the **theory of reasoned action**, strong norms about how you are expected to behave and strong beliefs that a certain outcome will occur will influence your behaviour.[19] In other words, your attitude about the behaviour and your norms about complying with the behaviour will lead you to behave in a specific way. For instance, if Carlos believes in the platform of the Conservative Party, helps out with the election for the Conservative Party, tries to coerce his friends to put up Conservative support signs in their yards, and all his friends know and expect him to vote Conservative, chances are his friends can predict his behaviour. Carlos will most likely vote Conservative.

Good examples of negative attitudes and negative judgments followed by negative treatment can be found in the workplace even if they are not vocalized. Denying promotion due to race or sex (although the reason is probably not explicitly stated), not hiring due to race, sex, or sexual orientation, and a host of other examples of discrimination may still occur at many workplaces even though they violate the Human Rights Act of Canada and the Canada Labour Code.

Of course, just because an individual holds an attitude about something does not mean this attitude will necessarily be reflected in that person's behaviour. For example, an employee who is racist may hide this racism knowing that there may be repercussions for any discriminatory behaviour. People may not engage in such behaviour because they know it is illegal (for example, firing someone because of sexual orientation), and intentions do not always materialize into behaviours.[20] The point is that having negative attitudes and making negative judgments will influence how we think about, and perhaps how we treat (or mistreat), others.

How can we avoid making negative judgments? First, remind yourself that you may be suffering from a bout of ethnocentrism. Your ways and ideas are not better, just different. Secondly, ask yourself "Am I thinking about this person in a stereotypical way?" Lastly, acknowledge differences as challenges, not barriers. A challenge is something that we can "take on" rather than a barrier that has to be broken or made to disappear.

Minimize Cultural Bloopers

An effective way of being culturally sensitive is to minimize actions that are likely to offend people from another culture because of differing values. Cultural bloopers are most likely to take place when you are visiting another country. The same bloopers, however, can also be committed with people from a different culture within your own country. To avoid these bloopers, you must carefully observe persons from another culture. Studying another culture through reading is also helpful.

E-commerce and other forms of internet communication have created new opportunities for creating cultural bloopers. Website developers and content providers must have good cross-cultural literacy, including an awareness of how information might be misinterpreted. Here is a sampling of potential problems:

- Numerical date formats are often used for convenience. However, to an American, 4/9/01 means April 9, 2001 (or 1901!), whereas many Europeans would interpret the same numerical expression as September 4, 2001.

- Colours on websites must be chosen carefully. For example, in some cultures purple is the colour of royalty, whereas in Brazil, purple is associated with death.
- Be careful of metaphors that may not make sense to a person for whom your language is a second language. Examples include "We've encountered an ethical meltdown" and "Our biggest competitor is over the hill."

International business specialist Rick Borelli recommends communicating your message directly in your customer's native tongue for a competitive advantage.[21] The translator, of course, must have good knowledge of the subtleties of the language to avoid a blooper. An English-to-French translator used the verb *baiser* instead of *baisser* to describe a program of lowering prices. *Baisser* is the French verb "to lower," whereas *baiser* is the verb "to kiss." Worse, in everyday language, *baiser* is a verb that refers to having intimate physical relationships!

Keep two key facts in mind when attempting to avoid cultural mistakes. One is that members of any cultural group show individual differences. What one member of the group might regard as an insensitive act, another might welcome. Recognize also that one or two cultural mistakes will not peg you permanently as a boor. Human Relations Skill-Building Exercise 8-3 will help you minimize certain cultural bloopers. The suggestions there will lead to cross-cultural skill development if practised in the right setting. During the next 30 days, look for an opportunity to relate to a person from another culture in the way described in these suggestions. Observe the reaction of the other person for feedback on your cross-cultural effectiveness.

Cultural Mistakes to Avoid with Selected Cultural Groups

Western Europe

Great Britain

- Asking personal questions. The British protect their privacy.
- Thinking that a business person from England is unenthusiastic when he or she says, "Not bad at all." English people understate positive emotion.
- Gossiping about royalty.

France

- Expecting to complete work during the French two-hour lunch.
- Attempting to conduct significant business during August—*les vacances* (vacation time).
- Greeting a French person for the first time and not using a title such as "sir" or "madam" (or monsieur, madame, or mademoiselle).

Italy

- Eating too much pasta, as it is not the main course.
- Handing out business cards freely. Italians use them infrequently.

Spain

- Expecting punctuality. Your appointments will usually arrive 20 to 30 minutes late.
- Making the American sign for OK with your thumb and forefinger. In Spain (and many other countries) this is vulgar.

Scandinavia (Denmark, Sweden, Norway)

- Being overly rank-conscious. Don't expect Scandinavians to pay close attention to a person's place in the hierarchy.
- Introducing conflict among Swedish work associates. Swedes go out of their way to avoid conflict.

Asia

All Asian

- Pressuring an Asian job applicant or employee to brag about his or her accomplishments. Asians feel self-conscious when boasting about individual accomplishments. They prefer to let the record speak for itself. In addition, they prefer to talk about group, rather than individual, accomplishments.

Japan

- Shaking hands or hugging Japanese (as well as other Asians) in public. Japanese consider the practices to be offensive.
- Not interpreting "We'll consider it" as a no when spoken by a Japanese business person. Japanese negotiators mean no when they say, "We'll consider it."
- Not giving small gifts to Japanese when conducting business. Japanese are offended by not receiving these gifts.
- Giving your business card to a Japanese businessperson more than once. Japanese prefer to give and receive business cards only once.

China

- Using black borders on stationery and business cards because black is associated with death.
- Giving small gifts to Chinese when conducting business. Chinese are offended by these gifts.
- Making cold calls on Chinese business executives. An appropriate introduction is required for a first-time meeting with a Chinese official.

Korea

- Saying no. Koreans feel it is important to have visitors leave with good feelings.

India

- Telling Indians you prefer not to eat with your hands. If the Indians are not using cutlery when eating, they expect you to do likewise.

(continued)

Mexico and Latin America

Mexico

- Flying into a Mexican city in the morning and expecting to close a deal by lunch. Mexicans build business relationships slowly.

Brazil

- Attempting to impress Brazilians by speaking a few words of Spanish. Portuguese is the official language of Brazil.

Most Latin American countries

- Wearing elegant and expensive jewellery during a business meeting. Most Latin Americans think people should appear more conservative during a business meeting.

NOTE: A cultural mistake for Canadians and Americans to avoid when conducting business in most countries outside North America is to insist on getting down to business quickly. Other stereotyped North American traits to avoid are aggressiveness, impatience, and frequent interruptions to get your point across. North Americans in small towns also like to build a relationship before getting down to business.

Summary

In this chapter, we have explored diversity in Canada. We have defined and looked at what a culture is and how culture is transmitted to others through acculturation and enculturation. Six dimensions of cultural values help us understand how cultures differ from one another: (1) individualism versus collectivism, (2) acceptance of power and authority, (3) materialism versus concern for others, (4) formality versus informality, (5) urgent time orientation versus casual time orientation, and (6) high-context versus low-context cultures (with an emphasis on body language). Many other cultural differences, such as religious practices, are also noteworthy. It is important to be alert to possible cultural differences.

Significant barriers to effective intercultural communication include our perceptual expectations and stereotyping, prejudice, and discrimination. Often stereotypes and prejudicial attitudes lead to discrimination, which can take a number of forms ranging in severity from negative feelings about a group to actual elimination of the group members. Other barriers include ethnocentrism, different verbal and nonverbal communication and use of symbols, and different norms and codes of conduct. Gender differences can also lead to misunderstanding between men and women at work as well as in other settings.

To improve your ability to span and conquer these barriers, you can use a variety of strategies to increase your intercultural competence. Actively seek knowledge and information about others different from you, demonstrate empathy and respect, don't be afraid to ask questions, and develop tolerance and sensitivity. Two other important strategies are to avoid negative judgments and avoid making cultural bloopers.

Questions and Activities

1. What do you feel are the main reasons for intolerance and prejudice? Support your views.
2. Several well-known companies conduct an *awareness week* to celebrate diverse groups such as Aboriginal groups or homosexuals. What is your opinion of the effectiveness of such activities for bringing about workplace harmony?
3. Have you been a victim of prejudice or discrimination? How did it feel? What was your reaction?
4. Many people are against the active recruitment of visible minorities and women in many professions. Should hiring be based solely on group membership or should the best person be hired regardless of race, ethnic origin, or gender? Support your opinion.
5. Differences in communication patterns between men and women have been identified. What impact will this information have on your communications with men and women?
6. Develop a list of what you perceive to be essential skills for working with others from different cultures or groups. Identify which skills you currently possess. How could you learn the other skills?
7. When you meet someone from another culture, what can you do to demonstrate that you respect that person's culture?
8. Many people speak loudly to deaf people, blind people, and those who speak a different language. Based on the information presented in this chapter, what mistakes are these people making?
9. Interview a person who has moved to Canada recently. What difficulties did he or she have after first arriving in Canada? What helped the person adjust to a new life in Canada?

Internet Skill Builder

Cultural Exploration

A useful way to learn about another culture is to discover new information, and the internet is a great source. Choose a culture you would like to learn more about. This culture could be anything you want, from same-sex orientation to a different ethnic group to a physical or mental challenge. To get started, use a search engine such as Yahoo, Excite, or Google and type in your choice. After examining several sites, bookmark your favourite site so that you can visit it frequently to learn more. You might even choose a language you don't speak and study it for a few minutes every day!

Weblinks

www-cgi.cs.cmu.edu/Web/Unofficial/Canadiana
This is the site for Canadiana, The Canadian Resource Page, with links to a variety of Canadian sites including government, entertainment, and so on.

www.tgmag.ca/magic/index.html
This is the Magic Assembling showcase where you can take a tour and explore the multicultural complexity of Metropolitan Toronto. There are also articles about different cultures and cultural traditions.

www.citzine.ca
This is Citzine, a youth site about being or becoming a Canadian citizen.

www.cic.gc.ca
From the Government of Canada, this is the Citizenship and Immigration department site.

Human Relations Case Study

THE ETHNOCENTRIC MARKETING ASSISTANT

Tamara graduated from a small college in her hometown and moved to a large city. With a diploma in marketing, she was particularly interested in the clothing industry. Although not exactly sure what she wanted to do, she was hired by a small clothing manufacturer in their shipping and receiving department. Here she assisted with packaging clothing for exporting to other countries. She also helped in receiving when different supplies arrived such as cloth and other sewing requirements. Tamara had a bubbly personality, always seemed to have fun at work, and was popular with her co-workers who were for the most part young, white, and also recent graduates. With her excellent work record and personality, she was promoted "upstairs" in two years as a marketing assistant to the head of marketing. As employees of a small company, everyone participated in all areas of the business. Ideas were freely exchanged between marketing, design, and manufacturing. Tamara was enthusiastic about her new job and let everyone know how exciting this was for her. She quickly engaged in conversation with everybody.

As part of her "cute" style, she developed nicknames for everyone, just as she had in shipping and receiving. She called her new boss "Chow Mein" instead of Chow Ling Su. As she whirred past people she gave affectionate pats to everyone. She often imitated the accent of the head of manufacturing, an older German-born man, and called him "Herbie" instead of Mr. Hermann as others did. She performed all of her duties enthusiastically and loved to tell jokes, sing, and chew gum while she worked. Although people often frowned at her antics, she seemed oblivious to any signals that her behaviour was any kind of problem. A couple of people had jokingly asked her to calm down a little and not to be continually so personal with them. Tamara just laughed it off. At Christmas, she gave out cards with Christian themes and kissed people while she dangled mistletoe over their heads. To Chow Ling Su, she asked, "Hey, what animal is it for you people this New Year?"

At her three-month performance appraisal she was told by Chow Ling Su, "You have some good knowledge of marketing, especially for the younger crowd, and we are pleased by many of your ideas. However, your behaviour leaves much to be desired. Your manner is insulting to many of us, and you have not changed even though many of us have asked you to do so. If you do not change, I fear that we may have to terminate your employment here."

Devastated, Tamara replied, "I don't understand, Chow Mein! I come to work on time, I help out, and my ideas have been adopted and appear to be working. What do you mean my manner is insulting? I treat everyone like old friends." Tamara burst into tears. "I don't understand what you mean. For over two years, I've been a good employee."

Questions

1. What cultural mistakes is Tamara making?
2. In what ways is Tamara displaying an ethnocentric attitude?
3. Offer Tamara several suggestions to improve her intercultural competence.
4. What basic communication skills do you feel that Tamara should use to improve her relations with her co-workers?

Developing Sensitivity to Other Cultures

With one person playing the role of Tamara and another playing the role of Chow Ling Su, continue the scene of the performance appraisal described above. Chow Ling Su will use appropriate communication skills to assist Tamara in developing cultural awareness. Tamara must also use good communication skills as she responds to the feedback of Chow Ling Su.

Handling Conflict and Being Assertive

Learning Outcomes

After studying the information and doing the exercises in this chapter, you should be able to

- understand why conflict between people takes place so often
- pinpoint several helpful and harmful consequences of conflict
- resolve conflict more effectively
- improve your negotiating skills
- practise various techniques to improve your assertiveness with others

Both on and off the job, we face a wide array of problems. Some of these problems include conflict with others. For example, Sunai is a mid-level manager. Another manager persists in verbally harassing her by telling her that she is incompetent. As they are both managers in different departments, they report to different supervisors. Sunai does her best to avoid this man, but it is not always possible. Over time, this continued hostility is getting to her. What is Sunai to do? As this behaviour is persisting, her only option is to confront the person directly. If the harassment continues, she may be able to go to Human Resources and find out her rights to work in a harassment-free workplace.

This situation illustrates the underlying nature of **conflict**, a condition that exists when two sets of demands, goals, or motives are incompatible. You cannot work both an eleven-to-seven and a nine-to-five schedule; and you cannot be engaged and not engaged at the same time. Such differences in demands often lead to a hostile or antagonistic relationship between two or more parties. A conflict can also be considered a dispute, a feud, a controversy, or a private war!

Conflict is important to study because it is far more complex than it appears on the surface. Many delicate human feelings are involved when two people are in conflict. The noted counselling psychologist Carl Rogers observed that most conflict between people includes four elements. First, each side thinks he or she is right and the other side is wrong. Second, communication breaks down as people do not hear each other. Third, there are distortions in perceptions as both sides ignore evidence that does not fit their viewpoint. Fourth, people distrust each other.[1]

A major purpose of this chapter is to describe ways of resolving conflict so that a win–win solution is reached. Both sides should leave the conflict feeling that their needs have been satisfied without resort to extreme behaviour. Both parties get what they deserve yet preserve the dignity and self-respect of the other side. Another purpose of this chapter is to explain assertiveness, because being assertive helps to prevent and resolve conflict.

Why So Much Conflict Exists

Many reasons exist for the widespread presence of conflict in all aspects of life. All of these reasons are related to the basic nature of conflict—the fact that not every person can have what he or she wants at the same time. As with other topics in this book, understanding conflict will help you develop a better understanding of why people act as they do. Here we describe six key sources of conflict.

Competition for Limited Resources

A fundamental reason you might experience conflict with another person is that not everybody can get all the money, material, supplies, or human help they want.

Conflict also ensues when employees are asked to compete for prizes such as bonuses based on individual effort, or for company-paid vacation trips. Because the number of awards is so limited, the competition becomes intense enough to be regarded as conflict. In some families, two or more children are pitted in conflict over the limited resources of money available for higher education.

Conflict stemming from limited resources has become prevalent as so many companies acquire other companies or decide to downsize. After one company takes over another, a decision is often made to eliminate a number of positions and to cut costs in other ways. People then squabble over which people should be entitled to hold on to their jobs and whose budget should be cut. In this instance, the positions in question and the money available become limited resources.

The Generation Gap and Personality Clashes

Various personality and cultural differences among people contribute to job conflict. Differences in age, or generation gaps, are one such factor. Generation gaps can lead to conflict because members of one generation may not accept values of another. Some observers see a clash between Baby Boomers, Generation X, and Baby Busters. The Baby Boomers are typically considered people born between 1947 and 1966, according to Canadian author David Foot, whereas Generation X is the group of late Boomers between 1960 to 1966. The Baby Busters are people born between 1967 and 1979. Generation Xers were launched into a world of climbing prices and often experienced an "overcrowded" world. This included crowded daycare, classrooms and portables that were too small, no room at the top for jobs since there were (and are) still so many Boomers in the workforce occupying high-end positions. Both Xers and Busters have had to start their work life in harder economic times when many companies have been trimming their workforces, merging, or downsizing. The Baby-Boom Echo generation, those born between 1980 to 1995, are just starting to enter the workforce.[2]

With such different birth times, these groups have experienced different environments, leading to differences between the generations and resulting in some stereotypes. Generation Xers have learned to look out for themselves and may be stereotyped by Boomers as being disrespectful of rules, not willing to "pay their dues," and being disloyal to employers. Generation X people see Boomers as worshipping hierarchy (layers of authority), being overcautious, and wanting to preserve the status quo.[3]

Cooperation is sometimes difficult to achieve between older and younger members of a department because older employees question the seriousness of purpose of the younger employees. Simultaneously, the younger workers may believe that the older workers are resistant to change and blindly loyal to the company.

Generation gaps as well as other forms of cultural diversity in the workplace have increased the potential for conflict. William L. Ury, a negotiation expert, says "Conflict resolution is perhaps the key skill needed in a diverse workforce."[4] When these conflicts are properly resolved, diversity lends strength to the organization because the various viewpoints each make an important contribution to solving a problem.

Many disagreements on the job stem from the fact that some people simply dislike each other. A **personality clash** is an antagonistic relationship between two people based on differences in personal attributes, preferences, interests, values, and styles. People involved in a personality clash often have difficulty specifying why they dislike each other. The end result, however, is that they cannot maintain an amiable work relationship. A strange fact about personality clashes is that people who get along well may begin to clash after working together for a number of years. Many business partnerships fold because the two partners eventually clash.

Diverse Teams

Conflict often surfaces as people work in teams whose members vary in many ways. Remembering William Ury's quotation above,[5] conflict resolution skills are imperative for teams with diverse members. Ethnicity, religion, and gender are three major factors that lead to clashes in viewpoints. Differing educational backgrounds and work specialties can also lead to conflict. Workers often shut out information that doesn't fit comfortably with their own beliefs, particularly if they do not like the person providing the information. When these conflicts are properly resolved, diversity lends strength to the organization because the various viewpoints make an important contribution to solving a problem. Groups that are reminded of the importance of effective communication and taught methods of conflict resolution can usually overcome the conflict stemming from mixed groups.[6]

The Building of Stone Walls

The slow and steady growth of a conflict situation has been likened by Richard J. Mayer to the building of a stone wall. The seed of the conflict is usually a minor incident that is not dealt with openly. The minor incident is called a *pinch*. Next, the person who was pinched unconsciously gathers data to support his or her view of the situation because of a need to be right. Much of the data are subject to perceptual distortion (seeing things in a way that fits our needs). As a result, a wall of minor incidents is built. The incidents eventually become an insurmountable obstacle (or stone wall) to honest and candid interaction with the *pincher*.[7]

A typical pinch is when an employee fails to share credit for a good idea he or she receives from a co-worker. The co-worker feels slighted and then looks for other incidents of the first person being dishonest. Communication breaks down between the two, and they become involved in frequent arguments. The employee who failed to share credit may be unaware of how or why the conflict began. If the pinched worker had confronted the issue early on, the conflict might not have festered.

Harassment

A substantial number of employees experience conflict because they are harassed by a manager, co-worker, or customer. In Canada, the Canada Labour Code, the Canadian Human Rights Act, and provincial and territorial human rights codes prohibit all types of harassment, including sexual harassment (which is dealt with in its own section below). The Canadian Human Rights Act, which applies to the federal government and federally regulated business, took effect in March 1978 and prohibits all harassment including harassment due to race, ethnicity, religion, sexual orientation, disability, or gender. The Canada Labour Code also establishes that all employees have the right to be free from any type of harassment and that employers must take steps to ensure a harassment-free workplace. The Canadian Employment Equity Act, 1995, was designed to ensure that no Canadians are denied jobs for reasons unrelated to their abilities and to help correct the employment disadvantages of four groups: women, members of visible minorities, aboriginal peoples, and persons with disabilities. These acts and codes attempt to ensure that no one will be harassed for any reason in the workplace and mandate that employers put into place policies and practices for fair and equitable treatment of all employees. If you are being harassed, whether sexually or otherwise, there are steps that you can take. The Canada Today feature below outlines some agreed upon steps that you can take to prevent or manage harassment.

Dealing with Harassment

What do you do if you feel you are being harassed by a co-worker (or worse yet, your manager)? You do not have to take it and you do not have to quit your job. Most organizations, large and small, typically have formal or informal policies and procedures. Do not be afraid to deal with the harassment.

Larger organizations typically have formal policies and procedures for dealing with all types of harassment. Most include a formal and informal complaint and resolution process based on the Ontario Human Rights Code or other provincial codes based on the Human Rights Act and formal Labour Codes.

In general, many harassment policies start with an informal complaint process. This process may include discussion with the person giving rise to the complaint, meeting with an organizational harassment adviser, or reporting the complaint to his or her immediate supervisor (or another supervisor if the immediate supervisor is the harasser). In many cases, resolution is accomplished at this informal level. Although it can be difficult to confront the person you feel is harassing you, this type of confrontation often successfully ends the behaviour. Being assertive, stating your case firmly, and if necessary stating that a formal complaint process will be initiated is often all that is required to end the harassment. The harassment adviser or other member of Human Resources may also be very helpful in planning a strategy to deal with the person.

A more formal process is usually initiated if the informal process is not successful. The formal process is most often activated with a written complaint. This written request should document all incidents. As such, it is important that if you feel you are being harassed, sexually or otherwise, it is imperative that you document all incidents of harassment. Although it can be difficult, you have to discuss the harassment with others who will investigate the complaint. However, your confidentiality will be respected and you must give permission if others become involved in the resolution process.

When a formal complaint has been made and investigated, the investigative team decides whether or not the complaint is substantiated. This team makes recommendations about further action, if any, to resolve the dispute.

In general, then, here are the steps that you can take:

- Record the incident(s) in detail. Make sure to record the names of any witnesses to the event.
- Often, confronting the person for smaller transgressions immediately works. Sometimes, the person may be unaware that you find a behaviour offensive. For example, a co-worker who continually calls you sweetie or tells racially discriminating jokes may not realize that this is offensive to you. Be assertive and say something like, "I would prefer that you do not tell such jokes in my presence. I find them offensive."
- If the person continues, you can then add, "If you persist in this (name the behaviour), I will have no choice but to report this matter to (name your supervisor). And follow through—idle threats will not change the behaviour.
- If the behaviour is very harassing (such as patting your behind, making lewd comments or overt sexual advances, destroying your personal property, and so on), go immediately to your supervisor. Again, make sure that you record the behaviour in writing including dates of the incidents. This may launch an informal investigation, but if the behaviour is severe, ask for an immediate formal investigation.
- If the workplace is not helpful, call the Labour Board or crisis centre in your area for immediate assistance. Remember that no one deserves to be harassed and you do not have to put up with it in any employment setting.
- You may also want to call a lawyer. Many organizations have an Employee Assistance Program and the consultation may be free of charge.

Sexual Harassment

Division XV.1 of Part III of the Canada Labour Code establishes that all employees have the right to be free of sexual harassment in the workplace and requires employers to take positive action to prevent sexual harassment in the workplace. The Code defines **sexual harassment** as

> any conduct, comment, gesture, or contact of a sexual nature that is likely to cause offence or humiliation to any employee or that might, on reasonable grounds, be perceived by that employee as placing a condition of a sexual nature on employment or on any opportunity for training or promotion.[8]

Harassment can include something as violent as rape or as subtle as making a sexually oriented comment about another person's body or appearance. Decorating the work area with pictures of nude people is another example of behaviour that can be categorized as sexual harassment. The most frequent form of harassment involves men against women, but harassment also takes the form of women sexually harassing men and people of the same sex harassing each other.

A Canadian Human Rights Tribunal identified three characteristics of sexual harassment. The first characteristic is that the encounters must be unsolicited and unwelcome to the complainant. An example of this type of behaviour is unwanted sexual remarks. The second characteristic is that the conduct continues despite the complainant's protests, or if it does stop, there are negative employment consequences, such as being denied a promised promotion. Third, any perceived cooperation by the complainant must be due to employment-related threats or promises.[9]

As a result of the Canadian Human Rights Act, each province has put in place legislation to protect employees from all types of harassment, including sexual harassment. For example, Ontario has its own Human Rights Code, which prohibits harassment, and employers are responsible to prevent and discourage harassment. If an employer fails to do so, the employee may file a complaint with the Ontario Human Rights Commission.[10]

Sexual harassment creates conflict because the harassed person has to make a choice between two incompatible motives. One motive is to get ahead or at least keep the job. But to satisfy this motive, the person is forced to sacrifice the motive of holding on to his or her moral values or preferences. This chapter's Canada Today feature presents suggestions for dealing with harassment. Human Relations Skill-Building Exercise 9-1 will help you identify situations that may be defined as harassment or discrimination.

Is This Harassment or Discrimination?

Divide up the class into small groups or even pairs. For each situation below, discuss whether or not the incident is harassment. Provide reasons for your viewpoint. Secondly, if you have time, discuss what the person should do about the situation.

1. Tina Wing works as a mechanic at a small garage. She is the first female mechanic hired and she is well qualified. There is only one staff washroom and on the walls are several posters of nude women. It is obvious that these posters have been up for years, but Tina finds them quite offensive. Is this sexual harassment?
2. Santos works as an underwriter in a large insurance company. Recently, a co-worker discovered that Santos is gay when she saw him with his partner at a wedding. Although Santos has never discussed his personal life with anyone, he is friendly and well-liked by most of his co-workers. This co-worker has let others know of Santos's sexual orientation and lately people have been whispering behind his back. In the lunchroom, he has heard some people blow "kisses" behind his back. When he turns around, everyone looks innocent although a few are giggling. Is this harassment?
3. Carla is a Native Canadian and has worked at the entry level in a large department store for several years. Her reviews have been excellent. Her manager stated in her most recent review, "Carla is a hard worker. She is friendly and professional with customers and returning customers often ask to deal with her. She is an asset to the store and goes beyond the call of duty in her responsibilities." A management trainee position came up that Carla applied for with the support and recommendation of her manager. Her application was not accepted with the reason given that Carla needed more experience. Carla then found out that a Caucasian person with much less training and only one year of retail experience had been accepted for the position. A friend told Carla that she was turned down because of her minority status. Has Carla been a victim of discrimination?

Competing Work and Family Demands

Balancing the demands of career and family life has become a major challenge facing today's workforce. The challenge is particularly intense for employees who are part of a two-wage-earner family—a group that represents approximately 62 percent of the workforce.[11] Attempting to meet work and family demands is a frequent source of conflict because the demands are often incompatible. Imagine having planned to attend your child's solo recital, and then being ordered at the last minute to work late because of an emergency.

The conflict over work versus family demands intensifies when the person is serious about both work and family responsibilities. The average professional working for an organization works approximately 55 hours per week, including five hours on weekends. Adhering to such a schedule almost inevitably results in some incompatible demands from work versus those from family members and friends. Conflict arises because the person wants to work sufficient hours to succeed on the job yet still have enough time for personal life.

Employers have taken major steps in recent years to help employees balance the competing demands of work and family. These programs help reduce conflict that arises from competing work and family demands. A sampling of these programs follows.

1. *Flexible work arrangements.* Many employers allow employees to use flexible work arrangements such as flextime, compressed work weeks, job sharing, and working from home. For example, flextime arrangements reduce stress and the "time crunch" many women feel as they try to balance home and work demands.[12] A related program is the compressed work week whereby the person works 40 hours in four days or less. Some employees prefer the compressed work week because it gives them longer weekends with their families. (For many others, however, ten-hour workdays create family problems.)

   The Royal Bank Financial Group, in a recent survey, found that allowing employees to utilize a variety of alternative work arrangements improved efficiency, morale, commitment, and customer service while reducing absenteeism. Forty-eight percent of the 1,700 Royal Bank Financial Group employees surveyed said that flexible work arrangements helped them deal with family responsibilities including child and elder care. The Royal Bank, one of Canada's largest employers, has over 1,100 job-share arrangements, more than any other company in Canada. Approximately 30 percent (more than 13,000) of the Royal Bank Financial Group's employees utilize some form of alternative work arrangement.[13]

2. *Family leave programs.* Family leave programs allow employees to take extended time off work, without pay, to meet family responsibilities. The employee's benefits continue while on leave, and the employee is guaranteed a job upon return. The leave applies to any combination of family and/or medical leaves. Recent legislation has extended parental leave up to one year.

3. *Dependent care programs.* Assistance in dealing with two categories of dependents—children and elderly parents—lies at the core of many pro-

grams and policies to help employees balance the demands of work and family. Many companies offer financial assistance for child care, including pre-tax expense accounts that allow employees to deduct child-care and elder-care expenses.

4. *Compassionate attitudes toward individual needs.* An informal policy that facilitates balancing of work and family demands leaves it to managers to decide what can be done to resolve individual conflicts. Yet managers cannot make arrangements with employees that would violate company policy. Being sensitive to individual situations could involve such arrangements as allowing a person time off to deal with a personal crisis. After the crisis is resolved the employee makes up the lost time in small chunks of extra work time.
5. *Recognition that work and personal life can be complementary.* A case history study of managers in a variety of companies revealed that some managers see work and personal life as complementing each other. The manager gets to know the goals and personal responsibilities of each member of the group and then helps each person achieve success on and off the job. A worker who needs to care for a dying parent, for example, might be able to work four days a week for a stretch and then make up the time later in the year. One positive result is that an individual with a satisfying personal life can produce more work in a shorter period of time than one who experiences work–family conflict.[14] As you have probably concluded, recognition that work and personal life can be complementary leads to taking individual cases into consideration.

The Good and Bad Sides of Conflict

Conflict over significant issues is a source of stress. We usually do not suffer stress over minor conflicts such as having to choose between wearing one sweater or another. Since conflict is a source of stress, it can have both positive and negative consequences to the individual. Like stress in general, we need an optimum amount of conflict to keep us mentally and physically energetic.

You can probably recall an incident in your life when conflict proved to be beneficial in the long run. Perhaps you and your partner or spouse hammered out an agreement over how much freedom each one has in the relationship. Handled properly, moderate doses of conflict can be advantageous. Some of the benefits that might arise from conflict are summarized in these key points:

1. *Talents and abilities may emerge in response to conflict.* When faced with a conflict, people often become more creative than they are in a tranquil situation. Assume that your company would no longer pay for your advanced education unless you used the courses to improve your job performance. You would probably find ways to accomplish such an end.
2. *Conflict can help you feel better because it satisfies a number of psychological needs.* By nature, many people like a good fight. As a socially acceptable substitute for attacking others, you might be content to argue over a dispute on the job or at home.

3. *As an aftermath of conflict, the parties in conflict may become united.* Two adolescents engaged in a fistfight may emerge bloodied but good friends after the battle. And two warring supervisors may become more cooperative toward each other in the aftermath of confrontation.
4. *Conflict helps prevent people in the organization from agreeing too readily with each other, thus making some very poor decisions.* **Groupthink** is the situation that occurs when group members strive so hard to get along that they fail to critically evaluate each other's ideas.

Despite the positive picture of conflict just painted, it can also have some detrimental consequences to the individual, the organization, and society. These harmful consequences of conflict make it important for people to learn how to resolve conflict:

1. *Prolonged conflict can be detrimental to some people's emotional and physical well-being.* As a type of stress, prolonged conflict can lead to such problems as heart disease and chronic intestinal disorders.
2. *People in conflict with each other often waste time and energy that could be put to useful purposes.* Instead of fighting all evening with your roommate, the two of you might fix up your shared space. Instead of writing angry email messages back and forth, two department heads might better invest that time in thinking up ideas to save the company money.
3. *The aftermath of extreme conflict may have high financial and emotional costs.* Sabotage—such as ruining machinery—might be the financial consequence. At the same time, management may develop a permanent distrust of many people in the workforce, although only a few of them are saboteurs.
4. *Too much conflict is fatiguing, even if it does not cause symptoms of emotional illness.* People who work in high-conflict jobs often feel spent when they return home from work. When the battle-worn individual has limited energy left over for family responsibilities, the result is more conflict. (For instance, "What do you mean you are too tired to go to the movies?" or "If your job is killing your appetite, find another job.")
5. *People in conflict will often be much more concerned with their own interests than with the good of the family, organization, or society.* A married couple in conflict might disregard the welfare of their children. An employee in the shipping department who is in conflict with his supervisor might neglect to ship an order. And a gang in conflict with another might leave a park or beach strewn with broken glass.[15]
6. *Workplace violence can erupt, including the killing of managers, previous managers, co-workers, and customers, as well as spouses and partners.* The number of violent incidents at work causing death or serious injury has risen dramatically in recent years.[16] Canada is in the top five countries reporting high numbers of workplace assaults and incidents of sexual harassment[17] Disgruntled employees, such as those recently fired, may attempt revenge by assassinating work associates. People involved in unresolved domestic disputes sometimes storm into a partner's workplace to physically attack him or her. Unresolved conflict and frustration from

financial, marital, or other domestic problems increase the odds of a person losing control of violent impulses at work.

7. *Conflict and anger sometimes lead to cyberstalking.* A new workplace threat is *cyberstalking,* the use of the internet, email, or other electronic communication devices to hound and harass another person. The majority of cyberstalkers are men, and most of their victims are women. Quite often, cyberstalking stems from a woman having terminated a relationship. However, cyberstalkers sometimes are disturbed enough to badger strangers. A study of the problem found that online harassment and threats sometimes lead to physical violence. The study also found that cyberstalkers can be as close as the next cubicle.[18]

Techniques for Resolving Conflicts with Others

Because of the inevitability of conflict, a successful and happy person must learn effective ways of resolving conflict. Here we concentrate on methods of conflict resolution that you can use on your own. Most of them emphasize a collaborative or win–win philosophy.

Confrontation and Problem Solving Leading to Win–Win

The most highly recommended way of resolving conflict is **confrontation and problem solving**. It is a method of identifying the true source of conflict and resolving it systematically. The confrontation in this approach is gentle and tactful rather than combative and abusive. Reasonableness is important because the person who takes the initiative in resolving the conflict wants to maintain a harmonious working relationship with the other party.

Imagine that Jason, the person working at the desk next to you, whistles loudly while he works. You find the whistling to be distracting and annoying; you think Jason is a noise polluter. If you don't bring the problem to Jason's attention, it will probably grow in proportion with time. Yet you are hesitant to enter into an argument about something a person might regard as a civil liberty (the right to whistle in a public place).

An effective alternative is for you to approach Jason directly in this manner:

You: Jason, there is something bothering me that I would like to discuss with you.

Jason: Go ahead, I don't mind listening to other people's problems.

You: My problem concerns something you are doing that makes it difficult for me to concentrate on my work. When you whistle it distracts me and grates on my nerves. It may be my hang-up, but the whistling does bother me.

Jason: I guess I could stop whistling when you're working next to me. It's probably just a nervous habit.

An important advantage of confrontation and problem solving is that you deal directly with a sensitive problem without jeopardizing the chances of forming a constructive working relationship in the future. One reason that the method works so effectively is that the focus is on the problem at hand, and not on the individual's personality.

Another approach to confrontation and problem solving is for each side to list what the other side should do. The two parties then exchange lists and select a compromise that both sides are willing to accept. Laying out each side's demands in writing is an effective confrontation technique, especially if the items on the list are laid out factually without angry comments included. As an example of this approach, here is a woman's list of demands concerning a conflict with her boyfriend:

- "Please don't introduce me as 'my current girlfriend.' It makes our relationship sound temporary.
- "Turn off the television set when we talk on the phone.
- "At least once in a while, give me priority over your family when we are scheduling a social event together.
- "Please open and close the car door for me when we are driving in your car."

All of the items on this list relate to consideration and respect, so they are part of the same conflict. The partner can then point out where he can grant concessions. Of course, he will have his own chance to produce a list.

The intent of confrontation and problem solving is to arrive at a collaborative solution to the conflict. The collaborative style reflects a desire to fully satisfy the desires of both parties. It is based on an underlying philosophy of **win–win**, the belief that after conflict has been resolved, both sides should gain something of value. The user of a win–win approach is genuinely concerned about arriving at a settlement that meets the needs of both parties, or at least does not badly damage the welfare of the other side. When a collaborative approach to resolving conflict is used, the relationships among the parties are built on and improved.

Here is an example of a win–win approach to resolving conflict. A manager granted an employee a few hours off on an occasional Friday afternoon because she was willing to be on call for emergency work on an occasional weekend. Both parties were satisfied with the outcome and both accomplished their goals.

Human Relations Skill-Building Exercise 9-2 gives you an opportunity to practise the win–win approach to conflict resolution. Confrontation and problem solving typically paves the way for getting to win–win.

Disarm the Opposition

The armament your criticizer has is valid negative criticism of you. The criticizer is figuratively clobbering you with knowledge of what you did wrong. If you deny that you have made a mistake, the criticism intensifies. A simple technique has been developed to help you deal with this type of manipulative criticism. **Disarm the opposition** is a method of conflict resolution in which you disarm the criticizer by agreeing with his or her criticism of you. The technique assumes that you have done something wrong.

Disarming the opposition capitalizes on the same principle that children often use in handling conflict or potential conflict with their parents. A child might say,

Win–Win Conflict Management

The class is organized into groups of six, with each group being divided into conflict-resolution teams of three each. The members of the team try to find a win–win solution to an issue separating the two sides. The team members are free to invent their own pressing issue or choose among the following:

Management wants to control costs by not giving cost-of-living adjustments in the upcoming year. The employee group believes that a cost-of-living adjustment is absolutely necessary.

The marketing team claims it could sell 250,000 units of a toaster large enough to toast bagels if the toasters could be produced at $15 per unit. The manufacturing group says it would not be feasible to get the manufacturing costs below $20 per unit.

Starbucks would like to build in a new location, adjacent to a historic district in one of the oldest cities in North America. The members of the town planning board would like the tax revenue and the jobs that the Starbucks store would bring, but they do not want a Starbucks next to the historic district.

After the teams have developed win–win solutions to the conflicts, the creative solutions can be shared with other teams.

"I spilled my drink on the sofa by mistake. Go ahead and punish me. I deserve it." Disarming the opposition works more effectively than counterattacking a person with whom you are in conflict.

Agreeing with criticism made of you by a superior is effective because by doing so you are then in a position to ask for that superior's help in improving your performance. Most managers realize that it is their responsibility to help employees overcome problems, not merely to criticize them. Imagine that you have been chronically late in submitting reports during the last six months. It is time for a performance review and you know you will be reprimanded for your tardiness. You also hope that your boss will not downgrade all other aspects of your performance because of your tardy reports. Here is how disarming the situation would work in this situation:

Your Boss: Have a seat. It's time for your performance review and we have a lot to talk about. I'm concerned about some things.

You: So am I. It appears that I'm having a difficult time getting my reports in on time. I wonder if I'm being a perfectionist. Do you have any suggestions?

Your Boss: I like your attitude. I think you can improve on getting your reports in on time. Maybe you are trying to make your reports perfect before you turn them in. Try not to figure out everything to four decimal places. We need thoroughness around here, but we don't want to overdo it.

Cognitive Restructuring

An indirect way of resolving conflict between people is to lessen the conflicting elements in a situation by viewing them more positively. According to the technique of **cognitive restructuring**, you mentally convert negative aspects into positive ones by looking for the positive elements in a situation.[19] How you frame or choose your thoughts can determine the outcome of a conflict situation. Your thoughts can influence your actions. If you search for the beneficial elements in a situation, there will be less area for dispute. Although this technique might sound like a mind game to you, it can work effectively.

Imagine that a co-worker of yours, Jennifer, has been asking you repeated questions about how to carry out a work procedure. You are about ready to tell Jennifer, "Go bother somebody else. I'm not paid to be a trainer." Instead, you look for the positive elements in the situation. You say to yourself, "Jennifer has been asking me a lot of questions. This does take time, but answering these questions is valuable experience. If I want to become a manager, I will have to help group members with problems."

After having completed this cognitive restructuring, you can then deal with the conflict more positively. You might say to Jennifer, "I welcome the opportunity to help you, but we need to find a mutually convenient time. That way, I can better concentrate on my own work."

Appeal to a Third Party

Now and then you may be placed in a conflict situation in which the other party either holds most of the power or simply won't budge. Perhaps you have tried techniques such as confrontation and problem solving or disarming the opposition, yet you cannot resolve your conflict. In these situations you may have to enlist the help of a third party with power—more power than you or your adversary has. Among such third parties are your common boss, union officials, or personnel managers. Taking your opponent to court is another application of the third-party technique.

In some situations, just implying that you will bring in a third party to help resolve the conflict situation is sufficient for you to gain advantage. One woman felt she was repeatedly passed over for promotion because of her sex. She hinted that if she were not given fairer consideration she would speak to the province's Human Rights Commission. She was given a small promotion shortly thereafter. Mediation, a formal type of third-party intervention, is discussed separately below.

Engage in Metacommunication

Many conflict situations take the form of poor communications between the parties involved. In these cases, resolving conflict and overcoming communication barriers come together. When confronted with a conflict involving communications, one response is to work around the problem by using one of the techniques already described in this chapter or in Chapter 7. A more typical response is to ignore the conflict or barrier by making no special effort to deal with it—a take-it-

or-leave-it approach to communication. Another possibility is to **metacommunicate**, or communicate about the conflicting part of your communications, to help overcome barriers or resolve a problem.

Suppose you are a team leader and one of the team members projects angry facial expressions and harsh gestures during your conversation about goals. You might say, "It looks like I'm not getting through to you. What do you dislike about our discussion?" The team member might say, "It's just that you're giving me tougher goals than the other team members. I think I'm being treated unfairly." By metacommunicating you have laid the groundwork to resolve the conflict over goals.

You can also use metacommunication to take the initiative about aspects of your communication that might create conflict. As a team leader facing heavy deadline pressures, you might say to a team member, "I might appear brusque today and tomorrow. Please don't take it personally. It's just that I have to make heavy demands on you because the team is facing a gruesome deadline."

Negotiation and Bargaining Tactics

Conflicts can be considered situations calling for **negotiating and bargaining**, conferring with another person to resolve a problem. When you are trying to negotiate a fair price for an automobile, you are also trying to resolve a conflict. At first the demands of both parties seem incompatible. After haggling for a while, you will probably reach a price that is satisfactory to both sides.

Negotiation has many applications in the workplace, including buying, selling, arriving at a starting salary or raise, and deciding on a relocation allowance. Negotiation may also take place with co-workers when you need their assistance. For example, you might need to strike a bargain with a co-worker to handle some of your responsibilities if you are faced with a temporary overload.

A sampling of five negotiating tactics to help you resolve conflict successfully is presented next. As with the other techniques of resolving conflict already presented, choose the ones that best fit your style and the situation.

Create a Positive Negotiating Climate

Negotiation proceeds much more swiftly if a positive tone surrounds the session. So it is helpful to initiate a positive outlook about the negotiation meeting. A good opening line in a negotiating session is, "Thanks for fitting this meeting into your hectic schedule." Nonverbal communication such as smiling and making friendly gestures helps create a positive climate.

In negotiating with co-workers for assistance, a positive climate can often be achieved by phrasing demands as a request for help. Most people will be more accommodating if you say to them, "I have a problem that I wonder if you could help me with." The problem might be that you need the person's time and mental energy. By giving that person a choice of offering you help, you have established a much more positive climate than by demanding assistance.[20]

Allow Room for Compromise but Be Reasonable

The basic strategy of negotiation is to begin with a demand that allows room for compromise and concession. Anyone who has ever negotiated the price of an automobile, house, or used furniture recognizes this vital strategy. If you are a buyer, begin with a low bid. (You say, "I'll give you $35 for that painting" when you are prepared to pay $70.) If you are the seller, begin with a high demand. (You say, "You can have this painting for $100" when you are ready to sell it for as low as $70.) As negotiations proceed, the two of you will probably arrive at a mutually satisfactory price. This negotiating strategy can also be used for such purposes as obtaining a higher starting salary or dividing property after a divorce or legal separation.

Common sense propels many negotiators to allow *too much* room for compromise. They begin negotiations by asking way beyond what they expect to receive, or offering far less than they expect to give. As a result of these implausible demands, the other side may become hostile, antagonistic, or walk away from the negotiations. Imagine that you've spotted a DVD player that you really want in a retail store. The asking price is $298.95. In an attempt to negotiate the price, you offer the store manager $98.95. Most likely the store owner will move on to the next customer. However, if you begin with a plausible offer such as $240, the store manager will likely take you seriously. Beginning with a plausible demand or offer is also important because it contributes to a positive negotiating climate.

Focus on Interests, Not Positions

Rather than clinging to specific negotiating points, keep your overall interests in mind and try to satisfy them. A negotiating point might be a certain amount of money or a concession that you must have. Remember that the true object of negotiation is to satisfy the underlying interests of both sides. The interests you and the other side are trying to protect might include money, lifestyle, power, or the status quo. For example, instead of negotiating for a particular starting salary,

Common sense propels many negotiators to allow **too much** room for compromise.

your true interests might be to afford a certain lifestyle. If the company pays all your medical and dental coverage, you can get by with a lower salary. Or your cost of living might be much lower in one city than in another. You can therefore accept a lower starting salary in the city with a lower cost of living.

Make a Last and Final Offer

In many circumstances, presenting a final offer will break a deadlock. You might frame your message something like this, "All I can possibly pay for your guitar is $280. You have my number. Call me when it is available at that price." Sometimes the strategy will be countered by a last and final offer from the other side: "Thanks for your interest. My absolute minimum price for this guitar is $300. Call us if that should seem OK to you." One of you will probably give in and accept the other person's last and final offer.

Allow for Face-Saving

We have reserved one of the most important negotiating and conflict-resolution strategies for last. Negotiating does not mean that you should try to squash the other side. You should try to create circumstances that will enable you to continue working with that person if it is necessary. People prefer to avoid looking weak, foolish, or incompetent during negotiation or when the process is completed. If you do not give your opponent an opportunity to save face, you will probably create a long-term enemy.

Face-saving could work in this way. A small-business owner winds up purchasing a computer, monitor, and printer for about twice what he originally budgeted. After the sale is completed, the sales rep says, "I know you bought a more professional rig than you originally intended. Yet I know you made the right decision. You will be able to do desktop publishing and save enough in printing costs to pay back the cost of the computer system in two years."

Use a Mediator

Some conflicts cannot be resolved between two parties, and a third party or **mediator** is required for successful resolution. For example, when two people refuse to listen to each other or refuse to see the "other side," chances are the conflict will not be resolved. **Mediation** is a formal method of conflict resolution that includes an objective third party. A mediator who has no vested interest in the resolution is more objective and will work to find a win–win outcome that will satisfy both parties.

Mediation is similar to, but not the same as, negotiation. In a mediation situation, an independent third party assists the involved parties in resolving the dispute on their own. Negotiation, on the other hand, often occurs between the parties and does not always involve a third person. A mediator helps the conflicting parties to clarify their solution choices, identifies possible resources, and assists in reaching decisions by recognizing each side's perspectives.[21] The mediator does not make the final decision but assists in finding possible alternatives that satisfy both sides in the dispute. Growing in popularity, **alternative dispute resolution** involves a professional mediator hired to help people arrive at a mutually acceptable solution. The goal in alternative dispute resolution is to arrive at a solution that both parties can agree to and feel that their goals have been achieved.

These professional mediators are often used in divorce situations as well as in business negotiations and other legal matters.

Developing Assertiveness

Several of the techniques for resolving conflict require assertiveness. Without forthrightness, confrontation and problem solving could not be achieved. Effective negotiation would also be difficult because assertiveness is required to carefully explain one's demands. Learning to express your feelings and make your demands known is also an important aspect of becoming an effective individual in general. Expressing your feelings helps you establish good relationships with people. If you aren't sharing your feelings and attitudes with other people, you will never get close to them.

Another benefit from being emotionally expressive, and therefore assertive, is that you get more of what you want in life. If you are too passive, people will neglect giving you what you want. Often it is necessary to ask someone when you want a raise, promotion, date, or better deal on a bank loan. Successful people usually make their demands known, yet they do not throw tantrums and are rarely bullies. (Exceptions to this general principle include some flamboyant trial lawyers and athletic coaches.)

Let's examine the nature of assertiveness in some detail, and then examine several techniques for building assertiveness. However, first take Human Relations Self-Assessment Quiz 9-1 to relate assertiveness to yourself.

Are You Nonassertive, Assertive, or Aggressive?

The following questionnaire is designed to give you tentative insight into your current tendencies toward submissiveness, assertiveness, or aggressiveness. As with other questionnaires presented in this book, the Assertiveness Scale is primarily a self-examination and discussion device. Answer each question Mostly True or Mostly False, as it applies to you.

	Mostly True	Mostly False
1. It is extremely difficult for me to turn down a sales representative when that individual is a nice person.	_______	_______
2. I express criticism freely.	_______	_______
3. If another person were being very unfair, I would bring it to that person's attention.	_______	_______

(continued)

	Mostly True	Mostly False
4. Work is no place to let your feelings show.	______	______
5. No use asking for favours; people get what they deserve on the job.	______	______
6. Business is not the place for tact; say what you think.	______	______
7. If a person looked as if he or she were in a hurry, I would let that person go in front of me in a supermarket line.	______	______
8. A weakness of mine is that I'm too nice a person.	______	______
9. If my restaurant bill is even 25¢ more than it should be, I demand that the mistake be corrected.	______	______
10. I have laughed out loud in public more than once.	______	______
11. I've been described as too outspoken by several people.	______	______
12. I am quite willing to have the store take back a piece of furniture that is scratched.	______	______
13. I dread having to express anger toward a co-worker.	______	______
14. People often say that I'm too reserved and emotionally controlled.	______	______
15. Nice guys and gals finish last in business.	______	______
16. I fight for my rights down to the last detail.	______	______
17. I have no misgivings about returning an overcoat to the store if it doesn't fit me properly.	______	______
18. If I have had an argument with a person, I try to avoid him or her.	______	______
19. I insist on my spouse (or roommate or partner) doing his or her fair share of undesirable chores.	______	______
20. It is difficult for me to look directly at another person when the two of us are in disagreement.	______	______
21. I have cried among friends more than once.	______	______
22. If someone near me at a movie kept up a conversation with another person, I would ask him or her to stop.	______	______
23. I am able to turn down social engagements with people I do not particularly care for.	______	______
24. It is in poor taste to express what you really feel about another individual.	______	______
25. I sometimes show my anger by swearing at or belittling another person.	______	______
26. I am reluctant to speak up in a meeting.	______	______
27. I find it relatively easy to ask friends for small favours such as giving me a lift to work when my car is being repaired.	______	______
28. If another person were talking very loudly in a restaurant and it bothered me, I would inform that person.	______	______
29. I often finish other people's sentences for them.	______	______
30. It is relatively easy for me to express love and affection toward another person.	______	______

(continued)

Scoring and Interpretation: Give yourself a point for each of your answers that agrees with the scoring key. If your score is 15 or less, it is probable that you are currently a nonassertive individual. A score of 16 through 24 suggests that you are an assertive individual. A score of 25 or higher suggests that you are an aggressive individual. Retake this quiz about 30 days from now to give yourself some indication of the stability of your answers. You might also discuss your answers with a close friend to determine if that person has a similar perception of your assertiveness. Here is the scoring key.

1. Mostly False
2. Mostly True
3. Mostly True
4. Mostly False
5. Mostly False
6. Mostly True
7. Mostly False
8. Mostly False
9. Mostly True
10. Mostly True
11. Mostly True
12. Mostly True
13. Mostly False
14. Mostly False
15. Mostly True
16. Mostly True
17. Mostly True
18. Mostly False
19. Mostly True
20. Mostly False
21. Mostly True
22. Mostly True
23. Mostly True
24. Mostly False
25. Mostly True
26. Mostly False
27. Mostly True
28. Mostly True
29. Mostly True
30. Mostly True

Assertive, Nonassertive, and Aggressive Behaviour

As implied above, **assertive** people state clearly what they want or how they feel in a given situation without being abusive, abrasive, or obnoxious. People who are assertive are open, honest, and "up-front" because they believe that all people have an equal right to express themselves honestly. Fred Pryor describes the type of assertive individual particularly needed in today's workplace:

> These pleasantly assertive workers are not intimidated by age or power or tradition. They have a calm, cool steadiness. They are their own persons. They don't wait to be asked for alternatives to "the way we do things here." They speak out when they think they have something to say that will benefit the organization and will add lustre to the bottom line.[22]

Assertive behaviour can be more fully understood by comparing it with that shown by two other types of people. **Nonassertive** people let things happen to them without letting their feelings be known. **Aggressive** people are obnoxious and overbearing. They push for what they want with almost no regard for the feelings of others.

Another way of explaining these differences is to say that the nonassertive person is stepped on and the aggressive person steps on others, while the assertive person deals with a problem in a mature and direct manner. Suppose a stranger invites you to accompany him or her to a party and you do not wish to go with that person. Here are the three ways of responding according to the three-way classification under discussion:

Assertive: Thank you for the invitation but I prefer not to go.

Nonassertive: I'm not sure, I might be busy. Could you call me again? Maybe I'll know for sure by then.

Aggressive: I'd like to go to a party, but not with you. Don't bother me again.

Gestures as well as words can communicate whether the person is being assertive, nonassertive, or aggressive. Exhibit 9-1 illustrates these differences.

Becoming More Assertive and Less Shy

There are a number of everyday actions a person can take to overcome shyness and lack of assertiveness. Shyness is a serious communication barrier for many individuals and can become part of feeling negative about oneself. **Shyness** can be defined as discomfort or an inhibition in interpersonal situations that interferes with the pursuit of personal or professional goals.[23] It has been estimated that as many as 40 percent of North Americans suffer from shyness, ranging from extreme to mild levels, at some point in their lives.[24] Extreme and prolonged shyness has been labelled **social phobia**. Estimates suggest that from three to twelve percent of the population have extreme shyness or social phobia.[25] The following techniques are most helpful for less severe cases of shyness. Even if the ones described here do not elevate your social skills, they will not backfire and cause you pain. After reading these techniques, you might be able to think of others that will work for you.[26]

Set a Goal Clearly establish in your mind in what ways you want to behave differently. Do you want to date more often? Speak out more in meetings? Be able to express dissatisfaction to co-workers? You can only overcome shyness by behaving differently; feeling differently is not enough.

Appear Warm and Friendly Shy people often communicate to others through their body language that they are not interested in reaching out to them. To overcome this impression, smile, lean forward, uncross your arms and legs, and unfold your hands.

exhibit 9-1

Assertive, Nonassertive, and Aggressive Gestures

Assertive

- Well-balanced
- Straight posture
- Hand gestures, emphasizing key words

Nonassertive

- Covering mouth with hand
- Excessive head nodding
- Tinkering with clothing or jewellery
- Constant shifting of weight
- Scratching or rubbing head or other parts of body
- Wooden body posture

Aggressive

- Pounding fists
- Stiff and rigid posture
- Finger waving or pointing
- Shaking head as if other person isn't to be believed
- Hands on hips

SOURCE: Donna E. Ledgerwood, "Workplace Relationships in the Federal Sector: Implications of Employees' Perceptions of Behavior," Presentation for Employees of Dallas Region United States Office of Personnel Management, 1989.

Make Legitimate Telephone Calls to Strangers Telephone conversations with strangers that have a legitimate purpose can help you start expressing yourself to people you do not know well. You might call numbers listed in classified ads to inquire about articles listed for sale. Try a positive approach: "Hello, my name is ____. I'd like to know about the condition of that piano you have for sale." Call the gas and electric company to inquire about a problem with your bill. Make telephone inquiries about employment opportunities in a firm of your choice. Call the library with reference questions. Call the municipal government office in your town with questions about local bylaws and regulations.

With practice, you will probably become more adept at speaking to strangers. You will then be ready for a more challenging self-improvement task.

Conduct Anonymous Conversations Try starting a conversation with a stranger in a safe setting such as a political rally, the waiting room of a medical office, a waiting line at the post office, or in a laundromat. Begin the conversation by addressing the common experience you are sharing at the time. Your conversation starters might resemble these:

- "I wonder if there will be any tickets left by the time we get to the box office?"
- "How long does it usually take before you get to see the doctor?"
- "Where did you get that laundry basket? I've never seen one so sturdy before."

Greet Strangers For the next week or so, greet every person you pass. Smile and make a neutral comment such as "How ya doing?" "Great day, isn't it?" Since most people are unaccustomed to being greeted by a stranger, you may get a few quizzical looks. Many other people may smile and return your greeting. A few of these greetings may turn into conversations. A few conversations may even turn into friendships. Even if the return on your investment in greetings is only a few pleasant responses, it will boost your confidence.

Use the Broken-Record Technique The assertion skill called *broken record* teaches you to persist until you get your way. **Broken-record technique** consists of calmly repeating your position over and over again without showing signs of anger or irritation. The person trying to persuade you will usually give up after a few minutes of hearing your "broken record." Acquiring this skill can help a shy person learn to say no, and not to give up after hearing the first no from another person. Basically, you keep repeating your "no" statement each time the person tries to get you to say "yes." A good one is to simply say, "No, I cannot" each time the person asks. Do not back down. When you repeat yourself over and over, the other person usually gives up!

Practise Being Decisive An assertive person is usually decisive, so it is important to practise being decisive. Some nonassertive people are even indecisive when asked to make a choice from a restaurant menu. They communicate their indecisiveness by asking their friend, "What are you going to have?" or asking the server, "Could you please suggest something for me?" or "What's good?" Practise quickly sizing up the alternatives in any situation and reaching a decision. This will help you be assertive and also project an image of assertiveness. Human Relations Skill-Building Exercise 9-3 is designed to improve decisiveness.

Treatments for the more debilitating types of shyness or social phobia include gradual exposure to feared situations, visualization (this involves visualizing the situation that arouses anxiety while practising relaxation techniques), learning positive self-talk, and learning how to cope with the anxiety of social situations and counselling. Many current treatments of social phobia, however, still rely on medication to ease anxiety, which may create dependence. Medication does not solve the problem and treatment should involve treating the social anxiety as a habit that can be changed.[27] Strategies like those mentioned earlier will help the shy or socially phobic person communicate with others and develop rich and meaningful relationships on and off the job.

Summary

Conflict occurs when two sets of demands, goals, or motives are incompatible. Such differences often lead to a hostile or antagonistic relationship between people. A conflict can also be considered a dispute, feud, or controversy.

Among the reasons for widespread conflict are (1) competition for limited resources; (2) generation gaps, personal differences, and personality clashes; (3) diverse teams; (4) the building of stone walls; (5) harassment including sexual harassment; and (6) competing work and family demands. The Canadian Human Rights Code prohibits all forms of harassment, including sexual harassment.

The benefits of conflict include the emergence of talents and abilities, constructive innovation and change, and increased unity after the conflict is settled. Among the detrimental consequences of conflict are physical and mental health problems, wasted resources, the promotion of self-interest, workplace violence, and cyberstalking.

Becoming More Assertive by Being Decisive

An important part of being assertive is to be decisive. To enhance your decisiveness, follow these steps:

1. Make a list of the requests people make of you that are a burden. Review the list and select one or two requests that you will refuse in the next week. Think about how you will politely, but firmly, inform someone of your need to say "no," then carry out your plan. What happened? Did you feel less guilty than you thought you would?
2. Review the requests you want to make of others to help you meet your own needs. Select one or two. Get clear in your mind what you specifically want. Formulate each request so that it is as reasonable as possible for the person you will ask, then make your request(s). Did you get a positive response? Are you happy with the support you obtained?

SOURCE: Adapted from Mel Silberman, with Freda Hansburg, *PeopleSmart: Developing Your Interpersonal Intelligence* (San Francisco: Berrett-Koehler Publishers, 2000), pp. 90–91.

Techniques for resolving conflicts with others include

1. Confrontation and problem solving leading to win–win—get to the root of the problem and resolve it systematically. The intention of confrontation and problem solving is to arrive at a collaborative solution to conflict.
2. Disarm the opposition—agree with the criticizer and enlist his or her help.
3. Cognitive restructuring—mentally convert negative aspects to positive ones by looking for the positive elements in the situation.
4. Appeal to a third party.
5. Use negotiation and bargaining tactics.
6. Use a mediator. Some conflicts may seem impossible to resolve and an objective third party with no vested interests may help find a mutually satisfying solution.

Negotiation and bargaining tactics include (1) create a positive negotiating climate; (2) allow room for compromise but be reasonable; (3) focus on interests, not positions; (4) make a last and final offer; and (5) allow for face-saving.

Several of the techniques for resolving conflict require assertiveness, or stating clearly what one wants and how one feels in a given situation. Being assertive also helps you develop good relationships with people and get more of what you want in life.

People can become more assertive and less shy by using techniques such as these:

1. Set a goal in relation to assertiveness.
2. Appear warm and friendly.
3. Make legitimate telephone calls to strangers.
4. Conduct anonymous conversations.
5. Greet strangers.
6. Use the broken-record technique (keep repeating your position without getting upset).
7. Practise being decisive.

Questions and Activities

1. Why are conflict resolution skills considered so important in a culturally diverse workplace?
2. What differences in goals might management and workers have that would lead to conflict?
3. Give an example from your own life of how competition for limited resources can breed conflict.
4. A manager invites a subordinate to dinner. The subordinate declines the offer, yet the manager repeats the invitation every week for five weeks. Is this persistent asking a form of sexual harassment? Explain.
5. Suppose a police officer catches you making a right turn on a red light without stopping. Which conflict-resolution method do you think would be best suited to handling the conflict with the officer? Explain.

6. Identify several occupations in which conflict-resolution skills are especially important.
7. You are dining in an expensive restaurant with a special person in your life. A person seated at the next table starts making a series of calls, in a loud voice, on his cellular telephone. You and your partner are upset about the calls interrupting your romantic dinner. Make up an assertive statement to tell the phone caller.
8. Some people with very successful careers are apparently aggressive, even to the point of being obnoxious. Why, then, is there an emphasis on being assertive on the job rather than aggressive?
9. How might extreme shyness interfere with personal and career goals?
10. Ask a successful person how much conflict he or she experiences in balancing the demands of work and personal life. Be prepared to report your findings in class.

Internet Skill Builder

Conflict Management Advice on the Web

Resolving conflict is such an important life activity that most people need all the help they can get. Search the web for advice about conflict resolution and see if you can acquire information to supplement the contents of this chapter. For this activity, you might first try a search engine that enables you to ask questions (e.g., "How do I resolve conflict?"), such as **www.AskJeeves.com**.

Weblinks

www.canada.justice.gc.ca
This is the website for Justice Canada. From this site, you can access the Canadian Human Rights Act, the Employment Equity Act, and articles written about them.

www.hrdc-drhc.gc.ca
From the site of Human Resources Development Canada you can access the Canada Labour Code.

www.shyness.com
Learn more about shyness—what it is, possible explanations, and treatment.

www.adrc.com
A Canadian site, this is the web home of the Alternate Dispute Resolution Centre.

www.hg.org/adr.htm
For more information on alternative dispute resolution, visit this site.

Human Relations Case Study

GENERATION X MEETS BABY BOOMER

After reading the case study and answering the questions that follow, try Human Relations Skill-Building Exercise 9-4.

While studying hotel and restaurant management at college, Cindy worked two part-time jobs: as a desk clerk at the Windmere Hotel and as a hostess at a restaurant. As graduation approached, Cindy sent résumés to many hotels around the country. She received a few encouraging responses, mostly advising her to contact the hotel after she had relocated to the area. In assessing her employment opportunities, Cindy decided that it would make sense to discuss a full-time position with the head manager at the Windmere. Much to Cindy's delight and amazement, the manager offered her a full-time position as assistant general manager. Cindy expressed a little hesitation about her ability to handle so much responsibility at this stage in her career. The manager assured Cindy that he had observed her handle difficult situations as a desk clerk and that she could easily become a competent assistant general manager. He also told Cindy that he and other staff members would be available to give her whatever assistance she needed.

Several weeks into her new position, Cindy felt confident that she was successfully handling her responsibilities, with one exception. The exception took the form of Stephanie, a night auditor with 20 years of experience at the Windmere. While attending high school, Stephanie worked part-time in housekeeping. Shortly after graduation, she married and became a parent. Cramped for money after her second child was born, Stephanie returned to the Windmere as the bell desk coordinator. She soon recognized that working during the day was not profitable because of the high child-care expenses she incurred. Stephanie transferred to the night auditor position, which she held for 14 years.

Stephanie was disturbed to learn that her new boss was Cindy, whom she described as "a Generation Xer half my age." Each night while auditing her boss's mistakes, Stephanie became increasingly frustrated. Finally, she decided to send Cindy an email message about her unacceptable performance, which initiated a series of emails sent back and forth between the two women:

> To: Cindy
> From: Stephanie
> I am starting to wonder if you are really qualified for your new position. I found loads of mistakes made by you and your staff in last night's audit. I knew this was going to happen! I have circled numerous errors from yesterday's transactions. Please fix them immediately.

> To: Stephanie
> From: Cindy
> Thank you for your ever so kind note! It is unfortunate you're having difficulty dealing with me in my new position. I *am* your boss, you know. I can imagine that this is a difficult thing for you to accept, but it's the truth. Be patient with me and my staff. We are not perfect!!!!

> To: Cindy
> From: Stephanie
> Your life as a student and part-time worker is over now. It's time you get cracking and take your new job a little bit more seriously. We've got a business to run here. Again, I remind you to inform your staff of their errors.

To: Stephanie
From: Cindy
We've got to stop meeting like this! Ha ha! Please forgive me. The desk clerks and I have been so wild and crazy that we haven't had a free minute to work. By the way, whatever transactions you have been referring to are no longer errors. If you would read the updated procedures manual you would know this. **Please** keep current on the many changes being made by management.

To: Cindy
From: Stephanie
Please find my letter of resignation in the envelope I placed on your desk this afternoon. Perhaps if the Windmere had hired an adult to replace Mr. Benton this would not have happened. Good luck finding a new night auditor who will stay with the hotel for 19.8 years. And one who was an entirely devoted employee.

Cindy thought to herself, "Did I do something terribly wrong, or am I dealing with a nut case? I wonder what I might have done differently. The general manager will not be too happy about Stephanie resigning."

Questions

1. What is the most likely source (or sources) of the conflict between Cindy and Stephanie?
2. What could Cindy have done to better resolve conflict with Stephanie?
3. What could Stephanie have done to better resolve conflict with Cindy?

SOURCE: Case researched by Nicole Harwood, Rochester Institute of Technology, May 1997.

Conflict Resolution

Imagine that before Stephanie resigned in a huff, Cindy took the initiative to resolve the conflict between them. One person plays the role of Cindy, who is exasperated with Stephanie's behaviour and wants to bring about a constructive working relationship. Another student plays the role of embittered Stephanie, who resents the fact that Cindy is her manager. The role play might be carried out with three pairs of students playing the two roles. Others in the class can provide constructive criticism about how well the conflict was managed.

Getting Along with Your Manager or Team Leader

Learning Outcomes

After reading the information and doing the exercises in this chapter, you should be able to

- recognize the impact your manager has on your future
- select several tactics for creating a favourable impression on your present or future manager
- select several tactics for dealing with your manager in a constructive manner
- prepare to deal effectively with a manager whom you perceive as being intolerable

Kevin, an accountant in receivables for a recycling company, had an idea that would save the company time and money when contracting out work to truck owners for the local recycling pickups. Some truck drivers took longer hours to run a route than other trucks from other companies. Current practice was that the truck owners billed the company for the number of hours the truck was en route. This practice resulted in a great deal of work for those in accounting, who had to tally hours monthly, often using scraps of paper that the drivers handed in. This system had led to serious errors in both overpaying and underpaying some drivers. Also, it was believed that some drivers were billing for hours that were not used or that drivers were taking too much time. On the other hand, some drivers with faster, state-of-the-art trucks were earning less than those with the older and slower rigs.

Kevin's idea was that each route should be averaged based on the last year of payment for each route and that each independent driver would be paid the same based on the yearly average. In this way, the route itself was the basis of the payment rather than the number of hours it took for each driver to complete the circuit. As well, by using averaging, areas where the pickups were bigger would be factored into the time that it took to complete the route. By simplifying the process, records could be quickly computerized and payments on time and more accurate.

Kevin, supported by his team leader, took the idea to the owner of the company. Upon hearing his idea, the owner stated, "Why, I like the idea in principle. I need to hear more and get more data. I'll have to let your team leader know how impressed I am with your work and creativity. Good work!" Upon hearing from the owner, Kevin's team leader commented on how well Kevin had done and that this would be included in his file for his next performance appraisal.

In this chapter we present a variety of strategies and tactics that lead to constructive relationships with an immediate superior, manager, or team leader. Getting along with your manager as well as co-workers is regarded by many as having good **political skills**, an interpersonal style that combines awareness of others with the ability to communicate well. People with political skill are charming and engaging, which inspires confidence, trust, and sincerity.[1] The strategies and tactics are grouped for convenience into three categories: creating a favourable impression on your manager, dealing with your manager directly, and coping with an intolerable manager.

Before reading further, take Human Relations Self-Assessment Quiz 10-1. It will sensitize you to the importance of getting along with your manager or team leader, even if you do not currently have one.

Human Relations Self-Assessment

Quiz 10-1

How Well Do You and Your Manager Communicate?

Here's a quick way to measure the quality of your communications with your immediate superior. If you are not currently working, think back to the last time you had a manager. Read the following statements and circle either A (*Agree*) or D (*Disagree*).

1.	I can ask for help without feeling embarrassed.	A	D
2.	My manager recognizes the good things that I do.	A	D
3.	I understand what my manager expects of me.	A	D
4.	My manager coaches me toward improvement when I need it.	A	D
5.	I am aware of the reasons for the major decisions my manager made recently.	A	D
6.	My manager understands my personal goals.	A	D
7.	I am aware of at least two specific things I can do to get a better rating at my next performance review.	A	D
8.	My manager lets me know when I've made a mistake without putting me down.	A	D
9.	I feel free to disagree with my manager when we talk.	A	D
10.	My manager is aware of the basic problems I have to cope with in doing my job.	A	D

Scoring and Interpretation: Count the number of A's you have circled. If you circled 10, your communication with your manager is excellent; 9 or 8 is good; 7 or 6, about average; 5 or less, needs improvement.

SOURCE: Adapted from *Practical Supervision*, Sample Issue, 1996.

Creating a Favourable Impression on Your Manager or Team Leader

The strategies and tactics in this section all help you create a favourable impression on the boss. The term *impression* refers to a true impression, not a false one. Following these straightforward suggestions helps you deserve a positive reputation.

Achieve Good Job Performance

Good performance remains the most vital strategy for impressing your manager. When any rational manager evaluates a group or team member's performance, the first question asked is "Is this employee getting the job done?" And you cannot get the job done if you are not competent.

Many factors contribute to whether you can become a competent performer. Among them are your education, training, personality characteristics, job experience, and special skills, such as being able to solve problems, resolve conflict, and organize your work. Much of this book discusses skills, techniques, and strategies that are designed to contribute to job competence.

An advanced way of displaying good job performance is to assist your manager or team leader with a difficult problem he or she faces. Your manager or team leader, for example, might need to know how to operate equipment outside his or her area of expertise. If you show your manager or team leader how to operate the equipment, he or she will think more highly of your job performance. Being part of a team means being helpful and cooperative to all team members including the team leader. In teams where each member may have a specialized skill including the leader, this type of assistance is essential to team success. If you demonstrate these characteristics, you are displaying good job performance as well as demonstrating good teamwork.

Display a Strong Work Ethic

A major factor contributing to good job performance is a strong **work ethic**, a firm belief in the dignity and value of work. People with a strong work ethic have strong internal motivation. An employee with a strong work ethic will sometimes be excused if his or her performance is not yet exceptional. This is true because the manager assumes that a strong work ethic will elevate performance eventually. A strong work ethic is more in demand today than ever because many organizations are thinly staffed. With fewer people performing the same amount of work, everybody has to work harder. The best overall way to display a strong work ethic is to work hard and enjoy the task. Six specific suggestions for demonstrating a strong work ethic follow.

1. *Work hard and enjoy the task.* By definition, a person with a strong work ethic works diligently and has strong internal motivation. The person may appreciate external rewards yet recognize the importance of any work that adds value to society.
2. *Demonstrate competence even on minor tasks.* Attack each assignment with the recognition that each task performed well, however minor, is one more career credit. A minor task performed well paves the way for your being given more consequential tasks.
3. *Assume personal responsibility for problems.* An employee with a problem will often approach the manager and say, "We have a tough problem to deal with." The connotation is that the manager should be helping the employee with the problem. A better impression is created when the employee says, "I have a tough problem to deal with, and I would like your advice." This statement implies that you are willing to assume responsibility for the problem and for any mistake you may have made that led to it.
4. *Assume responsibility for free-floating problems.* A natural way to display a strong work ethic is to assume responsibility for free-floating (nonassigned) problems. Taking on even a minor task, such as ordering lunch for a meeting that is running late, can enhance the impression one makes on a manager.

5. *Get your projects completed promptly*. A by-product of a strong work ethic is an eagerness to get projects completed promptly. People with a strong work ethic respect deadlines imposed by others. Furthermore, they typically set deadlines of their own that are even more tight than those imposed by their boss.
6. *Accept undesirable assignments willingly*. Another way of expressing a strong work ethic is to accept undesirable assignments willingly. Look for ways to express the attitude, "Whether or not this assignment is glamorous and fun is a secondary issue. What counts is that it is something that needs to be done for the good of the company."

Demonstrate Good Emotional Intelligence

A worker who deals effectively with the emotional responses of co-workers and customers is impressive, because feelings and emotions are a big challenge on the job. Such behaviour reflects emotional intelligence, defined in Chapter 5 in relation to dealing with anger. Emotional intelligence can also be regarded as the use of nonverbal cues, emotions, feelings, and mood. The person with good emotional intelligence recognizes and understands his or her own feelings and those of others.[2]

Demonstrating good emotional intelligence is impressive because it contributes to performing well in the difficult arena of dealing with feelings. A worker with good emotional intelligence would engage in such behaviours as (1) recognizing when a co-worker needs help but is too embarrassed to ask, (2) dealing with the anger of a dissatisfied customer, (3) recognizing that the boss is facing considerable pressure also, and (4) being able to tell whether a customer's "maybe" means "yes" or "no."

Be Dependable, Honest, and Ethical

Dependability is a critical employee virtue. If an employee can be counted on to deliver as promised, and to be at work regularly, that employee has gone a long way toward impressing the boss. A boss is uncomfortable not knowing whether an important assignment will be accomplished on time. If you are not dependable, you will probably not get your share of important assignments. Honesty is tied to dependability because a dependable employee is honest about when he or she will have an assignment completed.

Dependability and honesty are important at all job levels. One of the highest compliments a manager can pay an employee is to describe the employee as dependable. Conversely, it is considered derogatory to call any employee undependable. As one company president put it when describing a subordinate: "When he's great, he's terrific, but I can't depend on him. I'd rather he be more consistent even if he delivered fewer peak successes—at least I could rely on him."[3]

People who are *ethical* have high morals and treat others with respect and dignity. They do not engage in backstabbing or badmouthing their managers, team leaders, or co-workers. Ethical employees make sound judgments when completing their assignments and report their decisions to the manager. For example, if one of your responsibilities is to find out the costs of some new equipment, you get several quotes in a straightforward and honest manner. You do not engage in such activities as promising the company more favours later on if the price can be reduced, getting prices only from friends, or engaging in other questionable methods of "doing business." Such unethical conduct will reflect not only upon you, but upon your manager and company as well.

Ethical workers also do not mislead customers by stating a product is better than it really is or that an item can do more than stated in the product brochure. Lying about a product or pretending that something is a real "deal" or "steal" is also unethical. Dissatisfied customers who return with complaints about the item reflect poorly upon you, your manager, and your company. Lastly, "badmouthing" about competitors to customers is also considered unethical and many managers will not appreciate this behaviour. Remember that managers attend seminars, trade fairs, and the like where they do interact with competitors, and your manager may hear about your behaviour from the manager whose company you have been disparaging. Competition does not mean unfriendly relations.

Appreciate Your Manager's Strengths

You may not admire every boss you work for, particularly early in your career. Your young boss might be inexperienced and therefore less than ideal. Older managers you work for early in your career might be people who have been passed over for promotion many times. In other words, the company recognizes they are not the strongest supervisors. But they are usually competent enough to perform their jobs satisfactorily.

If you focus only on the weaknesses of your boss, you will probably communicate many negative nonverbal messages to that individual. For instance, when your boss is making general suggestions, you might display a bored expression on your face. Instead of thinking primarily about your boss's weakness, look for strengths. Look for answers to such questions as, "What knowledge does he or she have that can help me advance my career?" "What good points about my boss led to his or her promotion?" or "What do some of my co-workers see as my boss's strengths?" A case in point is Bruce, a young sales representative:

> Having recently graduated from business school, Bruce was fired up with modern techniques of selling, such as identifying the customer's most pressing problems. He was somewhat perplexed about why his boss, Arlie, was considered such an outstanding sales manager. He displayed few of the management techniques that Bruce had studied in school. Bruce then spoke to an aunt who worked in another department of the same company. "How come old Arlie is so highly regarded? He doesn't seem to know much about sales techniques or management." Bruce's aunt replied, "You could be right, Bruce. But Arlie knows how to read people and how to form good relationships. He's what is known as a good personal salesman."
>
> From that point on, Bruce began to look at techniques that Arlie used for forming good relationships with people. As he showed a sincere interest in learning more from Arlie, their relationship improved.

Show an Interest in Your Firm's Products or Services

Showing a genuine interest in your company and its products or services impresses superiors in both commercial and not-for-profit firms. This tactic works because so many workers do not identify with their employers. Many employees are not even familiar with what their organization is trying to accomplish. A natural opportunity for showing interest in your firm's products and services is to promote them. Find a way to promote your company's products or services and you will endear yourself to top management. The next step is to casually mention that you are actively using the product. As an administrative assistant working for a printer manufacturer told a vice president:

> My husband and I bought one of our desktop colour printers two years ago. We've become the neighbourhood print shop whenever somebody wants to prepare a fancy graphic. So far, the printer has never been back for service. Our neighbours are so impressed with the printer that two of them plan to buy one of their own.

Another way of showing an interest in your firm's product and services is to become familiar with the company website by visiting it regularly. In this way you can make informed comments about the website after speaking to key people about other matters. A question such as the following reflects legitimate interest: "How is the direct sale program over the internet going?"

Be a Good Organizational Citizen

An especially meritorious approach to impressing key people is to demonstrate **organizational citizenship behaviour**, the willingness to work for the good of the organization even without the promise of a specific reward. A good organizational citizen would do such things as assisting a person with a computer problem outside his or her team or department, or picking up a broken bottle on the company lawn. Organizational citizenship behaviour is increasing in importance as organizations face the challenge of global competition and the need for continuous innovation. The good organizational citizen goes above and beyond the call of duty.[4]

An effective way of being a good organizational citizen is to step outside your job description. Job descriptions are characteristic of a well-organized firm. If everybody knows what he or she is supposed to be doing, there will be much less confusion, and goals will be achieved. This logic sounds impressive, but job descriptions have a major downside. If people engage only in work included in their job description, the prevailing mentality becomes, "It's not my job." An effective way to impress your manager is therefore to demonstrate that you are not constrained by a job description. If something needs doing, you will get it done whether or not it is your formal responsibility.

An impressive way of stepping outside your job description is to anticipate problems, even when the manager had not planned to work on them. Anticipating problems is characteristic of a resourceful person who exercises initiative. Instead of working exclusively on problems that have been assigned, the worker is perceptive enough to look for future problems. Anticipating problems impresses most managers because it reflects an entrepreneurial, take-charge attitude.

Create a Strong Presence

A comprehensive approach to impressing your manager or team leader and other key people in the workplace is to create a strong presence, or keep yourself in the forefront. Such actions impress key people and simultaneously help advance your career. Stephanie Sherman, a career consultant, offers this advice for creating a strong presence:

- Get involved in high-visibility projects such as launching a new product or redesigning work methods. Even an entry-level position on such a project can be impressive.
- Get involved in teams because they give you an opportunity to broaden your skills and knowledge.
- Get involved in social and community activities of interest to top management, such as those sponsored by the company. Behave professionally and use your best manners.
- Create opportunities for yourself by making constructive suggestions about earning or saving money. Even if an idea is rejected, you will still be remembered for your initiative.
- Show a willingness to take on some of the tasks that your manager doesn't like to do but would be forced to do if you did not step in.[5]

Dealing Directly with Your Manager

To develop a good relationship with your manager, you need to create a favourable impression, as already described. You also need to focus directly on your relationship with your manager in terms of your work transactions with him or her. In this section we emphasize techniques geared toward transactions with the boss, rather than focusing on the impression you create. (Do not be concerned about overlap in the categories.)

Understand Your Manager

A crucial aspect of developing a good working relationship with the boss is to understand the boss, including the environment in which the boss works. An important starting point in understanding your manager is to recognize his or her style. A **style** is a person's way of doing things. Walter St. John identifies some questions that need to be answered to understand one's manager.[6]

1. What is your manager's position in the company hierarchy? What are his or her relationships with his or her manager?
2. What are your manager's blind spots, prejudices, pet peeves, and sore spots? What constitute positive and negative words to your manager?
3. Does your manager understand better as a reader (should you send a memo) or as a listener (should you tell him or her in person)?
4. Is your manager a morning or evening person? When is the best time of the day to approach your manager?

5. What is your manager's preference for getting things done?
6. What is most important to your manager?
7. What nonverbal signals does your manager communicate to you?

Finding answers to these questions, including understanding your manager's style, may involve discussions with co-workers as well as with the boss directly. Concentrate on "how" questions, such as "This is my first report for Julie. How does she like it done? Does she want a one-page summary at the beginning of the report or at the end?" Speaking to co-workers can also reveal what kinds of attitudes your boss expects you to have. For example, does the boss really believe that the customer is always right? Your question may also reveal that your manager is jumping to please a demanding superior. If this is true, you may be expected to do the same.[7]

Find Out What Your Manager Expects of You

You have little chance of doing a good job and impressing your manager unless you know what you are trying to accomplish. Work goals and performance standards represent the most direct ways of learning your manager's expectations. Review your work goals and ask clarifying questions. An example would be, "You told me to visit our major customers who are 60 days or more delinquent on their accounts. Should I also visit the three of these customers who have declared bankruptcy?" In addition to having a clear statement of your goals, it is helpful to know the priorities attached to them. In this way you will know which task to execute first.

A **performance standard** is a statement of what constitutes acceptable performance. These standards can sometimes be inferred from a job description. For example, part of the job description of a payroll specialist is to "calculate and maintain provincial and federal tax returns." The payroll specialist would therefore be meeting a standard by accurately computing these taxes. Performance standards are sometimes stated in quantitative terms, such as, "process an average of 50 medical insurance claims per day."

Bring Forth Solutions as Well as Problems

An advanced tactic for developing a good working relationship with your immediate superior is to bring solutions to your boss's attention, not just problems. Too often, group members ask to see their bosses only when they have problems requiring help. A boss under pressure may thus anticipate additional pressure when a group member asks for an appointment. The subordinate who comes forth with a solved problem is thus regarded as a welcome relief. In short, you can ease your manager's suffering by walking into his or her office and saying, "Here's what I did about that mess that was plaguing us yesterday. Everything is under control now."

Minimize Complaints

In the previous chapter we extolled the virtues of being open and honest in expressing your feelings and opinions. Nevertheless, this type of behaviour when carried to excess could earn you a reputation as a whiner. Few managers want to have a group member around who constantly complains about working conditions, co-workers, working hours, pay, and so forth. An employee who complains too loudly and frequently quickly becomes labelled a pill or a pest.

Another important reason a boss usually dislikes having a subordinate who complains too much is that listening to these complaints takes up considerable time. Most managers spend a disproportionate amount of time listening to the problems of a small number of ineffective or complaining employees. Consciously or unconsciously, a manager who has to listen to many of your complaints may find a way to seek revenge.

How then does an employee make valid complaints to the manager? The answer is to complain only when justified. And when you do offer a complaint, back it up with a recommended solution. Anyone can take potshots at something. The valuable employee is the person who backs up these complaints with a constructive action plan. Following are two examples of complaints, backed up by action plans for remedying the complaint:

- "I've noticed that several of us get very tired feet by the end of the working day. Maybe we could perform this work just as well if we sat on high stools."
- "We have a difficult time handling emergency requests when you are away from the department. I would suggest that when you will be away for more than one or two hours, one of us can serve as the acting supervisor. It could be done on a rotating basis to give each of us some supervisory experience."

Avoid Bypassing Your Manager

A good way to embarrass and sometimes infuriate your manager is to repeatedly go to his or her superior with your problems, conflicts, and complaints. Such bypasses have at least three strongly negative connotations. One is that you don't believe your boss has the power to take care of your problem. Another is that you distrust his or her judgment in the matter at hand. A third is that you are secretly launching a complaint against your manager.

The boss bypass is looked on so negatively that most experienced managers will not listen to your problem unless you have already discussed it with your immediate superior. There are times, however, when running around your manager is necessary; for example, when you have been unable to resolve a conflict directly with him or her (see the following section). But even under these circumstances, you should politely inform your manager that you are going to take up your problem with the next level of management.

In short, if you want to keep on the good side of your manager, bring all problems directly to him or her. If your boss is unable or unwilling to take care of the problem, you might consider contacting your boss's superior. Nonetheless, considerable tact and diplomacy are needed. Do not imply that your manager is incompetent, but merely that you would like another opinion about the issues at stake.

Suggest Improvements during the Performance Evaluation

An effective method of enhancing your relationship with your manager is to use the performance evaluation session as an opportunity to suggest a variety of work improvements. Making suggestions for improvement during the performance evaluation is logical because one purpose of an evaluation is to bring about improvements. After your manager has completed his or her agenda, volunteer ideas for such topics as these:

- Helping the department run more smoothly
- Making better use of your skills
- Saving time or money for the company
- Increasing productivity and quality[8]

Suggesting ideas of this nature communicates the fact that you perceive performance evaluation as an opportunity for both individual and company improvements. An attitude of this type will usually strengthen the relationship with your manager. If your company uses a peer evaluation system (as described in Chapter 1), look for an opportunity to make improvement suggestions to peers as well. However, also be aware that performance evaluations are not always the most positive of experiences as indicated by the Canada Today feature below.

Performance Appraisals—What Do They Really Accomplish?

Performance appraisals or performance evaluations are nearly universal in professionally managed organizations. A performance appraisal or evaluation usually involves a session where the employee sits down with an immediate supervisor (sometimes more than one) and reviews performance over a specified time. In some companies, such evaluations are used to decide upon such issues as promotions and pay or merit raises, and to plan for future performance changes. For the most part, these appraisals are a "top-down" process based on the ideas of what the manager thinks about the employee's past performance.

A 1997 survey of 2,004 Canadian workers, conducted by Watson Wyatt Worldwide, a consulting firm, discovered that performance appraisals are not an employee growth process but can actually be a disturbing and negative experience for many workers. According to this survey, only 57 percent of employees thought that they were evaluated fairly. Only 39 percent stated that the appraisal was useful for improving their performance (supposedly a major goal of evaluations and appraisals). Also of interest, only 42 percent reported that they had regular performance reviews. For many employees, performance appraisal time may be the only extensive communication with their upper-level managers. Fewer than two out of every five respondents in the survey stated that they talk with their leader or manager regularly about performance-related issues.

What can we conclude from this survey? First, many appraisals are a top-down meeting where the employer talks and the employee listens. Second, many of these appraisals are not done effectively, as they do not encourage better performance or allow employees any input or involvement in increasing their productivity. So while performance evaluations may be one avenue to impress your manager or team leader, such evaluations should not be the only time that you take an opportunity to do so. Instead, use a variety of the techniques that are discussed in this chapter.

SOURCE: Reprinted from an article appearing in the March 1999 issue of *CMA Management Magazine* by Tom Davis and Michael Landa, with permission of Certified Management Accountants of Canada.

Resolve Competing Demands of Two Managers

A substantial change in the modern workplace is that many workers report to more than one manager. A typical arrangement is for a person to report to a manager in his or her regular or *home* department. At the same time the person also reports to the head of a project, or task force, or team. Many people like this arrangement because it adds variety and excitement to the workday. An unfortunate consequence of having two bosses, however, is that you might be caught in conflict. One boss might make a demand that is incompatible with a demand made by the other boss. You might be asked to attend two meetings at the same time, or told by both bosses that some task has to be done immediately.

A recommendation for resolving the competing demands of two managers is to assemble a list of possible solutions that you can sell to both parties. After you have prepared your solutions, explain to both managers the pros and cons of each solution. Recommend which one you think would work best, and describe how it would be implemented. Get a reaction from each manager. After you have taken the steps just indicated, you and the two bosses might have a three-way discussion to resolve the issue.[9] The three of you might decide, for example, that the only way you can get both their projects done immediately is to hire an office temporary for the duration of the project.

Use Discretion in Socializing with Your Manager

A constant dilemma facing employees is how much and what type of socializing with the manager is appropriate. Advocates of socializing contend that off-the-job friendships lead to more natural work relationships. Opponents of socializing with the boss say that it leads to **role confusion** (being uncertain about what role you are carrying out). For example, how can your manager make an objective decision about your salary increase on Monday morning when he or she had dinner with you on Sunday? To avoid cries of favouritism, your boss might recommend you for a below-average increase.

One guideline to consider is to have cordial social relationships with the manager of the same kind shared by most employees. "Cordial" socializing includes activities such as company-sponsored parties, group invitations to the boss's home, and business lunches. Individual social activities, such as camping with the boss, double-dating, and so forth, are more likely to lead to role confusion.

Socializing should not include a casual romantic involvement. Romantic involvements between a superior and a subordinate are disruptive to work and morale. Co-workers usually suspect that the manager's special friend is getting special treatment and resent the favouritism.

What should you do if you and your boss seem suited for a long-term commitment? Why walk away from Mr. or Ms. Right? Our suggestion is that if you do become romantically involved, one of you should request a transfer to another department. Many office romances do lead to happy marriages and other long-term relationships. At the start of the relationship, however, use considerable discretion. Engaging in personal conversation during work time and holding hands in the company cafeteria are unprofessional and taboo.

Engage in Favourable Interactions with Your Manager

The many techniques described previously support the goal of engaging in favourable interactions with your manager. A study of interactions between bank employees and their supervisors showed that purposely trying to create a positive impression on the supervisor led to better performance ratings.[10] Although the finding is not surprising, it is reassuring to know that it is backed by quantitative evidence. Human Relations Self-Assessment Quiz 10-2 contains a listing of behaviours used by employees in the study to create positive interactions with their supervisors. Use these behaviours as a guide for skill building.

Although favourable interactions with a manager are valuable for relationship building, there are times when a group member has to deliver bad news. For example, you might have to inform the manager about a burst water pipe in the mainframe computer room or a bunch of customer complaints about a new product. You want to avoid being the messenger who is punished because he or she

Supervisor Interaction Checklist

Use the following behaviours as a checklist for achieving favourable interactions with your present manager or a future one. The more of these actions you are engaged in, the higher the probability that you are building a favourable relationship with your manager.

1. **Agree with your supervisor's major opinions outwardly even when you disagree inwardly.** ____
2. **Take an immediate interest in your supervisor's personal life.** ____
3. **Praise your supervisor on his or her accomplishments.** ____
4. **Do personal favours for your supervisor.** ____
5. **Do something as a personal favour for your supervisor even though you are not required to do it.** ____
6. **Volunteer to help your supervisor with a task.** ____
7. **Compliment your supervisor on his or her dress or appearance.** ____
8. **Present yourself to your supervisor as being a friendly person.** ____
9. **Agree with your supervisor's major ideas.** ____
10. **Present yourself to your supervisor as being a polite person.** ____

SOURCE: Adapted from Sandy J. Wayne and Gerald R. Ferris, "Influence Tactics, Affect, and Exchange Quality in Supervisor–Subordinate Interactions: A Laboratory Experiment and Field Study," *Journal of Applied Psychology*, October 1990, p. 494.

delivered bad news. Attempt to be calm and businesslike. Do not needlessly blame yourself for the problem. Mention that *we* (or *the company*) are facing a serious challenge. If possible, suggest a possible solution such as, "I have already investigated a backup computer service we can use until the damage is repaired."

Coping with a Problem Manager

Up to this point we have prescribed tactics for dealing with a reasonably rational boss. At some point in their careers many people face the situation of dealing with a problem manager—one who makes it difficult for the subordinate to get the job done. The problem is sometimes attributed to the boss's personality or incompetence. At other times, differences in values or goals could be creating the problem. However, also realize that some behaviours of managers go beyond problematic to more serious concerns about harassment or bullying. These suggestions are not designed to deal with this type of behaviour, and suggestions for these more serious behaviours were presented in Chapter 9. However, Exhibit 10-1 later in this section offers some suggestions if you perceive your manager as a bully. Our concern here is with constructive approaches to dealing with the delicate situation of working for a problem manager, not one who harasses or bullies you.

Re-evaluate Your Manager

As noted by J. Kenneth Matejka and Richard Dunsing, some problem managers are not really a problem. Instead, they have been misperceived by one or more group members. Some employees think they have problem managers when they simply have major role, goal, or value differences with their boss. (A role in this context consists of the expectations of the job.) The problem might also lie in conflicting personalities, such as being outgoing or shy. Another problem is conflicting perspectives, such as being detail-oriented as opposed to taking an overall perspective.

The differences just noted can be good or bad, depending on how they are viewed and used. For example, a detail-oriented group member working with an "overall perspective" boss can be a winning combination.[11]

Confront Your Manager about the Problem

A general-purpose way of dealing with a problem manager is to use confrontation and problem solving as described in Chapter 9. Because your manager has more formal authority than you, the confrontation must be executed with the highest level of tact and sensitivity. A beginning point in confronting a manager is to gently ask for an explanation of the problem. Suppose, for example, you believe strongly that your team leader snubs you because he or she dislikes you. You might inquire gently, "What might I be doing wrong that is creating a problem between us?"

Another situation calling for confrontation would be outrageous behaviour by the manager, such as swearing at and belittling group members. Since several members, or all group members, are involved, a group discussion of the problem might be warranted. You and your co-workers might meet as a group to discuss the impact of the manager's style on group morale and productivity. This tactic runs the risk of backfiring if the manager becomes defensive and angry. Yet career adviser Jim Miller believes it is worth the risk, because the problem of abuse will not go away without discussion.[12]

Confrontation can also be helpful in dealing with the problem of **micromanagement**, the close monitoring of most aspects of group member activities by the manager. "Looking over your shoulder" constantly is an everyday way of describing micromanagement. If you feel that you are being supervised so closely that it is difficult to perform well, confront the situation. Say something of this nature: "I notice that you check almost everything I do lately. Am I making so many errors that you are losing confidence in my work?[13] As a consequence, the manager might explain why he or she is micromanaging or begin to check on your work less frequently.

Learn from Your Manager's Mistakes

Just as you can learn from watching your manager do things right, you can also learn from watching him or her do things wrong. In the first instance, we are talking about using your manager as a positive model. "Modelling" of this type is an important source of learning on the job. Using a superior as a negative model can also be of some benefit. As an elementary example, if your manager criticized you in public, and you felt humiliated, you would have learned a good lesson in effective supervision: Never criticize a subordinate publicly. By serving as a negative example your manager has taught you a valuable lesson.

An unfortunate mistake some workers make is to yell at their manager when he or she has made a mistake (such as yelling at you in public).

Learning from a problem manager's mistakes can also occur when a manager or team leader is fired. Should your manager be fired, analyze the situation to avoid the mistakes he or she made. Enlist the help of others in understanding what went wrong. Did the manager get along poorly with the higher-level managers? Was the manager lacking in technical expertise? Did the manager not work hard enough? Did the manager commit ethical or legal violations such as sexual harassment or stealing company property? Whatever the reason, you will learn quickly what behaviour the company will not tolerate. If your manager was fired simply as a way to downsize or cut costs, there is still a lesson to be learned. Attempt to prove to the company that your compensation is a good investment for the company because your work is outstanding. In lean and mean times, your continued excellent performance may be your only ticket to promotion and continued employment!

What to Do When Your Manager Ignores Your Suggestions

One subtype of a problem manager is the one who ignores suggestions because he or she prefers to maintain the status quo. These managers see their jobs as simply running a smooth operation, and they perceive employees who continue to bring forth suggestions as troublemakers. The problem with not bringing forth innovative ideas is that you will never earn the reputation of being imaginative and ambitious.

exhibit 10 - 1

Is Your Boss a Bully?

Many managers might think of themselves as being very effective as they work hard to keep employees in line. These managers push employees, adjusting goals and micromanaging the tasks they assign to be completed. These are tough managers who may yell, insult, and patronize their subordinates. But when does "pushing hard" become bullying, and do you have to put up with it?

Bullying is any behaviour that intimidates, humiliates, or demeans you. If your boss yells at you and you just roll your eyes and it does not bother you, this might not be bullying. But if it does bother you, humiliate you, or stress you out, and you are the particular target, then you are being bullied. Bullying can range from personal insults and unjustified criticism to physically abusive or aggressive behaviour. Historically, bullying has gone on basically unchecked, often dismissed as a personality conflict or the strong management style of the supervisor. However, due to more public cases in Canada (such as the case of Pierre Lebrun, who went on a shooting spree at his workplace in Ottawa after being continually bullied by colleagues because of his speech impediment and facial tic), many companies are including behaviours like bullying under the same category as harassment in their policies, with the same consequences.

Here are a few suggestions if you feel you are being bullied by your manager (or even another co-worker), based on procedures for reporting and dealing with harassment:

- **Confront the person with his or her behaviour and the effect it is having upon you. Your manager may not have thought the behaviour was problematic, particularly if he or she has always treated employees in this fashion.**
- **Consult fellow workers. If the manager treats them as he or she treats you and they don't have a problem with it, you may need to re-evaluate your feelings. For example, if co-workers say, "Oh, she yells at everyone. After a while, you just ignore it, especially when you see the Christmas bonus cheques."**
- **Keep a log of all incidents. If you report the bullying, you will need the dates of the incidents as well as a clear and concise record of what happened. One recent case in Canada that did go to court awarded an RCMP officer over $90,000 in lost earnings and nervous shock after she was bullied by fellow officers and her immediate supervisor.**
- **Report the behaviour to the human resources department using company policies and procedures. It is up to Human Resources then to investigate your complaint and resolve the issue either formally or informally.**
- **Above all, remember that you do have rights. You do not have to tolerate a poisonous work environment. If you have questions, call your local Labour Board office or Human Rights Office.**

SOURCE: Lauren M. Bernardi, "Management by Bullying: The Legal Consequences," *Canadian Manager,* 26(3), Fall 2001, pp. 13–16.

A management research report offers several suggestions for coping with this form of problem manager. One approach is to implement your idea without his or her approval. If your idea works out well, your manager may embrace your suggestion. Another tactic is to cultivate your boss's superior. Tactfully tell your boss's boss about your innovative idea. He or she might support your idea and give you the green light to implement it.[14]

A real problem with cultivating your boss's boss is that a boss bypass is generally frowned upon. However, so long as you do not say or imply anything negative about your manager, it could be worth a try. You might say to his or her superior, "I have brought this to Ms. McHendry's attention, but she's too busy with other projects now to dig into my proposal."

What to Do When Your Manager Takes Credit for Your Accomplishments

Imagine that you have been assigned the job of making the arrangements for a company meeting. Everything runs so smoothly that at the banquet your manager is praised for his or her fine job of arranging the meeting. You smoulder while he or she accepts all the praise without mentioning that you did all the work. How should you handle a problem manager of this type—one who takes credit for your accomplishments?

Remember, first, that in one sense your manager does deserve much of the credit. Managers are responsible for the accomplishments and failures of their subordinates. Your boss had the good sense to delegate the task to the right person. Nevertheless, a self-confident manager would share the credit with you. To get the credit you deserve for your ideas and accomplishments, try these suggestions:

1. *Try a discreet confrontation.* The manager who is taking credit for your accomplishments may not realize that you are being slighted. A quiet conversation about the issue could prevent recurrences. You might gently ask, for example, "At what point do I get recognition for doing an assigned task well? I noticed that my name was not mentioned when our department received credit for setting up a new billing system." (It was you who did 95 percent of the work on the system.)
2. *Take preventive measures.* A sensible way to receive credit for your accomplishments is to let others know of your efforts while you are doing the work. This is more effective than looking for recognition after your manager has already taken credit for your accomplishments. Casually let others know what you are doing, including your boss's boss and other key people. In this way you will not sound immodest or aggressive—you are only talking about your work.
3. *Present a valid reason for seeking recognition.* By explaining why you want recognition, you will not seem unduly ambitious or pushy to your manager. You might say "I am trying to succeed in this company. It would help me to document my performance. Would it therefore be possible for my name to also appear on the report of the new billing system?"[15]

How to Work with a Disorganized Manager

Many well-organized people report to disorganized managers, creating the opportunity for tension and personality clashes. Under these circumstances, the well-organized subordinate faces the challenge of creating a good working relationship. In contrast, a well-organized boss is unlikely to put up with a disorganized subordinate for long. Given that the well-organized group member cannot readily fire the boss, he or she faces the task of forever compensating for the boss's disorganization. For example, many assistants have to spend time searching for the misplaced files of their boss—both hard-copy and disk files.

According to management consultant Deborah Zeigler, you can take several steps to facilitate a good working relationship with a disorganized manager.[16] Begin by identifying goals and priorities. Find out what the organization and department are attempting to accomplish, and what your boss expects of you. This basic information can be used as a wedge to encourage your boss to be better organized.

The second step is to communicate your concerns to your manager about how his or her work habits could be interfering with goal attainment. Tact and diplomacy are essential. You might say, for example, "I want to prepare a chart explaining our need for more salespeople, but I can't do it without the figures you promised me last week."

Third, rely on co-workers and others throughout the company to supplement your boss as an information source. When your manager is unavailable (disorganized people are often difficult to find) or does not have the information you need, network members might be able to help. In the example above, maybe somebody else can provide the figures you need.

A fourth step is to become familiar with your boss's primary problems in organization. If you know your manager has difficulty getting projects completed on time, step in well before the deadline to offer encouragement and assistance. You might present a chart to your boss estimating how close the project should be to completion. If you offer help, rather than criticism, your contribution will be valued.

How to Gently Get Away from Your Manager

Perhaps you have tried long and hard to develop a better working relationship with your manager but the situation is still intolerable. Three alternatives remain: You can wait for your manager to leave; you can leave the company; or you can look for a new job in the same firm. It generally makes the most sense to pursue the last course of action, particularly if you are satisfied with the firm.

The major strategy for getting away from your supervisor is to market yourself to other key managers in the company.[17] Make others aware of your accomplishments through such means as volunteering for committee work or getting your name in the company newsletter. Another method is to make personal contacts through such means as joining company teams or clubs.

While you are developing your contacts, speak to your manager about a transfer. Point out that although you are satisfied with your job, you value broad experience at this point in your career. Unfortunately, weak managers generally are reluctant to recommend subordinates for transfer.

Another recommended approach is to speak directly to the human resources department about your dilemma. Point out quietly that you want to be considered a candidate for transfer to another department. Suggest that you could make a bigger contribution if you worked for a manager who gave you more responsibility. However, never say anything derogatory about your present manager. Such a practice is strictly taboo.

A unifying theme exists to the aforementioned seven approaches for dealing with a problem manager. Continue to perform well despite your short-term problems. If your manager is indeed a poor performer or has a personality problem, top management is probably aware of the situation. You will be admired for your ability to cope with the situation. Performing poorly because you perceive your manager as a problem is self-defeating.

Summary

Developing a favourable relationship with your manager or team leader is the most basic strategy of getting ahead in your career. Your manager or team leader influences your future because he or she is often asked by other prospective superiors to present an opinion about your capabilities.

A general strategy for developing a good relationship with your manager or team leader is to create a favourable impression. Specific tactics of this type include these:

1. Achieve good job performance.
2. Display a strong work ethic.
3. Demonstrate good emotional intelligence.
4. Be dependable, honest, and ethical.
5. Appreciate your manager's strengths.
6. Show an interest in your firm's products or services.
7. Be a good organizational citizen.
8. Create a strong presence.

Many tactics for developing a good relationship with your manager or team leader require that you deal directly with him or her:

1. Try to understand your manager.
2. Find out what your manager expects of you.
3. Bring forth solutions as well as problems.
4. Minimize complaints.
5. Avoid bypassing your manager.
6. Suggest improvements during the performance evaluation.
7. Resolve competing demands of two managers.
8. Use discretion in socializing with your manager.
9. Engage in favourable interactions with your manager.

Coping with a manager you perceive to be a problem is part of getting along with him or her. Reevaluate your manager to make sure you have not misperceived him or her. It is important to confront your manager about your problem. Often this problem is a case of being micromanaged. Learning from your problem manager's mistakes is recommended, including if he or she is fired.

When your manager takes credit for your accomplishments, consider these tactics: discreetly confront your manager, take preventive measures by keeping others informed of work in progress, and present a valid reason for seeking recognition.

Working with a disorganized manager can lead to tension and a personality clash. Under these circumstances, tactfully explain how your manager's work habits create problems in attaining work goals. Rely on others to help you attain the information you need to accomplish work for your manager. Also, recognize your manager's biggest problems in organization and offer direct assistance.

When your relationship with your manager does not improve, it may be necessary to seek a transfer. The best method is to market yourself to other key managers in the company. This may involve establishing a network of contacts. Also, speak to your manager about a transfer without indicating your dissatisfaction, and present your case to the human resources department.

Questions and Activities

1. Suppose your manager reads this chapter. How might this influence the effectiveness of your using the strategies and tactics described here?
2. Identify three of the tactics described in this chapter that you are most likely to use. Explain.
3. Identify three of the tactics described in this chapter that you are least likely to use. Explain.
4. Is this chapter simply about "kissing up to the boss"? Explain.
5. Aside from suggestions in the text, how else can an employee show an interest in the firm's products or services?
6. Assuming team leaders don't have as much power as a regular manager, why is it still important to build a good relationship with your team leader?
7. Why is "creating a strong presence" considered a key strategy for getting ahead in the workplace?
8. Suppose you and a co-worker are best friends. Your friend gets promoted and becomes your manager. What should be your policy about socializing with this person?
9. What would your manager have to do before you would be willing to organize a group confrontation about his or her behaviour?
10. Interview an experienced manager. Ask his or her opinion about what an employee can do to create a favourable impression.

Internet Skill Builder

Management Skills for the Workplace

Visit **www.workforce.com**, the website of the American magazine *Workforce*. Scroll through the site with the goal of identifying three interpersonal skills that you think would be advantageous for you to develop to get along with your manager or team leader. Develop an action plan that will assist you in developing at least one of these skills. You may have to make some inferences as the articles may not be directly related to interpersonal skills for getting along with your boss.

Weblinks

www.cirb-ccri.gc.ca
This is the site for the Canada Industrial Relations Board. From this site you can see the latest additions to the Canada Labour Code and see what this board does in Canada.

www.mcb.co.uk/canada/raframe.htm
This is the website for the Canadian Management Forum, with all kinds of links and information about management in a wide field of industries.

Human Relations Case Study

THE PROBLEM MANAGER[18]

Read the case below and answer the questions that follow. Once you've done that, attempt Human Relations Skill-Building Exercise 10-1.

Kaled was a hard-working supervisor whose demonstrated ability gave him a strong shot at a middle-management position. One morning Kaled was reviewing next year's budget. He was distressed when he discovered that his budget was being cut and that he was losing one person in his department. "Sorry, things are tight and there's nothing we can do," said his manager, Ruth. Later, Kaled found out that Phil, another supervisor (whose division was doing poorly), was getting a budget increase. Kaled became furious and said to himself, "Of course Phil gets what he wants. He's always so buddy-buddy with Ruth."

Phil did regularly take time to chat with Ruth. He would ask about her grandchild and suggest having lunch together. Kaled had a cordial relationship with Ruth, but he mostly kept to himself and tended to his job.

Kaled thought over who in the company might be able to help him work out his dispute with Ruth. He remembered that he and the president had struck up an acquaintance when they met at a music concert several months ago. "Maybe if I talk to him," Kaled thought, "I can get my budget restored."

Kaled sent an email message to the president's office justifying why he wanted his budget and group member restored. The president thought Kaled's points were sound, and he requested that Ruth reverse her decision. Although miffed, Ruth complied with the president's request.

Kaled was relieved at first, but Ruth started making life miserable for him. Working over the problem in his head, Kaled thought there might be one way Ruth would change her attitude toward him. "Maybe a well-placed memo asking why Ruth was never available until 11:00 in the morning might work, or saying that I can't ever talk with her because she's always showing Phil photos of her grandchild."

Kaled sent another email to his "friend" the president, sending a copy to Ruth. He didn't hear from the president, but he did hear from Ruth. "I'm putting you on notice," she said, "for gross insubordination."

Kaled said calmly, "We'll see about that." He then returned to his office and put a call through to the president, who was in a day-long meeting. Finally, at 3:00 the president called and asked him to come to his office. "Ah, sweet revenge," thought Kaled.

"I understand you're not happy here, Kaled," said the president.

"But..." Kaled tried to protest.

"You know we would hate to lose someone as competent as you, but I do have some connections in other companies. I strongly suggest you let me help you find a suitable position elsewhere."

Questions

1. What errors in boss relationships did Kaled commit?
2. How might Kaled have attempted to improve his relationship with Ruth?
3. How should Kaled respond to the president's suggestion about looking for another job elsewhere?

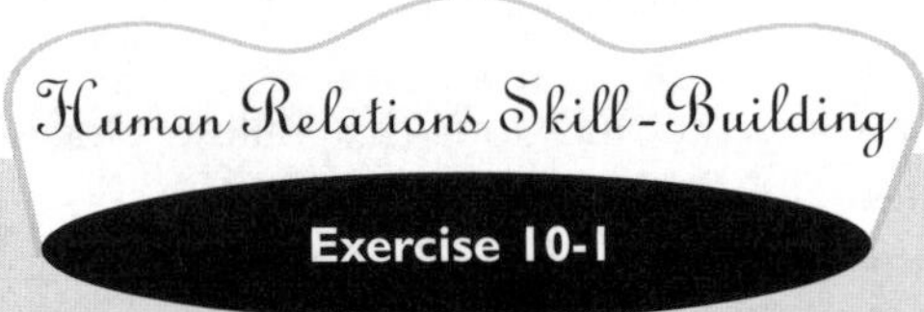

Discussing a Sensitive Issue with Your Manager

Assume Kaled decided to work directly with Ruth rather than go to the president with the budget controversy. Assume also that Kaled did learn about Phil receiving a budget increase. One student plays the role of Kaled, who is trying to get back in good graces with Ruth. Another student plays the role of Ruth, who has granted Kaled an appointment to further discuss the budget issue. The person who plays the role of Kaled should work diligently at creating a favourable impression on Ruth.

Getting Along with Co-workers and Customers

Learning Outcomes

After studying the information and doing the exercises in this chapter, you should be able to

- describe several strategies for developing good relationships with co-workers
- explain several strategies to deal with difficult people
- define groups and teams—their similarities and differences
- explain the process of team development using one model of team development
- explain several barriers that interfere with effective team behaviours
- list possible barriers to effective team development
- describe several methods to become an effective team member
- specify approaches to building good relationships with customers

Tammy was a copywriter at an advertising agency that was hard hit by a decline in client advertising. Her message to her work group was that advertising always runs in cycles. Tammy also noted that the bottom point had already been reached. She encouraged the team by reminding them that management was attempting to increase advertising activity outside the usual channels. Tammy proved to be right. The company soon landed a few big contracts to conduct direct-mail advertising. The payout to Tammy was that team spirit did not deteriorate, and two co-workers told Tammy they appreciated her support.

This brief anecdote illustrates the importance of making a deliberate effort to contribute to the welfare of group members. Tammy contributed to the team effort by encouraging her co-workers in times of trouble. Anyone with work experience is aware of the importance of getting along with co-workers and customers (including clients and patients). If you are unable to work cooperatively with others in the workplace, it will be difficult for you to do your job. You need their cooperation and support and they need yours. Furthermore, the leading reason employees are terminated is not poor technical skill but inability or unwillingness to form satisfactory relationships with others on the job.

In this chapter we describe a variety of approaches to help you build strong relationships with co-workers and customers. For convenience these strategies and tactics are classified into building good relations with co-workers, examining teams and developing team skills, and building good relationships with customers.

Building Good Co-worker Relationships

The approaches in this section are both *proactive* and *reactive*. In other words, there are really two ways to get along with others. You can lead in the spirit of cooperation—in other words, be proactive. Your second choice is to react to the behaviours of others in positive ways, even when the other person is being difficult. These are reactive strategies. In reality, each of us chooses and uses a variety of behaviours listed below to maintain harmonious workplace relations. Your job, then, is to pick and choose from these strategies and apply them to your advantage.

Develop Allies through Being Civil

People who are courteous, kind, cooperative, and cheerful develop allies and friends in the workplace. Practising basic good manners such as being pleasant and friendly is also part of being civil. While being civil may seem obvious to most of us, lack of such civility appears to be a growing concern in the workplace. Such incivility exists not just in violence or conflict, but in the "thousand small slings and arrows that day after day, eat away...."[1] Therefore, being civil may help you stand out in the face of such disrespectful or impolite behaviour. Being civil also involves not snooping, spreading malicious gossip, or weaseling out of group presents such as shower or retirement gifts. In addition, it is important to be available to co-workers who want your advice as well as your help in times of crisis.

Closely related to being civil is maintaining a positive outlook. Everyone knows that you gain more allies by being optimistic and positive than by being pessimistic and negative. Nevertheless, many people ignore this simple strategy for getting along well with others. Co-workers are more likely to solicit your opinion or offer you help when you are perceived to be a cheerful person.

From the supervisor's standpoint, an optimistic and positive employee is a greater asset than an employee with the opposite disposition. People who chronically complain are a drag on the morale of other employees in the office. People with a positive attitude tend to be asked first to try out new techniques and procedures. The reason is that they are more willing to accept change than are people with a negative outlook.

Make Other People Feel Important

A fundamental principle of fostering good relationships with co-workers and others is to make them feel important. Sheila Murray Bethela advises us to make use of the Please-Make-Me-Feel-Important concept. Visualize that everyone in the workplace is wearing a small sign around the neck that says, "Please make me feel important."[2] Although the leader has primary responsibility for satisfying this recognition need, co-workers also play a key role. One approach to making a co-worker feel important would be to bring a notable accomplishment of his or hers to the attention of the rest of the group. Human Relations Self-Assessment Quiz 11-1 gives you an opportunity to think through your tendencies to make others feel important.

Maintain Honest and Open Relationships

In human relations we attach considerable importance to maintaining honest and open relationships with other people. Giving co-workers frank but tactful answers to their requests for your opinion is one useful way of developing open relationships. Suppose that a co-worker asks your opinion about a memo that he intends to send to his boss. As you read it, you find it somewhat incoherent and filled with spelling and grammatical errors. An honest response to this letter might be: "I think your idea is a good one. But I think your memo needs more work before that idea comes across clearly."

As described in Chapter 7, accurately expressing your feelings also leads to constructive relationships. If you arrive at work upset over a personal problem and appearing obviously fatigued, you can expect some reaction. A peer might say, "What seems to be the problem? Is everything all right?" A dishonest reply would be, "Everything is fine. What makes you think something is wrong?" In addition to making an obviously untrue statement, you would also be perceived as rejecting the person who asked the question.

If you prefer not to discuss your problem, an honest response on your part would be, "Thanks for your interest. I am facing some problems today. But I think things will work out." Such an answer would not involve you in a discussion of

How Important Do I Make People Feel?

Indicate on a one-to-five scale how frequently you act (or would act if the situation presented itself) in the ways indicated below: very infrequently (VI); infrequently (I); sometimes (S); frequently (F); very frequently (VF). Circle the number underneath the column that best fits your answer.

	VI	I	S	F	VF
1. I do my best to correctly pronounce a co-worker's name.	1	2	3	4	5
2. I avoid letting other people's egos get too big.	5	4	3	2	1
3. I brag to others about the accomplishments of my co-workers.	1	2	3	4	5
4. I recognize the birthdays of friends in a tangible way.	1	2	3	4	5
5. It makes me anxious to listen to others brag about their accomplishments.	5	4	3	2	1
6. After hearing that a friend has done something outstanding, I shake his or her hand.	1	2	3	4	5
7. If a friend or co-worker recently received a degree or certificate, I would offer my congratulations.	1	2	3	4	5
8. If a friend or co-worker finished second in a contest, I would inquire why he or she did not finish first.	5	4	3	2	1
9. If a co-worker showed me how to do something, I would compliment that person's skill.	1	2	3	4	5
10. When a co-worker starts bragging about a family member's accomplishments, I do not respond.	5	4	3	2	1

Scoring and Interpretation: Total the numbers corresponding to your answers. Scoring 40 to 50 points suggests that you typically make people feel important; 16 to 39 points suggests that you have a moderate tendency toward making others feel important; 0 to 15 points suggests that you need to develop skill in making others feel important. Study this chapter carefully.

your personal problems. Also, you would not be perceived as rejecting your co-worker. The same principle applies equally well to personal relationships.

Follow Group Standards of Conduct

The basic principle to follow in getting along with co-workers is to follow **group norms**. These refer to the unwritten set of expectations for group members—what

people ought to do. Norms become a standard of what each person should do or not do within the group. Norms also provide general guidelines for reacting constructively to the behaviour of co-workers. Norms are a major component of the organizational culture, part of the values and beliefs of the firm that guide people's actions. In one firm, the norms and culture may favour hard work and high quality. In another firm, the norms and culture may favour a weaker work ethic.

Group norms also influence the social aspects of behaviour on the job. These aspects of behaviour relate to such things as the people to have lunch with, getting together after work, joining a company team, and the type of clothing to wear to work.

Workers learn about norms both through observation and direct instruction from other group members. If you do not deviate too far from these norms, much of your behaviour will be accepted by the group. If you deviate too far, you will be subject to much rejection and the feeling of being isolated. In some instances, you might even be subjected to verbal abuse if you make the other employees look bad.

Getting along too well with co-workers has its price as well. The risk of conforming too closely to group norms is that you lose your individuality. You become viewed by your superiors as "one of the office gang" rather than a person who aspires to move up in the organization.

Express an Interest in the Work of Others

Almost everyone is self-centred to some extent. Thus, topics of conversation that are favoured are ones closely related to people themselves, such as their children, friends, hobbies, work, or possessions. Sales representatives rely heavily on this fact in cultivating relationships with established customers. They routinely ask the customer about his or her hobbies, family members, and work activities. ("Say, how's your coin collection going?") You can capitalize on this simple strategy by asking co-workers and friends questions such as these:

- How is your work going? (*Highly recommended.*)
- How are things going for you?
- How did you gain the knowledge necessary for your job?
- How does the company use the output from your department?
- How does your present job fit in with your career plans?
- How did Leticia do in the county cat show?

A danger in asking questions about other people's work is that some questions may not be perceived as well-intentioned. There is a fine line between honest curiosity and snooping. You must stay alert to this subtle distinction.

Be a Good Listener

After you ask questions, you must be prepared to listen to the answers. The simplest technique for getting along with co-workers, friends, and acquaintances is to be a good listener. The topics you should be willing to listen to during working hours include job problems and miscellaneous complaints. Lunch breaks, coffee breaks, and after hours are better suited to listening to people talk about their personal lives, current events, sports, and the like.

Becoming an effective listener takes practice. As you practise your listening skills, try the suggestions offered in Chapter 7. The payoff is that listening builds constructive relationships both on and off the job. Too often, people take turns talking rather than listening to each other. The result is that neither party feels better as a result of the conversation.

Use Appropriate Compliments

An effective way of developing good relationships with co-workers and friends is to compliment something with which they closely identify, such as their children, spouse, hobbies, or pets. Paying a compliment is a form of **positive reinforcement**, rewarding somebody for doing something right. The right response is therefore strengthened, or reinforced. A compliment is a useful multipurpose reward.

Another way of complimenting people is through recognition. The suggestions made earlier about making people feel important are a way of recognizing people, and therefore compliments. Investing a small amount of time in recognizing a co-worker can pay large dividends in terms of cultivating an ally. Recognition and compliments are more likely to create a favourable relationship when they are appropriate. Appropriate in this context means that the compliment fits the accomplishment. Praise that is too lavish may be interpreted as belittling and patronizing.

Let's look at the difference between an appropriate and an exaggerated compliment over the same issue. An executive secretary gets a fax machine operating that was temporarily not sending messages.

> *Appropriate compliment*: Nice job, Stephanie. Fixing the fax machine took considerable skill. We can now resume sending important fax messages.

Exaggerated compliment: Stephanie, I'm overwhelmed. You're a world-class fax machine specialist. Are there no limits to your talents?

Observe that the appropriate compliment is thoughtful and is proportionate to what Stephanie accomplished. The exaggerated compliment is probably wasted because it is way out of proportion to the magnitude of the accomplishment.

Deal Effectively with Difficult People

A major challenge in getting along well with co-workers is to deal constructively with difficult people. These co-workers may be in your work group or team or elsewhere in your business or organization. A co-worker is classified as difficult if he or she is uncooperative, touchy, defensive, hostile, or even very unfriendly. Also, the various negative team roles that are discussed in a later section of this chapter describe behaviours of difficult co-workers. Here we present five widely applicable approaches to dealing with such individuals.

Take Problems Professionally, Not Personally

A key principle in dealing with a variety of personalities is to take what they do professionally, not personally. Difficult people are not necessarily out to get you. You may just represent a stepping-stone for them to get what they want.[3] For example, if a co-worker insults you because you need his help Friday afternoon, he probably has nothing against you personally. He might just prefer to become mentally disengaged from work on Friday afternoons. Your request distracts him from mentally phasing out of work as early as he would like.

Give Ample Feedback

The primary technique for dealing with counterproductive behaviour is to offer feedback to the difficult person regarding how his or her behaviour affects you. Focus on the person's behaviour rather than on characteristics or values. If a co-worker is annoying you by constantly pointing out potential disasters, say something to this effect: "I have difficulty maintaining my enthusiasm when you so often point out the possible negatives." Such a statement will engender less resentment than saying, "I find you to be a total pessimist, and it annoys me."

Use Tact and Diplomacy in Dealing with Annoying Behaviour

Co-workers who irritate you rarely do annoying things on purpose. Tactful actions on your part can sometimes take care of these annoyances without your having to confront the problem. Close your door, for example, if noisy co-workers are gathered outside. Or try one woman's method of getting rid of office pests: She keeps a file open on her computer screen and gestures to it apologetically when someone overstays a visit.

Sometimes subtlety doesn't work, and it may be necessary to diplomatically confront the co-worker who is annoying you. Jane Michaels suggests that you precede a criticism with a compliment. Here is an example of this approach: "You're one of the best people I've ever worked with, but one habit of yours drives me bananas. Do you think you could let me know when you're going to be late getting back to the office after lunch?"[4]

Use Humour

Nonhostile humour can often be used to help a difficult person understand how his or her behaviour is blocking others.[5] Also, the humour will help defuse conflict between you and that person. The humour should point to the person's unacceptable behaviour yet not belittle him or her. Imagine that Kevin (who in your opinion is a difficult person) says that he will not sign off on your report because instead of using the metric system you used imperial measures. You need Kevin's approval because the boss wants a consensus report from the group. You ask Kevin again the next day, and he still refuses to sign.

To gain Kevin's cooperation, you say: "I'm sorry we upset your scientific mind. But I swear on a stack of Bibles, one metre high, all future reports will use the metric system. Will you please affix your signature one centimetre below mine? By the way, did you see that 45-metre field goal the Alouettes kicker made in yesterday's game?" With a grin on his face, Kevin replies, "OK, give me the report to sign." (The touch of humour here indicates that you respect Kevin's desire to use the metric system, but you also acknowledge that it can sometimes be impractical.)

Reinforce Civil Behaviour and Good Moods

In the spirit of positive reinforcement, when a generally difficult person is behaving acceptably, recognize the behaviour in some way. Reinforcing statements would include "It's fun working with you today" and "I appreciate your professional attitude."

Listen and Respond

As usual, active listening improves many problems in human relations. Give the difficult person ample opportunity to express his or her concerns, doubts, anger, or other feelings. Then acknowledge your awareness of the person's position.[6] An example: "OK, you tell me that management is really against us and, therefore, we shouldn't work so hard." After listening, present your perspective in a way such as this: "Your viewpoint may be valid based on your experiences. Yet so far, I've found management here to be on my side." This exchange of viewpoints is less likely to lead to failed communication than if you are judgmental with a statement such as, "You really shouldn't think that way."

The tactics for dealing with difficult people just described require practice to be effective. Also, you may have to use a combination of the six tactics described in this section to deal effectively with a difficult person. The point of these tactics is not to out-manipulate or subdue a difficult person, but to establish a cordial and productive working relationship.

Face Maturely the Challenge of the Office Romance

As described in the discussion about socializing with the boss (Chapter 10), office romances can be disruptive to morale and productivity. Co-worker romances are a more widespread potential problem, because more romances take place between co-workers on the same level than between superiors and subordinates. As more women have entered the workforce in professional positions, and as professionals work longer hours, the office has become a frequent meeting place. Many companies have policies against managers dating people below them in the hierarchy, but few companies attempt to restrict same-level romantic involvements. Nevertheless, sensitivity is required to conduct an office romance that does not detract from one's professionalism.

Many companies are concerned about information leakage within their organization. If you date a person who has access to confidential information (such as trade secrets), management might be concerned that you are a security risk. You therefore might miss out on some opportunities for better assignments.

It is important not to abuse company tolerance of the co-worker romance. Do not invite the person you are dating to meals at company expense, take him or her on nonessential business trips, or create projects to work on jointly.

Strive to keep the relationship confidential and restricted to after hours. Minimize talking to co-workers about the relationship. Such behaviour as holding hands or kissing in public view is regarded as poor office etiquette.

Should your co-worker romance terminate, you face a special challenge. You must now work cooperatively with a person toward whom you may have angry feelings. Few people have the emotional detachment necessary to work smoothly with a former romantic involvement. Extra effort will therefore be required on both your parts.

Groups and Teams in the Workplace

The strategies that we have just discussed will assist you in getting along more effectively with co-workers, whether they are members of your work group, work team, or other members of your organization. Here we want to focus exclusively on teams and groups. With continued emphasis on the use of teams and groups in the workplace, you will also benefit from developing a better understanding of what work groups and teams are, the stages of group and team development, and strategies for you to become an effective team player. See the Canada Today box for a sample of Canadian companies that rely heavily on teams to meet organizational goals.

What Are Groups and Teams?

With such an emphasis in the workplace on working on teams and in groups, we need to be clear about what groups and teams are and how they differ. People often use the terms *group* and *team* interchangeably as if they were one and the same. You may talk about the group that you have to work with and say that the group has no team spirit. The next day, you may refer to the same group as your work team. However, we need to realize that the two terms are different. First, let's examine groups and then switch our focus to teams.

As you walk down any street downtown on a busy afternoon, you will see large numbers of people. Some of these people are obviously together; they may be holding hands, chatting with one another, or sitting at the same café table. You can also identify people who are alone even though they may be walking side by side. At the moment, these people are not part of any group, although they may be engaged in activities that are similar to those around them, such as standing in line at the bank machine, looking through the same outdoor sales rack, or watching a street musi-

Successful Companies That Rely on the "Team" Approach

Here is a small sampling of the companies in Canada that rely heavily on teams, particularly self-managed teams. Self-managed teams are specialized teams that assume all or most of the responsibility for their performance as well as doing their own performance reviews. Each team is responsible for all aspects of its performance. Leadership within the team may vary according to required tasks, or leadership may be done on a rotating basis. To be a truly self-managed team, the team must manage all tasks required for its performance. Many of these companies, such as Milltronics, gave their employees formal training to assist in the development of teams.

Investing in the team approach has paid off for many companies. The key is to train staff in the techniques of working effectively in groups. These skills are not hard to learn and usually involve basic communication skills, conflict resolution skills, skills in managing change, and decision-making and problem-solving skills. These companies are not presented in any type of order. The common thread is that teams are the core of how these companies "do business."

Company	***Location***	***Product***
Pratt and Whitney	Longueuil, Quebec	PW500 turbofan engine
Asea Brown Boveri Canada	Guelph, Ontario	power transformers
Siemens Milltronics	Peterborough, Ontario	measuring equipment
AMP of Canada	Markham, Ontario	electrical connectors and interconnection systems
Steelcase Canada Ltd.	Markham, Ontario	office furniture and equipment

SOURCES: Brian D. Harrison, Henry P. Conn, Barrie Whittaker, and James Mitchell, "Mobilizing Abilities Through Teamwork," *Canadian Business Review*, 21, 1994, pp. 20–24; and Steven L. Mcshane, *Canadian Organizational Behaviour* (Toronto: Richard D. Irwin Inc., 1995).

cian perform a song. A group is different from this kind of collection. A **group** consists of "*two or more people who are aware of each other, who both influence and are influenced by one another, who are engaged in an ongoing and relatively stable relationship, who share common goals, and who view themselves as belonging to the group.*"[7]

Let's examine each component of the definition so that we are clear as to what a group really is. First, a group consists of at least two people. Some researchers actually define a small group as consisting of three or more people.[8]

Being aware of each other and being influenced by each other means that group members have interdependence. The members depend on each other and therefore must communicate and interact. As we are well aware by now, this interaction will involve both verbal and nonverbal communication. Through communication, meanings and relationships are developed that establish a group context. For example, some groups develop special language or codes that only those within the group understand. In the group, members establish what are considered to be appropriate and inappropriate behaviours. For instance, you may have a group of friends who get together regularly for a meal. Is being late for the meal OK, or is a late entrance met with frowns of disapproval and a few sarcastic remarks?

Groups also share common **goals**. Some goals may be informal, such as friendship. Some goals may be more formal, such as raising a certain amount of money for a specific charity.

Last, people consider themselves to be part of the group. Group membership is deemed as important and necessary for the individual. If the group loses its importance for a member, the individual may opt out of the group or engage in other behaviours that may go against group rules or norms. You may have belonged to a group of friends in high school, but physical distance and new interests may diminish the importance of this group for you. On the other hand, some of these members may still live in your hometown, and so membership continues to be an important part of their lives.

So the question now is how do groups differ from teams?

A team starts out as a group but over time reaches a new level of quality. Special feelings are created among members, and a team creates its own processes and takes leadership for its own development and performance.[9] A work team, then, is a special kind of group that is usually brought together for a special task and has some special characteristics.[10]

- **A team is a diverse group of people.** In order to achieve its goal(s), a team is made up of people with specific abilities and resources. A group is often based on a more casual alliance. For instance, a marketing team may have members from finance, product development, as well as marketing specialists in advertising.
- **Members share leadership responsibility.** Because of the diversity of talents and abilities, each member must assume leadership as required for the task. For example, the individual from product development may assume a leadership role as he or she demonstrates and discusses the product for the rest of the team. At this point, this member gives direction to the other, less knowledgeable members.
- **A team creates an identity.** More than an ordinary group, teams develop specific self-images. This image creates cohesiveness and helps to motivate the team. Members begin to see themselves as the "Widget Creative Team."
- **Team efforts are interconnected.** A team continuously weaves and interconnects the efforts of individual team members to develop a tighter energy and higher focus than most groups have. Each team member's efforts become an integral part of the team effort.
- **Members work to achieve a mutually defined goal.** Like groups, teams also have goals. However, team goals involve more intensive communication to develop a consensus as to what the goals are and how they should be achieved. A team's goal may be to get the product on the shelves before the Christmas season. As such each member has his or her own goals to bring back to his or her own team and department.
- **The team works within the context of other groups and systems.** "A team affects and is affected by the context, situation, the environment, and the system within which it works."[11] While groups are affected the same way, the relationships within these systems are likely more critical to team functioning.

When these factors are put together, a **team** can be defined as "*a diverse group of people who share leadership responsibility for creating a group identity and an interconnected effort to achieve a mutually defined goal within the context of other groups and systems.*"[12] In general then, teams are often more tightly knit and cohesive, more focused on mutually defined goals, have more diverse members' backgrounds, and are usually formed for a specific purpose. There are many different types of teams in the workplace. Some teams, such as many task forces, have a formalized structure with a recognized leader (such as a chairperson or coordinator) and are temporary. Other teams are more informal, such as a teaching team at a college or a marketing team within an organization. Within any business or firm there may be many highly specialized teams, and employees may belong to more than one team. On the other hand, a small business may consist of one team. Successful small businesses often have a close group of people that work together to ensure continued company success.

How Teams and Groups Develop

Teams and groups do not "just happen." Teams, in particular, go through a series of developmental stages that can be identified. There are several theories of group development, including the four stages of group development by Tuckman[13] and the four phases of decision-making groups by Fisher.[14] We will examine the four stages of the Tuckman model, which includes the stages of forming, storming, norming, and performing. A fifth stage, adjourning, has been added to these four stages.[15]

The *forming stage* usually occurs when the group or team is new or there are a number of new members. Members are cautious and uncomfortable as they attempt to determine personal relationships and define their tasks. Little work is accomplished. Once the group or team has some idea about goals and responsibilities, the *storming stage* begins. During this stage, members may argue or become more emotional, and conflicts and differences of opinion emerge during team meetings. Important issues and ideas are tabled and emotions may run high. The *norming stage* can be identified as the period when conflicts are resolved and the group develops approaches for goal completion. The *performing stage* is entered when the group focuses its energy on tasks to attain goals. Decisions are reached, problems solved, and the group is now a fully functioning team.

A final stage can be added to this model: the *stage of adjourning*. Some teams, such as task forces and ad hoc committees, may be disbanded once the task has been completed or the goal has been reached. During adjournment, group members may experience several different emotions. They may be sad that the group is now about to be disbanded and may actually experience emotions similar to the grieving process. There may also be relief that the work is now completed and members can focus their energy elsewhere. Members may also feel proud of their accomplishments.[16]

It should be noted that team development does not always run a smooth course as these stages seem to suggest. In reality, the development may falter. For example, a team may quickly go through forming and storming and then get mired in the norming stage with conflicts. Some teams never to get beyond storming and other teams perform well for a period of time until conflict erupts or the team encounters an internal or external change. What we have presented here is a framework to assist you in understanding some of the processes that occur as teams develop, mature, and hopefully make efficient progress toward organizational goals.

Barriers to Effective Team-Building

Why don't teams always reach the performing stage? In other words, what are the barriers that slow teams down and inhibit team development and performance? Some of these barriers may be imposed upon the group by outside forces that the group may not be able to control (such as merging with another company). Other barriers are internal and result from group interaction and processes (such as new hires on the team and personal problems that interfere with working). Here we will review some of these barriers.

Time Constraints

When a work group or team does not have sufficient time to make a decision, complete goals or tasks, or solve a problem, the members may not put forth their best efforts. This type of pressure can create stress and work overload. Conflicts may erupt. As a result, the group may perform poorly.

Physical Barriers

Not all groups and teams work in conducive environments, as you may have experienced yourself—in classroom work groups, for example. A room that is too small, too hot, too cold, or too noisy, to name a few negative environmental barriers, makes work more difficult. Teams whose members are spread out geographically can have a difficult time getting together. These types of barriers need to be dealt with before team formation or else early in team development.

Inappropriate Group Size

Groups that are too large or groups that are too small, depending upon the purpose of the group or team, can create a barrier to effective performance. In a group that is too large, members may feel that they do not get enough opportunities for input. There may be more interpersonal conflict, and individual resources may not be fully utilized. Teams that do not have enough members may burn out the few active members. The size of the team should be related to the goals of the team.

Conflicting Goals of Group Members

When people join a team or group, they also bring different motives or goals with them. Some members may be there to sabotage any group efforts. Others may want to assume leadership or display power. Some people may want to put in as little effort as possible. Some team members may have **hidden agendas** that may ultimately interfere with team performance. Hidden agendas are personal goals that a member keeps to himself or herself and that may or may not be harmful to group efforts. The problem with personal agendas is that they work against open communication in the group and destroy trust within the group. Even members with positive goals and motives in mind may have differences over such issues as how the group should proceed, which goals should be given top priority, and how various tasks should be divided among members.

Roles That Interfere with Group Processes

In an ideal workplace, all team members value each other and treat each other and the team experience as valued parts of the job. Unfortunately, the reality is that some people also assume roles and play games in groups or teams that negatively affect the group. There are many reasons why people behave in these negative ways, ranging from inexperience in a team environment to darker motives such as a desire to hurt the organization itself. These roles hurt group members and group performance. Some of these roles are summarized here.[17] Near the end of the chapter, there are suggestions to assist you with dealing with difficult co-workers, including these types of difficult team members.

- **Dominator** This person demands attention, tries to control the discussion, interrupts, and tries to control others. He or she monopolizes the discussion and prevents the team from concentrating on its tasks.
- **Aggressor** Similar to the dominator, this person wants control. However, he or she puts down other team members, using sarcasm, name-calling, and other negative means to get what he or she wants.
- **The Put-Downer** Similar to the aggressor in some ways, this person is a little more subtle. He or she enjoys making others feel bad by poking fun or finding fault in others' ideas. This person can easily deflate enthusiasm in the team, as every idea has flaws and so do the people who offer them. This person can be passively aggressive and can engage in these behaviours while smiling the whole time!
- **The Know-It-All** This person thinks he or she knows everything (though often that's not the reality) and tries to impose the knowledge on the group. This person may use age, experience, education, or any other thing in his or her background to prove that he or she is correct and everyone else is wrong.
- **Distractor** While distraction can be useful when members are stressed, overuse of this role results in poor team performance. This person may clown around by teasing and joking, change topics and get the group off-task, and generally "act up." On a more aggressive side, this person can also distract the group by picking fights and watching "the fur fly" for fun. Often this person is not on the same page as everyone else on the team. Other team members end up helping this person catch up to everyone else, which slows down team progress.
- **Nonparticipator** This person can be a psychological deserter who may appear bored with or above the pettiness of group interaction. He or she may doodle, daydream, or in other ways nonverbally signal his or her lack of interest in the group work. These people can also be physical deserters by announcing they have to leave early, arriving late, not arriving at all, or arriving completely unprepared.
- **Recognition Seeker** This person gets the group off-task by boasting about accomplishments and tries to be the centre of the group's attention.

If not the centre of attention, this person pouts or becomes disruptive. He or she may try to hold side conversations or get recognition in other ways. While we all enjoy recognition for a job well done, this person demands constant recognition and praise.

- **The Mean and Unethical Player** This person can be unethical, dishonest, conniving, prejudicial, and nasty and behaves this way consistently. He or she may lie, cheat, take credit for others' efforts, belittle others, and engage in other unacceptable behaviours that harm team members, hurt team spirit, and discourage group efforts. For example, a person who continually makes sexist comments is belittling not only that person but the person's gender as well. This person can be very outward with his or her behaviour or may be sneakier as he or she tries to play one team member against another.
- **Special Interest Pleader** This person has outside interests and wants support from the group for these other interests. For example, as part of a sales team, you set up the meetings over the dinner hour when all the members are available and part of your responsibility is to provide supper. One team member keeps suggesting that you use a family member or friend to do the catering.
- **The "Yes, But" Player** This person is basically irresponsible for his or her part on the team. The behaviours of this person—always accompanied by excuses—include not finishing a task, being late, missing meetings, obtaining the wrong data, and doing the wrong thing. At first, these excuses may sound legitimate, but as time wears on, it becomes obvious this person is an irresponsible team member who refuses to do his or her part. For example, "I would have been here on time, but the traffic was bad"; then at the next meeting, "I tried to get here but the phone kept ringing"; followed at the next meeting with "I was so busy with my other work, I lost track of time"; and so on.
- **The Whiner/Complainer** This person undermines the entire spirit of the group with continual complaining and whining. Every idea from others is met with a list of reasons why the idea would never work. This person may complain about personal problems and other injustices that he or she is currently having to manage in his or her life.
- **The Super-Agreeable Player** This person never takes a stand. Perhaps afraid of hurting others' feelings or simply as a result of not caring, this person agrees with everyone. During discussion, this person will side with one person and then flip and side with someone else. This person has few original ideas and waffles on group decisions.

Competition Instead of Cooperation

In a society that values individualism, competitiveness, and "doing your own thing," cooperation may be difficult for some people. A barrier that hinders group and team work is a structure that fosters competition among group members instead of cooperation. Many well-meaning organizations have employee awards that go to a single individual rather than the entire team. People who want these awards may compete against their very own team members to achieve this recognition. Team awards foster cooperation among team members and are currently used in many organizations that foster the team approach.

Social Loafing

Have you ever been in a group or on a team where one or two members did very little work? These members were content to ride along for free and did very little to help the group obtain its goals. **Social loafing** is the tendency for people to perform at a lower level when working in groups than when working alone.[18] Social loafers do not try as hard in a group as they do when they are alone. Social loafing occurs more often when individual contributions are not monitored or identified in some way and in larger teams where individual efforts are less noticeable.[19] Witnessing such loafing and lack of effort can demoralize other team members and reduce motivation.

How to Become a More Effective Team Member

Now that you have an idea about the importance of teams in the workplace, the characteristics of teams, how teams develop, and some of the barriers to effective development, let's turn our focus onto strategies for becoming an effective team member or team player. A **team player** is one who emphasizes group accomplishment and cooperation rather than individual achievement and not helping others. You will have to be a team player if you wish to reach the pinnacle of power in your organization. Executives are expected to be good team players as well as individual decision makers.

Here we describe a representative group of behaviours that contribute to team play. In addition, engaging in such behaviour helps one be perceived as a team player.

1. **Share Credit with Co-Workers.** A direct method of promoting team play is to share credit for good deeds with other team members. Instead of focusing on yourself as the person responsible for a work achievement, point out that the achievement was the product of a team effort.
2. **Display a Helpful, Cooperative Attitude.** Working cooperatively with others is virtually synonymous with team play. Cooperation translates into such activities as helping another worker with a computer problem, covering for a teammate when he or she is absent, and making sure a co-worker has the input required from you on time. A general approach to cooperation is to exchange favours with teammates. A person's job, for example, might occasionally require that a large number of photocopies be made in a hurry. If the person in charge of making large batches of photocopies goes out of the way to take care of such a request, the person is owed a favour. A worker in the accounting department might be able to help the photocopy specialist get a tuition-assistance refund processed in a hurry.

   Exchanging favours as a method of building cooperation and teamwork remains effective only if these favours balance out in the long run. Can you think of any way in which an exchange of favours might be applied to a past or present job of yours?

Cooperation is so important to the smooth functioning of the workplace that it is often included as a factor in evaluating performance. Showing good cooperation with others contributes to a positive performance evaluation.

3. **Share Information and Opinions with Co-Workers.** Teamwork is facilitated when group members share information and opinions. This is true because one of the benefits of group effort is that members can share ideas. The result is often a better solution to problems than would have been possible for people working alone. The group thus achieves **synergy**—a product of group effort whereby the output of the group exceeds the output possible if the members worked alone.
4. **Provide Emotional Support to Co-Workers.** Good team players offer each other emotional support. Such support can take the form of verbal encouragement for ideas expressed, listening to a group member's concerns, or complimenting achievements. An emotionally supportive comment to a co-worker who appears to be under stress might be "This doesn't look like one of your better days. What can I do to help?"
5. **Follow the Golden Rule.** The ancient adage "Treat others the way you would like them to treat you" provides a firm foundation for effective team and group work. Although some may dismiss the golden rule as a syrupy platitude, it still works. For example, you would probably want someone to help you with a perplexing problem, so you take the initiative to help others when they need your expertise to solve a problem.
6. **To Establish Trust, Keep Confidential Information to Yourself.** Confidential information shared with you by a teammate should not be shared with others. Trust is essential to effective teamwork and can be exceedingly difficult to regain after a person is betrayed. Other teammates may also lose faith and trust in you if you breach even one member's trust.
7. **Avoid Actions That Could Sabotage or Undermine the Group or Team in Any Way.** Frequently criticizing group members directly or complaining about them to outsiders works against the best interest of the group. Members within the group, as well as the team or group leader, will most likely hear that you criticized them to an outsider, thus doing severe damage to your ability to work cooperatively with them.
8. **Engage in Shared Laughter.** Laughter is a natural team builder that enhances understanding and empathy, essential ingredients for team play. The individual can trigger laughter by making humorous comments related to a situation at hand, or making in-group jokes.
9. **Carefully Manage the Challenge of Being the Manager's Favourite.** A natural tendency is for a manager to rely most heavily on one or two team members who are the hardest working or most talented. Other team members may become envious of the "Boss's Pet." As a consequence, the favoured team member or members may find themselves alienated from the group. The favoured team player can soften the problem in two ways. First, he or she should not mention being favoured or brag about his or her relationship with the manager. Second, when receiving another plum

assignment from the manager (such as a trade show visit), the person might suggest that another team member deserves a turn at such an activity.

10. **Share the Glory.** You will make a poor team player if you try to grab all the glory for ideas that work and distance yourself from ideas that do not work. An effective team member wants all other members to succeed. You will stand out by praising the people you work with rather than hogging any praise for the team.[20]

11. **Avoid Backstabbing.** A special category of disliked behaviour is **backstabbing**, an attempt to discredit by underhanded means such as innuendo, accusation, or the like. A backstabber might drop hints to the boss, for example, that a co-worker performs poorly under pressure or is looking for a new job. Sometimes the backstabber assertively gathers information in order to backstab a co-worker. He or she might engage another worker in a derogatory discussion about the boss and then report the co-worker's negative comments back to the boss.

    Backstabbing tends to rise as the pressure for jobs increases. A career counsellor noted that during a period of intense job competition, "People seem inclined to stab before they get stabbed themselves."[21] An inference to be drawn here is that when jobs and promotions are in short supply, a person might be more inclined to backstab. The practice is still unethical, and it can backfire. A person who develops a reputation as a backstabber will receive poor cooperation from co-workers. The person might also be considered untrustworthy by management, thus stalling his or her own career.

Observing the 11 points just made and using your increased understanding of teams and groups in the workplace will help you become an effective team member. Recognize also that all other actions directed toward good co-worker relationships will also enhance team and group performance. Just as you may find yourself working with a difficult co-worker, you may also experience working with an uncooperative team member, such as one who takes on a negative role and then persists in this role. Exhibit 11-1 offers some suggestions for managing the difficult team member. Note the similarities between some of these strategies and the ones suggested earlier. The real goal to keep in mind is that you want to work effectively with the difficult person. You can pick and choose from a variety of ideas to assist you with this goal.

Building Good Relationships with Customers

Success on the job also requires building good relationships with both external and internal customers. *External customers* fit the traditional definition of customer that includes clients and guests. External customers can be classified as either retail or industrial. The latter represents one company buying from another, such as purchasing steel from a manufacturer. *Internal customers* are the people you serve within the organization, or those who use the output from your job. For example, if you design computer graphics, the other people in the company who receive your graphics are your internal customers.

exhibit 11-1

Oh, That Difficult Team Member!

Co-workers can be difficult, but what if you have to work with a difficult co-worker on your team? What do you do when a team member starts to behave in ways that hurt the team's progress? What if he or she challenges other members or treats them poorly? Too often we may sit quietly, perhaps feeling guilty or not knowing what to do. Or we may launch into our own attack or, even worse, side with the offender. If you say or do nothing, you have by your lack of intervention supported the inappropriate behaviour.

What should you do when this happens, or if you are the target of such behaviour? You do have choices! These choices range from mere acceptance to confrontation and expulsion from the group. As a rule of thumb, try the least intrusive methods first. Here are some suggestions for handling the difficult team member before the team suffers and loses all productivity. Many of these ideas rely on your ability to be assertive and to manage conflict well.

- **Accept the Behaviour.** Sometimes, your best strategy is to simply accept the behaviour. Some behaviours are not critical to either group climate or group functioning. For example, while you may find a co-worker's green hair offensive, it probably does not affect the brain underneath. Other behaviours may be annoying and downright irritating, but if they do not affect the team, then you should probably move on and accept the person.
- **Use Behaviour Modification.** Sometimes you can ignore the unacceptable behaviour and reward the good behaviour (remember positive reinforcement?). For example, a member who whines about things can be ignored when whining. Some people whine to get attention and ignoring it may eliminate it. When he or she finally says something positive, jump on it and praise it. Over time, the whining may disappear and this person may become a more positive spirit in the group.
- **Confront the Individual on a One-to-One Basis.** There are two ways to confront the person. The team leader (or assigned person) can talk to the person one-to-one outside team meetings or work to attempt to find a solution or terminate the behaviour. For example, an aggressive team member who continually challenges one group member may be best approached alone. A responsible and assertive (and maybe brave) team member who is the victim of such inappropriate comments or treatment may confront the person outside the team, saying, for example: "In meetings, you continually make reference to my big salary compared to yours. I fail to see the significance of this in relation to what we are doing. In the future, do not make such references." This type of confrontation may also work for members who are continually late, do poor quality work, or do not participate. If the reason for the behaviour is lack of understanding, lack of ability, or personal problems, it is much less embarrassing to deal with this in a one-to-one meeting than if the whole group is looking on with eager interest.
- **Confront the Person as a Team.** At times, it may be appropriate to deal with the person as a team. If team members have discovered an individual with a hidden agenda, or who has been lying, cheating, or otherwise acting unethically, group confrontation may be necessary. This may be especially important if this person has been playing team members off against each other. A united front may be your only recourse. Usually, a spokesperson is selected to start but others may have information to share as well. For example, "It has come to the team's attention that you have been lying to several of us about your progress with the computer support for this project. As a team, we would like to discuss this with

you and come up with an acceptable way to resolve this as quickly as possible so that we can all get back to work." Team confrontation may work best when it is the entire team that has been affected by the negative role or behaviour. If a member has continually made sexist remarks to all the female members, the entire team needs to present a united front that this is unacceptable conduct.

- **Go to Management.** When the first four suggestions have failed, you may need to seek the help of a higher authority. Team members who consistently fail to respond to other types of intervention may need more help to change their behaviour.
- **Expulsion.** When all else fails, you may have to expel the member. Your team may not have authority to do this, and in some environments it may be impossible. You do not want to resort to tricks like making the person's team life unbearable or taking on negative roles yourself, but many teams have been weighted down by poor team members. You may be able to expel the person by other sanctioned organizational methods. For example, a member who refuses to stop making harassing comments may be dealt with by using the harassment policy of your organization.

SOURCES: David W. Johnson and Frank P. Johnson, *Joining Together: Group Theory and Group Skills*, 3rd ed. (Englewood Cliffs, NJ: Prentice Hall, 1985); Gay Lumsden and Donald Lumsden, *Communicating in Groups and Teams: Sharing Leadership.* (Belmont, CA: Wadsworth Publishing Company, 1997).

The information already presented about getting along with your manager (in Chapter 10) and co-workers dealt with internal customers. Here we emphasize providing good service (or delight) to external customers. As usual, categories overlap and some techniques for serving external customers would also work well with internal customers, and vice versa. As shown in Exhibit 11-2, profits jump considerably as the customer is retained over time. And good service is the primary factor that keeps customers coming back. Time-tested suggestions for high-level customer service are presented next.[22]

exhibit 11-2

The Value of Customer Retention

Customer loyalty goes directly to the bottom line. Here are the financial consequences of increases in customer retention for various industries:

Industry	***Increase in Retention***	***Profit Increase***
Employer services such as payroll	4%	21%
Banking	5%	40%
Insurance	5%	60%
Laundry	5%	60%

SOURCE: Adapted from Theodore Garrison III, "The Value of Customer Service," in Rick Crandall, editor, *Celebrate Customer Service* (Corte Madera, CA: Select Press, 1999), p. 7.

1. *Establish customer satisfaction goals.* Decide jointly with your manager how much you intend to help customers. Find answers to questions such as the following: Is your company attempting to satisfy every customer within ten minutes of his or her request? Are you striving to provide the finest customer service in your field? Is your goal zero defections to competitors? Your goals will dictate how much and the type of effort you put into pleasing customers.
2. *Understand your customer's needs and place them first.* The most basic principle of selling is to identify and satisfy customer needs. Many customers may not be able to express their needs clearly. Also, they may not be certain of their needs. To help identify customer needs, you may have to probe for more information. For example, the associate in a consumer electronics store may have to ask, "What uses do you have in mind for your television receiver aside from watching regular programs? Will you be using it to display electronic photographs? Will you be using it to surf the internet?" Knowing such information will help the store associate identify which television set will satisfy the customer's needs.

   After you have identified customer needs, focus on satisfying them rather than doing what is convenient for you or your firm. Assume, for example, the customer says, "I would like to purchase nine reams of copier paper." The sales associate should not respond, "Sorry, the copying paper comes in boxes of ten, so it is not convenient to sell you nine reams." The associate might, however, offer a discount for the purchase of the full ten-ream box if such action fits company policy.
3. *Show care and concern.* During contacts with your customer, show concern for his or her welfare. Ask questions such as "How have you enjoyed the television set you bought here a while back?" or just "How are you feeling today?" After asking the question, project a genuine interest in the answer. A strictly business approach to showing care and concern is to follow up on requests. A telephone call or email to the requester of your service is usually sufficient follow-up. A follow-up is effective because it completes the communication loop between two people.
4. *Communicate a positive attitude.* A positive attitude is conveyed by factors such as appearance, friendly gestures, a warm voice tone, and good telephone communication skills. If a customer seems apologetic about making a heavy demand, respond, "No need to apologize. My job is to please you. I'm here to serve."
5. *Make the buyer feel good.* A fundamental way of building a customer relationship is to make the buyer feel good about himself or herself. Also, make the buyer feel good because he or she has bought from you. Offer compliments about the customer's healthy glow, or a report that specified vendor requirements (for an industrial customer). An effective feel-good line is "I enjoy doing business with you."
6. *Smile at every customer.* Smiling is a natural relationship builder and can help you bond with your customer. Smile several times during each customer contact, even if your customer is angry with your product or

service. Yet guard against smiling constantly or inappropriately, because your smile then becomes meaningless.

7. *Display strong business ethics.* Ethical violations receive so much publicity that one can impress customers by being conspicuously ethical. Look for ways to show that you are so ethical that you would welcome making your sales tactics public knowledge. Also, treat the customer the same way you would treat a family member or a valued friend.
8. *Be helpful rather than defensive when a customer complains.* As described earlier, look at a complaint professionally rather than personally. Listen carefully and concentrate on being helpful. The upset customer cares primarily about having the problem resolved, not whether you are at fault. Use a statement such as this one: "I understand that this mistake is a major inconvenience. I'll do what I can right now to solve the problem." Remember also that complaints that are taken care of quickly and satisfactorily will often create a more positive impression than mistake-free service.
9. *Cater to customers from diverse cultural backgrounds.* As discussed in Chapter 8, the increasing cultural diversity of Canada will continue to increase in the coming decades. This means that the customers whom we deal with will also be diverse, particularly in large urban areas such as Toronto, Vancouver, and Montreal. It has been estimated that by the year 2016 visible minorities will account for one-fifth of the Canadian population, with the majority living in Ontario.[23] In such a culturally diverse nation with a wide range of cultures and diverse groups, businesses also need to make changes to serve these diverse customers. For an example of such an awareness and service to a different culture, see the Canada Today feature on diversity management on the opposite page. By recognizing and appreciating cultural differences, businesses can develop strategies and methods to better serve different groups.
10. *Invite the customer back.* The Southern expression "Y'all come back, now!" is well suited for good customer service. Specific invitations to return may help increase repeat business. The more focused and individualized the invitation, the more likely that it will have an impact on customer behaviour. ("Y'all come back, now!" is sometimes used too indiscriminately to be effective.) Pointing out why you enjoyed doing business with the customer and what future problems you could help with is an effective technique.
11. *Avoid rudeness.* Although rudeness to customers is obviously a poor business practice, the problem is widespread. Rudeness by customer-contact personnel is a major problem from the employer's standpoint. Be aware of subtle forms of rudeness such as complaining about your job or working hours in front of customers. To elevate your awareness level about rudeness among customer-contact personnel, do Human Relations Self-Assessment Quiz 11-2.

All of the 11 points just made emphasize the importance of practising good human relations with customers. Good customer service stems naturally from practising good human relations. Human Relations Skill-Building Exercise 11-1 gives you an opportunity to practise two techniques for building customer relationships.

Diversity Management for Better Customer Service

Businesses today need to engage in "diversity management." Diversity management means that managers must pay attention to the diversity of their workers and the customers that use the business.

A good example of a business utilizing diversity management is National Grocers/Loblaws. Evolving demographics have led the company to change its hiring practices and occupational requirements. Hiring practices and occupational requirements are flexible depending on the location where the job will be. In one store locality, there had been an influx of Mandarin- and Cantonese-speaking immigrants who were unable to communicate with the store pharmacist. This meant lost revenue! To combat the communication barrier, another pharmacist was hired. The company required one additional occupational skill for this position—the ability to speak both Mandarin and Cantonese. After the position was filled, prescription and pharmacy revenues increased significantly.

This kind of flexibility in hiring practices to accommodate the diversity of customers is just one part of the new "diversity management" that Canadian businesses will need to implement to meet the challenges of an increasingly diverse population.[24]

Am I Being Rude?

Directions: Following is a list of behaviours of customer-contact workers that would be interpreted as rude by many customers. Indicate whether you have engaged in such behaviour in your dealings with customers—or whether you would be likely to do so if your job involved customer contact.

	Yes	*No*
1. I talk to a co-worker while serving a customer.	_______	_______
2. I conduct a telephone conversation with someone else while serving a customer.	_______	_______
3. I address customers by their first names without having their permission.	_______	_______
4. I address customers as "you guys."	_______	_______
5. I chew gum or eat candy while dealing with a customer.	_______	_______
6. I laugh when customers describe an agonizing problem they are having with one of our company's products or services.	_______	_______
7. I minimize eye contact with customers.	_______	_______

(continued)

	Yes	No
8. I say the same thing to every customer, such as "Have a nice day," in a monotone.	_______	_______
9. I accuse customers of attempting to cheat the company before carefully investigating the situation.	_______	_______
10. I hurry customers when my break time approaches.	_______	_______
11. I comment on a customer's appearance in a flirtatious, sexually oriented way.	_______	_______
12. I sometimes complain about or make fun of other customers when I am serving a customer.	_______	_______

Interpretation: The more of these behaviours you have engaged in, the ruder you are and the more likely it is that you are losing potential business for your company. If you have not engaged in any of these behaviours, even when faced with a rude customer, you are an asset to your employer. You are also tolerant.

Giving Good Customer Service

Role players in this exercise will demonstrate two related techniques for giving good customer service.

Scenario 1: Show care and concern. A sales representative meets with two company representatives to talk about installing a new information system for employee benefits. One of the company representatives is from the human resources department and the other from the telecommunications department. The sales representative will attempt to show care and concern for both company representatives during the same meeting.

Scenario 2: Make the buyer feel good. A couple, played by two role players, enters a new-car showroom to examine a model they have seen advertised on television. Although they are not in urgent need of a new car, they are strongly interested. The sales representative is behind quota for the month and would like to close a sale today. The rep decides to use the tactic "Make the buyer feel good" to help form a bond.

Summary

Getting along with co-workers is important for performing your job satisfactorily or better. Methods and tactics for building good co-worker relationships include the following:

1. Develop allies through being civil.
2. Make other people feel important.
3. Maintain honest and open relationships.
4. Follow group standards of conduct.
5. Express an interest in the work of others.
6. Be a good listener.
7. Use appropriate compliments.
8. Deal effectively with difficult people (including handling problems professionally, giving ample feedback, employing tact and diplomacy, using humour, reinforcing civil behaviour, and listening and responding).
9. Face maturely the challenge of the office romance.

An important part of getting along with co-workers is to understand the importance of teams and groups and to be able to effectively work as part of a team or group. Work teams are a special type of group that is brought together to perform specific tasks and goals. Groups and teams go through stages of development, which consist of forming, storming, norming, performing, and often, adjourning. Several barriers can inhibit team development, including time constraints, physical barriers, inappropriate group size, conflicting goals, roles that interfere with team progress, competing team members, and social loafing. Suggestions for being a good team player and working effectively on a team include these: share credit; display a helpful, cooperative attitude; share information; provide emotional support; follow the golden rule; keep confidential information to yourself; avoid actions that may sabotage the team; engage in shared laughter; share the glory; and avoid backstabbing.

Success on the job also requires building good relationships with both internal and external customers. Representative techniques for building constructive customer relationships include (1) establish customer-satisfaction goals, (2) understand customer needs, (3) show care and concern, (4) communicate a positive attitude, (5) make the buyer feel good, (6) smile at every customer, (7) display strong business ethics, (8) be helpful rather than defensive in response to complaints, (9) cater to customers from diverse cultural backgrounds, (10) invite the customer back, and (11) avoid being rude.

Questions and Activities

1. A critic of this chapter said, "A lot of ruthless people get ahead in business. So getting along with your co-workers may not really be that important." What do you think?

2. Identify three tactics described in this chapter that you think are the most relevant to entry-level workers for getting along with co-workers. Explain.
3. Make up an emotionally supportive statement to offer a co-worker whose wedding plans were cancelled one week before the marriage date.
4. Should companies have a policy about backstabbing? Explain.
5. What are the advantages of meeting a potential mate in the office rather than through friends or in public places such as bars or dances?
6. Many companies train employees in team skills. Why is such training essential for company success?
7. Many students dislike group assignments. What are some advantages and disadvantages of working in groups that you have experienced? Which strategies presented here would have helped you to overcome these disadvantages?
8. Have you ever been part of a team in the "performing" stage of development? If so, describe the experience to other classmates.
9. How might placing too much emphasis on being a good team player and fitting in with the group hurt a person's chances of becoming an executive?
10. If rudeness is so widespread today, why bother being polite and considerate on the job?

Internet Skill Builder

Interpersonal Skills for the Modern Workplace

Visit **www.canadianbusiness.com**, the website of *Canadian Business* magazine. Scroll through the site with the intent of identifying one of the recent articles that makes reference to a personal skill required for getting along with co-workers or customers. You may have to make some inferences, because you are not likely to find an article specifically on the topic of the interpersonal skills necessary for success.

Weblinks

www.workingwounded.com
This interesting site, hosted by Rob Rosner, author of the 1998 book *Working Wounded*, is about the "uncivil" workplace. It is devoted to tales about, and advice for, people who have to cope with workplaces that abound with uncivil behaviour.

www.flirtnow.com
This site features information on office romances and flirting in the workplace.

www.workteams.unt.edu
This is the site for the Center for the Study of Work Teams from the University of North Texas.

www.uiowa.edu/~grpproc
From the University of Iowa, this is the Center for the Study of Group Processes. From this site you can link to full-text articles from the journal *Current Research in Social Psychology*.

Human Relations Case Study

THE UNBALANCED TEAM

Bluestone Security Systems is one of the largest security systems distributors in its city, with annual sales of $20 million. Two years ago, Bill Scovia, vice-president of marketing and sales, reorganized the sales force. Previously, the sales force consisted of inside sales representatives (who took care of phone-in orders) and outside sales representatives (who called on accounts). The reorganization divided the outside sales force into two groups: direct sales and major accounts. The direct sales representatives were made responsible for small commercial customers and individual homeowners. As before, they would service existing customers and prospect for new accounts. Servicing existing customers usually involves adding fire protection to burglary protection and upgrading burglary systems.

In addition, Bluestone established a website to help sell its systems. A sales representative handling accounts generated by the website would receive one-half the ordinary commission. Although the representative would have to follow up on the web order or inquiry, top management felt that this would be an easy sale for a sales representative. The website was managed by a coordinator who would assign orders and inquiries to sales representatives in equal turns.

Three people who were direct sales representatives were promoted to major account executives. The account executives would service Bluestone's largest accounts, including prospecting for new business with these accounts. An example would be expanding the security system to a retailer's other stores. To promote teamwork and cooperation, Scovia assigned group sales quotas, including web sales, to account representatives. Collectively, their goal was to bring in 25 new large accounts per month, internet-generated sales included.

Given that the sales quota was a group quota, the account representatives were supposed to work together on strategy for acquiring new accounts. If a particular account executive did not have the expertise to handle his or her customer's problems, another account executive was supposed to offer help. Brian Marcus, for example, was the resident expert on the unique security problems of warehouses. If invited, Brian would join one of the two other account executives to call on a customer who owned a warehouse.

After the new sales organization had been in place 19 months, Elizabeth Kato, an account executive, was having lunch with Larry Starks, the manufacturing director at Bluestone. "I've about had it," said Elizabeth. "I'm tired of single-handedly carrying the team."

"What do you mean, you are single-handedly carrying the team?" asked Larry.

"You're a trusted friend, Larry. So let me lay out the facts. Each month the group is supposed to bring in 25 new sales. If we don't average those 25 sales per month, including web sales, we don't get our semi-annual bonus. That represents about 25 percent of my income. So a big chunk of my money comes from group effort.

"My average number of new accounts brought in for the last 12 months has been 14. And we are averaging about 21 sales per month. This translates into the other account execs averaging about seven sales among them. I'm carrying the group, but overall sales are still below quota. This means I didn't get my bonus last month.

"The other account execs are friendly and helpful in writing up proposals. But they just don't bring in their share of accounts."

Larry asked, "What does your boss say about this?"

"I've had several conversations with him about the problem. He tells me to be patient and to remember that the development of a fully balanced team requires time. He also tells me that I should develop a stronger team spirit. My problem is that I cannot pay my bills with team spirit."

Questions

1. What does this case illustrate about teamwork?
2. How effective is Elizabeth as a team player?
3. To what extent are Elizabeth's complaints justified?

Developing Self-Confidence and Leadership Skills

Learning Outcomes

After studying the information and doing the exercises in this chapter, you should be able to

- develop a strategy for increasing your self-confidence if you think it is desirable to do so
- understand the relationship of self-confidence to leadership
- identify a number of personal traits and characteristics of effective leaders
- identify a number of behaviours of effective leaders
- map out a tentative program for developing your leadership potential and skills

Katrina Makowski worked for several years as a member of the central support staff in a large law firm. One afternoon, office manager Georgette Dixon entered Katrina's work area. With a warm smile, she said, "Congratulations Katrina. On behalf of the rest of the managers in our firm, we are pleased to announce that you are the successful candidate for the team leader position of support services." Katrina said she was thrilled to accept the appointment, yet she asked, "Why me? I thought I was a real long-shot for this position. I'm not the most experienced support specialist in the group." Georgette replied, "Don't be so modest. You have managed many difficult situations very well. You're always on top of everything, take everything in stride, and maintain control. We want someone with your self-confidence in this team leader position."

The situation surrounding Katrina's promotion illustrates the importance of personal qualities to leadership—qualities such as a take-charge attitude, the ability to manage difficult situations, and self-confidence. While getting along with your manager, co-workers, and customers is essential for dealing effectively with people, if you wish to move up the "ladder" or work in supervisory positions, you will need to develop skills and abilities for assuming leadership roles.

Leadership occurs at all levels in an organization and can happen when people come to respect your opinion and personal characteristics and thus are influenced by you. Another way of becoming a leader is to be appointed to a formal position, such as supervisor or team leader, in which it is natural to exert leadership. Your greatest opportunity for exerting leadership, however, will come about from a combination of these methods of influence and learning the proper skills. You need to develop the "soft skills," as one author puts it. These skills include a blend of cognitive, emotional, and social skills as well as the managerial and technical skills required for a leadership position.[1] As a result, an individual with such appealing personal characteristics who is placed in a position of authority will find it relatively easy to exert leadership.

Our study of leadership will first focus on self-confidence because of its close relationship to, and requirement for, leadership. We then focus on the characteristics of leaders, their actions and attitudes, followed by an overview of how to develop your leadership potential, including some of those soft skills.

The Importance of Self-Confidence and Self-Efficacy

Self-confidence is necessary for leadership because it helps assure group members that things are under control. Assume you are a manager in a company that is rumoured to be facing bankruptcy. At a meeting you attend, the president tearfully confesses, "I'm sorry, I'm just no good in a crisis. I don't know what's going to happen to the company. I don't think I can get us out of this mess. Maybe one of you would like to try your hand at turning around a troubled company."

In this situation, company employees would feel insecure. Many would be so preoccupied with finding new employment that they couldn't concentrate on their work. You would want the president to behave in a confident, assured manner. Yet if the president were too arrogant about things, if he or she dismissed the problem too lightly, you might not feel secure then, either.

In other leadership situations as well, the leader who functions best is self-confident enough to reassure others and to appear in control. But if the leader is so self-confident that he or she will not admit errors, listen to criticism, or ask for advice, that too creates a problem. Human Relations Self-Assessment Quiz 12-1 provides some tentative insight into your level of self-confidence.

An appropriate amount of self-confidence is also important because it contributes to **self-efficacy**, the belief in one's capability to perform a task. Various studies have shown that people with a high sense of self-efficacy tend to have good job performance. They also set relatively high goals for themselves.[2] Self-efficacy is thus related to self-confidence but is tied more directly to performing a task. A straightforward implication of self-efficacy is that people who think they can perform well on a task do better than those who think they will do poorly.

An encouraging note is that self-efficacy can be boosted through training. In an experiment, 66 unemployed people participated in a self-efficacy workshop. The group included bookkeepers, clerks, teachers, skilled mechanics, and technicians. The workshop featured watching video clips of people successfully performing job-search behaviours, followed by encouragement from the trainer and peers. In contrast to unemployed people who did not attend the workshop, the people who were trained in self-efficacy became more involved in job searches.[3] Being involved in job searches included telephoning about a job and obtaining an interview.

Self-efficacy contributes to leadership effectiveness because a leader with high self-efficacy will usually believe that a task is doable. As a result, the leader can inspire others to carry out a difficult mission such as correcting a serious customer problem.

Developing Self-Confidence

Self-confidence is generally achieved by succeeding in a variety of situations. A confident sales representative may not be generally self-confident unless he or she also achieves success in activities such as taking exams, forming good personal relationships, navigating complex software, composing a letter, and displaying athletic skills.

Although this general approach to self-confidence building makes sense, it does not work for everyone. Some people who seem to succeed at everything still have lingering self-doubt. Low self-confidence is so deeply ingrained in this type of personality that success in later life is not sufficient to change things. Following are some specific strategies and tactics for building and elevating self-confidence. They will generally work unless the person has deep-rooted feelings of inferiority. The tactics and strategies are arranged approximately in the order in which they should be tried to achieve best results.

Human Relations Self-Assessment

Quiz 12-1

How Self-Confident Are You?

Indicate the extent to which you agree with each of the following statements: disagree strongly; disagree; neutral; agree; agree strongly.

	DS	D	N	A	AS
1. I frequently say to people, "I'm not sure."	5	4	3	2	1
2. I perform well in most situations in life.	1	2	3	4	5
3. I willingly offer advice to others.	1	2	3	4	5
4. Before making even a minor decision I usually consult with several people.	5	4	3	2	1
5. I am generally willing to attempt new activities for which I have very little related skill or experience.	1	2	3	4	5
6. Speaking in front of the class or other group is a frightening experience for me.	5	4	3	2	1
7. I sweat a lot when people challenge me or put me on the spot.	5	4	3	2	1
8. I feel comfortable attending a social event by myself.	1	2	3	4	5
9. I'm much more of a winner than a loser.	1	2	3	4	5
10. I am cautious about making any substantial change in my life.	5	4	3	2	1

Total score: ______________

Scoring and Interpretation: Calculate your total score by adding the numbers circled. A tentative interpretation of the scoring is as follows:
45–50: Very high self-confidence with perhaps a tendency toward arrogance
38–44: A high, desirable level of self-confidence
30–37: Moderate, or average, self-confidence
10–29: Self-confidence needs strengthening

Take an Inventory of Personal Assets and Accomplishments

Many people suffer from low self-confidence because they do not appreciate their own good points. Therefore, a starting point in increasing your self-confidence is to take an inventory of personal assets and accomplishments. This same activity was offered in Chapter 1 as a method of developing self-esteem. Personal assets should be related to characteristics and behaviours, rather than tangible assets such as an inheritance. Accomplishments can be anything significant in which you played a key role in achieving the results. Try not to be modest in preparing your list of assets and accomplishments. You are looking for any confidence-booster you can find.

Two lists prepared by different people will suffice to give you an idea of the kinds of assets and accomplishments that might be included:

Lillian
Good listener; most people like me; good handwriting; good posture; inquisitive mind; good at solving problems; good sense of humour; patient with people who make mistakes; better-than-average appearance. Organized successful fund drive which raised $30,000 for church; graduated tenth in high-school class of 500; achieved first place in industrial bowling league; daughter has an excellent career.

Angelo
Good mechanical skills; work well under pressure; good dancer; friendly with strangers; strong as an ox; good cook; can laugh at my own mistakes; great-looking guy; humble and modest. Made award-winning suggestion that saved company $25,000; scored winning goal in college basketball tournament; dragged child out of burning building.

The value of these asset lists is that they add to your self-appreciation. Most people who lay out their good points on paper come away from the activity with at least a temporary boost in self-confidence. The temporary boost, combined with a few success experiences, may lead to a long-term gain in self-confidence.

An important supplement to listing your own assets is hearing the opinion of others on your good points. This tactic has to be used sparingly, however, and mainly with people who are personal-growth-minded. A good icebreaker is to tell your source of feedback that you have to prepare a list of your assets for a human relations exercise (the one you are reading about right now!). Since that person knows of your work or your capabilities, you hope that he or she can spare a few minutes for this important exercise.

For many people, positive feedback from others does more for building self-confidence than does feedback from oneself. The reason is that self-esteem depends to a large extent on what we think others think about us. Consequently, if other people—whose judgment you trust—think highly of you, your self-image will be positive.

Develop a Solid Knowledge Base

A bedrock for projecting self-confidence is to develop a base of knowledge that enables you to provide sensible alternative solutions to problems. Intuition is very important, but working from a base of facts helps you project a confident image. Formal education is an obvious and important source of information for your knowledge base. Day-by-day absorption of information directly and indirectly related to your career is equally important. A major purpose of formal education is to get you in the right frame of mind to continue your quest for knowledge.

In your quest for developing a solid knowledge base to project self-confidence, be sensitive to the potential for abusing this technique. If you bombard people with quotes, facts, and figures, you are likely to be perceived as an annoying know-it-all.

Use Positive Self-Talk

A basic method of building self-confidence is to engage in **positive self-talk**, saying positive things about oneself to oneself. As explained by Jay T. Knippen and Thad B. Green, the first step in using positive self-talk is to objectively state the incident that is casting doubt about self-worth.[4] The key word here is *objectively*. Louis, who is fearful of poorly executing a report-writing assignment, might say, "I've been asked to write a report for the company, and I'm not a good writer."

The next step is to objectively interpret what the incident *does not* mean. Louis might say, "Not being a skilled writer doesn't mean that I can't figure out a way to write a good report, or that I'm an ineffective employee."

Next, the person should objectively state what the incident *does* mean. In doing this, the person should avoid put-down labels such as "incompetent," "stupid," "dumb," "jerk," or "airhead." All these terms are forms of negative self-talk. Louis should state what the incident does mean: "I have a problem with one small aspect of this job, preparing professional-level reports. This means I need to improve my report-writing skills."

The fourth step is to objectively account for the cause of the incident. Louis would say, "I'm really worried about writing a good report because I have very little experience in writing along these lines."

The fifth step is to identify some positive ways to prevent the incident from happening again. Louis might say, "I'll get out my textbook on business communications and review the chapter on report-writing," or "I'll enroll in a course or seminar on business report-writing."

The final step is to use positive self-talk. Louis imagines his boss saying, "This report is really good. I'm proud of my decision to select you to prepare this important report."

Positive self-talk builds self-confidence and self-esteem because it programs the mind with positive messages.[5] Making frequent positive messages or affirmations about the self creates a more confident person. An example would be, "I know I can learn this new equipment rapidly enough to increase my productivity within five days." If you do make a mistake, your positive self-talk might be, "It's taken me more time than usual to learn how to use this new equipment. I know I'll have the problem licked in a few days."

Positive self-talk contributes to self-confidence in another important way. According to Douglas Bloch, a writer and lecturer, teaching children to think positively about themselves by practising positive self-talk helps develop adult personalities capable of meeting life's challenges.[6]

Avoid Negative Self-Talk

As mentioned above, you should minimize negative statements about yourself in order to bolster self-confidence. A lack of self-confidence is reflected in statements such as, "I may be stupid but...," "Nobody asked my opinion," "I know I'm usually wrong, but...," and "I know I don't have as much education as some people, but...." Self-effacing statements like these serve to reinforce low self-confidence.

It is also important not to attribute to yourself negative, irreversible traits such as "idiotic," "ugly," "dull," "loser," and "hopeless."[7] Instead, look upon your weak points as areas for possible self-improvement. Negative self-labelling can do long-term damage to your self-confidence. If a person stops that practice today, his or her self-confidence may begin to increase.

Use Positive Visual Imagery

Assume you have a situation in mind in which you would like to appear confident and in control. An example would be a meeting with a major customer who has told you over the telephone that he is considering switching suppliers. Your intuitive reaction is that if you cannot handle his objectives without fumbling or appearing desperate, you will lose the account. An important technique in this situation is **positive visual imagery**, or picturing a positive outcome in your mind. To apply this technique in this situation, imagine yourself engaging in a convincing argument about retaining your customer as the primary supplier. Imagine yourself talking in positive terms about the good service your company offers and how you can rectify any problems.

Visualize yourself listening patiently to your customer's concerns and then talking confidently about how your company can handle these concerns. As you rehearse this moment of truth, create a mental picture of you and the customer shaking hands over the fact that the account is still yours.

Positive visual imagery helps you appear self-confident because your mental rehearsal of the situation has helped you prepare for battle. If imagery works for you once, you will be even more effective in subsequent uses of the technique.

Strive for Peak Performance

A key strategy for projecting self-confidence is to display **peak performance**. The term refers to much more than attempting to do your best. To achieve peak performance you must be totally focused on what you are doing. When you are in the state of peak performance you are mentally calm and physically at ease. Intense concentration is required to achieve this state. You are so focused on the task at hand that you are not distracted by extraneous events or thoughts.

The mental state achieved during peak performance is akin to a person's sense of deep concentration when immersed in a sport or hobby. On days when tennis players perform way above their usual game, they typically comment, "The ball looked so large today, I could read the label as I hit it." On the job, the focus and concentration allow you to sense and respond to relevant information coming from within you while impressing others by responding intelligently to their input.

Psychologist Charles Garfield says it is easy to detect those who have achieved or will achieve peak performance. Based on his study of more than 1,500 successful people, he concludes that peak performers have a mission in their work and lives. They have something they deeply care about to which they are fully committed.[8] Turning in peak performance helps you develop superior self-confidence, which projects through to others.

Sports psychologist James E. Loehr refers to peak performance as the ideal performance state. A person who achieves this state is able to attain exceptionally high performance while facing heavy pressure. A complex training program is required to attain the ideal performance state. The program includes identifying the right themes and keeping them alive on a daily basis. A person begins by identifying four areas for improvement, such as (1) insecurity, (2) defensiveness, (3) rigidity, and (4) pessimism. The person then converts these four weaknesses into strengths and makes them important life themes: (1) confidence, (2) openness, (3) flexibility, and (4) optimism. Anything a person does that reinforces one of these themes during a given day is entered in a log. For example, a person might make an optimistic comment to her manager about sales for the week. Tracking these themes brings them to life and allows for peak performance, or the ideal performance state.[9]

Bounce Back from Setbacks and Embarrassments

An effective self-confidence builder is to convince yourself that you can conquer adversities such as setbacks and embarrassments, thus being resilient. The vast majority of successful leaders have dealt successfully with at least one significant setback in their careers, such as being fired or demoted. In contrast, crumbling after a setback or series of setbacks will usually lower self-confidence. Two major suggestions for bouncing back from setbacks and embarrassments are presented next.

Get Past the Emotional Turmoil Adversity has enormous emotional consequences. The emotional impact of severe job adversity can rival the loss of a personal relationship. The stress from adversity leads to a cycle in which adversity is followed by stress, which is followed by more adversity. A starting point in dealing with the emotional aspects of adversity is to *accept the reality of your problem*. Admit that your problems are real and that you are hurting inside. A second step is *not to take the setback personally*. Remember that setbacks are inevitable so long as you are taking some risks in your career. Not personalizing setbacks helps reduce some of the emotional sting.

If possible, *do not panic*. Recognize that you are in difficult circumstances under which many others panic. Convince yourself to remain calm enough to deal with the severe problem or crisis. Also, *get help from your support network*. Getting emotional support from family members and friends helps overcome the emotional turmoil associated with adversity.

Find a Creative Solution to Your Problem An inescapable part of planning a comeback is to solve your problem. You often need to search for creative solutions, using the problem-solving and decision-making steps described in Chapter 3. Suppose a person faced the adversity of not having enough money for educational expenses. The person might search through standard alternatives such as applying for financial aid, looking for more lucrative part-time work, and borrowing from family members. Several students have solved this problem more creatively by asking strangers to lend them money as intermediate-term investments. An option the investors have is to receive a payback based on the future earnings of the students.

Leadership and Being a Leader

So far we have emphasized the importance of developing self-confidence so that you are able to provide leadership to others. **Leadership** is the process of bringing about positive changes and influencing others to achieve organizational goals. Self-confidence makes a contribution to leadership because people tend to be influenced by a person of high—but not unreasonable—self-confidence.

The key words in understanding leadership are *change* and *influence*. A leader often challenges the status quo and brings about improvements. A leader also influences people to do things, such as achieve a higher performance level, that they would not do in his or her absence. If influence is not exerted, then strictly speaking, there is no leadership.

Effective leadership at the top of organizations is necessary for their prosperity and even survival.[10] Effective leadership is also important throughout the organization, particularly in working with entry-level workers. Good supervision is needed to help employees deal with customer problems, carry out their usual tasks, and maintain high quality. The most rapidly growing form of leadership in the workplace is the team leader.

A **team leader** is a person who facilitates and guides the efforts of a small group, which is given some authority to govern itself. Many firms use work teams instead of traditional departments to accomplish work. For example, a work team might take care of various aspects of issuing an insurance policy. Instead of having power over the group, the team leader works with teammates to help them achieve their goals. Much of quality improvement in organizations takes place in teams.

Before studying the personal qualities and behaviours of effective leaders, take Human Relations Self-Assessment Quiz 12-2. The exercise will help you understand how ready you are to assume a leadership role. Taking the quiz will also give you insight into the type of thinking that is characteristic of leaders.

Traits and Characteristics of Effective Leaders

A major part of understanding leaders and leadership is to recognize that effective leaders have the "right stuff." In other words, certain inner qualities contribute to leadership effectiveness in a wide variety of situations. **Effectiveness** in this situation means that the leader helps the group or team accomplish its objectives without neglecting satisfaction and morale. The characteristics that contribute to effectiveness depend somewhat on the situation. A supervisor in a meat-packing plant may need some different characteristics from a supervisor of a medical office. The situation includes such factors as how experienced the people being supervised are, the job or tasks being performed, the company, and the cultural background of the employees. In the next several pages, we describe some of the more important traits and characteristics of leaders. Many of these characteristics and traits are capable of development and refinement.

Emotional Intelligence

Receiving more and more support is the idea that **emotional intelligence** is key to the development of a healthy personality, including one's ability to demonstrate effective leadership. The term, coined by Daniel Goleman, the author of two books and many articles on the subject, refers to a cluster of traits or abilities relating to the management and understanding of the emotional side of our lives.[11] These

Human Relations Self-Assessment

Quiz 12-2

Readiness for the Leadership Role

Indicate the extent to which you agree with each of the following statements. Use a one-to-five scale: (1) disagree strongly; (2) disagree; (3) neutral; (4) agree; (5) agree strongly. If you do not have leadership experience, imagine how you might react to the questions if you were a leader.

	Statement	
1.	It is enjoyable having people count on me for ideas and suggestions.	1 2 3 4 5
2.	It would be accurate to say that I have inspired other people.	1 2 3 4 5
3.	It's a good practice to ask people provocative questions about their work.	1 2 3 4 5
4.	It's easy for me to compliment others.	1 2 3 4 5
5.	I like to cheer people up even when my own spirits are down.	1 2 3 4 5
6.	What my team accomplishes is more important than my personal glory.	1 2 3 4 5
7.	Many people imitate my ideas.	1 2 3 4 5
8.	Building team spirit is important to me.	1 2 3 4 5
9.	I would enjoy coaching other members of the team.	1 2 3 4 5
10.	It is important to me to recognize others for their accomplishments.	1 2 3 4 5
11.	I would enjoy entertaining visitors to my firm even if it interfered with my completing a report.	1 2 3 4 5
12.	It would be fun for me to represent my team at gatherings outside our department.	1 2 3 4 5
13.	The problems of my teammates are my problems too.	1 2 3 4 5
14.	Resolving conflict is an activity I enjoy.	1 2 3 4 5
15.	I would cooperate with another unit in the organization even if I disagreed with the position taken by its members.	1 2 3 4 5
16.	I am an idea generator on the job.	1 2 3 4 5
17.	It's fun for me to bargain whenever I have the opportunity.	1 2 3 4 5
18.	Team members listen to me when I speak.	1 2 3 4 5
19.	People have asked me to assume the leadership of an activity several times in my life.	1 2 3 4 5
20.	I've always been a convincing person.	1 2 3 4 5
	Total score:	________

Scoring and Interpretation: Calculate your total score by adding the numbers circled. A tentative interpretation of the scoring is as follows:

- 90–100 High readiness for the leadership role
- 60–89 Moderate readiness for the leadership role
- 40–59 Some uneasiness with the leadership role
- 39 or less Low readiness for carrying out the leadership role

If you are already a successful leader and you scored low on this questionnaire, ignore your score. If you scored surprisingly low and you are not yet a leader or are currently performing poorly as a leader, study the statements carefully. Consider changing your attitude or your behaviour so that you can legitimately answer more of the statements with a 4 or a 5. Studying the rest of this chapter will give you additional insights into the leader's role that may be helpful in your development as a leader.

abilities include recognizing and managing your emotions, being able to self-motivate, controlling impulses, recognizing and managing others' emotions, and handling interpersonal relationships in an effective manner.[12] The traits and behaviours of emotional intelligence directly related to leadership include self-confidence, empathy, and visionary leadership.[13] Also, effective leaders demonstrate emotional calm in crises and control their negative emotions. Recent Canadian political blunders—verbal attacks on the United States—demonstrate that the inability to control emotions and not say whatever "pops" into one's head can have very negative repercussions. One example of such a blunder was the remark by MP Carolyn Parrish, who blurted out, "Damn Americans. I hate those bastards," unaware that she was being taped. This remark has jeopardized her re-election as a NATO association chair.[14]

Effective leaders are also able to read the nonverbal cues of others and strive to interpret them accurately. They can recognize emotions and empathize with the person experiencing the emotions. **Empathy** is the ability to place oneself in the other person's shoes. To empathize with another person you don't have to agree, but you do have to understand. As a team leader, you might ask a team member to work late one Thursday. The team member says, "That's my night to play bingo. Working is out of the question." You can understand how important bingo is to that person, and you express your understanding. Nevertheless, you emphasize the importance of the project. Passion for the work and the people is a particularly important aspect of emotional intelligence for leadership effectiveness. It is difficult to inspire others if you are not passionate about your major work activities.

Emotional intelligence can be developed through working on some of its components, such as finding work you are passionate about, developing self-confidence, and developing empathy. It is also important to develop the habit of trying to understand the feelings and emotions of people around you. Ask yourself such questions as "Why is the person feeling like this?", "What are the person's possible motives?", and "Why is this person telling me what he or she is telling me?" Effective leaders look beneath the surface to develop a deeper understanding of situations.

Trustworthiness

Group members consistently believe that leaders must display honesty, integrity, and credibility. Leaders themselves believe that honesty and integrity make a difference in their effectiveness. Researchers and observers also share these views. Warren G. Bennis, a leadership authority, interviewed more than 100 corporate leaders and 50 private-sector leaders during a 13-year period. One of the common threads he found was the capacity of leaders to generate and sustain trust. He observed a consistency among what leaders think, feel, and do. Bennis said it drives people crazy when bosses don't walk their talk.[15] How would you feel if you worked for a boss you couldn't trust?

Trust can be eroded in ways other than inconsistency and dishonesty. Bennis believes that the large disparity between the pay of top executives and that of lower-ranking workers damages trust. He contends that when CEOs of large corporations make 187 times the pay of average workers, it creates an "us versus them" mentality within the workforce rather than promoting teamwork.[16]

The importance of honesty also emerged in a study by the Center for Creative Leadership. Research showed that managers who become executive leaders are likely to espouse the following formula: "I will do exactly what I say I will do when I say I will do it. If I change my mind, I will tell you in advance so you will not be harmed by my actions."[17]

Ability to Perform the Group Task

The closer a leader is to the actual work of the group, the more skilled he or she must be with technical details. For example, the supervisor of internal auditing should be skilled at auditing. Being skilled in the actual work of the group can also be referred to as **technical competence**.

The truth of one widely held belief—that once you are a top-level leader you can leave technical details behind—is greatly exaggerated. Most successful people are still quite knowledgeable about the details of the field in which they found success. A recently appointed top executive of a major architectural and engineering firm had this to say about his new position: "I'm not going to be doing any design work on the boards and that's been true for a long time. But having a design sensibility is something you bring to the job every day, both in dealing with clients and in trying to help the people in the office do their work."[18]

Strong Work Motivation and High Energy

Leadership positions tend to be both physically and mentally demanding. A successful leader must be willing to work hard and long to achieve success. Many leaders appear to be driven by a need for self-fulfillment. Another fundamental reason strong work motivation is required for effectiveness is that a person has to be willing to accept the heavy responsibility that being a supervisor entails. As one department manager said, "Whoever thought being a manager would mean that I would have to fire a single parent who has three children to feed and clothe?"

Problem-Solving Ability and Openness to Experience

Mental ability and personality are important for leadership success. To inspire people, bring about constructive changes, and solve problems creatively, leaders need to be mentally sharp. Problem-solving and intellectual skills are referred to collectively as **cognitive factors**. The term *cognition* refers to the mental process or faculty by which knowledge is gathered.

A cognitive skill of major importance is *knowledge of the business,* or technical competence. An effective leader has to be technically or professionally competent in some discipline, particularly when leading a group of specialists. It is difficult for the leader to establish rapport with group members when he or she does not know what they are doing. A related damper on leadership effectiveness is when the group does not respect the leader's technical skill. Having good practical intelligence (*street smarts*) is also part of an effective leader's intellectual makeup. A leader with high practical intelligence could size up a good opportunity without spending an extensive amount of time analyzing what could possibly go wrong.

Closely related to cognitive skills is the personality characteristic of **openness to experience**, a positive orientation toward learning. People who have considerable openness to experience have well-developed intellects. Traits commonly associated with this dimension of the intellect include being imaginative, cultured, curious, original, broad-minded, intelligent, and artistically sensitive.

Charisma

An important quality for a high-level leader is **charisma**, a type of charm and magnetism that inspires others. Not every leader has to be charismatic, yet to be an effective leader you need some degree of this intangible personal quality.[19] A leader's charisma is determined by the subjective perception of him or her by other people. It is therefore impossible for even the most effective leaders to inspire and motivate everyone. Even popular business leaders are disliked by some of their employees. Charisma encompasses many traits and characteristics. Here we focus on vision, enthusiasm and excitement, and humour.

Vision

Top-level leaders need a visual image of where the organization is headed and how it can get there. The progress of the organization is dependent on the top executive having this vision. Effective leaders project ideas and images that excite people and therefore inspire employees to do their best. At a Conference Board of Canada conference in 2001, the new president of the board stated that leaders need the capacity to see the "bigger picture."[20] Leadership positions of lesser responsibility also call for some vision or that ability to see the bigger picture. Each work group in a progressive company might be expected to form its own vision, as in this vision statement: "We will become the best accounts receivable group in the entire desk-manufacturing industry."

Enthusiasm and Excitement

A psychoanalyst and Harvard Business School professor observes that leaders get excited about their work. Because of their contagious excitement, they stimulate group members.[21] Workers respond positively to enthusiasm, especially because enthusiasm may be perceived as a reward for good performance.

Enthusiasm is also effective because it helps build good relationships with group members. Verbal expressions of enthusiasm include such statements as "Great job" and "I love it." The leader can express enthusiasm nonverbally through gestures, nonsexual touching, and so forth.

Sense of Humour

Humour is a component of charisma and a contributor to leadership effectiveness. Humour helps leaders influence people by reducing tension, relieving boredom, and defusing anger.[22] The most effective form of humour by a leader is tied to the leadership situation. It is much less effective for the leader to tell rehearsed jokes. A key advantage of a witty, work-related comment is that it indicates mental alertness. A canned joke is much more likely to fall flat.

A sales manager was conducting a meeting about declining sales. He opened the meeting by saying, "Ladies and gentlemen, just yesterday I completed a computerized analysis of our declining sales. According to my spreadsheet analysis, if we continue our current trend, by the year 2005 we will have sales of negative $2,750,000. No company can support those figures. We've got to reverse the trend." The manager's humour helped dramatize the importance of reversing the sales decline.

Although inherited characteristics such as energy contribute to charisma, most people can develop some charismatic qualities. Exhibit 12-1 presents suggestions for acquiring more charisma.

The Entrepreneurial Spirit

An entrepreneurial leader assumes the risk of starting an innovative business. We ordinarily think of an entrepreneur as being self-employed because the person is a business owner. Yet the same entrepreneurial spirit can be applied as an employee. (This is much like the work habit technique of being self-employed psychologically.) A group leader with an entrepreneurial spirit would search for new activities for the group. The head of a manufacturing unit might say to the group, "Let's ask top management if we can take a shot at making this part that we now buy from a supplier."

The entrepreneurial spirit can also be expressed by reading trade publications and newspapers to keep up with what is happening in the industry. Talking with customers or others in the organization to keep aware of changing needs and requirements shows a spark of entrepreneurial thinking. The leader with an entrepreneurial spirit also visits other firms, attends professional meetings, and participates in educational programs.[23] All the activities just mentioned help the leader think of new activities for the group.

Behaviours and Skills of Effective Leaders

The personal traits, skills, and characteristics just discussed help create the potential for effective leadership. A leader also has to do things that influence group members to achieve good performance. The behaviours or actions of leaders described next contribute to productivity and morale in most situations.

Practise Strong Ethics

Being trustworthy as a leader facilitates the practice of strong (or good) **ethics**. Ethics is the study of moral obligation, or separating right from wrong. Ethical leadership is about doing the right thing by employees, customers, the environment, and the law.[24] Practising good ethics contributes to effective leadership for several reasons. Workers are more likely to trust an ethical than an unethical leader, which helps the leader gain the support of the group. Good ethics serves as a positive model for group members, thus strengthening the organization. Also, ethical leaders help group members avoid common ethical pitfalls in the work-

exhibit 12-1

Suggestions for Becoming More Charismatic

Following are a number of suggestions for behaving charismatically, all based on characteristics and behaviours often found among charismatic people.

1. *Communicate a vision.* A charismatic leader offers an exciting image of where the organization is headed and how to get there. A vision is more than a forecast because it describes an ideal version of the future of an entire organization or an organizational unit such as a department. The supervisor of paralegal services might communicate a vision such as, "Our paralegal group will become known as the most professional and helpful paralegal group in Alberta."
2. *Make frequent use of metaphors and analogies.* To inspire people, the charismatic leader uses colourful language and exciting metaphors and analogies. Develop metaphors to inspire people around you. To pick up the spirits of her maintenance group, a maintenance supervisor told the group, "We're a lot like the heating and cooling system in a house. A lot of people don't give us much thought, but without us their lives would be very uncomfortable."
3. *Inspire trust and confidence.* Make your deeds consistent with your promises. As mentioned earlier in this chapter, being trustworthy is a key leadership trait. Get people to believe in your competence by making your accomplishments known in a polite, tactful way.
4. *Be highly energetic and goal oriented.* Impress others with your energy and resourcefulness. To increase your energy supply, exercise frequently, eat well, and get ample rest. You can also add to an image of energy by raising and lowering your voice frequently and avoiding a slow pace.
5. *Be emotionally expressive and warm.* A key characteristic of charismatic leaders is the ability to express feelings openly. In dealing with team members, refer to your feelings at the time, such as "I'm excited because I know we are going to hit our year-end target by mid-October." Nonverbal emotional expressiveness, such as warm gestures and frequent touching (nonsexual) of group members also exhibits charisma.
6. *Make ample use of true stories.* An excellent way of building rapport is to tell stories that deliver a message.[25] Storytelling adds a touch of warmth to the teller and helps build connections among people who become familiar with the same story.
7. *Smile frequently, even if you are not in a happy mood.* A warm smile seems to indicate a confident, caring person, which contributes to a perception of charisma.[26]
8. *Be candid.* Practise saying directly what you want rather than being indirect and evasive. If you want someone to help you, don't ask, "Are you busy?" Instead ask, "Can you help me with a problem I'm having right now?"
9. *Make everybody you meet feel that he or she is quite important.* For example, at a company social gathering, shake the hand of every person you meet. Also, thank people frequently both orally and by written notes.
10. *Multiply the effectiveness of your handshake.* Shake firmly without creating pain, and make enough eye contact to notice the colour of the other person's eyes. When you take that much trouble, you project care and concern.
11. *Stand up straight and also use other nonverbal signals of self-confidence.* Practise good posture. Minimize fidgeting, scratching, foot tapping, and speaking in a monotone. Walk at a rapid pace without appearing to be panicked. Dress fashionably without going to the extreme that people notice your clothes more than they notice you.

12. *Be willing to take personal risks.* Charismatic leaders are typically risk takers, and risk taking adds to their charisma. Risks you might take would include suggesting a bright but costly idea and recommending that a former felon be given a chance in your firm.
13. *Be self-promotional.* Charismatic leaders are not shy. Instead, they toot their own horns and allow others to know how important they are. Without appearing self-absorbed, you, too, might let others know of your tangible accomplishments. Explain to others the key role that you played on your team or how you achieved a few tough goals.

place. Many of these unethical practices, as listed next, can lead to lawsuits against the company:

- Lying or misrepresenting facts
- Blaming others for your mistakes
- Divulging personal or confidential information to others in the company to promote yourself
- Permitting or failing to report violations of legal requirements
- Protecting substandard performers from proper discipline
- Condoning or failing to report theft or misuse of company property
- Suppressing grievances and complaints
- Covering up accidents and failing to report health and safety hazards
- Ignoring or violating higher management's commitments to employees
- Taking credit for the ideas of others[27]

To simplify a complex issue, an effective leader practises the golden rule: *Do unto others as you would have others do unto you*. Similarly, Steven Covey encourages leaders to follow natural principles such as doing only good things.[28] He urges corporate executives, for example, to establish only those goals that will benefit people.

Develop Partnerships with People

Leadership is now regarded as a long-term relationship, or partnership, between leaders and group members. According to Peter Block, in a **partnership** the leader and group members are connected in such a way that the power between them is approximately balanced. To form a partnership, the leader has to allow the group members to share in decision making. Four conditions are necessary to form a true partnership between the leader and group members:

1. *Exchange of purpose* The leader and team member should work together to build a vision.
2. *A right to say no* In a partnership each side has the right to say no without fear of being punished.
3. *Joint accountability* Each person takes responsibility for the success and failure of the group.

4. *Absolute honesty* In a partnership, not telling the truth to each other is an act of betrayal. When group members recognize that they have power, they are more likely to tell the truth because they feel less vulnerable to punishment.[29]

Help Group Members Reach Goals and Achieve Satisfaction

Effective leaders help subordinates in their efforts to achieve goals.[30] In a sense, they smooth out the path to reaching goals. One important way to do this is to provide the necessary resources to subordinates. An important aspect of a leader's job is to ensure that subordinates have the proper tools, equipment, and personnel to accomplish their objectives.

Another way of helping group members achieve goals is to reduce frustrating barriers to getting work accomplished. A leader who helps group members cut through minor rules and regulations would be engaging in such behaviour. In a factory, a supervisory leader has a responsibility to replace faulty equipment, make sure unsafe conditions are corrected, and see that troublesome employees are either rehabilitated or replaced.

Another important general set of actions characteristic of an effective leader is looking out for the satisfaction of the group. Small things sometimes mean a lot in terms of personal satisfaction. One office manager fought for better coffee facilities for her subordinates. Her thoughtfulness contributed immensely to their job satisfaction.

Giving group members emotional support is another effective way of improving worker satisfaction. An emotionally supportive leader would engage in activities such as listening to subordinates' problems and offering them encouragement and praise. Again, basic human relations skills contribute to leader effectiveness.

Set High Expectations

In addition to making expectations clear, it is important for leaders to set high expectations for group members. If you as a leader expect others to succeed, they are likely to live up to your expectations. This mysterious phenomenon has been labelled the **Pygmalion effect**. According to Greek mythology, Pygmalion was a sculptor and king of Cyprus who carved an ivory statue of a maiden and fell in love with it. The statue was soon brought to life in response to his prayers.

The point of the Pygmalion effect is that the leader can elevate performance by the simple method of expecting others to perform well. The manager's high expectations become a self-fulfilling prophecy. Why high expectations lead to high performance could be linked to self-confidence. As the leader expresses faith in the group members' ability to perform well, they become more confident of their skills.

Give Frequent Feedback on Performance

Effective leaders inform employees how they are progressing on the job. They know how to recognize progress and how to reward success. They give feedback on progress in such a manner as to encourage the employee to improve and use praise for things done right.[31]

Manage a Crisis Effectively

When a crisis strikes, that's the time to have an effective leader around. When things are running very smoothly, you may not always notice whether your leader is present. Effectively managing a crisis means giving reassurance to the group that things will soon be under control, specifying the alternative paths for getting out of the crisis, and choosing one of the paths.

Ask the Right Questions

As in the example just presented, leaders do not need to know all the answers. Instead, a major contribution can be to ask the right questions. Although being knowledgeable about the group task is important, there are many times when asking group members penetrating questions is more important. In today's complex and rapidly changing business environment, the collective intelligence of group members is needed to solve problems.[32] Asking questions, rather than giving answers, is the natural method of helping group members become better problem solvers. Here are sample questions a leader might ask group members to help them meet their challenges:

- What are you going to do differently to reduce by 50 percent the time it takes to fill a customer order?
- Top management is thinking of getting rid of our group and subcontracting the work we do to outside vendors. What do you propose we do to make us more valuable to the company?
- Can you figure out why the competition is outperforming us?

Be a Servant Leader

A humanitarian approach to leadership is to be a **servant leader**, one who serves group members by working on their behalf to help them achieve their goals, not the leader's goals. The idea behind servant leadership, as developed by Robert K. Greenleaf, is that leadership stems naturally from a commitment to service. Serving others, including employees, customers, and the community, is the primary motivation for the servant leader.[33] Servant leadership encompasses many different acts, all designed to make life easier or better for group members. Several acts of servant leadership are mentioned next.

A good starting point is for the leader to see himself or herself as a humble servant. ("I'm here to serve you.") Servant leaders also look for the opportunity to lend assistance directly to employees—for example, a supermarket manager bagging groceries during an unanticipated rush of business. On Lawrence Weinbach's first day as CEO of computer-maker Unisys Corp., he opened a door for an employee carrying a computer and picked up a piece of paper she dropped.[34] A servant leader would also provide the tools people need to accomplish their work, such as fighting for a budget big enough to cover expensive new equipment.

Although a servant leader is idealistic, he or she recognizes that one individual cannot accomplish everything. So the leader listens carefully to the array of problems facing group members and then concentrates on a few. As the head of a nurse's union told the group: "I know you are hurting in many ways. Yet I think that the work overload issue is the biggest one, so we will head into negotiations working on obtaining sensible workloads. After that we will work on job security."

This is by no means an exhaustive list of the behaviours and skills of an effective leader, but it is an excellent beginning. The Canada Today feature on page 326 lists six things that current leaders can do to keep their staff in the current climate of uncertainty. As a future (or perhaps current) leader, this may be of interest.

Developing Your Leadership Potential

How to improve your potential for becoming a leader is a topic without limits. Almost anything you do to improve your individual effectiveness will have some impact on your ability to lead others. If you strengthen your self-confidence, improve your memory for names, study this book carefully, read studies about leadership, or improve your physical fitness, you stand a good chance of improving your leadership potential. Six general strategies might be kept in mind if you are seeking to improve your leadership potential:

1. *Having general education and specific training* Almost any program of career training or education can be considered a program of leadership development. Courses in human relations, management, or applied psychology have obvious relevance for someone currently occupying or aspiring toward a leadership position. Many of today's leaders in profit and nonprofit organizations hold formal degrees in business. Specific training programs will also help you improve your leadership potential. Among them might be skill development programs in interviewing, employee selection, listening, assertiveness training, budgeting, planning, improving work habits, resolving conflict, and communication skills. After acquiring knowledge through study, you then put the knowledge into practice as a leader.
2. *Attending leadership development programs* A focused way of improving your leadership potential is to attend development programs designed specifically to improve your ability to lead others and develop self-confidence. A popular type of leadership development program called *outdoor training* places people in a challenging outdoor environment for a weekend or up to ten days. Participants are required to accomplish physical feats such as climbing a mountain, whitewater canoeing, building a wall, or swinging between trees on a rope.[35] Participants in these outdoor programs learn such important leadership skills and attitudes as teamwork, trusting others, and confidence in their ability to accomplish the seemingly impossible.
3. *Gaining leadership experience* No program of leadership improvement can be a substitute for leadership experience. Because leadership effectiveness depends somewhat on the situation, a sound approach is to attempt to gain

Six New Carrots, or How to Keep Your Staff Around

A Canadian book, *Values Shift: The New Work Ethic and What It Means for Business,* tries to tackle the problem of motivating and inspiring employees in a time when traditional values and ideas may no longer be valued by employees. What can leaders or managers do to keep employees in an era when promotions and big pay raises may not be possible? The authors have some interesting ideas on how to maintain and even excite current workers!

1. **Be proactive in offering workers a better work/life balance.** In the last 20 years, time spent on the job in a given year has increased by 163 hours while leisure time has declined by one-third. Freedom to take extended leave or sabbaticals has been identified as a key workplace benefit. Managers who help employees achieve better balance so that personal time can also be enjoyed will be seen as better leaders.
2. **Promote the sense of deeper cause.** Helping employees achieve deeper levels of satisfaction than just company profitability leads to happier and more motivated employees. Many companies, such as Americredit (including its Canadian location), give employees paid time for volunteer work, something that many find personally fulfilling.
3. **Promote professional growth and development.** Employees want the opportunity to learn and grow. A 1999 Gallup poll found that lacking such opportunity was one of the top three reasons for employee dissatisfaction. Managers who provide such opportunities including such activities as mentoring programs will be more successful.
4. **Treat employees like partners.** Workers who feel that their opinions and ideas matter enjoy their work more and are more likely to contribute enthusiastically and be more dedicated. Only 27 percent of employees in a 1999 Watson Wyatt Canada survey reported that they felt they were treated as valued business partners by their bosses.
5. **Encourage community-building in the workplace.** With longer work hours, technology in the workplace, flexible work hours, telecommuting, and other advances that tend to isolate people, many employees feel disconnected (and thus discontent) from the workplace and from each other. Leaders and workplaces who create opportunities for interaction will have happier employees.
6. **Start rebuilding trust.** Only 37 percent of employees rated the level of honesty in their organizations as high or very high. And only 14 percent felt that they could trust each other! Leaders not only need to work harder to gain the trust of their subordinates but also to work in ways that help employees trust each other.

What does this mean for you? Developing leadership skills and behaviours is very important. However, leadership takes place within organizational cultures, and it is obvious that not all organizations warmly embrace organizational goals and the leadership to guide employees to achieve these goals. Leadership is much more than management, and a more holistic approach is required if you are going to be an effective leader in today's organizations.

SOURCES: Pam Withers, "Managing Discontent," *BC Business*, January 2001, vol. 29(1), pp. 26–32. Used with permission of the author. This article is adapted from John P. Izzo and Pam Withers, *Values Shift: The New Work Ethic and What It Means for Business* (Prentice Hall Canada, 2000).

leadership experience in different settings. A person who wants to become an executive is well advised to gain supervisory experience in at least two different organizational functions (such as customer service and finance).

First-level supervisory jobs are an invaluable starting point for developing your leadership potential. It takes considerable skill to manage a fast-food restaurant effectively or to direct a public playground during the summer. A first-line supervisor frequently faces a situation in which subordinates are poorly trained, poorly paid, and not well motivated to achieve company objectives.

4. *Modelling effective leaders* Are you committed to improving your leadership skill and potential? If so, carefully observe a capable leader in action and incorporate some of his or her approaches into your own behaviour. You may not be able to or want to become that person's clone, but you can model (imitate) what the person does. For instance, most inexperienced leaders have a difficult time confronting others with bad news. Observe how a good confronter handles that situation and try that person's approach the next time you have some unfavourable news to deliver.
5. *Pursuing self-development of leadership characteristics and behaviour* Study the leadership characteristics and behaviours described in this chapter. As a starting point, identify several attributes you think you could strengthen within yourself given some self-determination. For example, you might decide that with effort you could improve your enthusiasm. You might also believe that you could be more emotionally supportive of others. It is also helpful to obtain feedback from reliable sources about which traits and behaviours you particularly need to develop.
6. *Becoming an integrated human being* A philosophical approach to leadership suggests that the model leader is first and foremost a fully functioning person. According to William D. Hitt, mastering the art of leadership comes with self-mastery. Leadership development is the process of self-development. As a result, the process of becoming a leader is similar to the process of becoming an integrated human being. For example, you need to develop values that guide your behaviour before you can adequately guide the behaviour of others.

   The model (or ideal) leader, according to Hitt, must possess six character traits: identity ("know thyself"), independence, authenticity, responsibility, courage, and integrity.[36] All of these traits have everyday meanings, but they can also have personal meanings. Part of becoming an integrated person is to answer such questions as, "What do I mean when I say I have integrity?" As we stated in the beginning of the chapter, this softer side or set of soft skills is an essential component of effective leadership.

Summary

Before most people can exert leadership, they need to develop an appropriate amount of self-confidence. Self-confidence is necessary for leadership because it helps assure group members that things are under control. A leader who is too self-confident, however, may not admit to errors, listen to criticism, or ask for advice. Also, you may appear insecure if you are too self-confident.

A general principle of boosting your self-confidence is to experience success (goal accomplishment) in a variety of situations. As you achieve one set of goals, you establish slightly more difficult goals, thus entering a success cycle. The specific strategies for building self-confidence described here are these:

1. Take an inventory of personal assets and accomplishments.
2. Develop a solid knowledge base.
3. Develop positive self-talk.
4. Avoid negative self-talk.
5. Use positive visual imagery.
6. Strive for peak performance.
7. Bounce back from setbacks and embarrassments.

Leadership is the process of bringing about positive changes and influencing others to achieve organizational goals. Effective leadership is needed at the top of organizations, but supervisors and team leaders also need to provide effective leadership. Effective leaders have the "right stuff."

Certain traits and characteristics contribute to leadership effectiveness in many situations. Among them are emotional intelligence; ability to perform the group task; strong work motivation and high energy; problem-solving ability and openness to experience; charisma (including vision, enthusiasm and excitement, and a sense of humour); and an entrepreneurial spirit.

Behaviours and skills of an effective leader (one who maintains high productivity and morale) include the following:

1. Practise strong ethics.
2. Develop partnerships with people (emphasizing power sharing).
3. Help group members reach goals and achieve satisfaction.
4. Set high expectations.
5. Give frequent feedback on performance.
6. Manage a crisis effectively.
7. Ask the right questions.
8. Be a servant leader.

Many activities in life can in some way contribute to the development of a person's leadership potential. Five recommended strategies for improving your leadership potential or leadership skills are (1) general education and specific training, (2) participation in leadership development programs, (3) acquisition of leadership experience, (4) modelling experienced leaders, (5) self-development of leadership characteristics and behaviour, and (6) becoming an integrated human being.

Questions and Activities

1. When you meet a person, how can you tell whether he or she is self-confident?
2. What is the difference between "trying your hardest" and achieving peak performance?
3. What positive self-talk can you use after you have failed on a major assignment?
4. How does the emphasis on developing strong ethics for leaders fit with the general stereotype of business executives?
5. Why is "ability to perform the group task" essential for a team leader?
6. Provide an example of something a leader motivated or inspired you to do that you would not have done without his or her presence.
7. Create a vision for your present or past employer (or any other company of your choosing).
8. Identify three areas in life in which being charismatic would help a person achieve his or her goals.
9. How might your current program of study contribute to your development as a leader?

Internet Skill Builder

Becoming More Charismatic

This chapter offered suggestions for becoming more charismatic. Search the internet for additional suggestions and compare them to suggestions in the text. Be alert to contradictions, and offer a possible explanation for them. Use a search phrase such as "how to become more charismatic." An all-encompassing phrase such as "developing leadership effectiveness" is unlikely to direct you to the information you need.

Weblinks

www.globalnode.com/users/stevenr/quiz/leader.htm
This is a leadership capability test. If you travel to the homepage, you can also access other tests. Beware: many of these tests are not valid or reliable, but they are fun!

http://greenleaf.org/home.html
This is a site about being a servant leader.

Human Relations Case Study

CHARISMATICALLY CHALLENGED COLLEEN

Twenty-seven-year-old Colleen McFerguson worked as a merchandising specialist for ValuMart, one of the largest international retail chains. Based in the United States, ValuMart also has a strong presence in Canada, Europe, Japan, and Hong Kong. Colleen began her employment with ValuMart as a cashier, and two years later she was invited into the training program for merchandising specialists.

Colleen performed well as a merchandising trainee in the soft-goods line. Her specialty areas included men's, women's, and children's clothing; linens and bedding; men's and women's jewellery; and home decorations. For several years in a row, Colleen received performance evaluation ratings of above average or outstanding. Among the write-in comments made by her supervisors were "diligent worker," "knows the tricks of merchandising," "good flair for buying the right products at the right price," and "fits right into the team."

Despite the positive performance appraisals supported with positive comments, Colleen had a gnawing discontent about her career at ValuMart. Despite five years of good performance, she was still not invited to become a member of the ValuTrackers, a group of merchandising and operations specialists who are regarded as being on the fast track to becoming future ValuMart leaders. The leaders hold high-level positions such as head merchandiser, regional vice-president, and store manager.

Several times when Colleen inquired about why she was not invited to join the ValuTrackers, she was told that she was not quite ready to be included in this elite group. She was also told not to be discouraged because the company still valued her contribution.

One day Colleen thought to herself, "I'm heading toward age 30, and I want a great future in the retail business now." So she convinced her boss, merchandising supervisor Evan Tyler, to set up a career conference with three people: Colleen, the boss, and her boss's boss, Heather Bridges, the area merchandising manager. She let Evan know in advance that she wanted to talk about her potential for promotion.

Evan started the meeting by saying, "Colleen, perhaps you can tell Heather and me again why you requested this meeting."

Colleen responded, "Thanks for asking, Evan. As I mentioned before, I'm wondering what you think is wrong with me. I receive a lot of positive feedback about my performance, but I'm not a ValuTracker. Also, you seem to change the subject when I talk about wanting to become a merchandising supervisor and eventually a merchandising executive. What am I doing wrong?"

Heather responded, "Evan and I frequently talk about the performance and potential of all our merchandising specialists. You're a good performer, Colleen, but you lack that little spark that makes a person a leader. You go about your job efficiently and quietly, but that's not enough. We want future leaders of ValuMart to make an impact."

Evan added, "I go along with Heather's comments. Another point, Colleen, is that you rarely take the initiative to suggest ideas. I was a little shocked by your request for a three-way career interview because it's one of the few initiatives you have taken. You're generally pretty laid-back."

"Then what do I have to do to convince you two that I should be a ValuTracker?" asked Colleen.

Heather replied, "Start acting more like a leader. Be more charismatic." Evan nodded in agreement.

Questions

1. What career advice can you offer Colleen McFerguson?
2. What might Colleen do to develop more charisma?
3. What is your opinion of the fairness of the ValuTracker program?

Choosing a Career and Developing a Portfolio Career

Learning Outcomes

After studying the information and doing the exercises in this chapter, you should be able to

- make a tentative career choice if you have not already done so
- identify skills that could serve as the basis for your career
- appreciate the complexity of choosing a career
- search for useful information about occupations and careers
- explain the basics of career switching and developing a portfolio career

Vincent Langlois was recently promoted to a supervising teller position in a bank, putting him on track to becoming a bank manager. Vincent enjoys his work and is proud of his accomplishments. Asked how he chose to launch his career as a teller, Vincent explained: "Four years ago as graduation was fast approaching, I didn't have a clue as to what aspect of business I would enter. One day it struck me that since I was on the internet for so many other purposes, perhaps I could use it to find a job. After surfing different directions, I hit Human Resources Development Canada's Job Bank. One of the jobs being advertised was a teller position. I had also heard that one way to get yourself known was to go into a nontraditional field. I thought being a male teller would be nontraditional, as most tellers are women.

"I figured that if I became a teller, maybe I would stand out because of being a man. Also, I always liked banks because the work they do is important. Next, I followed through by applying to the bank and I got it!"

Vincent's success in finding a career that is working for him illustrates a major theme of this chapter. For many people, finding the right career requires careful thinking and systematic effort. If you have not already chosen a career or are thinking of changing careers, this chapter is especially important. If you are content with your career, this chapter can be read with the intention of learning more about that vital part of your life. What a person does for a living is one of the key influences in his or her life. Your career is also a prime source of your self-concept and self-esteem.

The purpose of this chapter is to help you choose a career by describing systematic methods of career selection. For those who have already chosen a career field in general, this chapter may help you narrow down your career choice within your field. For example, a person entering the computer field might choose to emphasize those aspects of computers dealing heavily with people, such as computer sales or information systems.

Self-Knowledge and Choosing a Career

A **career** is a series of related job experiences that fit into a meaningful pattern. If you have a series of odd jobs all your working life, that is hardly a career. But if each job builds carefully on the previous one, we say you are "building a career." We assume that by making a sound initial choice of occupation, you will be on the first step toward building a real career. Chapters 14 through 16 provide information to help you advance in whatever career you have chosen.

A general strategy for making a sound career choice is to understand first the inner you, including what you have to offer. You then match that information with opportunities in the outside world. The Self-Knowledge Questionnaire presented in Chapter 1 asks many questions that are relevant to making a career choice. Almost any of the information provided by candid answers to those questions could help you make a sound career choice. Several specific illustrations are in order.

Question 1 asks, "How far have I gone in school?" If you answered, "Three years of high school," or "Four years of high school and two years of business school," you will need additional education to enter many fields. Among them are management, teaching, counselling, or social work.

Question 9 asks, "What aspect of these jobs did I enjoy?" Suppose you answered, "Anytime I was left alone to do some figuring or report writing I was happy. Thinking made me happy." Your answer could mean that you should search for a field in which working with ideas and data is more important than working with people or things. What about investigating laboratory work or financial analysis?

Question 31 asks, "What gives me satisfaction in life?" Suppose you answered, "Playing with my children, going fishing, and getting involved with my friends almost every day." However good for your mental health this answer might be, it certainly does limit the level of responsibility you can aspire to in most careers. A busy executive or professional person often comes out on the short end with respect to having ample time for family, fishing, and friends.

Some additional questions useful in clarifying the type of work you would prefer are presented in Human Relations Self-Assessment Quiz 13-1.

Learning More about Yourself

By candidly answering the questions that follow, you may be able to develop some new understanding about your career preferences. Try to write at least 25 words in response to each question, even if your answer is uncertain.

1. What kind of work would make me proud?

____

____

2. What would be a horrible way for me to make a living?

____

____

3. How important is a high income to me? Why?

____

____

4. How do I really feel about what other people think of the kind of work I do?

____

____

5. What kind of work would really be fun for me to do?

____

____

6. What kind of work would I be willing to do for ten consecutive years?

____

____

7. What kind of work would make me feel self-fulfilled?

____

____

8. What is my attitude toward doing the same thing every workday?

____

____

9. How do I really feel about being held responsible when things go wrong?

____

____

The Importance of Skills in Choosing a Career

In addition to other aspects of self-understanding, knowing which skills you possess—and enjoy performing—can be the basis for a successful career. A **skill** is a learned, specific ability to do something such as write a report, prepare a website, or troubleshoot software problems. A vast number of skills could be exercised in a career, including such skills as selling, calculating currency exchanges, and coaching workers. Identifying your skills is important both in choosing a career and in finding a job. Employers want to know what a job prospect can actually *do*, or what skills he or she possesses.

An enlightening perspective is that your best skill represents your **core competency**, or whatever you do best. But there is more to core competency than what is suggested in your job title.[1] Your core competency is the aspect of your job that you perform particularly well. As a collection agent, your core competency might be obtaining partial payments with accounts so long overdue that others consider them almost uncollectible. If you have developed a core competency early in your schooling or temporary work experience, making a sound career choice is easier. An adolescent with superior skill in explaining to others how to use electronic devices might have the necessary core competency for a career in technical writing. (A big part of a technical writer's job is preparing operating manuals for equipment.)

Julie Griffin Levitt has developed a useful way of identifying skills,[2] as outlined in Human Relations Self-Assessment Quiz 13-2. As you develop several of these skills to an above-average degree, they may become your core competency.

Skills Profile

Review the following skill areas and specific skills. In the space provided, write down each one you believe is a strong skill for you. You can also add a specific skill that was not included in the skill area listed at the left.

Skill Area	***Specific Skills***	***A Strong Skill for Me***
Communication	writing, speaking, knowledge of foreign language, telephone skills, persuasiveness, listening	___________
Creative	originating ideas, thinking up novel solutions	___________
Interpersonal relations	ability to get along well with others, being a team player, diplomacy, conflict resolution, understanding others	___________
Management	ability to lead, organize, plan, motivate others, make decisions, manage time	___________
Manual and mechanical	mechanically inclined, build, operate, repair, assemble, install, drive vehicles	___________
Mathematics	math skills, computers, analyzing data, budgeting, using statistical techniques	___________
Office	keyboarding, filing, business math, bookkeeping, using spreadsheets, word processing, database management, record keeping	___________
Sales	persuading others, negotiating, promoting, dressing fashionably	___________
Scientific	investigating, researching, compiling, systematizing, diagnosing, evaluating	___________
Service of customers	serving customers, handling complaints, dealing with difficult people	___________
Service of patients	nurturing, diagnosing, treating, guiding, counselling, consoling, dealing with emergencies	___________
Other skill area	______________________________	___________

SOURCE: Abridged and adapted from Julie Griffin Levitt, *Your Career: How to Make It Happen*, 2nd ed. (Cincinnati, Ohio: South-Western Publishing Co., 1990), pp. 19–21.

Getting Help from a Career Counsellor

In choosing a career or switching careers, an excellent method of learning more about yourself in relation to the world of work is to obtain help from a professional **career counsellor**. A counsellor usually relies on a wide variety of tests plus an interview to assist you in making a sound career choice. It is untrue that any single test will tell you what occupation you should enter. Tests are designed to provide useful clues, not to give you definite answers. Nor is it true that a career counsellor will tell you what occupation you should enter. Using tests and human judgment, the counsellor helps you become more aware of yourself and the alternatives that might suit your circumstances. This chapter emphasizes choosing a career by yourself. It is recommended, however, that you seek the help of a guidance counsellor, career counsellor, or counselling psychologist.

Interest Testing to Identify Careers of Interest

Career counselling emphasizes finding a career that suits a person's interests. The most widely used instrument for matching a person's interests with careers is the **Strong Interest Inventory (SII)**. The output of the SII is a computer-generated report that provides potentially useful information about making career choices.[3]

The SII asks 325 questions about your preferences (likes, dislikes, or indifferences) concerning occupations, school subjects, activities, amusements, and types of people. Exhibit 13-1 presents a sampling of such questions. A person's answers to these questions are used to compute three sets of scores: (1) general occupational themes, (2) basic interest scales, and (3) occupational scales.

exhibit 13 - 1

Type of Test Items Found on the Strong Interest Inventory

1.	Actor	L	I	D
2.	Aviator	L	I	D
3.	Architect	L	I	D
4.	Astronomer	L	I	D
5.	Athletic director	L	I	D
6.	Auctioneer	L	I	D
7.	Author of novel	L	I	D
8.	Author of scientific book	L	I	D
9.	Auto sales representative	L	I	D
10.	Auto mechanic	L	I	D

NOTE: In this section of the test, the subject indicates whether he or she would like (L), dislike (D), or be indifferent to (I) working in each occupation.

Scores on the Strong Interest Inventory

Each of the six occupational themes is associated with one or more basic interest scales as follows:

R Theme (Realistic) High scorers on this theme tend to be rugged, robust, practical individuals who are physically strong and frequently aggressive in outlook. The basic interest scales carrying the realistic theme are Agriculture, Nature, Adventure, Military Activities, and Mechanical Activities.

I Theme (Investigative) High scorers on this theme enjoy science and scientific activities, and are not particularly interested in working with others. They also enjoy solving abstract problems. The basic interest scales carrying the investigative theme are Science, Mathematics, Medical Science, and Medical Service.

A Theme (Artistic) High scorers on these themes are artistically oriented and like to work in settings where self-expression is welcome. The associated interest scales are Music/Dramatics, Art, and Writing.

S Theme (Social) High scorers on this theme are sociable, responsible, humanistic, and concerned with the welfare of others. The associated interest scales are Teaching, Social Service, Athletics, Domestic Arts, and Religious Activities.

E Theme (Enterprising) High scorers on this theme are skillful with words and use this capability to sell, dominate, and lead. The associated interest scales are Public Speaking, Law/Politics, Merchandising, Sales, and Business Management.

C Theme (Conventional) High scorers on this theme prefer the ordered activities, both verbal and numerical, that characterize office work. They are comfortable following the rules and regulations of a large firm. The associated interest scale is Office Practices.

The Strong Interest Inventory has 211 occupational scales, divided among the six general occupational themes and basic interest scales. For example, the following occupations are among those associated with the conventional theme and the office practices scales: accountant, banker, credit manager, business education teacher, food service manager, nursing home administrator, and secretary.

Interpreting the SII Profile

With the assistance of a counsellor, a person looks for patterns of high and low scores. High scores indicate interests similar to people in occupational areas and occupations, whereas low scores suggest the opposite. Assume that a person scores very high on the Office Practices Scale and high on the occupations of banker and credit manager. The same person also scores very low on the Investigative theme, the Medical Service Interest Scale, and the medical, technical, and respiratory therapist Occupational Scales. We conclude that this person would be happier as an office manager than as an ambulance medic!

Note that *interest* is not the same as *ability*. Some people may not have the mental aptitude and skills to do well in the occupations they would enjoy. Interest is but one important factor contributing to successful performance. Being interested in your field makes the biggest contribution to keeping you motivated.

Matching Your Career to Your Lifestyle

Another consideration in using self-knowledge to assist in choosing a career is to take into account your lifestyle preferences. Ideally, you should pursue a career that provides you with the right balance among work, leisure, and interaction with people. Some degree of compromise is usually necessary. If your preferred lifestyle is to take two-hour lunch breaks each workday, it would be difficult to attain a high level of responsibility. Executives, public relations specialists, and sales representatives who seem to spend considerable time at lunch are usually conducting business over their meal. They are not taking time out during the workday. If a cornerstone of your lifestyle is to remain in top physical and mental shape, you should probably avoid some of the high-pressure careers, such as ambulance paramedic or securities sales representative. On the other hand, you would want to avoid a career that provided too little challenge.

As just hinted, the term **lifestyle** can refer to many different key aspects of your life. In terms of making a career choice, it is helpful to regard lifestyle as the pattern by which a person invests energy into work and nonwork. Being the proverbial beach bum or ski bum is one lifestyle. So is being the 90-hour-a-week financial executive.

Today, an increasing number of people at different stages in their careers are making career choices that improve their chances of leading their preferred lifestyle. The general manager of a plant in a small town makes a revealing comment about modern lifestyles: "A number of years ago we couldn't get nearly the number of skilled people we needed to work here. The people who had a choice wanted to live in an area near a big city. Now we get loads of unsolicited résumés.

It seems that a lot of people want access to camping and fishing. I think they're also worried about crime and pollution in the cities."

The move toward a healthy balance between work and nonwork might also be considered part of the movement toward a higher quality of life. For some people, living in an $1,800-a-month studio apartment in Vancouver or Montreal represents a high quality of life. Such city dwellers would, of course, have to aspire to a very high-paying occupation to support their preference. How will your preferred lifestyle influence your career decision-making?

Another key aspect of matching your career to your lifestyle is to choose a career that enables you to achieve the right balance between work and personal life. People vary widely in what they consider the right balance. Individuals who want to be home at regular hours and on weekends, with very little travel, will usually have to avoid industrial sales or managerial work. On the other hand, individuals who prefer the excitement of breakfast meetings, weekend meetings, and travel might choose the two occupations just mentioned.

Flexible work schedules are a major mechanism for matching preferred lifestyle to career choice. Many people whose preferred lifestyle does not permit full-time work seek opportunities to work part-time. Others, whose preferred lifestyle is to minimize commuting and working outside the home, seek home-based careers that may involve teleworking. Be aware however, that some of these choices will lessen your opportunities in some areas of career choice.

An emerging trend of matching preferred lifestyle to career takes place at a later point in a person's career. As such, it is a method of modifying, rather than choosing, a career to fit a living pattern. **Downshifters** are workers who choose shorter hours and less-demanding work to allow more time for other activities. To achieve more happiness, these people ask their employers to be even more flexible about work hours and job demands. (A job that is too stressful can interfere with the ability to enjoy leisure.) What is your evaluation of the merits of downshifting? Would you want a shorter, easier job with less pay so that you can upshift in other areas of life?

Lastly, your career and job choices need to match your **values** and the things that are important to you in your life. While this may sound rather ideal, it is not unrealistic. If you value honesty and integrity, would you want to work for a company that has unethical business practices? The web can be a valuable source here. Many companies post mission statements that incorporate the values the company wishes to embrace as its best practice. On the opposite page is the credo of Johnson & Johnson, a large company with many locations including Canada. What values do you see in this credo? Does this company share some of your values?

Finding Out about Occupations

Whether or not you have already made a career choice, you should follow a fundamental rule of plotting your career—get the facts. Few people have valid information about careers they wish to pursue. A glaring example of occupational misinformation relates to the legal field. Many young people say, "I would like to be a lawyer. I'm good at convincing people. And I know I could sway a jury." Similarly, "I want to be a paralegal. I have the mind of a detective. I know I could break most of the tough cases I'd be given to research."

Johnson & Johnson: "Our Credo"

We believe our first responsibility is to the doctors, nurses and patients,
to mothers and fathers and all others who use our products and services.
In meeting their needs everything we do must be of high quality.
We must constantly strive to reduce our costs
in order to maintain reasonable prices.
Customers' orders must be serviced promptly and accurately.
Our suppliers and distributors must have an opportunity
to make a fair profit.

We are responsible to our employees,
the men and women who work with us throughout the world.
Everyone must be considered as an individual.
We must respect their dignity and recognize their merit.
They must have a sense of security in their jobs.
Compensation must be fair and adequate,
and working conditions clean, orderly and safe.
We must be mindful of ways to help our employees fulfill
their family responsibilities.
Employees must feel free to make suggestions and complaints.
There must be equal opportunity for employment, development
and advancement for those qualified.
We must provide competent management,
and their actions must be just and ethical.

We are responsible to the communities in which we live and work
and to the world community as well.
We must be good citizens–support good works and charities
and bear our fair share of taxes.
We must encourage civic improvements and better health and education.
We must maintain in good order the property we are privileged to use,
protecting the environment and natural resources.

Our final responsibility is to our stockholders.
Business must make a sound profit.
We must experiment with new ideas.
Research must be carried on, innovative programs developed
and mistakes paid for.
New equipment must be purchased, new facilities provided
and new products launched.
Reserves must be created to provide for adverse times.
When we operate according to these principles,
the stockholders should realize a fair return.

Permission to use credo, courtesy of Johnson & Johnson.

In reality, the work of a lawyer or paralegal includes the processing of much nonglamorous information. One example is figuring out how much money a bankrupt bakery owes to 27 different suppliers. Four general sources of occupational information are printed material and electronic information, computer systems, spoken information, and first-hand experience. Without this information it is difficult to find a good fit between yourself and existing opportunities.

Printed and Web-Based Information

Most libraries, bookstores, and Human Resources Development Canada centres are well supplied with information about career opportunities. One of the most comprehensive source documents of occupational information is the National Occupational Classification (NOC). The NOC replaces the Canadian Classification and Dictionary of Occupations (CCDO). It contains the classification structure and descriptions of 522 occupational groups that constitute the Canadian labour market. The index contains over 25,000 occupational titles divided into ten major classifications. For the various occupations it lists, there is information on employment requirements, type of work performed, education required to perform the job, and so on. The most recent update, NOC 2001, has added many new occupations, particularly in the areas experiencing high technological changes.

There are many general sourcebooks to assist individuals in gathering information on various careers. Also, try business magazines. For example, *Canadian Business* features articles about new job opportunities on a regular basis. These resources can be found in libraries, bookstores, and at Human Resources Development Canada offices or centres. Other sourcebooks include

- *Canada Employment Weekly* (contains over 500 career opportunities weekly)
- *Career Options*, a monthly magazine that can also be accessed over the internet at **www.cacee.com/coptions/2001**

An excellent sourcebook is *Job Futures 2000*, the most recent version of this valuable resource. *Job Futures 2000*, published by the Canadian Occupational Projection System of the Applied Research Branch and the Occupational and Career Division of Human Resources Development Canada (HRDC), includes four products. The first item is the *World of Work*, a new product that provides an overview of labour market trends and links them to career and educational choices. The second product, *Outlooks by Occupation*, provides general information on 211 occupational groups in Canada and has projections about how the labour market may change through 2004. The third product, *Outlooks by Fields of Study*, profiles 155 post-secondary fields of study. The fourth product, *Job Futures Companion,* is a step-by-step handbook on how to use *Job Futures*. These products are also available electronically on the internet at the HRDC website (**www.hrdc-drhc.gc.ca/JobFutures**).

Use of the internet's resources has been steadily growing in the past few years and will continue to do so in coming years. HRDC has an extensive site with several useful links, including an up-to-date Job Bank with literally thousands of postings. A career seeker can simply type in the job title sought, click onto geographical areas of interest, and read the list of available openings, many of which include contact names and salary schedules. HRDC also has extensive information on job skills, such as developing a résumé and preparing for a job interview. It is strongly recommended that you take a tour of this site and use it for job and career seeking. Two other sites of interest are WorkInfoNet and Campus WorkLink. Both sites offer job postings as well as information on acquiring job skills. WorkInfoNet has links to a vast array of career-related websites. Within this link are separate areas to explore, including jobs and recruiting, career planning, training, professional and community associations, and general information about the labour market. Campus WorkLink is also for job seekers as well as for employers wishing to hire new recruits. At this site, job seekers can post a résumé. Membership is free. A complete list of the site addresses mentioned here is provided at the end of this chapter. Another Canadian site, Career Discovery, is also very interesting and you can sign up for free (**www.careerdiscovery.ca**). There are many more sites that you can find on your own by typing in key words in your browser.

Computer-Assisted Career Guidance

Several career-guidance information systems have been developed for access by computer. The information contained in these systems is designed to help users plan their careers. Guidance information systems go one step beyond printed information because you can ask questions of (interact with) the computer. For instance, when you are keyed in on a specific occupation, you can ask "What is the promotion outlook?" and "What effect will technology have?"

A widely used career-guidance information system is DISCOVER, developed by the American College Testing Program and customized by ITP Nelson for use in Canada. Prior knowledge of computers is not required to use DISCOVER or other similar software. The system is intended for use by post-secondary students and by adults seeking a new career direction outside their current employment.[4]

The Canadian Work Preference Inventory is also widely used to assess a person's interests and match them with possible career options. The five categories of interests are those used in the National Occupational Classification's *Career Handbook*. These areas of interest include directive (taking control and being self-directed), innovative (like to explore, solve problems, and invent), methodical (prefer to work under direction and getting things done), objective (working with tools and equipment) and social preferences (like to be with and care for people). For example, a person high in directive—someone who likes to take charge and control—would prefer jobs where he or she can instruct others or give directions. This inventory can be used at the HRDC's Human Resources Centres and other career centres. Another widely used and recently updated career-guidance information system is Choices 2000, which can be used at no cost at many Human Resources Centres.

Speaking to People

An invaluable supplement to reading about occupations is speaking to people engaged in them. No matter what occupation interests you, search out a person actually employed in that kind of work. Most people welcome the opportunity to talk about themselves and the type of work they do. If you do not know anyone engaged in the career field that interests you, do some digging. A few inquiries will usually lead to a person you can contact. It is best to interview that person in his or her actual work setting to obtain a sense of the working conditions people face in that field.

Remember, however, that many people will probably say that although they are very happy in their work, there are better ways to make a living. Ask your dentist, doctor, lawyer, or plumber about his or her field, and you might be told, "Don't believe all those stories about people in this field being wealthy. We work long and hard for our money. And there's always the problem of people not paying their bills. I don't recommend that you enter this field."

Suppose you want to learn about the field of Total Quality Management, yet you do not know anyone who knows any person doing this kind of work. Try the cold-canvas method. Call one or two large companies and ask to speak to someone working in Total Quality. When you reach that department, indicate that you are trying to make a sound career choice and then proceed with your inquiry. The success ratio of this approach is remarkably high.

First-hand Experience

If you want to explore an occupation in depth, it is important to obtain some first-hand experience in that occupation. Part-time and temporary employment is particularly useful. One man who is a self-employed landscape consultant first tried out the field by working two summers for an established business. Some schools offer cooperative, or work-study, programs. However modest your cooperative employment, it can provide you with much valuable information. For instance, it is surprisingly helpful to observe whether or not people engaged in that type of work ever smile or laugh. If not, the work might be intense and dreary.

Temporary work in a field you might wish to enter could lead to a job offer. It is standard practice for employers to use part-time and temporary jobs as a way of screening prospective employees. A woman who is now a sales representative for a well-known business corporation presents this anecdote: "I took the most menial clerical position in the marketing department. My supervisor told her boss that I was a good worker—somebody who would give a fair shake to the company. Now I'm making more money and having more fun than I thought possible at my age."

A promising approach to gaining first-hand knowledge about a potential career is by directly observing a sampling of the career. **Job shadowing** is a way of gaining information about an occupation by spending a few hours with a professional in the workplace, observing first-hand what the job entails. Closely observing a professional in action will often lead to an enhanced understanding of what the work really entails. As practised at several schools, students get a four-hour shadowing opportunity at local business firms. Even when a student has chosen a career, the direct observation can help confirm that the choice was sound.[5]

Choosing a Growth Occupation

Another important type of occupational information for career selection relates to growth opportunities within the field. An advantageous way of choosing a career is to pursue an occupation that appears to have growth potential, *provided work in that field matches your interests*. Entering a rapidly growing field will not do a person much good if he or she does not like the work, because it will be difficult to perform well in the long run.

Using the growth-occupation strategy, the career seeker searches for a match between his or her capabilities and a growth occupation in a growth field. For example, a person who likes to provide support to others and to work extensively with computers might choose systems analyst (a growth occupation).

How do you identify growth occupations? One way is to use the sources described in the section about finding career information. For instance, visit the Human Resources Development Canada site and find out what jobs have the most listings. Also, check out current magazines that discuss hiring and job hunting on a fairly regular basis, such as *Computing Canada*, which recently listed hot jobs in the Canadian IT market, including project managers, data administrators, and software engineers.[6] Also, *Canadian Business* magazine often has helpful articles to guide you in some career choices and ideas.

Data, People, or Things

A helpful way of looking at career choices is to characterize jobs according to the amount of time devoted to data (or ideas), people, or things. The National Occupational Classification (NOC), published by Human Resources Development Canada, uses these categories of how time is spent on the job in describing all the occupational titles:

1. *Data/Information* Refers to working with facts, information, and ideas made from observations and interpretations. The activities involved in working with data are synthesizing, coordinating, analyzing, compiling, computing, copying, and comparing. Analyzing information generated by computers, for example, gives a person ample opportunity to work with data.
2. *People* Refers to working with human beings, and also to working with animals as if they were human. The activities involved in working with people are mentoring, negotiating, instructing, supervising, diverting, persuading, speaking/signalling, serving, and taking instructions/helping. A customer service representative would have ample opportunity to work with people, as the representative regularly handles customer complaints.
3. *Things* Refers to work with inanimate objects such as tools, equipment, and products. The activities involved in working with things are setting up, precision working, operating/controlling, driving/operating, manipulating, tending, feeding/offbearing, and handling. An office equipment repair technician would have ample opportunity to work with things while making service calls.

Most jobs involve a combination of dealing with data, people, and things. It is usually a question of the relative proportion of each dimension. Managers, for example, have high involvement with data and people and a low involvement with things. Registered nurses have an average involvement with all three.

Understanding one's preferences for working with data, people, and things sharpens a career choice. Job satisfaction is likely to increase when the individual engages in work that fits his or her relative interest in data, people, and things. A person with a balanced preference for all three would probably enjoy a position selling business equipment that also required substantial preparation of sales reports.

Developing a Portfolio Career and Career Switching

It is becoming increasingly common for people to either switch the emphasis of activities in their work or switch careers entirely. An example of switching the emphasis of activities would be a salesperson who is working with computers to shift to a new field in which he or she worked primarily with computers and did no selling. People modify their careers for a variety of reasons, all centring on the idea that something is missing in their present one. Here we look at two closely related approaches to changing direction in a career: developing a portfolio career and career switching.

Developing a Portfolio Career

Many people would like to change careers yet not be confined to focusing on one major type of job activity. To accomplish this, a growing number of people are developing a **portfolio career**, in which they use a variety of skills and earn money in several different ways. In addition to fulfilling a desire to diversify, a portfolio career helps many people when employment opportunities decrease and there are fewer full-time positions. According to the Statistics Canada Labour Force Survey, both full-time and part-time employment were on the increase in 2003.[7] It should also be noted that many people are choosing to work part-time rather than full-time.[8] To earn the equivalent of a full-time salary, many people are piecing together more than one part-time position. As more part-time positions pay benefits, working for more than one employer becomes more feasible.

According to career adviser Susan Larson, having a portfolio (or collection) of income-generating possibilities makes you more resistant to the effects of losing one job. You spread your risk by earning money in several ways. The career portfolio minimizes risks by accumulating groups of skills that can provide income. If one skill is not in demand, another might be.[9] A stenographer, for example, who also sold real estate might shift to full-time real estate sales if her company discontinued stenography. A common example of a skill portfolio is that of a person with a full-time position who has a part-time position requiring different skills. A department manager within a retail store might install satellite dishes as a part-time activity.

An important part of developing a portfolio career is keeping your occupational skills current. Suppose a person is able to translate documents from Japanese to English and English to Japanese, but is currently not working as a translator. Translation skills fade rapidly, so the bilingual person should continue to practise this skill at home.

When there are more jobs available than qualified candidates to fill them, it is easy to become smug and dismiss the relevance of a portfolio career. Part of effective career management, however, is to recognize that business cycles are inevitable. Recognize also that technological change can sometimes shrink a field. Many industrial sales reps, for example, have lost their positions in recent years because so much business-to-business selling now takes place over the internet (e-commerce).

Career Switching

From the perspective of career specialist Douglas T. Hall, the career of the 21st century will be driven more by the person than the organization. The ultimate career goal is psychological success that comes from attaining important goals such as achievement and family happiness. This stands in contrast to the older goal of climbing the corporate pyramid and making lots of money.[10] (Of course, this is still the major career goal for many people.) The new type of career emphasizes doing work that fits your major values in life. Whether in pursuit of psychological well-being or old-fashioned success, many people find it necessary to switch careers.

A major principle of career switching is to *be thorough*. Go through the same kind of thinking and planning that is recommended for finding a first career. Everything said in this chapter about choosing a first career is also relevant for choosing a later career. The advantage for the career switcher, however, is that the experienced person often has a better understanding of the type of work he or she does not want to do.

A new career should be *built gradually*. Few people are able to leave one career abruptly and step into another. For most people who switch careers successfully, the switch is more of a transition than an abrupt change. A constructive approach would be to take on a few minor assignments in the proposed new field and then search for full-time work in that field after building skill. An electronics technician, for example, might request to visit customers with sales representatives to facilitate a switch to industrial selling.

Sometimes an interim assignment can offer a person useful ideas for a complete career change or at least a different emphasis. One such possibility is to fill in for a person who is on a company-paid leave of absence, referred to as a *sabbatical*. Another possibility for an interim assignment is filling in for someone who is on family leave because of the birth or adoption of a child. Filling in for the boss, for example, can give a person a first-hand feel for managerial work.[11]

A major reason why many employees consider a new career is that they crave more independence. As a consequence, an increasingly popular path for the career switcher is to *move from salaried employment to self-employment*. In 2000, nearly one worker out of six was self-employed according to the Survey of Self-employment, indicating a strong growth in this career choice in Canada.[12] The prospective self-employed person needs to decide on which particular business to enter. For many people, self-employment means continuing to perform similar work, such as the company cafeteria manager entering the food catering business. Other formerly employed workers go into competition with their former employers, such as a print shop manager opening a print shop of her own. For those who lack specific plans of their own, prepackaged plans can be purchased. A sampling of these is listed in Exhibit 13-2.

Another self-employment possibility is to purchase a franchise, thus lowering the risk of a start-up business. Currently, franchises account for about one-third of retail sales in the United States and Canada. Yet franchises require a substantial financial investment, ranging from about \$6,000 to \$600,000. Another caution is that some franchise operators may work around 70 hours per week to earn about \$18,000 per year.

exhibit 13-2

A Sampling of Opportunities for Self-Employment, as Suggested by Entrepreneur Business Start-Up Guides

Computer-Based Businesses
Computer Consulting
Computer Repair Service
Electronic Bulletin Board Service
Laser Printing Recharging & Repair

Financial Services
Cheque Cashing Service
Financial Aid Services
Financial Broker
Real Estate Investment

Cleaning/Maintenance Businesses
Apartment Preparation Service
Damage Restoration
Garage Detailing Service
Parking Lot Striping & Maintenance

Services to Business
Collection Agency
Language Translation Service
Medical Billing
Mobile Bookkeeping

Personal Services
Private Investigator
Event Planning Service
Image Consulting
Operating a 900 Number

Foodservice Businesses
Coffeehouse
Food Court Restaurants
Mobile Frozen Yogurt
Mobile Restaurant/Sandwich Truck

Wholesale Businesses
Import/Export Business
Liquidated Goods Broker
Wholesale Distribution Business
Marketing a Family Recipe

Retail Businesses
Antique Sales & Restoration
Body Care Boutique
Pet Hotel & Grooming Service
Self-Storage Centre

Eight Suggestions for Career Preparation

Preparing for a career is closely related to choosing a career. To prepare is to make oneself ready to meet the challenges that lie ahead in whatever career you choose. Several of the points below[13] reinforce what you have already studied in this text or will study in Chapter 15.

1. *Be flexible.* You may have one career field in mind, such as business. Do not overlook the possibilities of applying your education and skills to a rapidly expanding field such as software development. Also, be flexible about the size of firm you hope to work for. Most of the job growth continues to take place in small and medium-sized firms.
2. *Develop interpersonal skills.* Good interpersonal skills, especially communication skills, are a foundation for many careers. Employers seek employees who speak and write well. Most jobs require contact with co-workers and customers, or working as part of a team—meaning that people skills are essential.

3. *Think globally.* Many jobs are becoming international jobs even if they do not involve travel. An increasing amount of business is being conducted with customers and suppliers from other countries. To capitalize on the globalization of business, polish your skills in your second language. (Some people may have to learn a second language for the first time.) It is also important to study the culture associated with your second language.
4. *Develop your information technology skills.* Computers have become an integral part of most jobs, including people-oriented jobs such as sales. Have you noticed how many outside-sales representatives work with laptop computers? Lack of computer skills, including recent technology tools, can be a career hindrance.
5. *Get an edge.* Although we may be on the verge of boom economic times, employers can still afford to be choosy. Any extra skill or knowledge can help distinguish you from other job applicants. Computer skills, foreign-language skills, and another degree are assets for most fields.
6. *Keep learning after you have chosen a field.* With technologies changing so rapidly, training has become a way of life in business and industry. Be prepared to take the initiative to acquire valuable new skills before the company offers you a training program.
7. *Be less concerned about promotions; it is what you know and how you apply it that really counts.* The corporate world today places much less emphasis on promotions than on acquiring skills and applying them well. *Promotion* in the new sense of the word often means getting to work on the most exciting projects and taking turns at being a team leader. Both of these activities can lead to higher compensation even if they do not lead to a change in job title.
8. *Strive for high-quality work.* Most employers assume that workers at all levels will strive to make high-quality goods and provide high-quality service. Many companies expect employees to apply quality principles to their work, so it is important to study books and articles about quality. Apply quality principles such as "Do it right the first time." Also, think of quality as simply being conscientious and terrific at what you do.

Summary

For many people, finding the right career requires careful thinking and systematic effort. What a person does for a living is one of the key influences in his or her life. Your career is also a prime source of your self-concept and self-esteem. A general strategy for making a sound career choice is first to understand the inner you, including what you have to offer.

Knowing which skills and abilities you possess and enjoy using can be the basis for a successful career. Your best skill is your core competency. Skill areas can be divided into the following areas: communication, creativity, interpersonal relations, management, manual and mechanical skills, mathematics, office skills, sales, scientific skills, service of customers, and service of patients.

Career counselling, including interest testing, can be helpful in making a good career choice. Ideally, a person should choose a career that meshes with his or her preferred lifestyle. A growing number of people are downshifting their careers to give themselves more time for leisure.

A recommended strategy for making a sound career choice is to gather valid occupational facts. The four sources to be consulted are printed and electronic information, computer-assisted guidance, knowledgeable people, and first-hand experience. The last category covers information gained from visiting places of work or from part-time or temporary employment. An advantageous way of choosing a career is to pursue an occupation that appears to have growth potential. Search for a match between your capabilities and interests and a growth occupation.

A helpful way of looking at occupations is to characterize every job by the proportion of time you devote to working with data, people, or things. It is best to choose an occupation or field that fits your preferences in these three work dimensions.

It is becoming increasingly common for people to either switch the emphasis of activities in their work or switch careers entirely. A portfolio career is one in which a person has a variety of skills that can be used to earn money in different ways. The skill portfolio is particularly useful when a person holds two or more part-time positions.

Career switching is necessary for many reasons including the pursuit of happiness. Switching careers follows many of the same principles as choosing a first career. A new career should be built gradually, often by phasing into the new career part-time. To satisfy a desire for independence, many people switch careers from being an employee to being self-employed.

At the same time you might be choosing a career, think of preparing for a career. Suggestions along these lines include these: be flexible; develop interpersonal skills; think globally; develop information technology skills; get an edge; keep learning; focus more on skills and knowledge than promotions; and strive for high-quality work.

Questions and Activities

1. How do you explain the fact that many students who are studying business still need to choose a career?
2. Now that you have read this chapter, what do you think you would do differently when choosing a career or career switching?
3. Which of the skills listed in Self-Assessment Quiz 13-2 do you think will take the longest time to develop? Why?
4. Why are technological skills important for career people who are not entering a technological field?
5. A friend of yours majoring in business administration will graduate in three months but still has no idea which career he (or she) would like to pursue. If you think this situation warrants concern, offer your friend some advice.
6. How might attempting to match your career to your lifestyle block your career progress?

7. What flaw do you detect in the strategy of choosing a career based on whether the field you select is a growth field?
8. In your own words, explain what is meant by a "portfolio career."
9. Which skills do you think would be the most important to develop before entering self-employment?
10. Speak to someone you think has a successful career to find out how that person made his or her career choice. Be ready to discuss your findings in class.

Internet Skill Builder

Finding a Career That Matches Your Interests

The chapter provided some information about vocational interests and careers. Search for additional information about identifying your vocational interests and matching them to a career. As a start, try such search phrases as "vocational interests," "occupational interests," and "matching career with interests." After your research is complete, speculate about how well any of your occupational interests match your field or contemplated field.

Weblinks

The weblinks in this chapter include job-related sites and those that post employment possibilities. There are many other related sites, so search away!

www.hrdc-drhc.gc.ca
This is the site for Human Resources Development Canada, a huge site with lots of resources for job seekers and career switchers. It includes a national Job Bank with literally thousands of jobs posted. The Electronic Labour Exchange is for job seekers and employers. Here, you create your skills profile, which is compared with a database of jobs; if you get a match, your profile is automatically forwarded to the employer. You will also find a wealth of counselling information, including guidance on résumé writing, job-finding tips, and so on.

www.workinfonet.ca
This site has links to Canadian career-related sites on the internet. It also offers separate sections of links for jobs and recruiting, career planning, professional and community associations, and labour market information.

www.headhunter.com
This site has a huge database of jobs on its job board and allows you to streamline your job search based on career field, education level, desired income, and even location. Many of the listings are from the United States, but there are thousands of Canadian jobs as well.

www.globecareers.com
A Canadian site, called Workopolis, with thousands of available jobs including jobs listed in *The Globe and Mail.*

www.employcanada.com
On this job centre site you can find or post jobs. You can also post your résumé free of charge.

Human Relations Case Study

After reading the case and answering the questions that follow, try Human Relations Skill-Building Exercise 13-1.

ALLISON'S DILEMMA

One year before entering college, Allison engaged her family, friends, and high-school guidance counsellor in helping her make a good career decision. Allison was asked by her guidance counsellor what activities in life she enjoyed the most. Allison's answer to this question provided her with a strong clue to a possible career path.

Allison responded thoughtfully, "I've really enjoyed my vacations with my parents. I've always been impressed with the way hotels and cruise ships operate. The people in charge are so polite, well dressed, and well spoken. I would enjoy working with people in the hotel and travel field. I also like the atmosphere of hotels. It's kind of in my blood."

With this initial hunch about a career prospect, Allison next conducted serious research. She investigated programs of study in hospitality and tourism. She also telephoned anybody she thought might know of someone working at a professional level this field.

Allison arranged interviews with two hotel managers and one assistant hotel manager. She also spoke to a friend's brother who had worked as a photographer on a few cruises. Based on these interviews and her own observations, Allison decided to major in hospitality and tourism upon entering college.

Three weeks before the first fall semester at college, Allison asked her parents to reserve dinnertime one Friday night for serious conversation. "What's on your mind, Allison?" asked her dad.

Allison replied, "Mom and Dad, I'm not so sure I want to go into the hospitality and tourism field. I think the work is great, but the sacrifice might be too big."

"What sacrifice?" asked her mother.

"The sacrifice," said Allison, "is that I couldn't lead a normal life. When my friends were off from work, I'd be working. When other people would be on vacation, I would be busier than ever. Another problem is that if you do a good job as a hotel manager, you're moved around from hotel to hotel.

"How could I ever lead a normal social life? How could I ever get married and raise children?"

Allison's dad asked, "Are you telling me that nobody in the hotel field has friends or family?"

"Maybe they have friends," said Allison, "but they must all be working at hotels or restaurants. These people are probably a culture of their own."

Allison's mom replied, "If you feel that strongly, pick another major. Just drop the whole idea. Find a field like office management where you could lead a normal life."

"It's not that simple," responded Allison. "I still want to enter the hospitality and tourism field. I know I would love the work. It's just the work schedule that might ruin it.

"I'm going to have to give my career choice a lot more thought."

Questions

1. How serious is the career choice problem facing Allison?
2. In what way is Allison facing a conflict?
3. What advice can you give Allison for deciding whether to pursue a career in hospitality and tourism?

Role Play: The Uncertain Career Seeker

The above case serves as background information for this role play. One person plays the role of Allison, who visits her guidance counsellor to mull over her career choice dilemma. Allison has considerable emotion about making a career choice. Another student plays the role of the guidance counsellor, who wants to both ask Allison the right questions and give her concrete advice. Run the role play for 10 to 15 minutes.

Conducting a Job Search

Learning Outcomes

After studying the information and doing the exercises in this chapter, you should be able to

- improve your chances of finding a suitable job
- target your job search and recognize what qualifications employers are seeking
- identify job-finding methods
- prepare an effective cover letter, résumé, and follow-up letter
- identify the types of employment tests and physical examinations an applicant is likely to take

Shefika Ahman is a marketing consultant with a large firm in Vancouver. She would like to move to Ontario where her aging parents live, so she is looking for a new job there that will allow her to spend more time with them and with her children. While she enjoys her present position, the travelling and long hours have taken their toll. With young children and being a new single parent, Shefika wants a company that promotes home–work balance through programs such as flextime and wellness programs.

First Shefika heads to the internet to several job bank sites. When she finds a job that sounds promising she stays on the internet and searches for information on the company at its own website (if it has one) as well as various newsgroups. If she is still intrigued, she then phones or emails career groups for women to find out how the company manages work–life balance and how flexible it is with working families. As she has found, some companies' promises of flexibility are only words and do not carry over into business practice. After three months of searching, she is flying to Ottawa for her first interview at a smaller company.

The job-search tactics of this professional illustrate an important point about finding a position: a systematic approach is advised. With careful planning and preparation (such as preparing answers to typical interview questions in advance), a job search is more likely to be successful. Job searches are important for several reasons. You may be starting your career; you may be tired of your present job; you may want to boost your career; or you might be downsized or fired. Another reason for conducting a job search is to find a new position within a large company. The purpose of this chapter is to provide the basic information you need to conduct a successful job search, including sources of job leads, preparation of a cover letter and résumé, and how to perform well in an interview. This chapter also presents a few fine points to help give you an edge over those who do the minimum necessary to find a suitable position. Although you probably already have some job-search knowledge, this chapter can be used as a refresher and a reminder to be systematic in searching for a new position.

Targeting Your Job Search

A job search begins with a reasonably flexible description of the type of job or jobs you are looking for. Flexibility is called for because with so many different jobs available, it is counterproductive to exclude possibilities by being too specific. A reasonable objective might be something of this nature: "I am searching for a job in the numerical field, with a large employer, located within 30 miles of here. I prefer accounting work. My minimum salary would be $575 per week."

Your chances of finding suitable employment are directly proportional to the number of positions that will satisfy your job objectives. One person with an interest in the literary field might only be willing to accept a job as a newspaper reporter—always a difficult position to find. Another person with the same background is seeking a job as (1) a newspaper reporter, (2) a magazine staff writer, (3) a copywriter in an advertising agency, (4) a communications specialist in a firm, or (5) a copywriter in a public relations firm. The second person has a better chance than the first of finding a job.

Closely tied in with the type of work you are seeking is the type of organization in which you would prefer to work. Unless you have had exposure to different types of organizations, you may have only tentative answers to this question. Questioning people who work for different types of organizations can provide you with some useful clues. A vital source of input about a prospective employer is present and past employees. Further, public tours can provide valuable tips about what it is like to work in a particular firm.

Visits to stores, restaurants, and government agencies will provide informal information about the general nature of working conditions in these places. Using the internet to find facts about a company has become standard practice. The internet search includes the firm's website as well as news stories about the company. Run your prospective company through your favourite search engines and see what you come up with.[1] As you begin your job search, ask yourself these questions to help you identify the type of organization that *might* be right for you:

- Would I feel more comfortable working in an office with hundreds of other people? Or would I prefer just a handful of co-workers?
- Would I prefer to work in a small town or in a busy metropolitan area?
- How important is access to stores and restaurants?
- Would it be best for me to work where I could rely on public transportation?
- Would I prefer an easygoing atmosphere or a highly competitive, "rat race" environment?
- How important are the social aspects of work to me? Would I be happy only in a place where I could meet prospective dates and make new friends?

Not every job candidate can afford to be so selective about a prospective employer. The more your skills are in demand, and the more prosperous the times, the more selective a person can be in choosing an employer.

Qualifications Sought by Employers

What you are looking for in an employer must be matched against what an employer is looking for in an employee. Job interviewers and employers do not all agree on the qualifications they seek in employees. Nevertheless, a number of traits, characteristics, skills, and accomplishments are important to many employers.[2]

The Conference Board of Canada's Corporate Council on Education has researched and identified an employability skills profile and has recently updated it.[3] Representatives from numerous Canadian companies have had input into developing this profile of skills, including Air Canada, Bell Canada, General Motors of Canada, IBM Canada, Nortel, Shell Canada, and Xerox Limited, to name just a few. The most recent profile of skills, Employability Skills 2000+, is presented in the Canada Today below. These skills are divided into three areas: fundamental

Qualifications Sought by Employers

Following is a list of qualifications widely sought by prospective employers. After reading each qualification, rate yourself on a 1-to-5 scale on the particular dimension.
1 = very low; 2 = low; 3 = average; 4 = high; 5 = very high.

1.	Appropriate education for the position under consideration, and satisfactory grades	1 2 3 4 5
2.	Relevant work experience	1 2 3 4 5
3.	Communication and other interpersonal skills	1 2 3 4 5
4.	Motivation and energy	1 2 3 4 5
5.	Problem-solving ability (intelligence) and creativity	1 2 3 4 5
6.	Judgment and common sense	1 2 3 4 5
7.	Adaptability to change	1 2 3 4 5
8.	Emotional maturity (acting professionally and responsibly)	1 2 3 4 5
9.	Teamwork (ability and interest in working in a team effort)	1 2 3 4 5
10.	Positive attitude (enthusiasm about work and initiative)	1 2 3 4 5
11.	Customer service orientation	1 2 3 4 5
12.	Information technology skills	1 2 3 4 5
13.	Internet research skills	1 2 3 4 5
14.	Willingness to continue to study and learn about job, company, and industry	1 2 3 4 5
15.	Likeability and sense of humour	1 2 3 4 5
16.	Dependability, responsibility, and conscientiousness (including good work habits and time management)	1 2 3 4 5

Interpretation: Consider engaging in some serious self-development, training, and education for items that you rated low or very low. If you accurately rated yourself as 4 or 5 on all the dimensions, you are an exceptional job candidate.

skills, teamwork skills, and personal management skills. According to the Council, these skills form the foundation of a high-quality Canadian workforce leading into the future. Human Relations Self-Assessment Quiz 14-1 lets you assess yourself in relation to some of the skills and qualifications sought by employers.

Job-Finding Methods

Two cornerstone principles of conducting a job campaign are (1) use several different methods and (2) keep trying. These two principles should be applied because

Employability Skills 2000+

The skills you need to enter, stay in, and progress in the world of work—whether you work on your own or as a part of a team.

These skills can also be applied and used beyond the workplace in a range of daily activities.

Fundamental Skills

The skills needed as a base for further development

You will be better prepared to progress in the world of work when you can:

Communicate
- read and understand information presented in a variety of forms (e.g., words, graphs, charts, diagrams)
- write and speak so others pay attention and understand
- listen and ask questions to understand and appreciate the points of view of others
- share information using a range of information and communications technologies (e.g., voice, email, computers)
- use relevant scientific, technological, and mathematical knowledge and skills to explain or clarify ideas

Manage Information
- locate, gather, and organize information using appropriate technology and information systems
- access, analyze, and apply knowledge and skills from various disciplines (e.g., the arts, languages, science, technology, mathematics, social sciences, and the humanities)

Use Numbers
- decide what needs to be measured or calculated
- observe and record data using appropriate methods, tools, and technology
- make estimates and verify calculations

Think & Solve Problems
- assess situations and identify problems
- seek different points of view and evaluate them based on facts
- recognize the human, interpersonal, technical, scientific, and mathematical dimensions of a problem
- identify the root cause of a problem
- be creative and innovative in exploring possible solutions
- readily use science, technology, and mathematics as ways to think, gain and share knowledge, solve problems, and make decisions
- evaluate solutions to make recommendations or decisions
- implement solutions
- check to see if a solution works, and act on opportunities for improvement

Personal Management Skills

The personal skills, attitudes, and behaviours that drive one's potential for growth

You will be able to offer yourself greater possibilities for achievement when you can:

Demonstrate Positive Attitudes & Behaviours
- feel good about yourself and be confident
- deal with people, problems, and situations with honesty, integrity, and personal ethics
- recognize your own and other people's good efforts
- take care of your personal health
- show interest, initiative, and effort

Be Responsible
- set goals and priorities balancing work and personal life
- plan and manage time, money, and other resources to achieve goals
- assess, weigh, and manage risk
- be accountable for your actions and the actions of your group
- be socially responsible and contribute to your community

Be Adaptable
- work independently or as a part of a team
- carry out multiple tasks or projects
- be innovative and resourceful: identify and suggest alternative ways to achieve goals and get the job done
- be open and respond constructively to change
- learn from your mistakes and accept feedback
- cope with uncertainty

Learn Continuously
- be willing to continuously learn and grow
- assess personal strengths and areas for development
- set your own learning goals
- identify and access learning sources and opportunities
- plan for and achieve your learning goals

Work Safely
- be aware of personal and group health and safety practices and procedures, and act in accordance with these

Teamwork Skills

The skills and attributes needed to contribute productively

You will be better prepared to add value to the outcomes of a task, project, or team when you can:

Work with Others
- understand and work within the dynamics of a group
- ensure that a team's purpose and objectives are clear
- be flexible: respect, be open to, and supportive of the thoughts, opinions, and contributions of others in a group
- recognize and respect people's diversity, individual differences, and perspectives
- accept and provide feedback in a constructive and considerate manner
- contribute to a team by sharing information and expertise
- lead or support when appropriate, motivating a group for high performance
- understand the role of conflict in a group to reach solutions
- manage and resolve conflict when appropriate

Participate in Projects & Tasks
- plan, design, or carry out a project or task from start to finish with well-defined objectives and outcomes
- develop a plan, seek feedback, test, revise, and implement
- work to agreed quality standards and specifications
- select and use appropriate tools and technology for a task or project
- adapt to changing requirements and information
- continuously monitor the success of a project or task and identify ways to improve

Employability Skills 2000+, Brochure 2000 E/F (Ottawa: The Conference Board of Canada, 2000), **www.conferenceboard.ca**

Creative Job-Finding Techniques

Job seekers often make the mistake of not exploring enough different methods for finding a job. After exploring a few conventional techniques, such as making a trip to the placement office, they sit back and wait for job offers to pour in. A better approach is to search for creative alternatives to finding a job. Think of every possibility, then sort out the workable from the unworkable later on. To accomplish this task, the class will be organized into brainstorming groups. The goal is to specify as large a number of job-finding techniques as possible. Follow the guidelines for brainstorming presented in Chapter 3, Exhibit 3-2.

After each group has assembled and edited its job-finding techniques, group leaders will present their findings to the rest of the class. Groups can then compare their job-finding suggestions.

most approaches to job finding are inefficient yet effective. *Inefficient* refers to the fact that a person might have to make many contacts to find just one job. Yet the system is *effective* because it does lead to a desired outcome—finding a suitable position.

Job-finding techniques are divided here into six types: (1) networking; (2) internet and résumé database services; (3) unsolicited letter campaigns; (4) telesearches; (5) placement offices, employment agencies, and career fairs; and (6) help-wanted ads.

Exhibit 14-1 presents the results of a survey of 344 corporate executives about where they found current employees. Although classified ads are the major source of employees, it is possible that a larger proportion of more recent hires were found through the internet. Human Relations Skill-Building Exercise 14-1 will help sensitize you to the many ways of finding a suitable position.

Networking (Contacts and Referrals)

By far the most effective method of finding a job is through personal contacts. **Networking** is the process of establishing a group of contacts who can help you in your career. Networking is particularly helpful because it taps you into the "insider system" or "internal job market." The internal job market is the large array of jobs that haven't been advertised and are usually filled by word of mouth or through friends and acquaintances of employees.

According to traditional wisdom, about 85 percent of job openings are in the hidden job market. The other 15 percent of jobs are advertised or registered with employment agencies and placement offices. Recent information such as that presented in Exhibit 14-1 suggests that the insider system is no longer so dominant. Nevertheless, the best way to reach the jobs in the hidden market is by getting someone to recommend you for one. When looking for a job, it is therefore important to tell every potential contact of your job search. The more influential the person, the better. Be specific about the type of job you are seeking. When workers are in short supply, some companies give cash bonuses and prizes to employees for referring job candidates to them.

exhibit 14-1

Sources of Employees According to Employers

Help-Wanted Ads	43%
Other	17%
Employee Referrals	13%
Employment Firms	12%
Temporary Firms	10%
Internet	5%

NOTE: Other studies typically find employee referrals to be a bigger source of candidates than help-wanted ads.

SOURCES: Information from Olsten Corporation survey reported in Mildred L. Culp, "Classifieds Still Important for Job Seekers," *WorkWise®*, syndicated column, August 29, 1999; and "Job Recruiters May Want to Go Online or Offline," Associated Press story, August 14, 2000.

To use networking effectively, it may be necessary to create contacts aside from those you already have. Networking is time-consuming, yet it is usually well worth the effort. A study of how unemployed people pursued networking indicated that people who are more extroverted and conscientious tried the hardest.[4] Liking people and being diligent pay off in terms of networking. Potential sources of contacts include these:

- Friends
- Parents and other family members
- Parents of friends
- Friends of parents
- Work associates
- Faculty and staff
- Former or present employer (if you hold a temporary job)
- Athletic team members and coaches
- Religious and community groups
- Trade and professional associations
- Career and job fairs

To capitalize on these contacts, it is helpful to carry business cards. You do not have to be employed to use a business card. Simply place on your card a notation such as, "Alex Catalino, accounting specialist, Winnipeg, Manitoba." Also include your geographic address, telephone number, and email address.

An important caution about networking: too many people are consuming too much of other people's time to help them with their job searches. Keep your request for assistance brief and pointed. Ask to reciprocate in any way you can. For example, you might prepare a chart or conduct research for a manager who gave you a job lead.

The Internet and Résumé Database Services

The internet is now a standard part of job hunting. For little or no cost, the job seeker can post a résumé or scroll through thousands of job opportunities. In the last chapter several of these sites were listed. For example, Headhunter.com and other sites mentioned in the previous chapter allow you to post an electronic résumé for no cost, or you can invest a few dollars and "locate" your résumé in a "better" area. If you are willing to move to another country, you can also visit many US or international résumé database sites such as Career Mosaic and E-Span. Résumé database sites allow employers to view résumés for potential employees. Employers usually pay some sort of fee to view these résumés and thus use these sites for serious employee searches. (Many of these sites can be found in the Weblinks section at the end of the chapter.)

Job hunting on the internet can lead to a false sense of security. Using the internet, a job search can cast a wide net, and hundreds of job postings can be explored. As a consequence, the job seeker may think that he or she can sit back and wait for a job offer to come through by email. In reality, the internet is just one source of leads that should be used in conjunction with other job-finding methods. Thousands of other job seekers can access the same job openings, and many of the positions listed have already been filled. Many employers hire résumé screening services (much like an employment agency) to sort through the thousands of posted résumés to find qualified applicants.

Unsolicited Letter Campaign

A standard and still current method of job finding is the **unsolicited letter campaign** or writing directly to a company you would like to work for. The plan is to come up with a master list of firms for whom you would like to work. You make up the list according to the categories most relevant to your situation, such as by indus-

try or geographic location. Your list can be developed through the internet by using search engines to access such categories as "furniture makers, Quebec." Business directories in libraries, such as those published by Dun and Bradstreet and Standard and Poor, provide full addresses and names of key people in the firms listed.

When writing the prospective employer, send the letter to a specific individual rather than Dear Sir, Madam, or Ms. The mailing should consist of a cover letter and résumé. A sensible approach is to scroll through company websites for employment information, as posted by most large employers. This approach automatically creates a contact person for you. Should somebody be interested in your letter, it could get you into the insider system. The person will either contact you directly or refer your letter and résumé to a hiring manager.

Telesearch

A related approach to the mail campaign is the **telesearch**, in which job leads are obtained by making unsolicited phone calls to prospective employers. The list of prospects can be assembled in the same manner as the mail campaign. Begin your inquiry into an organization by contacting the person who would be your boss if you landed the job you really want. A major goal of the telesearch is to establish direct contact with as many of these decision makers as you can.

It is best *not* to call an executive and ask if there are any openings. Such an inquiry invites a "no" response. Instead, use a brief presentation (about one minute) to attempt to arrange an interview:

> "Mr. Caldone, my name is Jack Paradise. I have three years of experience in your area of business and would like to drop by your office this week to discuss working for you. When would you have about 15 minutes to speak to me?"

This kind of approach is brief and direct, yet it ends in a way that makes it easier for the prospective employer to agree to an interview. If the person contacted has an opening or is interested in learning more about you, you will probably get the interview or be asked to send a résumé. Even if you fail to get an interview, you might be able to obtain a job lead from your contact. Inquire about other people who might be interested in hiring someone with your experience.

The telesearch, like the unsolicited letter campaign, is used to make the prospective employer want to meet you. Use the interview to make him or her want to hire you. Although the prospective employer cannot see you, smile and speak with confidence and enthusiasm. Approximately 100 telephone calls will be needed to land about five to ten interviews. Some prospects will telephone you at home, so have a professional-sounding outgoing message on your answering machine. (The same holds true for any job-finding method.)

Placement Offices, Employment Agencies, and Career Fairs

Your placement office is a primary avenue to finding a job. Even if you do not find a job through the placement office, you will still gain insight into the job-finding process. If recruiters visit your campus, you can gain valuable experience in being interviewed. Placement offices also offer helpful suggestions for preparing résumés and cover letters.

Employment agencies can also lead you to the right position. Employers use employment agencies to advertise jobs and screen applicants, particularly in large cities. Agencies tend to be more valuable for people with about five to ten years of work experience than for newcomers. Not to be overlooked, however, is that many employment agencies specialize in temporary help. After about nine months, a temporary job might become permanent. A concern expressed about employment agencies is that they sometimes encourage applicants to accept less-than-ideal positions just so the agency can earn a placement fee.

A variation of an employment agency is a *career agent*, who for a fixed fee works on behalf of his or her client (you). The career agent provides job-search and career counselling, and also has links with employers to help clients find positions. This service can be valuable if a career agent finds you a position you could not have found for free.

Career (or job) fairs function somewhat like a temporary placement office. A large number of employers may visit the fair to recruit employees. At the same time, a large number of applicants register at the fair and present their résumés. In addition to their direct value as a means of finding jobs, career fairs are also useful for learning about employment trends and the skills required for certain positions and for developing your network of career contacts.

Help-Wanted Ads in Newspapers, Magazines, and Trade Journals

A thorough job search includes a careful scanning of the help-wanted section of classified ads. Many people find good jobs through this method. Help-wanted ads are found in local and national newspapers, such as *The Globe and Mail*, the *Toronto Star*, and *The Edmonton Sun*. Professional and trade magazines such as *Personnel Journal* often contain ads searching for workers in the field of interest covered by the publication.

Because so many people respond to ads listing attractive-sounding jobs, this method yields relatively few job interviews. Four types of want ads can be identified: (1) open ads, (2) blind ads, (3) employment agency ads, and (4) catch ads.[5]

1. *Open ads* Open ads disclose considerable information about the position opening, including the name and phone number of the employer, the nature of the job and the company's business, and qualifications sought. Starting salary is sometimes mentioned. Consequently, open ads attract the largest number of applicants.
2. *Blind ads* These ads conceal the organization in which the advertised position is available but may contain other important information. The reader is requested to respond by sending a letter and résumé to a post office box or the newspaper. By placing a blind ad, the company does not have to deal with a large number of unqualified callers. Another reason the company uses a blind ad is to maintain secrecy with competitors and employees. One remote disadvantage of responding to a blind ad when currently employed is that the advertiser may be one's own employer.
3. *Employment agency ads* Placed by agencies, these ads list one or more job openings for their employer clients. Agencies tend to advertise their more attractive openings. These positions may be filled quickly, but the agency may encourage the job hunter to examine other possibilities. One of the

purposes of want ads placed by employment agencies is to enlarge their pool of qualified candidates.

4. *Catch ads* These ads promise unusually high-paying job opportunities without requiring specific job qualifications. Frequently these jobs involve selling difficult-to-sell merchandise, strictly on commission or with a modest weekly draw against commission. Respondents often find that they are required to sell home siding, food supplements, or magazine subscriptions. Furthermore, you might be asked to purchase the merchandise, which you will then attempt to sell to customers. These jobs are best suited for high risk takers.

In addition to being aware of the various job-finding methods, it is also important to consider *when* to begin a job search. In general, the bigger the job, the longer the job campaign. Finding a position within 30 days is exceptional, whereas a total search time of about six months is typical. You will usually need several months to prepare your résumé and cover letter, pursue all the methods described in this section, and wait to hear from employers. When people are in a particularly in-demand field, a position can sometimes be found in several days just by posting a résumé online. Even more quickly, some in-demand people are recruited away from their present employers without making any effort to conduct a job search.

Cover Letters

A résumé or job application form is necessary but not sufficient for conducting an intelligent job campaign. You also need a cover letter to accompany such documents. The cover letter multiplies the effectiveness of the résumé because it enables you to prepare a tailor-made, individual approach to each position you pursue. The most important purpose of the cover letter is to explain why you are applying for the position in question. Simultaneously, you try to convince the prospective employer why you should be considered. Here we look at two effective types of cover letters.

Attention-Getting Cover Letters

Most job seekers use the conventional approach for writing a letter, attempting to impress the prospective employer with their backgrounds. A more effective approach is to capture the reader's attention with a direct statement of what you might be able to do for the company. Keep this "what I can do for you" strategy paramount in mind at every stage of finding a job. It works wonders in the job interview, as it will in the rest of your career.

After you have stated how you can help the employer, present a one-page summary of your education and the highlights of your work experience. A sample cover letter is presented in Exhibit 14-2. Notice that the opening line is an attention-getter: "Without a good service department, a car dealership is in big trouble." You may not want to write an outrageous or flip cover letter, but it should have enough flair to attract the reader's attention.

Employment specialist Richard H. Beatty recommends a slightly different version of the attention-getting cover letter. He explains that an effective cover letter has five parts: an attention-grabbing introduction, a paragraph selling your value to the

exhibit 14-2

Sample Cover Letter

Date of letter

27 Buttercup Lane
Toronto Ontario M6P 2N5
Phone/Fax (416) 658-1000
jj@igs.net

Mr. Bart Bertrand
President
South View Dodge
258 Princess Blvd.
Toronto Ontario M1V 2P1

Dear Mr. Bertrand:

Without a good service department, a new-car dealership is in big trouble. An efficiency-minded person like myself who loves autos, and likes to help customers, can do wonders for your service department. Give me a chance, and I will help you maintain the high quality of after-sales service demanded by your customers.

The position you advertised in the *Sun* is an ideal fit for my background. Shortly, I will be graduating from Centennial College with an associate's degree in automotive technology. In addition, I was an automotive mechanics major at Harrison Vocational High.

My job experience includes three years of part-time general work at Manny's Petro Canada Service, and two years of clerical work at Brandon's Chrysler-Plymouth. Besides this relevant experience, I'm the proud owner of a mint condition 1980 sports coupe I maintain myself.

My enclosed résumé contains additional information about me. When might I have the opportunity to be interviewed?

Sincerely yours,

Jane Jenkins

employer, a background summary paragraph, a compelling follow-up action statement, and an appreciative close. Beatty recommends mentioning a personal contact as part of the attention-grabber,[6] for example: "Meg Atwood, your computer operations manager, mentioned that you are looking for a talented person to manage your website. I would very much like to talk to you about this position."

The T-Form Cover Letter

A novel format for a cover letter is one that systematically outlines how the applicant's qualifications match up against the job requirements posted in the position announcement.[7] The T-form (or column) approach gives the reader a tabular outline of how the applicant's background fits the position description. The T-form cover letter, presented in Exhibit 14-3, is also recommended because it has an attention-getting format.

exhibit 14-3

The T-Form Cover Letter

Nadir Simms
2127 Marketview Avenue
Downsview ON M1A W2C
Phone/Fax (416) 441-0761
gnc26@home.com

Sales Manager
Southeast Supply Corporation
200 Ashford Centre North, Suite 650
Toronto, ON M1V 2G6

Dear Sales Manager:

In response to your recent advertisement in the *Toronto Star* and on the EmployCanada website for telemarketing sales professionals, please consider the following:

Requirements	**My Qualifications**
Prior sales experience a must	Two years of full-time and part-time selling, including retail and magazine subscription renewals
Great communicator	Two different managers praised my communication skills; received an A in two communication skills courses
Self-motivated	Worked well without supervision; considered to be a self-starter
Reliable	Not one sick day in two years; never late with a class assignment

Your opportunity excites me, and I would be proud to represent your company. My résumé is enclosed for your consideration.

Sincerely,

Nadir Simms
enclosure

Preparing an Effective Job Résumé

The major purpose of a résumé is to help you obtain a job interview, not a job. A résumé is needed when you are applying as an outside candidate and often when seeking a transfer within a firm. Effective résumés are straightforward, factual presentations of a person's experiences, education, skills, and accomplishments. Yet a résumé is much like art. People have different ideas about what constitutes an effective résumé. To add to the confusion, some people spell "résumé" with the acute accents (résumé is a French word), and some without. A challenge in preparing an effective résumé is to suit many different preferences.

The issue of résumé length illustrates how employers hold different opinions about the best résumé format. A national survey of employers indicated that 24 percent said the résumé should be "no longer than one page"; 42 percent said "no longer than two pages," and 34 percent, "determined by information."[8]

A few general guidelines will be offered here to help you avoid serious mistakes. An overall perspective to keep in mind is, "If your résumé is not a winner, it's a killer."[9] Done properly, a résumé can lead to an interview with a prospective employer. Done poorly, it will block you from further consideration.

Three Types of Résumés

The three most commonly used résumé formats are the chronological, functional, and targeted. You might consider using one of these types, or a blend of them, based on the information about yourself you are trying to highlight. Whichever format you choose, you must include essential information.

The **chronological résumé** presents your work experience, education, and interests, along with your accomplishments, in reverse chronological order. A chronological résumé is basically the traditional résumé with the addition of accomplishments and achievements. Some people say the chronological résumé is too bland. However, it contains precisely the information that most employers demand, and it is easy to prepare.

The **functional résumé** organizes your skills and accomplishments into the functions or tasks that support the job you are seeking. A section of a functional résumé might read:

SUPERVISION: Organized the activities of five park employees to create a smooth-running recreation program. Trained and supervised four roofing specialists to help produce a successful roofing business.

The functional résumé is useful because it highlights the things you have accomplished and the skills you have developed. In this way, an ordinary work experience might seem more impressive. For instance, the tasks listed above under "supervision" may appear more impressive than listing the jobs "Playground supervisor" and "Roofing crew chief." One problem with the functional résumé is that it omits the factual information many employers demand. You might therefore appear to be hiding something about your background.

The **targeted résumé** focuses on a specific job target or position and presents only information about you that supports that target. Using a target format, an applicant for a sales position would list only sales jobs. Under education, the applicant would focus on sales-related courses such as communication skills and marketing. A targeted résumé is helpful in dramatizing your suitability for the position you are seeking. However, this résumé format omits other relevant information about you, and a new résumé must be prepared for each target position.

Whichever résumé format you choose, it is best to place your most saleable asset first.[10] If your work experience is limited, place education before work experience. If your skills are more impressive than your education or work experience, list them first.

A general-purpose résumé, following a chronological format, is presented in Exhibit 14-4. This person chose to place work experience before education.

exhibit 14-4

A General-Purpose Résumé

Jane Jenkins
27 Buttercup Lane
Toronto Ontario M6P 2N5
Phone/Fax (416) 658-1000
jj@igs.net

Qualification Summary	Experience in administrative support activities for automobile dealership. Education in office management and automotive repairs.
Job Objective	Management position in service department of new-car dealership.
Job Experience	
2001–present	Senior support specialist, Brandon-Chrysler Plymouth, Toronto. Responsible for receiving customer payments for service performed; preparing invoices; miscellaneous tasks as requested by service manager. • Set up database that saved space and reduced file-searching time.
1998–2001	Service station attendant, Manny's Petro Canada Service. Performed variety of light mechanical tasks such as assisting in brake relinings, installing mufflers and tailpipes, tune-ups, independent responsibility for lubrication and oil changes. • Increased sales of tires, batteries, and accessories by 18 percent during time periods on duty.
Formal Education	
1999–2001	Centennial College, Associate Degree, automotive technology, May 1998. Studied all phases of auto repair including computerized diagnostics, service department management. Attended school while working about 30 hours per week. Average grade, 92%.
1995–1999	Harrison Vocational Technical High School, Toronto. Graduated 10th in class of 137. Majored in automotive repair and maintenance. Also studied business education topics such as bookkeeping, business machines, and office systems and procedures.
Job-Related Skills	Word processing, spreadsheet analysis, development of databases. Can perform bookkeeping. Able to handle customer concerns and complaints in person or by phone. Know how to diagnose and repair wide range of automotive problems for domestic and imported vehicles.
Personal Interests and Hobbies	Enjoy automobile restoration and maintenance. Physical fitness enthusiast. Walt Disney movie buff. Read self-improvement books and current fiction; daily newspaper. Watch CNN and pro football on television.
References	On file with placement office at Centennial College. Permissible to contact present or former employer.

Although her résumé is chronological, it also allows room for accomplishments and skills. Many people have achieved good results with this format. However, do not restrict yourself. Investigate other résumé formats, including exploring software that provides the user with a résumé outline.

The references section of the résumé is another area where opinion varies. One approach is to list several references on the résumé, giving complete identifying information so the prospective employer can readily contact the references. A concern is that these references are often perceived as meaningless because you have identified friends. If you are a recent graduate, a slightly more objective approach is to indicate that references are on file in a placement office. References can also be provided with a cover letter or a follow-up letter. A sophisticated approach is to ask the prospective employer what type of references are preferred and then supply them promptly by email. Types of references include superiors, co-workers, and those outside work, such as athletic coaches and community leaders.

In preparing either a print or an electronic résumé, keep in mind that certain key words or references attract the attention of managers and specialists who scan résumés. The scanning may be done visually, electronically, or both. In today's market, key words and phrases include the following: *languages, computer, information technology, internet, e-commerce, e-tailing, experience, hard-working, overseas experience, flexible, task-oriented, team player,* and *customer-oriented.* A sensible tactic would be to mention those words that apply to you. Many of these words, such as *computer* and *team player,* are widely applicable.

The Electronic Résumé

A current development in résumé construction is to prepare one primarily for electronic databases. Many companies store résumés electronically, making it important to prepare one that is suitable for an electronic database. If a job search website calls for an electronic résumé, it can be entered into the right place on the web page. At other times an electronic résumé is printed and mailed to the employer, who in turn uses an optical scanner to enter the résumé in the company database. Note that attaching a word-processed résumé to an email is not the same as preparing an electronic résumé.

A distinguishing feature of an electronic résumé is that it contains keywords that fit the requirements of a keyword search. The job seeker should isolate keywords (nouns and adjectives) by placing them right under his or her name, address, and telephone numbers. Zane K. Quible recommends that keywords be selected from among the following information:[11]

- Title of jobs held by applicant
- Names of job-related tasks performed by the applicant
- Industry jargon such as "zero defects," "customer delight," or "just-in-time inventory management" (also acronyms such as JIT for "just in time")
- Special skills or knowledge possessed by the applicant
- Degrees earned
- High school program or college major (for college graduates, delete information about the high school program)
- High schools or colleges attended

- Special awards or honours received
- Nature of interpersonal skills the applicant possesses

Most of this information, of course, should also be included in a conventional printed résumé. Despite the increasing popularity of electronic résumés, the serious job hunter also needs a conventional (paper) one. Exhibit 14-5 (on page 371) illustrates an electronic résumé.

How to Handle the Job Objective Section

On the résumé, a **job objective** is the position you are applying for now or intend to hold in the future. A job objective is also referred to as a *job target* or a *position objective*. Although stating a job objective seems easy, it is a trouble spot for many résumé writers. Early in their careers many people feel compelled to state their long-range career objectives in the job objective section. A 21-year-old might state, "To become president of an international corporation." Certainly this is a worthy objective, but it is better to be more modest at the outset.

Employers will tend to interpret the job objective as a statement of your short-term plans. If you think your long-term objective should be stated, you might divide the section into "immediate objective" and "long-term objective." Current practice is to use the position under consideration as a job objective. Longer-term objectives can then be discussed during the job interview.

Another challenge with the job objective section is that your objective will often have to be tailored to the specific job under consideration. The job objective you have printed on your résumé may not fit exactly the job you are applying for. You might be considering a sales career. You find two good leads, one for selling an industrial product, and one for a consumer product. You would want your objective on one résumé to mention industrial sales, and on the other consumer sales.

By keeping your résumé on your computer, you can modify the objective section (and other sections as required) for a given job lead. Another approach is to omit the job objective section. Your cover letter can describe the link between you and the job under consideration. Notice how the cover letter in Exhibit 14-2 makes this link. (The same person, however, does include a job objective on her résumé.)

How Do You Write a Résumé When Your Background Does Not Fit the Position?

Job seekers sometimes lack the type of experience expected to qualify them for a position they seek. This lack of direct fit may occur when the applicant is switching fields or is entering the workforce after a long absence. In both instances it is helpful to emphasize skills and experience that would contribute to success in the job under consideration.

Assume a person with five years of experience as a bookkeeper applies for a sales representative position at an office equipment company. The bookkeeper is advised to make these types of entries on his or her résumé: "Five years of experience in working directly with office equipment including computers, fax machines, and high-speed copiers." "Able to size up equipment needs of accountants and bookkeepers." "Accustomed to negotiating budgets with managers."

Assume a person has 20 years of experience managing a household but has not worked outside the home. The candidate applies for an assistant manager position in a restaurant. The person should list relevant skills such as "Able to plan and prepare holiday meals and parties for large groups of people." The candidate is also advised to describe his or her volunteer work because such experience may be job-related. For example, "Coordinated church picnic for 250 people, including recruiting and supervising ten workers and raising the necessary funds."

exhibit 14-5

Electronic Résumé

Sara L. Adams
123 Elmwood Terrace
Vancouver BC V1G 2S2
(604) 332-1485 Fax (604) 372-4587
SLAdams@hmp.col

Keywords:	Accountant. Bookkeeper. Accounts receivable ledger. Accounts payable ledger. Financial reports. Business Administration. Lotus 1-2-3. Excel. Windows 2000. Word 2000. Team player. French. Supervision. President's Honour Roll. Superior oral communication skills. Superior written communication skills. Self-starter. Quick learner. Conscientious. Detail oriented. Reliable. Top 5 percent of class. IBM-compatible computers. Lakeville College, Winnipeg, MB.
Job objective:	To work as accountant or bookkeeper for private or public business, with eventual goal of becoming supervisor of bookkeeping or accounting, or office manager.
Education:	Lakeville College, Winnipeg, MB, 1996–1998 Accounting major. Associate's degree in Business Administration with High Honours. East Winnipeg High School, National Honour Society, 1992.
Experience:	London's Department Store, Vancouver, BC, 1992–present. Full-time for four years, then part-time while attending college. Performed bookkeeping and cashier activities. Maintained accounts receivable and accounts payable ledgers. Prepared variety of financial reports.
Key Accomplishment:	Developed a system of prompt payments which saved employer approximately $55,000 per year.
College Activities and Honours:	President of Accounting Club for two years. Team Leader of Student Misconduct Committee, President's Honour Roll, each semester, 1996–1998. Delta Phi Kappa Honorary, 1996–1998.

What about the Creative-Style Résumé?

Since employers receive so many résumés, it is difficult to attract an employer's attention. The solution offered to this problem is a creatively prepared résumé. A **creative-style résumé** is one with a novel format and design.

If done in a way to attract positive attention to oneself, creative-style résumés have merit. The generally accepted approach, however, is for résumés to be conservative. In one study, 93 percent of college recruiters surveyed preferred white or ivory colour for the résumé paper. For the entry-level job applicant, the conservative approach is the safest bet.[12] If you are applying for a position in which creative talent is a primary factor, the creative-style résumé is helpful. Creative-style résumés work well for a variety of jobs in a hip industry such as fashion or dot-com companies. A more conventional job requires a more conventional résumé. Human resource specialists often object to oversized résumés because they are difficult to fit into standard files.

Avoid making your résumé visually distracting in an attempt to be different, for instance by using more than three fonts. A useful suggestion is to print your résumé on grey paper with a half-inch white border. (Grey will probably not be disliked by people who prefer ivory.) In this way, your résumé will communicate a classy, distinctive quality while remaining easy to read.[13]

Do not confuse the *creative* résumé with the *created* résumé, in which you "create" facts to make a favourable impression. Many employers check facts presented on a résumé. Evidence of distortion of the truth or outright lying usually leads to immediate disqualification of the applicant. If you made the sandwiches at a sub shop, do not list your job title as "master chef" or "vice-president of operations." And résumé misinformation uncovered after the applicant is hired can lead to immediate dismissal.

Having a Successful Job Interview

A successful job campaign results in one or more employment interviews. Screening interviews are often conducted by telephone, particularly for customer-service positions requiring telephone skills. More extensive interviews are usually conducted in person. Many firms, however, also conduct group interviews in which the job candidates speak to several prospective work associates at the same time. Often the group interview is conducted in a casual environment, such as a restaurant or company cafeteria. The candidate may not be aware that meeting with the group is actually an interview and that he or she is being judged.

Another important development in employee interviewing is the **behavioural interview**, in which a candidate is asked how he or she handled a particular problem in the past. Examples of behavioural interview questions: "Describe a time when you didn't meet a deadline." "Tell me how you dealt with an angry customer. What was the problem and what was the outcome?"[14]

Becoming a skillful interviewee requires practice. You can acquire this practice as you go through the job-finding process. In addition, you can rehearse simulated job interviews with friends and other students. Practise answering the questions posed in Exhibit 14-6. You might also think of several questions you would not like to be asked and develop answers for them.

exhibit 14-6

Questions Frequently Asked of Job Candidates

The following questions are of the same basic type and content encountered in most employment interviews. Practise answering them in front of a friend, video camera, or mirror.

1. Why did you apply for this job?
2. What are your short-term and long-term goals?
3. What do you expect to be doing five years from now?
4. What are your strengths? areas for improvement?
5. Tell me about yourself.
6. How would other people describe you?
7. Why did you prepare for the career you did?
8. What makes you think you will be successful in business?
9. Why should we hire you?
10. Describe how well you work under pressure.
11. What has been your biggest accomplishment on the job?
12. What do you know about our firm?
13. Here's a sample problem. How would you handle it?

Videotaping the practice interviews is especially helpful because it provides feedback on how you handled yourself. In watching the replay, pay particular attention to your spoken and nonverbal communication skills. Then make adjustments as needed.

Suggestions for Performing Well in the Interview

A general guide for performing well in the job interview is to present a positive but accurate picture of yourself. Your chances of performing well in a job increase if you are suited for the job. Tricking a prospective employer into hiring you when you are not qualified is therefore self-defeating in terms of your career. The suggestions presented next will help you create a professional impact.

1. *Prepare in advance.* Be familiar with pertinent details about your background, including your employment history. Bring to the interview your social insurance number, driver's licence, résumé, and the names of references.[15] Prepare a statement in your mind of your uniqueness—what differentiates you from other job candidates. Sometimes the uniqueness is not strictly job related, such as being a champion figure skater. Being prepared in advance also means finding as much information about the company as you can. Many interviewers are impressed when candidates have thoroughly researched the company and can readily answer questions about the company such as products, locations, mission statement, and history of growth.

2. *Dress appropriately.* So much emphasis is placed on dressing well for job interviews that some people overdress. Instead of looking businesslike, they appear to be dressed for a wedding or a funeral. The safest tactic is to wear moderately conservative business attire when applying for most positions. Another important principle is to gear your dress somewhat to the type of prospective employer. If you have a job interview with an employer where sports attire is worn to the office regularly, dress more casually. Recognize also that dress standards have more latitude than in the past. If you are asked to wear business casual clothing to the interview, accept the suggestion.
3. *Focus on important job factors.* Inexperienced job candidates often ask questions about noncontroversial topics such as paid holidays, benefits, and company-sponsored social activities. All these topics may be important to you, but explore them after the basic issue—the nature of the job—has been discussed. In this way you will project a more professional image.
4. *Be ready for a frank discussion of your strengths and areas for improvement.* Almost every personnel interviewer and many hiring supervisors will ask you to discuss your strengths and areas for improvement (weaknesses). Everyone has weaknesses, or at least needs to improve in certain areas. To deny them is to appear uninsightful or defensive. However, you may not want to reveal weaknesses that are unrelated to the job (such as recurring nightmares or fear of swimming). A mildly evasive approach is to emphasize weaknesses that could be interpreted as strengths. A case in point: "Sometimes I'm too impatient when I see others do sloppy work."
5. *Do not knock former employers.* To justify looking for a new position, or having left a position in the past, job candidates often make negative statements about former employers. Employer-bashing makes one appear unprofessional. Take a positive approach by explaining what went wrong, such as a change in your job that left you without the opportunity to use the skills you were hired for.
6. *Ask a few good questions.* An intelligent interviewee asks a few good questions. An employment specialist for managers said, "The best way to impress somebody on an interview is to ask intelligent questions."[16] Here are a few questions worth considering:
   a. If hired, what kind of work would I actually be doing?
   b. What would I have to accomplish in this job to be considered an outstanding performer?
7. *Let the interviewer introduce the topic of compensation.* Often the interviewer will specify the starting salary and benefits to the interviewee, allowing little room for questioning. If asked what starting salary you are looking for, mention a realistic salary range—one that makes you appear neither desperate nor greedy. If the interviewer does not mention salary, toward the end of the interview ask a question such as, "By the way, what is the starting salary for this position?"
8. *Smile and exhibit a positive attitude.* People who smile during job interviews are more likely to receive a job offer.[17] It is also important to express a

positive attitude in other ways, such as agreeing with the interviewer and being impressed with facts about the company. If you want the job, toward the conclusion of the interview explain why you see a good fit between your qualifications and those demanded by the job. For example, "The way I see it, this job calls for somebody who is really devoted to improving customer service. That's me. I love to take good care of customers." Smiling also helps you appear relaxed.

9. *Emphasize how your skills can benefit the employer.* To repeat, an effective job-getting tactic is to explain to a prospective employer what you think you can do to help the company. Look for opportunities to make **skill-benefit statements**, brief explanations of how your skills can benefit the company.[18] Preparing these skill-benefit statements requires considerable self-examination. Practice is required to make the statements smoothly and confidently without appearing pompous or arrogant. If you were applying for a billing specialist position in a company that you knew was having trouble billing customers correctly, you might make this skill-benefit statement: "Here is how I would apply my skill and experience in setting up billing systems to help develop a billing system with as few bugs as possible: __________."
10. *Ask for the job and follow through.* If you want the job in question, be assertive. Make a statement such as, "I'm really interested. What is the next step in the process? Is there any other information I could submit that would help you complete your evaluation of me?" Part of asking for the job is to follow through. Mail a follow-up letter or send an email message within three working days after the interview. Even if you decide not to take the job, a brief thank-you letter is advisable. You may conceivably have contact with that firm in the future. A sample follow-up letter is shown in Exhibit 14-7 on page 376.

Psychological Testing and the Physical Examination

Psychological testing and the physical examination are two further challenges facing many job candidates who have made it through the interview. Psychological tests (sometimes called personnel or employment testing) can help both the employer and job candidate find a mutually satisfactory fit. The good fit is most likely to be found when the tests are accurate and fair and the candidate answers them accurately. It is best to take these tests with a positive, relaxed attitude. Being physically and mentally well rested is the best preparation. Specialists who develop the test profiles of successful candidates are not expecting an incredible display of human attributes. Also, psychological tests and the physical exam are but two factors in making hiring decisions.

Psychological Testing

Five types of personnel and psychological tests are widely used: achievement, aptitude, personality, interest, and integrity (honesty) tests. The fifth category is used

exhibit 14-7

Sample Follow-up Letter

27 Buttercup Lane
Toronto Ontario M6P 2N5
Phone/Fax (416) 658-1000
jj@igs.net

Date of writing letter

Mr. Bart Bertrand
President
South View Dodge
258 Princess Blvd.
Toronto Ontario M1V 2P1

Dear Mr. Bertrand:

Thank you for my recent chance to discuss the assistant service manager position with you and Mr. Ralph Alexander. It was illuminating to see what a busy, successful operation you have.

I was impressed with the amount of responsibility the assistant service manager would have at your dealership. The job sounds exciting and I would like to be part of the growth of the dealership. I realize the work would be hard and the hours would be long, but that's the kind of challenge I want and can handle.

My understanding is that my background is generally favourable for the position, but that you would prefer more direct experience in managing a service operation. Since the car repair and service business is in my blood, I know I will be a fast learner.

You said that about two weeks would be needed to interview additional candidates. Count on me to start work on July 1, should you extend me a job offer.

Sincerely,

Jane Jenkins

particularly in the retail and financial services industry. A recent trend in psychological testing is for the tests and application forms to be done by computer. The computer screening is popular with candidates and with employers because of its efficiency and apparent fairness. Test results, along with recommendations for hiring or not hiring, can be sent back to a client within ten minutes. Information about good applicants is readily transferred from one company location to another, such as between Blockbuster Video branches.[19]

1. *Achievement tests* sample and measure the applicant's knowledge and skills. They require applicants to demonstrate their competency on job tasks or related subjects. A person applying for a position as a paralegal might be given a test about real-estate and matrimonial law. Giving an applicant a sample of work to perform, such as making a sales pitch, is based on the same idea as a paper-and-pencil or computerized achievement test.
2. *Aptitude tests* measure an applicant's capacity or potential for performing satisfactorily on the job, given sufficient training. Mental-ability tests are the best-known variety of aptitude test. They measure ability to solve prob-

lems and learn new material. Mental-ability tests measure such specific aptitudes as verbal reasoning, numerical reasoning, and spatial relations (visualizing three dimensions). Scores on mental-ability tests are related to success in most jobs in which problem-solving ability is important.

3. *Personality tests* measure personal traits and characteristics that could be related to job performance. Among the many personal characteristics measured by these tests are conscientiousness, self-confidence, and emotional maturity. A recent development is to measure emotional intelligence, including such factors as impulse control and optimism. Personality tests have been the subject of heated controversy for many years. Critics are concerned that these tests invade privacy and are too imprecise to be useful. Nevertheless, personality factors have a profound influence on job performance. For example, conscientiousness is related to success in many different jobs.[20]
4. *Interest tests* measure preferences for engaging in certain activities such as mechanical, numerical, literary, or managerial work. They also measure a person's interest in specific occupations such as accountant, social worker, or sales representative. Interest tests are designed to indicate whether a person would enjoy a particular activity or occupation. They do not attempt, however, to measure a person's aptitude for that activity or occupation. The Strong Interest Inventory described in Chapter 13 is an interest test.
5. *Integrity (honesty) tests* are of two types: paper-and-pencil and polygraph tests (often referred to as lie-detector tests). Paper-and-pencil honesty tests ask people questions that directly or indirectly measure their tendency not to tell the truth. A direct question would be, "Should an employee be disciplined for stealing ten dollars' worth of supplies from the company?" (A dishonest person would answer no.) An indirect question would be, "Do you read the editorial page of the local newspaper every day?" (Only a dishonest person would answer yes. Almost nobody can claim a perfect record in this regard.)[21]

   Polygraphs record a person's internal physiological responses, such as heart rate and breathing rate, in response to questions. The level of emotional response to neutral questions is compared with responses to key questions. In Canada, polygraph tests might be used as a screening device by law enforcement agencies and some other employers when selecting candidates for particularly sensitive jobs. However, their use has been challenged on ethical grounds, and it should be noted that they are illegal in certain provinces, including Ontario.

The Physical Examination and Drug Testing

Employment-related medical examinations and drug testing are areas of controversy in many provinces. The Canadian Human Rights Commission and some provincial commissions have issued policies on medical examinations and drug and alcohol testing. Medical examinations should only be administered after a conditional offer of employment has been made, preferably in writing. Employment-related medical examinations are to be limited to determining the individual's ability to perform the essential duties of the job. The employer must disclose to the potential employee the use of medical examinations and drug testing prior to hiring.

Drug testing continues to be highly controversial provincially and federally. For example, a statement by the Ontario Human Rights Commission has validated concerns about this practice. According to the Ontario Human Rights Code, drug testing should only be used in industry to test for impairment in safety-sensitive operations or in industries that are subject to policies from another country, such as the trucking industry, which must abide by Canadian and American policies for vehicles crossing the border.[22]

Managing the Downside of Conducting a Job Search

For some people, finding a job is an easy task, particularly if they happen to be in a field in which the number of positions available is far greater than the number of job applicants. For many other people, the job search can be a mixed experience: some joy and some frustration. Much rejection can be expected. Few people are wanted by every employer. You have to learn to take rejection in stride, remembering that a good deal of personal chemistry is involved in being hired. Suppose the person doing the hiring likes you personally. You then have a much greater chance of being hired for the position than does another individual of comparable merit. If the interviewer dislikes you, the reverse is true.

Rejection and rudeness are frequently encountered in job hunting, which can easily create discouragement. Keep pressure on yourself to avoid slowing down because you are discouraged. Research documents the fact that assertive behaviours are associated with success in finding a job, even when the job hunter has average qualifications.[23] One study showed that unemployed people who maintain good control of their motivation through such means as goal setting are more likely to keep up the intensity of their job search. Also, job seekers who maintain control over anxiety and worry are more likely to keep trying.[24] Each lead processed takes you one step closer to finding work. And all you are looking for is one job.

Summary

Job search skills may be used at different stages in your career. The job search begins with a reasonably flexible statement of the type of job you are seeking (your job objective). Knowing what type of organization you would prefer to work for will help focus your job search. The qualifications listed in Self-Assessment Quiz 14-1 are frequently sought by employers; they should be kept in mind during the job search.

A systematic job search uses many job-finding methods, including networking (contacts and referrals); the internet and résumé database services; an unsolicited letter campaign; a telesearch; placement offices, employment agencies, and career fairs; and help-wanted ads. The number of job offerings on the internet continues to increase.

A cover letter should accompany a résumé and application form. An attention-getting cover letter should explain why you are applying for a particular position and identify your potential contribution to the employer. A T-form cover letter systematically outlines how the applicant's qualifications match up against the job requirements posted in the position announcement. The T-form approach gives the reader a tabular outline of how the applicant's background fits the position description.

The major purpose of a résumé is to help you obtain a job interview. There is no one best way to prepare a résumé. Effective résumés are straightforward, factual presentations of a person's experiences, skills, and accomplishments.

The chronological résumé presents your work experience, education, and interests, along with your accomplishments, in reverse chronological order. The functional résumé organizes your skills and accomplishments into the functions or tasks that support the job you are seeking. The targeted résumé focuses on a specific job or position, and presents only information that supports the target. A distinguishing feature of an electronic résumé is that it contains keywords that fit the requirements of a keyword search. Keywords should be placed right under the information identifying the individual.

The job objective on your résumé should describe the position you are seeking now or in the short-term future. When your credentials do not closely fit the position description, emphasize on your résumé those skills from other experiences that would help you succeed in the position. Creative-style résumés bring favourable attention to your credentials but should be used with discretion.

Rehearse being interviewed and then present yourself favourably but accurately in the interview. Specific interview suggestions include these: (1) prepare in advance; (2) dress appropriately; (3) focus on important job factors; (4) be prepared to discuss your strengths and areas for improvement; (5) do not knock former employers; (6) ask good questions; (7) let the interviewer introduce the topic of compensation; (8) smile and exhibit a positive attitude; (9) emphasize how your skills can benefit the employer; and (10) ask for the job and follow through.

Psychological testing may be part of the employment process, with five types of tests being widely used: achievement, aptitude, personality, interest, and integrity (or honesty) tests. The physical exam, including possible drug testing (a very controversial area), is another key step on the way to being hired.

Conducting a job campaign is typically inefficient but ultimately effective. Follow up every lead, and try not to take rejection and rudeness personally.

Questions and Activities

1. During times when there is a shortage of skilled workers, why is it still important to study how to conduct a job campaign?
2. Does it seem that most employers have unrealistic expectations of job candidates?
3. Which job-hunting technique is used most frequently by people you know? What accounts for its popularity?
4. Despite the widespread use of the internet for finding employment, the vast majority of executive positions are still filled by referrals or executive placement services. What might account for the limited use of the internet for filling executive positions?
5. What are some drawbacks of using the internet for employment opportunities?

6. Some job seekers send email messages instead of postal mail when conducting an unsolicited letter campaign. Identify an advantage and disadvantage of using email messages for this purpose.
7. What special challenges do voice-mail systems present for job seekers?
8. Given that people have so many different opinions about what makes an effective résumé, what kind of résumé should a job seeker prepare?
9. Many employers use telephone screening interviews before inviting a candidate for an in-person interview. What special communication challenges does this present for the job seeker?
10. Assume you are being interviewed for a position you really want, and the interviewer asks you several questions that could be considered in violation of employment law. How would you respond to his or her questions?

Internet Skill Builder

How Much Am I in Demand?

One of the most practical applications of the internet is for job finding. Use a job-finding site (see below) to find at least three jobs for which you might be qualified. Assuming that you would actually apply for the position, identify what you think is your strongest qualification. Do the same for your weakest qualification.

Weblinks

www.jobinterview.net
Preparing for the job interview.

Sites that have job postings and/or job finding tips:

Monster Board:	**www.monster.com**
Monster Board (Canada)	**www.monster.ca**
E-Span:	**www.espan.com**
CareerMosaic:	**www.careermosaic.com**
CareerBuilder:	**www.careerbuilder.com**
WorkInfoNet:	**www.workinfonet.ca**
Human Resources Development Canada:	**www.hrdc-drhc.gc.ca**
Job Shark:	**www.jobshark.com**

Human Relations Case Study

WHY ISN'T MY RÉSUMÉ GETTING RESULTS?

Kaled Naqui was working in the family business as a manufacturing technician while he attended career school. Although he got along well with his family members, Kaled wanted to find employment elsewhere so he could build a career on his own. Kaled's job objective was a position in industrial sales. He compiled a long list of prospective employers. He developed the list from personal contacts, classified ads in newspapers, and job openings on the internet. Kaled clipped a business card with a brief handwritten note to each résumé. The note usually said something to the effect, "Job sounds great. Let's schedule an interview at your convenience." The résumé is shown in Exhibit 14-8.

After mailing out 200 résumés, Kaled still did not have an interview. He asked his uncle and mentor, the owner of the family business, "Why isn't my résumé getting results?"

Questions

1. What suggestions can you make to Kaled for improving his résumé? Or does it require improvement?
2. What is your evaluation of Kaled's approach to creating a cover letter?

exhibit 14-8

Résumé of Kaled Naqui

Kaled Naqui
275 Birdwhistle Lane
Toronto Ontario M2M 2M2
(416) 614-7512 (Please call after 7 p.m. weekday nights)
Kaled@naqui.com

Objective

Long-range goal is Vice President of sales of major corporation. For now, industrial sales representative paid by salary and commission.

Job Experience

Five years experience in Naqui Industries as manufacturing technician, tool crib attendant, shipper, and floor sweeper. Voted as "employee of the month" twice.

Two years of experience in newspaper delivery business. Distributed newspapers door to door, responsible for accounts receivable and development of new business in my territory.

Education

George Brown College of Applied Arts and Technology, business administration major with manufacturing technology minor. Expect degree in June 2001. 68% average. Took courses in sales management and selling. Received a B+ in professional selling course.

Birdwhistle Lane High School, business and technology major, 1994–1998. Graduated 45th in class of 125. 82% average.

Skills and Talents

Good knowledge of manufacturing equipment; friends say I'm a born leader; have been offered supervisory position in Naqui Industries; real go getter.

References

OK to contact present employer except for my immediate supervisor, Jill Baxter, with whom I have a personality clash.

Developing Good Work Habits

Learning Outcomes

After studying the information and doing the exercises in this chapter, you should be able to

- appreciate the importance of good work habits and time management
- decrease any tendencies you might have toward procrastination
- develop attitudes and values that will help you become more productive
- develop skills and techniques that will help you become more productive
- overcome time-wasting practices

Employees of Eastman Kodak's finance department received an offer from their bosses earlier this year that probably seemed too good to be true. The workers were asked to attend meetings at which they could submit plans for eliminating the least productive and most annoying tasks from their jobs. The proposition was part of a program called Work-Out, borrowed from General Electric. Work-Out is built on the concept that individual workers, not managers, are best equipped to streamline their jobs and their companies.

As part of Work-Out, workers are expected to analyze their jobs and suggest ways to eliminate tasks they see as unnecessary, extraneous, or not valuable. Supervisors attend the sessions and are charged with deciding on the spot which tasks go and which stay.

Work-Out helps identify excess tasks that have built up over the years but have never been questioned. For example, some members of one department suggested reducing the frequency of certain arcane financial reports provided to the company's senior executives. The reports are now delivered quarterly rather than monthly.[1]

The Work-Out program at Kodak illustrates how workers are expected to look for ways to increase their productivity. Because good work habits and time management (including getting rid of unimportant work) improve productivity, they contribute to success in business. **Work habits** refer to a person's characteristic approach to work, including such things as organization, priority setting, and handling of paperwork and email. Poor work habits also interfere with social life because of such problems as cancelled social engagements or missed time with family.

People with good work habits tend to achieve greater career success and have more time to invest in their personal lives. They also enjoy their personal lives more because they are not preoccupied with unfinished tasks. Effective work habits are also beneficial because they eliminate a major stressor—the feeling of having very little or no control over your life. Being in control also leads to a relaxed and confident approach to work.

Good work habits and time management are more important than ever because of today's emphasis on **productivity**, the amount of quality work accomplished in relation to the resources consumed. Good work habits and time management lead to high personal productivity.

The goal of this chapter is to help you become a more productive person who is still flexible. Someone who develops good work habits is not someone who becomes so obsessed with time and so rigid that he or she makes other people feel uncomfortable. Ideally, a person should be well organized yet still flexible.

Information about becoming more productive is organized here into four related categories. One is overcoming procrastination, a problem that plagues almost everybody to some extent. The second is developing attitudes and values that foster productivity. The third category is the lengthiest: developing skills and techniques that lead to personal productivity. The fourth category deals with overcoming time wasters.

Dealing with Procrastination

The leading cause of poor productivity and career self-sabotage is **procrastination**, delaying a task for an invalid or weak reason. Procrastination is the major work-habit problem for most workers and students. Unproductive people are the biggest procrastinators, but even productive people have problems with procrastination. Think of all the people who fail to file their income tax returns on time even when the government owes them money.

Why People Procrastinate

People procrastinate for many different reasons. One is that we perceive the task to be done (such as quitting a job) as unpleasant. Another reason we procrastinate is that we find the job facing us to be overwhelming, such as painting a house. Another major cause of procrastination is a fear of the consequences of our actions.[2]

One possible consequence is a negative evaluation of your work. For example, if you delay preparing a report for your boss or instructor, that person cannot criticize its quality. Bad news is another negative consequence that procrastination can sometimes delay. If you think your personal computer needs a new disk drive, delaying a trip to the computer store means you will not have to hear the diagnosis: "Your disk drive needs replacement. We can do the job for about $300."

Another reason some people procrastinate is that they **fear success**. People sometimes believe that if they succeed at an important task, they will be asked to take on more responsibility in the future. They dread this possibility. Some students have been known to put off completing their degree requirements to avoid taking on the responsibility of a full-time position.

People frequently put off tasks that do not appear to offer a meaningful reward. Suppose you decide that your hard drive needs a thorough updating, including deleting inactive files. Even if you know this task should be done, the accomplishment of updated files might not be a particularly meaningful reward.

Many people often procrastinate as a way of rebelling against being controlled. Procrastination, used in this way, is a means of defying unwarranted authority.[3] Rather than submit to authority, a person might tell himself, "Nobody is going to tell me when I should get a report done. I'll do it when I'm good and ready."

Finally, some people procrastinate because they are perfectionists. They attempt to perfect a project before submitting it. As a result, the person procrastinates, not in beginning a project, but in letting go of it. When asked, "Have you finished that project?" the perfectionist replies, "No, there are a few small details that still need to be worked out." Being a perfectionist can also block starting new projects because the perfectionist will often want to keep working on the present project. Perfectionism comes in degrees: slight perfectionists may simply be extremely conscientious; heavy-duty perfectionists may be almost stalled in their actions. Human Relations Self-Assessment Quiz 15-1 gives you an opportunity to measure your degree of perfectionism.

Techniques for Reducing Procrastination

To overcome, or at least minimize, procrastination we recommend a number of specific tactics. A general approach, however, is simply to be aware that procrastination is a major drain on productivity. Being aware of the problem will remind you to take corrective action in many situations. When your accomplishment level is low, you might ask yourself, "Am I procrastinating on anything of significance?" The Canada Today feature that appears later in this chapter also offers some valuable tips on reducing your tendencies toward procrastination.

Human Relations Self-Assessment

Quiz 15-1

Am I a Perfectionist?

Below are some ideas held by some perfectionists. Which of these do you see in yourself? Rate how strongly you agree with each of the following statements on a scale of 0 to 4, with 4 indicating very strong agreement.

1. I have a great eye for details that others can miss. 0 1 2 3 4
2. I can get lost in details and forget the real purpose of the task. 0 1 2 3 4
3. I can get overwhelmed by too many details. 0 1 2 3 4
4. It stresses me when people don't want to do things the right way. 0 1 2 3 4
5. There is a right way and a wrong way to do most things. 0 1 2 3 4
6. I do not like my routine to be interrupted. 0 1 2 3 4
7. I expect a great deal from myself. 0 1 2 3 4
8. I expect no less of others than I expect of myself. 0 1 2 3 4
9. People should always do their best. 0 1 2 3 4
10. I am neat in my appearance. 0 1 2 3 4
11. Good grooming is important to me. 0 1 2 3 4
12. I do not like being seen before I have showered and dressed. 0 1 2 3 4
13. I do not like making mistakes. 0 1 2 3 4
14. Receiving criticism is horrible. 0 1 2 3 4
15. It is embarrassing to make mistakes in front of others. 0 1 2 3 4
16. Sharing my ideas with others makes me anxious. 0 1 2 3 4
17. I worry that my ideas are not good enough. 0 1 2 3 4
18. I do not have a great deal of confidence in myself. 0 1 2 3 4
19. I'm uncomfortable when my environment is untidy or disorganized. 0 1 2 3 4
20. When things are disorganized, it's hard for me to concentrate. 0 1 2 3 4
21. What others think about my home is important to me. 0 1 2 3 4
22. I have trouble making difficult decisions. 0 1 2 3 4
23. I worry that I may make the wrong decision. 0 1 2 3 4
24. Making a bad decision can be disastrous. 0 1 2 3 4

(continued)

25.	I often do not trust others to do the job right.	0 1 2 3 4
26.	I check the work of others to make sure it was done correctly.	0 1 2 3 4
27.	If I can control the process, it will turn out fine.	0 1 2 3 4
28.	I am a perfectionist.	0 1 2 3 4
29.	I care more about doing a quality job than others do.	0 1 2 3 4
30.	It's important to make a good impression.	0 1 2 3 4
	Score:	________

Under 20: Could be too casual about getting things right; may be not conscientious enough
Under 31: Probably not a perfectionist
31–60: Mild perfectionism
61–90: Moderate perfectionism
Over 91: Level of perfectionism that could lead to serious problems, including procrastination

SOURCE: Adapted with permission from Monica Ramirez Basco, *Never Good Enough: Freeing Yourself from the Chains of Perfectionism* (New York: The Free Press, 1999).

Calculate the Cost of Procrastination. You can reduce procrastination by calculating its cost.[4] One example is that you might lose out on obtaining a high-paying job you really want by not having your résumé and cover letter ready on time. Your cost of procrastination would include the difference in salary between the job you do find and the one you really wanted. Another cost would be the loss of potential job satisfaction.

Counterattack. Forcing yourself to do something overwhelming, frightening, or uncomfortable helps to prove that the task was not as bad as initially perceived.[5] Let's say you've accepted a new position but have not yet resigned from your present one because resigning seems so uncomfortable. Set up a specific time to call your manager, or his or her assistant, to schedule an appointment. Force yourself further to show up for the resignation appointment. After you break the ice with the statement, "I have something important to tell you," the task will be much easier.

Jump Start Yourself. You can often get momentum going on a project by giving yourself a tiny assignment to get started. One way to get momentum going on an unpleasant or overwhelming task is to set aside a specific time to work on it. If you have to write a report on a subject you dislike, you might set aside Saturday from 3 p.m. to 5 p.m. as your time to first attack the project. If your procrastination problem is particularly intense, giving yourself even a five-minute task, such as starting a new file, might help you gain momentum. After five minutes, decide whether to continue for another five minutes. The five-minute chunks will help you focus your energy.

Another way to create some momentum is to find a leading task to perform. A **leading task** is an easy warm-up activity.[6] If you were procrastinating about calling back an angry customer, you might first send an email message stating that you are investigating the problem and will telephone shortly.

Peck Away at an Overwhelming Task. Assume that you have a major project that does not have to be accomplished in a hurry. A good way of minimizing procrastination is to peck away at the project in 15- to 30-minute bits of time. Bit by bit the project will get down to manageable size and therefore not seem so overwhelming.

A related way of pecking away at an overwhelming task is to subdivide it into smaller units. For instance, you might break down moving into a series of tasks such as filing change-of-address notices, locating a mover, and packing books. Pecking away can sometimes be achieved by setting aside as little as five minutes to work on a seemingly overwhelming task. When the five minutes are up, either work five more minutes on the task or reschedule the activity for sometime soon.

Motivate Yourself with Rewards and Punishments. Give yourself a pleasant reward soon after you accomplish a task you would ordinarily procrastinate about. You might, for example, jog through the woods after having completed a tough take-home exam. The second part of this tactic is to punish yourself if you have engaged in serious procrastination. How about eating only oatmeal for five days?

Follow the WIFO Principle. Personal-effectiveness coach Shale Paul recommends that you use the technique of *worst in, first out* for dealing with unpleasant tasks you would prefer to avoid. After you finally get the task done, Paul says, "Chances are, you'll find that you spent nearly as much time worrying and rescheduling it as you did actually doing it." If the task sits high enough on your list of priorities, simply get it done and out of the way.[7] A related motivational principle is that, after completing the unpleasant task, moving on to a more pleasant (or less unpleasant) task functions as a reward.

Make a Commitment to Other People. Put pressure on yourself to get something done on time by making it a commitment to one or more other people. You might announce to co-workers that you are going to get a project of mutual concern completed by a certain date. If you fail to meet this date you may feel embarrassed.

Express a More Positive Attitude about Your Intentions. Expressing a more positive attitude can often lead to change in behaviour. If you choose words that express a serious intention to complete an activity, you are more likely to follow through than if you choose more uncertain words. If a co-worker says, "I *might* get you the information you need by next Friday," you probably won't be surprised if you don't receive the information by then. In contrast, if your co-worker says, "I *will*... Friday," there is less likelihood the person will procrastinate. Psychologist Linda Sapadin believes that you are less likely to procrastinate if you change your "wish" to "will," your "like to" to "try to," and your "have to" to "want to."[8]

Developing the Proper Attitudes and Values

Developing good work habits and time-management practices is often a matter of developing proper attitudes toward work and time. For instance, if you think that your job is important and that time is valuable, you will be on your way toward developing good work habits. In this section we describe a group of attitudes and values that can help improve your productivity through better use of time and improved work habits.

Become a Goal-Oriented Person and Value Your Time

Becoming goal-oriented is perhaps the first step in any serious program of improving work habits and time management. Being committed to a goal propels people toward good use of time. Imagine how efficient most employees would be if they were told, "Here is five days' worth of work facing you. If you get it finished in less than five days, you can have all that time saved to yourself." (One negative side effect, however, is that many employees might sacrifice quality for speed.)

As a consequence of being goal-oriented, successful people believe that their time is valuable. It is therefore difficult to engage them in idle conversation during working hours. As you proceed further into your career, the value of your time will usually increase. A person might choose to invest some discretionary time in career-building activities such as learning about team leadership or marketing on the internet.

Develop a Mission, Goals, and a Strong Work Ethic

A mission, or general purpose in life, propels you toward being productive. Assume that a person says, "My mission is to become an outstanding professional in my career and to be a loving, constructive parent." The mission serves as a compass to direct your activities, such as being well-organized in order to attain a favourable performance appraisal.

Goals are more specific than mission statements. The goals support the mission statement, but the effect is the same. Stephen Covey, a popularizer of time management techniques, expresses the importance of both a mission and goals in his phrase "Begin with the end in mind." He recommends you develop your mission statement by first thinking about what people who know you well would say at your funeral if you died three years from now. Also, list your various roles in life such as spouse, child, family member, professional, and soccer player. For each role, think of one or two major lifetime goals you have in that area. Then develop a brief mission statement describing your life's purpose that incorporates these goals.[9]

Say that your mission is to become an outstanding professional person. Your goals to support that mission might include achieving advanced certification in your field, becoming an officer in a professional organization, and making large donations to charity. When you're deciding how to spend your time each day, give top priority to goals related to your mission.

Closely related to establishing a mission and goals is developing a strong work ethic, as described in Chapter 12. Developing a strong work ethic may lead to even higher productivity than goal setting alone. For example, a goal of earning a high income might lead to some good work habits but not necessarily a high commitment to quality.

Value Good Attendance and Punctuality

On the job, in school, or in personal life, good attendance and punctuality are essential for developing a good reputation. Also, you cannot accomplish much if you are not present. Poor attendance and consistent lateness are the most frequent reasons for employee discipline. Furthermore, many managers interpret high absenteeism and lateness as signs of emotional immaturity.

Two important myths about attendance and punctuality should be challenged early in your career. One is that a certain number of sick days are owed an employee. Some employees who have not used up their sick days will find reasons to be sick at the end of the year. Another myth is that absence is preferred to lateness. Some employees believe, for example, that it is more honourable to be absent because of illness than late because of oversleeping. Consequently, the employee who oversleeps calls in sick rather than facing the embarrassment of arriving at work late..

Value Neatness, Orderliness, and Speed

Neatness, orderliness, and speed are important contributors to workplace productivity and therefore should be highly valued. An orderly desk, file cabinet, or work area does not inevitably signify an orderly mind. Yet orderliness does help most people become more productive. Less time is wasted and less energy is expended if you do not have to hunt for missing information. Knowing where information is and what information you have available is a way of being in control of your job. When your job gets out of control, you are probably working at less than peak efficiency.

Being neat and orderly helps you achieve good performance. Frequently breaking your concentration for such matters as finding a memo or a computer manual inhibits high performance.

Neatness is linked to working rapidly because clutter and searching for misplaced items consumes time. Employers emphasize speed today to remain competitive in such matters as serving customers promptly and bringing new products and services to the market. Speed is widely considered to be a competitive advantage. In the words of organizational consultant Price Pritchett:

> So you need to operate with a strong sense of urgency. Accelerate in all aspects of your work, even if it means living with a few more ragged edges. Emphasize *action*. Don't bog down in endless preparation trying to get things perfect before you make a move. Sure, high quality is crucial, but it must come quickly. You can't sacrifice speed. Learn to fail fast, fix it, and race on.[10]

The best approach to maintaining a neat work area and enhancing speed is to convince yourself that neatness and speed are valuable. You will then search for ways to be neat and fast, such as putting back a computer manual immediately after use or making phone conversations brief. The underlying principle is that an attitude leads to a change in behaviour.

Work Smarter, Not Harder

People caught up in trying to accomplish a job often wind up working hard, but not in an imaginative way that leads to good results. Much time and energy are thus wasted. If you develop the attitude of seeking to work smarter rather than harder, your productivity and satisfaction will increase. Let's look at an example of the difference between working harder and working smarter:

> A service technician checks his schedule to find that he has 35 service calls lined up for the week. If he takes the service calls in order of the time of their request, he will spend more than five full days crisscrossing his territory to visit customers. Taking the calls by time of request means that he will be working harder. In contrast, if he groups his calls according to proximity to each other, he can cover all customers in three and one-half days. The time savings comes from less travel time, thus allowing him to work smarter.[11]

An everyday application of working smarter, not harder, would be to telephone ahead to find out if a store has the merchandise you need rather than visiting the store to search for the merchandise. Similarly, many people save time shopping by making use of e-tailing and save visits to the library by searching for information over the internet.

Become Self-Employed Psychologically

A distinguishing characteristic of many self-employed people is that they care deeply about what they accomplish each day.[12] Most of their job activities directly or indirectly affect their financial health. Additionally, many self-employed people enjoy high job satisfaction because they have chosen work that fits their interests. Because of the factors just mentioned, the self-employed person is compelled to make good use of time. Also, the high level of job satisfaction typical of many self-employed people leads them to enjoy being productive.

If a person working for an employer regards his or her area of responsibility as self-employment, productivity may increase. To help regard employment by others as self-employment, keep this thought in mind: Every employee is given some assets to manage to achieve a good return on investment. If you managed the printing and copying centre for your company, you would be expected to manage that asset profitably.

Appreciate the Importance of Rest and Relaxation

A productive attitude to maintain is that overwork can be counterproductive and lead to negative stress and burnout. Proper physical rest contributes to mental alertness and improved ability to cope with frustration. Constant attention to work or study is often inefficient. It is a normal human requirement to take enough rest breaks to allow oneself to approach work or study with a fresh perspective. Each person has to establish the right balance between work and leisure within the bounds of freedom granted by the situation.

Neglecting the normal need for rest and relaxation can lead to **workaholism**, an addiction to work in which not working is an uncomfortable experience. Some types of workaholics are perfectionists who are never satisfied with their work and therefore find it difficult to leave work behind. In addition, the perfectionistic workaholic may become heavily focused on control, leading to rigid behaviour.

However, some people who work long and hard are classified as achievement-oriented workaholics who thrive on hard work and are usually highly productive.[13] Furthermore many people who work long and hard to be successful in their careers also intensely enjoy other activities. Warren Buffett, the legendary investor who is one of the world's richest people, carries an enormous workload. However, he is also a fanatic about bridge who regularly interrupts his workday to play bridge on the computer.

Time-Management Techniques

So far we have discussed improving productivity from standpoints of dealing with procrastination and developing the right attitudes and values. Skills and techniques are also important for becoming more productive. Here we describe some well-established methods of work-habit improvement, along with several new ones. For these techniques to enhance productivity, most of them need to be incorporated in our daily lives and practised regularly.[14] This is particularly true because many of these techniques are habits, and habits have to be programmed into the brain through repetition. The Canada Today feature (on page 393) offers some valuable tips on time management, organization, and procrastination from a well-known productivity consultant.

Clean Up and Get Organized

An excellent starting point for improving work habits and time management is to clean up your work area and arrange things neatly. Eliminate clutter by throwing out unnecessary paper and deleting computer files that will probably never be used again. According to one productivity expert, 80 percent of filed paperwork is never looked at again.[15] The idea is to learn to simplify the work area so that there are fewer distractions and the brain can be more focused. In addition, finding important files becomes easier. Getting organized includes sorting out which tasks need doing, including assignments and projects not yet completed. Getting organized can also mean sorting through the many small paper notes attached to the computer and on the wall.

A major reason a cleanup campaign is needed periodically is that many people have pack-rat tendencies. It is difficult to throw out tangible items (including paper, souvenir pens, and supply catalogues) because possessions give us a sense of security, status, and comfort.[16] A major cleanup principle is therefore to discard anything that is no longer valuable.

Plan Your Activities

The primary principle of effective time management is **planning**: deciding what you want to accomplish and what you will do to make it happen. The most elementary—and most important—planning tool is a list of tasks that need doing. Almost every successful person works from a to-do list. These lists are similar to the daily goals described in Chapter 2. Before you can compose a useful list, you need to set aside a few moments each day to sort out the tasks at hand.

Where Do You Put Your Lists? Some people dislike having small to-do lists stuck in different places. One reason is that these lists are readily lost among other papers. Many people therefore put lists on desk calendars or printed forms called *daily planners*. Software is also available to help you keep track of your activities.

How Do You Set Priorities? Faced with multiple tasks to do at the same time, it is possible to feel overwhelmed and freeze as a result. A time-tested prioritizing system is to use *A* to signify critical or essential items, *B* to signify important items, and *C* for the least important ones. Although an item might be regarded as a *C* (for example, refilling your stapler), it still has a contribution to make to your productivity and sense of well-being. Many people report that they obtain a sense of satisfaction from crossing an item, however trivial, off their list. Second, if you are at all conscientious, small undone items will come back to interfere with concentration. The key is to set priorities and follow some sort of system to assist you in accomplishing your tasks.

Tips for Increasing Productivity with Effective Time Management

Mark Ellwood, president of Pace Productivity, Toronto, is no stranger to the problems people have in maintaining a high level of productivity through time management. In 1989, Mr. Ellwood established Pace Productivity and designed his unique TimeCorder, a time-tracking system to assist in the development of sound time-management practices. His basic idea is that productive people are organized, manage procrastination, know how to use time effectively, manage paperwork and email, and are prepared to handle workplace challenges. As a consultant, he has helped many companies increase productivity by assisting employees in these areas. Companies that have benefited from his training include Metropolitan Life, the Royal Bank of Canada, Starbucks and Nortel, to name a few. Below is a list of some of the tips that he offers on his website. A visit to this site, found at **www.GetMoreDone.com,** will be well worth your time.

Some strategies for time management:

- Stop spending time on trivia such as recording a new voice-mail message daily.
- Block off time for important activities by making an appointment with yourself and keep it.
- Don't be a slave to technology. Leave your cell phone at home. People do not have to be able to reach you all of the time!
- Have the courage to say no.

Some strategies to manage paperwork:

- Create a block of time during non-prime time to handle paperwork. Schedule it and stick to it.
- Throw away previous drafts. They serve no purpose.
- Cut back on sending memos or emails. Use a phone call instead.
- Throw out last month's magazines when the new ones arrive.

Some strategies for handling email:

- Block off times to process your email. Twice per day should be enough.
- Check your spelling and grammar before sending email.
- Don't waste time reading unsolicited email, and if you are on a mailing list that you have no interest in, reply by writing "unsubscribe" or "remove" in the comment box.
- Don't attach large files without getting permission from the recipient of the email.

Some strategies to manage procrastination (not covered above):

- Make a deadline if you are procrastinating about making a decision and share the deadline with someone else. Stick to it.
- Make a game out of unpleasant tasks. Give yourself points as you complete it.
- Reward yourself for accomplishments. But if you do not finish by your deadline, do not take the reward anyway.
- Tailor your environment for work. Close your door and tidy your desk.

This information is presented with the permission of Mark Ellwood, Pace Productivity, Toronto, Ontario, Canada.

How Do You Schedule and Follow Through? To be effective, a to-do list must be an action tool. To convert your list into action, prepare a schedule of when you are going to do each of the things on the list. Follow through by doing things according to your schedule, checking them off as you go along.

Get Off to a Good Start

Get off to a good beginning, and you are more likely to have a successful, productive day. Start poorly, and you will be behind most of the day. According to Merrill Douglass, people who get going early tend to be in the right place at the right time more often, thus seeming to be lucky. "When you start early, you are lucky enough to get a good parking spot. You are lucky enough to avoid traffic jams. You are lucky enough to finish your job by the end of the day."[17] To get off to a good start regularly, it is important to start the day with the conscious intention of starting strong.

Make Good Use of Office Technology

In recent years, the productivity of office workers has increased because of effective use of information technology. Used properly, most high-tech devices in the office can improve productivity. Among the most productivity-enhancing devices are word processors, spreadsheets, voice mail, fax machines, photocopiers, and personal information managers. How you use these devices is the key to increased productivity. Several examples of enhanced productivity are described next.

Routine messages can be batched together and sent by email during non-peak hours. Routine voice-mail messages can be sent late in the day or at night, when the recipient is not likely to answer the phone. (You save time by not interacting with the person—but be careful not to neglect important relationship building.) Templates contained in word processing software save a lot of time when sending form letters that require only minor modification. A laptop computer can help you be much more productive during periods of potential downtime. While waiting in someone's office or in an airport or on the plane, you can spend your time answering correspondence. A rapidly growing approach to using information technology to improve your productivity is personal information manager (PIM) software. The purpose of such software is to help you organize your work, following many of the principles of time management. PIM software usually combines the functions of an address book, alarm clock, to-do list, telephone dialler, and notepad. Examples of PIM software are *Lotus Organizer*, *Sharkware Pro*, and *Sidekick*.

Concentrate on One Key Task at a Time

Effective people have a well-developed capacity to concentrate on the problem or person facing them, however surrounded they are with potential distractions. The best results from concentration are achieved when you are so absorbed in your work that you are aware of virtually nothing else at the moment. As described in Chapter 3, this is the flow experience. Another useful by-product of concentration is that it helps reduce absent-mindedness. If you really concentrate on what you are doing, the chances that you will forget what you intended to do diminish.

Note that the suggestion here is to concentrate on one *key* task at a time. As described later in this chapter, sometimes doing two or three minor tasks at the same time can help save time. But would you want a surgeon correcting your vision with a laser device to be placing a stock order on a cellular phone at the same time?

Streamline Your Work and Emphasize Important Tasks

As companies continue to operate with fewer workers than in the past, more nonproductive work must be eliminated. (Remember the story about Kodak's Work-Out program?) Every employee is expected to get rid of work that does not contribute to productivity or help customers. If you get rid of work that is of little consequence, you will have more time to concentrate on value-contributing tasks. Getting rid of such unproductive work is part of *re-engineering*, in which work processes are radically redesigned and simplified. Here are typical examples of work that does not add value:

- Email or paper messages that almost nobody reads
- Sending receipts and acknowledgments to people who do not need them
- Writing and mailing reports that nobody reads or needs
- Meetings that do not accomplish work, exchange important information, or improve team spirit
- Checking up frequently on the work of competent people

In general, to streamline or re-engineer your work, look for duplication of effort and waste for both you and your clients. An example of duplication of effort would be to routinely send people both emails and faxes covering the same topic. An example of waste would be to call a meeting for disseminating information that could easily be communicated by email.

Important (value-contributing) tasks are those in which superior performance could have a large payoff. No matter how quickly you take care of making sure that your store pays its bills on time, for example, this effort will not make your store an outstanding success. If, however, you concentrate your efforts on bringing unique and desirable merchandise into the store, this action could greatly affect your business success.

In following the *A-B-C* system, you should devote ample time to the essential tasks. You should not pay more attention than absolutely necessary to the *C* (trivial) items. Many people respond to this suggestion by saying, "I don't think concentrating on important tasks applies to me. My job is so filled with routine that I have no chance to work on the big breakthrough ideas." True, most jobs are filled with routine requirements. What a person can do is spend some time, perhaps even one hour a week, concentrating on tasks of potentially major significance.

Work at a Steady Pace

In most jobs, working at a steady clip pays dividends in efficiency. The spurt worker creates many problems for management. Some employees take pride in working rapidly, even when the result is a high error rate. At home, too, a steady pace is better than spurting. A spurt houseworker is one who goes into a flurry of activity every so often. An easier person to live with is someone who does his or her share of housework at an even pace throughout the year.

Another advantage of the steady-pace approach is that it accomplishes much more than putting out extra effort just once in a while. The completely steady worker would accomplish just as much the day before a holiday as on any Monday. That extra hour or so of productivity adds up substantially by the end of the year. Despite the advantages of maintaining a steady pace, some peaks and valleys in your work may be inevitable. Tax accounting firms, for example, have busy seasons.

Create Some Quiet, Uninterrupted Time

Many office workers find their days hectic, fragmented, and frustrating. Incessant interruptions make it difficult to get things done. The constant start-stop-restart pattern lengthens the time needed to get jobs done. Quiet time can reduce the type of productivity drain just described. To achieve quiet time, create an uninterrupted block of time enabling you to concentrate on your work. This could mean turning off the telephone, not accessing your email, and blocking drop-in visitors during certain times of the workday.

Quiet time is used for such essential activities as thinking, planning, getting organized, doing analytical work, writing reports, and doing creative tasks. One hour of quiet time might yield as much productive work as four hours of interrupted time.[18]

Quiet time is difficult to find in some jobs, such as those involving customer contact. An agreement has to be worked out with the manager about when and where quiet time can be taken.

Make Use of Bits of Time

A truly productive person makes good use of miscellaneous bits of time, both on and off the job. While waiting in line at a post office, you might update your to-do list; while waiting for an elevator, you might be able to read a brief report; and if you have finished your day's work ten minutes before quitting time, you can use that time to clean out a file. By the end of the year your productivity will have increased much more than if you had squandered these bits of time.

The trend referred to as "grazing" is a variation of making good use of bits of time. **Grazing** is eating meals on the run in order to make good use of time ordinarily spent on sitting down for meals. Many ambitious people today nibble at snacks rather than disrupt their work by visiting a restaurant. Grazing does have its disadvantages: You cannot network while grazing; eating while working can be bad for digestion; and it may deprive you of a needed rest break.

Stay in Control of Paperwork, the In-Basket and Email

Despite the major shift to the use of electronic messages, the workplace is still overflowing with printed messages, including computer printouts. Paperwork essentially involves taking care of administrative details such as correspondence, expense account forms, and surveys. Responding to email messages creates additional administrative details that require handling, even though it's *electronic work* rather than paperwork.

Unless you handle paperwork and email efficiently, you may lose control of your job or home life, which could lead to heavy stress. Ideally, a small amount of time should be invested in paperwork every day. Non-prime time (when you are at less than peak efficiency, but not overly fatigued) is the best time to take care of paperwork.

The in-basket remains the centre of paperwork. For many overwhelmed workers, the entire desktop becomes the in-basket. Four steps are particularly helpful in keeping an in-basket under control: (1) give attention to the in-basket every day; (2) sort in-basket items into an action file and a reading file; (3) take care of the action items as soon as possible; and (4) read items in the reading file during bits of time on the job or at home.

To refine your system of sorting paper and email messages a step further, classify each paper or email message as (1) do now, (2) do soon, (3) route or forward to someone else, (4) file or store, or (5) toss or delete. These five categories are a way of assigning priorities to messages.[19]

Use Multi-tasking for Routine Tasks

Personal productivity can sometimes be enhanced by doing two or more routine chores simultaneously. (Major tasks, however, require full concentration.) While exercising on a stationary bike, you might read work-related information; while commuting, listen to the radio for information of potential relevance to your job. While reading email, you might clean the outside of your computer; while waiting for a file to download, you might arrange your work area or read a brief report. Some of these uses you can find for bits of time, such as reviewing your to-do list as you ride the elevator, are actually multi-tasking.

While you are searching for productivity gains through multi-tasking, it is important to avoid rude or dangerous acts. It would be rude to do paperwork while on the telephone or sitting in class. It would be dangerous to engage in an intense conversation over the cellular phone while driving, and checking out email on a laptop or on-board computer would be even more dangerous because you would be forced to lose full eye contact with the road.

Overcoming Time Wasters

Another basic thrust to improved personal productivity is to minimize wasting time. Many of the techniques already described in this chapter help save time. The tactics and strategies described next, however, are directly aimed at overcoming the problem of wasted time.

Minimize Daydreaming

"Taking a field trip" while on the job is a major productivity drain. Daydreaming is triggered when the individual perceives the task to be boring—such as reviewing another person's work for errors. Brain research suggests that younger people are more predisposed to daydreaming than older people. Apparently, older people use neurons better to focus on tasks.[20]

Unresolved personal problems are an important source of daydreaming, thus blocking your productivity. This is especially true because effective time utilization requires good concentration. When you are preoccupied with a personal or business problem, it is difficult to give your full efforts to a task at hand. The solution is to do something constructive about whatever problem is sapping your ability to concentrate (as discussed in Chapter 4 about wellness and stress).

Avoid Being a Computer Goof-off or Cyberloafer

We are all aware of the productivity improvements possible when computers are used in the office. An unproductive use of computers, however, is to tinker with them to the exclusion of useful work. Many people have become intrigued with computers to the point of diversion. They become habituated to creating new reports, designing exquisite graphics, and making endless changes. Some managers spend so much time with computers that they neglect leadership responsibilities, thus lowering their productivity.

In addition to the problems just cited, internet surfing for purposes not strictly related to the job has become a major source of productivity loss. When the career website Vault.com surveyed more than 1,200 employees, 90.3 percent said they surfed non-work-related sites during the workday.[21]

The general message is straightforward: To plug one more potential productivity drain, avoid being a computer goof-off.

Keep Track of Important Names, Places, and Things

How much time have you wasted lately searching for such items as a telephone number you jotted down somewhere, your keys, or an appointment book? A supervisor suddenly realized he had forgotten to show up for a luncheon appointment. He wanted to call and apologize but was unable to locate the person's name and phone number. Standard solutions to overcoming these problems are to keep a wheel file (such as the type made by Rolodex) of people's names and companies. It is difficult to misplace such a file. Many managers and professionals store such information in a database or even in a word processing file. Such files are more difficult to misplace than a pocket directory.

Two steps are recommended for remembering where you put things. First, have a parking place for everything. This would include putting your keys and appointment book back in the same place after each use. Second, make visual associations. To have something register in your mind at the moment you are doing it, make up a visual association with that act. Thus, you might say, "Here I am putting my résumé in the back section of my canvas bag."

Set a Time Limit for Certain Tasks and Projects

Spending too much time on a task or project wastes time. As a person becomes experienced with certain projects, he or she is able to make accurate estimates of how long a project will take to complete. A paralegal might say, "Getting this will drawn up for the lawyer's approval should take two hours." A good work habit to develop is to estimate how long a job should take and then proceed with strong determination to get that job completed within the estimated time period.

A productive version of this technique is to decide that some low- and medium-priority items are worth only so much of your time. Invest that much time in the project, but no more. Preparing a file on advertisements that come across your desk is one example.

Schedule Similar Tasks Together: Clustering

An efficient method of accomplishing small tasks is to group them together and perform them in one block of time. Clustering of this type has several applications. If you are visiting an office supply store, think of what else you need there to avoid an unnecessary repeat visit. A basic way of scheduling similar tasks together is to make most of your telephone calls in relation to your job from 11:00 to 11:30 each morning. Or you might reserve the last hour of every workday for routine tasks such as responding to email and other correspondence.

Be Decisive and Finish Things

A subtle way of improving your personal productivity is to be decisive. Move quickly, but not impulsively, through the problem-solving and decision-making steps outlined in Chapter 3 when you are faced with a nonroutine decision. Once you have evaluated possible solutions to the problem, choose and implement one of them. Set a limit to how much time you will invest in arriving at a decision to a problem. Next, set a limit to the amount of time you will spend implementing your solution. If you are in charge of this year's office party committee, you might decide to hold the party at a particular location. Decide next on approximately how much time you should invest in the project, and stick to your limit.

Now that you have studied various ways to improve your personal productivity, do Human Relations Skill-Building Exercise 15-1. Incorporating many of these ideas in this chapter will help you achieve peak performance or exceptional accomplishment.

Summary

People with good work habits tend to be more successful in their careers than poorly organized individuals, and they tend to have more time to spend on personal life. Good work habits are more important than ever because of today's emphasis on productivity and quality.

Procrastination is the major work habit problem for most employees and students. People procrastinate for many reasons, including their perception that a task is unpleasant, overwhelming, or may lead to negative consequences. Fear of success can also lead to procrastination. Awareness of procrastination may lead to its control. Eight other techniques for reducing procrastination are (1) calculate the cost of procrastination; (2) counterattack the burdensome task; (3) jump-start yourself; (4) peck away at an overwhelming task; (5) motivate yourself with rewards and punishments; (6) follow the WIFO principle; (7) make a commitment to other people; and (8) express a more positive attitude about your intentions.

Developing good work habits and time-management practices is often a matter of developing proper attitudes toward work and time. Seven such methods are (1) become a goal-oriented person and value your time; (2) develop a mission, goals, and a strong work ethic; (3) value good attendance and punctuality; (4) value neatness, orderliness, and speed; (5) work smarter, not harder; (6) become self-employed psychologically; and (7) appreciate the importance of rest and relaxation.

The Personal Productivity Checklist

Each class member will use the four headings below (in the italics) to identify two areas where he or she is experiencing problems in developing productivity in the areas of work habits and time management. The problems could apply to work, school, or personal life.

In addition to identifying the problem area, each student will check off at least two solutions and then develop a brief action plan about how to overcome the problem by using these solutions. For instance, "One of my biggest problems is that I tend to start a lot of projects but finish very few of them. Procrastination is obviously a big problem area for me. Now that I am more aware of it, I am going to give myself a strict deadline for completing college papers. If I complete the paper before a deadline, I am going to reward myself with a new DVD."

Students then present their problems and action plans to the class. After each student has made his or her presentation, hold a class discussion to reach conclusions and interpretations about the problems revealed. For instance, it might be that one or two time-management problems are quite frequent.

	Especially applicable to me
Overcoming Procrastination	
1. Increase awareness of the problem.	________
2. Calculate cost of procrastination.	________
3. Jump-start yourself.	________
4. Peck away at an overwhelming task.	________
5. Motivate yourself with rewards and punishment.	________
6. Make a commitment to other people.	________
7. Express a more positive attitude about your intentions.	________
8. Use subliminal messages about overcoming procrastination.	________
Developing Proper Attitudes and Values	
1. Become a goal-oriented person and value your time.	________
2. Value good attendance and punctuality.	________
3. Value neatness, orderliness, and speed.	________
4. Develop an ethic of effectiveness and quality.	________
5. Work smarter, not harder.	________
6. Become self-employed psychologically.	________
7. Appreciate the importance of rest and relaxation.	________
Developing the Proper Skills and Techniques	
1. Clean up and get organized.	________
2. Plan your activities (including a to-do list with priority setting).	________

	Especially applicable to me
3. Get off to a good start.	________
4. Make good use of office technology.	________
5. Concentrate on one task at a time.	________
6. Streamline your work and emphasize important tasks.	________
7. Tackle distasteful tasks first.	________
8. Work at a steady pace.	________
9. Create some quiet, uninterrupted time.	________
10. Make use of bits of time.	________
11. Stay in control of paperwork and email.	________
Overcoming Time Wasters	
1. Minimize daydreaming.	________
2. Prepare a time log to evaluate your use of time.	________
3. Avoid being a computer goof-off.	________
4. Keep track of important names, places, and things.	________
5. Set a time limit for certain tasks and projects.	________
6. Be decisive and finish things.	________

Ten skills and techniques to help you become more productive are (1) plan your activities; (2) get off to a good start; (3) make good use of office technology; (4) concentrate on one key task at a time; (5) streamline your work and emphasize important tasks; (6) work at a steady pace; (7) create some quiet, uninterrupted time; (8) make use of bits of time; (9) stay in control of paperwork and email; and (10) use multi-tasking for routine tasks.

Six suggestions for overcoming time wasting are (1) minimize daydreaming; (2) avoid being a computer goof-off or cyberloafer; (3) keep track of important names, places, and things; (4) set time limits for certain tasks and projects; (5) schedule similar tasks together; and (6) be decisive and finish things.

Questions and Activities

1. In recent years, companies that sell desk planners and other time-management devices have experienced all-time peak demands for their products. What factors do you think created this boom?
2. What factors about a person's appearance might be accurate indicators of his or her work habits and time-management skills?
3. To what extent do athletes practise good work habits and time management during the game?

4. Some students contend that because they work best when they put things off until the last moment, procrastination probably will not hurt them in their career. What is wrong with their reasoning?
5. What type of bad work habits might result from having very low tendencies toward perfectionism?
6. Give an example of any work you have ever performed, or heard of someone else performing, that could be eliminated because it is unproductive.
7. What principle of work habits and time management described in this chapter helps explain that being unusually tidy and well-organized will not necessarily make a person successful?
8. Identify five bits of time you could put to better use.
9. Complaints are mounting that the frequent use of email and the internet is lowering productivity for many workers. What might be the problem?
10. Ask an experienced business person how he or she uses the computer to improve his or her work habits and time management. Be prepared to discuss your findings in class.

Internet Skill Builder

Boosting Productivity Online

The number of people online throughout the world continues to grow rapidly, with thousands of people getting started every day. Gather into small teams or work individually to identify ten ways in which the internet can increase personal productivity, either on the job or at home. To supplement your own thinking, you might search the internet for ideas on how the internet is supposed to boost productivity.

Weblinks

www.macleans.ca
This is the site for *Maclean's*, a Canadian weekly newsmagazine. Online articles often cover such topics as time management, procrastination, stress, and so on.

www.GetMoreDone.com
A site devoted to strategies for becoming more productive.

Human Relations Case Study

A CASE OF NOT GETTING IT DONE

Carol Winchester sat nervously outside the office of Daniel Delvin, a time-management consultant and personal coach. She kept thinking about how self-conscious she felt seeking professional help just because she was having a little trouble getting started on projects and finishing projects she had started. Carol said to herself, "This counsellor is going to think there's something really wrong with me just because I have a small procrastination problem."

Winchester's thought pattern was interrupted by a warm welcome from Daniel Delvin, a neatly dressed, middle-aged counsellor. With a smile and an extended hand, Delvin said, "Hi. You must be Carol Winchester. I'm Dan Delvin. Come in and have a seat near the coffee table. That's where we'll be talking." Delvin sat in a chair a few feet away from Winchester.

"What kind of help do you want from me?" asked Delvin.

"The reason I'm here," answered Winchester, "is that both my boss and my boyfriend think I'm a procrastinator—big time. I don't disagree entirely, but I don't think I'm quite the basket case they think I am."

Delvin replied, "I doubt you're a basket case, but I don't think you would be here if you weren't experiencing a little pain. Hurting a little bit and admitting that you have a problem are the beginning points for overcoming your problem. Let's get started, Carol, by you telling me about some of the ways in which you procrastinate."

"I've got a few horror stories to tell you," said Winchester with a nervous laugh. "A recent example is that it took me four months to make this appointment with you. [They both laugh.] I kept looking at my calendar and saying to myself that I was too busy to get help. I would pick up the phone to make an appointment. Then I would think of all the other things I needed to do. I finally set April 15 as an absolute firm date to call you. Then I realized I only had two more weeks to prepare my income tax forms for last year. I guess you could say that I even procrastinated on my income tax. But I finally did get it in on May 15, and the penalty amounted to only about $65. Those are two examples for you."

"Yes, they are two good examples. But I need more examples of your procrastination so I can better understand your problem."

"Okay, you asked for it," responded Winchester. "Lance, my boyfriend, whom I love very much, proposed to me one year ago. We were in a beautiful Greek restaurant called Acropolis. He pulled a ring out of the box. The group at the table across from us were watching intently. They were ready to clap when I said yes. Lance just assumed I would say yes. I didn't say yes, but I didn't say no. I just said I wasn't ready to make a decision that night.

"Two months later, when the engagement came up for about the tenth time in conversation, I did say yes. I know that by delaying my decision I took some of the romance out of Lance's proposal. His feelings are still a little hurt, but it didn't change his mind about wanting to marry me."

"Hold on a second," said Delvin. "Have you two agreed on a wedding date yet?"

"Lance has been pressing me a little, but I'm just not ready to be that specific about getting married."

"Let's switch channels now," said Delvin. "What about on the job? What has prompted your boss to think you have a major procrastination problem?"

"It would be fair to say that I need more time than most people to get my projects done. I'm the assistant sales promotion manager. I have to do things like make some of the arrangements for trade shows and work with printers to have brochures ready. My boss says that I wait so long to make arrangements for booking hotels that we often have to pay premium rates. I think he exaggerates that problem. I'm very thorough and that can be a big asset.

"A few times I've been late in getting computer disks ready for the printer so they can do their job on time. Yet, since we're supposed to be the customer, I think they should be adapting to our schedule. I can think of another recent example. We were going to hire a new assistant for the office. We all agreed she was the right person to do the job. My boss had to go out of town for an important sales meeting, so he told me to contact this woman and tell her about the job offer.

"I got so busy with other stuff that I didn't call her for a week. By that time she had accepted another job. My boss was upset and blamed losing her on my procrastination. My take on it is a little different. If that woman really wanted to work for us, she could have waited for the job offer instead of taking another position."

Delvin asked, "Carol, why do you think you procrastinate so much?"

Carol replied, "You're a little bit like my boss and my boyfriend. You assume that every time I delay doing something, it's procrastination. Sometimes something else very important comes up that prevents me from going down a particular path. At other times I might be just a little forgetful, like filing the taxes on time."

Questions

1. What do you see as some of the reasons behind Carol Winchester's procrastination?
2. What evidence do you find that Winchester might be defensive about her problem or denying its reality?
3. What advice can you offer Winchester for overcoming her procrastination problem?

Getting Ahead in Your Career

Learning Outcomes

After studying the information and doing the exercises in this chapter, you should be able to

- explain the new model of career advancement in organizations
- select several strategies and tactics for getting ahead in your career by taking control of your own behaviour
- select several strategies and tactics for advancing your career by exerting control over your environment
- recognize how to deal with the challenge of hidden barriers to career advancement

Chances are Prospect Associates Ltd., a consulting firm, won't ever offer Drew Melton a corner office and his pick of the company art collection. He started out as a copy-machine operator three years ago, and that's exactly where he is today. Yet Melton is not in a dead-end job. Two weeks after he was hired by Prospect Associates, Melton went to its president, Laura Henderson, and told her how he could run document production faster and faster. Henderson gave him the opportunity to run the operation his way.

"They're listening to my ideas, and that's why I'm making changes and contributing to the company," says Melton. Today he runs his own photocopy operation, dispensing advice to Prospect's harried consultants, who rely on his painstaking attention to detail to give their proposals a professional look.

The company president and Melton agree that he has advanced, although he has not climbed a corporate ladder. He has increased his contribution to the company by sharpening his skills and expanding the scope of his job. His salary has increased by more than 40 percent; he's respected by the company's professional staff; and there's no pressure on him to move up.[1]

Drew Melton's story is an example of how people are advancing their careers today using a blend of traditional tactics (such as displaying initiative) and modern tactics (growing within the job). In this chapter we focus on strategies, tactics, and attitudes that will help you achieve promotion or hold on to a position you enjoy. The same approaches will enable you to achieve **career portability**, the ability to move from one employer to another when necessary.

We have divided the vast information about career advancement into four sections. The first section describes the new model, or concept, of career advancement. The second section deals with approaches to managing or taking control of your own behaviour to advance or to retain a good position. The third section deals with approaches to exerting control over your environment to improve your chances for success. A brief section is also included on dealing with hidden barriers to career advancement.

The New Model of Career Advancement

Career advancement has acquired a shift in emphasis in recent years to accommodate new organizational structures. The major shift has been away from vertical mobility, or moving up the ladder, toward lateral growth, or advancing by learning more. Drew Melton's experience in expanding his position in the photocopy room illustrates the new model of career advancement. Here we look briefly at the key components of the new model of career advancement.

1. *More emphasis on horizontal growth.* As just mentioned, the major shift in career advancement has been toward more emphasis on learning new

skills and acquiring new knowledge in a position at the same organizational level. Many companies even give pay raises to employees who learn new job-related skills. Despite the emphasis on horizontal growth, many workers still aspire to climb the organizational ladder. Also, many companies offer promotion to a higher-level position as a reward for good performance.

2. *More emphasis on temporary leadership assignments.* In the traditional model of career advancement, an individual would strive to be promoted to a management or leadership position. The person would then hold on to that position unless demoted or fired. Today, many leadership positions are temporary, such as working as the head of a project to launch a new product. After the product is launched, the person might return to his or her position as a group member (individual contributor). Or a person might be assigned as a committee head because of his or her expertise. After the committee has completed its work, the person returns to a nonleadership position.
3. *Climbing the ladder of self-fulfillment.* For an increasing number of people, doing work that contributes to self-fulfillment is more important than a focus on promotion or earnings growth. To advance in your career would be to find work that provides more self-fulfillment. Individual preferences determine what type of work is self-fulfilling.
4. *Continuous learning.* According to career expert Douglas T. Hall, careers for the 21st century will consist of a series of short learning stages. *Career age*, or how long a person has been engaged in a type of work, will become more important than chronological age.[2] At one point in your career you might need to rapidly learn how to conduct research on the internet; at another stage, you might need to learn how to organize a trade show.
5. *Being promoted as much for learn-how as know-how.* Hall also predicts that in the 21st century, demand in the labour market will shift from those with know-how (present skills) to those with learn-how (learning capability).[3] A track record of being able to learn will give people the portability mentioned at the start of this chapter. Being able to learn rapidly makes continuous learning possible. The reason that learn-how is so important is that organizations face such rapid technological change.

The new model of career advancement is compatible with a modern definition of success. **Career success** as used here means attaining the twin goals of organizational rewards and personal satisfaction. Organizational rewards include such things as higher-ranking positions, more money, and challenging assignments. Personal satisfaction refers to enjoying, or liking, what you are doing. If your employer highly values your contribution and your job satisfaction is high, you are experiencing career success. However, success in general also includes accomplishments and satisfaction in personal life.

To begin relating career development to yourself, do Human Relations Self-Assessment Quiz 16-1.

The Career-Development Inventory

Career-development activities inevitably include answering some penetrating questions about yourself. Following are 12 representative questions to be found on career-development inventories. You may need several hours to do a competent job of answering these questions. After individuals have answered these questions by themselves, it may be profitable to hold a class discussion about the relevance of the specific questions. A strongly recommended procedure is for you to date your completed inventory and put it away for safekeeping. Examine your answers in several years to see (1) how well you are doing in advancing your career and (2) how much you have changed.

Keep the following information in mind in answering this inventory: People are generous in their self-evaluations when they answer career-development inventories, so you might want to discuss some of your answers with somebody who knows you well.

1. How would you describe yourself as a person?
2. What are you best at doing? worst?
3. What are your two biggest strengths or assets?
4. What are the two traits, characteristics, or behaviours of yours that need the most improvement?
5. What are your two biggest accomplishments?
6. Write your obituary as you would like it to appear.
7. What would be the ideal job for you?
8. What career advice can you give yourself?
9. Describe the two peak work-related experiences in your life.
10. What are your five most important values (the things in life most important to you)?
11. What goals in life are you trying to achieve?
12. What do you see as your niche (spot where you best fit) in the modern world?

Taking Control of Yourself

The unifying theme to the strategies, tactics, and attitudes described in this section is that you must attempt to control your own behaviour. You can advance your career by harnessing the forces under your control. Such a perspective is helpful because individuals have the primary responsibility for managing their own careers. The organization may help, but managing your career is your responsibility.

The following section concentrates on getting ahead by trying to control your external environment in some small way. Do not be concerned about overlap between the general categories of controlling yourself versus controlling the environment. Instead, focus on the meaning and application of the strategies and tactics. Recognize also that the information presented throughout this chapter will help you take responsibility for managing your career.

Develop Outstanding Interpersonal Skills

Getting ahead in business-related fields is exceedingly difficult unless you can relate effectively to other people. Workers are bypassed for promotion generally because someone thinks they cannot effectively be responsible for the work of others. Workers are more likely to be terminated for poor interpersonal skills than for poor technical skills.

Effective interpersonal or human relations skills refer to many specific practices. At a meeting, if you crack a joke that relieves tension and serves as an icebreaker, you are showing good interpersonal skills. If, as the team leader, you convince other team members to strive harder for quality, you are showing good interpersonal (and leadership) skills.

Chapters 7 through 12 of this book focused on important interpersonal skills such as communication, resolving conflict, being assertive, exerting leadership, behaving with self-confidence, and listening to customers.

Develop Expertise

A starting point in getting ahead is to develop a useful job skill. This tactic is obvious if one is working as a specialist, such as an insurance underwriter. Being skilled at the task performed by the group is also a requirement for being promoted to a supervisory position. After one is promoted to supervisor or another managerial job, expertise is still important for further advancement. It helps a manager's reputation to be skilled in such things as memo writing, computer applications, preparing a budget, and interviewing job candidates.

Although expertise in one's field is highly recommended, the workplace also demands that a person perform a variety of tasks outside that field. A recommended approach is to have depth in your primary field, but also to have breadth by having several lesser areas of expertise. A widespread example is that no matter what your specialty field, you are also expected to have information-technology skills.

Perform Well on All Your Assignments

Good job performance is the bedrock of a person's career. In rare instances a person is promoted on the basis of favouritism alone. In all other situations an employee must have received a favourable performance appraisal to be promoted. Before an employee is promoted, the prospective new boss asks, "How well did this person perform for you?" Carly Fiorina, now the top executive at Hewlett-Packard, offers this advice:

> Focus 100 percent on doing the job you have better than anybody else. I've seen a lot of high-flying people fall flat because they were so focused on the next job, they didn't get the current job done. Managers see performance as a measure of potential, not potential as a measure of performance.[4]

Performing well on all your assignments is also important because it contributes to the **success syndrome**, a pattern in which the worker performs one assignment well and then has the confidence to take on an even more difficult assignment. Each new assignment contributes to more self-confidence and more success. As you succeed in new and more challenging assignments, your reputation grows within the firm.

Create Good First Impressions

Every time you interact with a new person inside or outside your company, you create a first impression. Fair or not, these first impressions have a big impact on your career. If your first impression is favourable, you will often be invited back by an internal or external customer. Your first impression also creates a "halo" that may influence perceptions about the quality of your work in the future. If your first impression is negative, you will have to work extra hard to be perceived as competent later on.

Looking successful contributes to a positive first impression. Your clothing, your desk and office, and your speech should project the image of a successful, but not necessarily flamboyant, person. Your standard of dress should be appropriate to your particular career stage and work environment. Appropriate dress for an inventory specialist is not the same as for an outside salesperson dealing with industrial customers. Many salespeople and managers today maintain a flexible clothing style by such means as keeping a jacket and extra jewellery in the car or office. When an unanticipated meeting with a customer or some other special occasion arises, a quick modification of clothing style is possible.[5] Appearing physically fit is also part of the success image.

Projecting a sense of control is another key factor contributing to a positive first impression. Show that you are in control of yourself and the environment. Avoid letting your body language betray you—nonverbal messages are sent by fidgeting or rubbing your face. Make your gestures project self-assurance and purpose.[6] A verbal method of appearing in control is to make a positive assertion such as, "This is a demanding assignment and I welcome the challenge."

According to one theory of leadership, another reason first impressions are important is that the leader of a group quickly sizes up new members. Those who create a good impression become part of the in-group and are therefore given more favourable assignments and kept informed more regularly. Group members who do not create a good initial impression become part of the out-group and are treated much less favourably.[7]

Another key contributor to first impressions is a person's communication patterns and method of self-presentation. According to career coach Debra Benton, it is particularly important to avoid the following five self-defeating communication behaviours: (1) talking too fast, which makes what you say seem unimportant; (2) talking too much or giving more details than others want; (3) being too critical, or passing judgments about others; (4) being too self-critical or too revealing about your own inadequacies; and (5) displaying weak body language (see preceding) or using a weak tone of voice.[8]

Document Your Accomplishments

Keeping an accurate record of what you have accomplished on the job can be valuable when you are being considered for promotion, transfer, or assignment to a team or project. Documenting your accomplishments can also be used to verify new learning. In addition, a record of this type is also useful when your performance is being evaluated. You can show your manager what you have done for the organization lately. Many professional-level workers maintain a portfolio of their accomplishments, such as samples of successful work. The portfolio is much like that used by photographers, artists, and models when applying for a job and is gaining in popularity. Many colleges and universities have students design their portfolios in various courses. These portfolios can then be added to over time. Accomplishments do not have to be "on the job," as many skills are learned outside the office and should be included. Here are three examples of documented accomplishments from different types of jobs and a volunteer assignment:

1. A bank teller suggested one side door be modified to accommodate customers in wheelchairs. The number of physically disabled customers jumped 324 percent in two years.
2. A maintenance supervisor decreased fuel costs in her office by 27 percent in one year by installing ceiling fans.
3. A telephone service representative, working as a volunteer, designed and implemented a physical fitness program for mentally challenged youth for a weekend day-support program.

After documenting your accomplishments, it pays to advertise. Let key people know in a tasteful way of your tangible accomplishments. You might request an opportunity to make a presentation to your boss to review the status of one of your successful projects, or if it would be presumptuous for you to request a special meeting to discuss your accomplishments, use email for the same purpose.

Be Conventional in Your Behaviour

Although this book does not emphasize conformity to conventional norms of behaviour, they are of value in getting ahead. More precisely, by flouting tradition you could hurt your career. Areas in which conventional behaviour is expected by most employers include good attendance and punctuality, careful grooming, courtesy to superiors, an appropriate amount of smiling, good posture, adherence to company safety rules, and obeying authority. Employees who insist on being nonconformists in these areas do so at considerable risk to their career advancement.

Take a Creative Approach to Your Job

As emphasized in Chapter 3, being creative helps you get ahead in business. Your ideas must be backed up with concrete plans for their implementation. If you are associated with an innovative idea, and that idea pays dividends, your career might receive a big boost. For maximum benefit to your career, make innovative suggestions in areas that are likely to make money or save money. Here are two examples of suggestions along these lines:

- A worker at a law firm suggested that a paralegal and a lawyer should provide some free consulting hours to several charitable organizations in the city, as many wealthy individuals were involved in these organizations. As a result of her suggestion, the firm attracted several new wealthy clients.

- A worker at a publisher with a large mail-order business suggested the company produce books with a smaller trim size. The yearly savings in mailing and shipping costs were enormous.

Keep Growing through Continuous Learning and Self-Development

Given that continuous learning is part of the new model of career advancement, engaging in regular learning will help a person advance. Continuous learning can take many forms, including formal schooling, attending training programs and seminars, and self-study. It is particularly important to engage in new learning in areas of interest to the company, such as developing proficiency in a second language if the company has customers or employees in areas where that language is spoken. Many companies support continuous learning, making it easier for you to implement the tactic of growth through continuous learning. An example follows:

> As a major Canadian employer, Chrysler Canada Ltd. understands the need for people to become lifelong learners. One of their recent programs, called the Chrysler Canada Ltd.'s Windsor Experiment, had two purposes: (1) to identify best practices in apprenticeship training programs, and (2) to develop collaborations with various educational institutions to increase the number of workers who will be required in the automotive industry. In order to keep up with vast and fast technological changes, Chrysler also recognizes the need for constant retraining and upgrading of skills for current workers. To date, Chrysler Canada has had major achievements with this project, including: the opening of an automotive research and development centre with the University of Windsor; an electrical/electronics program in partnership with St. Clair College and the Canadian Auto Workers (CAW); and a reformed apprenticeship training program with St. Clair College that allows for more flexible scheduling to meet the needs of students.[9]

Self-development can include any type of learning but often emphasizes personal improvement and skill development. Improving your work habits or team leadership skills would be job-relevant examples of self-development.

Observe Proper Etiquette

Proper etiquette is important for career advancement because the pendulum has swung back toward a polite and mannerly business climate.[10] **Business etiquette** is a special code of behaviour required in work situations. The term *manners* has an equivalent meaning. Both etiquette and manners refer to behaving in an acceptable and refined way. In the digital era, etiquette is just as important as ever because of the new challenges that high-tech devices bring. For example, is it good etiquette to read the information on a co-worker's computer screen when visiting his or her cubicle? The globalization of business also creates challenges—for example, knowing whether handshakes are acceptable when visiting another country.[11]

Figuring out what constitutes proper etiquette and business manners requires investigation. One approach is to use successful people as models of behaviour or sources of information. Another approach is to consult a current book about business etiquette, such as the *Complete Business Etiquette Handbook.* Many of the suggestions offered in these books follow common sense, but many others would not be obvious to an inexperienced career person.

The basic rules of etiquette are to make the other person feel comfortable in your presence, to be considerate, and to strive not to embarrass anyone. Also, be cordial to all, remembering that everyone deserves our respect.[12] Specific guidelines stem from these basic rules. Exhibit 16-1 presents examples of good business etiquette and manners.

Develop a Proactive Personality

If you are an active agent in taking control of the forces around you, you stand a better chance of capitalizing on opportunities. Also, you will seek out opportunities such as seeing problems that need fixing. A **proactive personality** is one who is relatively unconstrained by his or her job description and freely effects change. People who are highly proactive identify opportunities and act on them, show initiative, and keep trying until they bring about meaningful change. A health and

exhibit 16-1

Business Etiquette and Manners

Below are 15 specific suggestions about office etiquette and business manners that should be considered in the context of a specific job situation. For example, the rule "Shouting is out" would not apply to traders on the floor of a stock exchange, where shouting is routine.

1. *Be polite to people in person.* Say "good morning" and "good night" to work associates at all job levels. Smile frequently. Offer to bring coffee or another beverage for a co-worker if you are going outside to get some for yourself.
2. *Write polite letters.* An important occasion for practising good etiquette is the writing of business and personal letters. Include the person's job title in the inside address; spell the person's name correctly. Use supportive rather than harsh statements. (For example, say "It would be helpful if you could" rather than "You must.") Avoid right-margin justification because it is much more severe looking than ragged right (uneven) text.
3. *Practise good table manners.* Avoid smacking your lips or sucking your fingers. If someone else is paying the bill do not order the most expensive item on the menu (such as a $150 bottle of Dom Pérignon champagne!). Offer to cut bread for the other person, and do not look at the bill if another person is paying.
4. *Remember names.* It is both good manners and good human relations to remember the names of work associates, even if you see them only occasionally.
5. *Treat males and females equally.* Amenities extended to females by males in a social setting are minimized in business settings today. During a meeting, a male is not expected to hold a chair or a door for a woman, nor does he jump to walk on the outside when the two of them are walking down the street. Many women resent being treated differently from males with respect to minor social customs. In general, common courtesies should be extended by both sexes to one another.
6. *Shouting is out.* Emotional control is an important way of impressing superiors. Following the same principle, shouting in most work situations detracts from your image.

7. *The host or hostess pays the bill.* An area of considerable confusion about etiquette surrounds business lunches and who should pay the cheque. The rule of etiquette is that the person who extends the invitation pays the bill. (Do you think this rule should be extended to social life?)

8. *Introduce the lower-ranking person to the higher-ranking person.* In other words, the higher-ranking person is the centre of attention, and others are introduced *to* him or her. For instance, you introduce the younger person *to* the older person: "[Older person's name], I'd like you to meet [younger person's name]." Similarly, co-workers are introduced *to* a client. Also, when introducing more than one person at a time, introduce higher-ranking people first; your boss's name should be mentioned before a co-worker's.

9. *Address superiors and visitors in their preferred way.* As the modern business world has become more informal, a natural tendency has developed to address people at all levels by their first names. It is safer to first address people by a title and their last name and then wait for them to correct you if they desire.

10. *Don't spread malicious gossip.* Although being a source of positive gossip brings you power in the office, spreading gossip that damages the reputation of another person is considered impolite. You could also become the recipient of a lawsuit.

11. *Make appointments with high-ranking people rather than dropping in.* It is taboo in most firms for lower-ranking employees to casually drop in on an executive.

12. *When another person is opening a door to exit a room or building, do not jump in ahead of him or her.* In recent years, many people have developed the curious habit of quickly jumping in past another person (moving in the opposite direction) who is exiting. Not only is this practice rude, it can lead to an uncomfortable collision.

13. *Be courteous about the copy machine.* If you are using the photocopier for a large run and someone approaches the machine wanting to copy one or two pages, allow that person to interrupt. When two people arrive at the copier machine simultaneously, the person with the smaller job goes first. When you're finished, refill the machine with paper and reset the machine.

14. *Forget about "air kissing" in the office.* Blowing kisses in the workplace is considered unprofessional. Unless you are going to kiss everyone in the office, kiss no one.

15. *Be sensitive to cross-cultural differences in etiquette.* When dealing with people from different cultures, regularly investigate possible major differences in etiquette. For example, using the index finger to point is considered rude in most Asian countries. The American sign for OK (thumb and index finger forming a circle) is considered a vulgarity in most other countries. Another example is that Finns are very private people, so don't ask questions about their private lives unless they bring up the topic first. Instead, talk about the safe topic of sports. Don't blow your nose in public in Belgium, where it is considered an offensive gesture. (It's not too cool elsewhere, either.)

Caution: Although all these points could have some bearing on the image you project, violation of any one of them would not necessarily have a negative impact on your career. It is the overall image you project that counts the most. Therefore, the general principle of being considerate of work associates is much more important than any one act of etiquette or manners.

SOURCES: Jim Rucker and Jean Anna Sellers, "Changes in Business Etiquette," *Business Education Forum,* February 1998, p. 45; "Business Etiquette: Teaching Students the Unwritten Rules," *Keying In,* January 1996, pp. 1–2; "Meeting and Greeting," *Keying In,* January 1996, p. 3; Lisa Lee Freeman, "Re-Finishing School," *Working Woman,* February 1999, pp. 84–85; compilation from other sources in Andrea Sachs, "Corporate Ps and Qs," *Time,* November 1, 1999, Special Business Section, p. 23.

safety specialist with a proactive personality, for example, might identify a health hazard others had missed, identify the nature of the problem, and ask management for funding to control the problem. Ultimately, this person's efforts in preventing major health problems would be recognized.

Managers prefer workers with proactive personalities because these workers become proactive employees—those who take the initiative to take care of problems. The modern employee is supposed to be enterprising. Instead of relying solely on the manager to figure out what work needs to be accomplished, he or she looks for projects to undertake.[13] The proactive employee, however, may clash with an old-fashioned manager who believes that an employee's job is strictly to follow orders.

A study conducted with nearly 500 men and women workers in diverse occupations examined the relationship between career success and a proactive personality. Proactive personality, as measured by a test, was related to salary, promotions, and career satisfaction.[14]

It may not be easy to develop a proactive personality, but a person can get started by taking more initiative to fix problems and attempting to be more self-starting. A proactive personality is perceived to have high control over situations.

Take Sensible Risks

An element of risk taking is necessary to advance very far in a career. Almost all successful people have taken at least one moderate risk in their careers. These risks include starting a new business with mostly borrowed money, joining a fledgling firm, or submitting a groundbreaking idea to management. Terrie M. Williams, founder of a public relations firm, believes that risk taking is the most essential ingredient in advancing a career. Not risking anything can mean risking even more, including inhibiting your career. Williams offers this explanation:

> When I'm approaching an important meeting, I sometimes find myself thinking, "I'm scared. I don't know if I can carry this off." Whenever I feel that way, I make a conscious effort to remind myself that being scared is good. It means I'm embarking on something new and different, and I can only go to the next level.[15]

Learn to Manage Adversity

Some adversity is almost inevitable in an ambitious person's career. It is difficult to get through a career without at least once being laid off, fired, demoted, transferred to an undesirable assignment, or making a bad investment. Company mergers and takeovers also contribute to adversity because so many people are laid off in the process or assigned to lesser jobs.

Personal resilience—the capacity to bounce back from setback—is necessary to overcome adversity. A general-purpose way of handling adversity is to first get emotional support from a friend or family member, and then solve the problem systematically. You can follow the decision-making steps described in Chapter 3.

Two other points about managing adversity are particularly relevant here. First, attempt not to be bitter and cynical about your problem. Bitterness and cynicism can freeze a person into inaction. Second, look to minimize the self-doubt that grows from a mental script called the *fear narrative*. According to Kenneth Ruge, this is a narrative in which you tell yourself that if you try again, something terrible will happen. "The word *can't* becomes the operative word and you become its prisoner." The best antidote is to create an opposite narrative whereby you think, "How can I use my imagination and creativity to move beyond this *can't* to achieve my goals?"[16]

Develop the Brand Called "You"

Well-known consultant Tom Peters urges all career-minded people to develop their credentials and their reputation to the extent that they stand out like a brand name. Although the analogy of each person becoming a recognizable brand name like Nike is far-fetched, the idea of becoming a trusted person with value is sound. As Peters sees it, you don't belong to any company for life, and your chief affiliation isn't any particular function or department (such as accounting). You are not defined by your job title or your job description. "Starting today, you are a brand."[17]

You begin developing brand You by identifying the qualities or characteristics that distinguish you from co-workers. What have you done recently to make You stand out? What benefit do you offer? Do you deliver high-quality work on time? Are you a creative problem solver? Next, you make yourself visible so you can cash in on your uniqueness (your brand). Almost all the ideas in this chapter will help you develop brand You!

The Canada Today feature on page 417 offers some other tips and ideas about developing your career.

Exerting Control over the Outside World

Here we emphasize strategies and tactics requiring you to exert some control over the outside environment. If you do not fully control it, at least you can try to juggle it to your advantage. For instance, "Find a Mentor" suggests that you search out a friendly and supportive person in your field who can help you advance in your career.

Develop a Flexible Career Path

Planning your career inevitably involves some form of goal setting. If your goals are laid out systematically to lead you to your ultimate career goal, you have established a career path. A **career path** is thus a sequence of positions necessary to achieve a goal.[18]

Here we describe two types of career paths. One type emphasizes climbing up the ladder in a traditional organization. The other emphasizes the horizontal movements that characterize the new model of career advancement.

The Traditional Career Path

A traditional (or vertical) career path is based on the assumption that a person will occupy a series of positions, each at a higher level of responsibility than the previous one. A person thus climbs the organizational ladder or hierarchy. If a career path is laid out in one firm, it must be related to the present and future demands of that firm. If you aspire toward a high-level manufacturing position, you would need to know the future of manufacturing in that company. Many US and Canadian firms, for example, plan to conduct more of their manufacturing in the

Pacific Rim or Mexico. If you were really determined, you might study the appropriate language and ready yourself for a global position.

Before establishing the goals on the career path, it is helpful to clarify your values. These are probably the same values that enabled you to choose a career in the first place. Questions to think about include these: "Can you name the three things most important to your job satisfaction? What do you really look for in a job? Do you want to be part of a team? To think creatively? Are you passionate about helping people and improving the world? Do you want to carefully follow directions, or do you prefer to decide which tasks are important?"[19]

While sketching out a career path you should list your personal goals. They should mesh with your work plans to help avoid major conflicts in your life. Some lifestyles, for example, are incompatible with some career paths. You might find it

Canadian Websites for Some Sound Career Advice

The internet is an excellent source for valuable ideas and strategies to help you develop and get ahead in your career. Below are a few Canadian sites and some advice and ideas.

Barbara Moses is a career-management consultant and author of two books on life career success. One of her interesting rules out of her 12 rules for success is that you need to become a career activist. A career activist is just that; someone who is vigilant and active in developing a career path. Identify and prepare for opportunities. Stay informed and alert. In other words, create your own opportunities rather than waiting for them to come to you. You can access many of her ideas at her website at **www.bbmcareerdev.com**.

From Queen's University, you can access a site with everything from ways to find a job to how to dress for that important interview. While it is for Queen's students, there are many helpful tips and ideas that make this site well worth the trip. Find it at **www.careers.queensu.ca/students/wecanhelp.asp**.

Tema Frank, author of *Canada's Best Employers for Women: A Guide for Job Hunters, Employees and Employers*, has an interesting website that includes the Employer of the Month, Employer News and, of course, Canada's best employers for women. Of course, good employers for women are usually also good employers for men. So don't avoid this one just because you are male. The site for Frank Communications can be found at **www.tcn.net/~frank**.

Chatelaine, a women's magazine available online, has a section on work, including archives of work-related articles. Many of the articles are written by women who have managed career problems such as balancing career and home life or changing careers. For example, one article, "Getting a Life" by Bonnie Schiedel, explains how she and four other women created the lives they wanted. The article was originally in the November 2001 issue of the magazine and you can read it at **www.chatelaine.com/work/read/article.jsp?content=667228**. The author moved her career and life from Toronto to a tiny town near Thunder Bay. An interesting read for people interested in career paths.

A site from Quebec that is excellent is **www.jobboom.com**. This site includes a Career and Orientation Profile, the Campbell Interest and Skills Survey, and other self-tests to help you in understanding yourself. Other sections include many career management sections including finding the right job for you, hot careers, and working for yourself. This site contains many valuable career development ideas and is also available in French.

SOURCE: Barbara Moses, "Career Intelligence: The 12 New Rules for Success," *Futurist*, Vol. 33, Issue 7, Aug/Sep 1999, pp. 28–36.

difficult to develop a stable home life (spouse, children, friends, community activities, garden) if you aspire to holding a sales position in the Far East.

Your career path is a living document and may need to be modified as your circumstances change.[20] Keep in mind changes in your company and industry. If becoming a branch manager is an important step in your career path, check to see if your company or industry still has branch managers. The changing preferences of your family can also influence your career path. A family that once wanted to stay put may now be willing to relocate, which could open up new possibilities on your career path.

Contingency ("what if?") plans should also be incorporated into a well-designed career path. For instance, "If I don't become an agency supervisor by age 35, I will seek employment in the private sector." Or, "If I am not promoted within two years, I will enroll in a business school program."

Lisa Irving, an ambitious 20-year-old, formulated the following career path prior to receiving an associate's degree in business administration. After she presented her tentative career path to her classmates, several accused Lisa of shooting for the moon. Lisa's career goals are high, but she has established contingency plans. Presented here as an example, not an ideal model, is Lisa's career path plan.

Work

1. Purchasing trainee for two years
2. Assistant purchasing agent for three years
3. Purchasing agent for five years (will join Purchasing Managers Association)
4. Purchasing supervisor for five years
5. Purchasing manager for six years
6. Manager, materials handling, for five years
7. Vice-president, procurement, until retirement

Personal Life

1. Rent own apartment after one year of working.
2. Attend university evenings until receive BBA in business administration.
3. Marry by age 30 (plan only one marriage).
4. Have one child by age 35.
5. Own and live in home with husband and child by age 38.
6. Volunteer work for Down's syndrome children.
7. Travel to India before age 50.

Contingency Plans

1. Will seek new employment by stage 3 if not promoted to purchasing agent.
2. If not promoted to vice-president by stage 6, will consider opening small retail business.
3. If I encounter sex discrimination at any stage, will look for employment with firm that has large government contracts (where discrimination is much less likely).
4. If I develop a stress disorder at any point, will seek nonsupervisory position in purchasing field.

Career paths can also be laid out graphically, as shown in Figure 16-1. One benefit of a career path laid out in chart form is that it gives a clear perception of climbing steps toward your target position. As each position is attained, the corresponding step can be shaded in colour or cross-hatched.

Most of the goals just mentioned include a time element, which is crucial to sound career management. Your long-range goal might be clearly established in your mind (such as owner and operator of a health spa). At the same time you must establish short-range goals (get any kind of job in health spa) and intermediate-range goals (manager of a health spa by age 30). Goals set far in the future that are not supported with more immediate goals may lose their motivational value.

The career path shown in Figure 16-1 features a steady progression of promotions, yet a reasonable number of years in each position. Such planning is realistic because promotions often take a long time to achieve.

The Horizontal Career Path

Many organizations today have structures that don't lend themselves to fixed career paths. Instead of plotting a series of moves over a long time period, many individuals can only make predictions about one or two years into the future. A significant feature of the horizontal career path is that people are more likely to advance by moving sideways than moving up. Or, at least, people who get ahead will spend a considerable part of their career working in different positions at or near the same level. In addition, they may occasionally move to a lower-level position to gain

Figure 16-1 A Traditional Career Path

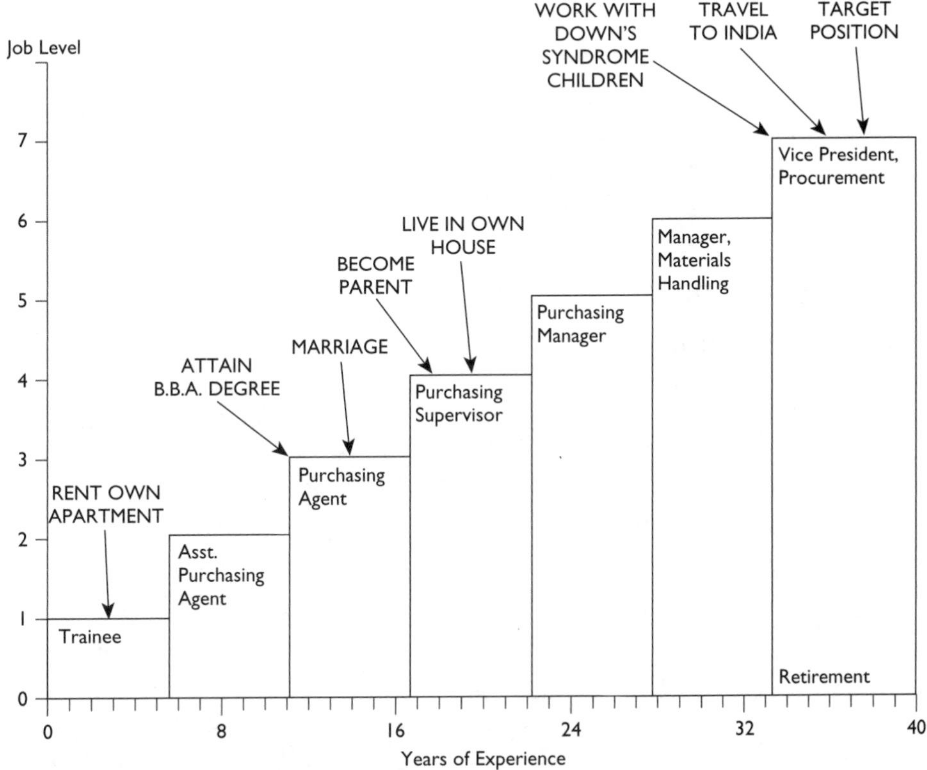

valuable experience. With a horizontal career path, the major reward is no longer promotion but the opportunity to gain more experience and increase job skills.

As with a traditional (or vertical) career path, a horizontal career path does not necessarily mean the person stays with the same firm. For example, a worker might spend three years in one company as an electronics technician, three years in another as an e-commerce coordinator, and then three years as a customer service specialist in a third company. All three positions would be approximately at the same level. The third company then promotes the individual to a much-deserved position as the marketing team leader. Following is a horizontal career path for Michael Wang, a career-school graduate who did attempt to make long-range predictions about his career.

Career

1. Electronics technician at office equipment company for three years
2. Computer repair technician for three years for computer company
3. Customer service representative for two years
4. Sales support specialist at computer company for three years
5. Marketing research specialist for two years
6. Outside sales representative for digital copying machine company for four years
7. Sales manager in small office equipment company for five years
8. Owner of electronic equipment servicing company for rest of career

Personal Life

1. Rent own apartment after one year of working.
2. Attend seminars to upgrade marketing and computer knowledge.
3. Study French with goal of becoming bilingual.
4. Purchase condo.
5. Marry by age 29.
6. Start raising family by age 31.
7. Run for county council by age 34.
8. Spend one month in Taiwan visiting relatives by age 36.
9. Begin investment program for children's education.

Contingency Plans

1. If cannot obtain experience as market research analyst, customer-service rep, or sales rep, will continue to develop as electronic technician.
2. If cannot find employment as sales manager, will attempt to become supervisor of electronic technicians.
3. If do not raise sufficient funds for starting own business, will continue in corporate job until retirement.

1. Will rent a duplex if purchasing condo is not feasible.
2. If unsuccessful in being elected to council, will do volunteer work for youths.
3. If not married by age 29, will continue to search for life partner beyond that age.

Figure 16-2 presents a horizontal career path. After you've studied the two types of career paths, do Human Relations Skill-Building Exercise 16-1.

Have an Action Plan to Reach Your Goals

As described in Chapter 2, a useful goal is backed up by a logical plan for its attainment. A recommended practice is to supplement your career path with a description of your action plans. Lisa Irving, the woman who wants to succeed in the purchasing field, might include an action plan of this nature:

> To become manager of materials handling, I will need to (1) perform in an outstanding manner as purchasing manager by such means as coordinating the billing system with the sales department, (2) engage in continuous self-study about the entire materials-handling field, (3) be active in the local purchasing association group, and (4) make sure that top management is aware of my talent and ambition.

Action plans can be drawn up in minute detail. As with any other aspect of career planning, however, avoid becoming too rigid in your thinking. Career paths and career plans are only tentative. A different path to your goal might fall right in your lap. Ten years from now, for instance, Lisa might receive a telephone call from an executive employment agency. The caller might say: "My client has engaged me to find a materials manager who is competent. Your name was given to us. Could you possibly meet me for lunch to discuss this exciting career opportunity?"

Practise Networking, Including Cyber-Networking

Developing a network of contacts was recommended in Chapter 14 as a method of finding a job. Currently the most popular career-advancement tactic, networking has several purposes. The contacts you establish can help you find a better position, offer you a new position, become a customer, become a valuable supplier, or help you solve difficult problems. People in your network can also offer you emotional support during periods of adversity.

Figure 16-2 A Horizontal Career Path

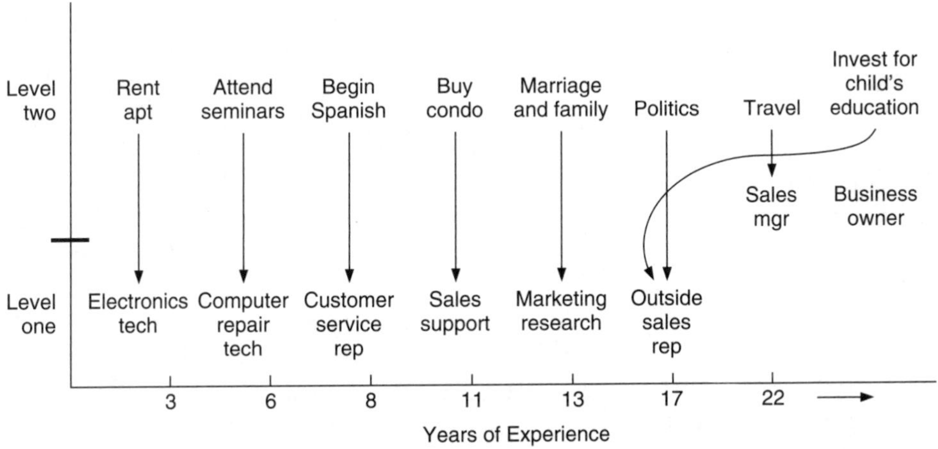

Career Pathing

1. Each class member will develop a tentative career path, perhaps as an outside assignment. About six volunteers will then share their paths with the rest of the class. Feedback of any type will be welcomed. Class members studying the career paths of others should keep in mind such issues as:
   - How logical does the plan appear?
   - Is this something the person really wants or is it simply an exercise in putting down on paper what the ambitious person is supposed to want?
   - How well do the individual's work plans mesh with personal plans?
2. Each class member will interview an experienced working person outside class about his or her career path. Most of the people interviewed will have already completed a portion of their path. They will therefore have less flexibility (and perhaps less idealism) than people just getting started in their careers. The conclusions reached about these interviews will make a fruitful class discussion. Among the issues raised might be these:
   - How familiar were these people with the idea of a career path?
   - How willing were they to talk about themselves?
   - Were many actual "paths" discovered, or did a series of jobs simply come about by luck or "fate"?

A recommended approach to networking is to keep a list of at least 25 people whom you contact at least once a month. The contact can be as extensive as a luncheon meeting or as brief as an email message. The starting point in networking is to obtain an ample supply of business cards. You then give a card to any person you meet who might be able to help you now or in the future. While first developing your network, be inclusive. Sandy Vilas says, "Remember the 3-foot rule—anyone within three feet of you is someone you can network with."[21] Later, as your network develops, you can strive to include a greater number of influential and successful people.

A substantial amount of social networking also takes place on the internet. The number of people potentially in your network is much greater if networking is done over the internet than if it is done locally and in person. The people in internet-based groups can also become valuable business contacts. Cyber-networking includes newsgroups, mailing lists, and chat rooms, as well as email. Newsgroups are part of the internet known as Usenet, which provides an enormous assortment of discussion forums. A good source of mailing lists useful for your purpose is **emailuniverse.com**, which has lists and other information about using email for business and networking. Corporate websites usually have a listing of contact people for a company, and it is possible that some of these people will become part of your network.[22]

Human Relations Skill-Building Exercise 16-2 recommends a systematic approach to networking to help you capitalize on its potential advantages.

Building Your Network

Networking can be regarded as the process of building a team that works with you to achieve success. You can start the following exercise now, but it will probably take your entire career to implement completely. To start networking, or to make your present networking more systematic, take the following steps:

Step 1. Jot down your top three goals or objectives for the coming three months, such as obtaining a new job or promotion, starting a small business, or doing a field research study.

1. ______________________________

____

2. ______________________________

____

3. ______________________________

____

Step 2. List family members, friends, or acquaintances who could assist you in meeting your goals or objectives. Prepare a contact card or database entry for each person on your list, including as many details as you can about the person, the person's family, friends, employers, and contacts.

Step 3. Identify what assistance you will request of your contact or contacts. Be realistic in light of your prior investment in the relationship. Remember, you have to be a friend to have a friend.

Step 4. Identify how you will meet your contact or contacts during the next month. Could it be for lunch, or at an athletic field, nightclub, sports club, recreational facility on campus, or cafeteria? Learn more about your contacts during your face-to-face meetings. In some cases you may have to use the telephone or email instead of an in-person meeting. Look for ways to mutually benefit from the relationship. At the beginning of each week, verify that you have made a small investment in building these relationships.

Step 5. Ask for the help you need. A network must benefit you. Thank the contact for any help given. Jot down in your planner a reminder to follow up with a call, letter, or email message to your contacts. In this way you will have less work to do before you make another request for help.

Step 6. For each person in your network, think of a favour, however small, you can return to him or her. Without reciprocity, a network fades rapidly.

SOURCE: Adapted and expanded from Cheryl Kitter, "Taking the Work out of Networking," Success Workshop, supplement to *The Pryor Report*, March 1998, pp. 1–2.

Achieve Broad Experience

Most people who land high-ranking positions are people of broad experience. Therefore, a widely accepted strategy for advancing in responsibility is to strengthen your credentials by broadening your experience. Workers who follow the new model of career advancement, as illustrated by the horizontal career path, are automatically achieving broad experience. It is best to achieve breadth early in your career because it is easier to transfer when one's compensation is not too high.

A major benefit of broad experience is that you achieve more career portability, allowing you to move to another employer should the need exist. The employability derives from being a more flexible person with a broader perspective. A person, for example, who has worked in both the underwriting (setting rates for risks) and the claims aspects of insurance would generally be well regarded by insurance companies.

Be Visible

A big career booster for many people is to call favourable attention to themselves and their accomplishments. You will recall that to develop the brand called You, a person must be visible to key people. Ways of gaining visibility include performing well on committee assignments, winning a suggestion award, performing well in a company-sponsored athletic event, getting an article published in a trade magazine, getting your name in the firm's newspaper, establishing a personal website that attracts attention, or distinguishing yourself in a community activity. Once you achieve visibility, you have a better chance of being noticed by an important person in the firm.

Find a Mentor

Most successful career people have had one or more mentors during their careers. A **mentor** is a more experienced person who guides, teaches, and coaches another individual. In years past, mentors were almost always higher-ranking people. Today mentors can be peers and even lower-ranking individuals. A lower-ranking individual, for example, can educate you on how other parts of the organization work—something you may need to know to advance.[23] A recent development in mentoring is to find a mentor from the contacts you make on the internet. After the person becomes your mentor, much of the mentoring can take place through email and messaging. (Busier mentors may prefer email because they can respond at their leisure.)

Mentor relationships are an important development process in many occupations. Some of the well-known ones are master–apprentice, physician–intern, teacher–student, and executive–junior executive. An emotional tie exists between the less-experienced person (the protégé) and the mentor. The mentor serves as a positive model and a trusted friend.

A modification and extension of mentoring is developing a **personal board of directors**, or a group of people who meet with you to discuss your career progress and problems you may be facing. Perhaps you would meet over a meal three times a year. A management consultant had this to say about his board of advisers:

> These are people who care about the business and about me personally. We meet once a month, and they beat up on me when I do strange things. None of them is reluctant to point out when I make mistakes, and they do it in a caring way. They have given me great advice. Some has hurt my feelings, but it helps me to reach my standards. They know my pursuit of excellence.[24]

The consultant in question meets once a month with his board of advisers, which is a lot to expect of busy people. However often you meet, some gesture of reciprocity on your part will help sustain the relationship. For example, you might help promote the products or services of your board of advisers.

Manage Luck

Few people do well in their careers without a good break along the way. Lucky events include your company's sudden expansion and therefore its need for people to promote into key jobs; your boss's resignation on short notice, leaving you to take over his or her job; or a boom in your business field, like the one the plastics recycling business is experiencing today.

To be lucky, you first have to clarify what you want. Otherwise, you may not recognize an opportunity when it comes your way. Assume you know that you want to become an officer in your trade association. Consequently, you will seize the opportunity when you hear that the group is looking for a new treasurer.

The strategy is not to simply wait for luck to come your way. In the words of Ray Kroc, founder of McDonald's: "Luck is a dividend of sweat. The more you sweat, the luckier you get."[25] You can manage luck to some extent by recognizing opportunities and taking advantage of them. The unlucky person is often the individual who, out of timidity, lets a good opportunity slip by. A good way of capitalizing on luck is to be ready to take advantage of opportunities when they come along. If you maintain a record of excellent work performance, and you strive to complete your program of studies, you will position yourself to take advantage of opportunities.

Balance Your Life

Balancing your life among the competing demands of work, social life, and personal interests can help you advance your career. As mentioned in several places in this book, having balance gives you additional energy and vitality, which will help you in your career. Without balance, a career person runs the risk of burnout and feeling that work is not worthwhile. Stephen Covey, the popular leadership and family-living guru, offers this perspective:

> Always being the last to leave the office does not make you an indispensable employee. In fact, those who work long hours for extended periods are prone to burnout. The trick is to have your priorities clear, honor your commitments and keep a balance in life.[26]

Dealing with Hidden Barriers to Advancement

Concern exists that many white women and people of colour of both sexes are held back from high-level promotions by a "glass ceiling." A **glass ceiling** is an invisible but difficult-to-penetrate barrier to promotion based on subtle attitudes and prejudices. As of September 1996, women held management positions in one-third of Canadian companies. Positions include owner, co-owner, CEO, chair, or partner. However, women only occupied 17 percent of senior management positions in Canada.[27] More recent statistics suggest that women in Canada and the United States are gaining ground in the area of management, with women in Canada accounting for 42 percent of all managerial jobs. However, male managers are still making more than their female counterparts.[28]

White women, women of colour, and men of colour face few barriers to advancement for one or two promotions. After that point their promotional opportunities are often limited. A study by the Conference Board of Canada found that women in management are still facing harassment and discrimination.[29]

An analysis of several factors contributing to the glass ceiling points to possible solutions to the problem that employers can pursue. A dominant factor is tradition. Men often promote men, and white people often promote white people, because they are familiar with them. Another reason for the glass ceiling is a lack of acceptance of women and minorities in key positions by top-level managers.[30] The acceptance problem depends somewhat on the type of industry. Industries such as financial services, transportation, publishing, and tobacco have women in more than 20 percent of corporate officer positions. In contrast, women in industries such as computers, textiles, and automotive constitute less than five percent of these positions.[31]

One strategy for overcoming the glass ceiling is to have patience. Barriers are lifting gradually in some companies and rapidly at others. As the workforce continues to become more diverse, additional promotional opportunities are open to women and minorities. Within five years from now the glass ceiling may be shattered, particularly as women and minorities gain middle-management experience.

Individuals who have strong evidence that they have been discriminated against can lodge a formal complaint with the company, and then with an outside agency. Filing discrimination charges is more effective if a person is denied a first promotion. It is more difficult to prove discrimination took place when a person is not offered an executive position. The reason is that executives are chosen according to intangible factors such as broad thinking ability and personal appeal.

Another strategy for overcoming these barriers is to enthusiastically apply all the other strategies and tactics found in this chapter. A glass ceiling may exist for most people, but not for every woman and every member of a minority group. An outstanding performer who is also perceived as having superior leadership characteristics, as discussed in Chapter 12, will often break through barriers to advancement.

Summary

Career advancement has witnessed a major shift in emphasis in recent years to accommodate the new organizational structures. This shift has involved less emphasis on vertical mobility and focuses more on lateral growth, or advancing by learning more. The new model also shows more emphasis on temporary leadership assignments, more self-fulfillment, continuous learning, and ability and willingness to learn.

One set of strategies and tactics for getting ahead can be classified as taking control of your own behaviour. Included are the following points:

1. Develop outstanding interpersonal skills.
2. Develop expertise.
3. Perform well on all your assignments.
4. Create good first impressions.
5. Document your accomplishments.
6. Be conventional in your behaviour.
7. Take a creative approach to your job.
8. Keep growing through continuous learning and self-development.
9. Observe proper etiquette.
10. Develop a proactive personality.
11. Take sensible risks.
12. Learn to manage adversity.
13. Develop the brand called *You*.

Another set of strategies and tactics for getting ahead centre on taking control of your environment, or at least adapting it to your advantage. The strategies include the following:

1. Develop a flexible career path.
2. Have an action plan to reach your goals.
3. Practise networking, including cyber-networking.
4. Achieve broad experience.
5. Be visible.
6. Find a mentor.
7. Manage luck.
8. Balance your life.

For some people, another part of managing a career is dealing with hidden barriers to advancement. These barriers take the form of a glass ceiling, an invisible but difficult-to-penetrate barrier to promotion based on subtle attitudes and prejudices. Diligently applying career-advancement strategies and tactics, including outstanding performance, can help overcome these barriers.

Questions and Activities

1. Explain in your own words the new model of career advancement in organizations.
2. What are some of the organizational rewards that a successful person can hope to attain?
3. Why not simply do a good job and forget about all the other strategies and tactics described in this chapter?

4. Some students in computer-related fields are now being recruited out of career schools and colleges to accept full-time employment. Some of the more talented students are even being recruited while in high school for full-time positions after they graduate. What career mistake could most of these students be making by failing to finish school?
5. In the beginning of their careers job seekers often comment that employers are looking for specialists, not generalists. Which career-advancement tactic does this comment support?
6. Describe an incident in which you or somebody you know displayed a proactive personality or was a proactive employee.
7. Identify several jobs for which observing good business etiquette would be particularly important.
8. Use the internet to search for a good career-advancement suggestion. Be prepared to share your findings with the class.
9. Identify several tactics you would be willing to use to become more visible in a large company.
10. Do you think glass ceilings are being broken in Canada? Why or why not?

Internet Skill Builder

The Glass Ceiling?

Some people think the glass ceiling prevents many qualified people from advancing in their careers; some people think the glass ceiling has cracked a little; and still others think it does not really exist. Use the internet to obtain recent information about the impact of the glass ceiling on career advancement. Speculate also about the extent to which the glass ceiling might affect you personally.

Weblinks

www.statcan.ca
A great site for statistics on Canada and the Canadian population.

http://strategis.ic.gc.ca
The site for Strategis Canada is devoted to Canadian business. The site contains information on employment, companies, and small businesses, to name just a few topics. From this site, you can also access the Canadian Management Network.

www.vault.com
A site with career advice.

www.ilo.org/public/english
This is the site for the International Labour Organization.

Human Relations Case Study

I'LL TAKE THAT OLD-TIME ECONOMY

Jeff Pequin, a 37-year-old accountant, worked for a paper company in Vancouver, British Columbia. The father of three, he was barely making enough money to get by, and he drove around in an old family car. He liked many aspects of his job, including a management team that treated its employees fairly. His work was not filled with excitement in the stable environment of the paper industry, but he had enough professional challenges to make the work interesting.

Pequin appreciated the fact that his job gave him enough time to spend with his family. Except when it was time to help prepare quarterly reports, Pequin was able to accomplish his work in about 45 hours per week. He also had enough free time to serve as an officer in the local chapter of the Institute of Management Accountants.

Despite his reasonable overall job satisfaction, a mild feeling of discontent kept running through Pequin's mind. People he read about, and many people he knew personally, were making it big in the New Economy. And he was stuck in the Old Economy.

As he explained to his wife over dinner at a Chinese restaurant one night: "Susie, I think that you, I, and the kids deserve better. Look at some of the Gen-X types who are making six- and seven-figure incomes in those dot-com companies. Look at the cars they drive: $60,000 SUVs, $150,000 sports cars, and exotic European convertibles. I love our old car, but it's approaching 150,000 kilometres."

Susie replied, "So what else about these dot-com types is bugging you?"

As he slowly exhaled, Jeff responded, "Those stock options are out of sight. I heard about a 26-year-old who sold some of the stock she accumulated through options and bought a $600,000 house for *cash*. I'm an accountant, so I should be a good money manager. Instead, we still have 22 years of payments left on our mortgage."

"So, what's really on your mind Jeff?" asked Sue.

"With your blessing, I'm starting a job search tomorrow," answered Jeff.

Starting that night, Jeff began exploring internet job sites and the classified advertisements in the Seattle newspapers. Over the next few days, Jeff also developed a list of employment agencies and executive placement services that specialize in finding talent for information technology–based companies.

Within three weeks, Jeff had four job offers. One position appeared to offer the greatest promise of excitement and wealth. He accepted a position as a controller at Homelectronics.com (a fictional, non-existent company), an e-tailer specializing in consumer electronics. He was offered a 12 percent pay hike over his salary at the paper company, plus stock options. At the time, dot-com companies were in big favour with many investors, and the future held great promise. Jeff had dreams of paying off his mortgage debt, buying a BMW, starting an investment program for the children's college expenses, and taking fabulous family vacations.

The first day on the new job at Homelectronics.com, Jeff was greeted hurriedly by the management team. He was assigned to a cubicle in a large, overcrowded room. As the controller, Jeff had a staff that consisted of one accountant, one bookkeeper, and an assistant shared with 10 other workers. Jeff shrugged off the uncomfortable surroundings as a natural part of being a new e-tailer.

Soon Jeff noticed that most of the company's financial information was in a state of chaos. When he asked the CEO about the problem, the CEO said, "We wouldn't have hired you if we didn't need somebody to clean up the mess. Besides, that's just paperwork. What's really important here is to grow our brand and our business."

As the days and weeks passed, Jeff became increasingly uncomfortable with what he saw at Homelectronics.com. He discovered that the company executives had been altering the financial statements for the bank and fabricating reasons for late payments to vendors. The company was also way behind on payments to advertisers, including other websites that served as links to Homelectronics.com. (The other websites were due commissions for referrals.)

Jeff was also perturbed about the standard operating procedure of charging customers' credit cards before the goods were even in stock—instead of when they were shipped. Several customers complained that they were paying interest on credit cards for home-entertainment centres they had not yet received.

Equally disturbing to Jeff was the fact that Homelectronics.com spent $3 in marketing and administrative costs for every $1 in sales. "They were doing virtual business with virtual money," he said.

Three months into his new job, Jeff realized he had made a mistake. In the pursuit of New Economy riches, he had jumped into a position that was giving him sleepless nights. As he explained to Sue, "The management team at Homelectronics.com is ethically challenged. If I jump ship right now, it might hurt my career. I wish I had never left that good old-time economy. I'm wondering whether to stick around for a while to see what happens, or should I start another job hunt right now?"

Questions

1. What career advice can you offer Jeff Pequin?
2. What should Jeff do about conducting a job search?
3. What career advice can you offer the top-management team at Homelectronics.com?

SOURCE: Some of the facts in this case are derived from Michelle Conlin, "Give Me that Old-Time Economy: Boomerang: Disenchanted dot-com Workers Return to Corporate America," *Business Week*, April 24, 2000, p. 99.

Glossary

Acculturation The process whereby one culture is modified by contact with another culture.

Achievement need The need to accomplish something difficult, to win over others.

Action plan A description of how a person is going to reach a goal.

Active listener A person who listens intensely, with the goal of empathizing with the speaker.

Addiction A compulsion to use substances or engage in activities that lead to psychological dependence and withdrawal symptoms when use is discontinued.

Aggressive Acting in an overbearing, pushy, obnoxious, and sometimes hostile manner.

Alternate dispute resolution A formalized type of mediation, usually involving a hired professional who mediates in a conflict.

Anger A feeling of extreme hostility, indignation, or exasperation.

Artifacts Personal objects that we select to personalize our environments.

Assertive Stating clearly what one wants or how one feels in a given situation without being abusive, abrasive, or obnoxious.

Backstabbing An attempt to discredit by underhanded means such as innuendo, accusation, or the like.

Balance theory An explanation of attraction, stating that people prefer relationships that are consistent or balanced.

Behaviour The tangible acts or decisions of people, including both their actions and words.

Behavioural interview A job interview in which the candidate is asked how he or she handled a particular problem in the past.

Behaviour modification (mod) A system of motivating people that emphasizes rewarding them for doing the right things and punishing them for doing the wrong things.

Beliefs The things that a person holds as true or false.

Bias A prejudgment toward another person or group based on something other than fact.

Blended family A family composed of adult partners and children from current and/or previous marriages.

Body image One's perception of one's body.

Body language Movements and gestures that reflect an individual's mood and feelings at any given moment.

Brainstorming A technique by which group members think of multiple solutions to a problem.

Brainwriting (or **solo brainstorming**) Arriving at creative ideas by jotting them down oneself.

Broken-record technique An assertive skill of calmly repeating one's position over and over again without showing signs of anger or irritation.

Burnout A condition of emotional, mental, and physical exhaustion, along with cynicism, in response to long-term job stressors.

Business etiquette A special code of behaviour required in work settings.

Cannabis A class of drugs, derived from the hemp plant, that generally produce a state of mild euphoria.

Career A series of related job experiences that fit into a meaningful pattern.

Career counsellor A specialist whose professional role is to provide counselling and guidance to individuals about their careers.

Career path A sequence of positions necessary to achieve a goal.

Career portability The ability to move from one employer to another when necessary.

Career success Attaining the twin goals of organizational rewards and personal satisfaction.

Carpal tunnel syndrome A condition that occurs when repetitive flexing and extension of the wrist causes the tendons to swell, thus trapping and pinching the median nerve.

Charisma A type of charm and magnetism that inspires others.

Chronemics How people perceive and use time.

Chronological résumé A job résumé that presents work experience, education, and interests, along with accomplishments, in reverse chronological order.

Co-culture A culture that exists within a larger culture.

Cognitive factors A set of skills, including problem-solving and intellectual skills.

Cognitive restructuring A way of dealing with conflict in which a person mentally converts negative aspects into positive ones by looking for the positive elements in a situation.

Collectivistic cultures Cultures that emphasize the importance of the group rather than individuals. People see themselves as members of a group rather than as separate individuals.

Communication The sending and receiving of messages.

Communication (information) overload A condition in which the individual is confronted with so much information to process that he or she becomes overwhelmed and therefore does a poor job of processing information.

Competence As part of wellness, the presence of both job skills and social skills, including the ability to solve problems and control anger.

Compulsiveness A tendency to pay careful attention to detail and to be neat.

Computer-mediated communication (CMC) Communication between people using the medium of computers.

Conflict A condition that exists when two sets of demands, goals, or motives are incompatible.

Confrontation and problem solving A method of identifying the true source of conflict and resolving it systematically.

Core competency With respect to a person, whatever he or she does best.

Creative-style résumé A job résumé with a novel format and design.

Creativity The ability to develop good ideas that can be put into practice.

Cultural sensitivity An awareness of and a willingness to investigate the reasons people of another culture act as they do.

Cultural training A set of learning experiences designed to help employees understand the customs, traditions, and beliefs of another culture.

Cultural values A set of central and enduring goals in life and ways of life that are important to a specific culture.

Culture A learned and shared system of knowledge, beliefs, values, attitudes, and norms.

Database A systematic way of storing files for future retrieval.

Decision making Selecting one alternative from the various solutions or courses of action that can be pursued.

Decision-making software Any computer program that helps the decision maker work through the problem-solving and decision-making steps.

Decoding The process whereby the receiver interprets the message and translates it into meaningful information.

Defensive communication The tendency to receive messages in such a way that our self-esteem is protected.

Denial The suppression of information that a person finds uncomfortable.

Depressant A drug that slows down vital body processes.

Depression A widespread emotional disorder in which the person has such difficulties as sadness, changes in appetite, sleeping difficulties, and a decrease in activities, interests, and energy.

Developmental opportunity A positive way of identifying a person's area of weakness (or need for improvement).

Differentiation of self Emotional security in which one is not desperate for signals of approval and affection from others.

Disarm the opposition A method of conflict resolution in which a person disarms the criticizer by agreeing with valid criticism directed at himself or herself.

Discrimination Unjustifiable negative behaviour directed towards members of a group.

Diversity awareness training A program that provides an opportunity for employees to develop the skills necessary to deal effectively with each other and with customers in a diverse environment.

Dopamine A neurotransmitter that is associated with pleasure and elation. (A *neurotransmitter* is a molecule that transports messages from one neuron in the brain to another across a synapse.)

Downshifter A worker who chooses shorter hours and less-demanding work to allow more time for other activities.

Downsizing (or **rightsizing**) A method of reducing the number of employees to save money and improve efficiency.

Effectiveness In relation to leadership, a situation in which the leader helps the group accomplish its objectives without neglecting satisfaction and morale.

Effectiveness ethic A focus on the need for excellent work and doing work the best way.

Emotional intelligence A cluster of traits related to the emotional side of life, including regulating emotions, controlling impulses, recognizing how others feel, and interpersonal communication skill.

Emotional labour The process of regulating both feelings and expressions to meet organizational goals.

Empathy Understanding another person's point of view, or placing oneself in another's shoes.

Encoding The process of organizing ideas into a series of symbols, such as words and gestures, designed to communicate with the receiver.

Enculturation The process whereby culture is transmitted from one generation to another.

Ethics A code of conduct that separates morally right actions from those that are wrong; also a study of moral obligation.

Ethnocentrism A belief or conviction that the way that one's own culture does things is superior to another culture's ways.

Expectancy theory of motivation An explanation of motivation stating that people will be motivated if they believe that their effort will lead to desired outcomes.

External locus of control A belief that external forces control one's fate.

Fear of success The belief that if one succeeds at an important task, one will be asked to take on more responsibility in the future.

Feedback Information that tells one how well one has performed and helps one make corrections where indicated.

Feeling-type individuals People who have a need to conform and who attempt to adapt to the wishes of others.

Fight-or-flight response The body's battle against a stressor that helps one deal with emergencies.

Flatlining Reducing middle management.

Flow experience Total absorption in one's work.

Forced-association technique The process of individuals or groups solving a problem by making associations between the properties of two objects.

Frustration A blocking of need or motive satisfaction, or a blocking of a need, wish, or desire.

Functional résumé A job résumé that organizes one's skills and accomplishments into the functions or tasks that support the job one is seeking.

Galatea effect Improving one's performance through raising one's own expectations.

Glass ceiling An invisible but difficult-to-penetrate barrier to promotion based on subtle attitudes and prejudices.

Goal An event, circumstance, object, condition, or purpose for which a person strives. Also, a conscious intention to do something.

Grazing Popular term for eating meals on the run to make use of time ordinarily spent sitting down for meals.

Group Two or more people who are aware of each other, influence each other, have a relationship, share common goals, and who view themselves as belonging to the group.

Group norms The unwritten set of expectations for group members—what people ought to do.

Groupthink The situation that occurs when group members strive so hard to get along that they fail to critically evaluate each other's ideas.

Grudge Unresolved or unrepressed anger felt toward someone who we believe has wronged us.

Hallucinogens A class of drugs that in small doses produce visual effects similar to hallucinations.

Hidden agenda Personal goals that are not shared with the group, which may interfere with team performance.

Human relations The art of using systematic knowledge about human behaviour to improve personal, job, and career effectiveness.

Information (or **communication**) **overload** A condition in which the individual is confronted with so much information to process that he or she becomes overwhelmed and therefore processes it poorly.

Insight A depth of understanding that requires considerable intuition and common sense.

Interference Noise in the communication process that distorts or blocks a message and leads to misinterpretation by the receiver.

Internal locus of control A belief that one is the primary cause of events happening to oneself.

Internet addiction (dependence) A condition whereby a person spends so much time on the internet that work and personal life often suffer, usually through neglect.

Interpersonal Anything relating to the interactions between and among people.

Intrinsic motivation The natural tendency to seek out novelty and challenges, to extend one's capacities, to explore, and to learn.

Intuition A method of arriving at a conclusion by a quick judgment or "gut feel."

Intuitive-type individuals People who prefer an overall perspective, or the big picture.

Job objective The position one is applying for now or a job one intends to hold in the future.

Job shadowing A way of gaining information about an occupation by spending a few hours with a professional in the workplace and observing first-hand what the job entails.

Lateral move Transferring to a job at the same level and approximate salary as the present one.

Lateral thinking Thought process whereby an individual seeks out many alternative solutions to a problem. Lateral thinking is creative and broad-based, as opposed to *vertical thinking,* which zeroes in on a single best solution.

Leadership The process of influencing others to achieve certain goals.

Leading task An easy warm-up activity that helps one get started on a project that one might otherwise procrastinate in doing.

Life-change units A scale of values assigned to the impact caused by certain life events, representing the average amount of social readjustment considered necessary to cope with a given change, such as the death of a spouse. The higher the number of life-change units, the greater the stress.

Lifestyle A person's typical approach to living, including moral attitudes, clothing preferences, and ways of spending money.

Maslow's need hierarchy A widely accepted theory of motivation emphasizing that people strive to fulfill needs. These needs are arranged in a hierarchy of importance: physiological, safety, belongingness, esteem, and self-actualization. People tend to strive for need satisfaction at one level only after satisfaction has been achieved at the previous one.

Mediation A type of conflict resolution whereby the two parties appeal to a third party to assist in arriving at a solution to the conflict.

Mediator A person who has received special training in order to assist two conflicting parties to arrive at a resolution that satisfies the needs of each party.

Mentors Bosses who take subordinates under their wings and guide, teach, and coach them.

Metacommunicate To communicate about the actual style of communicating or about how one is communicating. Often metacommunication involves clarifying the nonverbal elements of a message.

Micromanagement The close monitoring of most aspects of group members' activities by the manager.

Mirroring A form of nonverbal communication in which one person subtly imitates another, such as following the other person's breathing pattern.

Mixed signals Different messages to different audiences about the same topic.

Motive An inner drive that moves a person to do something.

Multicultural worker One who can work effectively with people of different cultures.

Narcotic A drug that dulls the senses, facilitates sleep, and becomes addictive with long-term use.

Need An internal striving or urge to do something. (Or a deficit within an individual that creates a craving for its satisfaction.)

Need for intimacy An explanation of love centring on the idea that people crave intimacy.

Negative affectivity A tendency to experience aversive (intensely disliked) emotional states.

Negative inquiry The active encouragement of criticism in order to use helpful information or exhaust manipulative criticism.

Negotiation and bargaining Conferring with another person to resolve a problem.

Networking The process of establishing a group of contacts who can help a person in his or her career.

Neurobiological disorders A quirk in the chemistry or anatomy of the brain that creates a disability.

Noise An unwanted interference that can distort or block a message.

Nonassertive Exhibiting a passive type of behaviour in which people let things happen to them without letting their feelings be known.

Nonpossessive relationship A relationship in which both people maintain separate identities and strive for personal fulfillment.

Nonverbal communication Sending messages other than by direct use of words, such as in writing and speaking with gestures.

Nonverbal feedback The signs other than words that indicate whether or not the sender's message has been delivered.

Norms A set of rules (usually unwritten) that set out guidelines for behaviour in a group setting.

Openness to experience A positive orientation toward learning.

Opiate A drug that dulls the senses, facilitates sleep, and is addictive with long-term use.

Organizational citizenship behaviour The willingness to work for the good of the organization, even without the promise of a specific reward.

Organizational culture The values and beliefs held by members of an organization.

Paradigm A model, framework, viewpoint, or perspective.

Paralanguage Vocal cues beyond the meaning of spoken words, including voice volume, tone, pitch, and intensity.

Paraphrase In listening, to repeat in one's own words what the sender says, feels, and means.

Participative leader A person in charge who shares power and decision making with the group.

Partnership In leadership, when the leader and group members are connected in such a way that the power between them is approximately balanced.

Peak performance The mental state necessary for achieving maximum results from minimum effort.

Peer evaluations A system in which co-workers contribute to an evaluation of a person's job performance.

Perfectionism A pattern of behaviour in which the individual strives to accomplish almost unattainable standards of flawless work.

Performance standard A statement of what constitutes acceptable performance.

Personal board of directors A group of people who meet with a person to discuss his or her career progress and problems faced.

Personality clash An antagonistic relationship between two people based on differences in personal attributes, preferences, interests, values, or styles.

Planning Deciding what needs to be accomplished and the actions needed to make it happen.

Political skills An interpersonal style that combines awareness of others with the ability to communicate well.

Portfolio career A career in which people use a variety of skills to earn money in several different ways.

Positive mental attitude A strong belief that things will work in one's favour.

Positive reinforcement Rewarding somebody for doing something right.

Positive self-talk Saying positive things about oneself to oneself to build self-confidence.

Positive visual imagery Picturing a positive outcome in one's mind.

Prejudice An unjustifiable negative attitude toward a group and its members.

Private self The actual person that one is.

Proactive personality A trait that leaves a person less constrained than others by forces in the situation, and that motivates him or her to bring about environmental change.

Problem A gap between what exists and what one wants to exist.

Procrastination Putting off a task for no valid reason.

Productivity The amount of quality work accomplished in relation to the resources consumed.

Proxemics The study of personal space.

Psychological hardiness Describes an individual who tends to profit from stressful situations instead of developing negative symptoms.

Psychotherapy A method of overcoming emotional problems through discussion with a mental health professional.

Public self What the person is communicating about himself or herself, and what others actually perceive about the person.

Pygmalion effect The mysterious phenomenon that occurs when group members succeed because their leader expects them to (i.e., a group tends to live up to the leader's expectations).

Quest fatigue The demoralization and disappointment that takes place when all one's efforts at finding a date or a mate fail.

Realistic goal One that represents the right amount of challenge for the person pursuing the goal.

Reflected appraisal Your view of yourself, based on the assessment of others.

Relaxation response A bodily reaction in which the person experiences a slower respiration and heart rate, lowered blood pressure, and lowered metabolism.

Resilience The ability to withstand pressure and emerge stronger for it.

Role ambiguity A condition in which a job holder receives confusing or poorly defined expectations.

Role conflict The state that occurs when a person has to choose between two competing demands or expectations.

Role confusion Uncertainty about the role one is carrying out. For example, socializing with one's boss may create fuzzy demarcation lines at work.

Role overload A burdensome work load that can lead to stress.

Role underload Having too little to do. Can sometimes create stress similar to that of role overload.

Seasonal affective disorder (SAD) A form of depression that develops during the fall and winter months and disappears as the days lengthen in the spring.

Self A person's total being or individuality.

Self-concept What one thinks of oneself; the person that one thinks one is.

Self-defeating behaviour A behaviour pattern in which the person intentionally or unintentionally engages in activities or harbours attitudes that work against his or her best interests.

Self-determining work Work that allows the person performing the task some choice in initiating and regulating his or her own actions.

Self-discipline The ability to work systematically and progressively toward a goal until it is achieved.

Self-disclosure The process of revealing one's inner self to others.

Self-efficacy The belief in one's capability to perform a task.

Self-esteem The sense of feeling worthwhile and the pride that comes from a sense of self-worth.

Self-respect How one thinks and feels about oneself.

Self-understanding Knowledge about oneself, particularly with respect to mental and emotional aspects.

Sensation-type individuals People who prefer routine and order.

Sensitivity Taking people's needs and feelings into account when dealing with them.

Servant leader A type of leader who serves group members by working on their behalf to help them achieve their goals, not the leader's goals.

Sexual harassment Behaviour of a sexual nature in the workplace that is offensive to an individual and that interferes with that person's ability to perform the job.

Shyness A feeling of discomfort, anxiety, or inhibition in social settings that ranges from mild to extreme.

Skill A learned, specific ability to perform a task competently (for example, writing a report, conducting a statistical analysis, or troubleshooting software problems).

Skill-benefit statement A brief explanation of how an individual's skills can benefit the company.

Social comparison Comparing ourselves to others around us, and obtaining information as to how similar or dissimilar we are to them.

Social exchange theory The idea that human relationships are based mainly on self- interest; therefore, people measure their social, physical, and other assets against a potential partner's.

Social loafing Individual efforts that are reduced by membership in a group or team.

Social phobia An extreme type of shyness that interferes with social relations.

Sponsor A higher-ranking individual who is favourably impressed with a person and therefore recommends him or her for promotion and choice assignments.

Stereotypes Separate and distinct categories for people based on broad generalizations and assumptions.

Stimulants A class of drugs that produce feelings of optimism and high energy.

Stress An internal reaction to any force that threatens to disturb a person's equilibrium.

Stress interview A deliberate method of placing a job applicant under considerable pressure and then observing his or her reactions.

Stressor The external or internal force that brings about the stress.

Strong Interest Inventory (SII) The most widely used instrument for matching a person's interests with careers.

Style A person's characteristic way of doing things.

Substance abuse The overuse of any substance that enters the bloodstream.

Substance dependence A compulsion to use substances or engage in activities that lead to psychological dependence, and to withdrawal symptoms when use is discontinued.

Success Used in this book to mean attaining the twin goals of organizational rewards and personal satisfaction.

Success syndrome A pattern in which the worker performs one assignment well and then has the confidence to take on even more difficult assignments.

Summarization The process of clarifying and condensing what a speaker has said in order to demonstrate understanding of the speaker's message.

Support system A group of people a person can rely on for encouragement and comfort.

Swim against the tide To advance one's career by taking an unconventional path to career success.

Synergy Energy that results from the combined efforts and contributions of individual team members.

Targeted résumé A job résumé that focuses on a specific job target or position and presents only information that supports the target.

Team A diverse group of people who share leadership responsibility for creating a group identity and an interconnected effort to achieve goals.

Team leader A person who facilitates and guides the efforts of a small group that is given some authority to govern itself.

Team player A person who emphasizes group accomplishment and cooperation rather than individual achievement and self-interest.

Technical competence In leadership, being skilled in the actual work of the group.

Technostress A stress reaction caused by an inability to cope with computer technologies in a constructive manner.

Telesearch A job search in which job leads are obtained through unsolicited phone calls to prospective employers.

Teleworking (telecommuting) A work arrangement in which employees work at a location outside the workplace, usually at home, full time or part time, and send output electronically to a central office.

Theory of reasoned action One theory that discusses the link between attitudes and behaviour.

Thinking-type individuals People who rely on reason and intellect to deal with problems.

Tolerance Awareness that cultural differences do exist, and the ability to cope with them through understanding and empathy.

Total Quality Management (TQM) A system of management in which all activities are directed toward satisfying external and internal customers.

Traditional mental set A fixed way of thinking about objects and activities.

Type A behaviour A pattern of being aggressively involved in a chronic, incessant struggle to achieve more in less time.

Unsolicited-letter campaign A job search method in which the job seeker sends letters to prospective employers without knowing if a job opening exists.

Value(s) A set of central and enduring goals in life and ways of living that a person feels are important, right, and true.

VDT stress An adverse physical and psychological reaction to prolonged work at a video display terminal.

Vertical thinking An analytical, logical thought process whereby an individual is seeking a single best solution to a problem. Narrower than *lateral thinking* because it results in fewer solutions.

Visualization As a stress-management technique, picturing oneself doing something one would like to do. In general, a method of imagining oneself behaving in a particular way in order to achieve that behaviour.

Wellness A formalized approach to preventive health care.

Win–win The belief that, after conflict has been resolved, both sides should gain something of value.

Workaholism An addiction to work in which not working is an uncomfortable experience.

Work ethic A firm belief in the dignity and value of work.

Work–family conflict A situation that occurs when the individual has to perform multiple roles: worker, spouse or partner, and often parent.

Work habits A person's characteristic approach to work, including such things as organization, handling of paperwork, and the setting of priorities.

Worst-case scenario The most dreadful result possible in a decision-making situation.

References

Chapter One

1. Timothy A. Judge and Shinichiro Watanabe, "Another Look at the Job Satisfaction–Life Satisfaction Relationship," *Journal of Applied Psychology*, December 1993, pp. 939–48.

2. An early study on this now well-accepted finding is E. Palmore, "Predicting Longevity: A Follow-up Controlling for Age," *The Gerontologist*, Winter 1969, pp. 247–50.

3. Leslie Fraught, "At Eddie Bauer You Can Work and Have a Life," *Workforce*, April 1997, p. 8.

4. Human Resources Development Canada, *Report of the Advisory Group on Working Time and the Distribution of Work* (Ottawa: 1994).

5. Dr. Linda Duxbury and Dr. Chris Higgins, *The 2001 National Work-Life Conflict Study: Report One*, Health Canada, published March 2002.

6. Human Resources Development Canada.

7. Dr. Linda Duxbury and Dr. Chris Higgins, *The 2001 National Work–Life Conflict Study: Report One*, Health Canada, March 2002.

8, 9. C.R. Snyder, "So Many Selves," *Contemporary Psychology*, January 1988, p. 77.

10. John Hattie, *Self-Concept* (Hillsdale, NJ: Erlbaum, 1992).

11. Marilyn E. Gist, "Self-Efficacy: Implications for Organizational Behaviour and Human Resource Management," *Academy of Management Review*, July 1987, pp. 472–85.

12. Thomas F. Cash, Barbara A. Winstead, and Louis H. Janda, "Your Body, Yourself," *Psychology Today*, July 1985, pp. 22–26.

13. Cited in Scott Sleek, "People Craft Their Self Image from Groups," *The APA Monitor*, November 1993, p. 22.

14. California State Department of Education, *Toward a State of Esteem*, Sacramento Department of Education, January 1990, p. 19.

15. Cited in Wayne Weiten and Margaret Lloyd, *Psychology Applied to Modern Life* (Pacific Grove, CA: Brooks/Cole Publishing, 1994), p. 51.

16. Randall Edwards, "Is Self-Esteem Really All That Important?," *The APA Monitor*, May 1995, p. 43.

17. Jon L. Pierce, Donald G. Gardner, Larry L. Cummings, and Randall B. Dunham, "Organization-Based Self-Esteem: Construct Definition, Measurement, and Validation," *Academy of Management Journal*, September 1989, p. 623.

18. Pierce, Gardner, Cummings, and Dunham, "Organization-Based Self-Esteem."

19. Lila L. Prigge and Charles M. Ray, "Social and Personality Development," in *The Hidden Curriculum* (*National Business Education Yearbook, No. 30*), 1992, p. 145.

20. Pierce, Gardner, Cummings, and Dunham, "Organization-Based Self-Esteem," p. 623.

21. Research mentioned in book review by E.R. Snyder in *Contemporary Psychology*, July 1998, p. 482.

22. Mona Charen, "'Teaching' Self-Esteem a Costly Failure," syndicated column, May 16, 1994.

23. Daniel L. Araoz, "The Manager's Self-Concept," *Human Resources Forum*, July 1989, p. 4.

24. "Self-Esteem: You'll Need It to Succeed," *Executive Strategies*, September 1993, p. 12.

25, 26. Roy F. Baumeister, *Escaping the Self: Alcoholism, Spirituality, Masochism, and Other Flights from the Burden of Selfhood* (New York: Basic Books, 1991).

Chapter Two

1. Phil Ebersole, "Our Work Ethic: Many Companies Thrive Despite What Polls Say," *Rochester Democrat and Chronicle,* March 10, 1997, p. 6 of *Monday Business.* Updated with telephone interview August 15, 2000.

2. Robert A. Baron, Bruce Earhard, and Marcia Ozier, *Psychology: Canadian Edition* (Scarborough, ON: Allyn and Bacon Canada, 1995).

3. David C. McClelland, *The Achieving Society* (New York: Van Nostrand Reinhold, 1961).

4. David C. McClelland and Richard Boyatzis, "Leadership Motive Pattern and Long-Term Success in Management," *Journal of Applied Psychology*, December 1982, p. 737.

5. Some of the research on risk taking and thrill seeking is reviewed in Karl Taro Greenfield, "Life on the Edge," *Time,* September 6, 1999, pp. 28–36.

6. Scott Hays, "Generation X and the Art of Reward," *Workforce,* November 1999, pp. 44–48.

7. The original statement of this famous explanation of human motivation is from Abraham H. Maslow, "A Theory of Human Motivation," *Psychological Review*, July 1943, pp. 370–96. See also Maslow, *Motivation and Personality* (New York: Harper & Row, 1954).

8. "Getting There: 1983 Success Magazine Goal-Setting Guide," *Success!*, January 1983, p. A10.

9. Patrick M. Wright, "Operationalization of Goal Difficulty as a Moderator of the Goal Difficulty–Performance Relationship," *Journal of Applied Psychology*, June 1990, p. 227.

10. P. Christopher Earley and Terri R. Lituchy, "Delineating Goals and Efficacy Effects: A Test of Three Models," *Journal of Applied Psychology*, February 1991, pp. 81–82.

11. Ian R. Gellatly and John P. Meyer, "The Effects of Goal Difficulty on Physiological Arousal, Cognition, and Task Performance," *Journal of Applied Psychology*, October 1992, p. 695.

12. Don VandeWalle and Larry L. Cummings, "A Test of the Influence of Goal Orientation on the Feedback-Seeking Process," *Journal of Applied Psychology*, June 1997, pp. 390–400.

13. Don VandeWalle, Steven P. Brown, William L. Cron, and John W. Slocum Jr., "The Influence of Goal Orientation and Self-Regulation Tactics on Sales Performance: A Longitudinal Field Test," *Journal of Applied Psychology,* April 1999, pp. 249–59.

14. "Employee Motivation: Set Them on Fire Without Burning Them Out," *Executive Edge,* August 1996, p. 10.

15. "Write Your Way to Goals," *Working Smart,* January 1999, p. 2.

16. William B. Werther Jr., "Workshops Aid in Goal Setting," *Personnel Journal,* November 1989, p. 34.

17. Stephen Sprinkel, "Not Having Fantasies Can Be Hazardous to Your Health, Counselor Says," *Gannett News Service*, April 10, 1982.

18. VandeWalle and Cummings, "A Test of the Influence of Goal Orientation," p. 392.

19. P. Christopher Earley, Terry Connolly, and Goran Ekegran, "Goals, Strategy Development, and Task Performance: Some Limits to the Efficacy of Goal Setting," *Journal of Applied Psychology*, February 1989, p. 24.

20. Edward L. Deci, James P. Connell, and Richard M. Ryan, "Self-Determination in a Work Organization," *Journal of Applied Psychology*, August 1989, p. 580.

21. Earley and Lituchy, "Delineating Goals and Efficacy Effects," p. 96.

22. Dov Eden and Joseph Kinnar, "Modeling Galatea: Boosting Self-Efficacy to Increase Volunteering," *Journal of Applied Psychology*, December 1991, pp. 770–80.

23. Bill Palmroth, "Aspire to Self-Organization," *The American Salesman*, 44(8), August 1999, pp. 26–30; Sherill Tapsell, "How Do I Know They're Working?," *Management*, 46(8), July 1999.

24. Tapsell, "How Do I Know They're Working?"

Chapter Three

1. *Employability Skills 2000+,* brochure (Ottawa: The Conference Board of Canada, 2000).

2. Daniel Goleman, *Working with Emotional Intelligence* (New York: Bantam, 1998).

3. Roger Frantz, "Intuition at Work," *Innovative Leader*, April 1997, p. 4.

4. Quoted in Bill Breen, "What's Your Intuition?," *Fast Company,* September 2000, p. 300.

5. Lisa A. Burke and Monica K. Miller, "Taking the Mystery out of Intuitive Decision Making," *Academy of Management Executive,* November 1999, p. 94.

6. "When to Go with Your Intuition," *Working Smart*, May 27, 1991, pp. 1–2.

7. Joanne Cole, "The Problem with Being Perfect," *Getting Results*, July 1997, p. 1.

8. John S. Hammond, Ralph L. Keeney, and Howard Rafia, "The Hidden Traps in Decision Making," *Harvard Business Review,* September–October 1998, p. 50.

9. The Myers-Briggs Type Indicator (MBTI) is published by Consulting Psychological Press, Inc., Palo Alto, CA 94306; David A. Whetton and Kim S. Cameron, *Developing Management Skills*, 2nd ed. (New York: HarperCollins, 1991), p. 66.

10. Adapted from John R. Schermerhorn, Jr., James G. Hunt, and Richard N. Osborn, *Managing Organizational Behavior*, 5th ed. (New York: John Wiley & Sons, 1994), p. 119.

11. Paul C. Nutt, "Surprising but True: Half the Decisions in Organizations Fail," *Academy of Management Executive,* November 1999, pp. 75–90.

12. "More on Problem Solving," *Personal Report for the Executive*, December 1, 1987, p. 4.

13. "Decision-Making Flaws," *Personal Report for the Executive*, February 15, 1988, pp. 5–6.

14. Cited in "Team Talent: Bringing Creativity on Board," *Supervisory Management,* April 1995, p. 7.

15. "Good Idea: Take Time to Think," Rochester, NY, *Democrat and Chronicle,* August 7, 2000, p. 8F.

16. Reprinted and updated with permission from Eugene Raudsepp with George P. Hough, Jr., *Creative Growth Games* (New York: Harcourt Brace Jovanovich, 1977).

17. Richard W. Woodman, John E. Sawyer, and Ricky W. Griffin, "Toward a Theory of Organizational Creativity," *The Academy of Management Review,* April 1993, pp. 293–321; Robert R. Godfrey, "Tapping Employee's Creativity," *Supervisory Management,* February 1986, pp. 17–18; Greg R. Oldham and Anne Cummings, "Employee Creativity: Personal and Contextual Factors at Work," *Academy of Management Journal,* June 1996, pp. 607–34; Mihaly Csikzentmihalyi, "If We Are So Rich, Why Aren't We Happy?," *American Psychologist,* October 1999, p. 824.

18. "Why Kids Beat Adults at Video Games: Two Types of Intelligence," *USA Weekend,* January 1–3, 1999, p. 5.

19. Teresa M. Amabile, "How to Kill Creativity," *Harvard Business Review,* September–October 1998, pp. 78–79.

20. Research cited in "What Happens in the Brain of an Einstein in the Throes of Creation?," *USA Weekend,* January 1–3, 1999, p. 11.

21. "Cows Now Count Sheep on Comfy Mattresses," Knight-Ridder, May 11, 1997.

22. Jerry Hirschberg, *The Creative Priority: Driving Innovative Business in the Real World* (New York: HarperBusiness, 1998).

23. Cited in Robert McGarvey, "Turn It On," *Entrepreneur*, November 1996, pp. 156–57.

24. Frederick D. Buggie, "Overcoming Barriers to Creativity," *Innovative Leader*, May 1997, p. 5.

25. R. Brente Gallupe et al., "Electronic Brainstorming and Group Size," *Academy of Management Journal*, June 1992, pp. 350–69.

26. "The Two-Person Technique," *The Pryor Report*, July 1992, p. 1; Michael LeBoeuf, *Imagineering: How to Profit from Your Creative Powers* (New York: Berkeley Books, 1985).

27. Quoted in Mark Hendricks, "Good Thinking: Knock Down the Barriers to Creativity—and Discover a Whole World of New Ideas," *Entrepreneur*, May 1996, p. 158.

28. "Be a Creative Problem Solver," *Executive Strategies*, June 6, 1989, pp. 1–2.

Chapter Four

1. Roger M. Mason, "Taking Health Care to Factory Floor Proves Smart Move for Growing Ontario Company," *Canadian Medical Association Journal*, 157(10), November 1997, pp. 1423–25.

2. Terry O'Neill, "Crunch Time for Families," *Citizen Centre Report,* 30(4), February 17, 2003, pp. 36–41.

3. Steve M. Jex, Terry A. Beehr, and Cathlyn K. Roberts, "The Meaning of Occupational Stress Items to Survey Respondents," *Journal of Applied Psychology*, October 1992, p. 623.

4. Dot Yandle, "Staying Well May Be up to You," *Success Workshop Folio* (a supplement to The Pryor Report Management Newsletter), February 1994, pp. 2–3.

5. Cary L. Cooper and Roy Pane (eds.), *Personality and Stress: Individual Differences in the Stress Process* (New York: John Wiley & Sons, 1991).

6. Statistics Canada, *Exercise Frequency, 1996–1997*, Catalogue No. 82F007XCB.

7. Statistics Canada, "How Healthy Are Canadians? 2001 Annual Report," *Health Reports*, Vol. 12(3), Catalogue No. 82-003-XIE.

8. Philip L. Rice, *Stress and Health: Principles and Practice for Coping and Wellness* (Monterey, CA: Brooks/Cole Publishing Company, 1987), pp. 353–54.

9. Jay Kimiecik, "Learn to Love Exercise," *Psychology Today,* January/February 2000, p. 20.

10. Stephenie Overman, "Rise and Sigh," *HR Magazine,* May 1999, p. 68.

11. Research cited in Overman, "Rise and Sigh," p. 70.

12. Canada's Food Guide to Healthy Eating, *Agriculture and Agri-Food Canada*, 1994.

13. W. Gifford Jones, MD, "The Doctor Game," *Peterborough Examiner*, January 9, 1997.

14. Susan McCullough, "Take the Bite out of the Lunch Crunch," *HR Magazine,* August 1998, pp. 55–62.

15. Statistics Canada, "How Healthy Are Canadians?"

16, 17. Emory L. Cowen, "In Pursuit of Wellness," *American Psychologist*, April 1991, p. 406.

18. Daniel Goleman, "Leadership That Gets Results," *Harvard Business Review,* March–April 2000, p. 80.

19. Research summarized in "Study: Sexes React Differently to Stress," *The Washington Post,* May 19, 2000. (Study published by Shelley Taylor, *Psychological Review,* 2000.)

20. Jeffrey R. Edwards, "A Cybernetic Theory of Stress, Coping, and Well-Being in Organizations," *Academy of Management Review,* April 1992, p. 248.

21. Research cited in "Mental Stress Is Linked to Blocked Blood Vessels," *APA Monitor,* February 1998, p. 7.

22. R. Douglas Allen, Michael A. Hitt, and Charles R. Greer, "Occupational Stress and Perceived Organizational Effectiveness: An Examination of Stress Level and Stress Type," *Personnel Psychology*, Summer 1982, pp. 359–70.

23. Raymond T. Lee and Blake E. Ashforth, "A Meta-Analytic Examination of the Correlates of Three Dimensions of Job Burnout," *Journal of Applied Psychology*, April 1996, p. 123.

24. Lee and Ashforth, "A Meta-Analytic Examination"; Joanne Cole, "An Ounce of Prevention Beats Burnout," *HRfocus,* June 1999, pp. 1, 14–15.

25. Patricia Chisholm, "Coping with Stress," *Maclean's*, January 8, 1996, p. 33.

26. Rabi S. Bhagat, "Effects of Stressful Life Events on Individual Performance and Work Adjustment Processes within Organizational Settings: A Research Model," *Academy of Management Review*, October 1983, pp. 660–71.

27. "Building Self-Esteem," **www.ashland.com/education/self-esteem/best_shot.html**.

28. Michael E. Cavanagh, "What You Don't Know about Stress," *Personnel Journal*, July 1988, p. 55.

29. Robert Oswalt and Kelly Silberg, "Self-Perceived Stress in College: A Survey," *Psychological Reports*, December 1995, p. 985.

30. T.M. Dembrowski and P.T. Costa, Jr., "Coronary-Prone Behavior: Components of the Type A Pattern and Hostility," *Journal of Personality*, 55, 1987, pp. 211–35; Ray H. Rosenman, *Type A Behavior and Your Heart* (New York: Fawcett, 1975).

31. Peter Y. Chen and Paul E. Spector, "Negative Affectivity as the Underlying Cause of Correlations between Stressors and Strains," *Journal of Applied Psychology*, June 1991, p. 398.

32. Paul E. Spector, Peter Y. Chen, and Brian J. O'Connell, "A Longitudinal Study of Relations between Job Stressors and

Job Strains While Controlling for Prior Negative Affectivity and Strains," *Journal of Applied Psychology,* April 2000, p. 216.

33, 34. Marilyn L. Fox, Deborah J. Dwyer, and Daniel C. Ganster, "Effects of Stressful Job Demands and Control on Physiological and Attitudinal Outcomes in a Hospital Setting," *Academy of Management Journal*, April 1993, pp. 290–91.

35. John Schaubroeck and Deryl E. Merritt, "Divergent Effects of Job Control on Coping with Work Stressors: The Key Role of Self-Efficacy," *Academy of Management Journal,* June 1997, pp. 738–54.

36. Terry O'Neill, "Crunch Time for Families," *Citizen Centre Report*, 30(4) February 17, 2003.

37. Craig Bond, *Technostress: The Human Cost of the Computer Revolution* (Reading, MA: Addison Wesley, 1984), p. 16.

38. James D. Brodzinski, Robert P. Scherer, and Karen A. Goyer, "Workplace Stress: A Study of the Internal and External Pressures Placed on Employees," *Personnel Administrator*, July 1989, pp. 77–78.

39. Alicia A. Grandey, "Emotion Regulation in the Workplace: A New Way to Conceptualize Emotional Labor," *Journal of Occupational Health Psychology,* Vol. 5, No. 1, 2000, pp. 95–110.

40. Michele Conlin, "Is Your Office Killing You? Sick Buildings Are Seething with Molds, Monoxide—and Worse," *Business Week,* June 5, 2000, pp. 114–28.

41. "Making Stress Work for You," *Executive Strategies*, October 3, 1989, p. 5.

42. Philip Morgan and H. Kent Baker, "Building a Professional Image: Dealing with Job Stress," *Supervisory Management*, September 1985, p. 38.

43. John Roger and Peter McWilliams, *Wealth 101: Getting What You Want—Enjoying What You've Got* (Los Angeles: Prelude Press, 1993).

44. "Canadian Workers among Most Stressed," *Worklife* (14)2, 2002.

45. Herbert Benson (with William Proctor), *Beyond the Relaxation Response* (New York: Berkley Books, 1995), pp. 96–97.

46. Sue McDonald, "Take a Deep Breath," *The Cincinnati Enquirer*, October 24, 1995, p. D3.

47. Quoted in "Forget about Eliminating Stress; Learn to Live with It Instead," Knight-Ridder story, October 5, 1999.

Chapter Five

1. John Wareham, *Wareham's Way: Escaping the Judas Trap* (New York: Atheneum, 1983), p. 107.

2. Thomas A. Widiger and Allen J. Frances, "Controversies Concerning the Self-Defeating Personality Disorder," in Rebecca C. Curtis, ed., *Self-Defeating Behaviors* (New York: Plenum Press, 1989), p. 304.

3. Seth Allcorn, "The Self-Protective Actions of Managers," *Supervisory Management*, January 1989, pp. 3–7.

4. Connirae Andreas and Steve Andreas, *Heart of the Mind* (Moab, UT: Real People Press, 1991).

5. J. Madeleine Nash, "Addicted," *Time*, May 5, 1997, pp. 69–76.

6. Statistics Canada, *Health Reports*, Vol. 12, No. 3, April 2001, Ottawa: Ministry of Industry, Catalogue No. 82-003.

7. The Federal, Provincial, and Territorial Advisory Committee on Population Health, *Statistical Report on the Health of Canadians*. Prepared for the Meeting of Ministers of Health, September 1999. Statistics Canada, Catalogue No. 82-570-X1E.

8. Jonathan A. Segal, "Alcoholic Employees and the Law," *HRMagazine*, December 1993, pp. 87–88.

9. The Federal, Provincial, and Territorial Advisory Committee on Population Health.

10. Michael E. Cavanagh, "Myths Surround Alcoholism," *Personnel Journal*, February 1990, pp. 112–21.

11. Based mostly on Harriet B. Braiker, "What All Career Women Need to Know about Drinking," *Working Woman*, August 1989, p. 72.

12. The Federal, Provincial, and Territorial Advisory Committee on Population Health.

13. Robert A. Baron, Bruce Earhard, and Marcia Ozier, *Psychology: Canadian Edition* (Scarborough, ON: Allyn and Bacon Canada, 1995).

14. "University Student Drug Use and Lifestyle," Addiction Research Foundation, news release, February 2, 1995.

15. The Federal, Provincial, and Territorial Advisory Committee on Population Health.

16. Scott Sleek, "Isolation Increases with Internet Use," *APA Monitor,* September 1998, pp. 1, 30.

17. Carol Potera, "Trapped in the Web," *Psychology Today,* March/April 1998, p. 72.

18. Andrew J. DuBrin, *Bouncing Back: How to Handle Setbacks in Your Work & Personal Life* (Englewood Cliffs, NJ: Prentice Hall, 1982), pp. 85–102; Melba Colgrove, Harold H. Bloomfeld, and Peter McWilliams, *How to Survive the Loss of a Love* (New York: Bantam Books, 1976).

19. "Understanding Depression," Canadian Mental Health Association, Vancouver, October 1993.

20. Statistics Canada, *Health Reports.*

21. Anthony J. Levitt, Michael H. Boyle, Russell T. Joffe, and Zillah Baumal, "Estimated Prevalence of the Seasonal Subtype of Major Depression in a Canadian Community Sample," *Canadian Journal of Psychiatry,* (45)7, September 2000, pp. 650–54.

22. John Lawrie, "Coping with Depression on the Job," *Supervisory Management*, June 1992, pp. 6–7.

23. Peggy Stuart, "Tracing Workplace Problems to Hidden Disorders," *Personnel Journal*, June 1992, p. 84. Our discussion of neurobiological disorders is based on the Stuart article.

24. Jennifer M. Jones, Susan Bennett, Marion P. Olmsted, Margaret L. Lawson, and Gary Rodin, "Disordered Eating

Attitudes and Behaviours in Teenaged Girls: A School-based Study," *Canadian Medical Association Journal, (165)*5, September 4, 2001, pp. 547–53.

25. Susan McClelland, "Distorted Images," *Maclean's,* August 14, 2000, pp. 41–43.

26. Terry O'Neill, "Death Wish 1: Dying to Be Skeletal," *Report/Newsmagazine (Alberta Edition),* January 21, 2002, pp. 48–50.

27. Information from The National Eating Disorder Information Centre, **www.nedic.ca**.

28. Jones et al., "Disordered Eating Attitudes and Behaviours."

29. Daniel Goleman, *Emotional Intelligence: Why It Can Matter More Than IQ* (New York: Bantam Books, 1995).

30. Fred Pryor, "Is Anger Really Healthy?," *The Pryor Report Management Newsletter*, February 1996, p. 3.

31. John Cloud, "Classroom for Hotheads," *Time,* April 10, 2000, p. 53.

Chapter Six

1. Diane Swanbrow, "The Paradox of Happiness," *Psychology Today*, July/August 1989, p. 38.

2. The major sources of information for this list are Mihaly Csikzentmihalyi, "Finding Flow," *Psychology Today*, July/August 1997, pp. 46–48, 70–71; Swanbrow, "The Paradox of Happiness"; Martin Seligman, *What You Can Change and What You Can't* (New York: Knopf, 1994); Maury M. Breecher, "C'mon Smile!" *Los Angeles Times*, October 3, 1982.

3. David Meyers, *The Pursuit of Happiness* (New York: Morrow, 1997); Black and McCafferty, "The Age of Contentment," p. 6.

4. Based on research conducted by Tim Kasser, department of psychology, the University of Rochester, 1994.

5. Martin Seligman, "Don't Diet, Be Happy," *USA Weekend*, February 4–6, 1994, p. 12.

6. Steven Reiss, "Secrets of Happiness," *Psychology Today,* January/February 2001, pp. 50–52, 55–56.

7. Richard Carlson, *You Can Be Happy No Matter What: Five Principles Your Therapist Never Told You*, revised edition (Novato, CA: New World Library, 1997).

8. Ibid., p. 71.

9. Howard Halpern, "Single or Married People Share Same Joys and Problems," syndicated column, November 12, 1988.

10. Quoted in Gary Soulsman, "Looking for Love in All the Right Places," *The Wilmington News Journal*, syndicated story, May 4, 1991.

11. John M. Darley, Sam Glucksberg, and Ronald A. Kinchla, *Psychology*, 4th ed. (Englewood Cliffs, NJ: Prentice Hall, 1988), p. 681.

12, 13. Daniel Goleman, "Making a Science of Why We Love Isn't Easy," *The New York Times,* syndicated story, July 23, 1986.

14. Pam Janis, "The Science of Sex," *USA Weekend*, March 29–31, 1996, pp. 16–17; Theresa Crenshaw, *Guide to the Ingredients in Our Sex Soup* (New York: Putnam, 1996).

15. Jeannette Lauer and Robert Lauer, "Marriages Made to Last," *Psychology Today*, June 1985, p. 24.

16. Robert J. Sternberg, *Love Is a Story* (New York: Oxford University Press, 1998); Sternberg, "What's Your Love Story?," *Psychology Today,* July/August 2000, pp. 52–59.

17. John Gottman and Sybil Carrere, "Welcome to the Love Lab," *Psychology Today,* September/October 2000, pp. 42–43.

18. Andrew Christensen and Neil Jacobensen, *Reconcilable Differences* (New York: Guilford Press, 2000).

19. Statistics Canada, "Husband-Wife Families, Distribution and Average Income by Earner Category," Catalogue No. 13-215-X1B (Ottawa: 1997).

20. Janet E. East and Judith A. Frederick, "Working Arrangements and Time-Stress," *Canadian Social Trends*, Winter 1996, pp. 14–19.

21. Terry O'Neill, "Crunch Time for Families," *Citizen Centre Report 30*(4), February 17, 2003, pp. 36–41.

22. "What Makes Women Healthy or Unhealthy?," Final Report, Vol. 2, *Canada Health Action: Building on the Legacy: An Overview of Women's Health*.

23. Steven R. Covey, "Decide Your Priorities," *USA Weekend*, December 31, 1993–January 2, 1994, p. 9.

24. Harville Hendrix, "Love and Marriage," *Family Circle* syndicated story, March 17, 1990.

25. Cited in Murray Dubin, "The Knack of Marriage: You Can Learn the Skills, Say Those Rooting for Coupledom," *Philadelphia Inquirer* syndicated story, August 22, 2000.

26. Research reported in "Listen and Improve Relations," *The Pryor Report*, May 1994, p. 12.

27. Diane Vaughan, "The Long Goodbye," *Psychology Today*, July 1987, p. 39.

28. Francesca M. Cancian, *Love in America: Gender and Self-Development* (Cambridge, England: Cambridge University Press, 1987).

29. Peter D. Kramer, *Should You Leave?* (New York: Morrow, 1997).

Chapter Seven

1. Our communication model is a condensation of a widely used model. An example of such a model is Robert E. Coffee, Curtis W. Cook, and Phillip L. Hunsaker, *Management and Organizational Behaviour* (Burr Ridge, IL: Irwin, 1994), pp. 197–200.

2. Joseph A. DeVito, *Messages: Building Interpersonal Communication Skills*, 3rd ed. (New York: HarperCollins, 1996).

3, 4. Albert Mehrabian, *Silent Messages: Implicit Communication of Emotions and Attitudes*, 2nd ed. (Belmont, CA: Wadsworth, 1981).

5. Irene Hanson Frieze, Josephine E. Olson, and June Russell, "Attractiveness and Business Success: Is It More Important for

Women or Men?," paper presented at the Academy of Management, Washington DC, August 1989.

6. N.M. Henley, *Body Politics: Power, Sex and Nonverbal Communication* (Englewood Cliffs, NJ: Prentice-Hall, 1977).

7. Edward T. Hall, "Proxemics—A Study of Man's Spatial Relationships," in *Man's Image in Medicine and Anthropology* (New York: International Universities Press, 1963); Pauline E. Henderson, "Communication without Words," *Personnel Journal*, January 1989, pp. 28–29.

8. Joann Ellison Rodgers, "Flirting Fascination," *Psychology Today*, January–February, 1999.

9. Merrill E. Douglass, "Standing Saves Time," *Executive Forum*, July 1989, p. 4.

10. Roger E. Axtell, *Do's and Taboos of Hosting International Visitors* (New York: John Wiley and Sons, 1989).

11. Research cited in Marco R. della Cava, "In the Blink of an Eye, Researcher Learns about Humans," *Gannett News Service*, May 7, 1988.

12. *Body Language for Business Success: 77 Ways to Get Results Using Nonverbal Communication,* special report from the National Institute of Business Management, McLean, Virginia, July 1989.

13. Ed McDaniel and Peter A. Anderson, "International Patterns of Tactile Communication: A Field Study," *Journal of Nonverbal Behaviour*, 22(1), pp. 59–75.

14. Jeffrey Jacobi, *The Vocal Advantage* (Upper Saddle River, NJ: Prentice-Hall, 1996).

15. Betty S. Johnson, "Communication in a Changing Environment," in *The Changing Dimensions of Business Education* (Reston, VA: National Business Education Association, 1997), pp. 112.

16. S.C. Gwynne and John F. Dickerson, "Lost in the E-mail," *Time*, April 21, 1997, p. 89.

17. KPMG Canada, 1997 Telecommuting Survey [online], available at **www.kpmg.ca/hr/telcmut.htm**.

18. Statistic quoted in Lorraine Anthony, "'Telecommuting' trend hasn't taken off," *Peterborough Examiner,* February 21, 2003, A6.

19. Daniel Araoz, "The Effective Boss," *Human Resources Forum*, November 1989, p. 4.

20. Rodger W. Griffeth, "Information Overload: A Test of the Inverted U Hypothesis with Hourly and Salaried Employees," *Academy of Management Best Papers Proceedings*, p. 234.

21. Sharon Lund O'Neill, "An Empowered Attitude Can Enhance Communication Skills," *Business Education Forum,* April 1998, pp. 28–30.

22. Suzette Haden Elgin, *Genderspeak* (New York: Wiley, 1993).

23. Judy E. Pickens, "Terms of Equality: A Guide to Bias-Free Language," *Personnel Journal*, August 1985, p. 24. The basic idea for Table 6–1 stems from the same source.

24, 25. Darrell W. Donakowski and Victoria M. Esses, "Native Canadians, First Nations, or Aboriginals: The Effect of Labels on Attitudes Toward Native Peoples," *Canadian Journal of Behavioural Science*, 28(2), 1996, pp. 86–91.

26. Janice Alessandra and Tony Alessandra, "14 Telephone Tips for Ernestine," *Management Solutions*, July 1988, pp. 35–36; Donna Deeprose, "Making Voice Mail Customer Friendly," *Supervisory Management*, December 1992, pp. 7–8; Steven Daly and Nathaniel Wice, *Alt.Culture* (New York: HarperCollins, 1996).

27. Jean Mausehund and R. Neil Dortch, "Presentation Skills in the Digital Age," *Business Education Forum,* April 1999, pp. 30–32.

28. Daniel Araoz, "Right-Brain Management (RBM): Part 2," *Human Resources Forum*, September 1989, p. 4.

Chapter Eight

1. Joseph A. Devito, *Messages*, 3rd ed. (New York: HarperCollins College Publishers, 1996).

2. Geert Hofstede, *Culture's Consequences: International Differences in Work-Related Values* (Beverly Hills, CA: Sage, 1980; updated and expanded in "A Conversation with Geert Hofstede," *Organizational Dynamics,* Spring 1993, pp. 53–61; Jim Kennedy and Anna Everest, "Put Diversity in Context," *Personnel Journal,* September 1991, pp. 50–54.

3. Geert Hofstede, *Culture's Consequences: International Differences in Work-Related Values* (Beverly Hills, CA: Sage, 1980).

4. Ibid.; Geert Hofstede, *Cultures and Organizations* (London: McGraw Hill, 1991).

5. Lee. G. Bolman and Terrence E. Deal, "Leading and Managing: Effects of Context, Culture, and Gender," *Educational Administration Quarterly*, 28, 1992, pp. 314–29; Stuart Schmidt and Ryh-Song Yeh, "The Structure of Leader Influence: A Cross-National Comparison," *Journal of Cross-Cultural Psychology*, 23, 1992, pp. 251–64.

6, 7. Hofstede, *Culture's Consequences*.

8. S. Gaines, Jr., "Relationships among Members of Cultural Minorities," in J.T. Wood and S.W. Duck, eds., *Understanding Relationship Processes, 6: Off the Beaten Track: Understudied Relationships* (Thousand Oaks, CA: Sage, 1995) pp. 51–88.

9. E.T. Hall, *Beyond Culture* (Garden City, NY: Doubleday, 1976).

10. Quoted in "Discrimination Is Brain's Way," *Los Angeles Times* story, May 7, 1995.

11. Ronald P. Philipchalk, *Invitation to Social Psychology* (Orlando, FL: Harcourt Brace and Company, 1995).

12. Roger E. Axtell, *Do's and Taboos of Hosting International Visitors* (New York: John Wiley and Sons, 1989) p. 118.

13. Pashaura Singh, "Sikh Traditions in Ontario," *Polyphony*, 12, 1990, pp. 130–36.

14. John Gray, *Men Are from Mars, Women Are from Venus* (New York: HarperCollins, 1992).

15. Mary Crawford, *Talking Difference: On Gender and Language* (Newbury Park, CA: Sage Publications, 1995).

16. Deborah Tannen, *Talking from 9 to 5* (New York: William Morrow, 1994); Tannen, *You Just Don't Understand* (New York: Ballentine, 1990); Gray, *Men Are from Mars*; Tannen, "The Power of Talk: Who Gets Heard and Why," *Harvard Business Review*, September–October 1995, pp. 138–48.

17. Gillian Flynn, "White Males See Diversity's Other Side," *Workforce*, February 1999, p. 52.

18. Arvind V. Phatak, *International Dimensions of Management* (Boston: Kent, 1983), p. 167.

19. I. Ajzen and M. Fishbein, *Understanding Attitudes and Predicting Social Behaviour* (Englewood Cliffs, NJ: Prentice Hall, 1980).

20. J.E. Alcock, D.W. Carment, and S.W. Sadava, *A Textbook of Social Psychology* (Scarborough, ON: Prentice Hall Allyn & Bacon Canada, 1998).

21. Rick Borelli, "A Worldwide Language Trap," *Management Review*, October 1997, pp. 52–54.

Chapter Nine

1. Carl Rogers, "Dealing with Psychological Tensions," *Journal of Applied Behavioural Science*, (1), 1956, pp. 12–13.

2, 3. David K. Foot with Daniel Stoffman, *Boom, Bust and Echo* (Toronto: Macfarlane Walter & Ross, 1996).

4. Quoted in Sybil Evans, "Conflict Can Be Positive," *HRMagazine*, May 1992, p. 50.

5. Evans, "Conflict Can Be Positive."

6. Angela Pirisi, "Teamwork: The Downside of Diversity," *Psychology Today*, November/December 1999, p. 18.

7. Richard J. Mayer, *Conflict Management: The Courage to Confront* (Columbus, OH: Batelle Press, 1990).

8. Human Resources Development Canada, Information on Labour Standards, Pamphlet 12—Sexual Harassment [online], available at **http://info.load-otea.hrdc-drhc.ca/~lsweb/harassmen.htm**.

9. H.F. Schwind, H. Das, W. Werther, and K. Davis, *Canadian Human Resource Management*, 4th ed. (McGraw-Hill Ryerson Canada, 1995).

10. "Human Rights in Employment," pamphlet prepared by the Canadian Human Rights Commission, 1992.

11. Garnett Picot and John Myles, "Children in Low-Income Families," *Canadian Social Trends*, Autumn 1996.

12. "Women's Stress Eased by Flextime," *The Globe and Mail*, January 8, 1997.

13. "Flexible Work Lessons 'Struggle to Juggle,'" *Worklife Report*, 11(2), pp. 8–9, 1998.

14. Stewart D. Friedman, Perry Christensen, and Jessica DeGroot, "Work and Life: The End of the Zero-Sum Game," *Harvard Business Review*, November–December 1998, pp. 119–29.

15. John D. Arnold, *When Sparks Fly: Resolving Conflicts in Your Organization* (New York: McGraw-Hill, 1993).

16. Shari Caudron, "Workplace Violence," *Workforce*, August 1998, pp. 44–52.

17. International Labour Organization, "Violence on the Job—A Global Problem," press release, Monday, July 20, 1998, at **www.us.ilo.org/news/prsrls/violence.html**.

18. Kenneth Kaye, *Workplace Wars and How to End Them: Turning Personal Conflicts into Productive Teamwork* (New York: Amacom, 1994).

19. "Beware of Cyberstalking—The Latest Workplace Threat," *HRfocus*, April 2000, p. S3; **www.usdoj.gov/criminal/cybercrime/cyberstalking.htm**.

20. Joseph D. O'Brian, "Negotiating with Peers: Consensus, Not Power," *Supervisory Management*, January 1992, p. 4.

21. Joseph P. Folger, Marshall Scott Poole, and Randall K. Stutman, *Working Through Conflict: Strategies for Relationships, Groups, and Organizations*, 4th ed., (Reading, MA: Addison Wesley Longman Inc., 2001).

22. Adapted from Fred Pryor, "Become 'Pleasantly Assertive,'" *The Pryor Report*, January 1992, p. 3.

23, 24, 25. Lynne Henderson and Philip Zimbardo, "Shyness," *Encyclopedia of Mental Health* (San Diego, CA: Academic Press, 1998).

26. Philip Zimbardo, *Shyness: What It Is, What to Do about It* (Reading, MA: Addison-Wesley, 1977), pp. 220–26; Kevin Shyne, "Shyness: Breaking through the Invisible Barrier to Achievement," *Success*, July 1982, pp. 14–16, 36–37, 51.

27. Henderson and Zimbardo, "Shyness."

Chapter Ten

1. Gerald R. Ferris, Pamela L. Perrewé, William P. Anthony, and David C. Gilmore, "Political Skill at Work." *Organizational Dynamics*, Spring 2000, p. 25.

2. Robert Epstein, "The Key to Our Emotions," *Psychology Today*, July/August 1999, p. 20.

3. William A. Cohen and Nuritt Cohen, "Get Promoted Fast," *Success*, July/August 1985, p. 6.

4. George A. Neuman and Jill R. Kickul, "Organizational Citizenship Behaviors: Achievement Orientation and Personality," *Journal of Business and Psychology*, Winter 1998, pp. 263–64.

5. Anita Bruzzese, "Get the Boss to Take Notice of You," *Gannett News Service*, April 21, 1997.

6. Walter D. St. John, "Successful Communications between Supervisors and Employees," *Personnel Journal*, January 1983, p. 76.

7. John J. Gabarro and John P. Kotter, "Managing Your Boss," *Harvard Business Review*, May–June 1993, p. 152. (HBR Classic reprint of article originally published in January–February 1980.)

8. "Using Evaluation Time to Improve Your Own Job," *Success Workshop* (Supplement to Pryor Report), May 1996, p. 2.

9. Jay T. Knippen, Thad B. Green, and Kurt M. Sutton, "How to Handle Problems with Two Bosses," *Supervisory Management*, August 1991, p. 7.

10. Sandy J. Wayne and Gerald R. Ferris, "Influence Tactics, Affect, and Exchange Quality in Supervisor-Subordinate Interactions: A Laboratory Experiment and Field Study," *Journal of Applied Psychology*, October 1990, pp. 487–99.

11. J. Kenneth Matejka and Richard Dunsing, "Managing the Baffling Boss," *Personnel*, February 1989, p. 50.

12. Quoted in Kathleen Driscoll, "Is a Tyrannical Boss Getting You Down? Don't Be Afraid to Confront Her," Rochester, NY, *Democrat and Chronicle*, June 14, 1995, p. 10B.

13. "How's the View Back There?," *Working Smart*, December 1996, p. 1.

14. Matejka and Dunsing, "Managing the Baffling Boss."

15. *How to Win at Organizational Politics—Without Being Unethical or Sacrificing Your Self-Respect* (New York: The Research Institute of America, January 1985), pp. 7–8.

16. "How to Work with a Disorganized Boss," *The Office Professional*, January 1994, pp. 1, 3–4.

17. D. Keith Denton, "Survival Tactics: Coping with Incompetent Bosses," *Personnel Journal*, April 1985, p. 68.

18. Adapted from George Milite, "Office Politics: It's Still out There," *Supervisory Management*, July 1992, pp. 6–7.

Chapter Eleven

1. Chris Lee, "The Death of Civility," *Training*, July 1999, p. 26.

2. Sheila Murray Bethela, *Making a Difference* (New York: G.P. Putnam's Sons, 1989).

3. Dru Scott, *Customer Satisfaction: The Other Half of Your Job* (Los Altos, CA: Crisp Publications, 1991), p. 16.

4. Jane Michaels, "You Gotta Get Along to Get Ahead," *Woman's Day*, April 3, 1984, p. 60.

5. Kaye Loraine, "Dealing with the Difficult Personality," *Supervision*, April 1989, pp. 6–8.

6. Sam Deep and Lyle Sussman, *What to Say to Get What You Want* (Reading, MA: Addison Wesley, 1995).

7. J.E. Alcock, D.W. Carment, and S.W. Sadava, *A Textbook of Social Psychology*, 4th ed. (Scarborough, ON: Prentice Hall Allyn & Bacon Canada, 1998).

8. Isa N. Engleberg and Dianna R. Wynn, *Working in Groups: Communication Principles and Strategies* (New York: Houghton Mifflin Company, 1997).

9. D.C. Kinlaw, *Developing Superior Work Teams: Building Quality and the Competitive Edge* (Lexington, MA: Lexington Books, 1991).

10. Gay Lumsden and Donald Lumsden, *Communicating in Groups and Teams: Sharing Leadership*, 2nd ed. (Belmont, CA: Wadsworth Publishing Company, 1997).

11, 12. Ibid., p. 15.

13. B. Tuckman and M. Jensen, "Stages of Small-Group Development," *Group and Organizational Studies*, 2, 1977, pp. 419–27.

14. B.A. Fisher, "Decision Emergence: Phases in Group Decision Making," *Speech Monographs*, 37, 1977, pp. 53–66.

15, 16. Marilyn E. Laiken, *The Anatomy of High Performing Teams: A Leader's Handbook* (Toronto: OISE Press, 1994).

17. Engleberg and Wynn, *Working in Groups;* Lumsden and Lumsden, *Communicating in Groups and Teams.*

18. R. Albanese and D.D. Van Fleet, "Rational Behaviour in Groups: The Free-Riding Tendency," *Academy of Management Review,* 10, 1985, pp. 565–81; Jennifer George, "Extrinsic and Intrinsic Origins of Perceived Social Loafing in Organizations," *Academy of Management Journal,* 35, 1992, pp. 191–202.

19. Steven L. McShane, *Canadian Organizational Behaviour* (Toronto: Richard D. Irwin Inc., 1995).

20. E.G. Bauer, "Are You a Good Team Player?," *Working Together,* sample issue, Dartnell Corporation, undated.

21. Tony Lee, "Competition for Jobs Spawns Backstabbers and a Need for Armor," *The Wall Street Journal*, November 3, 1993, p. B1.

22. Linda Thornburg, "Companies Benefit from Emphasis on Superior Customer Service," *HRMagazine,* October 1993, pp. 46–49; "Getting Closer to the Customer," *Getting Results,* August 1997, p. 8; "Complaints Are Good for You," *Working Smart,* June 1996, p. 1; Theodore Garrison III, "The Value of Customer Service," in Rick Crandall, ed., *Celebrate Customer Service* (Corte Madera, CA: Select Press, 1999), pp. 3–22.

23. Jennifer Chard and Viviane Renaud, "Visible Minorities in Toronto, Vancouver, and Montreal," *Canadian Social Trends*, Autumn 1999, pp. 20–25.

24. Bernadette Lynn, CMA, "Diversity in the Workplace: Why We Should Care," *CMA Management Accounting Magazine*, 70(5), June 1996, pp. 9–12.

Chapter Twelve

1. Felicity Somerset, "The Softer Side of Leadership," *CMA Management,* October 2001, Vol. 75(7), pp. 12–14.

2. Marilyn E. Gist and Terence R. Mitchell, "Self-Efficacy: A Theoretical Analysis of Its Determinants and Malleability," *Academy of Management Review*, April 1992, pp. 183–211.

3. Dov Eden and Arie Aviram, "Self-Efficacy Training to Speed Reemployment: Helping People to Help Themselves," *Journal of Applied Psychology*, June 1993, pp. 352–60.

4. Jay T. Knippen and Thad B. Green, "Building Self-Confidence," *Supervisory Management*, August 1989, pp. 22–27.

5. Wolf J. Rinke, "Maximizing Management Potential by Building Self-Esteem," *Management Solutions*, March 1988, p. 6.

6. Douglas Bloch, *Positive Self-Talk for Children* (New York: Bantam, 1993).

7. Philip G. Zimbardo, *Shyness: What It Is, What to Do about It* (New York: Jove/HBJ, 1977), p. 209.

8. Work cited in Michael Rozek, "Can You Spot a Peak Performer?," *Personnel Journal*, June 1991, p. 77.

9. James E. Loehr, *Stress for Success* (New York: Evans, 1997).

10. Genevieve Capowski, "Anatomy of a Leader: Where Are the Leaders of Tomorrow?," *Management Review*, March 1994, pp. 10–17.

11. Daniel Goleman, *Emotional Intelligence* (New York: Bantam Books, 1995).

12. Goleman, *Emotional Intelligence.*

13. Daniel Goleman, "Leadership That Gets Results," *Harvard Business Review,* March–April 2000, p. 80.

14. Daniel LeBlanc, "NATO Job Could Be Yanked from MP Parrish, *The Globe and Mail*, March 6, 2003, p. A6.

15. Cited in Julie Cohen Mason, "Leading the Way into the 21st Century," *Management Review*, October 1992, p. 19.

16. Richard M. Hodgetts, "A Conversation with Warren Bennis on Leadership in the Midst of Downsizing," *Organizational Dynamics*, Summer 1996, p. 75.

17. Morgan W. McCall, Jr., and Michael M. Lombardo, *Off the Track: Why and How Successful Leaders Get Derailed*, technical report 21 (Greensboro, NC: Center for Creative Leadership, 1983), p. 11.

18. "Architectural Firm Picks New President," *The New York Times*, May 21, 1981, p. D2.

19. Edwin A. Locke and Associates, *The Essence of Leadership: The Four Keys to Leading Successfully* (New York: Lexington/ Macmillan, 1991), pp. 32–34.

20. Felicity Somerset, "The Softer Side of Leadership."

21. Abraham Zaleznik, *The Managerial Mystique: Restoring Leadership in Business* (New York: Harper & Row, 1989).

22. Shari Caudron, "Humour Is Healthy in the Workplace," *Personnel Journal*, June 1992, p. 63.

23. Andrew J. DuBrin, *Leadership: Research Findings, Practice, and Skills* (Boston, MA: Houghton Mifflin, 1995), pp. 12–13.

24. "Ethics—Business Educators Teach Students to... Do the Right Thing!", *Keying In*, January 1997, p. 1.

25. Elizabeth Weil, "Every Leader Tells a Story," **www.fastcompany.com/online/15/rftf.html** (accessed May 6, 1999).

26. Suggestions 7, 9, and 10 are from Roger Dawson, *Sources of Power Persuasion* (Upper Saddle River, NJ: Prentice Hall, 1992), pp. 181–83.

27. Robert B. Maddux and Dorothy Maddux, *Ethics in Business: A Guide for Managers* (Los Altos, CA: Crisp Publications, 1994).

28. George W. Fotis, "Interactive Personal Ethics," *Management Review*, December 1996, p. 46; "Covey Proposes Principle-Based Leadership," *Management Review*, September 1995, pp. 20–21.

29. Peter Block, *Stewardship: Choosing Service over Self-Interest* (San Francisco: Berrett-Koehler Publishers, 1993), pp. 27–32.

30. Robert T. Keller, "A Test of the Path-Goal Theory of Leadership with Need for Clarity as a Moderator in Research and Development Organizations," *Journal of Applied Psychology*, April 1989, pp. 208–12.

31. "Motivating Personnel: A Condition Essential to Business Growth." Federal Office of Regional Development (Quebec), Dec. 1995.

32. Ronald A. Heifetz and Donald L. Laurie, "The Work of Leadership," *Harvard Business Review*, January–February 1997, p. 124.

33. Robert K. Greenleaf, *The Power of Servant Leadership: A Journey into the Nature of Legitimate Power and Greatness* (San Francisco: Berrett-Koehler Publishers, Inc., 1998).

34. "Blueprint for a Servant Leader," *Executive Strategies,* March 2000, p. 7.

35. Jennifer J. Laabs, "Team Training Goes Outdoors," *Personnel Journal*, June 1991, p. 59.

36. William D. Hitt, *The Model Leader: A Fully Functioning Person* (Columbus, OH: Battelle Press, 1993).

Chapter Thirteen

1. "Your Personal Core Competency," *Executive Strategies,* February 1996, p. 11.

2. Updated from Julie Griffin Levitt, *Your Career: How to Make It Happen,* 2nd ed. (Cincinnati, OH: South-Western College Publishing, 1990), pp. 11–21.

3. The description of the Strong Interest Inventory is based on James G. Clawson, John P. Kotter, Victor A. Faux, and Charles C. McArthur, *Self-Assessment and Career Development*, 3rd ed. (Englewood Cliffs, NJ: Prentice Hall, 1992), pp. 125–35.

4. *DISCOVER for Colleges and Adults*, The American College Testing Program, ITP Nelson Canada, updated regularly.

5. Carol Klieman, " 'Shadowing' Offers a Few Hours of On-the-Job Learning," *Chicago Tribune* (Jobs Section), September 28, 1997, p. 1.

6. Patricia Macinnis, "Job Hunting 101," *Computing Canada,* January 17, 2003, p. 26.

7. Statistics Canada, "Labour Force Survey," *The Daily,* March 7, 2003.

8. Statistics Canada, "Part-time by Choice," *The Daily,* Friday, November 24, 2000.

9. Quoted in Kathleen Driscoll, "Portfolio Career May Be the Way to Reinvent Your Future," Rochester, NY, *Democrat and Chronicle*, February 17, 1997, p. 5.

10. Douglas T. Hall, "Protean Careers of the 21st Century," *Academy of Management Executive*, November 1996, p. 8.

11. Mildred Culp, "Filling In Can Boost Career, but Be Wary of Guarantees," syndicated column, February 20, 2000.

12. Statistics Canada, The Survey of Self-Employment, abstract, January 29, 2002, Catalogue No. 71M0017XCB.

13. "Seven Tips for Career Preparation," *NBEA Keying In*, November 1993, p. 8; Anne Fisher, "Six Ways to Supercharge Your Career," *Fortune*, January 13, 1997, pp. 46–47.

Chapter Fourteen

1. "Reference Check Mates," *Working Woman,* August 2000, p. 84.

2. Based in part on Bob Weinstein, "What Employers Look For," in *The Honda How to Get a Job Guide* (*Business Week's Guide to Careers*, 1985), p. 24; Julie Griffin Levitt, *Your Career: How to Make It Happen* (Cincinnati, OH: South-Western, 1990), pp. 129–31.

3. *Employability Skills Profile 2000+*, The Conference Board of Canada, May 2000, **www.conferenceboard.ca.**

4. Connie R. Wanberg, Ruth Kanfer, and Joseph T. Banas, "Predictors and Outcomes of Networking Intensity among Unemployed Job Seekers," *Journal of Applied Psychology,* August 2000, pp. 491–503.

5. Robert D. Lock, *Job Search: Career Planning Guidebook, Book II* (Pacific Grove, CA: Brooks/Cole, 1988), pp. 34–35.

6. Richard H. Beatty, *The Perfect Cover Letter* (New York: John Wiley and Sons, 1997).

7. Based on form used by Garett Associates, Alexandra, Virginia.

8. Mary Alice Griffin and Patricia Lynn Anderson, "Résumé Content," *Business Education Forum*, February 1994, p. 11.

9. Peggy Schmidt, "When to Start Looking for a Job," *Business Week's Guide to Careers*, February 1986, p. 71.

10. R. Neil Dortch, "Résumé Preparation," *Business Education Forum*, April 1994, pp. 47–48.

11. Zane K. Quible, "Job Seeking Process," in *The Changing Dimensions of Business Education* (Reston, VA: National Business Education Association, 1997), p. 176.

12. Dortch, p. 47.

13. "Quick Career Booster," *WorkingSmart,* January 1998, p. 3.

14. "Helping Students Prepare for New Interviewing Tactics," *Keying In,* January 2000, pp. 1, 5.

15. Seth Godin, ed., *The 1994 Information Please Business Almanac & Desk Reference* (Boston: Houghton Mifflin, 1994), p. 354.

16. "Talking with Lynn Bignell about Job Hunting," *Working Smart*, November 1991, p. 7.

17. Susan Kleinman, "Is Your Attitude Killing Your Career?," *Cosmopolitan*, May 1994, p. 225.

18. Ellen Forman, "Surviving under the Microscope," *Sun-Sentinel* syndicated story, April 21, 1997; Nancy K. Austin, "The New Job Interview: Beyond the Trick Question," *Working Woman*, March 1996, pp. 23–24.

19. "Screening by Computer Speeds Hiring Process," Knight-Ridder, August 6, 2000.

20. Orlando Behling, "Employee Selection: Will Intelligence and Conscientiousness Do the Job?," *Academy of Management Executives,* February 1998, pp. 77–88.

21. Larry Reynolds, "Truth or Consequences," *Personnel*, January 1991, p. 5; Paul R. Sackett, Laura R. Burris, and Christine Callahan, "Integrity Testing for Personnel Selection: An Update," *Personnel Psychology*, Autumn 1989, p. 493.

22. Ontario Human Rights Commission, Policy on Drug and Alcohol Testing, **www.ohrc.on.ca/en_text/publications/drug-alcohol-policy.shtml**.

23. Mark J. Schmitt, Elise L. Amel, and Ann Marie Ryan, "Self-Reported Assertive Job-Seeking Behaviors of Minimally Educated Job-Hunters," *Personnel Psychology*, Spring 1993, p. 119.

24. Connie R. Wanberg, Ruth Kanfer, and Maria Rotundo, "Unemployed Individuals: Motives, Job-Search Competencies, and Job-Search Constraints as Predictors of Job Seeking and Reemployment," *Journal of Applied Psychology,* December 1999, pp. 897–910.

Chapter Fifteen

1. Ben Rand, "Kodak Workers Asked to Cut Waste," Rochester, NY, *Democrat and Chronicle,* October 2, 2000, pp. 1A, 4A.

2. Theodore Kurtz, "10 Reasons Why People Procrastinate," *Supervisory Management*, April 1990, pp. 1–2.

3. Ibid., p. 2.

4. Alan Lakein, *How to Gain Control of Your Time and Your Life* (New York: Wyden Books, 1973), pp. 141–51.

5. "Don't Procrastinate," *Practical Supervision*, January 1989, p. 3.

6. Robert M. Meier and Susan Sheffler, "The Perils of Perfectionism," *Success!*, September 1984, p. 14.

7. Cited and quoted in "Get with It: Nip Your Procrastination Right in the Bud," *Entrepreneur,* September 1998, p. 94.

8. Linda Sapadin, *It's about Time! The Six Styles of Procrastination and How to Overcome Them* (New York: Viking, 1996).

9. Stephen R. Covey with Elaine Pofeldt, "Why Is This Man Smiling?," *Success,* January 2000, pp. 38–40.

10. Price Pritchett, *The Employee Handbook of New Work Habits for a Radically Changing World* (Dallas, TX: Pritchett and Associates, Inc., 1997), p. 11.

11. "Be Efficient—Get Organized," *Working Smart*, March 1994, p. 8.

12. Raymond P. Rood and Brenda L. Meneley, "Serious Play at Work," *Personnel Journal*, January 1991, p. 90.

13. Mildred L. Culp, "Working Productively with Workaholics While Minimizing Legal Risks," syndicated column, Passage Media, 1997.

14. Jolene D. Scriven, "Teaching Time Management," *Business Education Forum,* February 1996, p. 19.

15. Quoted in "On-Job Disorder, Clutter Wastes Time, Money; Tame It," Knight-Ridder story, January 24, 2000.

16. Odette Pollar, "So, You Are Called a Packrat!" *The Pryor Report,* March 1996, p. 9.

17. Merrill Douglass, "Timely Time Tips: Ideas to Help You Manage Your Time," *Executive Management Forum*, September 1989, p. 4.

18. Douglass, "Timely Time Tips," p. 4.

19. Kara Swisher, "Paper Chastening," *Working Woman,* May 1999, p. 90.

20. Paul Chance, "The Wondering Mind of Youth," *Psychology Today*, December 1988, p. 22.

21. Reported in Alan Cohen, "No Web for You," *Fortune Small Business,* October 2000, p. 56.

Chapter Sixteen

1. Adapted from Donna Fenn, "Best Career Advancement: Bottoms Up," *Inc. Magazine Archives* [online], available at **www.inc.com/incmagazine/archives/07930581.html.**

2. Douglas T. Hall, "Protean Careers of the 21st Century," *Academy of Management Executive*, November 1996, p. 9.

3. Ibid., p. 10.

4. Freestanding quote in *Executive Strategies,* June 1999, p. 2.

5. Jacquelyn Lynn, "Apparel Perils: 'Dress for Success' Isn't So Cut and Dried Anymore," *Entrepreneur,* June 1999, p. 36.

6. "First Impressions: You Have to Make Them Count," *Executive Strategies*, December 1992, p. 10.

7. Jim Harris, *Getting Employees to Fall in Love with Your Company* (New York: AMACOM, 1996), p. 87.

8. Quoted in "Career Breakers," Rochester, NY, *Democrat and Chronicle*, March 29, 1999, p. 1F.

9. Kurtis Kitagawa, "Chrysler Canada Ltd.'s Windsor Experiment: Benchmarking against Global Best Practices," The Conference Board of Canada, August 1998.

10. Robert Half, "Etiquette for Success," *New Accountant*, January 1990, p. 27; "Good Manners: Why They Matter in the Nineties," *Executive Strategies*, November 1992, p. 10.

11. Andrea Sachs, "Corporate Ps and Qs," *Time* (Select Business Section), November 1, 1999, p. 23.

12. "Business Etiquette: Teaching Students the Unwritten Rules," *Keying In,* January 1996, p. 2.

13. Donald J. Campbell, "The Proactive Employee: Measuring Workplace Initiative," *Academy of Management Executive,* August 2000, pp. 52–66.

14. Scott E. Seibert, J. Michael Crant, and Maria L. Kraimer, "Proactive Personality and Career Success," *Journal of Applied Psychology,* June 1999, pp. 416–27.

15. "When the Knot in Your Stomach Is a *Good* Thing," *Executive Strategies,* July 1996, p. 5.

16. "The Bounce-Back Factor: Regain Lost Confidence and Charge Ahead," *Executive Strategies,* June 1997, p. 6.

17. Tom Peters, "The Brand Called You: You Can't Move Up If You Don't Stand Out," *Fast Company,* August/September 1997, pp. 83–94. The quotation is from p. 86.

18. Ray J. Friant, Jr., "Leadership Training for Long-Term Results," *Management Review*, July 1991, pp. 52–53.

19. Deb Koen, "Identifying Values Clarifies Career Goals," Rochester, NY, *Democrat and Chronicle,* June 4, 2000.

20. "Check Your Career Cadence," *Executive Strategies*, November 1993, pp. 7–8.

21. Quoted in "Network Your Way Up," *Working Smart,* February 1997, p. 4.

22. "Networking on the Internet," *Keying In,* January 1998, pp. 1, 6.

23. Marshall Loeb, "The New Mentoring," *Fortune*, November 27, 1995, p. 213.

24. Michele Himmelberg, "Wisdom from the Ancients: Learn from a Career Mentor," *The Orange County Register,* syndicated story, March 26, 2000.

25. Quoted in "The Secret to Being Lucky," *Success Workshop* (Supplement to *Pryor Report*), March 1996, p. 1.

26. Stephen Covey, "How to Succeed in Today's Workplace," *USA Weekend*, August 29–31, 1997, pp. 4–5.

27. "She's the Boss," *Canadian Business*, September 1996, pp. 43–46.

28. Randall Poe and Carol Lee Courter, "Glass Ceiling Shows a Few Cracks," *Across the Board*, Vol. 35, Issue 2, February 1998, p. 5.

29. "Business Notes," *Maclean's*, June 26, 2000, Vol. 113, Issue 26, p. 28.

30. Barbara Ettorre, "Breaking the Glass... or Just Window Dressing?," *Management Review*, March 1992, pp. 16–22.

31. Catalyst, "The Facts, Ma'am," p. 88; Rose Mary Wentling, "Breaking Down Barriers to Women's Success," *HRMagazine,* May 1995, pp. 81–83.

Index